The Spiritual Life

ALSO BY HENRI NOUWEN

Aging
Behold the Beauty of the Lord
Beyond the Mirror
Clowning in Rome
Compassion
Creative Ministry
A Cry for Mercy
The Genesee Diary
Heart Speaks to Heart
In the Name of Jesus
Life of the Beloved
Lifesigns
Love in a Fearful Land
Out of Solitude
Reaching Out
The Return of the Prodigal Son
The Road to Daybreak
Walk with Jesus
With Open Hands
The Wounded Healer

WITH MICHAEL J. CHRISTIANSEN
AND REBECCA J. LAIRD

Spiritual Direction
Spiritual Formation
Discernment

The Spiritual Life

Eight Essential Titles by Henri Nouwen

HENRI NOUWEN

HarperOne
An Imprint of HarperCollins*Publishers*

HarperOne

FIRST EDITION

Designed by Yvonne Chan
Illustrations by Yvonne Chan
Author photograph on page 666 by Kevin Dwyer

Library of Congress Cataloging-in-Publication Data
Names: Nouwen, Henri J. M., author.
Title: The spiritual life : eight essential titles by Henri Nouwen / Henri Nouwen.
Description: San Francisco : HarperOne, 2016. | Includes index.
Identifiers: LCCN 2016006046 | ISBN 9780062440105 (paperback)
Subjects: LCSH: Spiritual life—Catholic Church. | BISAC: RELIGION / Spirituality. |
    RELIGION / Christian Life / Spiritual Growth. | RELIGION / Christianity / General.
Classification: LCC BX4705.M542 A25 2016 | DDC 248.4/82—dc23 LC record available
    at http://lccn.loc.gov/2016006046

16 17 18 19 20 RRD(C) 10 9 8 7 6 5 4 3 2 1

CONTENTS

Making All Things New

An Invitation to the Spiritual Life

*In gratitude for ten joyful years with students
and faculty of the Yale Divinity School*

Do not worry; do not say, "What are we to eat? What are we to drink? How are we to be clothed?" . . . Your heavenly Father knows you need them all. Set your hearts on his kingdom first . . . and all these other things will be given you as well.

—Matthew 6:31–33

MAKING ALL THINGS NEW
CONTENTS

INTRODUCTION

IN THIS BOOK I would like to explore what it means to live a spiritual life and how to live it. In the midst of our restless and hectic lives we sometimes wonder, "What is our true vocation in life?" "Where can we find the peace of mind to listen to the calling voice of God?" "Who can guide us through the inner labyrinth of our thoughts, emotions, and feelings?" These and many similar questions express a deep desire to live a spiritual life, but also a great unclarity about its meaning and practice.

I have written this book, first of all, for men and women who experience a persistent urge to enter more deeply into the spiritual life but are confused about the direction in which to go. These are the people who "know" the story of Christ and have a deep desire to let this knowledge descend from their minds into their hearts. They have a vague sense that such "heart-knowledge" can not only give them a new sense of who they are, but can even make all things new for them. But these same people often feel a certain hesitation and fear to enter on this uncharted path, and often wonder if they are not fooling themselves. I hope that, for them, this small book offers some encouragement and direction.

But I also want to speak, although indirectly, to the many for whom the Christian story is unfamiliar or strange but who experience a general desire for spiritual freedom. I hope that what is written for Christians is written in such a way that there is enough space for others to discover anchor-points in their own search for a spiritual home. This can only be a true book for Christians when it addresses itself also to those whose many questions about the meaning of life have remained open-ended. The authentic spiritual life finds its basis in the human condition, which all people—whether they are Christians or not—have in common.

As the point of departure, I have chosen Jesus' words "Do not worry." Worrying has become such a part and parcel of our daily life that a life without worries seems not only impossible, but even undesirable. We have a suspicion that to be carefree is unrealistic and—worse—dangerous. Our worries motivate us to work hard, to prepare ourselves for the future, and to arm ourselves against impending threats. Yet Jesus says, "Do not worry; do not say, 'What are we to eat? What are we to drink? How are we to be clothed?' . . . Your heavenly Father knows you need them all. Set your hearts on his kingdom first . . . and all these other things will be given you as well." With this radical and "unrealistic" counsel, Jesus points to the possibility of a life without worries, a life in which all things are being made new. Since I hope to describe the spiritual life in which the Spirit of God can recreate us as truly free people, I have called this book *Making All Things New*.

I have divided my reflections into three parts. In the first part, I want to discuss the destructive effects of worrying in our daily lives. In the second part, I plan to show how Jesus responds to our paralyzing worries by offering us a new life, a life in which the Spirit of God can make all things new for us. Finally, in the third part, I want to describe some specific disciplines which can cause our worries slowly to lose their grip on us, and which can thus allow the Spirit of God to do his recreating work.

I

"All These Other Things"

Introduction

THE SPIRITUAL LIFE is not a life before, after, or beyond our everyday existence. No, the spiritual life can only be real when it is lived in the midst of the pains and joys of the here and now. Therefore we need to begin with a careful look at the way we think, speak, feel, and act from hour to hour, day to day, week to week, and year to year, in order to become more fully aware of our hunger for the Spirit. As long as we have only a vague inner feeling of discontent with our present way of living, and only an indefinite desire for "things spiritual," our lives will continue to stagnate in a generalized melancholy. We often say, "I am not very happy. I am not content with the way my life is going. I am not really joyful or peaceful, but I just don't know how things can be different, and I guess I have to be realistic and accept my life as it is." It is this mood of resignation that prevents us from actively searching for the life of the Spirit.

Our first task is to dispel this vague, murky feeling of discontent and to look critically at how we are living our lives. This requires honesty, courage, and trust. We must honestly unmask and courageously confront our many self-deceptive games. We must trust that our honesty and courage will lead us not to despair, but to a new heaven and a new earth.

More so than the people of Jesus' day, we of the "modern age" can be called worrying people. But how does our contemporary worrying actually manifest itself? Having looked critically at my own life and the lives of those around me, two words emerge as descriptive of our situation: filled and unfulfilled.

Filled

ONE OF THE most obvious characteristics of our daily lives is that we are busy. We experience our days as filled with things to do, people to meet, projects to finish, letters to write, calls to make, and appointments to keep. Our lives often seem like overpacked suitcases bursting at the seams. In fact, we are almost always aware of being behind schedule. There is a nagging sense that there are unfinished tasks, unfulfilled promises, unrealized proposals. There is always something else that we should have remembered, done, or said. There are always people we did not speak to, write to, or visit. Thus, although we are very busy, we also have a lingering feeling of never really fulfilling our obligations.

The strange thing, however, is that it is very hard not to be busy. Being busy has become a status symbol. People expect us to be busy and to have many things on our minds. Often our friends say to us, "I guess you are busy, as usual," and mean it as a compliment. They reaffirm the general assumption that it is good to be busy. In fact, those who do not know what to do in the near future make their friends nervous. Being busy and being important often seem to mean the same thing. Quite a few telephone calls begin with the remark, "I know you are busy, but do you have a minute?" suggesting that a minute taken from a person whose agenda is filled is worth more than an hour from someone who has little to do.

In our production-oriented society, being busy, having an occupation, has become one of the main ways, if not *the* main way, of identifying ourselves. Without an occupation, not just our economic security but our very identity is endangered. This explains the great fear with which many people face their retirement. After all, who are we when we no longer have an occupation?

More enslaving than our occupations, however, are our preoccupations. To be *pre*-occupied means to fill our time and place long before we are there. This is worrying in the more specific sense of the word. It is a mind filled with "ifs." We say to ourselves, "What if I get the flu? What if I lose my job? What if my child is not home on time? What if there is not enough food tomorrow? What if I am attacked? What if a war starts? What if the world comes to an end? What if . . . ?" All these "ifs" fill our minds with anxious thoughts and make us wonder constantly what to do and what to say in case something should happen in the future. Much, if not most, of our suffering is connected with these preoccupations. Possible career changes, possible family conflicts, possible illnesses, possible disasters, and a possible nuclear holocaust make us anxious, fearful, suspicious, greedy, nervous, and morose. They prevent us from feeling a real inner freedom. Since we are always preparing for eventualities, we seldom fully trust the moment. It is no exaggeration to say that much human energy is invested in these fearful preoccupations. Our individual as well as communal lives are so deeply molded by our worries about tomorrow that today hardly can be experienced.

Not only being occupied but also being preoccupied is highly encouraged by our society. The way in which newspapers, radio, and TV communicate their news to us creates an atmosphere of constant emergency. The excited voices of reporters, the predilection for gruesome accidents, cruel crimes, and perverted behavior, and the hour-to-hour coverage of human misery at home and abroad slowly engulf us with an all-pervasive sense of impending doom. On top of all this bad news is the avalanche of advertisements. Their unrelenting insistence that we will miss out on something very important if we do not read this book, see this movie, hear this speaker, or buy this new product deepens our restlessness and adds many fabricated preoccupations to the already existing ones. Sometimes it seems as if our society has become dependent on the maintenance of these artificial worries. What would happen if we stopped worrying? If the urge to be entertained so much, to travel so much, to buy so much, and to arm ourselves so much no longer motivated our behavior, could our society as it is today still function? The tragedy is that we are indeed caught in a web of false expectations and contrived needs. Our occupations and preoccupations fill our external and internal lives to the brim. They prevent the Spirit of God from breathing freely in us and thus renewing our lives.

Unfulfilled

BENEATH OUR WORRYING lives, however, something else is going on. While our minds and hearts are filled with many things, and we wonder how we can live up to the expectations imposed upon us by ourselves and others, we have a deep sense of unfulfillment. While busy with and worried about many things, we seldom feel truly satisfied, at peace, or at home. A gnawing sense of being unfulfilled underlies our filled lives. Reflecting a little more on this experience of unfulfillment, I can discern different sentiments. The most significant are boredom, resentment, and depression.

Boredom is a sentiment of disconnectedness. While we are busy with many things, we wonder if what we do makes any real difference. Life presents itself as a random and unconnected series of activities and events over which we have little or no control. To be bored, therefore, does not mean that we have nothing to do, but that we question the value of the things we are so busy doing. The great paradox of our time is that many of us are busy and bored at the same time. While running from one event to the next, we wonder in our innermost selves if anything is really happening. While we can hardly keep up with our many tasks and obligations, we are not so sure that it would make any difference if we did nothing at all. While people keep pushing us in all directions, we doubt if anyone really cares. In short, while our lives are full, we feel unfulfilled.

Boredom is often closely linked to resentment. When we are busy, yet wondering if our busyness means anything to anyone, we easily feel used, manipulated, and exploited. We begin to see ourselves as victims pushed around and made to do all sorts of things by people who do not really take us seriously as human beings. Then an inner anger starts to develop, an anger which in time settles into our hearts as an always fretting companion. Our hot anger gradually becomes cold anger. This "frozen anger" is the resentment which has such a poisoning effect on our society.

The most debilitating expression of our unfulfillment, however, is depression. When we begin to feel not only that our presence makes little difference but also that our absence might be preferred, we can easily be engulfed by an overwhelming sense of guilt. This guilt is not connected with any particular action, but with life itself. We feel guilty being alive. The realization that the world might be better off without the soft drink, the deodorant, or the nuclear submarine, whose production fills the working hours of our life, can lead us to the despairing question, "Is my life worth living?" It is therefore not so surprising that people who are praised by many for their successes and accomplishments often feel very unfulfilled, even to the point of committing suicide.

Boredom, resentment, and depression are all sentiments of disconnectedness. They present life to us as a broken connection. They give us a sense of not-belonging. In interpersonal relations, this disconnectedness is experienced as loneliness. When we are lonely we perceive ourselves as isolated individuals surrounded, perhaps, by many people, but not really part of any supporting or nurturing community. Loneliness is without doubt one of the most widespread diseases of our time. It affects not only retired life but also family life, neighborhood life, school life, and business life. It causes suffering not only in elderly people but also in children, teenagers, and adults. It enters not only prisons but also private homes, office buildings, and hospitals. It is even visible in the diminishing interaction between people on the streets of our cities. Out of all this pervading loneliness many cry, "Is there anyone who really cares? Is there anyone who can take away my inner sense of isolation? Is there anyone with whom I can feel at home?"

It is this paralyzing sense of separation that constitutes the core of much human suffering. We can take a lot of physical and even mental pain when we know that it truly makes us a part of the life we live together in this world. But when we feel cut off from the human family, we quickly lose heart. As long as we believe that our pains and struggles connect us with our fellow men and women and thus make us part of the common human struggle for a better future, we are quite willing to accept a demanding task. But when we think of ourselves as passive bystanders who have no contribution to make to the story of life, our pains are no longer growing pains and our struggles no longer offer new life, because then we have a sense that our lives die out behind us and do not lead us anywhere. Sometimes, indeed, we have to say that the only thing we remember of our recent past is that we were very busy, that everything seemed very urgent, and that we could hardly get it all done. *What* we were doing we have forgotten. This shows how isolated we have become. The past no longer carries us to the future; it simply leaves us worried, without any promise that things will be different.

Our urge to be set free from this isolation can become so strong that it bursts forth in violence. Then our need for an intimate relationship—for a friend, a lover, or an appreciative community—turns into a desperate grabbing for anyone who offers some immediate satisfaction, some release of tension, or some temporary feeling of at-oneness. Then our need for each other degenerates into a dangerous aggression that causes much harm and only intensifies our feelings of loneliness.

Conclusion

I HOPE THAT these reflections have brought us a little closer to the meaning of the word *worry* as it was used by Jesus. Today worrying means to be occupied and preoccupied with many things, while at the same time being bored, resentful, depressed, and very lonely. I am not trying to say that all of us are worried in such an extreme way all the time. Yet, there is little doubt in my mind that the experience of being filled yet unfulfilled touches most of us to some degree at some time. In our highly technological and competitive world, it is hard to avoid completely the forces which fill up our inner and outer space and disconnect us from our innermost selves, our fellow human beings, and our God.

One of the most notable characteristics of worrying is that it fragments our lives. The many things to do, to think about, to plan for, the many people to remember, to visit, or to talk with, the many causes to attack or defend, all these pull us apart and make us lose our center. Worrying causes us to be "all over the place," but seldom at home. One way to express the spiritual crisis of our time is to say that most of us have an address but cannot be found there. We know where we belong, but we keep being pulled away in many directions, as if we were still homeless. "All these other things" keep demanding our attention. They lead us so far from home that we eventually forget our true address, that is, the place where we can be addressed.

Jesus responds to this condition of being filled yet unfulfilled, very busy yet unconnected, all over the place yet never at home. He wants to bring us to the place where we belong. But his call to live a spiritual life can only be heard when we are willing honestly to confess our own homeless and worrying existence and recognize its fragmenting effect on our daily life. Only then can a desire for our true home develop. It is of this desire that Jesus speaks when he says, "Do not worry. . . . Set your hearts on his kingdom first . . . and all these other things will be given you as well."

II

"His Kingdom First"

Introduction

JESUS DOES NOT respond to our worry-filled way of living by saying that we should not be so busy with worldly affairs. He does not try to pull us away from the many events, activities, and people that make up our lives. He does not tell us that what we do is unimportant, valueless, or useless. Nor does he suggest that we should withdraw from our involvements and live quiet, restful lives removed from the struggles of the world.

Jesus' response to our worry-filled lives is quite different. He asks us to shift the point of gravity, to relocate the center of our attention, to change our priorities. Jesus wants us to move from the "many things" to the "one necessary thing." It is important for us to realize that Jesus in no way wants us to leave our many-faceted world. Rather, he wants us to live in it, but firmly rooted in the center of all things. Jesus does not speak about a change of activities, a change in contacts, or even a change of pace. He speaks about a change of heart. This change of heart makes everything different, even while everything appears to remain the same. This is the meaning of "Set your hearts on his kingdom first . . . and all these other things will be given you as well." What counts is where our hearts are. When we worry, we have our hearts in the wrong place. Jesus asks us to move our hearts to the center, where all other things fall into place.

What is this center? Jesus calls it the kingdom, the kingdom of his Father. For us of the twentieth century, this may not have much meaning. Kings and kingdoms do not play an important role in our daily life. But only when we understand Jesus' words as an urgent call to make the life of God's Spirit our priority can we see better what is at stake. A heart set on the Father's kingdom is also a heart set on the spiritual life. To set our hearts on the kingdom therefore means to make the life of the Spirit within and among us the center of all we think, say, or do.

I now want to explore in some depth this life in the Spirit. First we need to see how in Jesus' own life the Spirit of God manifests itself. Then we need to discern what it means for us to be called by Jesus to enter with him into this life of the Spirit.

Jesus' Life

THERE IS LITTLE doubt that Jesus' life was a very busy life. He was busy teaching his disciples, preaching to the crowds, healing the sick, exorcising demons, responding to questions from foes and friends, and moving from one place to another. Jesus was so involved in activities that it became difficult to have any time alone. The following story gives us the picture: "They brought to him all who were sick and those who were possessed by devils. The whole town came crowding round the door, and he cured many who were suffering from diseases of one kind or another; he also cast out many devils. . . . In the morning, long before dawn, he got up and left the house, and went off to a lonely place and prayed there. Simon and his companions set out in search of him, and when they found him they said, 'Everybody is looking for you.' He answered, 'Let us go elsewhere, to the neighboring country towns, so that I can preach there too, because that is why I came.' And he went all through Galilee, preaching in their synagogues and casting out devils" (Mark 1:32–39).

It is clear from this account that Jesus had a very filled life and was seldom if ever left alone. He might even appear to us as a fanatic driven by a compulsion to get his message across at any cost. The truth, however, is different. The deeper we enter into the Gospel accounts of his life, the more we see that Jesus was not a zealot trying to accomplish many different things in order to reach a self-imposed goal. On the contrary, everything we know about Jesus indicates that he was concerned with only one thing: to do the will of his Father. Nothing in the Gospels is as impressive as Jesus' single-minded obedience to his Father. From his first recorded words in the Temple, "Did you not know that I must be busy with my Father's affairs?" (Luke 2:49), to his last words on the cross, "Father, into your hands I commit my spirit" (Luke 23:46), Jesus' only concern was to do the will of his Father. He says, "The Son can do nothing by himself; he can do only what he sees the Father doing" (John 5:19). The works Jesus did are the works the Father sent him to do, and the words he spoke are the words the Father gave him. He leaves no doubt about this: "If I am not doing my Father's work, there is no need to believe me . . ." (John 10:37); "My word is not my own; it is the word of the one who sent me" (John 14:24).

Jesus is not our Savior simply because of what he said to us or did for us. He is our Savior because what he said and did was said and done in obedience to his Father. That is why St. Paul could say, "As by one man's disobedience many were made sinners, so by one man's obedience many will be made righteous" (Romans 5:19). Jesus is the obedient one. The center of his life is this obedient relationship with the Father. This may be hard for us to understand, because the word *obedience* has so many negative connotations in our society. It makes us think of authority figures who impose their wills against our desires. It makes us remember unhappy childhood events or hard tasks performed under threats of punishment. But none of this applies to Jesus' obedience. His obedience means a total, fearless listening to his loving Father. Between the Father and the Son there is only love. Everything that belongs to the Father, he entrusts to the Son (Luke 10:22), and everything the Son has received, he returns to the Father. The Father opens himself totally to the Son and puts everything in his hands: all knowledge (John 12:50), all glory (John 8:54), all power (John 5:19–21). And the Son opens himself totally to the Father and thus returns everything into his Father's hands. "I came from the Father and have come into the world and now I leave the world to go to the Father" (John 16:28).

This inexhaustible love between the Father and the Son includes and yet transcends all forms of love known to us. It includes the love of a father and mother, a brother and sister, a husband and wife, a teacher and friend. But it also goes far beyond the many limited and limiting human experiences of love we know. It is a caring yet demanding love. It is a supportive yet severe love. It is a gentle yet strong love. It is a love that gives life yet accepts death. In this divine love Jesus was sent into the world, to this divine love Jesus offered himself on the cross. This all-embracing love, which epitomizes the relationship between the Father and the Son, is a divine Person, coequal with the Father and the Son. It has a personal name. It is called the Holy Spirit. The Father loves the Son and pours himself out in the Son. The Son is loved by the Father and returns all he is to the Father. The Spirit is love itself, eternally embracing the Father and the Son.

This eternal community of love is the center and source of Jesus' spiritual life, a life of uninterrupted attentiveness to the Father in the Spirit of love. It is from this life that Jesus' ministry grows. His eating and fasting, his praying and acting, his traveling and resting, his preaching and teaching, his exorcising and healing, were all done in this Spirit of love. We will never understand the full meaning of Jesus' richly varied ministry unless we see how the many things are rooted in the one thing: listening to the Father in the intimacy of perfect love. When we see this, we will also realize that the goal of Jesus' ministry is nothing less than to bring us into this most intimate community.

Our Lives

OUR LIVES ARE destined to become like the life of Jesus. The whole purpose of Jesus' ministry is to bring us to the house of his Father. Not only did Jesus come to free us from the bonds of sin and death, he also came to lead us into the intimacy of his divine life. It is difficult for us to imagine what this means. We tend to emphasize the distance between Jesus and ourselves. We see Jesus as the all-knowing and all-powerful Son of God who is unreachable for us sinful, broken human beings. But in thinking this way, we forget that Jesus came to give us his own life. He came to lift us up into loving community with the Father. Only when we recognize the radical purpose of Jesus' ministry will we be able to understand the meaning of the spiritual life. Everything that belongs to Jesus is given for us to receive. All that Jesus does we may also do. Jesus does not speak about us as second-class citizens. He does not withhold anything from us: "I have made known to you everything I have learned from my Father" (John 15:15); "Whoever believes in me will perform the same works as I do myself" (John 14:12). Jesus wants us to be where he is. In his priestly prayer, he leaves no doubt about his intentions: "Father, may they be one in us, as you are in me and I am in you. . . . I have given them the glory you gave to me, that they may be one as we are one. With me in them and you in me, may they be so completely one that the world will realize . . . that I have loved them as much as you love me. Father, I want those you have given me to be with me where I am, so that they may always see the glory you have given me. . . . I have made your name known to them and will continue to make it known, so that the love with which you loved me may be in them, and so that I may be in them" (John 17:21–26).

These words beautifully express the nature of Jesus' ministry. He became like us so that we might become like him. He did not cling to his equality with God, but emptied himself and became as we are so that we might become like him and thus share in his divine life.

This radical transformation of our lives is the work of the Holy Spirit. The disciples could hardly comprehend what Jesus meant. As long as Jesus was present to them in the flesh, they did not yet recognize his full presence in the Spirit. That is why Jesus said: "It is for your own good that I am going because unless I go, the Advocate [the Holy Spirit] will not come to you; but if I do go, I will send him to you. . . . When the Spirit of truth comes he will lead you to the complete truth, since he will not be speaking as from himself but will say only what he has learned; and he will tell you of the things to come. He will glorify me, since all he tells you will be taken from what is mine. Everything the Father has is mine; that is why I said: All he tells you will be taken from what is mine" (John 16:7, 13–15).

Jesus sends the Spirit so that we may be led to the full truth of the divine life. *Truth* does not mean an idea, concept, or doctrine, but the true relationship. To be led into the truth is to be led into the same relationship that Jesus has with the Father; it is to enter into a divine betrothal.

Thus Pentecost is the completion of Jesus' mission. On Pentecost the fullness of Jesus' ministry becomes visible. When the Holy Spirit descends upon the disciples and dwells with them, their lives are transformed into Christ-like lives, lives shaped by the same love that exists between the Father and the Son. The spiritual life is indeed a life in which we are lifted up to become partakers of the divine life.

To be lifted up into the divine life of the Father, the Son, and the Holy Spirit does not mean, however, to be taken out of the world. On the contrary, those who have entered into the spiritual life are precisely the ones who are sent into the world to continue and fulfill the work that Jesus began. The spiritual life does not remove us from the world but leads us deeper into it. Jesus says to his Father, "As you sent me into the world, I have sent them into the world" (John 17:18). He makes it clear that precisely because his disciples no longer belong to the world, they can live in the world as he did: "I am not asking you to remove them from the world, but to protect them from the evil one. They do not belong to the world any more than I belong to the world" (John 17:15–16). Life in the Spirit of Jesus is therefore a life in which Jesus' coming into the world—his incarnation, his death, and resurrection—is lived out by those who have entered into the same obedient relationship to the Father which marked Jesus' own life. Having become sons and daughters as Jesus was Son, our lives become a continuation of Jesus' mission.

"Being in the world without being of the world." These words summarize well the way Jesus speaks of the spiritual life. It is a life in which we are totally transformed by the Spirit of love. Yet it is a life in which everything seems to remain the same. To live a spiritual life does not mean that we must leave our families, give up our jobs, or change our ways of working; it does not mean that we have to withdraw from social or political activities, or lose interest in literature and art; it does not require severe forms of asceticism or long hours of prayer. Changes such as these may in fact grow out of our spiritual life, and for some people radical decisions may be necessary. But the spiritual life can be lived in as many ways as there are people. What is new is that we have moved from the many things to the kingdom of God. What is new is that we are set free from the compulsions of our world and have set our hearts on the only necessary thing. What is new is that we no longer experience the many things, people, and events as endless causes for worry, but begin to experience them as the rich variety of ways in which God makes his presence known to us.

Indeed, living a spiritual life requires a change of heart, a conversion. Such a conversion may be marked by a sudden inner change, or it can take place through a long, quiet process of transformation. But it always involves an inner experience of oneness. We realize that we are in the center, and that from there all that is and all that takes place can be seen and understood as part of the mystery of God's life with us. Our conflicts and pains, our tasks and promises, our families and friends, our activities and projects, our hopes and aspirations, no longer appear to us as a fatiguing variety of things which we can barely keep together, but rather as affirmations and revelations of the new life of the Spirit in us. "All these other things," which so occupied and preoccupied us, now come as gifts or challenges that strengthen and deepen the new life which we have discovered. This does not mean that the spiritual life makes things easier or takes our struggles and pains away. The lives of Jesus' disciples clearly show that suffering does not diminish because of conversion. Sometimes it even becomes more intense. But our attention is no longer directed to the "more or less." What matters is to listen attentively to the Spirit and to go obediently where we are being led, whether to a joyful or a painful place.

Poverty, pain, struggle, anguish, agony, and even inner darkness may continue to be part of our experience. They may even be God's way of purifying us. But life is no longer boring, resentful, depressing, or lonely because we have come to know that everything that happens is part of our way to the house of the Father.

Conclusion

"HIS KINGDOM FIRST." I hope that these words have received some new meaning. They call us to follow Jesus on his obedient way, to enter with him into the community established by the demanding love of the Father, and to live all of life from there. The kingdom is the place where God's Spirit guides us, heals us, challenges us, and renews us continuously. When our hearts are set on that kingdom, our worries will slowly move to the background, because the many things which made us worry so much start to fall into place. It is important to realize that "setting your heart on the kingdom" is not a method for winning prizes. In that case the spiritual life would become like winning the jackpot on a TV game show. The words "all other things will be given you as well" express that indeed God's love and care extend to our whole being. When we set our hearts on the life in the Spirit of Christ, we will come to see and understand better how God keeps us in the palm of his hand. We will come to a better understanding of what we truly need for our physical and mental well-being, and we will come to experience the intimate connections between our spiritual life and our temporal needs while journeying through his world.

But this leaves us with a very difficult question. Is there a way to move from our worry-filled life to the life of the Spirit? Must we simply wait passively until the Spirit comes along and blows away our worries? Are there any ways by which we can prepare ourselves for the life of the Spirit and deepen that life once it has touched us? The distance between the filled yet unfulfilled life on the one hand, and the spiritual life on the other, is so great that it may seem quite unrealistic to expect to move from one to another. The claims that daily living makes on us are so real, so immediate, and so urgent that a life in the Spirit seems beyond our capabilities.

My description of the worry-filled life and the spiritual life as the two extremes of the spectrum of living was necessary to make clear what is at stake. But most of us are neither worrying constantly nor absorbed solely in the Spirit. Often there are flashes of the presence of God's Spirit in the midst of our worries, and often worries arise even when we experience the life of the Spirit in our innermost self. It is important that we gradually realize where we are and learn how we can let the life of God's Spirit grow stronger in us.

This brings me to the final task: to describe the main disciplines which can support us in our desire to have our worries lose their grip on us, and to let the Spirit guide us to the true freedom of the children of God.

III

"Set Your Hearts"

Introduction

THE SPIRITUAL LIFE is a gift. It is the gift of the Holy Spirit, who lifts us up into the kingdom of God's love. But to say that being lifted up into the kingdom of love is a divine gift does not mean that we wait passively until the gift is offered to us. Jesus tells us to set our hearts on the kingdom. Setting our hearts on something involves not only serious aspiration but also strong determination. A spiritual life requires human effort. The forces that keep pulling us back into a worry-filled life are far from easy to overcome. "How hard it is," Jesus exclaims, ". . . to enter the kingdom of God!" (Mark 10:23). And to convince us of the need for hard work, he says, "If anyone wants to be a follower of mine, let him renounce himself and take up his cross and follow me" (Matthew 16:24).

Here we touch the question of discipline in the spiritual life. A spiritual life without discipline is impossible. Discipline is the other side of discipleship. The practice of a spiritual discipline makes us more sensitive to the small, gentle voice of God. The prophet Elijah did not encounter God in the mighty wind or in the earthquake or in the fire, but in the small voice (see 1 Kings 19:9–13). Through the practice of a spiritual discipline we become attentive to that small voice and willing to respond when we hear it.

From all that I said about our worried, over-filled lives, it is clear that we are usually surrounded by so much inner and outer noise that it is hard to truly hear our God when he is speaking to us. We have often become deaf, unable to know when God calls us and unable to understand in which direction he calls us. Thus our lives have become absurd. In the word *absurd* we find the Latin word *surdus*, which means "deaf." A spiritual life requires discipline because we need to learn to listen to God, who constantly speaks but whom we seldom hear. When, however, we learn to listen, our lives become obedient lives. The word *obedient* comes from the Latin word *audire*, which means "listening." A spiritual discipline is necessary in order to move slowly from an absurd to an obedient life, from a life filled with noisy worries to a life in which there is some free inner space where we can listen to our God and follow his guidance. Jesus' life was a life of obedience. He was always listening to the Father, always attentive to his voice, always alert for his directions. Jesus was "all ear." That is true prayer: being all ear for God. The core of all prayer is indeed listening, obediently standing in the presence of God.

A spiritual discipline, therefore, is the concentrated effort to create some inner and outer space in our lives, where this obedience can be practiced. Through a spiritual discipline we prevent the world from filling our lives to such an extent that there is no place left to listen. A spiritual discipline sets us free to pray or, to say it better, allows the Spirit of God to pray in us.

I will now present two disciplines through which we can "set our hearts on the kingdom." They can be considered as disciplines of prayer. They are the discipline of solitude and the discipline of community.

Solitude

WITHOUT SOLITUDE IT is virtually impossible to live a spiritual life. Solitude begins with a time and place for God, and him alone. If we really believe not only that God exists but also that he is actively present in our lives—healing, teaching, and guiding—we need to set aside a time and space to give him our undivided attention. Jesus says, "Go to your private room and, when you have shut your door, pray to your Father who is in that secret place" (Matthew 6:6).

To bring some solitude into our lives is one of the most necessary but also most difficult disciplines. Even though we may have a deep desire for real solitude, we also experience a certain apprehension as we approach that solitary place and time. As soon as we are alone, without people to talk with, books to read, TV to watch, or phone calls to make, an inner chaos opens up in us. This chaos can be so disturbing and so confusing that we can hardly wait to get busy again. Entering a private room and shutting the door, therefore, does not mean that we immediately shut out all our inner doubts, anxieties, fears, bad memories, unresolved conflicts, angry feelings, and impulsive desires. On the contrary, when we have removed our outer distractions, we often find that our inner distractions manifest themselves to us in full force. We often use the outer distractions to shield ourselves from the interior noises. It is thus not surprising that we have a difficult time being alone. The confrontation with our inner conflicts can be too painful for us to endure.

This makes the discipline of solitude all the more important. Solitude is not a spontaneous response to an occupied and preoccupied life. There are too many reasons not to be alone. Therefore we must begin by carefully planning some solitude. Five or ten minutes a day may be all we can tolerate. Perhaps we are ready for an hour every day, an afternoon every week, a day every month, or a week every year. The amount of time will vary for each person according to temperament, age, job, lifestyle, and maturity. But we do not take the spiritual life seriously if we do not set aside some time to be with God and listen to him. We may have to write it in black and white in our daily calendar so that nobody else can take away this period of time. Then we will be able to say to our friends, neighbors, students, customers, clients, or patients, "I'm sorry, but I've already made an appointment at that time and it can't be changed."

Once we have committed ourselves to spending time in solitude, we develop an attentiveness to God's voice in us. In the beginning, during the first days, weeks, or even months, we may have the feeling that we are simply wasting our time. Time in solitude may at first seem little more than a time in which we are bombarded by thousands of thoughts and feelings that emerge from hidden areas of our mind. One of the early Christian writers describes the first stage of solitary prayer as the experience of a man who, after years of living with open doors, suddenly decides to shut them. The visitors who used to come and enter his home start pounding on his doors, wondering why they are not allowed to enter. Only when they realize that they are not welcome do they gradually stop coming. This is the experience of anyone who decides to enter into solitude after a life without much spiritual discipline. At first, the many distractions keep presenting themselves. Later, as they receive less and less attention, they slowly withdraw.

It is clear that what matters is faithfulness to the discipline. In the beginning, solitude seems so contrary to our desires that we are constantly tempted to run away from it. One way of running away is daydreaming or simply falling asleep. But when we stick to our discipline, in the conviction that God is with us even when we do not yet hear him, we slowly discover that we do not want to miss our time alone with God. Although we do not experience much satisfaction in our solitude, we realize that a day without solitude is less "spiritual" than a day with it.

Intuitively, we know that it is important to spend time in solitude. We even start looking forward to this strange period of uselessness. This desire for solitude is often the first sign of prayer, the first indication that the presence of God's Spirit no longer remains unnoticed. As we empty ourselves of our many worries, we come to know not only with our mind but also with our heart that we never were really alone, that God's Spirit was with us all along. Thus we come to understand what Paul writes to the Romans, "Sufferings bring patience . . . and patience brings perseverance, and perseverance brings hope, and this hope is not deceptive, because the love of God has been poured into our hearts by the Holy Spirit which has been given to us" (Romans 5:4–6). In solitude, we come to know the Spirit who has already been given to us. The pains and struggles we encounter in our solitude thus become the way to hope, because our hope is not based on something that will happen after our sufferings are over, but on the real presence of God's healing Spirit in the midst of these sufferings. The discipline of solitude allows us gradually to come in touch with this hopeful presence of God in our lives, and allows us also to taste even now the beginnings of the joy and peace which belong to the new heaven and the new earth.

The discipline of solitude, as I have described it here, is one of the most powerful disciplines in developing a prayerful life. It is a simple, though not easy, way to free us from the slavery of our occupations and preoccupations and to begin to hear the voice that makes all things new.

Let me give a more concrete description of how the discipline of solitude may be practiced. It is a great advantage to have a room or a corner of a room—or a large closet!—reserved for the discipline of solitude. Such a "ready" place helps us set our hearts on the kingdom without time-consuming preparations. Some people like to decorate such a place with an icon, a candle, or a simple plant. But the important thing is that the place of solitude remain a simple, uncluttered place. There we dwell in the presence of the Lord. Our temptation is to do something useful: to read something stimulating, to think about something interesting, or to experience something unusual. But our moment of solitude is precisely a moment in which we want to be in the presence of our Lord with empty hands, naked, vulnerable, useless, without much to show, prove, or defend. That is how we slowly learn to listen to God's small voice. But what to do with our many distractions? Should we fight these distractions and hope that thus we will become more attentive to God's voice? This does not seem the way to come to prayer. Creating an empty space where we can listen to God's Spirit is not easy when we are putting all our energy into fighting distractions. By fighting distractions in such a direct way, we end up paying more attention to them than they deserve. We have, however, the words of Scripture to which to pay attention. A psalm, a parable, a biblical story, a saying of Jesus, or a word of Paul, Peter, James, Jude, or John can help us to focus our attention on God's presence. Thus we deprive those "many other things" of their power over us. When we place words from the Scriptures in the center of our solitude, such words—whether a short expression, a few sentences, or a longer text—can function as the point to which we return when we have wandered off in different directions. They form a safe anchoring place in a stormy sea. At the end of such a period of quiet dwelling with God we may, through intercessory prayer, lead all the people who are part of our lives, friends as well as enemies, into his healing presence. And why not conclude with the words that Jesus himself taught us: the Our Father?

This is only one specific form in which the discipline of solitude may be practiced. Endless variations are possible. Walks in nature, the repetition of short prayers such as the Jesus prayer, simple forms of chanting, certain movements or postures — these and many other elements can become a helpful part of the discipline of solitude. But we have to decide which particular form of this discipline best fits us, to which we can remain faithful. It is better to have a daily practice of ten minutes solitude than to have a whole hour once in a while. It is better to become familiar with one posture than to keep experimenting with different ones. Simplicity and regularity are the best guides in finding our way. They allow us to make the discipline of solitude as much part of our daily lives as eating and sleeping. When that happens, our noisy worries will slowly lose their power over us and the renewing activity of God's Spirit will slowly make its presence known.

Although the discipline of solitude asks us to set aside time and space, what finally matters is that our hearts become like quiet cells where God can dwell, wherever we go and whatever we do. The more we train ourselves to spend time with God and him alone, the more we will discover that God is with us at all times and in all places. Then we will be able to recognize him even in the midst of a busy and active life. Once the solitude of time and space has become a solitude of the heart, we will never have to leave that solitude. We will be able to live the spiritual life in any place and any time. Thus the discipline of solitude enables us to live active lives in the world, while remaining always in the presence of the living God.

Community

THE DISCIPLINE OF solitude does not stand alone. It is intimately related to the discipline of community. Community as discipline is the effort to create a free and empty space among people where together we can practice true obedience. Through the discipline of community we prevent ourselves from clinging to each other in fear and loneliness, and clear free space to listen to the liberating voice of God.

It may sound strange to speak of community as discipline, but without discipline community becomes a "soft" word, referring more to a safe, homey, and exclusive place than to the space where new life can be received and brought to its fullness. Wherever true community presents itself, discipline is crucial. It is crucial not only in the many old and new forms of the common life but also in the sustaining relationships of friendship, marriage, and family. To create space for God among us requires the constant recognition of the Spirit of God in each other. When we have come to know the life-giving Spirit of God in the center of our solitude and have thus been able to affirm our true identity, we can also see that same life-giving Spirit speaking to us through our fellow human beings. And when we have come to recognize the life-giving Spirit of God as the source of our life together, we too will more readily hear his voice in our solitude.

Friendship, marriage, family, religious life, and every other form of community is solitude greeting solitude, spirit speaking to spirit, and heart calling to heart. It is the grateful recognition of God's call to share life together and the joyful offering of a hospitable space where the recreating power of God's Spirit can become manifest. Thus all forms of life together can become ways to reveal to each other the real presence of God in our midst.

Community has little to do with mutual compatibility. Similarities in educational background, psychological make-up, or social status can bring us together, but they can never be the basis for community. Community is grounded in God, who calls us together, and not in the attractiveness of people to each other. There are many groups that have been formed to protect their own interests, to defend their own status, or to promote their own causes, but none of these is a Christian community. Instead of breaking through the walls of fear and creating new space for God, they close themselves to real or imaginary intruders. The mystery of community is precisely that it embraces *all* people, whatever their individual differences may be, and allows them to live together as brothers and sisters of Christ and sons and daughters of his heavenly Father.

I would like to describe one concrete form of this discipline of community. It is the practice of listening together. In our wordy world we usually spend our time together talking. We feel most comfortable in sharing experiences, discussing interesting subjects, or arguing about current issues. It is through a very active verbal exchange that we try to discover each other. But often we find that words function more as walls than as gates, more as ways to keep distance than to come close. Often—even against our own desires—we find ourselves competing with each other. We try to prove to each other that we are worth being paid attention to, that we have something to show that makes us special. The discipline of community helps us to be silent together. This disciplined silence is not an embarrassing silence, but a silence in which together we pay attention to the Lord who calls us together. In this way we come to know each other not as people who cling anxiously to our self-constructed identity, but as people who are loved by the same God in a very intimate and unique way.

Here—as with the discipline of solitude—it is often the words of Scripture that can lead us into this communal silence. Faith, as Paul says, comes from hearing. We have to hear the word from each other. When we come together from different geographical, historical, psychological, and religious directions, listening to the same word spoken by different people can create in us a common openness and vulnerability that allow us to recognize that we are safe together in that word. Thus we can come to discover our true identity as a community, thus we can come to experience what it means to be called together, and thus we can recognize that the same Lord whom we discovered in our solitude also speaks in the solitude of our neighbors, whatever their language, denomination, or character. In this listening together to the word of God, a true creative silence can grow. This silence is a silence filled with the caring presence of God. Thus listening together to the word can free us from our competition and rivalry and allow us to recognize our true identity as sons and daughters of the same loving God and brothers and sisters of our Lord Jesus Christ, and thus of each other.

This example of the discipline of community is one out of many. Celebrating together, working together, playing together—these are all ways in which the discipline of community can be practiced. But whatever its concrete shape or form, the discipline of community always points us beyond the boundaries of race, sex, nationality, character, or age, and always reveals to us who we are before God and for each other.

The discipline of community makes us persons; that is, people who are sounding through to each other (the Latin word *personare* means "sounding through") a truth, a beauty, and a love which is greater, fuller, and richer than we ourselves can grasp. In true community we are windows constantly offering each other new views on the mystery of God's presence in our lives. Thus the discipline of community is a true discipline of prayer. It makes us alert to the presence of the Spirit who cries out "Abba," Father, among us and thus prays from the center of our common life. Community thus is obedience practiced together. The question is not simply, "Where does God lead me as an individual person who tries to do his will?" More basic and more significant is the question, "Where does God lead us as a people?" This question requires that we pay careful attention to God's guidance in our life together and that together we search for a creative response. Here we come to see how prayer and action are indeed one, because whatever we do as a community can only be an act of true obedience when it is a response to the way we have heard God's voice in our midst.

Finally, we have to keep in mind that community, like solitude, is primarily a quality of the heart. While it remains true that we will never know what community is if we never come together in one place, community does not necessarily mean being physically together. We can well live in community while being physically alone. In such a situation, we can act freely, speak honestly, and suffer patiently, because of the intimate bond of love that unites us with others even when time and place separate us from them. The community of love stretches out not only beyond the boundaries of countries and continents but also beyond the boundaries of decades and centuries. Not only the awareness of those who are far away but also the memory of those who lived long ago can lead us into a healing, sustaining, and guiding community. The space for God in community transcends all limits of time and place.

Thus the discipline of community frees us to go wherever the Spirit guides us, even to places we would rather not go. This is the real Pentecost experience. When the Spirit descended on the disciples huddling together in fear, they were set free to move out of their closed room into the world. As long as they were assembled in fear they did not yet form community. But when they had received the Spirit, they became a body of free people who could stay in communion with each other even when they were as far from each other as Rome is from Jerusalem. Thus, when it is the Spirit of God and not fear that unites us in community, no distance of time or place can separate us.

Conclusion

THROUGH THE DISCIPLINE of solitude we discover space for God in our innermost being. Through the discipline of community we discover a place for God in our life together. Both disciplines belong together precisely because the space within us and the space among us are the same space.

It is in that divine space that God's Spirit prays in us. Prayer is first and foremost the active presence of the Holy Spirit in our personal and communal lives. Through the disciplines of solitude and community we try to remove—slowly, gently, yet persistently—the many obstacles which prevent us from listening to God's voice within us. God speaks to us not only once in a while but always. Day and night, during work and during play, in joy and in sorrow, God's Spirit is actively present in us. Our task is to allow that presence to become real for us in all we do, say, or think. Solitude and community are the disciplines by which the space becomes free for us to listen to the presence of God's Spirit and to respond fearlessly and generously. When we have heard God's voice in our solitude we will also hear it in our life together. When we have heard him in our fellow human beings, we will also hear him when we are with him alone. Whether in solitude or community, whether alone or with others, we are called to live obedient lives, that is, lives of unceasing prayer— "unceasing" not because of the many prayers we say but because of our alertness to the unceasing prayer of God's Spirit within and among us.

CONCLUSION

MY ORIGINAL QUESTIONS were, "What does it mean to live a spiritual life?" and "How do we live it?" In this book I have described the spiritual life as the active presence of God's Spirit in the midst of a worry-filled existence. This life becomes a possibility when, by the disciplines of solitude and community, we slowly create some free inner space in our filled lives and so allow God's Spirit to become manifest to us.

We live in a worry-filled world. We find ourselves occupied and pre-occupied with many things, while at the same time feeling bored, resentful, depressed, and very lonely. In the midst of this world the Son of God, Jesus Christ, appears and offers us new life, the life of the Spirit of God. We desire this life, but we also realize it is so radically different from what we are used to that even aspiring to it seems unrealistic. How, then, can we move from fragmentation to unity, from many things to the one necessary thing, from our divided lives to undivided lives in the Spirit? A hard struggle is required. It is the struggle to allow God's Spirit to work in us and recreate us. But this struggle is not beyond our strength. It calls for some very specific, well-planned steps. It calls for a few moments a day in the presence of God when we can listen to his voice precisely in the midst of our many concerns. It also calls for the persistent endeavor to be with others in a new way by seeing them not as people to whom we can cling in fear, but as fellow human beings with whom we can create new space for God. These well-planned steps, these disciplines, are the concrete ways of "setting your hearts on his kingdom," and they can slowly dismantle the power of our worries and thus lead us to unceasing prayer.

The beginning of the spiritual life is often difficult not only because the powers which cause us to worry are so strong but also because the presence of God's Spirit seems barely noticeable. If, however, we are faithful to our disciplines, a new hunger will make itself known. This new hunger is the first sign of God's presence. When we remain attentive to this divine presence, we will be led always deeper into the kingdom. There, to our joyful surprise, we will discover that all things are being made new.

ACKNOWLEDGMENTS

DURING THE PAST few years, various friends have asked me, "What do you mean when you speak about the spiritual life?" Every time this question has come up, I have wished I had a small and simple book which could offer the beginning of a response. Although there are many excellent books about the spiritual life, I still felt that there was a place for a text which could be read within a few hours and could not only explain what the spiritual life is but also create a desire to live it. This feeling caused me to write this book. Many of the ideas have been expressed before by others as well as by myself, but I hope and pray that the way they are brought together here will be of help to those who feel "filled but unfulfilled."

I want to express my sincere thanks to the Passionist Sisters of Our Lady of Calvary retreat house in Farmington, Connecticut, who by their kindness and hospitality created the quiet space in which this book could be written. I am also grateful for the good advice and enthusiastic support of John Shopp and his colleagues at Harper & Row, and for the generous help of John Mogabgab, Robert Moore, and Wil Rikmanspoel in making the manuscript ready for publication. I owe a special word of thanks to the many students of the Yale Divinity School whose insightful criticisms on the first draft made me rewrite many parts of this text. Finally, I want to say thanks to Henry Morris, who suggested the title to me. I hope that all of us who worked together on this book will find that it was worthwhile ministry.

The Way of the Heart

The Spirituality of the Desert Fathers and Mothers

To John Mogabgab

THE WAY OF THE HEART
CONTENTS

PROLOGUE

IN TWENTY YEARS we will celebrate the second millennium of the Christian Era. But the question is: "Will there be anything to celebrate?" Many voices wonder if humanity can survive its own destructive powers. As we reflect on the increasing poverty and hunger, the rapidly spreading hatred and violence within as well as between countries, and the frightening buildup of nuclear weapons systems, we come to realize that our world has embarked on a suicidal journey. We are painfully reminded of the words of John the Evangelist:

> The Word . . . the true light . . . was coming into the world . . . that had its being through him, and the world did not know him. He came to his own domain and his own people did not accept him (John 1:9–11).

It seems that the darkness is thicker than ever, that the powers of evil are more blatantly visible than ever, and that the children of God are being tested more severely than ever.

During the last few years I have been wondering what it means to be a minister in such a situation. What is required of men and women who want to bring light into the darkness, "to bring good news to the poor, to proclaim liberty to captives and to the blind new sight, to set the downtrodden free, to proclaim the Lord's year of favor" (Luke 4:18–19)? What is required of a man or a woman who is called to enter fully into the turmoil and agony of the times and speak a word of hope?

It is not difficult to see that in this fearful and painful period of our history we who minister in parishes, schools, universities, hospitals, and prisons are having a difficult time fulfilling our task of making the light of Christ shine into the darkness. Many of us have adapted ourselves too well to the general mood of lethargy. Others among us have become tired, exhausted, disappointed, bitter, resentful, or simply bored. Still others have remained active and involved—but have ended up living more in their own name than in the Name of Jesus Christ. This is not so strange. The pressures in the ministry are enormous, the demands are increasing, and the satisfactions diminishing. How can we expect to remain full of creative vitality, of zeal for the Word of God, of desire to serve, and of motivation to inspire our often numbed congregations? Where are we supposed to find nurture and strength? How can we alleviate our own spiritual hunger and thirst?

These are the concerns I should like to address in the following pages. I hope to offer some ideas and some disciplines that may be of help in our efforts to remain vital witnesses of Christ in the coming years; years that no doubt will be filled with temptations to unfaithfulness, a comfortable self-centeredness, and despair.

But where shall we turn? To Jacques Ellul, William Stringfellow, Thomas Merton, Teilhard de Chardin? They all have much to say, but I am interested in a more primitive source of inspiration, which by its directness, simplicity and concreteness, can lead us without any byways to the core of our struggle. This source is the *Apophthegmata Patrum*, the *Sayings of the Desert Fathers*. The Desert Fathers, who lived in the Egyptian desert during the fourth and fifth centuries, can offer us a very important perspective on our life as ministers living at the end of the twentieth century. The Desert Fathers—and there were Mothers, too— were Christians who searched for a new form of martyrdom. Once the persecutions had ceased, it was no longer possible to witness for Christ by following him as a blood witness. Yet the end of the persecutions did not mean that the world had accepted the ideals of Christ and altered its ways; the world continued to prefer the darkness to the light (John

3:19). But if the world was no longer the enemy of the Christian, then the Christian had to become the enemy of the dark world. The flight to the desert was the way to escape a tempting conformity to the world. Anthony, Agathon, Macarius, Poemen, Theodora, Sarah, and Syncletica became spiritual leaders in the desert. Here they became a new kind of martyr: witnesses against the destructive powers of evil, witnesses for the saving power of Jesus Christ.

Their spiritual commentaries, their counsel to visitors, and their very concrete ascetical practices form the basis of my reflections about the spiritual life of the minister in our day. Like the Desert Fathers and Mothers, we have to find a practical and workable response to Paul's exhortation: "Do not model yourselves on the behavior of the world around you, but let your behavior change, modeled by your new mind. This is the only way to discover the will of God and know what is good, what it is that God wants, what is the perfect thing to do" (Romans 12:2).

To structure my reflections, I will use a story told about Abba Arsenius. Arsenius was a well-educated Roman of senatorial rank who lived at the court of Emperor Theodosius as tutor to the princes Arcadius and Honorius. "While still living in the palace, Abba Arsenius prayed to God in these words, 'Lord, lead me in the way of salvation.' And a voice came saying to him, 'Arsenius, flee from the world and you will be saved.' Having sailed secretly from Rome to Alexandria and having withdrawn to the solitary life (in the desert) Arsenius prayed again: 'Lord, lead me in the way of salvation' and again he heard a voice saying, 'Arsenius, flee, be silent, pray always, for these are the sources of sinlessness.'"[1] The words *flee, be silent* and *pray* summarize the spirituality of the desert. They indicate the three ways of preventing the world from shaping us in its image and are thus the three ways to life in the Spirit.

My first task is to explore what it means for us to flee from the world. This raises the question of solitude. My second task is to define silence as an essential element of a spirituality of ministry. Finally, I want to challenge you with the vocation to pray always.

---

1 Benedicta Ward, trans., *The Sayings of the Desert Fathers* (London & Oxford: Mowbrays, 1975), 8.

Solitude

Introduction

ST. ANTHONY, THE "FATHER of monks," is the best guide in our attempt to understand the role of solitude in ministry. Born around 251, Anthony was the son of Egyptian peasants. When he was about eighteen years old he heard in church the Gospel words, "Go and sell what you own and give the money to the poor . . . then come and follow me" (Matthew 19:21). Anthony realized that these words were meant for him personally. After a period of living as a poor laborer at the edge of his village, he withdrew into the desert, where for twenty years he lived in complete solitude. During these years Anthony experienced a terrible trial. The shell of his superficial securities was cracked and the abyss of iniquity was opened to him. But he came out of this trial victoriously—not because of his own willpower or ascetic exploits, but because of his unconditional surrender to the Lordship of Jesus Christ. When he emerged from his solitude, people recognized in him the qualities of an authentic "healthy" man, whole in body, mind, and soul. They flocked to him for healing, comfort, and direction. In his old age, Anthony retired to an even deeper solitude to be totally absorbed in direct communion with God. He died in the year 356, when he was about one hundred and six years old.

The story of St. Anthony, as told by St. Athanasius, shows that we must be made aware of the call to let our false, compulsive self be transformed into the new self of Jesus Christ. It also shows that solitude is the furnace in which this transformation takes place. Finally, it reveals that it is from this transformed or converted self that real ministry flows. I therefore propose to explore these three aspects of St. Anthony's life in the hope of uncovering the problems as well as the opportunities in our ministry.

The Compulsive Minister

THOMAS MERTON WRITES in the introduction to his *The Wisdom of the Desert*:

> Society . . . was regarded [by the Desert Fathers] as a shipwreck from which each single individual man had to swim for his life. . . . These were men who believed that to let oneself drift along, passively accepting the tenets and values of what they knew as society, was purely and simply a disaster.[1]

This observation leads us straight to the core of the problem. Our society is not a community radiant with the love of Christ, but a dangerous network of domination and manipulation in which we can easily get entangled and lose our soul. The basic question is whether we ministers of Jesus Christ have not already been so deeply molded by the seductive powers of our dark world that we have become blind to our own and other people's fatal state and have lost the power and motivation to swim for our lives.

Just look for a moment at our daily routine. In general we are very busy people. We have many meetings to attend, many visits to make, many services to lead. Our calendars are filled with appointments, our days and weeks filled with engagements, and our years filled with plans and projects. There is seldom a period in which we do not know what to do, and we move through life in such a distracted way that we do not even take the time and rest to wonder if any of the things we think, say, or do are *worth* thinking, saying, or doing. We simply go along with

---

1 Thomas Merton, *The Wisdom of the Desert* (New York: New Directions Publishing Corp., 1960), 3.

the many "musts" and "oughts" that have been handed on to us, and we live with them as if they were authentic translations of the Gospel of our Lord. People must be motivated to come to church, youth must be entertained, money must be raised, and above all everyone must be happy. Moreover, we ought to be on good terms with the church and civil authorities; we ought to be liked or at least respected by a fair majority of our parishioners; we ought to move up in the ranks according to schedule; and we ought to have enough vacation and salary to live a comfortable life. Thus we are busy people just like all other busy people, rewarded with the rewards which are rewarded to busy people!

All this is simply to suggest how horrendously secular our ministerial lives tend to be. Why is this so? Why do we children of the light so easily become conspirators with the darkness? The answer is quite simple. Our identity, our sense of self, is at stake. Secularity is a way of being dependent on the responses of our milieu. The secular or false self is the self which is fabricated, as Thomas Merton says, by social compulsions. "Compulsive" is indeed the best adjective for the false self. It points to the need for ongoing and increasing affirmation. Who am I? I am the one who is liked, praised, admired, disliked, hated or despised. Whether I am a pianist, a businessman or a minister, what matters is how I am perceived by my world. If being busy is a good thing, then I must be busy. If having money is a sign of real freedom, then I must claim my money. If knowing many people proves my importance, I will have to make the necessary contacts. The compulsion manifests itself in the lurking fear of failing and the steady urge to prevent this by gathering more of the same—more work, more money, more friends.

These very compulsions are at the basis of the two main enemies of the spiritual life: anger and greed. They are the inner side of a secular life, the sour fruits of our worldly dependencies. What else is anger than the impulsive response to the experience of being deprived? When my sense of self depends on what others say of me, anger is a quite natural reaction to a critical word. And when my sense of self depends on what I can acquire, greed flares up when my desires are frustrated. Thus greed and anger are the brother and sister of a false self fabricated by the social compulsions of an unredeemed world.

Anger in particular seems close to a professional vice in the contemporary ministry. Pastors are angry at their leaders for not leading and at their followers for not following. They are angry at those who do not come to church for not coming and angry at those who do come for coming without enthusiasm. They are angry at their families, who make them feel guilty, and angry at themselves for not being who they want to be. This is not an open, blatant, roaring anger, but an anger hidden behind the smooth word, the smiling face, and the polite handshake. It is a frozen anger, an anger which settles into a biting resentment and slowly paralyzes a generous heart. If there is anything that makes the ministry look grim and dull, it is this dark, insidious anger in the servants of Christ.

It is not so strange that Anthony and his fellow monks considered it a spiritual disaster to accept passively the tenets and values of their society. They had come to appreciate how hard it is not only for the individual Christian but also for the church itself to escape the seductive compulsions of the world. What was their response? They escaped from the sinking ship and swam for their lives. And the place of salvation is called desert, the place of solitude. Let us now see what this solitude did to them.

The Furnace of Transformation

WHEN ANTHONY HEARD the word of Jesus, "Go and sell what you own and give the money to the poor . . . then come and follow me," he took it as a call to escape from the compulsions of his world. He moved away from his family, lived in poverty in a hut on the edge of his village, and occupied himself with manual work and prayer. But soon he realized that more was required of him. He had to face his enemies—anger and greed—head-on and let himself be totally transformed into a new being. His old, false self had to die and a new self had to be born. For this Anthony withdrew into the complete solitude of the desert.

Solitude is the furnace of transformation. Without solitude we remain victims of our society and continue to be entangled in the illusions of the false self. Jesus himself entered into this furnace. There he was tempted with the three compulsions of the world: to be relevant ("turn stones into loaves"), to be spectacular ("throw yourself down"), and to be powerful ("I will give you all these kingdoms"). There he affirmed God as the only source of his identity ("You must worship the Lord your God and serve him alone"). Solitude is the place of the great struggle and the great encounter—the struggle against the compulsions of the false self, and the encounter with the loving God who offers himself as the substance of the new self.

This might sound rather forbidding. It might even evoke images of medieval ascetical pursuits from which Luther and Calvin have happily saved us. But once we have given these fantasies their due and let them wander off, we will see that we are dealing here with that holy place where ministry and spirituality embrace each other. It is the place called solitude.

In order to understand the meaning of solitude, we must first unmask the ways in which the idea of solitude has been distorted by our world. We say to each other that we need some solitude in our lives. What we really are thinking of, however, is a time and a place for ourselves in which we are not bothered by other people, can think our own thoughts, express our own complaints, and do our own thing, whatever it may be. For us, solitude most often means privacy. We have come to the dubious conviction that we all have a right to privacy. Solitude thus becomes like a spiritual property for which we can compete on the free market of spiritual goods. But there is more. We also think of solitude as a station where we can recharge our batteries, or as the corner of the boxing ring where our wounds are oiled, our muscles massaged, and our courage restored by fitting slogans. In short, we think of solitude as a place where we gather new strength to continue the ongoing competition in life.

But that is not the solitude of St. John the Baptist, of St. Anthony or St. Benedict, of Charles de Foucauld or the brothers of Taizé. For them solitude is not a private therapeutic place. Rather, it is the place of conversion, the place where the old self dies and the new self is born, the place where the emergence of the new man and the new woman occurs.

How can we gain a clearer understanding of this transforming solitude? Let me try to describe in more detail the struggle as well as the encounter that takes place in this solitude.

In solitude I get rid of my scaffolding: no friends to talk with, no telephone calls to make, no meetings to attend, no music to entertain, no books to distract, just me—naked, vulnerable, weak, sinful, deprived, broken—nothing. It is this nothingness that I have to face in my solitude, a nothingness so dreadful that everything in me wants to run to my friends, my work, and my distractions so that I can forget my nothingness and make myself believe that I am worth something. But that is not all. As soon as I decide to stay in my solitude, confusing ideas, disturbing images, wild fantasies, and weird associations jump about in my mind like monkeys in a banana tree. Anger and greed begin to show their ugly faces. I give long, hostile speeches to my enemies and dream lustful dreams in which I am wealthy, influential, and very attractive—or poor, ugly, and in need of immediate consolation. Thus I try again to run from the dark abyss of my nothingness and restore my false self in all its vainglory.

The task is to persevere in my solitude, to stay in my cell until all my seductive visitors get tired of pounding on my door and leave me alone. The "Isenheim Altar" painted by Grünewald shows with frightening realism the ugly faces of the many demons who tempted Anthony in his solitude. The struggle is real because the danger is real. It is the danger of living the whole of our life as one long defense against the reality of our condition, one restless effort to convince ourselves of our virtuousness. Yet Jesus "did not come to call the virtuous, but sinners" (Matthew 9:13).

That is the struggle. It is the struggle to die to the false self. But this struggle is far, far beyond our own strength. Anyone who wants to fight his demons with his own weapons is a fool. The wisdom of the desert is that the confrontation with our own frightening nothingness forces us to surrender ourselves totally and unconditionally to the Lord Jesus Christ. Alone, we cannot face "the mystery of iniquity" with impunity. Only Christ can overcome the powers of evil. Only in and through him can we survive the trials of our solitude. This is beautifully illustrated by Abba Elias, who said: "An old man was living in a temple and the demons came to say to him, 'Leave this place which belongs to us,' and the old man said, 'No place belongs to you.' Then they began to scatter his palm leaves about, one by one, and the old man went on gathering them together with persistence. A little later the devil took his hand and pulled him to the door. When the old man reached the door, he seized the lintel with the other hand crying out, 'Jesus, save me.' Immediately the devil fled away. Then the old man began to weep. Then the Lord said to him, 'Why are you weeping?' and the old man said, 'Because the devils have dared to seize a man and treat him like this.' The Lord said to him, 'You had been careless. As soon as you turned to me again, you see I was beside you.'"[2] This story shows that only in the context of the great encounter with Jesus Christ himself can a real authentic struggle take place. The encounter with Christ does not take place before, after, or beyond the struggle with our false self and its demons. No, it is precisely in the midst of this struggle that our Lord comes to us and says, as he said to the old man in the story: "As soon as you turned to me again, you see I was beside you."

We enter into solitude first of all to meet our Lord and to be with him and him alone. Our primary task in solitude, therefore, is not to pay undue attention to the many faces which assail us, but to keep the eyes of our mind and heart on him who is our divine savior. Only in the context of grace can we face our sin; only in the place of healing do we dare to show our wounds; only with a single-minded attention to Christ can we give up our clinging fears and face our own true nature. As we come to realize that it is not we who live, but Christ who lives in us, that he is our true self, we can slowly let our compulsions melt away and begin to experience the freedom of the children of God. And then we can look back with a smile and realize that we aren't even angry or greedy any more.

What does all of this mean for us in our daily life? Even when we are not called to the monastic life, or do not have the physical constitution to survive the rigors of the desert, we are still responsible for our own solitude. Precisely because our secular milieu offers us so few spiritual disciplines, we have to develop our own. We have, indeed, to fashion our own desert where we can withdraw every day, shake off our compulsions,

---

2 Benedicta Ward, trans., *The Sayings of the Desert Fathers* (London & Oxford: Mowbrays, 1975), 61.

and dwell in the gentle healing presence of our Lord. Without such a desert we will lose our own soul while preaching the gospel to others. But with such a spiritual abode, we will become increasingly conformed to him in whose Name we minister.

The very first thing we need to do is set apart a time and a place to be with God and him alone. The concrete shape of this discipline of solitude will be different for each person depending on individual character, ministerial task, and milieu. But a real discipline never remains vague or general. It is as concrete and specific as daily life itself. When I visited Mother Teresa of Calcutta a few years ago and asked her how to live out my vocation as a priest, she simply said: "Spend one hour a day in adoration of your Lord and never do anything you know is wrong, and you will be all right." She might have said something else to a married person with young children and something else again to someone who lives in a larger community. But like all great disciples of Jesus, Mother Teresa affirmed again the truth that ministry can be fruitful only if it grows out of a direct and intimate encounter with our Lord. Thus the opening words of St. John's first letter echo down through history: "Something . . . we have heard, and we have seen with our own eyes; that we have watched and touched with our hands: the Word, who is life—this is our subject" (1 John 1:1).

Solitude is thus the place of purification and transformation, the place of the great struggle and the great encounter. Solitude is not simply a means to an end. Solitude is its own end. It is the place where Christ remodels us in his own image and frees us from the victimizing compulsions of the world. Solitude is the place of our salvation. Hence, it is the place where we want to lead all who are seeking the light in this dark world. St. Anthony spent twenty years in isolation. When he left it he took his solitude with him and shared it with all who came to him. Those who saw him described him as balanced, gentle, and caring. He had become so Christlike, so radiant with God's love, that his entire being was ministry.

Let me now try to show how a compassionate ministry flows from a transformed self.

A Compassionate Ministry

ANTHONY'S LIFE AFTER he had emerged from his period of total isolation was blessed by a rich and varied ministry. People from many walks of life came to him and asked for advice. The solitude that at first had required physical isolation had now become a quality of his heart, an inner disposition that could no longer be disturbed by those who needed his guidance. Somehow his solitude had become an infinite space into which anyone could be invited. His advice was simple, direct, and concrete: "Someone asked him: 'What must one do in order to please God?' The old man replied, 'Pay attention to what I tell you: whoever you may be, always have God before your eyes; whatever you do, do it according to the testimony of the holy Scriptures; in whatever place you live, do not easily leave it. Keep these three precepts and you will be saved.'"[3]

To Abba Pambo, who asked him, "What ought I to do?" the old man said: "Do not trust in your own righteousness, do not worry about the past, but control your tongue and your stomach." And looking into the future, Anthony said with words which have an eerie timeliness: "A time is coming when men will go mad, and when they see someone who is not mad, they will attack him saying, 'You are mad, you are not like us.'"[4] Through the struggle with his demons and the encounter with his Lord, Anthony had learned to diagnose the hearts of people and the mood of his time and thus to offer insight, comfort, and consolation. Solitude had made him a compassionate man.

Here we reach the point where ministry and spirituality touch each other. It is compassion. Compassion is the fruit of solitude and the basis of all ministry. The purification and transformation that take place in solitude manifest themselves in compassion.

Let us not underestimate how hard it is to be compassionate. Compassion is hard because it requires the inner disposition to go with others to the place where they are weak, vulnerable, lonely, and broken. But this is not our spontaneous response to suffering. What we desire most is to do away with suffering by fleeing from it or finding a quick cure for it.

---

3 Ward, *Sayings of the Desert Fathers*, 2.
4 Ward, *Sayings of the Desert Fathers*, 2–5.

As busy, active, relevant ministers, we want to earn our bread by making a real contribution. This means first and foremost doing something to show that our presence makes a difference. And so we ignore our greatest gift, which is our ability to enter into solidarity with those who suffer.

It is in solitude that this compassionate solidarity grows. In solitude we realize that nothing human is alien to us, that the roots of all conflict, war, injustice, cruelty, hatred, jealousy, and envy are deeply anchored in our own heart. In solitude our heart of stone can be turned into a heart of flesh, a rebellious heart into a contrite heart, and a closed heart into a heart that can open itself to all suffering people in a gesture of solidarity.

If you would ask the Desert Fathers why solitude gives birth to compassion, they would say, "Because it makes us die to our neighbor." At first this answer seems quite disturbing to a modern mind. But when we give it a closer look we can see that in order to be of service to others we have to die to them; that is, we have to give up measuring our meaning and value with the yardstick of others. To die to our neighbors means to stop judging them, to stop evaluating them, and thus to become free to be compassionate. Compassion can never coexist with judgment because judgment creates the distance, the distinction, which prevents us from really being with the other.

Much of our ministry is pervaded with judgments. Often quite unconsciously we classify our people as very good, good, neutral, bad, and very bad. These judgments influence deeply the thoughts, words, and actions of our ministry. Before we know it, we fall into the trap of the self-fulfilling prophecy. Those whom we consider lazy, indifferent, hostile, or obnoxious we treat as such, forcing them in this way to live up to our own views. And so, much of our ministry is limited by the snares of our own judgments. These self-created limits prevent us from being available to people and shrivel up our compassion.

"Do not judge and you will not be judged yourselves" is a word of Jesus that is indeed very hard to live up to. But it contains the secret of a compassionate ministry. This becomes clear in many stories from the desert. Abba Moses, one of St. Anthony's followers, said to a brother: "To die to one's neighbor is this. To bear your own faults and not to pay attention to anyone else wondering whether they are good or bad. Do no harm to anyone, do not think anything bad in your heart towards anyone, do not scorn the man who does evil, do not put confidence in him who does wrong to his neighbor, do not rejoice with him who injures his neighbor. . . . Do not have hostile feelings towards anyone and do not let dislike dominate your heart."[5] And with the typically graphic imagery of the desert, everything is summarized with the words: "It is folly for a man who has a dead person in his house to leave him there and go to weep over his neighbor's dead."[6]

Solitude leads to the awareness of the dead person in our own house and keeps us from making judgments about other people's sins. In this way real forgiveness becomes possible. The following desert story offers a good illustration: "A brother . . . committed a fault. A council was called to which Abba Moses was invited, but he refused to go to it. Then the priest sent someone to say to him, 'Come, for everyone is waiting for you.' So he got up and went. He took a leaking jug, filled it with water, and carried it with him. The others came out to meet him and said to him, 'What is this, Father?' The old man said to them, 'My sins run out behind me, and I do not see them, and today I am coming to judge the error of another.' When they heard that they said no more to the brother but forgave him."[7]

What becomes visible here is that solitude molds selfrighteous people into gentle, caring, forgiving persons who are so deeply convinced of their own great sinfulness and so fully aware of God's even greater mercy that their life itself becomes ministry. In such a ministry there is hardly any difference left between doing and being. When we are filled with God's merciful presence, we can do nothing other than minister because our whole being witnesses to the light that has come into the darkness. Here are two desert stories that show this tender, compassionate ministry.

"Of Abba Ammonas, a disciple of Anthony, it is said that in his solitude he 'advanced to the point where his goodness was so great that he took no notice of wickedness.' Thus, having become bishop, someone brought a young girl who was pregnant to him, saying, 'See what this un-

---

5 Ward, *Sayings of the Desert Fathers*, 120–21.
6 Ward, *Sayings of the Desert Fathers*, 120–21.
7 Ward, *Sayings of the Desert Fathers*, 117.

happy wretch has done; give her a penance.' But he, having marked the young girl's womb with the sign of the cross, commanded that six pairs of fine linen sheets should be given her, saying, 'It is for fear that, when she comes to give birth, she may die, she or the child, and have nothing for the burial.' But her accusers resumed, 'Why did you do that? Give her a punishment.' But he said to them, 'Look, brothers, she is near to death; what am I to do?' Then he sent her away and no old man dared accuse anyone any more."[8]

This story illustrates beautifully how the compassionate person is so aware of the suffering of others that it is not even possible for him or her to dwell on their sins. The second story makes clear how extremely careful and sensitive is a compassionate minister.

"Three old men, of whom one had a bad reputation, came one day to Abba Achilles. The first asked him, 'Father, make me a fishing-net.' 'I will not make you one,' he replied. Then the second said, 'Of your charity make one, so that we have a souvenir of you in the monastery.' But he said, 'I do not have time.' Then the third one, who had a bad reputation, said, 'Make me a fishing-net, so that I may have something from your hands, Father.' Abba Achilles answered him at once, 'For you, I will make one.' Then the two other old men asked him privately, 'Why did you not want to do what we asked you, but you promised to do what he asked?' The old man gave them this answer, 'I told you I would not make one, and you were not disappointed, since you thought that I had no time. But if I had not made one for him, he would have said, "The old man has heard about my sin, and that is why he does not want to make me anything," and so our relationship would have broken down. But now I have cheered his soul, so that he will not be overcome with grief.'"[9]

Here indeed is ministry in its purest form, a compassionate ministry born of solitude. Anthony and his followers, who escaped the compulsions of the world, did so not out of disdain for people but in order to be able to save them. Thomas Merton, who described these monks as people who swam for their life in order not to drown in the sinking ship of their society, remarks:

---

8 Ward, *Sayings of the Desert Fathers*, 23.
9 Ward, *Sayings of the Desert Fathers*, 24–25.

They knew that they were helpless to do any good for others as long as they floundered about in the wreckage. But once they got a foothold on solid ground, things were different. Then they had not only the power but even the obligation to pull the whole world to safety after them."[10]

Thus in and through solitude we do not move away from people. On the contrary, we move closer to them through compassionate ministry.

Conclusion

IN A WORLD that victimizes us by its compulsions, we are called to solitude where we can struggle against our anger and greed and let our new self be born in the loving encounter with Jesus Christ. It is in this solitude that we become compassionate people, deeply aware of our solidarity in brokenness with all of humanity and ready to reach out to anyone in need.

The end of Anthony's story shows him, after years of compassionate ministry, returning to his solitude to be totally absorbed in direct communion with God. One of the desert stories tells us about a certain old man who asked God to let him see the Fathers. God heard his prayer and the old man saw them all except Anthony. "So he asked his guide, 'Where is Abba Anthony?' He told him in reply that in the place where God is, there Anthony would be."[11] It is very important for us to realize that Anthony concluded his life in total absorption in God. The goal of our life is not people. It is God. Only in him shall we find the rest we seek. It is therefore to solitude that we must return, not alone, but with all those whom we embrace through our ministry. This return continues until the time when the same Lord who sent us into the world calls us back to be with him in a never-ending communion.

10 Merton, *Wisdom of the Desert*, 23.
11 Ward, *Sayings of the Desert Fathers*, 6.

2

Silence

Introduction

WHEN ARSENIUS, THE Roman educator who exchanged his status and wealth for the solitude of the Egyptian desert, prayed, "Lord, lead me into the way of salvation," he heard a voice saying, "Be silent." Silence completes and intensifies solitude. This is the conviction shared by the Desert Fathers. A charming story about Abbot Macarius makes the point quite well. "Once the abbot Macarius, after he had given the benediction to the brethren in the church at Scete, said to them, 'Brethren, fly.' One of the elders answered him, 'How can we fly further than this, seeing we are here in the desert?' Then Macarius placed his finger on his mouth and said, 'Fly from this.' So saying, he entered his cell and shut the door."[1]

Silence is the way to make solitude a reality. The Desert Fathers praise silence as the safest way to God. "I have often repented of having spoken," Arsenius said, "but never of having remained silent." One day Archbishop Theophilus came to the desert to visit Abba Pambo. But Abba Pambo did not speak to him. When the brethren finally said to Pambo, "Father, say something to the archbishop, so that he may be edified," he replied: "If he is not edified by my silence, he will not be edified by my speech."[2]

---

1 James O. Hannay, *The Wisdom of the Desert* (London: Methuen, 1904), 206.
2 Benedicta Ward, trans., *The Sayings of the Desert Fathers* (London & Oxford: Mowbrays, 1975), 69.

Silence is an indispensable discipline in the spiritual life. Ever since James described the tongue as a "whole wicked world in itself" and silence as putting a bit into the horse's mouth (James 3:3, 6) Christians have tried to practice silence as the way to self-control. Clearly silence is a discipline needed in many different situations: in teaching and learning, in preaching and worship, in visiting and counseling. Silence is a very concrete, practical, and useful discipline in all our ministerial tasks. It can be seen as a portable cell taken with us from the solitary place into the midst of our ministry. Silence is solitude practiced in action.

In this reflection I would like first to show how wordy our world has become. Then I want to describe the great value of silence in this wordy world. Finally I hope to indicate how silence can be a sign of God's presence in the different forms of ministry.

Our Wordy World

OVER THE LAST few decades we have been inundated by a torrent of words. Wherever we go we are surrounded by words: words softly whispered, loudly proclaimed, or angrily screamed; words spoken, recited, or sung; words on records, in books, on walls, or in the sky; words in many sounds, many colors, or many forms; words to be heard, read, seen, or glanced at; words which flicker off and on, move slowly, dance, jump, or wiggle. Words, words, words! They form the floor, the walls, and the ceiling of our existence.

It has not always been this way. There was a time not too long ago without radios and televisions, stop signs, yield signs, merge signs, bumper stickers, and the ever-present announcements indicating price increases or special sales. There was a time without the advertisements which now cover whole cities with words.

Recently I was driving through Los Angeles, and suddenly I had the strange sensation of driving through a huge dictionary. Wherever I looked there were words trying to take my eyes from the road. They said, "Use me, take me, buy me, drink me, smell me, touch me, kiss me, sleep with me." In such a world who can maintain respect for words?

All this is to suggest that words, my own included, have lost their creative power. Their limitless multiplication has made us lose confidence in words and caused us to think, more often than not, "They are just words."

Teachers speak to students for six, twelve, eighteen, and sometimes twenty-four years. But the students often emerge from the experience with the feeling, "They were just words." Preachers preach their sermons week after week and year after year. But their parishioners remain the same and often think, "They are just words." Politicians, businessmen, ayatollahs, and popes give speeches and make statements "in season and out of season," but those who listen say: "They are just words . . . just another distraction."

The result of this is that the main function of the word, which is communication, is no longer realized. The word no longer communicates, no longer fosters communion, no longer creates community, and therefore no longer gives life. The word no longer offers trustworthy ground on which people can meet each other and build society.

Do I exaggerate? Let us focus for a moment on theological education. What else is the goal of theological education than to bring us closer to the Lord our God so that we may be more faithful to the great commandment to love him with all our heart, with all our soul, and with all our mind, and our neighbor as ourselves (Matthew 22:37)? Seminaries and divinity schools must lead theology students into an ever-growing communion with God, with each other, and with their fellow human beings. Theological education is meant to form our whole person toward an increasing conformity with the mind of Christ so that our way of praying and our way of believing will be one.

But is this what takes place? Often it seems that we who study or teach theology find ourselves entangled in such a complex network of discussions, debates, and arguments about God and "God-issues" that a simple conversation with God or a simple presence to God has become practically impossible. Our heightened verbal ability, which enables us to make many distinctions, has sometimes become a poor substitute for a single-minded commitment to the Word who is life. If there is a crisis in theological education, it is first and foremost a crisis of the word. This is not to say that critical intellectual work and the subtle distinctions it requires have no place in theological training. But when our words are no longer a reflection of the divine Word in and through whom the world has been created and redeemed, they lose their grounding and become as seductive and misleading as the words used to sell Geritol.

There was a time when the obvious milieu for theological education was the monastery. There words were born out of silence and could lead one deeper into silence. Although monasteries are no longer the most common places of theological education, silence remains as indispensable today as it was in the past. The Word of God is born out of the eternal silence of God, and it is to this Word out of silence that we want to be witnesses.

Silence

SILENCE IS THE home of the word. Silence gives strength and fruitfulness to the word. We can even say that words are meant to disclose the mystery of the silence from which they come.

The Taoist philosopher Chuang Tzu expresses this well in the following way:

> The purpose of a fish trap is to catch fish and when the fish are caught, the trap is forgotten. The purpose of a rabbit snare is to catch rabbits. When the rabbits are caught, the snare is forgotten. The purpose of the word is to convey ideas. When the ideas are grasped, the words are forgotten. Where can I find a man who has forgotten words? He is the one I would like to talk to.[3]

"I would like to talk to the man who has forgotten words." That could have been said by one of the Desert Fathers. For them, the word is the instrument of the present world and silence is the mystery of the future world. If a word is to bear fruit it must be spoken from the future world into the present world. The Desert Fathers therefore considered their

---

3 Thomas Merton, *The Way of Chuang Tzu* (New York: New Directions, 1965), 154.

going into the silence of the desert to be a first step into the future world. From that world their words could bear fruit, because there they could be filled with the power of God's silence.

In the sayings of the Desert Fathers, we can distinguish three aspects of silence. All of them deepen and strengthen the central idea that silence is the mystery of the future world. First, silence makes us pilgrims. Secondly, silence guards the fire within. Thirdly, silence teaches us to speak.

SILENCE MAKES US PILGRIMS

Abba Tithoes once said, "Pilgrimage means that a man should control his tongue." The expression "To be on pilgrimage is to be silent" (*peregrinatio est tacere*), expresses the conviction of the Desert Fathers that silence is the best anticipation of the future world.[4] The most frequent argument for silence is simply that words lead to sin. Not speaking, therefore, is the most obvious way to stay away from sin. This connection is clearly expressed by the apostle James: ". . . every one of us does something wrong, over and over again; the only man who could reach perfection would be someone who never said anything wrong—he would be able to control every part of himself" (James 3:2).

James leaves little doubt that speaking without sinning is very difficult and that, if we want to remain untouched by the sins of the world on our journey to our eternal home, silence is the safest way. Thus, silence became one of the central disciplines of the spiritual life. St. Benedict, the father of the monastic life in the West and the patron saint of Europe, puts great emphasis on silence in his Rule. He quotes the Psalmist who says, "I will keep a muzzle on my mouth . . . I will watch how I behave and not let my tongue lead me into sin" (Psalm 39:1). St. Benedict not only warns his brothers against evil talk, but also tells them to avoid good, holy, edifying words because, as it is written in the book of Proverbs, "A flood of words is never without its faults" (Proverbs 10:19). Speaking is dangerous and easily leads us away from the right path.

The central idea underlying these ascetic teachings is that speaking gets us involved in the affairs of the world, and it is very hard to be in-

---

4 Ward, *The Sayings of the Desert Fathers*, 198.

volved without becoming entangled in and polluted by the world. The Desert Fathers and all who followed in their footsteps "knew that every conversation tended to interest them in this world, to make them in heart less of strangers here and more of citizens."[5]

This might sound too unworldly to us, but let us at least recognize how often we come out of a conversation, a discussion, a social gathering, or a business meeting with a bad taste in our mouth. How seldom have long talks proved to be good and fruitful? Would not many if not most of the words we use be better left unspoken? We speak about the events of the world, but how often do we really change them for the better? We speak about people and their ways, but how often do our words do them or us any good? We speak about our ideas and feelings as if everyone were interested in them, but how often do we really feel understood? We speak a great deal about God and religion, but how often does it bring us or others real insight? Words often leave us with a sense of inner defeat. They can even create a sense of numbness and a feeling of being bogged down in swampy ground. Often they leave us in a slight depression, or in a fog that clouds the window of our mind. In short, words can give us the feeling of having stopped too long at one of the little villages that we pass on our journey, of having been motivated more by curiosity than by service. Words often make us forget that we are pilgrims called to invite others to join us on the journey. *Peregrinatio est tacere.* "To be silent keeps us pilgrims."

SILENCE GUARDS THE FIRE WITHIN

A second, more positive, meaning of silence is that it protects the inner fire. Silence guards the inner heat of religious emotions. This inner heat is the life of the Holy Spirit within us. Thus, silence is the discipline by which the inner fire of God is tended and kept alive.

Diadochus of Photiki offers us a very concrete image: "When the door of the steambath is continually left open, the heat inside rapidly escapes through it; likewise the soul, in its desire to say many things, dissipates its remembrance of God through the door of speech, even though everything it says may be good. Thereafter the intellect, though lacking

---

5 Hannay, *Wisdom of the Desert*, 205.

appropriate ideas, pours out a welter of confused thoughts to anyone it meets, as it no longer has the Holy Spirit to keep its understanding free from fantasy. Ideas of value always shun verbosity, being foreign to confusion and fantasy. Timely silence, then, is precious, for it is nothing less than the mother of the wisest thoughts."[6]

These words of Diadochus go against the grain of our contemporary life-style, in which "sharing" has become one of the greatest virtues. We have been made to believe that feelings, emotions, and even the inner stirrings of our soul have to be shared with others. Expressions such as "Thanks for sharing this with me," or "It was good to share this with you," show that the door of our steambath is open most of the time. In fact, people who prefer to keep to themselves and do not expose their interior life tend to create uneasiness and are often considered inhibited, asocial, or simply odd. But let us at least raise the question of whether our lavish ways of sharing are not more compulsive than virtuous; that instead of creating community they tend to flatten out our life together. Often we come home from a sharing session with a feeling that something precious has been taken away from us or that holy ground has been trodden upon. James Hannay, commenting on the sayings of the Desert Fathers, writes:

> The mouth is not a door through which any evil enters. The ears are such doors as are the eyes. The mouth is a door only for exit. What was it that they [the Desert Fathers] feared to let go out? What was it which someone might steal out of their hearts, as a thief takes the steed from the stable when the door is left open? It can have been nothing else than the force of religious emotion.[7]

What needs to be guarded is the life of the Spirit within us. Especially we who want to witness to the presence of God's Spirit in the world need to tend the fire within with utmost care. It is not so strange that many

---

6 Diadochus of Photiki, "On Spiritual Knowledge and Discrimination: One Hundred Texts," in *The Philokalia*, vol. 1, compiled by St. Nikodimos of the Holy Mountain and St. Makarios of Corinth, trans., eds., G.E.H. Palmer, Phillip Sherrard, Kallistos Ware (London & Boston: Faber & Faber, 1979), 276.

7 Hannay, *Wisdom of the Desert*, 205–6.

ministers have become burnt-out cases, people who say many words and share many experiences, but in whom the fire of God's Spirit has died and from whom not much more comes forth than their own boring, petty ideas and feelings. Sometimes it seems that our many words are more an expression of our doubt than of our faith. It is as if we are not sure that God's Spirit can touch the hearts of people: we have to help him out and, with many words, convince others of his power. But it is precisely this wordy unbelief that quenches the fire.

Our first and foremost task is faithfully to care for the inward fire so that when it is really needed it can offer warmth and light to lost travelers. Nobody expressed this with more conviction than the Dutch painter Vincent van Gogh:

> There may be a great fire in our soul, yet no one ever comes to warm himself at it, and the passersby only see a wisp of smoke coming through the chimney, and go along their way. Look here, now what must be done? Must one tend the inner fire, have salt in oneself, wait patiently yet with how much impatience for the hour when somebody will come and sit down—maybe to stay? Let him who believes in God wait for the hour that will come sooner or later.[8]

Vincent van Gogh speaks here with the mind and heart of the Desert Fathers. He knew about the temptation to open all the doors so that passersby could see the fire and not just the smoke coming through the chimney. But he also realized that if this happened, the fire would die and nobody would find warmth and new strength. His own life is a powerful example of faithfulness to the inner fire. During his life nobody came to sit down at his fire, but today thousands have found comfort and consolation in his drawings, paintings, and letters.

As ministers our greatest temptation is toward too many words. They weaken our faith and make us lukewarm. But silence is a sacred discipline, a guard of the Holy Spirit.

---

8 Vincent van Gogh, *The Complete Letters of Vincent van Gogh*, vol. 1 (Greenwich, Connecticut: New York Graphic Society, 1959), 197.

SILENCE TEACHES US TO SPEAK

The third way that silence reveals itself as the mystery of the future world is by teaching us to speak. A word with power is a word that comes out of silence. A word that bears fruit is a word that emerges from the silence and returns to it. It is a word that reminds us of the silence from which it comes and leads us back to that silence. A word that is not rooted in silence is a weak, powerless word that sounds like a "clashing cymbal or a booming gong" (1 Corinthians 13:1).

All this is true only when the silence from which the word comes forth is not emptiness and absence, but fullness and presence, not the human silence of embarrassment, shame, or guilt, but the divine silence in which love rests secure.

Here we can glimpse the great mystery in which we participate through silence and the Word, the mystery of God's own speaking. Out of his eternal silence God spoke the Word, and through this Word created and recreated the world. In the beginning God spoke the land, the sea, and the sky. He spoke the sun, the moon, and the stars. He spoke plants, birds, fish, animals wild and tame. Finally, he spoke man and woman. Then, in the fullness of time, God's Word, through whom all had been created, became flesh and gave power to all who believe to become the children of God. In all this, the Word of God does not break the silence of God, but rather unfolds the immeasurable richness of his silence.

By entering into the Egyptian desert, the monks wanted to participate in the divine silence. By speaking out of this silence to the needs of their people, they sought to participate in the creative and recreative power of the divine Word.

Words can only create communion and thus new life when they embody the silence from which they emerge. As soon as we begin to take hold of each other by our words, and use words to defend ourselves or offend others, the word no longer speaks of silence. But when the word calls forth the healing and restoring stillness of its own silence, few words are needed: much can be said without much being spoken.

Thus silence is the mystery of the future world. It keeps us pilgrims and prevents us from becoming entangled in the cares of this age. It guards the fire of the Holy Spirit who dwells within us. It allows us to speak a word that participates in the creative and recreative power of God's own Word.

The Ministry of Silence

WE ARE NOW left with the question of how to practice a ministry of silence in which our word has the power to represent the fullness of God's silence. This is an important question because we have become so contaminated by our wordy world that we hold to the deceptive opinion that our words are more important than our silence. Therefore it requires a strenuous discipline to make our ministry one that leads our people into the silence of God. That is the task Jesus has given us. The whole of Jesus' ministry pointed away from himself to the Father who had sent him. To his disciples Jesus said, "The words I say to you I do not speak as from myself; it is the Father, living in me, who is doing this work" (John 14:10). Jesus, the Word of God made flesh, spoke not to attract attention to himself but to show the way to his Father: "I came from the Father and have come into the world and now I leave the world to go to the Father (John 16:28). I am going to prepare a place for you . . . so that where I am you may be too" (John 14:2–3). In order to be a ministry in the Name of Jesus, our ministry must also point beyond our words to the unspeakable mystery of God.

One of our main problems is that in this chatty society, silence has become a very fearful thing. For most people, silence creates itchiness and nervousness. Many experience silence not as full and rich, but as empty and hollow. For them silence is like a gaping abyss which can swallow them up. As soon as a minister says during a worship service, "Let us be silent for a few moments," people tend to become restless and preoccupied with only one thought: "When will this be over?" Imposed silence often creates hostility and resentment. Many ministers who have experimented with silence in their services have soon found out that silence can be more demonic than divine and have quickly picked up the signals that were saying: "Please keep talking." It is quite understandable that most forms of ministry avoid silence precisely so as to ward off the anxiety it provokes.

But isn't the purpose of all ministry to reveal that God is not a God of fear but a God of love? And couldn't this be accomplished by gently and carefully converting the empty silence into a full silence, the anxious silence into a peaceful silence, and the restless silence into a restful silence, so that in this converted silence a real encounter with the loving Father could take place? What a power our word would have if it could enable people to befriend their silence! Let me describe a few concrete ways in which this might happen.

SILENCE AND PREACHING

Our preaching, when it is good, is interesting or moving, and sometimes both. It stimulates mind and heart and thus leads to a new insight or a new feeling. This is both valuable and necessary. But there is another option, one which is especially appropriate when we work with small groups. There is a way of preaching in which the word of Scripture is repeated quietly and regularly, with a short comment here and there, in order to let that word create an inner space where we can listen to our Lord. If it is true that the word of Scripture should lead us into the silence of God, then we must be careful to use that word not simply as an interesting or motivating word, but as a word that creates the boundaries within which we can listen to the loving, caring, gentle presence of God.

Most people who listen to a sermon keep their eyes directed toward the preacher, and rightly so, because he or she asks for attention to the word that is being spoken. But is it also possible for the word to be spoken in such a way that it slowly moves attention away from the pulpit to the heart of the listener and reveals there an inner silence in which it is safe to dwell.

The simple words "The Lord is my shepherd" can be spoken quietly and persistently in such a way that they become like a hedge around a garden in which God's shepherding can be sensed. These words, which at first might seem to be no more than an interesting metaphor, can slowly descend from the mind into the heart. There they may offer the context in which an inner transformation, by the God who transcends all human words and concepts, can take place. Thus, the words "The Lord is my shepherd" lead to the silent pastures where we can dwell in the loving presence of him in whose Name the preacher speaks. This meditative preaching is one way to practice the ministry of silence.

SILENCE AND COUNSELING

Counseling is understood by many to be a way in which one person listens to another and guides him or her to better self-understanding and greater emotional independence. But it is also possible to experience the relationship between pastor and counselee as a way of entering together into the loving silence of God and waiting there for the healing Word. The Holy Spirit is called the divine Counselor. He is actively present in the lives of those who come together to discern God's will. This is why human counselors should see as their primary task the work of helping their parishioners to become aware of the movements of the divine Counselor and encouraging them to follow these movements without fear. In this perspective, pastoral counseling is the attempt to lead fearful parishioners into the silence of God, and to help them feel at home there, trusting that they will slowly discover the healing presence of the Spirit.

This suggests that the human counselor needs to be very sensitive to the words of Scripture as words emerging from God's silence and directed to specific people in specific circumstances. When a word from Scripture is spoken by a counselor at that particular moment when the parishioner is able to hear it, it can indeed shatter huge walls of fear and open up unexpected perspectives. Such a word then brings with it the divine silence from which it came and to which it returns.

SILENCE AND ORGANIZING

Finally, I would like to stress the importance of silence in the ways a minister organizes his own life and that of others. In a society in which entertainment and distraction are such important preoccupations, ministers are also tempted to join the ranks of those who consider it their primary task to keep other people busy. It is easy to perceive the young and the elderly as people who need to be kept off the streets or on the streets. And ministers frequently find themselves in fierce competition with people and institutions who offer something more exciting to do than they do.

But our task is the opposite of distraction. Our task is to help people concentrate on the real but often hidden event of God's active presence in their lives. Hence, the question that must guide all organizing activity in a parish is not how to keep people busy, but how to keep them from being so busy that they can no longer hear the voice of God who speaks in silence.

Calling people together, therefore, means calling them away from the fragmenting and distracting wordiness of the dark world to that silence in which they can discover themselves, each other, and God. Thus organizing can be seen as the creation of a space where communion becomes possible and community can develop.

These examples of silence in preaching, counseling, and organizing are meant to illustrate how silence can help to determine the practical shape of our ministry. But let us not be too literal about silence. After all, silence of the heart is much more important than silence of the mouth. Abba Poemen said: "A man may seem to be silent, but if his heart is condemning others he is babbling ceaselessly. But there may be another who talks from morning till night and yet he is truly silent."[9]

Silence is primarily a quality of the heart that leads to ever-growing charity. Once a visitor said to a hermit, "Sorry for making you break your rule." But the monk answered, "My rule is to practice the virtue of hospitality towards those who come to see me and send them home in peace."[10]

Charity, not silence, is the purpose of the spiritual life and of ministry. About this all the Desert Fathers are unanimous.

Conclusion

THIS BRINGS ME to the end of my reflection on silence. In our chatty world, in which the word has lost its power to communicate, silence helps us to keep our mind and heart anchored in the future world and allows us to speak from there a creative and recreative word to the present world. Thus silence can also give us concrete guidance in the practice of our ministry.

---

9 Ward, *Sayings of the Desert Fathers*, 143.
10 Jean Bremond, *Les Pères Du Désert*, vol. 2 (Paris: Libraire Victor Lecoffre, 1927), 371.

There is little doubt that the Desert Fathers believed that simply not speaking is a very important practice. Too often our words are superfluous, inauthentic, and shallow. It is a good discipline to wonder in each new situation if people wouldn't be better served by our silence than by our words. But having acknowledged this, a more important message from the desert is that silence is above all a quality of the heart that can stay with us even in our conversation with others. It is a portable cell that we carry with us wherever we go. From it we speak to those in need and to it we return after our words have born fruit.

It is in this portable cell that we find ourselves immersed in the divine silence. The final question concerning our ministry of silence is not whether we say much or little, but whether our words call forth the caring silence of God himself. It is to this silence that we all are called: words are the instrument of the present world, but silence is the mystery of the future world.

Prayer

Introduction

WHEN ARSENIUS HAD asked for the second time, "Lord, lead me to the way of salvation," the voice that spoke to him not only said, "Be silent" but also, "Pray always." To pray always—this is the real purpose of the desert life. Solitude and silence can never be separated from the call to unceasing prayer. If solitude were primarily an escape from a busy job, and silence primarily an escape from a noisy milieu, they could easily become very self-centered forms of asceticism. But solitude and silence are for prayer. The Desert Fathers did not think of solitude as being alone, but as being alone with God. They did not think of silence as not speaking, but as listening to God. Solitude and silence are the context within which prayer is practiced.

The literal translation of the words "pray always" is "come to rest." The Greek word for rest is *hesychia*, and hesychasm is the term which refers to the spirituality of the desert. A hesychast is a man or a woman who seeks solitude and silence as the ways to unceasing prayer. The prayer of the hesychasts is a prayer of rest. This rest, however, has little to do with the absence of conflict or pain. It is a rest in God in the midst of a very intense daily struggle. Abba Anthony even says to a fellow monk that it belongs "to the great work of a man . . . to expect temptations to his last breath." *Hesychia*, the rest which flows from unceasing prayer, needs to be sought at all costs, even when the flesh is itchy, the world alluring, and the demons noisy. Mother Theodora, one of the Desert Mothers, makes this very clear: ". . . you should realize that as soon as you intend to live in peace, at once evil comes and weighs down your soul through *accidie* [sense of boredom], faintheartedness, and evil thoughts. It also attacks your body through sickness, debility, weakening of the knees, and all the members. It dissipates the strength of soul and body, so that one believes one is ill and no longer able to pray. But if we are vigilant, all these temptations fall away."[1]

Although weakness of the knees is not likely to be our main complaint, we ministers have no lack of excuses, often very sophisticated ones, for staying away from prayer. For us, however, prayer is as important as it was for the early Desert Fathers. Let me therefore explore the role of prayer in our daily lives. I will first express my suspicion that we tend to see prayer primarily as an activity of the mind. Then I would like to present the prayer of the hesychasts as a prayer of the heart. Finally, I want to show how this prayer of the heart calls for a discipline in order to make it the center of our daily ministry.

The Prayer of the Mind

VERY FEW MINISTERS will deny that prayer is important. They will not even deny that prayer is the most important dimension of their lives. But the fact is that most ministers pray very little or not at all. They realize that they should not forget to pray, that they should take time to pray, and that prayer should be a priority in their lives. But all these "shoulds" do not have the power to carry them over the enormous obstacle of their activism. There is always one more phone call, one more letter, one more visit, one more meeting, one more book, and one more party. Together these form an insurmountable pile of activities. The contrast between the great support for the idea of prayer and the lack of support for the practice of it is so blatantly visible that it becomes quite easy to believe in the ruses of the evil one which Amma Theodora described in such vivid detail.

---

1 Benedicta Ward, trans., *The Sayings of the Desert Fathers* (London & Oxford: Mowbrays, 1975), 71.

One of these demonic ruses is to make us think of prayer primarily as an activity of the mind that involves above all else our intellectual capacities. This prejudice reduces prayer to speaking with God or thinking about God.

For many of us prayer means nothing more than speaking with God. And since it usually seems to be a quite one-sided affair, prayer simply means talking to God. This idea is enough to create great frustrations. If I present a problem, I expect a solution; if I formulate a question, I expect an answer; if I ask for guidance, I expect a response. And when it seems, increasingly, that I am talking into the dark, it is not so strange that I soon begin to suspect that my dialogue with God is in fact a monologue. Then I may begin to ask myself: To whom am I really speaking, God or myself?

Sometimes the absence of an answer makes us wonder if we might have said the wrong kind of prayers, but mostly we feel taken, cheated, and quickly stop "this whole silly thing." It is quite understandable that we should experience speaking with real people, who need a word and who offer a response, as much more meaningful than speaking with a God who seems to be an expert at hide-and-seek.

But there is another viewpoint that can lead to similar frustrations. This is the viewpoint that restricts the meaning of prayer to thinking about God. Whether we call this prayer or meditation makes little difference. The basic conviction is that what is needed is to think thoughts about God and his mysteries. Prayer therefore requires hard mental work and is quite fatiguing, especially if reflective thinking is not one of our strengths. Since we already have so many other practical and pressing things on our minds, thinking about God becomes one more demanding burden. This is especially true because thinking about God is not a spontaneous event, while thinking about pressing concerns comes quite naturally.

Thinking about God makes God into a subject that needs to be scrutinized or analyzed. Successful prayer is thus prayer that leads to new intellectual discoveries about God. Just as a psychologist studies a case and seeks to gain insight by trying to find coherence in all the available data, so someone who prays well should come to understand God better by thinking deeply about all that is known about him.

In thinking about God, as with speaking to God, our frustration tolerance is quite low, and it does not take much to stop praying altogether. Reading a book or writing an article or sermon is a lot more satisfying than this mental wandering into the unknown.

Both these views of prayer are the products of a culture in which high value is placed on mastering the world through the intellect. The dominating idea has been that everything can be understood and that what can be understood can be controlled. God, too, is a problem that has a solution, and by strenuous efforts of the mind we will find it. It is therefore not so strange that the academic gown is the official garb of the minister, and that one of the main criteria for admission to the pulpit is a university degree.

This, of course, does not mean that the intellect has no place in the life of prayer, or that theological reflection and prayer are mutually exclusive. But we should not underestimate the intellectualism of the mainstream North American churches. If the public prayers of ministers inside as well as outside of church buildings are any indication of their prayer life, God is certainly busy attending seminars. How can we possibly expect anyone to find real nurture, comfort, and consolation from a prayer life that taxes the mind beyond its limits and adds one more exhausting activity to the many already scheduled ones?

During the last decade, many have discovered the limits of the intellect. More and more people have realized that what they need is much more than interesting sermons and interesting prayers. They wonder how they might really experience God. The charismatic movement is an obvious response to this new search for prayer. The popularity of Zen and the experimentation with encounter techniques in the churches are also indicative of a new desire to experience God. Suddenly we find ourselves surrounded by people saying, "Teach us to pray." And suddenly we become aware that we are being asked to show the way through a region that we do not know ourselves. The crisis of our prayer life is that our minds may be filled with ideas of God while our hearts remain far from him. Real prayer comes from the heart. It is about this prayer of the heart that the Desert Fathers teach us.

The Prayer of the Heart

HESYCHASTIC PRAYER, WHICH leads to that rest where the soul can dwell with God, is prayer of the heart. For us who are so mind-oriented it is of special importance to learn to pray with and from the heart. The Desert Fathers can show us the way. Although they do not offer any theory about prayer, their concrete stories and counsels offer the stones with which the later Orthodox spiritual writers have built a very impressive spirituality. The spiritual writers of Mount Sinai, Mount Athos, and the *startsi* of nineteenth-century Russia are all anchored in the tradition of the desert. We find the best formulation of the prayer of the heart in the words of the Russian mystic Theophan the Recluse: "To pray is to descend with the mind into the heart, and there to stand before the face of the Lord, ever-present, all-seeing, within you."[2] All through the centuries, this view of prayer has been central in hesychasm. Prayer is standing in the presence of God with the mind in the heart; that is, at that point of our being where there are no divisions or distinctions and where we are totally one. There God's Spirit dwells and there the great encounter takes place. There heart speaks to heart, because there we stand before the face of the Lord, all-seeing, within us.

We have to realize that here the word heart is used in its full biblical meaning. In our milieu the word heart has become a soft word. It refers to the seat of the sentimental life. Expressions such as "heartbroken" and "heartfelt" show that we often think of the heart as the warm place where the emotions are located in contrast to the cool intellect where our thoughts find their home. But the word heart in the Jewish-Christian tradition refers to the source of all physical, emotional, intellectual, volitional, and moral energies.

From the heart arise unknowable impulses as well as conscious feelings, moods, and wishes. The heart, too, has its reasons and is the center of perception and understanding. Finally, the heart is the seat of the will: it makes plans and comes to good decisions. Thus the heart is the central and unifying organ of our personal life. Our heart determines our per-

---

2 Timothy Ware, ed. *The Art of Prayer: An Orthodox Anthology* (London: Faber & Faber, 1966), 110.

sonality, and is therefore not only the place where God dwells but also the place to which Satan directs his fiercest attacks. It is this heart that is the place of prayer. The prayer of the heart is a prayer that directs itself to God from the center of the person and thus affects the whole of our humanness.

One of the Desert Fathers, Macarius the Great, says, "The chief task of the athlete [that is, the monk] is to enter into his heart."[3] This does not mean that the monk should try to fill his prayer with feeling, but that he should strive to let his prayer remodel the whole of his person. The most profound insight of the Desert Fathers is that entering into the heart is entering into the kingdom of God. In other words, the way to God is through the heart. Isaac the Syrian writes: "Try to enter the treasure chamber . . . that is within you and then you will discover the treasure chamber of heaven. For they are one and the same. If you succeed in entering one, you will see both. The ladder to this Kingdom is hidden inside you, in your soul. If you wash your soul clean of sin you will see there the rungs of the ladder which you may climb."[4] And John Carpathios says: "It takes great effort and struggle in prayer to reach that state of mind which is free from all disturbance; it is a heaven within the heart [literally 'endocardial'], the place, as the Apostle assures us, 'where Christ dwells in us' (2 Cor. 13:5)."[5]

The Desert Fathers in their sayings point us toward a very holistic view of prayer. They pull us away from our intellectualizing practices, in which God becomes one of the many problems we have to address. They show us that real prayer penetrates to the marrow of our soul and leaves nothing untouched. The prayer of the heart is a prayer that does not allow us to limit our relationship with God to interesting words or pious emotions. By its very nature such prayer transforms our whole being into Christ precisely because it opens the eyes of our soul to the truth of ourselves as well as to the truth of God. In our heart we come to see ourselves as sinners embraced by the mercy of God. It is this vision that makes us cry out, "Lord Jesus Christ, Son of the living God, have

---

3 Macarius the Great, cited in Irenée Hausherr, *The Name of Jesus*, trans. Charles Cummings (Kalamazoo, MI: Cistercian Publications, Inc. 1978), 314.

4 Macarius the Great, cited in Hausherr, *The Name of Jesus*, 314.

5 John Carpathios, cited in Hausherr, *The Name of Jesus*, 314.

mercy on me, a sinner." The prayer of the heart challenges us to hide absolutely nothing from God and to surrender ourselves unconditionally to his mercy.

Thus the prayer of the heart is the prayer of truth. It unmasks the many illusions about ourselves and about God and leads us into the true relationship of the sinner to the merciful God. This truth is what gives us the "rest" of the hesychast. To the degree that this truth anchors itself in our heart, we will be less distracted by worldly thoughts and more single-mindedly directed toward the Lord of both our hearts and the universe. Thus the words of Jesus, "Happy the pure in heart: they shall see God" (Matthew 5:8), will become real in our prayer. Temptations and struggles will remain to the end of our lives, but with a pure heart we will be restful even in the midst of a restless existence.

This raises the question of how to practice the prayer of the heart in a very restless ministry. It is to this question of discipline that we must now turn our attention.

Prayer and Ministry

HOW CAN WE, who are not monks and do not live in the desert, practice the prayer of the heart? How does the prayer of the heart affect our daily ministry?

The answer to these questions lies in the formulation of a definite discipline, a rule of prayer. There are three characteristics of the prayer of the heart that can help us to formulate this discipline:

- The prayer of the heart is nurtured by short, simple prayers.
- The prayer of the heart is unceasing.
- The prayer of the heart is all-inclusive.

NURTURED BY SHORT PRAYERS

In the context of our verbose culture it is significant to hear the Desert Fathers discouraging us from using too many words: "Abba Macarius was asked 'How should one pray?' The old man said, 'There is no need at all to make long discourses; it is enough to stretch out one's hand and say, "Lord, as you will, and as you know, have mercy." And if the conflict grows fiercer say: "Lord, help." He knows very well what we need and he shows us his mercy.'"[6]

John Climacus is even more explicit: "When you pray do not try to express yourself in fancy words, for often it is the simple, repetitious phrases of a little child that our Father in heaven finds most irresistible. Do not strive for verbosity lest your mind be distracted from devotion by a search for words. One phrase on the lips of the tax collector was enough to win God's mercy; one humble request made with faith was enough to save the good thief. Wordiness in prayer often subjects the mind to fantasy and dissipation; single words of their very nature tend to concentrate the mind. When you find satisfaction or compunction in a certain word of your prayer, stop at that point."[7]

This is a very helpful suggestion for us, people who depend so much on verbal ability. The quiet repetition of a single word can help us to descend with the mind into the heart. This repetition has nothing to do with magic. It is not meant to throw a spell on God or to force him into hearing us. On the contrary, a word or sentence repeated frequently can help us to concentrate, to move to the center, to create an inner stillness and thus to listen to the voice of God. When we simply try to sit silently and wait for God to speak to us, we find ourselves bombarded with endless conflicting thoughts and ideas. But when we use a very simple sentence such as "O God, come to my assistance," or "Jesus, master, have mercy on me," or a word such as "Lord" or "Jesus," it is easier to let the many distractions pass by without being misled by them. Such a simple, easily repeated prayer can slowly empty out our crowded interior life and create the quiet space where we can dwell with God. It can be like a ladder along which we can descend into the heart and ascend to God. Our choice of words depends on our needs and the circumstances of the moment, but it is best to use words from Scripture.

This way of simple prayer, when we are faithful to it and practice it at regular times, slowly leads us to an experience of rest and opens us to God's active presence. Moreover, we can take this prayer with us into a

---

6 Ward, *Sayings of the Desert Fathers*, 111.
7 John Climacus, cited in Hausherr, *The Name of Jesus*, 286.

very busy day. When, for instance, we have spent twenty minutes in the early morning sitting in the presence of God with the words "The Lord is my Shepherd" they may slowly build a little nest for themselves in our heart and stay there for the rest of our busy day. Even while we are talking, studying, gardening, or building, the prayer can continue in our heart and keep us aware of God's ever-present guidance. The discipline is not directed toward coming to a deeper insight into what it means that God is called our Shepherd, but toward coming to the inner experience of God's shepherding action in whatever we think, say, or do.

UNCEASING

The second characteristic of the prayer of the heart is that it is unceasing. The question of how to follow Paul's command to "pray without ceasing" has had a central place in hesychasm from the time of the Desert Fathers to nineteenth-century Russia. There are many examples of this concern from both ends of the hesychastic tradition.

During the period of the Desert Fathers, there was a pietistic sect called the Messalians. These were people who had an overly spiritualized approach to prayer and considered manual work condemnable for a monk. Some of the monks of this sect went to see Abba Lucius. "The old man asked them, 'What is your manual work?' They said, 'We do not touch manual work but as the Apostle says, we pray without ceasing.' The old man asked them if they did not eat and they replied they did. So he said to them, 'When you are eating who prays for you then?' Again he asked them if they did not sleep and they replied they did. And he said to them, 'When you are asleep, who prays for you then?' They could not find any answer to give him. He said to them, 'Forgive me, but you do not act as you speak. I will show you how, while doing my manual work, I pray without interruption. I sit down with God, soaking my reeds and plaiting my ropes, and I say, "God, have mercy on me; according to your great goodness and according to the multitude of your mercies, save me from my sins."' So he asked them if this were not prayer and they replied it was. Then he said to them, 'So when I have spent the whole day working and praying, making thirteen pieces of money more or less, I put two pieces of money outside the door and I pay for my food with the rest of the money. He who takes the two pieces of money prays for me when I am eating and when I am sleeping; so, by the grace of God, I fulfill the precept to pray without ceasing.'"[8]

This story offers a very practical answer to the question "How can I pray without ceasing while I am busy with many other things?" The answer involves the neighbor. Through my charity my neighbor becomes a partner in my prayer and makes it into unceasing prayer.

In the nineteenth century, when the problems with the Messalians did not exist, a more mystical response was given. We find it in the famous story about a Russian peasant called *The Way of the Pilgrim*. It begins as follows: "By the grace of God I am a Christian man, but by my actions a great sinner . . . On the twenty-fourth Sunday after Pentecost I went to church to say my prayers there during the Liturgy. The first Epistle of St. Paul to the Thessalonians was being read, and among other words I heard these—'*Pray without ceasing*' [1 Thessalonians 5:17]. It was this text, more than any other, which forced itself upon my mind, and I began to think how it was possible to pray without ceasing, since a man has to concern himself with other things also in order to make a living."[9] The peasant went from church to church to listen to sermons but did not find the answer he desired. Finally he met a holy *staretz* who said to him: "'Ceaseless interior prayer is a continual yearning of the human spirit towards God. To succeed in this consoling exercise we must pray more often to God to teach us to pray without ceasing. Pray more, and pray more fervently. It is prayer itself which will reveal to you how it can be achieved unceasingly; but it will take some time.'"[10] Then the holy *staretz* taught the peasant the Jesus Prayer: "Lord Jesus Christ, have mercy on me." While traveling as a pilgrim through Russia, the peasant repeats this prayer thousands of times with his lips. He even considers the Jesus Prayer to be his true companion. And then one day he has the feeling that the prayer by its own action passes from his lips to his heart. He says: ". . . it seemed as though my heart in its ordinary beating began

---

8 Ward, *Sayings of the Desert Fathers*, 102.
9 R. M. French, trans., *The Way of the Pilgrim* (New York: The Seabury Press, 1965), 1.
10 French, *The Way of the Pilgrim*, 2–3.

to say the words of the Prayer within at each beat . . . I gave up saying the Prayer with my lips. I simply listened carefully to what my heart was saying."[11]

Here we learn of another way of arriving at unceasing prayer. The prayer continues to pray within me even when I am talking with others or concentrating on manual work. The prayer has become the active presence of God's Spirit guiding me through life.

Thus we see how, through charity and the activity of the Prayer of Jesus in our heart, our whole day can become a continual prayer. I am not suggesting that we should imitate the monk Lucius or the Russian pilgrim, but I do suggest that we, too, in our busy ministry should be concerned to pray without ceasing, so that whatever we eat, whatever we drink, whatever we do at all, we do for the glory of God. (See 1 Cor. 10:31). To love and work for the glory of God cannot remain an idea about which we think once in a while. It must become an interior, unceasing doxology.

ALL-INCLUSIVE

A final characteristic of the prayer of the heart is that it includes all our concerns. When we enter with our mind into our heart and there stand in the presence of God, then all our mental preoccupations become prayer. The power of the prayer of the heart is precisely that through it all that is on our mind becomes prayer.

When we say to people, "I will pray for you," we make a very important commitment. The sad thing is that this remark often remains nothing but a well-meant expression of concern. But when we learn to descend with our mind into our heart, then all those who have become part of our lives are led into the healing presence of God and are touched by him in the center of our being. We are speaking here about a mystery for which words are inadequate. It is the mystery that the heart, which is the center of our being, is transformed by God into his own heart, a heart large enough to embrace the entire universe. Through prayer we can carry in our heart all human pain and sorrow, all conflicts and agonies, all torture and war, all hunger, loneliness, and misery, not because of

11 French, *The Way of the Pilgrim*, 19–20.

some great psychological or emotional capacity, but because God's heart has become one with ours.

Here we catch sight of the meaning of Jesus' words, "Shoulder my yoke and learn from me, for I am gentle and humble in heart, and you will find rest for your souls. Yes, my yoke is easy and my burden light" (Matthew 11:29–30). Jesus invites us to accept his burden, which is the burden of the whole world, a burden that includes human suffering in all times and places. But this divine burden is light, and we can carry it when our heart has been transformed into the gentle and humble heart of our Lord.

Here we can see the intimate relationship between prayer and ministry. The discipline of leading all our people with their struggles into the gentle and humble heart of God is the discipline of prayer as well as the discipline of ministry. As long as ministry only means that we worry a lot about people and their problems; as long as it means an endless number of activities which we can hardly coordinate, we are still very much dependent on our own narrow and anxious heart. But when our worries are led to the heart of God and there become prayer, then ministry and prayer become two manifestations of the same all-embracing love of God.

We have seen how the prayer of the heart is nurtured by short prayers, is unceasing and all-inclusive. These three characteristics show how the prayer of the heart is the breath of the spiritual life and of all ministry. Indeed, this prayer is not simply an important activity, but the very center of the new life which we want to represent and to which we want to introduce our people. It is clear from the characteristics of the prayer of the heart that it requires a personal discipline. To live a prayerful life we cannot do without specific prayers. We need to say them in such a way that we can listen better to the Spirit praying in us. We need to continue to include in our prayer all the people with and for whom we live and work. This discipline will help us to move from a distracting, fragmentary, and often frustrating ministry toward an integrating, holistic, and very gratifying ministry. It will not make ministry easy, but simple; it will not make it sweet and pious, but spiritual; it will not make it painless and without struggles, but restful in the true hesychastic sense.

Conclusion

IN OUR MIND-ORIENTED world, we will need a serious discipline to come to a prayer of the heart in which we can listen to the guidance of Him who prays in us. The great emphasis on prayer in ministry is not meant as an incentive to be less involved with people or to leave untouched our society with its many struggles. Prayer as understood by the hesychasts helps us to discern which of our ministerial activities are indeed for the glory of God and which are primarily for the glory of our unconverted ego. The prayer of the heart offers us a new sensitivity that enables us to separate the chaff from the wheat in our ministry and thus to become much less ambiguous witnesses of Jesus Christ.

The prayer of the heart is indeed the way to the purity of heart that gives us eyes to see the reality of our existence. This purity of heart allows us to see more clearly, not only our own needy, distorted, and anxious self but also the caring face of our compassionate God. When that vision remains clear and sharp, it will be possible to move into the midst of a tumultuous world with a heart at rest. It is this restful heart that will attract those who are groping to find their way through life. When we have found our rest in God we can do nothing other than minister. God's rest will be visible wherever we go and whoever we meet. And before we speak any words, the Spirit of God, praying in us, will make his presence known and gather people into a new body, the body of Christ himself.

EPILOGUE

THE QUESTION WITH which I started this exploration of desert spirituality and contemporary ministry was: "How can we minister in an apocalyptic situation?" In a period of history dominated by the growing fear of a war that cannot be won and an increasing sense of impotence, the question of ministry is very urgent.

As a response to this question I have presented the words, "Flee from the world, be silent and pray always," words spoken to the Roman aristocrat Arsenius who asked God how to be saved. Solitude, silence, and unceasing prayer form the core concepts of the spirituality of the desert. I consider them to be of great value for us who are ministers as we approach the end of the second millennium of Christianity.

Solitude shows us the way to let our behavior be shaped not by the compulsions of the world but by our new mind, the mind of Christ. Silence prevents us from being suffocated by our wordy world and teaches us to speak the Word of God. Finally, unceasing prayer gives solitude and silence their real meaning. In unceasing prayer, we descend with the mind into the heart. Thus we enter through our heart into the heart of God, who embraces all of history with his eternally creative and recreative love.

But does not this spirituality of the desert close our eyes to the cruel realities of our time? No. On the contrary, solitude, silence, and prayer allow us to save ourselves and others from the shipwreck of our self-destructive society. The temptation is to go mad with those who are mad and to go around yelling and screaming, telling everyone where to go, what to do, and how to behave. The temptation is to become so involved in the agonies and ecstasies of the last days that we will drown together with those we are trying to save.

Jesus himself has warned us:

> "Take care that no one deceives you; because many will come using my name and saying, 'I am the Christ,' and they will deceive many. You will hear of wars and rumors of wars; do not be alarmed, for this is something that must happen, but the end will not be yet. For nation will fight against nation, and kingdom against kingdom. There will be famines and earthquakes here and there . . . many will fall away; men will betray one another and hate one another. Many false prophets will arise; they will deceive many, and with the increase of lawlessness, love in most men will grow cold; but those who stand firm to the end will be saved. This Good News of the kingdom will be proclaimed to the whole world as a witness to all the nations. And then the end will come" (Matthew 24:4–14).

These words of Jesus have a striking relevance. It is our great task to stand firm to the end, to proclaim the Good News to the whole world, and to hold on to him who rose victorious from the grave. The raging torrents of our tumultuous times have made it very hard not to lose sight of the light and not to let ourselves drift away into the darkness. The powers and principalities not only reveal their presence in the unsettling political and economic situation of our day but also they show their disruptive presence in the most intimate places of our lives. Our faithfulness in relationships is severely tested, and our inner sense of belonging is questioned again and again. Our anger and greed show their strength with added vehemence, and our desire to indulge ourselves in the despairing hedonism of the moment proves to be stronger than ever.

Yes, the dangers are very real. It is not impossible that we might become false prophets shouting, "Look, here is the Christ" or "He is there" (Matthew 24:23). It is not impossible that we might deceive people with our self-made assurances, and that not only others' love but also our own might grow cold. Our compulsive, wordy, and mind-oriented world has a firm grip on us, and we need a very strong and persistent discipline not to be squeezed to death by it.

By their solitude, silence, and unceasing prayer the Desert Fathers show us the way. These disciplines will teach us to stand firm, to speak words of salvation, and to approach the new millennium with hope, courage, and confidence.

When we have been remodeled into living witnesses of Christ through solitude, silence, and prayer, we will no longer have to worry about whether we are saying the right thing or making the right gesture, because then Christ will make his presence known even when we are not aware of it.

Let me conclude with one more desert story.

"Three Fathers used to go and visit blessed Anthony every year and two of them used to discuss their thoughts and the salvation of their souls with him, but the third always remained silent and did not ask him anything. After a long time, Abba Anthony said to him: 'You often come here to see me, but you never ask me anything,' and the other replied, 'It is enough to see you, Father.'"[1]

This story is a fit ending to this book. By the time people feel that just seeing us is ministry, words such as these will no longer be necessary.

---

1 Benedicta Ward, trans., *The Sayings of the Desert Fathers* (London & Oxford: Mowbrays, 1975), 6.

ACKNOWLEDGMENTS

THIS BOOK FOUND its beginning in a seminar at Yale Divinity School on the spirituality of the desert. It was one of the most stimulating seminars I have ever been part of. We were five women and eleven men. We represented very different religious traditions: Unitarian, Disciples of Christ, Baptist, Presbyterian, Dutch Reformed, Christian Reformed, Episcopalian, Roman Catholic, and Greek Orthodox. In age we ranged from early twenties to late forties and in geographical background from the United States to Ireland, Holland and Australia. Together we tried to discover what the Desert Fathers and Mothers of the fourth century have to say to men and women who want to be ministers of Jesus Christ in the twentieth century.

As we exchanged ideas and experiences in response to the stories from the desert, we gradually came to see the "way of the heart" as the way that united us in spite of our many historical, theological, and psychological differences. It was this discovery that encouraged me to present "the way of the heart" as Convocation lectures at Perkins School of Theology in Dallas and at the National Convention of Pastoral Counselors in Denver. I am very grateful for the many responses I received during these occasions.

A special word of thanks goes to Virginia Yohe and Carol Plantinga for their secretarial assistance, to Stephen Leahy, Phil Zaeder, Fred Bratman, and Robert Moore for their editorial comments, to John Eudes Bamberger for his encouragement, and to Jim Antal for offering his beautiful photograph for the jacket.

I would also like to express my deep gratitude to all the members of the seminar: George Anastos, Kim Brown, Colman Cooke, Susan Geissler, Frank Gerry, Christine Koetsveld, Joseph Núñez, Robert Parenteau, Donald Postema, Kathy Stockton, Marjorie Thompson, Steven Tsichlis, Joshua Wootton, and Mich Zeman. Their many rich and varied responses to the words from the desert enabled me to present the book as a book for all who are committed to the Christian ministry.

I dedicate this book to John Mogabgab, who taught the course with me. I do so in gratitude not only for his invaluable contributions to the seminar and this book, but also, and most of all, for the five years during which we worked together at Yale Divinity School. His deep friendship and support have made these years a true gift of God.

Intimacy

To John Eudes

INTIMACY
CONTENTS

INTRODUCTION

THE SOURCES OF the following chapters are many: teaching, counseling, discussing, chatting, partying, celebrating, and most of all just being around. Each chapter is written because someone—a student, a teacher, a minister, a priest, a religious brother or sister—asked a question. I wrote on different occasions, for different people, with different questions in mind. I wrote not to solve a problem or to formulate a theory but to respond to men and women who wanted to share their struggles in trying to find their vocation in this chaotic world.

Looking back on the variety of questions and concerns that confronted me, I saw a unity in the many subjects that justifies bringing them together in one book. First of all, there is a unity of perspective, which is pastoral. Although the language and the approach might be considered psychological, the perspective is that of a priest who wonders how to understand what he sees in the light of God's work with people. Secondly, there is a unifying theme. It has become increasingly clear to me that underlying the many concerns there was one main question: "How can I find a creative and fulfilling intimacy in my relationship with God and my fellow human beings?" How can one person develop a fruitful intimacy with another person? What does intimacy mean in the life of a celibate priest or in a community of religious? How can we be intimate with God during moments of celebration or silent prayer?

It is not surprising that many of these questions are raised in a university milieu, dominated by young adults. Erik Erikson has stressed how the careful balance between intimacy and distance is the most crucial psychological task of those coming out of their adolescence and trying to develop lasting and productive relationships. Today, however, the struggle for intimacy is no longer limited to one age group. In the midst of a competitive and demanding world, people of all ages have become painfully aware of their deep-seated desire for a place of intimacy. This desire is felt as much by married people and by priests and religious committed to a celibate life as it is by dating students.

Therefore this book can be considered a book about the inner life. It does not deal with the burning issues that have become such a real part of our daily life: inflation, unemployment, crime, hunger, poverty and the threat of nuclear war. But it tries to address itself directly to what seems to pervade all these problems to some degree: people's seldom articulated and often unrecognized desire for a real home in this world. For that reason, I would like to call this a book about intimacy.

THE CONTEXT

1

From Magic to Faith

Religious Growth in Psychological Perspective

DURING THE YEAR we are exposed to many events, trivial and significant, which usually don't raise questions unless we pay some special attention to them:

A paratrooper, Captain Ridgway, rowed from Cape Cod to Ireland with his friend. Overwhelmed by the greatness of the ocean and the incredible forces of nature, he found that the medal given to him by the Cape Codders kept him together and gave him words to pray.

One priest, smiling, said to another priest as they left a packed college church at the end of the semester, "The finals are the best proof that man is basically religious."

Little Johnny says, "Hey, Dad, you can't make President Kennedy alive. But God can, can't He? Cause he can do everything!" And we think: "Isn't little Johnny cute?"

You read about an astronaut, symbol of modern science, smuggling a cross into orbit, and you just don't know what to think about it.

Or you meet a student, coming from a deeply religious family where God was the source of strength and happiness, suddenly asking questions so deep and fundamental that everything that had happened before seems completely irrelevant to him.

Then you read about a group of young men leaving their good jobs, their comfortable homes and sometimes even their families to go to the most desperate places of this world, to live with people they don't even as yet know.

What about all this? Magic or Faith? Superstition or contact with ultimate reality? Something to avoid or to aspire to? To clarify these questions let us look at the life of a man from the time he is folded in the safe womb of his mother to the moment he is walking around, broad-shouldered, with his thumbs pushed behind his leather belt, curiously looking around at this world and what lies beyond. We will call this trip "from Magic to Faith." We all make this trip, and it might be worthwhile to look at it from a distance.

In each phase of a man's life we will stress one particular aspect of our development which is a constituent of a mature religious sentiment.

A. THE FIRST FIVE YEARS OF LIFE

During the first five years of life we have to take three big steps out of the magical world in which we are born.

I. During the first 18 months we come to the somewhat frustrating discovery that we are not the center of the world.

Most of you will agree that there are people and things outside of us which will continue to exist even when we don't. This is, however, not so self-evident as it seems. It is only through a long and often frustrating experience that we are able to discover the objective world. As a baby in the mother's womb, everything is there for us; mother is a part of ourself. Later, it can be quite a painful experience to discover that our cry does not create the milk, that our smile does not produce the mother, that our needs do not evoke their own satisfaction. Only gradually do we discover our mother as the other, as not just a part of ourself. Every time we experience that we are not ruling the world by our feelings, thoughts and actions, we are forced to realize that there are other persons, things and events which have their autonomy.

Therefore, the first step out of the magical world is the discovery of an objective reality. It can happen that we reach this objectivity only partially. Although we slowly unfold and become able to stand on our own feet and point to the things around us as objective realities available for our curious mind, this may not happen so easily in the religious dimension. Many mature, successful men in this life often might still treat God as part of themselves. God is the factotum which comes in handy in times of illness, shock, final exams, in every situation in which we feel insecure. And if it does not work, the only reaction may be to cry louder. Far from becoming the Other, whose existence does not depend on mine, he might remain the easy frame which fits best around the edges of my security. Great anxiety, caused by internal or external storms, can sometimes force us to regress to this level of religion. This regression may even save our life, as it did Captain Ridgway's. It gives us something to hold on to, a medal or a candle which can keep us together. It may be a very helpful form of religion; but certainly it is not a mature form of religion.

II. The second step out of our magical world is the formation of the language. Somewhere between our 18th month of life and our 3rd birthday we started mumbling our first sounds which slowly developed into words, sentences, and a language. Although it may be disappointing that there are things around us which do not belong to us, by words we can take revenge, because our first words give us a mysterious power over things. Like an American who is excited to discover that his first French word, *garçon*, really brings the waiter to his table, the child experiences not so much the mastery of words but mastery of objects. It takes quite a while before we can detach the word from the object and give it a symbolic function.

The magical word gives us power not only over objects but also over our own instinctual impulses. Before we had words we couldn't resist the temptation of grabbing flowers in daddy's garden. But by the word "flower" we became able to substitute the act of grabbing and touching, and with our hands clasped together at our back we could then say: "nice flower, no touch."[1]

Well, religion is full of words. Long litanies, exclamations and often-repeated formulas play a very important role in many religions. What concerns us here is that this use of words often does not transcend the magical phase. Instead of being the free and creative expression of deep

---

1 Selma H. Fraiberg, *The Magic Years* (Charles Scribner's Sons: 1959).

realities communicable to our fellow man, the words may become a substitute for reality, a subtle form of power over the capricious movements of our gods, our devils, or our own impulses.

Is there not something of this magical world left in us if we feel that we will be saved if we say our prayers every day, or if we at least keep the custom of the three Hail Marys before going to bed? It seems difficult to overcome this word-magic. We feel pretty good if we have fulfilled our obligation, mumbled our table prayers, raced through our rosary or recited our breviary. We seem to be saying, "God cannot do anything to us now. We did what he asked us to do, and now it is his turn to pay us back." Our prayers give us some power over God, instead of engaging us in a real dialogue.

III. The third step out of the magical world is the formation of our conscience. This is the great event between our third and fifth years. When we had learned that objects existed outside ourselves which kept existing even if we did not, and when we had experienced that words were not omnipotent tools to manipulate the world around us, we were still confronted with a much more important step: the step from daddy to us. "I am not going to hit my nasty little sister, not because Daddy does not like that, but because I don't like it, because it is bad." The external disciplinary agent, daddy, mommy, priest, etc., slowly is converted into an internal policeman.

Conscience becomes possible by the process of identification. We develop the capacity to interiorize certain aspects of the personality of another person, to make them a part of ourselves. In the case of moral development, we take over judgments, standards and values of beloved persons and incorporate them into our own personality.

Or is there something else happening at the same time? During those first four years of life we felt that daddy could do everything, that he was omnipotent, that he could solve all the problems and lift all the weights. In our fantasy daddy is the greatest athlete in the world, he builds houses, writes books, creates bicycles and is able to get everything for me, if only he wants to. Well, we became disappointed sooner or later. Daddy turns out to be a square, after all. We couldn't really depend on him any longer. How could we solve this problem?

Interiorization might not solve the whole problem. The need for an omnipotent Father who gives us love, shelter and protection, in whose arms we can hide and feel safe, might simply be too intense. The magical father couldn't be done without, we needed him too much, and therefore,.he stayed with us in another name: GOD. And so we thought that if daddy could not make President Kennedy live again, at least God could do it.

When Sigmund Freud wrote his *Future of an Illusion,* he irritated and deeply disturbed the faithful, by saying that religion is the continuation of infantile life and that God is the projection of the ever-present desire for shelter.

Freud's task was to cure people, that is, to make them become more mature. And looking at the many people in his office in Vienna who suffered from their religion more than they were saved by it, he tried to unmask their projections. The psychiatrist Rumke summarizes Freud's position when he writes: "When man matures completely he realizes that his God image, often a father-God image, is a reincarnation of the infantile worldly father, loved and feared. God is apparently no more than a projection. If that which blocks his growth is taken away, the image fades. Man distinguishes good from evil according to his own standards. He has conquered the remainder of his neurosis, which was all that his religion was."[2] What is important in this context is that Freud was not altogether wrong. We often stay in this magical and infantile world in which God is as nice to have around as the comforting blanket of Linus in "Peanuts." For many, religion is really not very much more than Freud found it to be, and for all of us, so many of our religious experiences are clothed in images of childhood that it is often very difficult to say where our infantilism ends and our religion begins.

It seems appropriate here to ask a critical question: Is the idea of God an infantile prolongation of our ideal father image, or is our receptivity to the child-father idea the result of our more profound and primary relationship with God? Indeed the basic criticism of Freud proposed by the German psychiatrist Binswanger is a reversal: God is not the prolongation of the child's relationship with his dad, but the child's feeling for

2 H. C. Rümke, *The Psychology of Unbelief* (Sheed & Ward: 1962).

his dad is a concretizing of an idea born of his most fundamental relation to his Creator. In other words, we couldn't love our father if God had not loved us first. But here we have left the field of psychology.[3]

In one way we have to agree with Freud: in so far as our God is a pure surrogate for our conscience and a preventative to the development of a rational mind, a mature self and an autonomous individual, it is only a sign of good health and insight to throw our God out as a disease called neurosis. It is even sad to notice how few have the courage to do this.

Healthy development means a gradual movement out of the magical world. Even when the development takes place in other areas, our religion easily remains on this immature level. In that case, God remains the magical pacifier whose existence depends on ours. Prayers remain tools to manipulate him in our direction and religion is nothing more than a big, soft bed on which we doze away and deny the hardships of life. Our religious sentiment will never be mature 1) if God is not the Other, 2) if prayer is not a dialogue, and 3) if religion is not a source of creative autonomy.

B. SCHOOL AGE: 5–12 YEARS

When we were about five years old we went to school. In the small unit of our family the most essential behavioral patterns were pretty well established. Our first experiences of trust, happiness, fear, friendship, joy and disappointment and our first reactions to these experiences took place in our parental home. But then we entered a new world. In school we met other boys and girls who also had parents and homes, and then we had to find out if what we learned at home really worked. In many ways our years in grade school were years in which our major patterns of behavior were fortified, modified, enlarged or disrupted, years in which we experienced success and failure in a larger society than we were used to during the first years of our lives.

Religion in our society is generally a private affair. As soon as we heard about the new math, the history of man, as soon as we learned how to do things ourselves and how to be master of our world, the chance was great that religion became isolated as a separate reality, good for Sunday

3 H. C. Rümke, *The Psychology of Unbelief.*

and the pious hour of the week but not really related to all the new things we heard about this and other worlds. Allport says maturity comes only when a growing intelligence somehow is animated by the desire not to suffer arrested development, but to keep pace with the intake of relevant experience. "In many people, so far as the religious sentiment is concerned, this inner demand is absent. Finding their childhood religion to have comforting value and lacking outside pressure, they cling to an essentially juvenile formulation."[4]

A mature religion is integral in nature—that means that it is flexible enough to integrate all new knowledge within its frame of reference and keep pace with all the new discoveries of the human mind. It indeed takes the cross into the space craft. Going to school means starting on the road to science, and if religion does not follow the same road with an open and critical eye, the grown man who flies the ocean in superjets might be religiously still content with his tricycle. Essential for mature religion is the constant willingness to shift gears, to integrate new insights and to revise our positions.

C. ADOLESCENCE: 12–18 YEARS

With adolescence, we entered into a new and very critical phase of our development. Some of us might have experienced a sudden and dramatic change, others gradually entered the new realities hardly noticing the entry.

Suddenly or gradually, we were confronted with the fact that not only is life outside of us very complicated but life inside of us is just as complicated, or even more so. Until this time we were very curious about all the things going on around us, were excited by all the new things we saw and heard; but then we sensed deep and, often, very strange and disturbing feelings inside. New, often dark, urges seemed to push us without our understanding. We were overwhelmed by feelings of intense joy and happiness, so much so that we didn't know what it meant. Or we were victims of a wish to die, to kill, to hurt, to destroy. We felt that we were torn apart sometimes by the most conflicting feelings and ideas; love and hate, desire to embrace and desire to kill; desire to give and desire to take.

---

4 Gordon Allport, *The Individual and His Religion* (Macmillan: 1950).

Perhaps we touch here one of the most important crossroads of our religious development. The question is: can we accept and understand our inner conflicts in such a way that by clarification and understanding they become a source of maturation of our religious sentiment? Very often we fail. Very often religion has become identified with cleanliness, purity, the perfect life—and every feeling which seems to throw black spots on our white sheet seems to be antireligious. In that case we cannot allow ourselves to have strong sexual urges and cruel fantasies and aggressive desires. Religion says: "No!" Do not curse, do not steal, do not kill, do not masturbate, do not gossip, do not, do not, do not . . . Then teachers who tell us to be nice, obedient and lovable start to irritate us no end. Nobody really seems to understand this strange new world of internal feelings which make us feel solemnly unique but, at the same time, horribly lonesome.

Many of us remember how deeply we wanted understanding, how difficult it was to express ourselves and how few people really were close to us. A feeling of shame and guilt often made us feel terribly lonesome and we felt that we were hypocrites whom nobody would love if they really knew how we felt. Many things are possible in this period. We might feel that religion was so oppressive and depressive, so far away from all our experience, so authoritarian and negativistic that the only way of resolving the conflict was to break away from it. Some became sick of the shouting priest in the pulpit, others never felt any understanding for their disturbing feelings or could no longer stand the obvious hypocrisy of many churchgoers, and many dropped away—some slowly, others in open rebellion.

But there is another reaction, perhaps more harmful. This is the tendency to deny and repress drastically the other side, the dark wishes, the unwelcome shadow. Then we are saying, "After all, we are clean, pure, sinless, and we want to keep our record spotless." We want to stay in complete control of ourselves, never have an evil thought, never curse, never get drunk, never fail, but always remain perfect, saintly and, in a way, so self-content that we don't leave anything to God to be saved. We walk through life as if we had swallowed an Easter candle, rigid and tense, always afraid that things will get out of hand.

This reaction is just as harmful as open rebellion, or even more so, because it blocks our way to religious maturation. But there is a way to maturity in which we can say, "Sure, I have weak spots but that does not make me weak. I have ugly thoughts but that does not make me ugly." This is the realization that we have to tolerate the weeds in order to have good wheat. If we try to eradicate all the weeds we might also pull out the precious wheat. A man who is never mad nor angry can never be passionately in favor of anything either. A man who never loses his temper might have nothing worthwhile to lose after all; he who is never down seldom enjoys himself either. He who never takes a risk might never fail, but he also will never succeed.

It is very difficult for each of us to believe in Christ's words, "I did not come to call the virtuous, but sinners. . . ." Perhaps no psychologist has stressed the need of self-acceptance as the way to self-realization so much as Carl Jung. For Jung, self-realization meant the integration of the shadow. It is the growing ability to allow the dark side of our personality to enter into our awareness and thus prevent a one-sided life in which only that which is presentable to the outside world is considered as a real part of ourselves. To come to an inner unity, totality and wholeness, every part of our self should be accepted and integrated. Christ represents the light in us. But Christ was crucified between two murderers and we cannot deny them, and certainly not the murderers who live in us.

This is a task for life, but during our adolescence we had a real chance to test our religious sentiment in this respect. The conflict is obvious; the solution is not rebellion nor repression, but integration.

D. THE YOUNG ADULT

Meanwhile, we went to college. What happens in college? College is the period between homes. We have left our parental home and have not yet committed ourselves to a home of our own. We have gone a safe distance from all things Mom and Dad always had to say but we also keep a safe distance from those who want to take away this wonderful vacation from home life. We don't have to worry any more about how to find a compromise between our own ideas and feelings and those of our parents, but on the other hand, we are not yet responsible to any one person in particular. We feel that the time of being educated is over but we are not quite ready to start educating others. In short, we live between two homes, and in a certain way this is the period of the greatest freedom of our life.

In college we also develop a new way of thinking. We learn a scientific approach; the key term is: hypothesis; the criterion: probability; and the tool: experimentation. Only on the basis of an experiment are we willing to accept and reject, and only with a sense of relativity do we want to speak about certainty. For our religious development the college years can become the most ideal time to make our religious ideas and values from "second-hand fittings into first-hand fittings" (Allport). We may develop enough self-acceptance and creative distance to do some responsible experimentation.

During the college years, a new important aspect of a mature religious sentiment can develop: "I can be sure without being cocksure" (Allport). As we enter college we take with us many religious concepts and ideas which seemed obvious, and which we never questioned. The question is, whether or not we have the courage to put question marks behind many things; if we can allow ourselves to doubt without losing all grounds. Only he who feels safe in this world can take risks, only he who has a basic trust in the value of life is free to ask many questions without feeling threatened. Trust creates the possibility of a religion of search, which makes a commitment possible without certainty. By the basic trust in the meaning of life we are able to live with a hypothesis, without the need of absolute certainty.

The man who never had any religious doubts during his college years probably walked around blindfolded; he who never experimented with his traditional values and ideas was probably more afraid than free; he who never put to a test any of dad's and mom's advice probably never developed a critical mind; and he who never became irritated by the many ambiguities, ambivalences and hypocrisies in his religious milieu probably never was really satisfied with anything either. But he who did, took a risk. The risk of embarrassing not only his parents but also his friends, the risk of feeling alienated from his past and of becoming irritated by everything religious, even the word "God." The risk even of the searing loneliness which Jesus Christ suffered when He cried, "God, my God, why have you forsaken me?"

In college we can often discover, with pain and frustration, that a mature religious man is very close to the agnostic, and often we have difficulty in deciding which name expresses better our state of mind: agnostic or searching believer. Perhaps they are closer than we tend to think.

E. THE ADULT MAN

One facet of adulthood which has special significance for our religious attitude is that the mature adult mind is characterized by a unifying philosophy of life. If we could look at our daily life from above, we might wonder what we are so busy for, so excited about, so concerned with. We might ask with Alfie, "After all, what is it all about?" And if there is no real answer to this question, the most honest reaction might be: boredom. Many people who no longer see the meaning of their lives, their daily, often utterly dull, activities, feel bored. Boredom is the dullness of life felt all the way to your stomach. It is the lukewarm quality of daily life, which manifests itself in the repetition of the "I don't care" phrase. Now if we ask ourselves what boredom really means we might say, "It is the isolation of experience." That is to say, we have an experience in life which in no way seems to be connected with the past or the future. Every day seems to be just another day, indifferent, colorless and bleak, just like every other day. This is the mentality in which we need "kicks"—very short, artificially induced upheavals which, for a while, pull us out of our boredom without really giving any meaning to past or future.

Boredom is the disconnected life, filled with thousands of different words, ideas, thoughts and acts which seem like so many pieces of garbage in stagnant waters. Boredom, which so easily leads to depression, often can become a pervasive feeling, a creeping temptation, difficult to shake off. And certainly, if we have finished school and have a family and a job, this feeling of deep boredom might overwhelm us with the question, "So what?" Now we have everything, and we will be dead, gone and forgotten in a couple of years, perhaps only remembered because of our oddities and idiosyncracies!

It is in this perspective that a mature, religious sentiment fulfills a creative function. Because it has a unifying power, it brings together the many isolated realities of life and casts them into one meaningful whole. The thousand disconnected pieces fall together and show a pattern which we couldn't see before. All the individuals in the card section of the stadium don't seem to make sense to each other, but from a certain distance, and in a certain perspective, they form a very meaningful word. Just so in a unifying perspective, the many facets of life prove to belong together and point in a definite direction. That is what we refer to if we say that a mature religion gives meaning to life, gives direction, reveals a goal and creates a task to be accomplished. It can make us leave job, country and family to dedicate our life to the suffering poor. It can make us bury ourselves in silence, isolation and contemplation in a Trappist monastery.

This new perspective is what we can call faith. It does not create new things but it adds a new dimension to the basic realities of life. It brings our fragmented personality into a meaningful whole, unifies our divided self. It is the source of inspiration for a searching mind, the basis for a creative community and a constant incentive for an on-going renewal of life.

So we come to the end of our trip from Magic to Faith. We started folded up in our mother's womb, one with the world in which we lived. We slowly unfolded out of the magical unity into an autonomous existence, in which we discovered that we were not alone but stood in a constant dialogue with our surroundings; and we ended by bringing together all the varieties of life in a new unity—not that of Magic but that of Faith.

INTIMACY AND
SEXUALITY

2

The Challenge to Love

ALTHOUGH I AM not writing from the Iron Mountain, I would like to consider this chapter as a "Report on the Possibility and Desirability of Love." For the question is not, What should I do if I find myself in deep love with another stranger in this world? but rather, Can this love ever be a reality at all? Many are asking themselves if we are doomed to remain strangers to each other. Is there a spark of misunderstanding in every intimate encounter, a painful experience of separateness in every attempt to unite, a fearful resistance in every act of surrender? Is there a fatal component of hate in the center of everything we call love?

We probably have wondered in our many lonesome moments if there is one corner in this competitive, demanding world where it is safe to be relaxed, to expose ourselves to someone else, and to give unconditionally. It might be very small and hidden. But if this corner exists, it calls for a search through the complexities of our human relationships in order to find it.

How do we go about this? Our plan is first to describe carefully and understand the two main forms of existing, the form of power and the form of love, or in other words, the taking form and the forgiving form, and secondly to examine how these forms are related to destruction and to creation. Only then are we ready to ask the crucial question: Is love a utopian dream or a possibility within our reach?

A. The Taking Form

OUR ATTENTION GOES first to the taking form of existence, which is the form of power. Let me start by introducing the man who suffers from a constant fear that everything is too much for him. Everything, I mean. It just seems that he is no longer able to keep the many pieces of his life together in a meaningful unity. He is nervous and trembling, tense and restless, and he has lost his usual ability to concentrate and create. He says, "I can't function any longer. Everybody likes me, my friends think a lot of me—but they don't really know me. If they found out who I really am and how I really feel, they wouldn't want to look at me any longer. I know that I often hate instead of love, that I sometimes want to hurt instead of cure, to kill instead of heal. You know, I am a hypocrite." Few people will say this. Perhaps we sometimes say it to ourselves and find ourselves caught in a prison of fear. "If they really knew us, they would stop loving us." It is the fear of being trapped, of being taken.

Let us have a closer look at this all-pervasive taking form.[1] When you take a teacup by its handle, you can keep it at a distance and look at it from all sides. You can make it an obedient instrument in your hands. You can manipulate it in any direction you want. You have complete control over it, for it is in your hands, your power. Many of our human relationships are of this order. When you are mad at a four year old and take him by his ear and shake his head like a teacup, he feels offended, humiliated, treated like an object. When in a hazing party, you take a freshman by his nose, pull his leg, or pinch his cheeks, he feels taken. But worse than these physical forms is the mental form in which we can take our fellow man. We can take him by his vulnerable spot, his hidden weakness, and make him an object at which we can look from a distance, which we can turn around and lead to the place we want it to go. You see how this form of taking is a form of power. It has the structure of black-mailing, in which we keep the other's weakness behind our back, until the moment we can use it against him at the time he blocks our way.

There are too many illustrations in our life to deny the dominating

---

1 Cf., Ludwig Binswanger, *Grundformen und Erkenntnis Menschlichen Daseins* (Max Niehans Verlag Zürich: 1953), 266–281.

role of this taking form of existence. When you sit together and talk in a free and relaxed fashion about a friend you like very much, it might happen that a stranger walks in and says: "Who are you talking about? About Mary? Oh, that sexpot . . ." You freeze. Mary has become an object, a thing, a piece of conversation, and the dialogue dies and often is perverted into a verbal combat. When a psychologist revels in discovering that his patient is a classic example of an obsessive neurotic and sends him home with the new label, gratified by his good diagnosis, he takes him by his weakness and substitutes classification for cure. When people go through your life history to check your past and find your weak spot which can be used against you, should you move in a direction opposite of their power, they operate in the taking form. The Russian author, Daniel, one of the victims of a recent writers' trial, describes in vivid terms how the revelation of a dark spot in someone's past can drive him into isolation, despair and finally total disintegration. Knowing someone's past can be the most lethal weapon in human relationships, which can bring about shame, guilt, moral and even physical death.

But we don't need such dramatic examples. Is not every student, who fills out application forms for graduate schools, and every professor, who writes letters of recommendation, obedient to the taking structure of our life? We are judged, evaluated, tested, and graded, diagnosed and classified from the time our parents compared our first walk with a little neighbor's. Gradually, as time goes on, we realize that our permanent record is building its own life, independent of ours. It is really not so amazing that we often feel caught, taken, and used for purposes not our own. The main concern then becomes not who I am but who I am considered to be, not what I think, but what others think of me.

In this taking existence we find ourselves operating in terms of power, motivated by fear. We are armed to our teeth, carefully following the movements of the other, waiting to hit back at the right moment and in the vulnerable spot. If we don't, we just might miss the right job, the good grad school, the assignment in Alaska (which we had hoped for during the Vietnam crisis), or even the man or woman we hoped to marry. And so, often in very subtle forms we envelop ourselves in the cocoon of our taking world.

Even understanding people, which seems the opposite of taking them, becomes stained by power. "Psychological understanding" then means having an idea about the hidden motives of people. It is like saying: "You don't have to tell me. I know that fellow." Hours of therapy and counseling can be wasted by the client trying to figure out what technique the counselor uses. Isn't this true also for many dating relationships? Sometimes it seems that a boy feels more relaxed in the classroom than when he is alone with a girl. Instead of feeling free to give his affection, express freely his moods and concerns to the girl he loves, he is more self-conscious than ever, wants to make the right remark at the right time, and is everything but spontaneous. What looks from a distance like love is often, at a closer look, fear. I am saying, "I don't want to become a pawn, to be pushed around. I want to keep control over the situation. And after all — it is always better to drop than to be dropped."

All this leaves us with the suspicion that the reality which we call "love" is nothing other than a blanket to cover the real fact that a man and a woman conquer each other in a long, subtle skirmish of taking movements in which one is always the winner who manipulates the other in the patterns of his or her life. Love seems to be unmasked as another taking of our fellow man and exercising of our subtle but pervasive power over him.

If this is true, destruction becomes an inescapable aspect of our existence, for the taking form of life means that our weakness can always be held against us and that there is no place in life where we are safe. Thomas Merton in his study about nonviolence has shown how this taking mode of existence is based on the concept of the irreversibility of evil. Your mistakes, failures, and offenses are unchangeable elements on the record of your life. Evil then is definitive and unchangeable. The only solution for the irreversible is its destruction. If evil cannot be reversed and forgiven, the only thing those living the taking mode can do with it is to cut it out, to uproot it, to burn it to ashes. In its full consequences this means that tenderness, sympathy, and love can only be considered as weaknesses to be eliminated, and that every mistake is final and unforgiveable. Then a misplaced gesture becomes a haunting memory, a bitter word creates an excruciating remorse, and a faithless moment leads to despair and destruction of life.

These are the dynamics of war and hate. If we look at the thousands of people suffering in mental institutions, the millions of children crushed in the conflict between their parents, the endless number of people separated from each other and left alone, we wonder if anybody can ever escape the taking form of our existence. It is the form of power which brings destruction unless the power is ours.

In this perspective, imprisoned in the vicious circle of taking, power and final destruction, we find ourselves doomed to the impossibility of love. Not without sarcasm in his voice, the man of power will say: "Love, peace and forgiveness are the dreams of those who have not yet entered the vicious circle. But wait until the day when their most primitive impulse to survive will speak its irresistible language. Then they will not only take life, they will grab it."

B. The Forgiving Form, Which Is the Form of Love

BUT THE MAN who dared to trust us said: "If my friends found out who I really am and how I really feel, they would not look at me any longer, they would spit on me and leave me alone with my hypocrisy." This man has drastically broken through the closed circle. Somehow he has jumped far beyond the reasonable and has broken through the walls of shame. He has believed that confession is a possibility. When a man cries, when the walls of his self-composure break down and he is able to express his deepest despair, weakness, hate and jealousy, his meanness and inner division, he somewhere believes that we will not take and destroy him. As if a voice told him: "Don't be afraid to tell."

Maybe we remember the few occasions in our life in which we were able to show someone we love our real self: not only our great successes but also our weaknesses and pains, not only our good intentions but also our bitter motives, not only our radiant face but also our dark shadow. It takes a lot of courage, but it might just open a new horizon, a new way of living. It is this breaking through the closed circle, often described as a conversion experience, which may come suddenly and unexpectedly or slowly and gradually. People might call us a crazy idealist, an unrealistic dreamer, a first class romanticist, but it does not touch us very deeply because we know with a new form of certainty which we had never experienced before that peace, forgiveness, justice, and inner freedom are more than mere words. Conversion is the discovery of the possibility of love.

How can we understand this loving form of existence in which the taking form is transcended? Love is not based on the willingness to listen, to understand problems of others, or to tolerate their otherness. Love is based on the mutuality of the confession of our total self to each other. This makes us free to declare not only: "My strength is your strength" but also: "Your pain is my pain, your weakness is my weakness, your sin is my sin." It is in this intimate fellowship of the weak that love is born. When the exposure of one's deepest dependency becomes an invitation to share this most existential experience, we enter a new area of life. For in this sharing of weakness violence can be overcome. When we are ready to throw stones—words can be as sharp as stones—someone just may have the courage to cry out: "He who is without sin, let him throw the first stone."

If we are willing to believe that the wheat can only come to full maturity if we allow the weeds to exist in the same field, we don't have to be afraid of every conflict and avoid every argument. It is here where love creates a smile, and where humor can be soft instead of cynical. You know the situation. John and Sally walk in the park. After a ten minute exposition by John about Hegel, Kierkegaard, Camus, Sartre and some other of his recent authors, there is a long silence. Sally asks, "John, do you care for me?" John becomes a little irritated, "Sure I do, but I wanted to know what you think about existentialism." Sally: "John I don't want to marry a philosopher. I want to marry you." John becomes mad. "Don't be so silly and stupid, if we can't have a decent conversation, how can we ever get along?" Sally: "There is little more to love than a decent conversation, and I just don't want to be another of your classmates."

Well, they had a short walk that evening. But perhaps later they could laugh about it and say, "At least we were not afraid to show our real feelings." If John and Sally would have been only sweet, understanding and agreeing with each other they might have doubted if they really were free to love. And it is exactly there, where love becomes visible.

Let us examine some characteristics of love. Love first of all is *truthful*. In the fellowship of the weak the truth creates the unshakable base on which we feel free to move. Truth means primarily the full acceptance of our basic human condition, which says that no man has power over any other man. Faithfulness is only possible if constantly guided by the truth of the human situation which prevents us from fictitiousness, shallowness, and simulation.

The second characteristic of love is its *tenderness*. Perhaps nowhere does it become so clear that love transcends the taking form than in its tenderness. In love hands don't take, grasp or hold. They caress. Caressing is the possibility of human hands to be tender. The careful touch of the hand makes for growth. Like a gardner who carefully touches the flowers to enable the light to shine through and stimulate growth, the hand of the lover allows for the full self-expression of the other. In love the mouth does not bite, devour or destroy. It kisses. A kiss is not to take in, but to allow for the full and fearless surrender. In love the eyes don't trap the stranger's body through a sartrian keyhole, nor do they arouse shame by the feeling of being exposed as Noah felt when his son Ham looked at his naked body; but in love the eyes cover the other's body with the warm radiation of an admiring smile as an expression of tenderness.

Finally and most importantly, love asks for a total *disarmament*. The encounter in love is an encounter without weapons. Perhaps the disarmament in the individual encounter is more difficult than international disarmament. We are very able to hide our guns and knives even in the most intimate relationship. An old bitter memory, a slight suspicion about motives, or a small doubt can be as sharp as a knife held behind our back as a weapon for defense in case of attack. Can we ever meet a fellow man without any protection? Reveal ourselves to him in our total vulnerability? This is the heart of our question. Are man and woman able to exclude the power in their relationship and become totally available for each other? When the soldier sits down to eat he lays down his weapons, because eating means peace and rest. When he stretches out his body to sleep he is more vulnerable than ever. Table and bed are the two places of intimacy where love can manifest itself in weakness. In love men and women take off all the forms of power, embracing each other in total disarmament. The nakedness of their body is only a symbol of total vulnerability and availability.

When the physical encounter of men and women in the intimate act of intercourse is not an expression of their total availability to each other, the creative fellowship of the weak is not yet reached. Every sexual relationship with built-in reservations, with mental restrictions or time limits, is still part of the taking structure. It means "I want you now, but not tomorrow. I want something from you, but I don't want *you*." Love is limitless. Only when men and women give themselves to each other in total surrender, that is, with their whole person for their whole life, can their encounter bear full fruits. When through the careful growth of their relationship men and women have come to the freedom of total disarmament, their giving also becomes for-giving, their nakedness does not evoke shame but desire to share, and their ultimate vulnerability becomes the core of their mutual strength. New life is born in the state of total vulnerability—this is the mystery of love. Power kills. Weakness creates. It creates autonomy, self-awareness and freedom. It creates openness to give and receive in mutuality. And finally it creates the good ground on which new life can come to full development and maturity. This explains why the highest safeguard for the physical, mental and spiritual health of the child is not primarily the attention paid to the child but the unrestricted love of the parents for each other.

If the taking form of existence were the only possibility, destruction would be our fate. But if love can be found, creation can exist. Because love is based, as Merton says, on the belief in the reversibility of evil. Evil then is not final and unchangeable. Ghandi's concept of nonviolence was essentially based on his conviction that forgiveness could change every enemy into a friend, that in hatred love is hidden, in despair hope, in doubt faith, in evil good, in sin redemption. Love is an act of forgiving in which evil is converted to good and destruction into creation. In the truthful, tender, and disarmed encounter of love man is able to create. In this perspective it becomes clear that the sexual act is a religious act. Out of the total disarmament of man on his cross, exposing himself in his extreme vulnerability, the new man arises and manifests himself in freedom. Is it not exactly in this same act of self-surrender that we find our highest fulfillment which expresses itself in the new life we create? Religion and sexuality, which in the past have been so often described as opponents, merge into one and the same reality when they are seen as an expression of the total self-surrender in love.

C. The Possibility of Love

HAVING DESCRIBED THE taking form and the loving form, the form which can destroy by power and the form which can create through forgiving, we have to return to our original question: "Is love a utopian dream or a possibility within our reach?" Let us start here by saying that our life is often a very painful fluctuation between the two desires to take and to forgive. We want to be ambitious and competitive but sometimes we want to forgive. We want strength and successes, but sometimes we feel a desire to confess our other side. We want to kill, but also to cure, to hurt but also to help. Although the world in which we live keeps suggesting that realism is an outlook on life based on power, confusing but at the same time attractive prophets keep saying that there is another possible alternative, the alternative of love. They all seem to ask for conversion, change of mind. But we don't know if we really can take the risk.

And we have good reasons to be afraid. Love means openness, vulnerability, availability and confession. When our friend says, "If my friends found out how I really feel, if I would show my real self, then they would no longer love me but hate me"—he speaks about a real possibility. It is very risky to be honest, because someone just might not respond with love, but take us by our weak spot and turn it against ourselves. Our confession might destroy us. Revealing our past failures and present ambivalences can make us losers. We can be thrown away in a gesture of contempt. This is not only a possibility but a cruel fact in the lives of many who feel that love and forgiveness is a utopian fantasy of flower children.

It is obvious that the taking structure is so much a part of our existence that we cannot avoid it. Don't ask the telephone operator how she is feeling today. Don't start a conversation about the prayer life of the man from whom you want to buy some stamps at the post office. Don't ask your teacher about his sexual behavior. You destroy human communication because you want to play a game without rules, which means no game at all. We are wise enough to prefer in most situations the taking form. Wise as the oyster who keeps his hard shell tightly closed to protect his tender and vulnerable self. Our problem therefore is not how we can completely annihilate the taking structure of life but whether there is any possibility at all to transcend that structure, to open our shell even when it is only somewhat, somewhere, somehow, sometime.

How often is the intimate encounter of two persons an expression of their total freedom? Many people are driven into each other's arms in fear and trembling. They embrace each other in despair and loneliness. They cling to each other to prevent worse things from happening. Their sleep together is only an expression of their desire to escape the threatening world, to forget their deep frustration, to ease for a minute the unbearable tension of a demanding society, to experience some warmth, protection, and safety. Their privacy does not create a place where they both can grow in freedom and share their mutual discoveries, but a fragile shelter in a storming world.

But can it be anything else, we wonder, if the only real and final solution to life is death. If we don't know where we come from or where we are going, if life is a trembling little flame between two darknesses, if we are thrown into this existence only to be swallowed by it, then being secure seems more pathological than real. In that case there is nothing else left for us to do but to try to survive and use all possible power to keep the flame burning. Is this cowardice? Perhaps. But it often seems better to be a coward than to be dead.

Here the psychologist stops and the philosopher finishes his last sentences with a question mark. Here we also should stop—unless someone is able to cut through the vicious circle. Indeed, it seems that sometimes in the depths of our despair and in the loneliness of our prison, we do not become hardened and bitter but open and sensitive for the voice of a new man. Those who want to hear him can hear him and those who want to read him can read him. To many he is a source of irritation and anger, for a few a sign of hope. In ecstasy the new man proclaims.

Something which has existed since the beginning, that we have
heard and have seen with our own eyes; that we have watched and
touched with our hands: . . . this is our subject. . . . God is light, there
is no darkness in him at all. . . . If we live our lives in the light, as he
is in the light, we are in union with one another . . . (1 John 1:1–7).

Suddenly everything is converted into its opposite. Darkness into light,
enslavement into freedom, death into life, taking into giving, destruction
into creation and hate into love. With an irresistible strength the voice
breaks through the vicious circle of our existence saying:

Let us love one another since love comes from God . . . (1 John 4:7).
In love there can be no fear, but fear is driven out by perfect love:
because to fear is to expect punishment, and anyone who is afraid
is still imperfect in love (1 John 4:18). (But) God is greater than
our heart (1 John 3:20). We have to love, because he loved us first
(1 John 4:19).

What else does this mean besides the redeeming revelation that love
is a possibility? Perhaps the best definition of revelation is the uncovering
of the truth that it is safe to love. The walls of our anxiety, our anguish,
our narrowness are broken down and a wide endless horizon is shown.
"We have to love, because he loved us first." It is safe to embrace in
vulnerability because we both find ourselves in loving hands. It is safe
to be available because someone told us that we stand on solid ground.
It is safe to surrender because we will not fall into a dark pit but enter a
welcoming home. It is safe to be weak because we are surrounded by a
creative strength.

To say and live this is a new way of knowing. We are not surrounded
by darkness but by light. He who knows this light will see it. The cripple
will walk, the deaf hear, the mute speak, the blind see, and the mountains move. Someone has appeared to us and said: The sign of love is
the sign of weakness: A baby wrapped in swaddling clothes and lying in
a manger. That is the glory of God, the peace of the world and the good
will of all men.

I could not find any other language than this to express that love has become a possibility. If there is a need for a new morality it is the morality which teaches us the fellowship of the weak as a human possibility. Love then is not a clinging to each other in the fear of an oncoming disaster but an encounter in a freedom that allows for the creation of new life. This love cannot be proved. We can only be invited to it and find it to be true by an engaging response. As long as we experience the Christian life as a life which puts restrictions on our freedom of expression, we have perverted and inverted its essence. The core message of Christianity is exactly this message of the possibility of transcending the taking form of our human existence. The main witness of this message is Jesus who in the exposure of his total vulnerability broke through the chains of death and found his life by losing it. He challenges us to break through the circle of our imprisonment. He challenges us to face our fellow man without fear and to enter with Him in the fellowship of the weak, knowing that it will not bring destruction but creation, new energy, new life, and—in the end—a new world.

INTIMACY AND
PRAYER

3

Student Prayers: Between Confusion and Hope

WHEN WE ASK about the prayerlife of today's college student we ask to enter into a very intimate world. It is the world where the student faces the ultimate meaning of his existence and tries to relate to what stretches beyond the limits of his birth and death. Entering this world can only happen on invitation. Every form of force will harm this most sensitive area of life and even ruin the same realities which we want to understand.

But why enter at all? Shouldn't this most private domain remain private at all cost? Yet what sounds like respect and protection of a man's individuality might in fact be a fearful avoidance to experience the deepest possible level of human communication. A man who wants to share his prayer wants to share his life, and not just as a sequence of events, emotions and thoughts. He wants to share a moment in which the question of the meaning of existence can be raised. And perhaps it is exactly in the sharing of his prayer that a man is able to reveal his God to his fellow man.

Based on this conviction, some university students asked their friends to write a prayer. There was no sampling involved, no systematic selection, no careful divisions into groups, college years or family background. The most simple question was asked: "Are you willing to write a prayer?" The response to this question was the first discovery: "Yes. Yes, I would like to try. Nobody asked me before, but I would like to write a prayer and I will ask my friends too." Friends asked friends and within two months a collection grew of 41 prayers written by students of both sexes, with a wide variety of attitudes and views on life. Some students were used to praying, others never prayed. Some lived with an easy familiarity in the house of God, others wondered if the word "God" made any sense at all. Some took life as a happy selection of good things, others as a torture chamber with closed windows. Some were regular churchgoers, others never went or had stopped going because of boredom or unbelief. But all wrote a prayer and wanted others to read it. And while the collection went from hand to hand, evoking many different reactions, students found themselves reading a prayerbook, which is a rather exceptional kind of book to read on today's college campus.

In this study I would like to present these prayers, not to draw any general conclusion about the religious life of the students, but simply as one of the many witnesses of man's ongoing search for meaning. One of the students who read all the prayers with great care and sensitivity wrote: "A personal prayer falls always, I think, between disciplines or definitions. Something lurks behind the words too personal, too elusive to get at with any system of rigorous analysis. Despite this difficulty a reader can understand and describe what is going on in a particular prayer, and with maturity, sensitivity and attention he may come to understand much of that which lies beneath the words and phrases strung together to make up that prayer."[1] With this same attitude I hope to be able to describe the world of prayer as visible through this collection.

But is there any perspective within which we can place this wide variety of individual expressions? After studying the prayers it seemed that they touched two extreme experiences: the experience of total confusion and self-doubt in which the student finds himself asking for clarity and self-understanding and the experience of a strong and definitive hope, characterized by self-awareness, self-acceptance and the expectance of greater things to come. We find the praying student somewhere between these poles of confusion and hope. So also can we locate in a tentative way the divergent prayers. Taking them together we even can see a movement out of the prison of self-doubt to the freedom of self-confirmation. And moving between these two poles we encounter many Gods, with many faces and many tasks. Most visible in this collection are the following Gods:

1 R. Bradley.

1. "The Clarifying God"
2. "The Banned God"
3. "The Big Buddy God"
4. "The Compassionate God"
5. "The Beautiful God"
6. "The Giving God"
7. "The Coming God"

1. THE CLARIFYING GOD

Under the mask of a self-assertive attitude many students hide deep feelings of confusion. Bombarded by millions of contradicting stimuli, confronted with opposing viewpoints, ideals and desires, they often feel lost in the stream of events and feelings and wonder who they are and where they are going. Many are persecuted by the question: "Can I do anything meaningful in this mad world, which speaks one day about nonviolence and the other day about revolution, one day about a crusade in Europe and the other day about murder in Vietnam?" In the middle of all this confusion they have lost track of their ideas, feeling and emotions and have become entangled in the complexity of their internal life.

When these students pray they are confronted with their own confusion. "What can I do?" or "What do I want?" is a question, but a more basic question is "What do I feel?" And this confusion of mind and cluttering of feelings can lead to an inability to experience the many differentiations in life. Joy and sadness, anger and thankfulness, love and hate seem to blend into a paralyzing lump of unidentifiable emotions. The result is often apathy, dullness, fatigue. Overstimulated, overexposed, overfed with ideals and slogans stretched in too many different directions, nothing else can be said than: "I don't care." A dull passivity has become the only possible attitude. While students are preparing themselves for a great Mardi Gras, one of them prays:

Well, here we are, another Mardi-Gras weekend—for some a time
of fun, enjoyment, thoughtfulness and forgetfulness, and for some a
time of depression and anger.

But for me neither: and that just about sums up the whole apathetic slump. It is serious and has gotten to the point where its causes—the library, the war, the ugliness, the jokes, the intolerance—have broken most enthusiasm to the point where drifting is the only thing possible.

I don't think that I like drifting—oh, not a rat race, just some enthusiasm, some interest, and then I can at least pursue something, even though that something may be shaded.

Please help everyone to find enthusiasm and interest.

Out of his dullness and apathy this student asks for articulation and differentiation to find some new handles and directions in the labyrinth of the inner life and rediscover himself within some clear boundaries of identifiable experiences.

This confusion often leads to a very negative self-evaluation. Many students experience vaguely self-contempt, even self-hate. They have lost self-respect and are angry with their own unknown self. You cannot love what you do not know and how can you love yourself, when the only thing you experience is a deep pit of intermingled impulses, feelings, emotions and ideas, of which you are more victim than master. Out of this confusion one student prays:

Help me find and cherish myself—to solve the problems of myself and others, to more clearly see the direction in which I'm going. It has been so cloudy and jerky—sometimes I wonder if I'm progressing at all—and sometimes I wonder if I can. Remove this doubt I have about myself—or better let me see the doubt and lack of confidence for what it is, and in removing it, learn more of it. I can see in my actions how my doubt and lack of confidence come out. I hide it well, but hiding it makes me worry all the more. Help me remove this self-consciousness which makes me second-guess myself. Let me cease to try to impose a definition on myself, but to act and think naturally. Let me see that all are to be respected, many are to be loved, and some must be fought—and that all men are more than I think they are.

And even praying itself becomes nearly an impossibility. There is so little distance and so much cloudiness that praying creates guilt and enters in the vicious circle of a growing self-devaluation.

> Lord, I don't really feel like praying. I'm confused, everything is confused. I don't know what I'll be doing next year—I don't even know for sure what I want to be doing next year, or what I should be doing. I feel guilty praying—turning to you at a time like this because I feel two-faced to pray only when I need help and not to pray when I don't.

But somewhere there is a spark of light, hardly noticeable and very subtle. The attitude of praying can sometimes create that little bit of distance which is the beginning of self-knowledge. Praying, if it is anything more than a narcissistic self-complaint, involves someone else, another who is not just me. And in this way we can see that the expression of confusion can become the beginning of its solution. Praying then means creating distance and God's answer is given in the praying act. One student after a long prayer filled with spiritual dizziness and self-doubt writes this short post-scriptum:

> This must be a prayer, because it has done something already. As you think about things, they become clearer, and kind of fall into place. I don't think that thinking about problems ever solves any alone, but at least gives a basis for further action and further thought.

Here the clarifying God reveals himself. Here the first step is set out of confusion. Here a road becomes visible and man can at least start to walk on his own feet. New channels of energy become available and the result of this prayer is that a man can feel that he can do something himself. The student's post-script is a beautiful echo of Anton Boisen's conviction: "I do believe in prayer. I believe that its chief function is—to find out what is wanted of us and to enable us to draw upon sources of strength which will make it possible for us to accomplish our task whatever it may be."[2]

---

2 Anton Boisen, *Out of the Depth* (Harper & Brothers: 1960), 111.

Prayer opens our eyes for ourselves and through clarification enables us to step forward in the direction of hope.

2. THE BANNED GOD

Sometimes the step out of confusion means a step away from God. It is not seldom that man found internal rest and harmony once he had the courage to shake off his torturing God. His present Godless life feels like a liberation after years of painful and humiliating occupation. This experience of change is a conversion experience in reverse, but with the same psychological effects: new internal freedom, growing self-respect, new hope. For some students their God-ridden past is filled with memories of scrupulosity, guilt-feelings, fear for punishment, unbearable responsibilities and unlivable expectations. They felt surrounded by a wall of prohibitions and deprived by God's cruel omnipotence, omniscience and omnipresence from their own self-respect. Exposed in their miserable nakedness to God's intruding eye they were like men robbed of their most intimate identity. For these individuals the murder of their God was an experience of conversion, and the way to self-discovery, self-respect, self-awareness and self-affirmation. They had to have the courage to ban their tyrannical God and to claim back their own most personal individuality.

Therefore, prayer to a nonexisting God, the banned God, is not an embarrassing joke, but a deep and sincere expression of a paradise gained. Such a prayer can show how thin the edge is between agnosticism and Christian faith. The banning of God has created a new peace of mind and a fearless heart. One student prays:

> When I speak to you I strongly suspect that You aren't "out there" now and never were. I have lost You and I feel better for it because You diminished me and wouldn't let me be myself. I always felt I had to consider what You wanted me to do, what image or state of perfection You demanded.
>
> Since the time of our separation I've grown more selfish. I'm concerned a lot with myself, with my own development as a human being. I suppose I still want to be perfect, but not for my own sake, nor to please You. What matters now are the others.

This is a real prayer. What makes it a prayer? It is a dialogue, a conversation. That means that here one is not rigid, closed, bitter and cynical, but open to a response, willing to listen and available for growth. It is the same student who prays:

> If and when I find You again—and I'm certainly leaving myself open
> to that—I just know that I'll find You in the Others and in my Self.
> Who knows, maybe You are what is best in each of us.

God has become an obstacle in man's desire to be good for his neighbor. Instead of the way to the other, He is in the way. A prayer to such a God becomes an act of cowardice or just weakness. A student painfully aware of the contradiction involved in his praying attitudes describes his conversion from God to men as follows:

> There just doesn't seem to be any real reason to pray—I don't say
> prayers any more. I'm still not really convinced that there is such
> a thing as a God. You don't achieve or receive anything aside from
> your own ambitions and work or from another. Thanking people in-
> volved in a specific situation seems much more relevant than thank-
> ing God.

There is someone more important than God, that is man. God-talk is boring, trivial, fruitless and vicious. It keeps us away from what really matters. With a new found freedom a student says:

> I can't be bothered with the trivial things the church worries about.
> It just seems a waste of time.

In all these prayers, or nonprayers, God is experienced as blocking the way to the self and therefore to the other. The prayer for self-discovery is a prayer asking God to leave, sometimes forcing him to get out of the way in order to find freedom and self. So a man steps out of his confusion by banning a suffocating God from his existence.

3. THE BIG BUDDY GOD

In a seemingly drastic contrast with the banned God, we encounter in the student-prayers the big-buddy-God. It is the God with whom you can talk with an easy-going familiarity. In a remarkable way God combines the qualities of a playmate and a cure-all. He is like a big-brother, part of the family, but stronger and willing to solve with a friendly smile the worries of the baby-boy. You can speak with him in a shoulder slapping way and brag about him when you need some support in your self-esteem. You can count on Him every moment and you can forget about your own problems, since He is around all the time, never too tired to help out. One prayer to this big-buddy-God reads as follows:

> Lord, there are an awful lot of things that bug me lately. The real uncertainty of next year, especially all the people I snub every day—as a result of a lot of stagnant relationships. Really, Lord, I'm a pretty imperfect specimen—basically, Lord, help me to keep trying to love a little bit better and to be a little bit more open to others. Also, Lord, help me to become what You want me to become. Help me to choose the right law school, the right wife, and the right job—make money insignificant—Also remember the guys at home, the guys at school, those getting married and those in Vietnam.
>
> So, Lord, I'm going to play handball now, and I'd like to ask just one more thing of You, that is, help me to live more vibrantly what I believe or at least what I think I believe. Help me to take serious every event in life especially every person, and understand it or him, not condemn it or him. Okay?
>
> P.S. Thanks for dying on the cross for me and my friends.

The casual tone of this prayer is like that of a boy comfortably sitting on daddy's lap. There are many problems, but they don't cut deep, they don't really hurt. They hardly touch the heart of the praying man. If there is confusion, it is confusion of an external nature, which doesn't cause internal turmoil but which can be dealt with by a direct request for help with the unshakable conviction that everything will be okay soon.

This attitude comes close to what William James calls the once-born, healthy-minded type of religion. It is the religion of the man "who's soul is of this sky-blue sort, whose affinities are rather with flowers and birds and all enchanting innocencies than with dark human passions, who can think no ill of man or God, and in whom religious gladness, being in possession from the outset, needs no deliverance from any antecedent burden."[3] William James does not hide his suspicion about this "ultra-optimistic form of the once-born philosophy."[4] He points up the superficial nature of a religion in which all evil is externalized and not recognized as a part of man asking for conversion. This superficiality of the once-born-minded is also obvious in this prayer:

Hey, Big Man. Things are in a sorry state right now. The whole country is in an uproar. You know, I never really thought about it much. I mean in terms of affecting me. Martin Luther King was kind of off in the distance. He was a rabble-rouser. He confronted the people with something new, different and unpleasant. It made me stop and think. I don't have any conclusions though. I don't imagine You like this mess we've gotten ourselves in, but help us out of it, please?

Remarkable here is that the student himself is more or less aware of his own uninvolvement and aloof distance. But although he recognizes vaguely his lack of personal responsibility he still expects the solution to come from his big-buddy-Jesus.

If we analyse both prayers more closely we see that we can hardly discover any real hope. These prayers are still on the level of wish-fulfillment. Wishes are concrete; "They have specific objects and articulate contents."[5] The wish wants something very specific and belongs more to the surprise level of Santa Claus than to the personalistic level of faith.

---

3 William James, *The Varieties of Religious Experience* (Enlarged edition. University Books: 1963), 80.
4 James, *The Varieties of Religious Experience*, 362.
5 See Paul Pruyser, "Phenomenology and Dynamics of Hoping," *Journal for the Scientific Study of Religion* 3:86–96 (Fall 1963) and, *A Dynamic Psychology of Religion* (Harper & Row: 1968), 166–170.

The big-buddy prayers which we quoted are filled with wishes and expect God to surprise man soon with his great divine gift. These prayers therefore, are still far away from self-knowledge, self-acceptance and hope. Although they seem so opposite from the prayers to the banned God, they are very close to them when we see them on the continuum from confusion to hope. This kind of prayers is free from confusion, but not by facing the problems, but by banning them or not allowing them to enter into the inner life. The internal rest of the man who has shaken off the bothersome God is just as superficial as the relaxed attitude of him who talks to God as a divine playmate.

4. THE COMPASSIONATE GOD

In the long row of prayers there is a turning point where a new perspective is breaking through. No entangling confusion nor easy rest, but the beginning of something different pointing to hope, vaguely, hesitantly and tentatively, but clearly recognizably. These prayers can best be called antiheroic prayers. They ask for a creative passivity in a demanding competitive world.

They are the crying out of a man who uses grades as a measure for success, success as a basis of promotion and promotion as a criterion of human value. They also are a protest against the desires to become a star, to be worshiped for exceptional results, or honored for bravery. They are prayers to a compassionate God, who does not ask for heroic martyrdom, but wants to embrace a weak man.

Father, I ask not that you give me strength nor bravery, nor humility, nor courage. These are but words, straining futilely to compress and to define that which was meant to be open. The more I grasp for these man-made ideas, the more I fail. In the end all words, all exhortations seem little more than hollow clatter. When I listen to these words my life becomes a task, a challenge—and always I fail. Such thinking urges me to "try a little harder." And I fail again. And so on in an endless circular parade both led and followed by proud men.

Perhaps this frustration is your silent voice begging me to stop, to let you carry my "burden." Whenever I do stop, there is no burden.

Then I sense your presence in the stillness, a stillness flowing far beneath the sterile incongruency of man alone.

I should ask for nothing, just wait for you to give. But I am impatient and must ask. Father, help me to receive the peace which you constantly offer; help me to hear the frozen stillness of your harmony; help me to be passive; help me to accept; help me to stop.

This sounds like a prayer of an exhausted circus dancer who feels that he can lose balance at any moment and fall from the thin rope in the middle of a roaring crowd. It is the voice of a tired man, tired from the unceasing request to do better, to try harder, to climb higher. It is the cry of a man doubting if he will be able to keep pace with the fast-moving world, and fearful of falling apart under the growing burden of his demanding milieu.

This praying man wants to stop, to surrender in the soft caressing hands of an understanding God, to fall asleep in safe arms, to cry without fear, to let go, relax his tense muscles and rest long and deep, forgetting the cold, cruel and hostile world. In many ways this prayer represents an anti-climax to the banner-waving type of Christianity, in which the brave heroic youth willing to give his life for his commanding God was extolled as an example for all lukewarm believers. It is the other side of the man stimulated and challenged from many pulpits to fight his way through this dangerous world and secure through utmost efforts everlasting rewards in the future-life.

But perhaps we are shortsighted when we only see here a reaction to a triumphalistic past. Perhaps we find here the nucleus of the new mystic, the beginning of a prayer which is not the result of human concentration, but of the emptiness created for the divine Spirit. We can catch a glimpse of this new mysticism when we recognize the new sense of humility shining through the antiheroic prayer. They are smiling prayers, in which man asks for a little bit of happiness, a little bit of beauty, a little bit of meaning in life. One student prays:

I don't want to live in vain—Make me live for something—I'm no hero. I don't really have whatever it is that makes a hero. But I don't want to be a coward. I don't want to be afraid when the time for courage arrives. Let me do something. Let me do it in my own quiet unheroic way. If I can just be remembered as being a good man, as being a distinct and different man, I will feel that I did not waste my life. If I feel that my living here, that the very fact that I existed and lived on earth, meant something to someone, I will be happy. Let me be remembered by someone. Let me help someone—Don't permit me to just exist as another human being. Make me live. I don't want to live in vain.

The beauty is modesty. The fatigue is less obvious here. The humble desire to be of some good to someone is central. But there very well might have been a purifying experience which made this prayer possible. There is a new rest and freedom not the result of repression or avoidance, but based on the humble recognition of man's important but small place in the face of his Creator.

5. THE BEAUTIFUL GOD

On our way out of confusion we have passed the point where something new was breaking through. In the prayers to the compassionate God we discovered a new openness, a new receptivity which gave room to a creative relationship to the "reality of the unseen" (William James). And although there was still much reaction against the spy-God, the cry for compassion and understanding also meant an opening of the senses for new experiences.

We now come to a group of prayers which can be seen as a dramatic plea for sensitivity. In these prayers students ask to be in touch with what is real, to experience in depth the world which surrounds us and to feel united with the vital sources of life. They look for oneness and a liberation from the painful sense of alienation. They want to touch, taste, smell, hear and see what is beyond their own lonesomeness and surrender to the unspeakable beauty of the divine. They are prayers to the beautiful God, beautiful in a sensual way, in which the analytical distance is broken down in an ecstatic joy making God into a bodily experience. The alienation out of which these prayers are born is most dramatically verbalized by the student who writes:

Alone while in class
Alone with my friends
Alone in a pressing crowd
Where to turn to shelter this all embracing shell?
The world is without life — no longer a friend
The trees sticky leaves, children;
All seem — only unreal.
They out there. I am apart.

Out of this isolation the impulse to dive back into the womb of existence speaks its urging language. These prayers are like prayers of the American Indians who aspired not to be master over the world or to rule creation in God's name but only to merge with nature and experience the participation with the creative forces of life. In their masks the face of man merges with the body of a lizard or snake and in their rituals they hoped to reach the sense of their brotherly place in nature.

This same desire is visible in some of the students who let their hair grow free, dress in a loose unrestrained way, speak about beautiful things and beautiful people and eat the seeds which help them enter in the passive state where colors and sounds embrace them with a tender touch. Central is the desire to step away from the meager emotions of a technocratic society in which superficiality leads to boredom and the breaking of contact with the mysterious powers of reality. And this brings us to a new prayer:

Help us to see that which is real. A reality. Help us to lie under a tree and enjoy the grass and sky and wind, to have a definitive feeling, perhaps simple, perhaps deep, to think wildly, openly, to stretch.

To hold a hand and mean it, to appreciate beauty, to experience a relationship, a joy, a satisfaction, a sadness, a desperation, an exhaustion. To feel close to an idea, an ideal, and to ourselves. To feel part of a country, a person and the earth. To rise out of the depths of desperation and self-made alienation, and to be close once again to you. These are what we can grasp, these are real. These are experiences. That is our prayer, Lord. To be aware, to rise up, to realize, to understand and to care.

Perhaps more than any of the others this prayer expresses one of the deepest desires of the contemporary student faced with a dismembered and broken reality in which he has to find his place, but which often seems more threatening than inviting. In a milieu that tries to refine the senses through ingenuous instruments, the student wonders if he can trust his own body and if his senses are able to bring him in contact with the reality in which he lives. But as soon as the touch of sensitivity dawns upon him a new vibration pervades him. A girl prays:

> Just to hear . . . the annoying buzz of haunting alarm clocks through the thin walls of those who live nearby.
> Just to see . . . a friend who has waited to walk with me over to class, and that look on his face when I've done it again, but I don't know what.
> Just to smell . . . the freshness of a spring morning when the sun is warm and winter has passed: when the flowers are budding and the grass is moist.
> Just to feel . . . the refreshment of an afternoon shower; the softness of a baby duck; the sand between my toes; the thrill of a tender kiss.
> Just to taste . . . not only a snack or a meal, but the sweet and bitter of life; and to love with my entirety the who that they are, whether ugly or gracious or right or sad.

Students like this girl are filled with the experience of new life, new beauty and new energy. They say "Yes" to all that is, and in their humble recognition of their own fragility they open themselves to the splendor of their beautiful God. A new ray of hope is coming through.

6. THE GIVING GOD

The antiheroic prayers showed a first hesitant appreciation of the little things. In the prayers to the compassionate God, a creative passivity became visible and the last two prayers revealed the deep desire to merge with the beautiful God and to experience a new sense of unity and belonging. We are far away from the confused state of mind, with which we started this analysis, but still not arrived at what we can call Christian hope.

The plea for sensitivity with the desire to feel deeply embedded in reality was still in many ways a plea of the lonesome, somewhat isolated man. The need to merge, to be one, to belong, often reveals a regressive impulse, which cannot tolerate the distinction between the praying man and his world, between himself and the other, between his weakness and God's strength. Often it seems as if the quest for belonging means a fear of being different and an unwillingness to claim the individuality of the self. The identity of the praying person, therefore, has not yet a clear form and a prayer for sensitivity can sound somewhat preoccupied. Its God is more a protective device than the giving other.

Obviously we only speak about differences in degree, but in the prayers to the beautiful God, God is hardly recognized as the other who is free to give or not to give. He is more an indispensable source of warmth always available to offer comfort. But once God is recognized as the other who gives in freedom, man is able to think. Sensitivity is a condition to experience God's gifts, but thanks includes also the willingness to recognize the distance between the giver and the receiver.

When man is able to thank he is able to know his limitations without feeling defensive and to be self-confident without being proud. He claims his own powers and at the same time he confesses his need for help. Thanking in a real sense avoids submissiveness as well as possessiveness. It is the act of a free man who can say: I thank you. Here I and you are two different persons with different identities who can enter in an intimate relationship without losing their own selves. An act of free thanking requires a careful balance between closeness and distance. Too much closeness can lead to a self-effacing dependency, too much distance to an overevaluation of the self with a defensive pride.

Many of the student prayers are so self-centered, so full of deep personal concern, or so craving for sympathy and protection that there is not enough distance to say thanks. But there are exceptions in which a new freedom is visible and a prayer becomes a hymn of thanksgiving.

Lord, thank You for life, love and people.
Dear Lord, thank You for the beautiful day, for the flowers, for the
   birds, for my family, for my friends, for me.
for all that has been—thanks
for all that will be—yes!

In thanks man is open and moves outward. In confusion all the attention
is drawn inward in an attempt to unravel the complexities of the internal
world, hardly leaving any possibility to say thanks. In confusion man clings
to himself, in thanks he stretches out his hands and points to the source of
new energy, new life, new love. Thanks then can even become possible in
a sad world. One student concludes a long prayer with the words:

What can I say but thank You; in the middle of bad it has never been
   so good.

Here thanks can shake off the depression of the present and make hope
a possibility.

7. THE COMING GOD

When many students were asked to read the prayers and to give their reactions to them there was an almost unanimous attraction to one prayer
which we consider a prayer to the coming God. Although different students could sympathize with many strong positive or negative affects,
expressed in the collection, the attitude communicated through form
and content by this prayer called "hope" was immediately recognized as
the most desirable, most modern and most Christian.

I hope that I will always be for each man what he needs me to be.
I hope that each man's death will always diminish me, but that fear
   of my own will never diminish my joy of life.
I hope that my love for those whom I like will never lessen my love
   for those whom I do not.
I hope that another man's love for me never be a measure of my love
   for him.

I hope that every man will accept me as I am, but that I never will.

I hope that I will always ask for forgiveness from others, but will never need be asked for my own.

I hope that I will find a woman to love, but that I will never seek one.

I hope that I will always recognize my limitations, but that I will construct none.

I hope that loving will always be my goal, but that love will never be my idol.

I hope that every man will always have hope.

Here we find ourselves as far away as possible from confusion. Here we listen to a man who stands on solid ground and points into the future. He knows where he is and looks with expectation towards the things to come. The structure and thought of this prayer show a great self-confidence carefully integrated with a deep sense of humility. The prayer illustrates in a beautiful way some of the basic dynamics of the attitude of the mature Christian.

In comparison with the painful self-preoccupation, which we found in the prayer of the confused student, we see here a great sense of self-awareness, self-acceptance. There are clear, but not rigid lines which mark the personality. In this attitude of hope we see a man well defined but always available for redefinition. In comparison with the prayers to the banned God, there is no artificial rest created by a negative conversion but a free dialogue without need to defend. In hope God is no obstacle, but the way to human love. In comparison with the prayers to the big-buddy-God, there is no easy optimism nor simplistic wish-fulfilling thinking. The hope expressed is on a very personal level and never concretized in toy-like desires. Man does not ask the coming God for favors, but opens himself to a deepening of an interpersonal relationship, which depends on two persons, and can never be forced. In comparison with the antiheroic prayers to the compassionate God, there is no feeling of fatigue or reaction against an overdemanding society. In hope man does not react to a frustrating past, but reaches forward to a promising future. In comparison with the prayers to the beautiful God, the praying man here is less alienated and more self-composed. There is no desire to merge with God, but to strengthen the own identity. In hope man does not ask to vanish and lose himself in the embracing arms of a protecting God, but he experiences his being different as a creative possibility. In comparison with the prayers to the giving God, thanks is less explicitly formulated, but constantly presupposed. Real hope is impossible without the deep awareness that life is a gift and holds endless promises.

So we see in the prayer to the coming God the attitude of hope as an attitude of self-awareness and self-acceptance from which man enters in a creative dialogue with his living God, constantly leaving behind his past and stretching forward to a future which he experiences as an inexhaustible source of new life.

WE TRIED TO enter into the intimacy of the student prayer-life. We did this on invitation by studying the prayers written by the student himself and offered for evaluation. By seeing the whole collection as a move out of confusion towards mature hope we wanted to prevent ourselves from labeling the different student prayers as more or less "good" or "bad." We only wanted to understand where the student could be located in his search for meaning and a God whom he can call his God. The distinctions between the different God's were perhaps too artificial, but they were intended to make it easier to recognize the intimate moves of man to come closer to himself and the God of his faith.

4

Pentecostalism on Campus

SINCE THE PENTECOSTAL movement has become a vivid reality on some university campuses, many active participants, as well as distant observers, have asked, "Is this healthy or dangerous, something to be encouraged or something to be avoided?"

Various students who experienced the gift of tongues, who felt the Real Presence of the Holy Spirit and for whom a new world of feelings has opened itself, expressed their change: "It is a tremendous experience. It is new, unique, full of joy and peace. I am different, that is for sure. Only one who has surrendered can really understand what I am talking about. Many problems I have long been struggling with just seemed to vanish, became like an empty shell falling off. Heavy burdens became feather-light things; hostile attitudes converted to deep sympathy. People whom I once feared are now my friends. Those whom I hated I can love, those who were masters are partners. I know with a deep certainty that God has spoken to me in a new way."

But sometimes the same students will tell you the other side of their feelings: "I wonder if it is all real, if it is really me. It is like another world which is not mine; one so overwhelming that it seems unreal. Once in a while, after a prayer meeting when I am by myself, I feel lonesome and depressed. Will it last? Perhaps it is just for a short time and then my problems will come back. I wonder if it is really good for me."

The same ambivalence is expressed by outsiders. They see people pray, sing, and read together; they see their happiness, joy and new convictions; but they wonder how real or healthy it is. And since this is all so close, it seems very difficult to find the distance to understand without falling into a fanatic rejection and ridicule on the one hand or an uncritical enthusiasm on the other.

This essay is an attempt to clarify certain issues and to be of some help in an honest evaluation. I will use, besides my own observations and discussions with students, the study by Kilian McDonnell, O.S.B., "The Ecumenical Significance of the Pentecostal Movement."[1] I will approach the subject from three perspectives.

A Historical Perspective

ALTHOUGH PENTECOSTALISM WAS originally found among people with a low economic status and closely related with the nonliturgical churches (such as the Assembly of God Church), since 1955 a new wave of Pentecostalism has entered the more prosperous communities, inspired many intellectuals, and established itself in such liturgical churches as the Lutheran and Episcopalian.

McDonnell, who studies the rising Pentecostalism with a group of anthropologists, is probably the most informed and knowledgeable theologian in this area. Considering it as "the fastest growing movement within the Christian tradition"[2] he asks himself, "How can the Pentecostals with so few means form such apostolic Christians while our liturgies rich in theological content and tradition fail to communicate the urgency of evangelization to the faithful?" Do our liturgies develop a sense of community? Do they form a congregation which acts, prays, listens, sings and sorrows together, a true community of the redeemed? Have the Roman Catholics become comfortable with the too-oft-extolled beauties of the Roman Liturgy (sobriety, grandeur, clarity, objectivity, lapidary formulations, fixity of form, supranational appeal—the list reads as though drawn up by an enemy) and failed to notice that, in every liturgical instance and in every cultural context, sobriety and objectivity may not be virtues to emphasize,

---

1 Kilian McDonnell, O.S.B., "The Ecumenical Significance of the Pentecostal Movement," *Worship* (December 1966).
2 McDonnell, "The Ecumenical Significance of the Pentecostal Movement," 609.

that grandeur amidst poverty may be an indictment, that supranational appeal may, in fact, be a species of Roman liturgical colonialism?

Pentecostals are in many lands the fastest-growing Christian denomination. Why? "Undoubtedly the answer involves many factors, but this much we know. Our liturgies have failed."[3] And McDonnell even wonders whether "St. Paul would not feel more at home in the free fervor of a Pentecostal meeting than in the organized dullness of our liturgical celebrations."[4] There is no doubt about one thing. The rapidly growing interest in the Pentecostal prayer meeting at university-campus reveals an intensive need, a long-hidden frustration which manifests itself in the sudden breakthrough of a form of behavior which is rather unusual in a student-community.

It is difficult to imagine how a Catholic university looked in the twenties and thirties. About the University of Notre Dame, where John F. O'Hara was the prefect of religion, Joe Hoffman writes: "O'Hara gave Notre Dame its enormous standing within the Catholic populace of the United States as a place where the solid practice of Catholicism could be found. His goals were clear-cut and defined: Mass, Communion, frequent confession, devotion to the Blessed Sacrament and to Mary. His methods were novenas in preparation for Christmas, Easter, Mother's Day, and exams. There were processions, hours of adoration, the rosary, first Friday devotions, and all of them were popular. Freshmen arriving on campus were immediately indoctrinated into the system. By means of the Religious Bulletin, which was read as much beyond the campus as by the students, O'Hara hammered at students foibles, suggested means for advancing in the spiritual life, gave timely notice of approaching religious events, commented on the spiritual significance of the news of the day, presented points of character development, gave short instructions on ideals, corrected student abuses, and answered difficulties. It was spiritual reading in tabloid form. O'Hara kept statistics on religious practice, published religious surveys and was keenly aware of the tempo and mentality of the student body. He was extremely successful."[5]

---

3 McDonnell, "The Ecumenical Significance of the Pentecostal Movement," 622–623.
4 McDonnell, "The Ecumenical Significance of the Pentecostal Movement," 615
5 Joseph Hoffman, C.S.C., unpublished article.

Today the picture is completely different. A university is no longer a place with easygoing students who consider their four years as a relatively relaxed time with abundant opportunity for prayer, sports, social life and extracurricular activities; rather, it is a very ambitious and competitive institution. Today, students often look upon their four years as a race in which only the fittest survive. In the educational revolution of the post-Sputnik era, academic excellence became the key word.

But competition demands a price. Most students take the challenge and are able to utilize the new pressures in a useful and often creative way. But many do not, and instead they often develop an excessive amount of anxiety and tension and experience a painful lonesomeness which they hide beneath the surface of seemingly well-adjusted behavior. The university community now counts hundreds of very lonesome men who consider their neighbors more as rivals than as friends. For many, their roommate is a stranger and their classmate a threat. "Everyone for himself, and God for us all." That seems most safe. Knowledge becomes a weapon by which you stay in school, avoid the Army, win a fellowship, and make a career. And the Church does not seem to help very much. Going through a time of reevaluation and extreme self-criticism, she offers more questions than answers. Instead of a safe home, she is more a source of deep discomfort for a man who looks for a solid support in a tumbling world.

In this context the Pentecostal movement very well can be understood as a revival, a rekindling of the devotional Church, or the revenge of a repressed sentiment. Everyone who enters a Pentecostal meeting is suddenly confronted with all that seems to be at odds with a "typical" university student. In the midst of the congregation, students witness how their lonesomeness and insecurity have been overcome by the gift of the Holy Spirit. One who never had a friend and always felt afraid now feels free to share his deepest thoughts and desires with his fellow man. Long struggles with most embarrassing problems are wiped away by the infusion of God's Spirit. Sadness is changed to joy, restlessness to peace, despair to inner content, and separation to togetherness.

On a campus where people stay relatively distant from each other, the most intimate ideas are shared and the barriers to communication are broken. Where men hardly touch each other, they embrace and hold each other in a free physical contact. They lay hands on each other's shoulders and heads, pray aloud for each other's needs, and let themselves be led by deep spiritual impulses to which they surrender in ecstatic joy and happiness. The new feelings are so great and overpowering that they cannot be caught in human concepts or words, but break through in ecstatic sounds varying in tone and intensity and expressing a prayer of total surrender and praise, saying with Jeremiah, "Ah, Lord, I don't know how to speak." Hands, eyes and mouth express unknown happiness, openness and joy. Young men move up and down in the pleasant rhythm of biblical songs, or are quiet in a long and contemplative silence. So intense is the exchange that many feel a new, warm intensity pervading their whole persons. Their hands radiate new power and a soft and tender breeze touches their skins. Joy and happiness may break through in tears and sweat and the intensity of the prayer may lead to a happy and satisfying experience of physical exhaustion caused by total surrender.

The Spirit has come. He who asks will receive and feel that God is not a strange God. He will taste again His sweetness, hear His internal call, and be able to love Him with his whole person, body and soul, without any reservation.

A Psychological Perspective

HOW CAN WE evaluate this new movement? We can understand it as a revival of the devotional Church and as a reaction of a repressed religious sentiment in a cool and competitive world. But is it healthy or sick? Does it cure or make wounds? It is very difficult to give an outright answer, but perhaps some considerations may be of help.

Does it heal or hurt? There is no doubt that many people who surrendered to this experience get a tremendous and often very sudden relief from their mental and spiritual pains. Problems they have been struggling with for years are wiped away in a moment and lose their unbearable weight. The questions are: Are they cured or covered? Is the real human conflict resolved or "snowed under" by the overwhelming power of a new experience?

We know that electroshock, an artificially induced emotional experience, can cover a depression for many years but does not cure it. It may make us forget our problems for some years, but, in fact, it delays the process of cure by not using the human qualities to heal. One might wonder if the miraculous effect of the Pentecostal experience is not in a certain way like a shock treatment. If a young man or woman suddenly feels redeemed from deep mental suffering, they might, in fact, paralyze their internal human ability to overcome their problem, and when the pains recur later on they might be more discouraged than before.

If we use sleeping pills, we certainly will fall asleep but, at the same time, we can kill our own capacities to find physical rest and become quite dependent on these external forces. And, if the Pentecostal experience in many cases gives this sudden freedom, sudden friendship, sudden happiness and joy, we might prevent the gradual development of our internal capacities to develop meaningful, lasting friendships, to enjoy happiness, and to tolerate frustrations. Many people who have had deep, internal religious experiences (during retreats, cursillos, novitiates, etc.) all can witness to the fact that they relieved many pains for a while, but that the real test came later when there were no feelings to depend on, no experiences to count on. The task lies in the desert where God is not feelable and naked faith is all we have.

The Pentecostal experience might take away (even permanently) certain real problems, but it is very doubtful that it will cure deep mental suffering. It might only cover it up and delay the attempt for a real cure.

Can it be dangerous? For many people, perhaps even for most, it hardly seems to be dangerous. It might be even beneficial to a certain extent, especially for those who through retreats, cursillos and other religious practices have become exposed to the inner feelings that are in line with the Pentecostal experience. But for some it is dangerous—very dangerous.

First of all, for those who are not prepared, every inducement of a strong emotion can break and do serious harm. The Christian tradition has been deeply convinced of the importance of preparation. Christ did not come to this world before a long preparation of His people. We do not celebrate Christmas without Advent, nor Easter without Lent. And

St. Paul distinguishes between Christians who still need spiritual milk and those who are ready for solid food. The whole mystical tradition stresses the need for purification in order to enter into intimacy with God and the danger of unprepared exposure to divine powers.

Several students showed remarkable signs of anxiety and confusion. They were so overwhelmed by these new feelings that they lost their hold on reality. They found they could no longer study nor concentrate on their daily work; they felt a pushing urge to share with others. In some cases, physical and mental exhaustion were visible, and people felt on the edge of a physical or mental breakdown. This is dangerous and may lead to psychotic reaction, which needs hospitalization and special psychiatric help in order to be cured. These are exceptional cases, but still no less a source of concern.

Secondly, there are those who strongly desire to have the gifts of the Spirit but do not feel able to come to the real experience. They wonder why others are so happy, and they are not; why others can speak in tongues and they cannot; why others feel free to embrace each other, and they do not. More than ever before, they feel like outsiders or even outcasts. And they wonder, "What is wrong with me that I do not receive the gifts?" Feelings of guilt and depression can result from this, and many may feel more lonesome than before. For those who ask but do not receive, the Pentecostal movement can create real dangers.

There is a heavy responsibility on the leaders of the movement. Emotion, and certainly religious emotions, need careful direction, careful guidance, and careful care.

Does it create community? Who could deny this? The free and easy way in which the participants relate to each other, talk, sing and pray together should convince everybody that here a real, new community is formed. Still there are some questions here. By suddenly breaking through the barriers of shyness and distance, many have given away their privacy. Many have shown their deepest self to their fellow man and laid themselves open for the other. They have stripped themselves of their reservations and inhibitions and have shared their most intimate feelings, ideas and thoughts with others. In a way they have merged their personality with their friends and given up their otherness.

But, is this real community? One who has given away so much of himself creates an unquenchable need to be constantly together with the other to whom he has given himself, in order to feel a whole person. Many students who actively participated in the prayer meetings felt terribly lonesome during the vacation and felt a deep urge and desire to be with their friends again. Instead of creating the freedom to leave the group and to go out and work, many want to remain in the safe protection of the togetherness where they can really feel at home.

The lack of distance and the stress on intimacy make the creative community hardly possible. A good liturgy always should be characterized by a subtle balance between closeness and distance. It should offer different modes and levels of participation and many ways of religious experience. Perhaps it seldom did before and is only thought of as a distant, cool reality. But in the Pentecostal movement on campus, closeness has become so central that there is little room left for those who want to retain some distance and keep an intimacy for themselves.

In this context the danger is real that the Pentecostal movement creates a situation in which there is a growing desire to reinforce the feelings of oneness and togetherness, which makes the community highly self-centered and hinders the development of the autonomous Christian who does not depend on the other to feel his own commitments. A real community is for stretching out. The Pentecostal community tends to be bent over inwards, and, without so wanting or aspiring, to become an in-group, developing the idea of a spiritual elite (as the cursillo did) with a subtle handling of the terms "we" and "they."

Are the prayer meetings all spontaneous? The informal, somewhat casual character of the Pentecostal meetings suggests that the real leadership is given to the Holy Spirit. But on closer observation, the meetings are found to be much more organized. There is a certain program that reappears in most Pentecostal meetings: First, witnesses, songs, readings, which prepare for the baptism of the Spirit. Then there is some time allotted for free conversation in which people share their experiences. Finally, after offering more prayers, songs and readings, the laying on of the hands takes place, leading to a climax in the speaking in tongues and the praising of the Lord in ecstatic forms of happiness and joy. This all could not take place without strong and very influential leaders.

But here a new question arises. Who accepts responsibility or authority? The "leaders" refer immediately to the Spirit as the great leader. To the question "Can't the experience be very dangerous for some people?" they would reply, "The Holy Spirit cannot do dangerous things. He is a healing force." In this way the "leaders" refuse explicit leadership, responsibility and authority, confiding in the immediate intervention of God. But in so doing they tend to neglect a definite responsibility, not only in terms of preparation and the actual event but also in terms of the long-range consequences that these experiences will have on the ongoing development of the spiritual life of the people involved.

A Theological Perspective

AN ACTIVE PARTICIPANT of the Pentecostal movement will probably pay very little attention to a psychological approach to his experience. He might even feel psychology to be a hindrance to the free movements of the Spirit.

But this immediately raises the question of the theological significance of the Pentecostal movement. Most remarkable is the conviction of the immediate intervention of the Holy Spirit in human life. During the meetings the "leaders" often explain how he who is willing to surrender and ask for God's coming will experience the eruption of the Spirit in this human world and allow Him to take over the initiative. "Pentecostalism was, and to a degree remains, more a movement than a church," McDonnell has said.[6] We cannot speak about a Pentecostal doctrine, and perhaps it is for this reason that Pentecostalism so easily becomes a part of different religious institutions to which it adapts itself quite easily. For entering the Catholic Church, Pentecostalism could establish contact at the sacramental level by showing "the relation of the sacramental life to personal holiness and practical piety."[7]

---

6 McDonnell, "The Ecumenical Significance of the Pentecostal Movement," *op. cit.*, 623.

7 McDonnell, "The Ecumenical Significance of the Pentecostal Movement," *op. cit.*, 621.

It is, therefore, understandable that Pentecostalism brings people back to their religious practices. Often students who did not "practice their religion" return to confession, Communion, and their lost devotion to Our Lady and the rosary. In no way does Pentecostalism seem to threaten the Catholic orthodoxy. The opposite seems true. In the eyes of many, it seems to point to a reinforcing of the basic Roman Catholic doctrines and beliefs.

But it is exactly here where many theologians raise questions. For, while not denying any Catholic doctrine or practice, the Pentecostals within the Catholic Church act in a way which does not take into account the major development of the recent renewal in Catholic theology. A deeper understanding of the incarnation leads to a rethinking of the humanity of God. More and more it has become clear that God reveals Himself to man through man and his world and that a deeper understanding of human behavior leads us to a deeper understanding of God. The new insights of psychology, sociology, anthropology and so forth are no longer feared as possible threats to the supernatural God, but more as an invitation to theological reflection on the new insights and understandings. Vatican II strongly supported this humanization of the Church, and the new theology was a great encouragement to mobilize all the human potentialities in the different levels of human life as being the most authentic way to understand the voice of God to His people. The new theology was "discovered" by a deeper understanding of the createdness of the world, by discerning that there is a task of Christian secularization. It was exactly this that the first Christians did: demythologize Caesar and the State. The more we make the world what it ought to be, a created reality with tremendous potentialities for growth, the more this world calls for Him, who is Uncreated. And in this sense secularization is possible only by faith.

In the perspective of this trend in theology, which also encourages more social action and "worldly" involvement, the Pentecostal trend seems a step back. It calls for God's immediate intercession outside the human potentials. In a way it seems that God does not use man, unless as a passive instrument which is the victim of the struggle between demonic and divine forces. The devil is an alien power invading man, and so is the

Spirit. The question then becomes, "Who is possessing me?" But possession, good or evil, remains a passive state; it does not give full credit to the basic Christian idea that we are created to create, and to realize our deepest human potentialities in the service of our fellow men, in the love of whom we discover the Spirit of God.

Having discussed the Pentecostal movement as a revival of the devotional Church, as a religious reaction to a world with a heavy stress on achievement, and as raising many psychological and theological questions, the critical tone might have overshadowed a deeper concern about a valid religious experience. We might have overlooked that in one way the Pentecostal movement is an invitation to a deeper search. It made God a living God, a real experience, an actual event. Whereas the whole field of theological education is desperately looking for ways to bring theology from "brain level to guts level," the Pentecostals certainly do it. And it is no surprise that many envy those who experience the presence of God as an undeniable reality. Is it not just this that all the forms of renewal (liturgical, social, clerical, etc.) are trying to do—to make religious life something vibrant, a living source of constant inspiration?

The new wave of Pentecostalism on campus obviously answers a burning need in many students. It worries many who are concerned about the effects on the mental health of some of the participants, it places a heavy responsibility on the leaders of the movement, and it disturbs many theologians; but it also offers a chance to come to a new realization of the crucial importance of valid religious experience as an authentic part of the Christian life. It would be a pity if we missed this chance by a hasty judgment and an intolerant condemnation.

INTIMACY AND COMMUNITY

5

Depression in the Seminary

IT IS NOT too long ago that the stereotype of the seminarian offered the picture of a very nice, sweet boy, somewhat talkative, easily excited about such innocent things as a recent article, naive, inexperienced especially in matters of sex, but always good-natured, friendly, smiling, and ready to help even when not asked.

That stereotype is changing rapidly. What we see today is far from an easy-going, optimistic young man. We are struck by quite different characteristics. We are more likely to find a problem-ridden, struggling student who takes himself, his world and his future very seriously, who wants to debate and discuss many issues, who is seldom relaxed, but inclined to experience his youth as a long and dark tunnel the end of which he does not see.

And whereas we tended to think of the seminary as a place with joyful, self-confident people, now a visitor might find it to be a place with troubled, doubting people, pervaded with a general atmosphere of depression. Although we are stereotyping and therefore simplifying, we cannot avoid the growing conviction that depression is one of the most surprising symptoms in our seminary communities. If it is true that depression is considered as one of the main problems of the college student, this is even more the case if we consider the seminarian of today. For not only a distant look but even many intensive discussions with seminarians leave one with the feeling that a heavy cloud, undefined and mysterious, is darkening the life of the seminary.

And many staff members find themselves amazed and deeply disappointed when they discover that after years of conscious modernization and liberalization, after many efforts to open a closed system to free an unfree institution, they find their students sad instead of happy, unfriendly and moody instead of good-natured, closed and suspicious instead of open and communicative. This seemingly strange phenomenon demands our special attention today. Our main question is: What is the relationship between formation and depression? And, as no clinician will ever advise any therapeutic measure without a careful and specific diagnosis, we will first try to understand the nature of the depression and its correlation with different new techniques in formation. Then we will try to make some suggestions which might help us in our task to overcome this painful and often destructive symptom.

I. Diagnostic Considerations

THERE IS NO doubt that we who are seminary staff members find ourselves in a very complex situation, actually in the middle of a paradox. We are giving to people who come to us for formation the freedom to educate themselves. We are taking away structures from people who want to be formed through channeling their unstructured drives. We have become deeply convinced that the highly regimented seminary life belongs definitely to the past, but also we have discovered that many new freedoms do not always give the desired satisfaction. In this context we have to face the problem of seminary depression.

I propose to discuss this problem in two ways: as a problem of identity for the students and staff, and as a problem of new educational methods.

A. DEPRESSION AS AN IDENTITY PROBLEM

1. A Problem of Student Identity

Staff-members are dealing with students who realize that they have not yet fully developed their potentialities, who experience a tremendous amount of energy, and who have only a vague idea in which direction they want to go. The students all hope to find three things:

a) Competence, which enables them to cope with the demands of society.

b) Control, which provides them with channels for their unruly impulses.

c) Vocation, which gives them the conviction that they are called to do what they felt vaguely attracted to.

Some will discover that they are not intelligent enough to become competent, some will find that their deepest desires point in a direction other than celibate community life, and many will recognize that they are not called for the work they felt inclined to in the beginning. But it is certain that all are looking for a structure, clear, explicit and articulated, in which they can test themselves and be tested by others in order to allow the necessary decisions for their future life. If this is true we immediately become aware of a severe identity crisis in terms of competence, impulse control and vocation.

a) If a seminarian wants competence he finds himself involved in one of the most difficult fields to feel competent in — theology. The questions of theology vary from questions regarding specific issues all the way to the question of whether theology is a field for study at all. Very few students feel proud of theology as their discipline in the way a lawyer, doctor, sociologist, or psychologist is proud of his field, and most often they hope to become competent in other areas of study besides theology in order to feel like valuable members of society.

b) If a seminarian wants to find control for his strong drives and impulses, he finds himself in a situation where many taboos are questioned and in which he finds many ambiguous signals regarding the expression of his erotic desires. What has vanished is clarity. A student who pronounced temporary vows and dates a girl on the side is not expelled from the seminary, but rather it is suggested to him in many ways that it might be good to have some dating experience before he makes up his mind. Not too long ago the so-called "particular friendships" were a subject of concern to many faculty members, and of ridicule to the students who did not really know what their superiors were so concerned about. But today the staff has become afraid to even warn against particular friendships whereas many students find themselves in energy-devouring personal relationships with roommates or friends and are sometimes made very anxious due to the obvious sexual feelings which have come to their awareness. Overt homosexual relations which ten years ago were mostly a part of the fantasy of the staff now at times have become a part of the student's problems.

c) If a student comes to deepen his vocation, he finds that hardly anybody can tell him what it means to be a priest. We might even say that the closer he comes to ordination the vaguer his ideas about the priesthood become. When he entered the seminary, he perhaps wanted to be a man like his uncle-priest, his teacher-priest, or like one of the priests he admired, but while going through the years of formation he is exposed to so much questioning, doubting and personal failures that he starts wondering more and more if he should give the most explicit unchangeable commitment to the most undefined and unclear profession. At the same time he wonders who is calling whom. Ten years ago it was clear that the church called and that it was an honor, privilege and election to be ordained to the priesthood. The representatives of the church made it clear: "If you don't live up to the expectations, we ask you to leave." But now the student seems to say to the church: "If you don't live up to my expectations I am leaving." And in many subtle ways it is communicated to the student that nobody wants to lose him and that he can make more demands on the church than the church on him. And although it might seem that this form of student power is attractive to the seminarian, the fact of the matter is that nobody wants to enter a profession which does not contain a demanding call.

So we see that precisely in the three main areas of seminary formation, Competence, Control and Vocation, the student feels frustrated. He feels like a man without a respected discipline, surrounded by ambiguous signals concerning his impulse control and preparing himself for a vocation which has become subject to endless questioning. Slowly the idea crawls up to him that the most unpopular thing to do these days is to become a priest. For a young man, full of energy, ambition and generosity, commitment to an unappreciated, nonchallenging and unclear life seems no commitment at all. And it is not difficult to see that this identity crisis can become the source of a painful depression.

2. A Problem of Staff Identity

The problem, however, is not just a student problem. The new attitudes of the faculty also explain part of this strange feeling of a collective depression. In a somewhat complicated and seldom recognized way, the democratization of student-faculty relations cause unexpected conflicts. Not too long ago seminaries were places with many rules, usually strict observance and a clear-cut division of authority. There was a lot of rebellion and anger caused by this structure, but students knew to whom to show their anger and against whom to rebel. There was usually a clear system of reward and punishment and students knew what to expect when they took a risk and were caught in the act—frequently a very innocent act of trespassing some quite irrelevant rule. But then someone came to them and said: "It is up to you, if you want to go to Mass or not, if you want to stay in bed or not, go to parties or not, date girls or not, stay up all night or not, come to the recreation or not. You know what you are supposed to do. It is up to your own conscience to do it." Most good, willing and idealistic staff members don't always see what this means. Many times it simply means, "We expect you to do all these things and follow all these rules, but we will not enforce them. We trust you and your own judgment. We hope you won't disappoint us."

The result of this new attitude is the situation of sin without the possibility of doing penance. Seminarians now act in many ways which they know that their superiors don't like, but nobody says anything, nobody objects, reprimands or punishes. They only look disappointed, personally offended, and are saying with their eyes: "I thought I could trust you, but now you do this to me." If a man has nobody to punish him when he feels he deserves it, he starts punishing himself. It is this inward-turned hostility which causes the depression which has become such a pervasive mood in many seminarians. And many staff members are surprised and even bitterly disappointed that all their generous gifts of freedom to the students are not accepted with a joyful thanks, but result in an often loaded and chokingly unfree student-staff relationship. We should take a closer look at this phenomenon. Two aspects seem important: a) The personalized punishment, and b) The verbal and non-verbal communication of doubts.

a. The Personalized Punishment

The staff very often is disappointed that the students don't live up to the expectations. Students prove less generous than the faculty hoped. They take advantage of their new freedom, do not express thanks for it, but only ask for more. Superiors and other faculty members very often feel personally hurt, and although their hands are itching to slap the student in the face, they feel too liberal to do so, and have to resort to a very subtle and often harmful form of punishment, such as: speaking about lack of trust, sudden inappropriate anger about very small things, looking somber and heavy, and communicating on a very personal level that they are offended and that the students make their life miserable. And just as no child can adequately react to his mother who instead of punishing the child for breaking a glass, says, "Don't you love mama more than to do this to me?", so a student does not know how to handle this highly personalized form of punishment. He can only feel guilty and unable to do anything about it. And that is what creates this tense and choking feeling which takes the humor out of relationships and makes everyone hypersensitive to each other.

b. Communication of Doubts

The second aspect of the student-staff relationship which can lead to depression is the way in which the staff communicates its own problems. Many faculty members are questioning the same basic values the students are questioning. They realize that the student problems are not just problems related to their own individual growing pains, but to the growing pains of the whole church. And many seminary teachers are doubting if it is good to encourage a young, intelligent man to become a priest in a community full of confusion and worries. They are asking themselves: "Am I really making a man happy by encouraging him to persevere in the seminary? Can I really give a meaningful answer to his question of what it means to be a priest in a modern world? Does it really make sense to advise him to commit himself for life to a status in which sexual intimacy cannot be striven for? Can I take the responsibility, even when it is a partial responsibility, for anybody's choice of a profession which is in the middle of drastic change?"

These doubts and this anguish do not remain unnoticed by students. In many verbal and nonverbal ways these existential questions enter into the student-faculty relationship. Identification is still the main process by which a man finds his vocation in life. Strong convincing personalities, who give an attractive visibility to their way of life, are the most powerful influences on a young man's life choice. Who wants to become a doctor when his teachers don't believe that they can cure, who wants to be coached by a coach who does not believe that he can win a game, who wants to become a teacher when his professor is only bitter about his students? And who wants to become a priest if he lives with priests who question the foundations of their commitment: the nature of the priesthood, the church, the incarnation and the concept of God. And although these questions are not always personal questions, they are so much a part of the general atmosphere of religious life today that only a stubborn isolationist can completely stay away from them.

Therefore we might wonder if many faculty members who encourage their students to discuss their problems in an open exchange of ideas and adopt the role of understanding listeners themselves, do not in fact, although not intentionally, pass on their burden. And students might experience this as if they are told: "You might like to have a try at the problems which we did not find an answer for ourselves." It might even be possible that many forms of liberalization in today's seminary formation are felt by the students to be testimony of the incapacity to offer meaningful structures on the side of the staff. Many seminarians, who have participated in year-long discussions on about every possible basic subject are showing signs of fatigue, disappointment, confusion and even hostility. Some even feel cheated, as if they had wasted their time groping with questions which don't lead anywhere and are doomed to create frustration.

And so we find not only depression related to the identity crisis of the students but also related to the identity crisis of the staff. It is exactly the mutual reinforcement of many doubts, uncertainties and worries which makes it so difficult to lift the hovering cloud above the seminary. If we now will try to analyze some of the new trends in seminary formation we have to try to understand the temptation of creating a vicious circle of depression which is very difficult to break.

B. DEPRESSION AND THE NEW EDUCATIONAL METHODS

Having discussed the seminary depression as a problem of identity of students as well as staff members, we now should have a closer look at some new educational techniques to explore their possible relationships with this phenomenon. We will limit our discussion to two new approaches in seminary education which have become very popular in practically all modern seminaries in the United States as well as in Europe: I will call them dialogue and small-group living. And although you might experience it as a rather painful process, I propose to analyze these new methods in some detail to show some of the most overlooked complications of these methods. It might be important to say at this point that I do not try in any way to question or minimize the value of these methods. I only hope to point out the many hidden traps of which we have to be aware in order to avoid them.

1. Dialogue and Depression

The word dialogue is used here in a very general way. It is meant to embrace many forms of behavior described in terms such as: encounter, open discussion, talking things through, being open to each other, and it indicates a high level of verbal communication. In this analysis we want to focus on the verbal aspects of the dialogue.

The growing emphasis on the value of verbal communication of students with each other and their faculty is based on two usually unarticulated presuppositions which are usually taken for granted. They are, first, that free and open sharing of ideas and feelings brings people closer together, and, secondly, that a high degree of verbal interchange facilitates existential decisions by clarifying the issues involved.

Our first question therefore is: Does verbal communication bring people closer together? Although words are meant to communicate, they very often are used as a curtain to prevent communication. You probably remember that one of the best ways to succeed in an oral exam is to keep talking to prevent the professor from asking more questions, or to keep him talking, allowing him to suggest the answer before you have to confess your ignorance. In many discussions words are used to fill a fearful silence, to prevent the real questions from being asked or the painful issues from being touched. Many parliamentary discussions are aimed more at delaying the problem than at coping with it. Hours of talk in the United Nations, which to an outsider seem trivial and artificial, fulfill the highly useful function of preventing a dangerous encounter. Although this seems obvious on a large scale we seldom are aware of these same dynamics if we encourage our students to discuss their problems. But let us not forget that students who are constantly subject to grading and evaluation are in many ways afraid of each other and usually hyper-self-conscious. They are often so caught up in questioning their own adequacy that they are hardly open to allowing anybody to enter into the sensitive area of their personality, where they experience doubts and confusions. When you observe a discussion of students carefully, you will often find yourselves in the midst of many verbal harnesses, which are often more restraining the more words are used. If you don't believe it, just see what happens when someone is interrupted. The only one who usually brings the subject back to the moment of interruption is the speaker himself. Very seldom someone else says: "Sorry, you were talking about your trip through the mountains when John came in. How did things go on?" If the storyteller himself does not pick up the subject again, the conversation shifts to other subjects without pain.

What do people do when others are speaking? Well, very often they are busy preparing their own story, or deciding upon their own position. If someone remarks: "The assassination of Senator Kennedy was the result of a communist conspiracy," the usual reaction to that statement is the internal question: "Do I agree or not?" Instead of trying to better understand the speaker's position, the listener is thrown back on himself, and is busy figuring out his own position. And as soon as this position is verbally expressed, the rest of the dialogue is often a constant attempt to defend it, and to avoid defeat. Very often you will see people convincing themselves and their peers of an idea which they only hesitantly formulated in the beginning. The sadness of this story is that people often enter the discussion freely and relatively open-minded, and leave it very opinionated, with the meager satisfaction that they could not be convinced of the opposite and that they won a battle even when there was basically nothing to win.

All I am trying to say is that verbal interchange between students does not always bring them closer together. It might just as well separate them. Seminarians who have been encouraged to dialogue with the suggestion that this will create a better community can become very disappointed and even hostile when they find that a year of discussion did not take away their feelings of loneliness and alienation. Often enough they find an unexpected contrast between the result of many discussions and the main reason why they engaged themselves in the first place. And sometimes they feel more like strangers after than before the dialogue started. It is not difficult to see how a feeling of failure and depression can come forth from this experience.

Our second question is: How far does the clarification of pertinent issues help to solve existential problems? Here we touch a very painful source of frustration. For insight into a problem and the ability to cope with it are two different things. If seminarians discuss the meaning of the priesthood, celibacy, the institutional church, the death of God, etc., this might help them to think more clearly about these issues and to see the different ramifications of the problems, but if they expect to solve their very personal questions: Should I become a priest, live a celibate life, remain within the institutional church, and believe in a living God, then long discussions can become an excruciating experience. I have followed a year-long discussion by seminarians who hoped to make a decision on celibacy before the approaching date of the ordination. It was sad to see how these students became more and more entangled in a complex net of arguments, ideas and concepts and found themselves lost in a labyrinth of theological turnpikes, highways and sideroads, with a growing anger that they never came to that mysterious center where the answer was supposed to lie waiting for them.

What is really happening here? What would you think about a boy and a girl spending an hour a day to find convincing arguments that they love each other? You know these discussions are the best argument that they should not marry each other, if they don't want to enter into a rigid, stiff relationship, with a total lack of spontaneity.

Discussion requires a certain distance from the subject which allows you to see the many aspects of the issues, and gives you the opportunity to be analytical about it. But analysis means a temporary delay of participation. And only on the level of participation, existential decisions are made. Nobody becomes a priest because of three or four convincing arguments. Nobody commits himself to the celibate life because of Rahner, Schillebeeckx or Sydney Callahan. Theology, psychology and sociology don't offer solutions for existential crises, and everyone who suggests this enhances frustration, especially in the case of young men who have not yet fully experienced the limitation of the ratio.

There is a tragic and humorous note to the fact that, whereas in many seminaries there is a growing adoration for explicit intellectual awareness and an increasing emphasis on "knowing what you do," the non-religious youth is burning incense, practicing meditation, and eating seed, to reach a higher degree of participation with the basic sources of life. Meanwhile our liturgies have become more talkative and verbose, and incense and other stimuli, auditory and visual, are scorned as being a part of an old magic.

But what we see is that the seminarians feel caught in the ropes of their dialogues and, seeing no end in terms of decision-making, they become disappointed, moody and depressed.

2. Small Group Living and Depression

Besides a growing emphasis on dialogue and discussion we find in many formation programs a shift from large, sometimes anonymous, groups of students living together in one building, to the more intimate, small groups, which often are called teams.

The team approach is an obvious reaction to a very impersonal kind of living in which the students went through many years of formation without ever being able to establish meaningful relationships with their fellow students or faculty. By dividing the large group into small teams, the possibility of real fraternities is created and a new form of community living envisioned. But here also, just as in the case of dialogue and discussion, things don't always work out in the expected direction. Let us try to understand some of the difficulties involved with the team approach.

a) The first problem is the simple fact that seminarians cannot avoid each other any longer. In a large group, where small, informal subgroups usually develop, there exists the possibility of staying away from irritating people, of keeping distant from others who seem to operate on a different wavelength, and of moving more or less freely in and out. In a team you are very close to a few fellows, and many of your activities are under the critical eyes of your team members, even when you don't feel attracted to them. If you do not show up at a team meeting, this not only will be noticed, but also criticized as a sign of lack of interest or commitment to the group. If you do not speak in a gathering people wonder why you are so silent. Whatever you do or don't do can become highly charged by very personal connotations. It is obvious therefore that team living is much more demanding than living in a large group, and asks for a much greater maturity.

b) The second problem is related to the confusion about the meaning of a team. The word team is usually used to indicate the cooperation of a small group of people who by coordination of their different skills are better able to fulfill a certain task. The common task is what determines the nature of the team. If the team does not function well, this will be reflected in the quality of the work.

In a formation setting, however, the team often is not task-oriented. The team wants to create the best possible living conditions for its members. It is more like a family unit to which you return after a busy day of work. And here the problems start, because the team in this setting easily becomes self-oriented instead of task oriented, and the problems of the team are not any longer related to questions raised by the nature of the work to be done but to questions raised by the nature of the interpersonal relationships. And in this case many team meetings tend to degenerate into amateur group therapy, in which members try to explore their feelings toward each other, and encourage each other to put on the table many things which much better could remain in the drawer. Team meetings in this case can become highly charged, and instead of moving away from individual concerns to a common concern, they can become self-centered to the point of narcissism.

We have to realize that the students involved are already very self-conscious, considering their age, their academic life and their ambivalent feelings toward their future profession. And although it might be very important that individual anxiety and confusion be expressed at certain times, the main purpose of the whole formation is to encourage students to grow away from this self-interest and to become free and open, to be really interested in the life and concerns of their fellowmen.

It is true that a culture which does not allow regression at times can ruin people. Without sleep man cannot live, but the real things usually don't happen during sleep. Crying, talking about yourself, and defenseless expression of feelings of love and hate are very important for the mental health of man, but they all are temporary regressions which can only be meaningful in terms of an ensuing progression. In formation regression should be allowed and even encouraged at times, but never considered as an ideal to strive for. The ideal remains not to be concerned with yourself, not to cry, not to express all your emotions, but to forget your own problems, and to do the work which calls for your attention and interest. Therefore, I feel that a team in which regressive forms of behavior are encouraged is vitiating its own purpose.

c) This brings us to the final problem with the team, which is related to intimacy. Lonesomeness is often experienced on a very deep and painful level by adolescents and young adults. The tendency exists to look for a solution to this problem by establishing very demanding and often exhausting friendships. These friendships can be clinging and immature and based on primitive needs. One of the tasks of formation is to stimulate the student not to let himself be guided by these impulsive needs, but to come to a mature self-awareness and self-confidence, in which friendship can develop as a giving and forgiving relationship and in which feelings of lonesomeness can be understood and accepted in a mature way.

Therefore it is very important to prevent the team from becoming a clique which is allowed to act on primitive needs and desires. This is difficult because the stresses on many students are so intense that they often have inexhaustable needs for intimacy, and clinging friendships. But this is often encouraging the unrealistic fantasy that the true, real, faithful friend is somewhere waiting, able to take away all the feelings of frustration. A man who lives in the seminary or enters the priesthood with this fantasy is doomed to be a very unhappy man. And if the team becomes a way to satisfy this unrealistic desire for intimacy, much harm can be done.

So we can see that team living is a very special and delicate enterprise which demands the special attention of those who are responsible for formation. The main danger is that a task-oriented team degenerates into a self-oriented clique in which sticky relationships drain the psychic energy of the students and allow regressive behavior. In this situation students easily become peevish, very demanding and irritable. They tend to ask for more attention than anybody can give and for more sympathy than anybody can show. They speak more about love than is healthy, enjoy in a very subtle way their own loneliness, and show basically all the symptoms of a spoiled child. And the most common universal and contagious symptom of this regressive behavior is depression, the feeling of not being understood, loved or liked, and the desire to be pitied by those for whom they feel a strange mixture of hostility and love. And so small-group living can easily, in complete contrast with its intention, degenerate into a very depressing way of living. Most remarkable is that the feelings involved are often so vague and all-pervasive that the seminarians themselves and even the staff have great difficulty in identifying the source of the problem.

APPENDIX: THE PROBLEM OF FATIGUE
Before finishing this diagnostic section, I would like to consider one of the most visible symptoms related to the problem of dialogue and small-group living. A remarkable number of seminarians complain about an inappropriate degree of fatigue. Although they can sleep as long as they want, they look very tired. Their eyelids feel heavy and they experience their bodies as something they carry around. The philosopher might say: "They have their bodies more than they are their bodies." When they wake up in the morning they don't feel relaxed, but are very much aware of themselves lying on the bed as a heavy load. Even dressing becomes like a job that asks concentration and special energy. This so-called neurotic fatigue is the result of a way of living which is characterized by hyperawareness, by which man does not rely any longer on his automatic

processes, but wants to know what he does from moment to moment. Just as a man who wants to be aware of his breathing is in danger, and one who wants to control his heartbeat cannot live, a seminarian who speaks all the time about friendship, love and community might miss the opportunity to experience any of these realities. This lack of participating life is usually related to an often unconscious anxiety. Somehow man in that state of fatigue has temporarily lost his basic confidence that life is good and worth living and acts as if he has to be constantly awake, always prepared for unexpected traps and dangers.

This form of fatigue can be harmful because it easily brings the students into a vicious circle which he can hardly break. His depression makes him tired, and his fatigue makes him depressed, and so on. I do not want to suggest that all or most seminarians show this symptom, but some of them do, and recognizing its nature might prevent us from saying: "Come on, take a good rest and don't study for a day," because instead of helping him, that sort of advice might make it worse.

This finishes our diagnostic section, in which we discussed the problem of depression as a problem of identity of students and staff and as a problem related to the new educational methods, dialogue and small-group living. As an often visible symptom of depression, we focused on the neurotic fatigue. All this leaves us with many questions. The temptation now is to say: "Perhaps we should go back to the good old days, with the early hours, long meditation, the rites of discipline and the whole clearcut system of reward and punishment." Before we make that mistake we should raise the question of therapy.

II. Therapeutic Consideration

AFTER OUR RATHER long diagnosis we might wonder if the new trends in seminary education are really as promising as we hoped them to be. If openness to many basic questions, the new democratic forms of government, the emphasis on dialogue and small-group living result in a funereal atmosphere or a collection of intelligent grumpies, we could become somewhat suspicious about being modern.

But this is a temptation, the famous temptation, of using the weak spots in renewal as an argument for conservatism. If anything is clear it is that the seminary life as we knew it ten years ago is gone, never to return. And what is even more clear is that it took courage, imagination, and a great sensitivity to our changing world to start new ways in the preparation for the priesthood and the religious life. And it would be easy, cheap and dishonest to point to the mistakes of those who took the risks of new experiments. Every form of experimentation is bound to yield some unexpected problems. If they were expected, it probably was not a real experiment to begin with.

But we also have to try to account for the problems. And when we explained how new student-staff relationships and new educational approaches have their painful drawbacks, we did not want to suggest that the new ways are the wrong ways, but that they can perhaps be smoothed a little bit by a better understanding of the dynamics involved.

Therefore, our task now is to formulate an "antidepressive regime," that is, guidelines which might help to alleviate the depressive reactions to many creative initiatives. Before mentioning, however, any specific guidelines we should formulate the principle on which all guidelines rest. That principle is that all formation has as its primary task to offer a meaningful structure which allows for a creative use of the student's energies. Structure is the key word of formation and the criterion of any educational guideline. Structure allowing one to judge which feelings to trust and which feelings to distrust, which ideas to follow and which to reject. Structure providing unity to the many seemingly disconnected emotions and ideas of the student. Structure which helps to decide which plan is just a fancy and which contains the seed for a workable project. Structure, which offers the possibility to organize the day, plan the year, and steer the course of life.

Our problems today are not related to the fact that we are too modern, too liberal or too progressive, but that we do not have as yet the meaningful structures through which we can help the student give form to his many as yet undirected and unfocused potentialities.

In the context of this principle we now will try to formulate some guidelines. We will do this in terms of student-faculty identity and in terms of the new educational methods.

A. STRUCTURE AND THE IDENTITY PROBLEM

A student who is struggling with his identity in terms of competence, control and vocation will never find this if the staff to whom he daily relates does not claim in a clear and defined way its own role. This role is a role of authority. If a staff member has no authority at all a student cannot relate to him as a student. The main guideline here is that the staff has to be authoritative without becoming authoritarian. Authoritative simply means that the source of the staff member's authority lies in his competence, maturity and faith. He knows his field, is able to cope with the tensions of life and believes that he is called to do a meaningful work. This is the kind of authority that is inner-directed and does not need to rely on quotes from popes, bishops or superiors in order to give a sense to desires. An authoritarian man needs the rules to live, an authoritative man lives in such a way that the rules become obvious. Students want to be criticized, reprimanded and even punished. They ask for it if you can hear their language. But the authority by which this happens should be based not on subjective feelings and ideas, not on abstract rules and regulations, but on a critical, competent and objective understanding of the students' behavior.

Conflicts, frictions and differences of opinion don't have to be avoided. They are a part of formation. But only when the faculty claims its own authority and insists on it, will the student be able to identify himself, evaluate his own experiments in life and take a firm stand there where he feels solid ground. And such a student is not depressed.

B. STRUCTURE AND THE NEW EDUCATIONAL METHODS

Our second guideline is related to dialogue and small-group living in the seminary. Both are highly moral activities which require someone who is able to take the responsibility. If it is true that a discussion can unite as well as separate, and that a small group can be task-oriented as well as self-centered, we are involved in very sensitive areas of life which cannot be left to the process of trial and error. If nobody accepts this responsibility, emotions, ideas and plans will be like water which is not guided by a riverbed but splashes in all directions destroying land instead of irrigating it. He who accepts responsibility will be able to provide creative channels through which life can become purposive. Therefore our guideline here is that such sensitive processes as dialogue and group living require a well-defined responsibility in order to be effective.

This responsibility usually means that some form of leadership has to exist by which structure can be brought to dialogue and group processes. Let me mention different ways in which this leadership can function.

a) Good leadership can prevent group processes from becoming amateur forms of group therapy. The expression of love and hate, anger and frustration, hostility and erotic desires, without special control, careful supervision and well-defined goals is dangerous and tends to harm people more than help them.

b) Good leadership can foster at times of crisis the right atmosphere to discuss certain existential issues. Such a discussion can have a temporary value. When the leader is not just an equal participant, but represents more than an individual opinion, he can make it clear to the students that they are on safe ground and they are protected against dangerous traps.

c) Good leadership keeps the communication in a group free and open. Nobody can be forced to enter a discussion if he does not want it. Many people just don't have anything to say or are not ready to say it. And subtle pressure to participate in a dialogue can take away the freedom of people to determine their own degree of intimacy.

Considering these aspects of good leadership it seems that the essential idea is that discussions and group living can only bring people closer together if they are already together in some way. Leadership means the representation of some level of community within which these processes can take place in a creative way. The leader's authority can be seen as an expression of the authority which belongs to the community in the first place. The task of a leader, therefore, can be seen as safeguarding the boundaries of the community and judging which ideas, feelings and actions can be handled within these boundaries and which not. And people will feel much freer to express themselves when they know that they will be warned when they trespass.

Therefore, good leadership offers an antidepressive regime by bringing the loaded question into the safe context of a community. And this brings us to our conclusion which finally allows us to ask what a religious community can be.

THE RELIGIOUS COMMUNITY

After these "therapeutic" considerations in which structure was the key word, we finally had to bring in the term community. Perhaps this is the most widely used term in recent discussions about religious life evoking feelings of great excitement as well as feelings of utter boredom. Up to this point we have tried to avoid this word in order to take a more critical look at the underlying dynamics. But by way of conclusion we need to bring this big word back to our attention and ask ourselves what it means in the context of the problem of seminary depression.

Religious community is *ecclesia*, which means called out of the land of slavery to the free land. It is constantly moving away from the status quo, searching for what is beyond the here and now. As soon as the community becomes sedentary, it is tempted to lose its faith and worship the house-gods instead of the one true God who is leading it in a pillar of fire.

If we speak about vocation we have to ask first of all if the community has a vocation that means experiencing itself as being called out of Egypt, the land of depression, to a new as yet undiscovered country. It seems that some communities have lost their élan and have become so enchanted by the beautiful oasis which they found on their way that they settled for that and forgot their real call.

I think that the vocation of the individual seminarian can be seen as a participation in the vocation of the community. When many students leave the seminary these days, this might very well be due to the fact that they have not been able to find the vocation in which they can participate. Instead they found a group of people very preoccupied with internal conflicts, wrapped up in small, insignificant debates about rituals, rules and authorities, and remarkably blind to the fact that most of their energy is spoiled by trivia while the world is on the verge of committing suicide. These self-centered communities tend to throw the student back on himself and encourage him to be very reflective, suggesting that vocation is an internal inspiration which cannot be discovered unless through endless self-scrutiny. This causes the seminarian to take himself much too seriously and to ask his superiors to pay constant attention to his most individual needs and desires. I think that the problem usually is not with the students who want to give their best, nor with the faculty who are willing to do anything for their students, but with the community at large, which has lost its most basic conviction that its existence is mandatory because it is called to fulfill a task nobody else will fulfill.

There is no lack of generosity. There is so much of it that everyone who can mobilize it and channel it can make mountains move and oceans hold their waves. I am convinced that a community which feels called to do a most difficult task, which asks for great sacrifices and great self-denial in order to do the work of God which is obvious and self-evident, will have no problems at all in finding people who want to join in the challenging enterprise. He who promises hard work, long hours, and much sacrifice will attract the strong and generous but he who promises protection, success and all the facilities of an affluent society will have to settle for the weak, the lazy and the spoiled. It is sad to say, but it is not always the weak and the lazy who leave our seminaries, but often the strong and the generous who had too much to give to do their best in an easy life.

The task of the religious community is to constantly move away out of the comfortable situation and to look for areas where only one who is willing to give his life wants to go. This can be everything: education, hospital work, mission work, etc. But as soon as any of these enterprises starts to become very profitable and successful we should know that this is a state of temptation and a challenge to cut the ties again, and to move on to new areas. And much of the depression we discovered in our diagnosis might be considered in the final analysis as a sign that the community is tempted to stop being *ecclesia* and to lose contact with the pillar of fire. A religious community can only survive when it stays in contact with this fire. It is the same fire which was the symbol of the new community on the day of Pentecost. Instead of huddling together and clinging to each other in fear, the apostles opened their doors, stepped into the world and went out in different directions. They knew that they were carried and supported by more than just the psychological experience of sympathy and friendship.

That is what Jesus indicated to the hard-headed Peter when He asked him three times: "Do you love Me more than these others do?" Jesus meant *agape*, not *phileia*. It took Peter a while to understand the difference. But Jesus meant that only this Divine love, *agape*, would make it possible for him to fulfill his vocation. Because this vocation meant that he would not any longer put on his own belt and walk where he liked, but stretch out his hands and let somebody else put a belt around him, and take him where he would rather not go (John 21:18). Only by growing old would Peter be able to do this. The formation in the seminary is meant to allow this growth to the mature man who strengthened by the new love is able to understand that the cross is no longer a sign of depression but a sign of hope.

INTIMACY AND
THE MINISTRY

6

The Priest and His Mental Health

IF YOU WERE ever present at the admission of a severely disturbed patient to a mental hospital, you might have been surprised by some of the questions asked by the psychiatrist. Instead of asking: "What is the problem?" or "What is bothering you?" he sometimes says: "Can you tell me what time it is, do you know what day it is, what month is this, what year is this?" Then he inquires: "What is the name of this town and what country are we in?" And finally he asks: "What is your name, who are your friends, and what job do you have?"

Why does a doctor ask all these obvious questions? He wants to know if the patient knows: when he is, where he is, and who he is. Because basic to man's mental health is that he is oriented in time, place, and person, or—to say the same—that man is realistically aware of himself.

But what is most basic to our mental health is also crucial in all levels of our behavior. The painful and difficult problems in our life are always related to essentials. We cannot exist without being loved, but nevertheless to love and to be loved remains our main concern through life. In the same way, being oriented in time, place, and person is at the root of our mental health. As we grow up and are confronted with new bits of reality every day of our life, this remains a constant challenge, especially for those whose world is in the midst of turmoil, subjected to severe reevaluation and extreme self-criticism. That is our world, and perhaps especially the world of the priest. The question: "When, where and who am I?" might after all not be easy to answer when asked by the priest in the modern world. Suddenly and painfully confronted with new and confusing realities, he might lose his orientation. And this means that his mental health is threatened.

Therefore, I will discuss the mental health of the priest in the world in terms of healthy timing, healthy spacing, and healthy self-understanding, and show how problems in these three areas can become a source of mental suffering for the priest in the modern world.

1. Healthy Timing

HEALTHY TIMING IS perhaps one of the most obvious and nevertheless least understood problems for priests. Let us have a look at two forms of timing: long-range timing and short-term timing.

Long-range timing refers to the way a priest uses his days, weeks, and months in the perspective of an effective life plan. I don't think that it is an exaggeration to say that many newly ordained priests leave the seminary with great ambitions, high aspirations and often zealous expectations. The excited new priest tends to jump into his pastoral activities as a true follower of Pelagius. He very soon can become the victim of what by distant observers has been called "A redemption complex." He is almost omnipresent, as far as his territory goes. No Bible group, no P.T.A. meeting, no Boy Scouts practice, Holy Name gathering, social, financial or pious meeting exists without his being there. He talks with almost everyone who wants to talk with him, gives advice to troubled parishioners, counsels couples, teaches classes to grade, trade and high school, and is constantly available for everybody's needs, except perhaps his own. He seldom refuses an invitation, seldom says no, and seldom withdraws to his private room. And he receives his rewards. He is popular, well-liked by his parishioners. They call him nice, kind, and understanding, and say: "This man is really giving himself for his people. He at least understands what is going on. He is different from the old pastor. This young man is available for us, all the time." Indeed, all the time. With a certain pride he tells his colleagues that he hardly gets more than five hours sleep a night, that he never has an opportunity to read a book except his breviary, that he does not even have an hour free to play a game of golf.

Well, you know what this is: The redemption complex in full bloom. But how long does it last? Two, four or five years, perhaps, then things start to look different. He has not been able to change the world around him as he had hoped, people are not so much different from the way they were during his first year. The same old problems keep coming up, but they don't look so exciting anymore. No new books or ideas have entered his room, Then, slowly, but sometimes very pervasively, a feeling of dullness and boredom can creep in and the question comes up: "What am I doing after all? Nothing is really changing and I am getting tired of activities, people, and myself."

Fatigue—physical, because of lack of sleep; mental, because of lack of motivation; and spiritual, because of lack of inspiration—takes over and leads to neutral resignation, growing irritation, or even to eroding depression.

We can call this unhealthy long-range timing. The so-popular, inspiring, creative priest has become, in a few years, an irritated, empty, routine, tired man, who keeps repeating to himself, if not on the pulpit, that since Jesus Christ nothing really has changed, and that there is nothing new under the sun. And many priests who were the hope of the diocese or the star of the order become bitter and disappointed men; some clinging to the priesthood to keep some sort of a home, others leaving it in the hope of starting a new life somewhere else.

But this is still somewhat exceptional. Much more common is the unhealthy short-term timing. Short-term timing refers to the way a priest uses his hours during one day. It seems to me that it is extremely important that the priest has a time to work and a time to relax. There are ways of living in which it is difficult to say whether a person is creating or recreating. A priest who lives in the rectory all day and is surrounded by his colleagues, in a way, is always in his office. People can call him every hour of the day and he is never completely outside the work atmosphere. On the other hand, he can rest at very unusual hours and is always also in his home where he eats, sleeps, plays and prays. So there is very little definition of time. This can result in a feeling of being always busy day and night, without really either working hard or resting well. He has some scheduled activities, but otherwise his work is pretty well at random. The priest is never very certain about what he will be doing during the next hours. To a man with a high sense of duty, this can become extremely frustrating. The lack of gratification can result in a feeling of: "I did not do enough" and impels him to do more in his free hours, with the effect that his disappointment with himself only increases.

When the distinctions between day and night, work and play, duty and hobby, become fuzzy, life loses its rhythm and becomes poorly defined. Such "unhealthy living" may kill inspiration and creativity by making a man the victim rather than the organizer of his time. He is always on the go and seldom stops to reflect on the meaning and effectiveness of his busy life. And sometimes it seems that he is afraid to stand still and think, afraid to discover that being busy and tired is quite something else from being useful.

It is clear that this problem is closely related to celibacy. A priest never leaves home to go to work and never comes back after having fulfilled his daily task, to find someone who helps him take some distance. He is always at home and never at home; he is always at work and never at work, and he wears his uniform always without any distinction of time or kind of activity. This unhealthy short-term timing also can soon lead to fatigue as a constant complaint and to boredom as a constant mood.

In short, healthy timing is essential for the physical, mental and spiritual health of the priest, not only in terms of the long-range effectiveness in his life as a priest, but also in terms of his creativity and inspiration in daily life.

2. Healthy Spacing

BESIDES A HEALTHY use of time, a healthy use of place is of great importance for the mental health of the priest. We can speak about healthy spacing. Seminarians, diocesan and religious priests mostly live in houses where they share all the various aspects of their lives under one roof. One of the critical problems of the Catholic seminary today is called its "total institutionalization." This means that every level of living of the student—his religious formation, his academic training, his social life and his physical education—are all institutionalized and under the same roof, the same rule, and the same authority. The one, very defined milieu pervades and covers all the levels of the life of the student.

And this is not only true of the seminary, but in many ways also of the religious community life and of the rectory life. It seems that there is only one organization which can compete with the Catholic church in terms of total institutionalization, and that is the military.

The priest or seminarian often finds himself in a situation which is experienced as suffocating. If he eats or drinks, plays or prays, sleeps or stays up at night, studies or day dreams, goes to a movie or to a play, all his activities are directly or indirectly under the same authority. He is enclosed.

One of the reasons why a man in the business or academic world is often able to tolerate considerable frustration is exactly related to the fact that he does not find his demanding boss back in his private home, that in his interracial committee he can be leader; that if he goes on a vacation with his wife and children he has authority and responsibility which is different from his authority and responsibility in his profession; that when he goes to the country club he can temporarily forget his conflict with his wife and his problems with his kids. In other words, there are different roofs under which he lives: his home, his office, his cottage, his country club, his church, all representing different realities of life with different authorities and responsibilities. They indicate different levels of living, not completely separated, but distinct enough to be able to function as a mechanism to prevent, compensate, or take away many strains and pressures of daily life. If your superior is bugging you, you at least don't have to face him all day. If you always have to smile and be nice as a tourist guide, you at least can be mad and angry at home for a while. If you cannot say what you think about your secretary in your office, you at least have a chance to let your steam off with your friends in the bar. Different places and different spaces. That can create a healthy balance.

The seminarian or priest often lacks this variation. Whatever he thinks, feels, does, says or writes is finally under the critical eye of the same authority or string of authorities. A parish pastor not only expects his assistant to do responsible professional work between 8 and 5, he also wants him to play bridge with him once a week, to socialize with some of his friends, to join him for a dinner party and perhaps even play golf with him. But he also may expect him not to drink too much beer, not to see *Blow-up*, not to talk with prostitutes on the street, not to wear a tie, not to buy a Thunderbird, and not to receive girls in his room. This is what might be called spiritual suffocation and causes many seminarians and priests to feel caught in a web of unclear relations from which they cannot free themselves without tearing loose. Leaving the priesthood can then become a way to get some fresh air.

Closely related to healthy spacing is the problem of authority vs. responsibility. The question is: "To what extent are we boss under our own roof?" First of all, in the Catholic church we are very quick to delegate responsibility but very slow to delegate authority. Many sermons, lectures, and talks are aimed at convincing us of the tremendous responsibility of the priest in the modern world. But the authority which belongs to this responsibility is not always a part of the package. A priest is responsible for the good atmosphere in the house, but he cannot always change the rules; responsible for a meaningful liturgy, but he cannot experiment very much; responsible for good teaching, but he has to follow the prescribed sequence of subjects, and especially responsible for good advice, but he does not feel free to give his own opinion because he has to represent someone else's authority instead of his own. In reality, this means that in a setting of total institutionalization every sphere of life is controlled from one central point. This has its advantages. After all, the general of an army cannot win a war if he has only partial command over his troops or if that command only lasts from 8 in the morning until 5 in the evening. The question for a priest, however, is whether he is really at war.

But there is another perhaps more complicated problem. That is the problem of the shadow government. Those who have authority do not always know how much they really have. Often they suffer from lack of clarity. The superior of a house does not know how far he can go because a bishop is watching him somewhere; the bishop does not know how far he can go because the apostolic delegate is looking over his shoulder, and the apostolic delegate is not sure exactly what Rome thinks. The problem is not that some have more authority than others, but that there is no clarity and that the further one gets from the problem the thicker the clouds become. Perhaps a lot of fear and anxiety about authority is not so much related to power but to the cloudiness of power, which leaves the responsible people always hanging shadowy in the air. Nobody knows who is really saying what and the further away from home the vaguer and the more anonymous people become. This is what I mean by the shadow government, which causes this constant referral to eternity, where all lines melt together in a quasi-sacred mystery that cannot be touched.

In short, healthy spacing not only refers to healthy defining of places and rooms, but also, connected with that, to healthy clarification of responsibilities and authority which belong to the different roofs under which we live.

3. Healthy Self-Understanding

BUT AFTER ALL this, we still have not arrived at the core of the matter. More fundamental than healthy timing and healthy spacing is healthy self-understanding. In this tumbling and changing world the priest is faced with the most central question: "Who am I?" The rapidly diminishing number of vocations to the priesthood all over the world is dramatically showing that along with the whole church, the priest has entered into an identity crisis. He is asking himself: "Who am I and what can I do?"

In discussing the priest's reality orientation in terms of person, we will make a distinction between his individual and his professional identity.

A. If someone's individual identity crisis concerns the basic levels of his personality he suffers from a severe pathology. Deep depression, obsessive compulsive action, and different forms of psychotic behavior indicate that psychiatric help and sometimes hospitalization are needed. Although perhaps few priests suffer from these severe forms of identity confusion, this basic problem is, in some degree, the problem of every man—but perhaps more of every priest.

How does the priest see himself in his relationship with his fellowman? How does he relate privacy to fellowship, intimacy to social intercourse? Essentially, human existence is "being together." I am not alone in the world but I share this world with others. To be able to live a healthy life in this world which judges me and asks me to play a role according to my physical identity, two things are necessary. First, that I must have my own inner privacy where I can hide from the face of the challenging world; and secondly, I must establish a hierarchy of relationships with this same world. In the inner circle of my life I find him or her who is closest to me. Around this circle of intimacy I find the circle of family and dear friends. Then, at a somewhat larger distance, I locate relatives, and acquaintances and, even further away, the associates in business and work. Finally, I am aware of the vast circle of people that I don't know by name but who in some vague way also belong to this world, which I can call *my* world. Thus, I am surrounded by expanding circles on the threshold of which I station guards, who carefully check whom they allow to enter into a closer intimacy with me. I don't say to the bus driver what I can say to my colleagues. I don't say to my friends what I can say to my parents. But there is a place where nobody can enter, where I am completely by myself, where I develop my own most inner privacy. This is the place where I can meet God, who by His incarnation has thrown off his otherness. The possibility for a man to hide from the face of the world is a condition for the formation of any community. A man who does not have privacy cannot be a part of a community.

It is exactly here that the priest has problems. Very often he has lost his private life, where he can be with himself; nor has he a hierarchy of relationships with guards on the thresholds. Being friendly to everybody, he very often has no friends for himself. Always consulting and giving advice, he often has nobody to go to with his own pains and problems. Not finding a real intimate home in his house or rectory, he often rambles through the parish to find people who give him some sense of belonging and some sense of a home. The priest, who is pleading for friends needs his parishioners more than they need him. Looking for acceptance, he tends to cling to his counselees, and depend on his faithful. If he has not found a personal form of intimacy where he can be happy, his parishioners become his needs. He spends long hours with them, more to fulfill his own desires than theirs. In this way he tends to lose the hierarchy of relationships, never feels safe, is always on the alert, and finally finds himself terribly misunderstood and lonesome.

The paradox is that he who has been taught to love everyone, in reality finds himself without any friends; that he who trained himself in mental prayer often is not able to be alone with himself. Having opened himself to every outsider, there is no room left for the insider. The walls of the intimate enclosure of his privacy crumble and there is no place left to be with himself. The priest who has given away so much of himself creates an inexhaustable need to be constantly with others in order to feel that he is a whole person.

And here the priest is in a crisis situation. Without a spiritual life and a good friend he is like a sounding brass or a tinkling cymbal. This might impress you as an old-fashioned sermon, unless you realize that the question underneath is: "Who guides him who has to guide his people?" No psychotherapist will feel competent to help people if he himself is not willing to constantly reevaluate his own mental health with professional help. But which priest has a spiritual director who helps him to find his way through the complexities of his and others' spiritual lives? There are hundreds of priests who are able theologians, good preachers, excellent organizers, brilliant writers, highly competent sociologists, psychologists, mathematicians and philosophers; but how many are there who can help their fellowmen and especially, their fellow priests, in their most individual spiritual needs? Those seem to be as seldom as white crows. Perhaps one of the most urgent questions remains: "Who is the pastor for the priest?"

B. This brings us to our final and perhaps most specific concern, the professional identity of the priest. Healthy self-understanding not only means a healthy understanding of yourself as an individual in the world, but also a healthy understanding of yourself as a professional man.

The first and most obvious question seems to be: Do we actually have a profession? We live in a society which is characterized by a rapidly growing professionalization. We see a growing number of professionally trained people: doctors, psychiatrists, psychologists, social workers, lawyers, judges, architects, engineers, and nearly every year new professions seem to create themselves. In the psychiatric field we now speak about music therapists, group-therapists, occupational therapists, etc. Everyone has his own specialty, with his own training and his own place in the team of the professions. Where does this leave the priest? What is his speciality? What is his own unique contribution? Is it not true that many priests feel extremely frustrated because they feel that they know a little bit of everything but are not really good in anything? Many feel that they are amateur counselors, amateur social workers, amateur psychologists, amateur group leaders and amateur teachers, but when and where are they really pros? And it is not surprising that many priests are very uncomfortable in a professional milieu, and, in spite of their four or five years of post-graduate training, feel more at ease with the so-called "simple people."

Priests have pretty good reasons to feel this way. A doctor, after four years of theoretical training, needs at least two years of internship under close supervision before he is allowed to practice by himself. A psychologist cannot start his independent work before at least two years of practical training in a very controlled supervisory setting. A social worker does not earn his title without many years of very strict guidance in his professional field. But what about a priest? Most priests study four years of theology and then jump right into the pastoral work without any internship whatsoever. And of those who have a pastoral year only very few receive the needed supervision to make their experience in practice a real learning experience. Who supervised their sermons carefully? Who critically studied and discussed their pastoral conversations? Who helped them to express in the liturgy something meaningful through their hands, voice and eyes? And especially, who helped them to consider the relevance of their knowledge and information—stored up during four years of theory—for their very specific relationship with the confused teenager, the searching college student, the doubtful husband, the despairing father or the depressed widow? Who helped them to ask if their pastoral expectations are realistic or if their desires and needs are tolerable? Who taught them to make intelligent choices and accept possible failures? Who explored with them their limitations, and who taught them to handle the complicated authority problems in relationships with superiors as well as with parishioners? Who inspired them to do more study and research in their own field, and who finally guided them in the integration of new experience? In short, who made them real professionals?

The sociologist, Osmund Schreuder, writes: "The crisis in regard to the priesthood in our time seems to be related to the professional under-development of this occupation."[1] If this is true, we face a mental health problem because a man who permanently doubts his own competence can hardly be considered mentally healthy.

A second question is: Even if our work is professional, is it a reward-ing profession? A professional man who works hard and is creative, re-ceives his rewards. People tell him how they appreciate his work. They praise him, give him a higher salary, and offer him a promotion. And the visible and tangible rewards make him appreciate his profession more. What about the priest? Many priests seem to experience their work as simply filling a position which happened to be open. They are not there because of the specific professional skill which they can apply to that specific situation but they are there because no other priest was there for the job. And once in the job, nobody really cares what he does. As long as he doesn't do stupid things, does not write letters to the editor and does not generally disrupt the existing order, he doesn't hear anything. The reward of the quiet priest is silence from above.

Few religious authorities praise their men. They expect them to do their job and not to ask for a "thank you." Perhaps many priests have even denied themselves the desire to be praised, thanked, paid and ap-preciated. Some distorted view on obedience seems to forbid a desire for gratification and satisfaction. It is amazing to see how few priests can accept a real compliment. They are not used to it and feel somewhat embarrassed, as if they are not allowed to be complimented. But when all the gratification you get out of your study is your grades at the end of the semester, you are less mentally healthy than when you enjoy your study daily and have a good grade on top of that. Daily life in the latter case, is fun. In the former case, you have a lot of pain for the sake of a little gratification. If a priest does not enjoy his daily pastoral work and is only hoping for God's grade at the end of his life, his mental health is in danger. And so is his most important task of bringing life and happiness to his fellowman.

---

1 Osmund Schreuder, "Het professioneel karakter van het geestelijk ambt," *Dekker en van de Vegt* (Nijmegen 1964), 7.

There is one form of gratification which is most absent in the daily life of the parish priest, and that is the gratification of his professional theological discipline. Every professional man knows that his task is not only to keep informed in his field, but also to offer a creative contribution to it. The doctor and psychologist know that while working with people they are helping them best when at the same time they are looking for new insights for the sake of their discipline. A doctor who sees hundreds of allergic patients might, by a systematic way of treating them, not only serve his patients but also his science.

Are there pastors who realize that the people they are working with every day form one of the main sources for their theological understanding? Since God became man, man became the main source for the understanding of God. The parish is just as much a field of research for the priest as the hospital is for the doctor. Perhaps nobody made us so much aware of the need of this empirical theology as the Protestant mental-hospital chaplain, Anton Boisen, who wrote: "Just as no historian worthy of the name is content to accept on authority the simplified statement of some other historian regarding the problem under investigation, so I have sought to begin, not with ready made formulations contained in books, but with the living human documents and with actual social conditions in all their complexity."[2]

The priest is confronted every day with living human documents, and if he is able to read and understand them and make them a constant source for his theological reflection, his life can always be new, surprising, inspiring and creative. There is no human problem, human conflict, human happiness, or human joy, which cannot lead to a deeper understanding of God's work with man.

In this way his profession asks him to remain responsible for God, to keep God alive always changing and always the same, as man himself. And it is here that the priest can find himself at the heart of his profession.

Healthy self-understanding. This was our last and main concern. Healthy understanding of our own individual self realistically related to the other on the basis of a sound spiritual life and a sense for inti-

---

2 Anton Boisen, *The Exploration of the Inner World* (Harper & Brothers: 1962), 185.

macy, and healthy understanding of our professional self, which gives us a humble, gratifying, and scholarly place in the team of the helping professions.

THIS BRINGS US to the end of this orientation session. Is the priest oriented in time, place and person? Does he know when he is, where he is and who he is? Our roaring days are threatening his balance, balance between private and public life, between places to be reserved and places to be shared, between contemplation and action, between study and work. This threat creates anxiety. And this hurts. But if the wounds are understood, it might very well be a constructive anxiety. Then an honest diagnosis serves a good prognosis.

7

Training for the Campus Ministry

DURING THE SECOND World War, many army chaplains, Protestant and Catholic, were faced with a very difficult question: How to be a pastor without a church? In the field there is no pulpit to speak from, no altar to stand behind, no bible class to direct, no discussion group to lead. Many felt like carpenters who had lost their tools. They had to ask themselves, "Can I do something without anything but myself? Can I be a priest without a collar, a book, or a chalice?" In this emergency situation, thousands of men ran to the quickly organized seminars to get some basic training in this new field work.

Perhaps our University campuses today are like the battlefields of the Second World War. The familiar channels through which we could function and reach thousands of students, are leaking or completely broken down. Religious bulletins, processions, rosaries and holy hours are strange memories that evoke a smile. Chapels have become less popular places to visit. Masses and other celebrations only attract a small section of the campus population. Bible clubs, discussion groups, and retreats are liked, perhaps by many, but we wonder for how long. And as time goes on we feel ourselves victims of a religious strip tease in which students are insisting we remove one vestment of office after another, as if to say: "We want to see you naked, and then we will see what you are worth."

In short: We cannot rely on old channels and prepared roads, but we are thrown back on our most personal resources and faced with a great deal of anxiety. To use the image of Erwin Goodenough: The curtains through which we communicated with the divine, are torn down and we wonder if we can live without them.[1]

In the middle of this confusion we ask for training. But can we speak about training if we are not clear about its object? What does it mean to be a campus minister? If we are able to delineate the role of the campus minister, we also will be able to lay bare the main areas for training. Therefore, I propose first to raise two questions closely related to one another.

1. How can the priest be an efficient and skillful pastor in a campus community?
2. How can he remain a whole and integrated man in a milieu which is constantly changing and by its own nature repeatedly challenging his own commitment?

You will probably realize that the second question is much more important than the first, however seldom asked. But let us start where the question is asked and then break through to the level where it hurts. Then, finally, we are free to ask the last question.

3. What is the best way to prepare a man for this special ministerial task?

I. The Efficient and Skillful Campus Minister

ALTHOUGH THE FACULTY and other personnel related to the university also ask for his attention, the main pastoral concern of the campus minister is the student. We will focus on the pastoral care for the student.

For most students, the patterns of life were pretty clear and well-defined during their high-school years. Home and school were closely related and many customs, practices, rules, and regulations, although often criticized in their particular form, were seldom questioned on a basic level. There were many problems, but problems could be solved. There were many questions, but every question had an answer. There were many stupid teachers, but the smart ones knew what they were talking about.

---

1 Erwin R. Goodenough, *The Psychology of Religious Experiences* (Basic Books: 1965).

But at college things became different. Being away from home, without strong anchors in the family tradition, and without a clear goal on the horizon, the student starts drifting. Familiar answers do not work anymore, long cherished beliefs lose their obviousness, and carefully built structures crumble, sometimes suddenly, sometimes gradually. And in this new milieu where science sets the tone, where research is the main approach and hypothesis the main model, certainty becomes the most suspected attitude and the question mark, the most respected symbol. But asking questions is a fearful thing. The answer might be No. Do I have anything to hope for in my future? Yes or No? Is love a real human possibility? Yes or No? Is there anybody who cares for anybody except himself? Yes or No? And finally: Is life worth living? Yes or No? Asking these questions is a dangerous thing to do. Many may prefer to stay away from them and do their daily business because it seems much safer to hold to "the way they think and act at home" than to rock the boat in such a stormy sea. But if the student used to the microscope, familiar with Skinner boxes and proud of his computer techniques, avoids asking these questions about the core values which give meaning to any tool at all, he takes the risk of becoming an unhappy genius, a man who knows everything except why he lives.

It is in this milieu that the campus priest has to be a pastor. What should he be able to offer to the student? I propose to discuss this under three titles: *a climate, a word, a home.*

1. A CLIMATE

Perhaps the real desire of many students is not primarily to find an answer to the deep and often painful questions related to the meaning of being but to find a climate in which he is allowed to ask these questions without fear. Most amazing about many Christian milieux is the great taboo on asking questions. You know how questions about the divinity of Christ, the virginity of Mary, the priesthood of women, the advisability of abortion, and even about a good selection process for bishops might not be just food for an interesting discussion but would spoil many meals in a rectory. These questions seem to be more than interesting; they are dangerous and explosive. Questioning the morality of war, the value of academic progress, the meaning of monogamy may cause people to throw stones through your windows because all these questions suggest that the safe little playpen we have set up for ourselves might be nothing more than a subtle form of self-deception. But if we are so afraid to face a question which comes from without, how much more threatening will the question be which comes from within? Is it really worth eating and drinking, studying and fighting, living and being? We know that the most common form of mental suffering on campuses today is depression. Depression is caused by questions which cannot be asked and which are swallowed and inverted into the experience of deep guilt. The question, "Why do I live?" is turned into a castigating self-doubt, "Is it worthwhile to live?"

Can the priest tolerate this question? Can he offer a climate in which the most basic doubts can be expressed without fear, where the most sacred realities can be unveiled without creating the need to defend, where despair can be allowed to be despair without the need to fill the threatening holes? Can he accept agnosticism? That is, can he accept the fact that we do not know the reality in which we live? A man who lives in a scientific milieu has to learn to be happy with a little bit of knowledge. Goodenough states: "The true agnostic is not interested in whether man can ever 'know' the truth as a whole; what he wants is to find out a little more than he knows now."[2]

If Christianity is not a panacea for every doubt, ignorance, and impotence, it might create the possibility of being an agnostic without being afraid, of being happy without a cure-all and safe without a playpen. Gordon Allport considers as one of the attributes of a mature religion *"its heuristic character."* He writes, "A heuristic belief is one that is held tentatively until it can be confirmed, or until it helps us discover a more valid belief."[3] If this characteristic can develop anywhere, it should on a college campus. But what is needed is a climate to allow searching without fear, and questioning without shame. The first demand of a question is not to be answered but to be accepted. Then the problem of faith can become the mystery of faith and the problem of God, the mystery of

---

2 Goodenough, *The Psychology of Religious Experiences,* 182.
3 Gordon Allport, *The Individual and His Religion* (Macmillan), 72.

God. As long as the priest considers atheism as the only alternative for orthodoxy and unbelief as the only alternative for dogma, every question put to him will be felt as a threat and every doubt as an attack calling for defense. But his faith tells him that growth can only take place when belief and unbelief, doubt and faith, hope and despair can exist together. It is only slowly that a student is willing to realize this, and he will never be able to do it unless there is someone to offer him a fearless climate.

2. A WORD

Many have already said, since St. Paul, that faith comes from hearing, and that the word of God is all we have to give. But few were wise enough, as was St. Paul, to realize that not every word is for everyone, that some need milk and others solid food. Diagnosis has been one of the weakest qualities in the pastoral field. What doctor would give all his pills to all his patients? What psychologist would administer all his tests to all his clients? What counselor would give all his advice to all his counselees? Their training is geared to diagnosis, based on the insight that not everything is good for everyone, and that help only can be given on the basis of the clinical understanding of the unique needs of our fellowman. But it is sad to see that so much pastoral activity is based on the supposition that all the good words are good for everyone. And often the pastor behaves like a poor salesman who wants to sell the whole church as a package at once to everyone he happens to meet.

Much pastoral phoniness is related to the inability to be clinical in pastoral contact and pastoral conversation. Not everyone needs encouragement, not everyone asks for correction, not everyone is ready to be invited to prayer or to hear the name of God. Some ask for silence, some for a single word, some need instruction, some just understanding, some want a smile, some a severe hand, some need support, and some need to be left alone. Perhaps much of today's anti-clericalism on campuses is related to the insensitivity of men whose vocation is to care for the most individual need. If anybody is aware of his own individuality and unique needs, it is the student who is studying to find *his* place in *his* world. The fact that many prefer a psychologist to a priest is less related to the different ideas they have to offer than it is to the fact that the one thinks diagnostically and clinically and the other often globally and generally. And therefore, the campus minister should be able to offer a word which is an honest response to the unique and highly individual needs of the students.

3. A HOME

The third and perhaps most difficult thing to offer is a home where some degree of intimacy can be experienced. In our modern highly demanding, and competitive university, which is everything but a Schola—a place to be free—many students suffer from an intense feeling of loneliness. They are very self-conscious, constantly on their watchtower to register carefully all the movements of their surroundings, hyper-alert to the reactions of their teachers and fellow students. They have their antennas out to pick up all those signs which can suggest the way to good grades, good letters of recommendation, good grad schools, and good jobs. For many, it has become a matter of life and death because they know that if you can't carry books, there will be little else than rifles to carry. Many experience some sense of self-contempt and have lost the ability to be with themselves. In this highly stress-filled situation, intimacy has become nearly impossible for many students. And although in this searching time of life there is a heightened desire for warmth, tenderness, and disarmed relaxation, for many students their roommate is more a stranger than a buddy, their classmates more rivals than friends, their teachers more authorities than guides. This craving for intimacy is perhaps one of the most central concerns for the campus minister. How can he, in some way, somewhat satisfy this nearly inexhaustible need?

The answer is obvious but at the same time immense. It is the creation of a community where the student can experience some sense of belonging. If the years of free search are not surrounded by some form of intimacy and lived in some form of community, the search may be bitter instead of mild, narrow-minded instead of mature, cold and calculated instead of open and receptive.

There are many ways in which we have tried and do try to form these communities: discussion groups, weekends, retreats or advances, many forms of celebration and most of all the Eucharist. Crucial to all these forms seems to be the creation of a healthy balance between closeness and distance. The campus minister can be the guardian of this very subtle balance. This is very difficult because the need for intimacy can be so strong that it finds expression in a suffocating embrace. Different forms of intense mutual confession, sharing of feelings, and repeated physical contact may seem a good sign on a campus which counts so many alienated students but, in fact, can create cliques instead of community, stickiness instead of freedom, and even fear instead of love. In this desire to experience some oneness, students might cling to each other instead of freely communicating. And if the campus minister sees a growing interest in Pentecostalism, cursillos, group-dynamics, and very informal liturgies, he should not only ask himself to what extent do these new groups satisfy obvious present needs, but also to what extent will they offer in the long run the freedom and maturity the student is looking for.

In the many new experiments in liturgy on campus, the balance between closeness and distance seems to be essential for the maturation of the Christian. A good liturgy is a liturgy with full participation without a pressure to participate, a liturgy with free expression and dialogue without an urge to be too personal, a liturgy where man is free to move in closer or to take more distance without feeling that he is offending people, and a liturgy where physical contact is real but does not break through the symbolic boundaries. I don't think there will ever be a single good liturgy. The personality of the minister, the nature of the students, and the climate of the place ask for many different forms. But much more important then the particular format, canon, language, or gesture is the careful balance between closeness and distance which allows the Christian community to be intimate *and* open, to be personal *and* hospitable, to receive the daily core-group as well as the occasional visitors, to be nurturing as well as apostolic.

The problem of intimacy is very often experienced as the core problem of the emotional life of the young adult. His relationships with female as well as male friends often can be clouded by painful anxieties. Closeness is desirable as well as fearful, and it asks for a careful guide to find a vital balance which can lead to a life in which one can be committed and open-minded at the same time.

Summarizing the special skills which can make the campus minister an efficient and skillful pastor we might say: He should offer a climate, in which the student can raise basic questions without fear, a word which is an honest response to his individual needs, and a home where he can experience intimacy with a vital balance between closeness and distance.

II. The Spirituality of the Campus Minister

BUT ALL WE have said until this moment seems rather trivial and superficial if we consider it just in terms of skills for efficient ministry. I hope you have already become aware of the fact that, all the way through, the minister himself is involved most personally, most individually, and often most painfully. If our real concern is the making of the "whole man," "the mature Christian," we cannot avoid the question: How can the minister himself become and remain a whole and integrated man in a community which is constantly changing and by its own nature constantly challenging his commitment?

In many ways the campus community is the most demanding and tiring place for a minister to work. Every four years his parish is completely de-and-repopulated. Each time he is once again faced with a new wave of searching, questioning, critical men and women who usually have mixed feelings when they are invited to contact the priest. Over and over again, he is asked to respond to the powerful feelings of doubt, aggression and loneliness and to act as guide in the intensive struggle for self-discovery and meaning in life. This means a constant request for honesty, authenticity, openness, and a nearly bottomless availability. And when he finally, often after a long time, has received confidence and established some community, he will find that graduation is often the end of it all. Students go away and keep going away. The minister stays. Except for some cards at Christmas, he does not hear very much any more and thanks are seldom expressed. He knows that students have to leave; he even knows that they should not become too attached to the school or to him and that an education to independence sometimes also includes a renunciation of thanks; but he also knows how much it hurts when people, in whom he has invested so much of his own self, leave him. How often can a man build with care and patience a personal relationship with people who will be running away so soon only to look back at their college years as a part of their necessary preparation for life? For the student, college is just a temporary phase; for the minister, it is a way of living. And finally, how much questioning can a man take? Can he allow people to ask him all the time: Why are you a priest? Why do you believe in God? Why do you pray? Can he allow himself to be flexible all the time and willing to shift gears, to incorporate new ideas, to scrutinize new criticism and to question again his basic convictions? But this is exactly what happens, when students ask questions because every question about the meaning of life is, at the same time, a question about the meaning of the ministry. The question, "Why do I live?" is at the same time the question, "Why are you a priest?" It is obvious that not only the student but also, and perhaps even more, the minister realizes that his own existence is at stake.

If it is true that a psychiatrist who works closely with people in conflicts has to watch his own emotional life very carefully, then this is even more the case for a priest who is in daily contact with ultimate questions of life and death. And just as X-rays can heal and hurt us, exposure to these questions can have good but also dangerous effects. It is not so surprising that campus ministers are often suffering from a considerable amount of stress and need serious pastoral care more than anybody else. Although every campus minister has his own personality and therefore asks for individual guidance, there seem to be some main problem areas which allow generalization. We will discuss these under three titles: silence, friendship, and insight.

1. SILENCE

A university is not only a place for intellectual pursuits but also for a good amount of intellectualization; not only a place for rational behavior but also for elaborate rationalization. It is probably not only the most verbal place but also the most wordy and talkative place. And religion is not exempt from this phenomenon. The campus minister is exposed to a nearly unbelievable amount of words, arguments, ideas, concepts, and abstractions. How can he separate the sense from the nonsense, the holy words from the crazy ones? This problem is tremendous not only for the student but just as much for the minister who might fall into the temptation of adoring the products of man's consciousness, trying to catch even the divine in the net of his explicit awareness. He can become entangled in the ropes of his own sentences and unable to be moved by the great Power which is beyond his capacity to articulate.

And often the drama of the campus minister is that, trapped by the need to understand and to be understandable, he loses communication with the realities which—as he himself knows—are transcendent to his mind.

In this context the campus minister needs silence. Silence means rest, rest of body and mind, in which we become available for Him whose heart is greater than ours. That is very threatening; it is like giving up control over our actions and thoughts, allowing something creative to happen not by us but to us. Is it so amazing that we are so often tired and exhausted, trying to be masters of ourselves, wanting to grasp the ultimate meaning of our existence, struggling with our identity? Silence is that moment in which we not only stop the discussion with others but also the inner discussions with ourselves, in which we can breathe in freely and accept our identity as a gift. "Not I live, but He lives in me." It is in this silence that the spirit of God can pray in us and continue his creative work in us. We never will find God in students unless it is God within us who recognizes Himself in them. Without silence the Spirit will die in us and the creative energy of our life will float away and leave us alone, cold, and tired. Without silence we will lose our center and become the victim of the many who constantly demand our attention.

2. FRIENDSHIP

The second urgent need of the campus minister is friendship. Here we enter a very difficult area because it is the most sensitive one. But it has to be said that the campus minister who depends for friendship on students is in a very dangerous situation not just because of the fact that students will leave him after some years but more because friendship with students often paralyzes the possibility of being their pastor. If the student community becomes the main source of the personal gratification and satisfaction of the priest, he easily becomes the victim of fluctuating sympathies and preferences and quickly loses his freedom. If he needs students to fill his emotional needs, he clings to them and is not able to maintain the distance which allows him to be different. And as soon as students experience his great desire to be intimate with them, to know details of their lives, to be invited to their parties and closely involved with their daily ups and downs, they lose the possibility of relating to him in a creative way.

The campus minister needs privacy, a home where he is not with students, and where he is free for himself. Just as no doctor could stay healthy if he would only see patients, and no psychiatrist could stay "whole" if his private life and that of his clients would merge, so no campus minister will ever be able to function well over a long period of time if he would always be with students. It might seem that student problems are urgent and that they require immediate attention, but let us first of all ask ourselves, "Do they really need us more than we need them?" The campus priest needs a home, a place where he can live with friends and have his own intimacy. Only then will he keep from drowning in the high and low waves of the fluctuating life of the university.

3. INSIGHT

Besides silence and friendship, insight is one of the main constituents of the spirituality of the campus minister. By insight, we mean a sound perspective of the minister on the significance of his own priesthood. Although much suffering of today's priests derives from distorted emotions, we should not overlook the importance of a clear understanding of his task in the society of today. For many priests, it is not so much their needs for friendship and sympathy which limit their pastoral freedom as their theological outlook on their own existence. I just wonder how many guilt feelings of today's priests are related to their concept of God, their view of revelation, and their ideas about Jesus Christ and his church. If the campus minister thinks that *he* is responsible for the faith on campus, if he thinks that it is his task to bring as many students as possible to the sacraments, and if he thinks that the students' way to heaven is somehow related to their membership in the church, he can be sure that the campus is going to be his purgatory. Because not only can feelings influence thoughts, but thoughts can also create very deep and powerful emotions. In the mind of a priest for whom sacramentality is, in practice, identical with the reception of the sacraments, the growing unpopularity of confession and communion must create a considerable amount of anxiety and perhaps even self-reproach. For a man to whom the recognition of Jesus Christ as Savior is the criterion of the fruitfulness of his priestly service, a modern college campus cannot do anything but cause deep-seated guilt feelings and much unhappiness. And if the satisfaction of the campus minister is dependent on a growing conversion of students to his creed and belief, his work can hardly be more than suffocating.

Many priests are deeply concerned today. Faced with the rapid changes in church attitudes, they worry and even panic, sometimes to the point of declaring the days as wicked, the students as degenerate, and Christianity as burning its last candle. The question is: Are these concerns really pastoral concerns, or are they rather more signs of little faith? Perhaps we are too easily caught in the narrowness of our own theological insights. They can make us anxious instead of free, unbelievers instead of faithful, suspicious instead of trustful.

Can the priest dedicate himself fully to a so-called nonreligious student without the hidden condition or hope for a future conformity to his belief? In an academic community, people are very sensitive to the slightest form of pressure—hyper-sensitive even. The most guarded freedom is the freedom of thought. Although we are committed to God-*Logos* who came to free us from the God-*Anangke*,[4] that is, to the Word of God who liberated us from the chains of our pressing needs, it is very difficult to allow God's Word to be completely free. Often we do not feel comfortable with a free moving Spirit and prefer a so-called realistic limitation and control. But the Truth is to set us free. A growing insight through study of the Word and a deepening understanding of our own task as witnesses of this Word can prevent us from being a victim of our own narrow-mindedness.

Silence, friendship, and insight are three aspects of the spirituality of the campus priest which seem important if he wants to become and

---

4 Sigmund Freud, *The Future of an Illusion* (Doubleday Anchor Books. New York), 97.

remain a "whole" and integrated man. If he wants to be a skillful and efficient minister who can offer a climate, a word, and a home for his students, he will soon find that without silence, friendship, and insight his fruitfulness will be very short-lived and temporary.

III. Training for the Campus Ministry

THE TWO QUESTIONS, how to be skillful and how to be whole, proved to be closely related. Together they not only delineate a picture of an ideal, perhaps utopian, campus minister, but they also circumscribe the main fields of training. This brings us to the final question: How should the training of the campus minister take place?

There are many settings in terms of time and place within which we can envision a training situation. We can think of a one-day-a-week program extending over a whole year, of a series of intensive workshops, of a full-time summer program, and ideally of a whole year of pastoral internship.

Programs of this nature preferably should be planned on the campuses. If this is not possible other training fields, such as general and mental hospitals, educational centers, prisons, and industrial schools, could also be considered. But essential for every setting is that it offers supervised pastoral experience, that is, pastoral experience which through careful control becomes available for supervision by a competent and specially educated pastor.

Many future ministers are like people who have learned Spanish in school. They are able to read and perhaps even to write Spanish, but when they come to Mexico the best they can do is stutter. What they need is not just experience but also someone who constantly corrects their mistakes, makes them aware of their own idiosyncrasies, and suggests new ways of expression according to the culture in which they find themselves. Experience without supervision can lead to the adaptation of poor patterns of behavior which are very difficult to shake off. It can create narrow-mindedness because it tends to make us settle on the first thing which seems to work. Then the pastor becomes like the conceited foreigner who says: "As long they know what I am saying, who cares what mistakes I make?" But this just might be the reason that he always will remain a foreigner. Pastoral work is more than a language. It asks for our ability to touch the most sensitive areas of life, and requires us not only to understand the highly individual needs of the other but also the many complex responses of the self. Just as no surgeon would start operating after only having read books, no pastor should touch the soft and tender internal life of his fellowman with the great books and the powerful ideas he brought with him from the classroom. Let me give you an example:

A young deacon in Holland paid a house visit to a middle aged couple and explained to them in convincing terms that birth control was no longer any problem, that they had no reason to be concerned about their son who had stopped going to church, that celibacy would go out the window within a decade and that most devotions were perfect examples of magic. After his exposition the mother of the house thought for a while and then said meditatively: "Nothing really has changed." "How do you mean?" asked the deacon. "Well," she mused, "twenty years ago the priests told us what we should do and believe. Now, with the same intolerance, they tell us what we should not do and not believe. After all the problem is still the same."

If this deacon wants to be sensitive to the real needs of his parishioner and if he wants to come to a better understanding of his own preoccupations he will be helped by supervised pastoral experience. Let us have a closer look now, first at the nature of the supervisory process and secondly at the kind of pastoral experience which can become available for supervision.

A. THE NATURE OF THE SUPERVISORY PROCESS

It is obvious that supervision is a very delicate art, which not only requires sensitivity, and a special understanding of the dynamics of the human relationships, but also demands careful preparation for the difficult task of individual professional guidance. It is sad to say that within the field of Catholic pastoral education there are only very few men who can claim for themselves the title of pastoral supervisor. To show the importance of supervision we will look at three of its characteristics.

1. An Antiprojective Regime

First of all supervision is an antiprojective regime. The most striking characteristic of supervision is the constant invitation to take back our projections. The center of attention is the trainee. And although the trainee might explain his problems easily as the problem of the older pastor, the rigid institution, the unfatherly bishop, the anticlericalism of the students, the supervisor will ask him: "But what about you?" There are many ways to project. But seldom are we made aware of our inclination to draw people or situations into the picture behind which we can hide ourselves. What the supervisor does is to bring us right back to the center of the problem: me.

2. A School for Alternatives

Secondly, supervision is a school for alternatives. Every pastor has his own strengths and qualities. It is obvious that he will use and develop them as best he can. One will feel at ease in the pulpit, another in the classroom, a third in youth groups and a fourth in individual counseling. The question is whether our qualities might not become temptations to narrow us down to only those fields to which we feel most inclined. Professional training means a training which broadens our ways of pastoring and offers us possible alternatives. It gives us the freedom to act differently in different situations based not just on our inclination but on the understanding of the particular situation. Through supervision we are invited to face the weaker aspects of our behavior. The supervisor is saying: "There are many ways of being a good pastor. I know that this is the way in which you feel most comfortable, which is most easy to you, so let us forget this way for a moment and have a look at other possible ways." If a man uses his strong capacities too much he is in danger of having his other potentials become paralyzed or at least underdeveloped. If he feels too much at ease with a specific pattern of behavior the danger exists that the learning process will stop.

Supervision never gives lasting satisfaction. It is an ongoing process of opening new possibilities. This opening is a most painful process. It gives you the feeling that everything can be done differently and that it is at least immature not to consider the other possibilities.

Therefore, supervision seems to be only consistent in its inconsistencies. It forces one constantly to move away from what is safe. It is a very frustrating process. The supervisor often seems to consider his student as cream. He doesn't mind in what direction he churns him, he's only interested in the butter which is the result of all his stirring.

As a school for alternatives, supervision creates distance. It says: "Stop, have a look at yourself, and think." The tendency to act on the spur and the impulse of the moment is so great that blindness to alternatives can result. But after good supervision we know at least, that although we are taking one road there are other roads which we did not choose. We know that distance is possible without causing separation, and that involvement is possible without causing blindness.

3. The Way to Basic Questions

Finally, supervision is the way to ask the basic questions. Supervision is not a problem-solving device in which the supervisor advises his student what to do in difficult cases. It rather offers the freedom and opportunity to ask the basic questions. Very often the minister invests much time and energy in problems which are peripheral and accidental, without questioning the suppositions on which his actions are based. Many problems can be used to hide the real question. The question: What should I say to this student? can cover up the question: Why do I want to say something to him at all? The question: How can I reach as many students as possible? can cover up the question: Why should I reach so many students? The question: How can I make the liturgy attractive? can hide the question: What does attractiveness mean when speaking about liturgy? The question: How can I be a good witness for Christ? can disregard the question: Does Christ really mean anything to me? And finally the question: How can I be a good priest? can avoid the question: Do I really want to be a priest? Through supervision we might finally have the courage to touch the heart of the matter and to ask the basic questions. And this brings us back to where we started: Asking basic questions is the privilege of the mature Christian. So we see supervision as an antiprojective regime, as a school for alternatives and as a way to ask the basic questions.

B. THE PASTORAL EXPERIENCE

But what has to be supervised? That is our final problem. The answer seems simple: pastoral experience. But how does pastoral experience become available for supervision? By control, by creative limitation. Franz Alexander calls psychotherapy a controlled life experience. Training for the ministry can very well be called a controlled pastoral experience. Doing many different things can be helpful as well as damaging, but doing just a few things under close supervision is priceless. Talking with hundreds of people about God may be fine, but analyzing one conversation word for word is a learning experience. Not only learning how to talk, but also learning how to understand myself in the interaction with my fellowman. The great importance of pastoral training is the opportunity for the minister to experience himself as a professional person in a controlled setting. To struggle with one's own professional self in a situation in which every aspect of one's daily ministerial practice becomes subject to supervision is a way of learning, unique and practically unknown in the tradition of Catholic theological education. It is especially the controlled experience which makes this pastoral experience different from so many other experiences in the field.

About a decade ago some Hollanders started to build a miniature Dutch city in which the tallest church tower did not come higher than a man's waist, the famous public buildings of the country were knee-high, the great rivers could be crossed in one step and the whole world in which we live could be overlooked in one glance. This miniature city soon became one of the greatest tourist attractions and not just for children as was planned, but for adults as well. The sensation seems to be the controlled life experience. People suddenly were able to see themselves as a part in a larger setting of which the structure and the boundaries were visible. This is what makes supervised pastoral experience so exciting. It is a pastoral experience in miniature, through which we are able to see where we stand and where we go. If we want to prepare ourselves to live and work in the complex university community it is important to start by looking at it from some distance and to make us familiar with the complex map of student life, so that we will not get lost, once we enter it fully.

WE WILL FINISH as we started. The minister preparing himself for work on the campus is like an army chaplain entering the battlefield for the first time. Anticipatory anxiety is to be expected. This anxiety can paralyze efficient work and endanger the integration of the personality but by careful training this same anxiety can become constructive instead of destructive and a source of great pastoral creativity instead of distress. A minister who is prepared for his task can enter a university community even when it is in great turmoil, without fear. He is free. With a realistic confidence in his abilities, with a sense of inner harmony and most of all with the trust in the value of his service, he can be a free witness for God, who can strengthen hope, fulfill love, and make joy complete.

CONCLUSION

INTIMACY WAS THE main theme which brought together the otherwise so different subjects of this book. In the context of man's development from the magic oneness of the small child to the faithful oneness of the adult Christian we discussed the intimate relationships possible between man and woman, man and man, man and God. We also tried to show the problem of the student trying to find his own place within the religious community and finally we analyzed the situation of the contemporary minister who is called to guide others in their search for meaning without losing his own home.

It does not seem an exaggeration to say that this book was primarily concerned about the inner life of man. This might seem a somewhat unpopular emphasis in a time in which the social problems are so pressing that much attention for the "stirrings of the soul" easily suggests a pietistic preoccupation with the self.

But if man really has to love his neighbor as himself there seems to be a good reason to wonder if man today is able enough to relate to himself in a creative way and to live from the center of his existence.

During the past years many concerned idealistic men returned from their social actions in the fields, the ghettos and the slums with the painful realization that the courage to continue and the will to persevere can not depend on the gratification which they received from their involvement. There were hardly any visible results, very few words of thanks and not seldom suspicion and hostility. Many were thrown back on themselves and had to ask: "Why should I do all this, when nobody asks me to do it, when many call me naive, and when most people remain completely indifferent towards my great desire to make a better world?" The answer to this question will never come unless man is able to live from his center and feel at home with his own self. Consciously or unconsciously many young people practicing Yoga, reading Zen and intrigued by new forms of meditation are asking for a new spirituality and are looking for a guide.

The churches, in many ways entangled in their own structural problems, often seem hardly ready to respond to this growing need to live a spiritual life. The tragedy is that many find the church more in the way to God than the way to God, and are looking for religious experiences far away from the ecclesiastical institutions. But if we read the signs well, we are on the threshold of a new area of spiritual life, the nature and ramifications of which we can hardly foresee. Hopefully, we will not be distracted by the trivia of churchy family-quarrels and overlook the great questions which really matter. Hopefully, we will be sensitive enough to feel the gentle breeze by which God makes His presence known. (1 Kings 19:13).

ACKNOWLEDGMENTS

THIS BOOK IS born out of a two-year "visit" to the University of Notre Dame. The many friendships with students and teachers made it very easy for me to overcome the feeling of being a guest and to fully participate in the intense life of this fast-developing campus, which not only reflects but also stimulates the many turbulent changes in feelings, thoughts and actions of modern society.

Without the stimulation and support of many students the following chapters never would have been written. Special thanks are due to Frank Allman, Ray Novaco, Dwight Norwood, Bob Bradley, Joe Ahearn, Mike McCarty, Greg Milmoe and Joseph Wissink, who by their honest reactions, criticisms and corrections helped me to think and rethink, to write and rewrite.

In the preparation of the chapters about the ministry I found great help in the lively discussions with the Holy Cross priests of the University of Notre Dame. In particular I am grateful to Louis Putz, Joe Hoffmann, Joe Simons, David Burrell, John Gerber, Ralph Dunn, Jim Burtchaell, John Dunne, Claude Pomerleau and Don McNeill. By their great sympathy they made me part of their life and community and in many ways tuned me in to the different problems of the priest on campus.

I also would like to express my great thankfulness to the many faculty members and their wives who encouraged me to write and took away the hesitancies of the foreigner in me. John and Mary Alice Santos, Don and Christine Costello, John and Martha Borkowski, and Charles and

Carol Allen, offered through their friendship many insights which are expressed in the following pages.

I owe much to Joe Collins for his careful revisions of the manuscript.

Finally, I am grateful to Linda Papas and Mrs. M. J. van der Meer for their secretarial work.

This book is dedicated to John Eudes Bamberger, monk and psychiatrist, eminent guide through the complexities of the inner life.

The Living Reminder

Service and Prayer in Memory of Jesus Christ

To the alumni of Yale Divinity School whose continuing interest and support is a source of great encouragement for its students and faculty.

THE LIVING REMINDER
CONTENTS

Exploring Connections

WHAT ARE THE spiritual resources of ministers? What prevents them from becoming dull, sullen, lukewarm bureaucrats, people who have many projects, plans, and appointments but who have lost their heart somewhere in the midst of their activities? What keeps ministers vital, alive, energetic and full of zeal? What allows them to preach and teach, counsel and celebrate with a continuing sense of wonder, joy, gratitude, and praise?

These are the questions of this book. They concern the relationship between the professional and the personal life of those who want to work in the service of the Gospel. They call for a careful exploration of the connections between ministry and spirituality.

Ministry is service in the name of the Lord. It is bringing the good news to the poor, proclaiming liberty to captives and new sight to the blind, setting the downtrodden free and announcing the Lord's year of favor (Luke 4:18). Spirituality is attention to the life of the spirit in us; it is going out to the desert or up to the mountain to pray; it is standing before the Lord with open heart and open mind; it is crying out, "Abba, Father"; it is contemplating the unspeakable beauty of our loving God.

We have fallen into the temptation of separating ministry from spirituality, service from prayer. Our demon says: "We are too busy to pray; we have too many needs to attend to, too many people to respond to, too many wounds to heal. Prayer is a luxury, something to do during a free hour, a day away from work or on a retreat. The few who are exclusively

concerned with prayer—such as Trappists, Poor Clares, and some isolated hermits—are really not involved in ministry. They are set free for
single-minded contemplation and leave Christian service to others." But
to think this way is harmful; harmful for ministers as well as for contemplatives. Service and prayer can never be separated; they are related to
each other as the Yin and Yang of the Japanese Circle.

In this book I want to explore the connection between ministry and
spirituality and show how service is prayer and prayer is service. After
considerable thought, I felt that the best way to set about this exploration
would be to look at ministry as "remembrance" and at the minister as a
living reminder of Jesus Christ. In both the Old and New Testament "to
remember" has a central place. Abraham Joshua Heschel says: "Much of
what the Bible demands can be comprised in one word, 'Remember.'"[1]
And Nihls Dahl, speaking about early Christianity, says: "The first obligation of the apostle vis-à-vis the community—beyond founding it—is
to make the faithful remember what they have received and already
know—or should know."[2] So it is in keeping with the core of the biblical
tradition to look at ministry in the context of remembrance. Therefore,
I will discuss our spiritual resources by looking at the minister as a reminder: first, as a healing reminder, second as a sustaining reminder,
third as a guiding reminder. The terms healing, sustaining, and guiding
have been discussed in a masterful way by Seward Hiltner in his *Preface
to Pastoral Theology*.[3] In the following three chapters I would like to use
the same terms to express my great indebtedness to Seward Hiltner as my
teacher and to share my conviction that spiritual resources can be sought
and found in the heart of our ministry. Moreover, these terms will help to
establish a connection between our present-day concerns with the spiritual life and the many new insights into interpersonal relationships that
we have received from the social sciences in recent decades and incorporated into the practice of the ministry.

---

1 Abraham Joshua Heschel, *Man is not Alone* (New York: Farrar, Straus & Giroux,
  1951), 161.
2 Nihls Dahl, "Anamnesis: Memory and Commemoration in Early Christianity," *Studia
  Theologica*, 1 (1947), 75.
3 Seward Hiltner, *Preface to Pastoral Theology* (New York: Abingdon Press, 1954).

The Minister as a Healing Reminder

Introduction

LET ME START with a story about Elie Wiesel. In 1944, all the Jews of the Hungarian town of Sighet were rounded up and deported to concentration camps. Elie Wiesel, the now famous novelist, was one of them. He survived the holocaust and twenty years later returned to see his home town again. What pained him most was that the people of Sighet had erased the Jews from their memory. He writes:

> I was not angry with the people of Sighet . . . for having driven out their neighbors of yesterday, nor for having denied them. If I was angry at all it was for having forgotten them. So quickly, so completely . . . Jews have been driven not only out of town but out of time as well.[1]

This story suggests that to forget our sins may be an even greater sin than to commit them. Why? Because what is forgotten cannot be healed and that which cannot be healed easily becomes the cause of greater evil. In his many books about the holocaust, Elie Wiesel does not remind us of Auschwitz, Buchenwald, and Treblinka to torture our consciences with heightened guilt feelings, but to allow our memories to be healed

---

1 Elie Wiesel, *Legends of Our Time* (New York: Holt, Rinehart and Winston, 1968), 123, 128.

and so to prevent an even worse disaster. An Auschwitz that is forgotten causes a Hiroshima, and a forgotten Hiroshima can cause the destruction of our world. By cutting off our past we paralyze our future: forgetting the evil behind us we evoke the evil in front of us. As George Santayanna has said: "He who forgets the past is doomed to repeat it."

With this in mind I would like to discuss how the minister as a reminder is first of all a healer who, by healing our wounded past, can open up a new future. I will touch on three areas: the wounds, the healing, and the healer.

The Wounds

THE FRENCH WRITER-POLITICIAN André Malraux writes in his *Anti-Memoirs,* "One day it will be realized that men are distinguishable from one another as much by the forms their memories take as by their characters."[2] This is a very important observation. The older we grow the more we have to remember, and at some point we realize that most, if not all, of what we have is memory. Our memory plays a central role in our sense of being. Our pains and joys, our feelings of grief and satisfaction, are not simply dependent on the events of our lives, but also, and even more so, on the ways we remember these events. The events of our lives are probably less important than the form they take in the totality of our story. Different people remember a similar illness, accident, success, or surprise in very different ways, and much of their sense of self derives less from what happened than from how they remember what happened, how they have placed the past events into their own personal history.

It is not surprising, therefore, that most of our human emotions are closely related to our memory. Remorse is a biting memory, guilt is an accusing memory, gratitude is a joyful memory, and all such emotions are deeply influenced by the way we have integrated past events into our way of being in the world. In fact, we perceive our world with our memories. Our memories help us to see and understand new impressions and give them a place in our richly varied life experiences.

---

2 André Malraux, *Anti-Memoirs* (New York: Bantam Books, 1970), 125.

I have always been fascinated by the way immigrants, especially Dutchmen respond to the U.S.A. when they come here for the first time. The first way they make themselves feel at home in their new country is to look at things which remind them of the old country. Then they start to see all the things which are larger, bigger, wider, and heavier than at home. Finally, often after several years, they begin to compare things within the country: the East with the West, the city with the countryside. When that happens then they are at home. Then they have built up a large enough store of memories in the U.S.A. to compare its different parts and aspects.

These observations show how crucial our memory is for the way we experience life. This is why, in all helping professions—such as medicine, psychiatry, psychology, social work—the first questions are always directed to the memory of the patient or client. "Please tell me your story. What brought you here? What are the events which led you to this place here and now?" And it is clear that what doctors and therapists hear about are not just events but memories of events.

It is no exaggeration to say that the suffering we most frequently encounter in the ministry is a suffering of memories. They are the wounding memories that ask for healing. Feelings of alienation, loneliness, separation; feelings of anxiety, fear, suspicion; and related symptoms such as nervousness, sleeplessness, nail-biting—these all are part of the forms which certain memories have taken. These memories wound because they are often deeply hidden in the center of our being and very hard to reach. While the good memories may be present to us in outer signs such as trophies, decorations, diplomas, precious stones, vases, rings, and portraits, painful memories tend to remain hidden from us in the corner of our forgetfulness. It is from this hidden place that they escape healing and cause so much harm.

Our first and most spontaneous response to our undesirable memories is to forget them. When something painful has happened we quickly say to ourselves and to each other: "Let's forget it, let's act as if it did not happen, let's not talk about it, let's think about happier things." We want to forget the pains of the past—our personal, communal, and national traumas—and live as if they did not really happen. But by not remembering them we allow the forgotten memories to become independent forces that can exert a crippling effect on our functioning as human beings. When this happens, we become strangers to ourselves because we cut down our own history to a pleasant, comfortable size and try to make it conform to our own daydreams. Forgetting the past is like turning our most intimate teacher against us. By refusing to face our painful memories we miss the opportunity to change our hearts and grow mature in repentance. When Jesus says, "It is not the healthy who need the doctor, but the sick" (Mark 2:17), he affirms that only those who face their wounded condition can be available for healing and so enter into a new way of living.

The Healing

HOW ARE WE healed of our wounding memories? We are healed first of all by letting them be available, by leading them out of the corner of forgetfulness and by remembering them as part of our life stories. What is forgotten is unavailable, and what is unavailable cannot be healed. Max Scheler shows how memory liberates us from the determining power of forgotten painful events. "Remembering," he says, "is the beginning of freedom from the covert power of the remembered thing or occurrence."[3]

If ministers are reminders, their first task is to offer the space in which the wounding memories of the past can be reached and brought back into the light without fear. When the soil is not plowed the rain cannot reach the seeds; when the leaves are not raked away the sun cannot nurture the hidden plants. So also, when our memories remain covered with fear, anxiety, or suspicion the word of God cannot bear fruit.

To be a reminder requires a dynamic understanding of the lives and behavior of those who need to be reminded, an understanding which offers insight into the many psychic forces by which painful memories are rejected. Anton Boisen, the father of the Movement for Clinical Pastoral Education, pleaded for this dynamic understanding when he proposed a

---

3 Max Scheler, *On the Eternal in Man,* trans. Bernard Noble (New York: Harper and Brothers, 1960), 41.

"theology through living human documents." Many pastoral theologians and psychologists have deepened this understanding with the help and inspiration of the contemporary behavioral sciences.

During the past few decades theological educators have become increasingly convinced of the importance of this dynamic approach to ministry, and the many centers for Clinical Pastoral Education have made great contributions in this direction. But today, in the seventies, new questions are being heard. Has the great emphasis on the complex psychodynamics of human behavior not created a situation in which ministers have become more interested in the receiver of the message than in the message itself? Have we not become more immersed in the language of the behavioral sciences than in the language of the Bible? Are we not talking more about people than about God, in whose name we come to people? Do we not feel closer to the psychologist and psychiatrist than to the priest? Sometimes these questions have an accusatory and self-righteous tone, but often they are raised with an honest desire to move forward with a full appreciation of what has been learned. Such questions challenge us to look beyond the task of accepting. Accepting is only one aspect of the process of healing. The other aspect is connecting.

The great vocation of the minister is to continuously make connections between the human story and the divine story. We have inherited a story which needs to be told in such a way that the many painful wounds about which we hear day after day can be liberated from their isolation and be revealed as part of God's relationship with us. Healing means revealing that our human wounds are most intimately connected with the suffering of God himself. To be a living memory of Jesus Christ, therefore, means to reveal the connections between our small sufferings and the great story of God's suffering in Jesus Christ, between our little life and the great life of God with us. By lifting our painful forgotten memories out of the egocentric, individualistic, private sphere, Jesus Christ heals our pains. He connects them with the pain of all humanity, a pain he took upon himself and transformed. To heal, then, does not primarily mean to take pains away but to reveal that our pains are part of a greater pain, that our sorrows are part of a greater sorrow, that our experience is part of the great experience of him who said, "But was it not ordained that the Christ should suffer and so enter into the glory of God?" (cf. Luke 24:26)

By connecting the human story with the story of the suffering servant, we rescue our history from its fatalistic chain and allow our time to be converted from *chronos* into *kairos*, from a series of randomly organized incidents and accidents into a constant opportunity to explore God's work in our lives. We find a beautiful example revealing this connection in Martin Luther's letter of counsel to Elector Frederick of Saxony. He writes:

> When, therefore, I learned, most illustrious prince, that Your Lordship has been afflicted with a grave illness and that Christ has at the same time become ill in you, I counted it my duty to visit Your Lordship with a little writing of mine. I cannot pretend that I do not hear the voice of Christ crying out to me from Your Lordship's body and flesh and saying: "Behold I am sick." This is so because such evils as illness and the like, are not borne by us who are Christian, but by Christ himself, our Lord and Saviour, in whom we live. . . . [4]

All of ministry rests on the conviction that nothing, absolutely nothing, in our lives is outside the realm of God's judgment and mercy. By hiding parts of our story, not only from our own consciousness but also from God's eye, we claim a divine role for ourselves; we become judges of our own past and limit mercy to our own fears. Thus we disconnect ourselves not only from our own suffering but also from God's suffering for us. The challenge of ministry is to help people in very concrete situations—people with illnesses or in grief, people with physical or mental handicaps, people suffering from poverty and oppression, people caught in the complex networks of secular or religious institutions—to see and experience their story as part of God's ongoing redemptive work in the world. These insights and experiences heal precisely because they restore the broken connection between the world and God and create a new unity in which memories that formerly seemed only destructive are now reclaimed as part of a redemptive event.

---

4 Martin Luther, *Letters of Spiritual Counsel*, ed. and trans. Theodore G. Tappert, *Library of Christian Classics*, vol. 18 (Philadelphia: The Westminster Press, 1955), 27.

The Healer

THE MINISTER, AS a living memory of God's great deeds in history, is called to heal by reminding people of their wounded past and by connecting their wounds with the wounds of all humanity, redeemed by the suffering of God in Christ. But what are the implications of such a viewpoint for the personal life of the minister? The temptation is strong to ask the "how" question: "How do I become a living memory of God; how do I accept and connect; how do I lift up the individual story into the divine history?" These questions are temptations insofar as they avoid the more basic question: "Who am I as a living memory of God?" The main question indeed is not a question of doing, but a question of being. When we speak about the minister as a living re-minder of God, we are not speaking about a technical specialty which can be mastered through the acquisition of specific tools, techniques, and skills, but about a way of being which embraces the totality of life: working and resting, eating and drinking, praying and playing, acting and waiting. Before any professional skill, we need a spirituality, a way of living in the spirit by which all we are and all we do becomes a form of reminding.

One way to express this is to say that in order to be a living reminder of the Lord, we must walk in his presence as Abraham did. To walk in the presence of the Lord means to move forward in life in such a way that all our desires, thoughts, and actions are constantly guided by him. When we walk in the Lord's presence, everything we see, hear, touch, or taste reminds us of him. This is what is meant by a prayerful life. It is not a life in which we say many prayers, but a life in which nothing, absolutely nothing, is done, said, or understood independently of him who is the origin and purpose of our existence. This is powerfully ex-pressed by the nineteenth-century Russian Orthodox *staretz*, Theophan the Recluse:

> Into every duty a God-fearing heart must be put, a heart con-stantly permeated by the thought of God; and this will be the door through which the soul will enter into active life. . . . The essence

is to be established in the remembrance of God, and to walk in his presence.[5]

Thus Theophan the Recluse stresses that our mind and heart should be exclusively directed to the Lord and that we should see and understand the world in and through him. This is the challenge of the Christian and especially that of the minister. It is the challenge to break through our most basic alienation and live a life of total connectedness.

The strategy of the principalities and powers is to disconnect us, to cut us off from the memory of God. It is not hard to see how many of our busy actions and restless concerns seem to be disconnected, reminding us of nothing more than the disorder of our own orientation and commitment. When we no longer walk in the presence of the Lord, we cannot be living reminders of his divine presence in our lives. We then quickly become strangers in an alien land who have forgotten where we come from and where we are going. Then we are no longer the way to the experience of God, but rather *in* the way of the experience of God. Then, instead of walking in God's presence we start walking in a vicious circle, and pulling others into it.

At first sight this may seem rather pious and unrealistic, but not for long. The emphasis on ministry as a profession that has dominated our thinking during the past several decades may have led us to put too much confidence in our abilities, skills, techniques, projects, and programs. In so doing, we have lost touch with that reality with which we are called to connect, not so much by what we do, but by who we are.

In recent years I have become more and more aware of my own tendency to think that the value of my presence depends on what I say or do. And yet it is becoming clearer to me every day that this preoccupation with performing in fact prevents me from letting God speak through me in any way he wants, and so keeps me from making connections prior to any special word or deed.

---

5 Theophan the Recluse in Igumen Chariton, *The Art of Prayer,* ed. by Timothy Ware (London: Faber and Faber, 1966), 85, 98.

In no way am I trying to minimize or even to criticize the importance of training for the ministry. I am simply suggesting that this training will bear more fruit when it occurs in the context of a spirituality, a way of life in which we are primarily concerned, not to be with people but to be with God, not to walk in the presence of anyone who asks for our attention but to walk in the presence of God—a spirituality, in short, which helps us to distinguish service from our need to be liked, praised, or respected.

Over the years we have developed the idea that being present to people in all their needs is our greatest and primary vocation. The Bible does not seem to support this. Jesus primary concern was to be obedient to his Father, to live constantly in his presence. Only then did it become clear to him what his task was in his relationships with people. This also is the way he proposes for his apostles: "It is to the glory of my Father that you should bear much fruit and then you will be my disciples" (John 15:8). Perhaps we must continually remind ourselves that the first commandment requiring us to love God with all our heart, all our soul, and all our mind is indeed the first. I wonder if we really believe this. It seems that in fact we live as if we should give as much of our heart, soul, and mind as possible to our fellow human beings, while trying hard not to forget God. At least we feel that our attention should be divided evenly between God and our neighbor. But Jesus' claim is much more radical. He asks for a single-minded commitment to God and God alone. God wants all of our heart, all of our mind, and all of our soul. It is this unconditional and unreserved love for God that leads to the care for our neighbor, not as an activity which distracts us from God or competes with our attention to God, but as an expression of our love for God who reveals himself to us as the God of all people. It is in God that we find our neighbors and discover our responsibility to them. We might even say that only in God does our neighbor become a neighbor rather than an infringement upon our autonomy, and that only in and through God does service become possible.

At first this may appear to contradict the widely shared perspective which maintains that we come to know God only through relationships with our neighbors, and that service to the neighbor is also service to God (cf. Matt. 24:34–40). This viewpoint is firmly rooted in our personal experience and so has an immediacy which is convincing. And it is indeed true that God may meet us in the neighbor. But it is crucial for our ministry that we not confuse our relationship with God with our relationships with our neighbors. It is because God first loved us that we can love our neighbors rather than demand things of them. The first commandment receives concreteness and specificity through the second; the second commandment becomes possible through the first. The first and second commandments should never be separated or made mutually exclusive, neither should they be confused or substituted one for the other. That is why the second commandment is equal to the first, and that is why all ministry is based on our personal and communal relationship with God. This is what Dietrich Bonhoeffer says in his books, *The Communion of Saints* and *The Cost of Discipleship*. It is also the core idea of Thomas Merton's writings, and it was the intuition of all the great Christian leaders, who considered a growing intimacy with Christ the source of all their actions.

And so, to be living reminders of God we must be concerned first of all with our own intimacy with God. Once we have heard, seen, watched, and touched the Word who is life, we cannot do other than be living reminders. Once our lives are connected with his, we will speak about him, sing his praise, and proclaim his great deeds, not out of obligation but as a free, spontaneous response. In order for this response to be lasting and oriented to the felt needs of those to whom we minister, we need discipline, formation, and training. But these can do little more than offer channels for the lived experience of God.

Conclusion

IN THIS DISCUSSION of the minister as a healing reminder, I have stressed three points. First of all, ministers heal by reminding. Second, they remind by accepting the wounds of our individual pasts and by connecting them with the wounds of all humanity suffered by God himself. Finally, this reminding happens not so much because of what ministers say or do but by how their own lives are intimately connected with God in Jesus Christ. This means that to be a healing reminder requires a spirituality, a spiritual connectedness, a way of living united with God. What does this imply for the daily life of the minister?

It implies that prayer, not in the sense of *prayers*, but in the sense of a prayerful life, a life lived in connection with Christ, should be our first and overriding concern.

It implies that in a life of connectedness with Christ the needs of our neighbors and the nature of our service are disclosed.

It implies that all training and formation are intended to facilitate this disclosure, and that the insights of the behavioral sciences should be seen as aids in this process.

It implies that prayer cannot be considered external to the process of ministry. If we heal by reminding each other of God in Christ, then we must have the mind of Christ himself to do so. For that, prayer is indispensable.

Finally, it implies that what counts is not our lives, but the life of Christ in us. Ultimately, it is Christ in us from whom healing comes. Only Christ can break through our human alienation and restore the broken connections with each other and with God.

The Minister as a Sustaining Reminder

Introduction

LET ME START again with Elie Wiesel. In *The Town Beyond the Wall*[1] and *A Beggar in Jerusalem*,[2] Wiesel evokes in a masterful way the sustaining power of friendship. In both books it is not simply from a friend but from the memory of a friend that the sustaining power flows.

In *The Town Beyond the Wall* it is Michael who lives through torture but avoids madness because Pedro, his absent friend, lives in his memory and so sustains him in the midst of his agony. And in *A Beggar in Jerusalem* it is David who is sustained in his struggles by the memory of his friend Katriel, killed during Israel's Six-Day War. This is a crucial theme in Wiesel's writings. He wants us to remember not only the wounds but also the great affectionate bonds of our life stories. Just as the memory of past wounds can prevent us from repeating the evil that wounded us, so also the memory of love can nurture us in our day-to-day struggles. In his novels Wiesel expresses the profound truth that memory not only connects us with our past but also keeps us alive in the present. He touches here a mystery deeply anchored in the biblical tradition. When Israel remembers God's great acts of love and compassion, she enters into these great acts themselves. To remember is not simply to look back at past events; more importantly, it is to bring these events into the present and

---

1 Elie Wiesel, *The Town Beyond the Wall* (New York: Atheneum, 1964).
2 Elie Wiesel, *A Beggar in Jerusalem* (New York: Random House, 1970).

celebrate them here and now. For Israel, remembrance means participation. Brevard S. Childs writes: "The act of remembering serves to actualize the past for a generation removed in time from those former events in order that they themselves can have an intimate encounter with the great acts of redemption. . . . Although separated in time and space from the sphere of God's revelation in the past, through memory the gulf is spanned, and the exiled people share again in redemptive history."[3]

It is central to the biblical tradition that God's love for his people should not be forgotten. It should remain with us in the present. When everything is dark, when we are surrounded by despairing voices, when we do not see any exits, then we can find salvation in a remembered love, a love which is not simply a wistful recollection of a bygone past but a living force which sustains us in the present. Through memory, love transcends the limits of time and offers hope at any moment of our lives.

This is the message of the Bible. This is the message which Elie Wiesel puts in the context of the agonies of our century. This also is the message which forms the core of our lives as ministers of the Gospel of Jesus Christ. Therefore, I will speak now about the minister as a sustaining reminder. Again, three aspects present themselves to us: the sustenance, the sustaining, and the sustainer.

The Sustenance

ONE OF THE mysteries of life is that memory can often bring us closer to each other than can physical presence. Physical presence not only invites but also blocks intimate communication. In our preresurrection state our bodies hide as much as they reveal. Indeed, many of our disappointments and frustrations in life are related to the fact that seeing and touching each other does not always create the closeness we seek. The more experience in living we have, the more we sense that closeness grows in the continuous interplay between presence and absence.

In absence, from a distance, in memory, we see each other in a new way. We are less distracted by each other's idiosyncracies and are better able to see and understand each other's inner core.

3　Brevard S. Childs, *Memory and Tradition in Israel* (London: SCM Press, 1962), 56, 60.

When I am away from home, I often express myself in letters in a much more intimate way than when I am with my family. And when I am away from school, students often write letters in which they say things they were never able to express when I was around.

In memory we are able to be in touch with each other's spirit, with that reality in each other which enables an always deepening communication. There is little doubt that memory can distort, falsify, and cause selective perception. But that is only one aspect of memory. Memory also clarifies, purifies, brings into focus, and calls to the foreground hidden gifts. When a mother and father think of their children who have left home, when a child remembers his parents, when a husband and wife call each other to mind during long periods of absence, when friends recall their friends, it is often the very best that is evoked and the real beauty of the other that breaks through into consciousness. When we remember each other with love we evoke each other's spirit and so enter into a new intimacy, a spiritual union with each other. At the same time, however, the loving memory always makes us desire to be in touch again, to see each other anew, to return to the shared life where the newly found spirit can become more concretely expressed and more deeply embedded in the mutuality of love. But a deeper presence always leads again to a more purifying absence. Thus the continuous interplay between presence and absence, linked by our creative memory, is the way in which our love for each other is purified, deepened and sustained.

This sustaining power of memory becomes most mysteriously visible in God's revelation in Jesus Christ. Indeed it is in memory that we enter into a nurturing and sustaining relationship with Christ. In his farewell discourse Jesus said to his disciples, "It is for your own good that I am going, because unless I go, the Advocate will not come to you; . . . But when the Spirit of truth comes he will lead you to the complete truth" (John 16:7, 13). Here Jesus reveals to his closest friends that only in memory will real intimacy with him be possible, that only in memory will they experience the full meaning of what they have witnessed.

They listened to his words, they saw him on Mount Tabor, they heard him speak about his death and resurrection, but their ears and eyes remained closed and they did not understand. The Spirit, his spirit, had not yet come, and although they saw and heard, smelled and touched him, they remained distant. Only later when he was gone could his true Spirit reveal itself to them. In his absence a new and more intimate presence became possible, a presence which nurtured and sustained in the midst of tribulations and which created the desire to see him again. The great mystery of the divine revelation is that God entered into intimacy with us not only by Christ's coming, but also by his leaving. Indeed, it is in Christ's absence that our intimacy with him is so profound that we can say he dwells in us, call him our food and drink, and experience him as the center of our being.

That this is far from a theoretical idea becomes clear in the lives of people like Dietrich Bonhoeffer and Alfred Delp[4] who, while in Nazi prisons waiting for death, experienced Christ's presence in the midst of his absence. Bonhoeffer writes: "The God who is with us is the God who forsakes us (Mark 15:34). . . . Before God and with God we live without God."[5] Thus the memory of Jesus Christ is much more than the bringing to mind of past redemptive events. It is a life-giving memory, a memory which sustains and nurtures us here and now and so gives us a real sense of being rooted amidst the many crises of daily life.

The Sustaining

HOW DOES A ministry as a sustaining memory of Jesus Christ take shape? From what has been said about the maturing interplay between absence and presence, it is clear that we need to look more closely at the ministry of absence. We are living in a culture and social climate which places a great and positive emphasis on presence. We feel that being present is a value as such, and almost always better than being

---

4 Delp, a Jesuit theologian and commentator on social issues in economic and political life for the periodical *Stimmen der Zeit*, was imprisoned by the Nazis in July, 1944. Tried and sentenced to death the following January, he died on February 2, 1945, two months before Bonhoeffer was executed. Delp's prison writings may be found in the third volume of his collected papers: *Christus und Gegenwart*, vol. 3: *Im Angesicht des Todes* (Frankfort am Main: Verlag Josef Knecht, 1949).

5 Dietrich Bonhoeffer, *Letters and Papers from Prison*, ed. by Eberhard Bethge (New York: Macmillan and Co., 1972), 360.

absent. Being present constitutes much of our occupation as ministers: present to patients and students, at services, at Bible groups, at all sorts of charitable meetings, at parties, at dinners, at games—and just present in the streets of our town.

Although this ministry of presence is undoubtedly very meaningful, it always needs to be balanced by a ministry of absence. This is so because it belongs to the essence of a creative ministry constantly to convert the pain of the Lord's absence into a deeper understanding of his presence. But absence can only be converted if it is first of all experienced. Therefore, ministers do not fulfill their whole task when they witness only to God's presence and do not tolerate the experience of his absence. If it is true that ministers are living memories of Jesus Christ, then they must search for ways in which not only their presence but also their absence reminds people of their Lord. This has some concrete implications. It calls for the art of leaving, for the ability to be articulately absent, and most of all for a creative withdrawal. Let me illustrate this with the ministry of visitation and the ministry of the Eucharist.

In our ministry of visitation—hospital visits and home visits—it is essential for patients and parishioners to experience that it is good for them, not only that we come but also that we leave. In this way the memory of our visit can become as important, if not more important, than the visit itself. I am deeply convinced that there is a ministry in which our leaving creates space for God's spirit and in which, by our absence, God can become present in a new way. There is an enormous difference between an absence after a visit and an absence which is the result of not coming at all. Without a coming there can be no leaving, and without a presence absence is only emptiness and not the way to a greater intimacy with God through the Spirit.

The words of Jesus: "It is for your good that I leave" should be a part of every pastoral call we make. We have to learn to leave so that the Spirit can come. Then we can indeed be remembered as a living witness of God. This shows the importance of being sensitive to the last words we speak before we leave a room or house; it also puts the possibility of a prayer before leaving into a new light.

Not only in pastoral visits but also, and even more so, in the celebration of the sacraments, we need to be aware of the importance of a ministry of absence. This is very central in the Eucharist. What do we do there? We eat bread, but not enough to take our hunger away; we drink wine, but not enough to take our thirst away; we read from a book, but not enough to take our ignorance away. Around these "poor signs" we come together and celebrate. What then do we celebrate? The simple signs, which cannot satisfy all our desires, speak first of all of God's absence. He has not yet returned; we are still on the road, still waiting, still hoping, still expecting, still longing. We gather around the table with bread, wine, and a book to remind each other of the promise we have received and so to encourage each other to keep waiting in expectation for his return. But even as we affirm his absence we realize that he already is with us. We say to each other: "Eat and drink, this is his body and blood. The One we are waiting for is our food and drink and is more present to us than we can be to ourselves. He sustains us on the road, he nurtures us as he nurtured his people in the desert." Thus, while remembering his promises in his absence we discover and celebrate his presence in our midst.

The great temptation of the ministry is to celebrate only the presence of the Lord while forgetting his absence. Often the minister is most concerned to make people glad and to create an atmosphere of "I'm OK, you're OK." But in this way everything gets filled up and there is no empty space left for the affirmation of our basic lack of fulfillment. In this way God's presence is enforced without connection with his absence. Almost inevitably this leads to artificial joy and superficial happiness. It also leads to disillusionment because we forget that it is in memory that the Lord is present. If we deny the pain of his absence we will not be able to taste his sustaining presence either.

Therefore, every time ministers call their people around the table, they call them to experience not only the Lord's presence but his absence as well; they call them to mourning as well as to feasting, to sadness as well as to joy, to longing as well as to satisfaction.

And so the Eucharist is a memorial of the Lord's death and resurrection, a memorial which sustains us here and now. As we are being reminded we are nurtured. As we become aware of his absence we discover his presence, and as we realize that he left us we also come to know that he did not leave us alone.

So we see that sustaining calls for a patient and humble attitude, an attitude in which we do not create false gaiety, easy excitement, or hollow optimism. The minister is not called to cheer people up but modestly to remind them that in the midst of pains and tribulations the first sign of the new life can be found and a joy can be experienced which is hidden in the midst of sadness.

Therefore, a sustaining ministry requires the art of creative withdrawal so that in memory God's Spirit can manifest itself and lead to the full truth. Without this withdrawal we are in danger of no longer being the way, but *in* the way; of no longer speaking and acting in his name, but in ours; of no longer pointing to the Lord who sustains, but only to our own distracting personalities. If we speak God's word, we have to make it clear that it is indeed God's word we speak and not our own. If we organize a service, we have to be aware that we cannot organize God but only offer boundaries within which God's presence can be sensed. If we visit, we have to remember that we only come because we are sent. If we accept leadership it can only be honest if it takes the form of service. The more this creative withdrawal becomes a real part of our ministry the more we participate in the leaving of Christ, the good leaving that allows the sustaining Spirit to come.

The Sustainer

WHAT ARE THE implications of the ministry of sustaining for the personal life of the minister? Perhaps we need to reconsider a little our ideas about availability. When absence is a part of our ministry, we have to relativize our view of the value of availability. We ministers may have become so available that there is too much presence and too little absence, too much staying with people and too little leaving them, too much of us and too little of God and his Spirit. It is clear that much of this is connected with a certain illusion of indispensability. This illusion needs to be unmasked.

From all I have said about the minister as a sustaining reminder, it becomes clear that a certain unavailability is essential for the spiritual life of the minister. I am not trying to build a religious argument for a game of golf, a trip to a conference, a cruise to the Caribbean, or a sabbatical. These arguments have been made and they all strike me as quite unconvincing in the midst of our suffering world. No, I would like to make a plea for prayer as the creative way of being unavailable.

How would it sound when the question, "Can I speak to the minister?" is not answered by "I am sorry, he has someone in his office" but by "I am sorry, he is praying." When someone says, "The minister is unavailable because this is his day of solitude, this is his day in the hermitage, this is his desert day," could that not be a consoling ministry? What it says is that the minister is unavailable to me, not because he is more available to others, but because he is with God, and God alone—the God who is our God.

My spiritual director at the abbey of the Genesee spent one day a week in a small hermitage on the property of the abbey. I remember that his absence had a comforting effect on me. I missed his presence and still I felt grateful that he spent a whole day with God alone. I felt supported, nourished, and strengthened by the knowledge that God was indeed his only concern, that he brought all the concerns of the people he counseled into his intimate relationship with God, and that while he was absent he was, in fact, closer to me than ever.

When our absence from people means a special presence to God, then that absence becomes a sustaining absence. Jesus continuously left his apostles to enter into prayer with the Father. The more I read the Gospels, the more I am struck with Jesus' single-minded concern with the Father. From the day his parents found him in the Temple, Jesus speaks about his Father as the source of all his words and actions. When he withdraws himself from the crowd and even from his closest friends, he withdraws to be with the Father. "In the morning, long before dawn, he got up and left the house, and went off to a lonely place and prayed there" (Mark 1:35). All through his life Jesus considers his relationship with the Father as the center, beginning, and end of his ministry. All he says and does he says and does in the name of the Father. He comes from the Father and returns to the Father, and it is in his Father's house that he wants to prepare a place for us.

It is obvious that Jesus does not maintain his relationship with the Father as a means of fulfilling his ministry. On the contrary, his relationship with the Father is the core of his ministry. Therefore, prayer, days alone with God, or moments of silence, should never be seen or understood as healthy devices to keep in shape, to charge our "spiritual batteries," or to build up energy for ministry. No, they are all ministry. We minister to our parishioners, patients, and students even when we are with God and God alone.

It is in the intimacy with God that we develop a greater intimacy with people and it is in the silence and solitude of prayer that we indeed can touch the heart of the human suffering to which we want to minister.

Do we really believe this? It often seems that our professional busy-ness has claimed the better part of us. It remains hard for us to leave our people, our job, and the hectic places where we are needed, in order to be with him from whom all good things come. Still, it is in the silence and solitude of prayer that the minister becomes minister. There we remember that if anything worthwhile happens at all it is God's work and not ours.

Prayer is not a way of being busy with God instead of with people. In fact, it unmasks the illusion of busy-ness, usefulness, and indispensability. It is a way of being empty and useless in the presence of God and so of proclaiming our basic belief that all is grace and nothing is simply the result of hard work. Indeed, wasting time for God is an act of ministry, because it reminds us and our people that God is free to touch anyone regardless of our well-meant efforts. Prayer as an articulate way of being useless in the face of God brings a smile to all we do and creates humor in the midst of our occupations and preoccupations.

Thinking about my own prayer, I realize how easily I make it into a little seminar with God, during which I want to be useful by reading beautiful prayers, thinking profound thoughts and saying impressive words. I am obviously still worried about the grade! It indeed is a hard discipline to be useless in God's presence and to let him speak in the silence of my heart. But whenever I become a little useless I know that God is calling me to a new life far beyond the boundaries of my usefulness.

We can say therefore that ministry is first and foremost the sharing of this "useless" prayer with others. It is from the still point of prayer that we can reach out to others and let the sustaining power of God's presence be known. Indeed, it is there that we become living reminders of Jesus Christ.

Conclusion

IN OUR DISCUSSION of the minister as a sustaining reminder, three ideas have been dominant. First, we sustain each other in the constant interplay between absence and presence. Second, a sustaining ministry asks ministers to be not only creatively present but creatively absent. Third, a creative absence challenges ministers to develop an ever growing intimacy with God in prayer and to make that the source of their entire ministry.

This means that to be a sustaining reminder we must make our own the words of Jesus: "It is for your own good that I am going, because unless I go the Advocate [the Holy Spirit] will not come to you" (John 16:7).

What does all this suggest for our daily lives as ministers?

It suggests that we need to explore not only ways of being present to people but also ways of being absent.

It suggests that in the way we visit, preach, and celebrate we must keep struggling with the question of how to be the way, without being *in* the way.

It suggests that prayer can never be considered a private affair. Rather, it belongs to the core of ministry and, therefore, is also subject to education and formation.

It suggests that it is important to look at our daily calendars again and schedule some useless time in the midst of our busy work. We ought to schedule our time with God with the same realism that we schedule our time with people.

Finally, it suggests that amidst so many "useful" people we should try to keep reminding ourselves of our basic uselessness and so bring a smile and a little humor to all we do.

The Minister as a Guiding Reminder

Introduction

THE FIRST WORD belongs again to the great reminder, Elie Wiesel. In his novel *The Gates of the Forest* Wiesel tells the story of Gregor. Having survived the holocaust, Gregor finds himself in Paris, seeking a new future after the horrendous trials of his past. There, on the advice of a friend and not without reluctance, he visits the rabbi. When the rabbi asks what Gregor expects of him, the answer is, "Make me able to cry."

> The Rebbe shook his head. "That is not enough. I shall teach you to sing. Grown people don't cry, beggars don't cry. . . . Crying is for children. Are you still a child, and is your life a child's dream? No, crying's no use. You must sing."
>
> "And you, Rebbe? What do you expect of me?"
>
> "Everything."
>
> And when Gregor started to protest, the Rebbe added, "Jacob wrestled with the angel all night and overcame him. But the angel implored him: Let me go, dawn is approaching. Jacob let him go; to show his gratitude the angel brought him a ladder. Bring me this ladder."
>
> "Which one of us is Jacob?" asked Gregor. "And which the angel?"
>
> "I don't know," said the Rebbe with a friendly wink. "Do you?"
>
> Gregor got up and the Rebbe took him to the door. "Promise to come back," he said, holding out his hand.

"I'll come back."

"Will you come to our celebrations?"

"Yes."[1]

This pastoral visit has much to say. Elie Wiesel, who gives to Gregor many autobiographical traits, expresses in this dialog his hope in a new future. Beyond tears there is singing, beyond sadness there is celebration, beyond the struggle there is the ladder given in gratitude by an angel. The rabbi is the living reminder of a faithful God. When in the same conversation Gregor asks, "After what happened to us, how can you believe in God?", the Rabbi responds, "How can you *not* believe in God after what has happened?"[2] The God who wrestles with us also gives us a ladder to a new future. Wiesel, who does not want us to forget the past, does not want us to lose faith in the future either. Harry James Cargas says of Wiesel: "He knows that each of us is an inheritor of the entire past while being the beginning point for all the future."[3] And so Wiesel, the great reminder, becomes a hopeful guide.

There is little doubt that it was the Hasidic tradition with its deep faith in God that enabled Wiesel to speak about hope after the holocaust. During his early youth, Hasidism had impregnated Wiesel's heart, mind, and soul and given him a memory of God which could not be erased, even by the holocaust. It proved to be his saving guide in the years of grief and mourning.

Ministers, as living reminders of Jesus Christ, are not only healers and sustainers, but also guides. The memory that heals the wounds of our past and sustains us in the present also guides us to the future and makes our lives continuously new. To be living reminders means to be prophets who, by reminding, point their people in a new direction and guide them into unknown territory. Therefore, I would like to speak now about the minister as a guiding reminder. Again, three areas call for our attention: the guidance, the guiding, and the guide.

---

1 Elie Wiesel, *The Gates of the Forest* (New York: Holt, Rinehart and Winston, 1966), 198.

2 Wiesel, *The Gates of the Forest*, 198.

3 Harry James Cargas, *In Conversation with Elie Wiesel* (New York: Paulist Press, 1976), 121–22.

The Guidance

GOOD MEMORIES OFFER good guidance. We all have had the experience that in times of distress, failure, and depression it is the good memories which give us new confidence and hope. When the night is dark and everything seems black and fearful, we can hope for a bright new day because we have seen a bright day before. Our hope is built on our memories. Without memories there are no expectations. We do not always realize that among the best things we can give each other are good memories: kind words, signs of affection, gestures of sympathy, peaceful silences, and joyful celebrations. At the time they all may have seemed obvious, simple, and without many consequences, but as memories they can save us in the midst of confusion, fear, and darkness.

When we speak about guiding memories we do not necessarily refer to a conscious remembering, an explicit reflection on events in the past. In fact, most of our memories guide us in a prereflective way. They have become flesh and blood in us. Our memories of trust, love, acceptance, forgiveness, confidence, and hope enter so deeply into our being that indeed we become our memories. The fact that we are alive, that our hearts beat, our blood flows, our lungs breathe, is a living memory of all the good care that came our way. It is primarily such incarnate, pulsating memories that carry us through our dark moments and give us hope. These memories might be dormant during our normal day-to-day living, but in times of crisis they often reveal their great revitalizing power.

It is to these conscious and unconscious memories that the great prophets in history have appealed. The prophets of Israel guided their people first of all by reminding them. Hear how Moses guides his people: "Remember how Yahweh led you out of Egypt . . . follow his ways and pay reverence to him" (cf. Deuteronomy 8:2–14). "Do not mistreat strangers, remember that once you were a stranger" (cf. Exodus 22:20; Deuteronomy 10:19). Listen to the indignant Isaiah: "Stir your memories again, you sinners, remember things long past. I am God unrivalled, God who has no like. From the beginning I foretold the future, and predicted beforehand what is to be" (Isa. 46:8–10).

By reminding their people of the misery of slavery and the liberating love of God, the prophets of Israel motivated them to move forward, and challenged them to honor their memory by their behavior. As living reminders of God's care and compassion, they unmasked the stifling and narrow-minded viewpoints of their contemporaries and again disclosed the vision that inspired their forefathers and that still offers constant guidance in the continuing search for salvation.

In Jesus this prophetic ministry finds its fullest expression. In his teaching he reminds his contemporaries of their own history, confronts them with their limited views, and challenges them to recognize God's guiding presence in their lives. He evokes the memory of Elijah and Elisha, Jonah and Solomon. He tries to break through the fearful resistance of his followers and open their hearts to the unlimited love of his Father. Everything Jesus tells his disciples about the need for repentance and the love of the Father he tells them so that they will remember during the difficult times ahead. "I have told you all this so that when the time comes, you will remember" (John 16:4).

And so they did. As Jesus reminded his disciples of the Father, so the disciples remind each other and their followers of Jesus. In memory of Jesus they speak, preach, witness, and break bread; in memory of Jesus they find the strength to live through tribulations and persecutions. In short, it is the memory of Jesus that guides them and offers them hope and confidence in the midst of a failing culture, a faltering society, and a dark world.

So our memories give us guidance. They are the blueprint for our future. They help us to move forward faithful to the vision which made us leave the land of slavery, and obedient to the call which says that the promised land is still ahead of us.

The Guiding

HOW DO MINISTERS, as living memories of Jesus Christ, guide their people in the concrete circumstances of everyday life? Two ways of guiding suggest themselves in the context of this discussion on memory: confronting and inspiring. It may be surprising to think of confrontation as a form of guidance, but a prophetic ministry which guides toward a new future requires the hard, painful unmasking of our illusions: the illusion that "we have arrived," that we have found the final articulation of our faith, and that we have discovered the life-style which best gives shape to our ideals. We are constantly tempted to replace the original vision with a rather comfortable interpretation of that vision. It is this complacent and stifling narrowing down of the vision to our own needs and aspirations that all reformers have confronted with their prophetic ministries. Benedict in the sixth century, Francis in the twelfth, Martin Luther in the sixteenth, John Wesley in the eighteenth, and people such as Dorothy Day and Mother Theresa today—all of them have confronted the ways in which the great vision has become blurred and has lost its convincing appeal. Guidance requires the breaking down of these false walls and the removal of obstacles to growth. People caught in mental and spiritual chains cannot be guided.

But guidance demands more than confrontation. It requires recapturing the original vision, going back to the point from which the great inspiration came. In this sense all reformers are revisionists, people who remind us of the great vision. Benedict recaptured the vision of community, Francis recaptured the vision of poverty, Luther recaptured the vision of God's undeserved grace, Wesley recaptured the vision of a living faith, and today many prophets are recapturing the vision of peace and justice. They all have moved backwards, not in sentimental melancholy but in the conviction that from a recaptured vision new life can develop. The French have an imaginative expression: *recular pour mieux sauter,* to step back in order to jump farther. Ministers who guide step back in order to touch again the best memories of their community and so to remind their people of the original vision. The paradox of progress is that it occurs by conserving the great memory which can revitalize dormant dreams.

Thus the minister guides by confronting and inspiring. Confrontation challenges us to confess and repent; inspiration stirs us to look up again with new courage and confidence.

How might such confrontation and inspiration express themselves in our daily ministry? I will limit myself to only one concrete suggestion:

tell a story. Often colorful people of great faith will confront and inspire more readily than the pale doctrines of faith. The Epistle to the Hebrews does not offer general ideas about how to move forward but calls to mind the great people in history: Abel, Enoch, Noah, Abraham, Sarah, Isaac, Jacob, Moses, and many others. And then it says, "With so many witnesses in a great cloud on every side of us, we too, then, should throw off everything that hinders us, especially the sin that clings so easily, and keep running steadily in the race we have started" (Hebrews 12:1).

We guide by calling to mind men and women in whom the great vision becomes visible, people with whom we can identify, yet people who have broken out of the constraints of their time and place and moved into unknown fields with great courage and confidence. The rabbis guide their people with stories; ministers usually guide with ideas and theories. We need to become storytellers again, and so multiply our ministry by calling around us the great witnesses who in different ways offer guidance to doubting hearts.

One of the remarkable qualities of the story is that it creates space. We can dwell in a story, walk around, find our own place. The story confronts but does not oppress; the story inspires but does not manipulate. The story invites us to an encounter, a dialog, a mutual sharing.

A story that guides is a story that opens a door and offers us space in which to search and boundaries to help us find what we seek, but it does not tell us what to do or how to do it. The story brings us into touch with the vision and so guides us. Wiesel writes, "God made man because he loves stories."[4] As long as we have stories to tell to each other there is hope. As long as we can remind each other of the lives of men and women in whom the love of God becomes manifest, there is reason to move forward to new land in which new stories are hidden.

The Guide

WHAT ARE THE implications of this understanding of guidance for the spiritual life of ministers? They are many, and they all cut deeply into our way of being attentive to the world. But they all point to the need to

4 Wiesel, *The Gates of the Forest*, flyleaf.

be in touch with the source from which the guiding inspiration comes. It is clear from what we have already said that we cannot guide others by a simple argument, some casual advice, a few instructions, or an occasional sermon. Prophecy confronts and inspires only insofar as prophets are indeed speaking from the vision which guides their own lives day and night. It is in the encounter with the prophetic minister that strength is found to break out of myopic viewpoints and courage is given to move beyond safe and secure boundaries.

I have asked many people for counsel in my own personal and professional life. The more I reflect on this, the more I realize that I experience guidance and hope, not because of any specific suggestion or advice but because of a strength far beyond their own awareness which radiated from my counselors. On the other hand, I have tried to help many people and have been increasingly surprised that I often gave strength when I least expected to and received grateful notes when I thought that I had been of no help at all. It seems that we often reveal and communicate to others the life-giving spirit without being aware of it. One of the most comforting remarks I ever heard was: "I wish you could experience yourself as I experience you. Then you would not be so depressed." The great mystery of ministry is that while we ourselves are overwhelmed by our own weaknesses and limitations, we can still be so transparent that the Spirit of God, the divine counselor, can shine through us and bring light to others.

How then can we be spiritual people through whom God's divine counselor and guide can become manifest? If we really want to be living memories, offering guidance to a new land, the word of God must be engraved in our hearts; it must become our flesh and blood. That means much more than intellectual reflection. It means meditating and ruminating on God's word—chewing it or, as the Psalmist puts it, "murmuring" it day and night. In this way the word of God can slowly descend from our mind into our heart and so fill us with the life-giving Spirit. This "total" meditation on the Word of God lies deeply embedded in the rabbinic as well as the Christian tradition. Jean Leclercq, the Benedictine medieval scholar, writes:

> . . . to meditate is to read a text and to learn it "by heart" in the fullest sense of this expression, that is, with one's whole being: with the body since the mouth pronounced it, with the memory which fixes it, with the intelligence which understands its meaning and with the will which desires to put it in practice.[5]

This meditation on God's Word is indispensable if we want to be reminders of God and not of ourselves, if we want to radiate hope and not despair, joy and not sadness, life and not death. Since the greatest news is that the Word has become flesh, it is indeed our greatest vocation and obligation to continue this divine incarnation through daily meditation on the word.

While any specific prayer technique is secondary to our obligation to meditate, and although every individual has to find his own way, a disregard for techniques in prayer is just as unwise as a disregard for techniques and skill in pastoral care. The history of Jewish and Christian spirituality shows that our most precious relationship, our relationship with God, cannot simply be left to our spontaneous outpourings. Precisely because God is central to our lives, our relationship with him calls for formation and training, including skills and methods. Therefore, it is sad that most ministers have more hours of training in how to talk and be with people than how to talk and be with God. There are even seminaries which feel that the question of how to pray is not a question to which the faculty can respond. Yet how can we guide people with God's word if that word is more a subject for discussion and debate than for meditation? It is not the disembodied word that guides, but the word that pervades our whole earthly being and manifests itself in all we do and say.

One simple and somewhat obvious technique is memorization. The expression "to know by heart" already suggests its value. Personally

---

5 Jean Leclercq, *The Love of Learning and the Desire for God: A Study of Monastic Culture* (New York: Fordham University Press, 1961), 21, 22.

I regret the fact that I know so few prayers and psalms by heart. Often I need a book to pray, and without one I tend to fall back on the poor spontaneous creations of my mind. Part of the reason, I think, that it is so hard to pray "without ceasing" is that few prayers are available to me outside church settings. Yet I believe that prayers which I know by heart could carry me through very painful crises. The Methodist minister Fred Morris told me how Psalm 23 ("The Lord is my shepherd") had carried him through the gruesome hours in the Brazilian torture chamber and had given him peace in his darkest hour. And I keep wondering which words I can take with me in the hour when I have to survive without books. I fear that in crisis situations I will have to depend on my own unredeemed ramblings and not have the word of God to guide me.

Perhaps the 1970s offer us a unique chance to reclaim the rich tradition of schooling in prayer. All spiritual writers, from the desert fathers to Teresa of Avila, Evelyn Underhill, and Thomas Merton, have stressed the great power and central importance of prayer in our lives. Theophan the Recluse expresses this forcefully when he says:

Prayer is the test of everything; prayer is also the source of everything; prayer is the driving force of everything; prayer is also the director of everything. If prayer is right, everything is right. For prayer will not allow anything to go wrong.[6]

If this is true, then it is obvious that prayer requires supervision and direction. Just as verbatim reports of our conversations with patients can help us to deepen our interpersonal sensitivities, so a continuing evaluation of our spiritual life can lead us closer to God. if we do not hesitate to study how love and care reveal themselves in encounters between people, then why should we shy away from detailed attention to the relationship with him who is the source and purpose of all human interactions? The fact that many of the spiritual movements of our day seem to be irresponsible, manipulative, and even downright dangerous for the

---

6 *The Art of Prayer,* 51.

mental and physical health of the people involved, makes it urgent that the spiritual life of ministers and future ministers not be left to their own uninformed experimentations.

There is little doubt that seminaries and centers for Clinical Pastoral Education are challenged to incorporate the spiritual formation of the students into their programs. This will be far from easy and there are many pitfalls, but denying the increasing spiritual needs of students and ministers will only backfire in the form of a growing amateurism in this most sensitive area of contemporary experience.

Many ministers today are excellent preachers, competent counselors, and good program administrators, but few feel comfortable giving spiritual direction to people who are searching for God's presence in their lives. For many ministers, if not for most, the life of the Holy Spirit is unknown territory. It is not surprising, therefore, that many unholy spirits have taken over and created considerable havoc. There is an increasing need for diagnosticians of the soul who can distinguish the Holy Spirit from the unholy spirits and so guide people to an active and vital transformation of soul and body, and of all their personal relationships.[7] This gift of discernment is a gift of the Spirit which can only be received through constant prayer and meditation.

Thus the spiritual life of the minister, formed and trained in a school of prayer, is the core of spiritual leadership. When we have lost the vision, we have nothing to show; when we have forgotten the word of God, we have nothing to remember; when we have buried the blueprint of our life, we have nothing to build. But when we keep in touch with the life-giving spirit within us, we can lead people out of their captivity and become hope-giving guides.

Conclusion

I HAVE TRIED to make three points in this discussion of the minister as a guiding reminder. First, our hope in the future is built on our conscious and unconscious memories. Second, guiding takes place by unmasking the illusion of present comfort and reminding people of the original vi-

---

7 *The Art of Prayer,* 119.

sion. Third, this vision becomes flesh and blood by an unceasing meditation on the Word of God.

All this means that to be guiding ministers, we must be prophets who, by appealing to memories, encourage our fellow human beings to move forward. Let me summarize what this says about our lives as ministers.

It says that we need to think about ways to make our individual and collective memories a source of guidance.

It says that we should look at guidance as a form of prophecy.

It says that we should rediscover the art of storytelling as a ministerial art.

It says that meditation is indispensable for a real incarnation of the Word of God in our lives.

Finally, it says that we need to explore ways to introduce schooling in prayer into pastoral education.

A Professing Profession

WHEN I FINISHED writing these chapters about the minister as a living reminder of Jesus Christ, I realized that, in fact, I had discussed the minister as pastor, as priest, and as prophet. As pastors, ministers heal the wounds of the past; as priests, they sustain life in the present; and as prophets, they guide others to the future. They do all of this in memory of him who is, who was, and is to come. When I became aware of how traditional I had been, I felt a little embarrassed at first. But then I realized that, after all, my only real task had been to be a reminder of what we already know.

What I have tried to do is to look at the biblical roles of ministry in the context of the new developments in pastoral psychology and thus to unite two aspects of the ministry as a profession. Profession as we conceive of it today primarily suggests training, skill, expertise, and a certain specialization. Theological education in recent decades has made a major contribution toward establishing the ministry as a profession in a highly professionalized world. But "profession" also refers to professing, witnessing, proclaiming, announcing. This professing side of our ministerial life, which is deeply rooted in our biblical heritage, requires formation as well. Profession as expertise and profession as proclamation can never be separated without harm. When we profess our faith in Christ without any ministerial expertise, we are like people shouting from the mountaintop without caring if anyone is listening. But when we are skillful experts who have little to profess, then we easily become lukewarm technicians who squeeze God's work between 9 A.M. and 5 P.M.

One of our most challenging tasks today is to explore our spiritual resources and to integrate the best of what we find there with the best of what we have found in the behavioral sciences. When psychiatrists, psychologists, medical doctors, and other professionals ask us, "Tell me, how are you different from us?" we must be able to hear that question as a challenge to transcend the boundaries of our technocratic society and to proclaim with renewed fervor that the Lord is risen, is risen indeed. The temptation remains to forget our proclaiming task and to settle for an easy professionalism. But I am convinced that deep in our heart there is a voice that keeps calling us back to the hard but joyful task of proclaiming the good news.

Let me conclude with the story of the disenchanted rabbi who:

> was weary of threatening sinners with the wrath of Yahweh . . . and of comforting the meek with his goodness. And so, deserting his synagogue, he set off on his wanderings in disguise. He came to an old woman who lay dying in her drafty hovel. "Why was I born," asked the old woman, "when as long as I can remember nothing but misfortune has been my lot?" "That you should bear it," was the disguised rabbi's reply, and it set the dying woman's mind at rest. As he drew the sheet over her face, he decided that from then on he would be mute. On the third day of his wanderings, he encountered a young beggar girl, carrying her dead child on her back. The rabbi helped to dig the grave; shrouding the tiny corpse in linen, they laid it in the pit, covered it up, broke bread, and to the beggar girl's every word the rabbi answered with gestures. "The poor thing got nothing, neither pleasure nor pain. Do you think it was worth his being born?" At first the rabbi in disguise made no move, but when the girl insisted, he nodded. Thereupon he decided to be deaf as well as dumb. He hid away from the world in a cave. There he met no one, only a ferret. Its foot was hurt, so the rabbi bound it with herbs; whereupon the ferret brought his tasty seeds. The hermit prayed, the tiny beast wiggled its nose, and the two grew fond of one another. One afternoon a condor plummeted from a great height, and as the ferret was basking in the sun at the mouth of the cave, carried it off

before the rabbi's eyes. At that, the rabbi thought to himself that it would be better if he closed his eyes too. But since—blind, dumb, and deaf—he could do nothing but wait for death, which, he felt, it was not seemly to hasten, he girded his loins and returned to his congregation. Once again he preached to them on the subject of good and evil, according to Yahweh's law. He did what he had done before and waxed strong in his shame."[1]

We often may want to run away from our home to hide out and play deaf, dumb, and blind for a while. But we are ministers. Not only dying and lonely people but even little ferrets remind us of that. And so we keep returning to our people, faithful to our vocation, and growing strong in humility and love.

---

1 George Konrad, *The Case Worker* (New York: Harcourt Brace Jovanovich, 1974), 130–31.

ACKNOWLEDGMENTS

THE CONTENT OF this book was first presented in the form of three lectures at the International Conference of the Association for Clinical Pastoral Education and the Canadian Association for Pastoral Education.

I am grateful to Vernon Kuehn for inviting me to the conference and to Robert Bilheimer, director of the Institute for Ecumenical and Cultural Research in Collegeville, Minnesota, for offering me a quiet place, a peaceful time, and a gentle community in which to work. I also want to thank Fred Hofheinz and the staff of the Lilly Endowment for their encouragement and financial support.

I owe a special word of thanks to Jack Jerome, Jim Mason, and Bud Kaicher for their skillful typing of the manuscript, to Phil Zaeder for his sound advice, and to Sylvia Zaeder and Stephen Leahy for their editorial assistance.

Finally, I want to express my deep appreciation to my friend and assistant John Mogabgab whose many insights and suggestions helped me to give this book its final form.

¡Gracias!

A Latin American Journal

*To all who bear witness to the presence of the
suffering Christ in Latin America*

¡GRACIAS!

CONTENTS

INTRODUCTION

In Search of a Vocation

THIS JOURNAL IS the personal report of my six-month sojourn in Bolivia and Peru. I wrote it in an attempt to capture the countless impressions, feelings, and ideas that filled my mind and heart day after day. It speaks about new places and people, about new insights and perspectives, and about new joys and anxieties. But the question that runs through all its pages and binds the many varied fragments together is: "Does God call me to live and work in Latin America in the years to come?" This vocational question has guided me in the selection of issues to comment upon, it has directed me in my observations, and it has deeply influenced my responses to what I have seen and heard. This journal, therefore, is neither a travel diary, nor an analysis of Latin American conditions, nor a critical study of political and religious movements. Even though I often mention interesting sights, describe distressing living conditions, and comment on the impact of political and religious currents, I do not claim more expertise than the expertise that comes from an honest search for a new vocation. This journal records a six-month journey toward discernment. In the midst of all the travels, language studies, conversations, and encounters, I tried to discern God's voice; and in the midst of the great variety of my inner responses, I tried to find the way to be obedient to that voice.

The question: "Does God call me to Latin America?" was not a new question for me. From the day I left Holland to teach pastoral theology at Yale Divinity School, I had been wondering about the connection between the northern and the southern parts of the American continent. Somehow I felt that teaching future ministers in the United States about God's mysterious work with people could not be done unless the word "people" included the millions of Spanish-and Portuguese-speaking human beings whose destiny is intimately linked with that of their English-speaking brothers and sisters. Somehow, I knew that God's voice could not be heard unless it would include the voices of the men, women, and children of Latin America. With this "knowledge," I made short visits to Mexico, Chile, and Paraguay, and took some language training in Bolivia. Although these excursions led only to piecemeal involvements and limited commitments, they deepened my conviction about the spiritual unity of the American continent.

Finally, after ten years, I felt free enough to confront directly the question that had haunted me for so long. I left the Divinity School, moved in temporarily with my Trappist friends at the Abbey of the Genesee in upstate New York, and started to prepare myself for a more systematic discernment of a possible vocation in Latin America. Meanwhile, the Maryknoll fathers in Peru had invited me to make Peru the center of my activities. They suggested, however, that I first go to Bolivia for some additional language training. Thus, in October 1981, I flew to Peru to get to know my Maryknoll hosts and from there to Cochabamba, Bolivia, for a three-month course designed to improve my Spanish. In January 1982, I returned to Peru for three months of orientation "in the field." It is these six months, from October 1981 to March 1982, that this journal records. In it, I tried to impose some order on the myriad experiences that were part of this journey. But, most of all, I have tried to find an answer to the question: "Does God call me to live and work in Latin America in the years to come?"

I am very glad that I can share this search for a new vocation with others, because I know that all who love God strive constantly to hear his voice more clearly. I therefore hope that telling my story will offer encouragement to others to tell theirs.

1

October

The Lord of the Miracles

Sunday, October 18
Lima, Peru

THANKS BE TO God for bringing me here. The closer I came to the day of departure, the more convinced I was that going to Latin America was indeed the thing to do. Off and on the thought occurred to me that I was not ready for this change. I felt too tired, too preoccupied with personal struggles, too restless, too busy, too unprepared. But as the day of departure drew closer, I felt a growing sense of call. What had seemed little more than an adventure now presented itself as a vocation.

I left the Abbey of the Genesee in upstate New York on Sunday, October 11, for a one-week visit to Yale Divinity School in New Haven, where I had taught for ten years. It proved to be an important week, in which all the contacts, discussions, prayers, and celebrations helped me to listen more carefully to God's call, to let go of what was past, and to look forward to a totally new ministry. It seems paradoxical, but the expressions of friendship at Yale of former students and colleagues, and the deep personal conversations, gave me a profound sense of mission. I realized that I was not going just because it seemed like a good idea, but because those who love me most sent me on my way with affection, support, and prayers. The more I realized that I was truly loved, the more

I felt the inner freedom to go in peace and to let all inner debate about motivation subside.

The Eucharistic celebration on Friday afternoon meant more to me than I can express in words. I had a strong sense of community, and an awareness that this community will stay with me wherever I go. The Lord himself brought us together and has made it clear to us that we are One in him and that this unity will allow us to be free, courageous, and full of hope. Whatever my experience in Latin America will bring to me, it will be part of a body formed in love and it will reverberate in all its members. The Body and Blood of our Lord Jesus Christ are indeed food for eternal life, a life that liberates us to live without fear and to travel without apprehension.

John Vesey drove me to the airport. He had come from Brooklyn to spend the last day in New Haven with me to help me pack. Our friendship started in Bolivia in the summer of 1972, when I was there for language training, and we have stayed in touch ever since. Having just returned from a seven-year ministry in Paraguay, he expressed his enthusiasm for my decision to return to Bolivia for more training and to join the Maryknoll fathers in Peru. His strong sense of God's guidance in our lives and his deep awareness of the beauty of the Divine in the midst of this dark world convinced me more than ever that it was good to go.

Monday, October 19

On the airplane to Lima, I spoke with the woman next to me. She told me that she was returning home with her mother, who had undergone three operations in the United States. "Is your mother better now?" I asked. "Oh yes, she is totally cured," she said with fervent conviction, "and the whole family is waiting at the airport to welcome her home." After a few minutes of silence, she wanted to know my reasons for going to Peru. When I told her that I was a priest planning to work with the Maryknoll missioners, her face changed dramatically. She leaned over to me, grabbed my hand, and whispered in an agonized way: "Oh Father, mother has cancer and there is little hope for her."

The first thing I learned about Peruvians was that they have an unlimited trust in priests. Even though the Church certainly has not earned such unconditional respect during the last centuries, the people of Peru give their confidence to their priests without hesitation. This impression was strongly affirmed on Sunday morning, when I found myself in the huge crowd on the Plaza de Armas, welcoming the procession of *el Señor de los milagros* (the Lord of the Miracles). As soon as the bystanders realized that I was a priest, they let go of their inhibitions, handed me their children to lift above the crowds, and told me about their joys and sorrows.

Peru: from the moment I entered it, I felt a deep love for this country. I do not know why. I did not feel this when I went to Chile or Bolivia in the past. But looking at the busy streets of Lima, the dark open faces and the lively gestures, I felt embraced by a loving people in a way I had not known before. Walking through the busy streets, looking at the men, women, and children in their penitential dress—purple habits with white cords—and sensing the gentle spirit of forgiveness, I had the strange emotion of homecoming. "This is where I belong. This is where I must be. This is where I will be for a very long time. This is home." Everything seemed easy. Thousands of people, but no pressing crowds; countless voices, but no shouts or cries; a multitude of faces, but no anger or frustration. I had never experienced this before. The obvious explanation is that I saw Peru for the first time on the feast day of the Lord of the Miracles, a day celebrated with a procession characterized by repentance and quiet prayer. But for me it was a day of comfort and consolation, a day on which the decision to come to this country was affirmed.

I felt as though the crowds of Lima were embracing me and showering me with the affection I had missed during the past months. It seemed as if the whispering crowds, the gentle movements of the bearers of the picture of the Lord of the Miracles, and the uninhibited smiles of the children all said to me: "Do not be afraid, the Lord loves all of us . . . you too."

Yes, I saw the Lord! How strange was that first day in Lima. In the central square, with its many balconies, thousands of people had gathered. On one balcony, president Fernando Belaúnde Terry stood waiting to pay homage to the Christ being carried into his presence. On another, the mayor was ready to hand the key of the city to the Lord of the Miracles; and on a third balcony, the church dignitaries stood to bless the image of the Crucified. Who was bowing to whom? Who was using whom? Who was trying to win votes, admiration, or sympathy? Who knows? But the people applauded the One whom they trusted and left the president, the mayor, and the bishops to their own speculations. New bouquets of flowers were continually brought to the platform on which the Image of Christ slowly moved through the crowds. When I lifted up a little Peruvian girl and showed her the Lord of the Miracles, I felt that the Lord and the little girl were both telling me the same story: presidents, mayors, and bishops come and go, but our God continues to enter our lives and to invite children to climb on the shoulders of adults and recognize him.

On the evening of this first day in Peru, I had the sensation that I had been here for a long time and that all that I had heard and seen had a deep and old familiarity. Everything whispered, "Welcome home, my friend."

Tuesday, October 20

It took only a few hours to be immersed in the real questions. Monsignor Alberto Koenigsknecht introduced me to them without knowing he was doing so. Alberto, a Maryknoller, is the prelate of the diocese of Juli in the Altiplano. He is staying at the Maryknoll Center house in Lima to organize a day of prayer to protest the attacks against the Christian community in his prelature. On August 15, the Institute for Rural Education was ransacked. On September 19, dynamite exploded in the entrance of Alberto's home and a note was found with a death threat.

Alberto was careful in his explanation. "We do not know who did it and why it was done, but it certainly was well planned." In August 1979, a pastoral week was held in the diocese of Juli. This meeting showed a strong and unwavering commitment to the poor and the oppressed. The final text says: "We decide to commit ourselves to the poor, that is, to those who form the oppressed class, those who depend on their work but do not have the means to live a dignified life, since they are exploited by others who deny them their rights." These are very strong words when spoken or written in and about Peru, and it certainly is possible that the recent attacks and death threat are among the responses.

Alberto spoke to the underminister of justice, but received little support. An investigation was promised, but nothing happened. And now it is the Church's turn to respond. In a few weeks, on November fifteenth, Christians of Peru will be called to Juli to express solidarity with the poor and to give a clear sign that attacks and death threats are not going to change the chosen direction. Alberto realized that he was taking a risk, but he felt that he had to do it. Gustavo Gutiérrez, the father of liberation theology, and his staff were consulted. It had become evident that a clear sign was needed to show the strength of the Church's commitment.

I sense that all of this might be just the beginning of a long road of suffering. Similar things have happened in El Salvador, similar things are happening in Guatemala, and the small rumblings in Peru seem to belong to that same awakening of the people of God in Latin America.

Wednesday, October 21

Pete Byrne, the superior of the Maryknoll fathers in Peru, drove me to the Ciudad de Dios (the City of God). "This is the parish where you will live and work when you come back from language school," he said with excitement. "You will love it. Now it all looks strange and unfamiliar to you, but it won't take long for you to feel part of the people here. They will love you and you will love them." Pete drove his car through the crowds gathering around the marketplace and took me to the Pamplona Alta section, where Maryknoll missioners Pete Ruggere, Tom Burns, and Larry Rich are living.

I was struck not only by the obvious poverty of the people, but also by their dignity. They care for what they own, and they manage to keep little gardens in the midst of this dry, sandy, and dusty place. Thousands of people live here—125,000—but there is space between houses as well as between people. The area is poor, very poor, but not depressing. It is full of visible problems, but not without hope.

Later in the day an elderly laywoman dressed as a nun—Maria is her name—told me about the beginning of the Ciudad de Dios. Ciudad de Dios was the result of a popular invasion on Christmas Eve 1954. Maria remembered that day with a sense of pride. She belonged to the founding fathers and mothers. On that Christmas night, thousands of people illegally occupied the barren land and immediately started to develop it. The government had no choice but to comply and eventually help, and now there is the City of God with countless brick houses, a large church, a school, and several medical posts.

The invasion of Ciudad de Dios was one of the first in a long series of similar invasions. Poverty and lack of land forced a constant migration from the countryside to the city. The Indian migrants first lived with relatives and friends; but when they became too numerous and desperate for a space and a livelihood, they organized themselves and seized the barren desert land surrounding the city. Today Lima has a large belt of "young towns," many of which are the result of these illegal land seizures.

Pamplona Alta, which belongs to the same parish, developed a few years after Ciudad de Dios was founded. From the many little shacks visible on the bare hills beyond Pamplona Alta, it is clear that invasions — although on a much smaller scale — are still taking place today.

Pete Ruggere welcomed me to the house where I would stay in January. It consists of brick walls, a cement floor, and a roof put together with pieces of wood, plastic, and straw. "It gets wet here when it rains," Pete observed, "but it seldom rains." We visited the neighbors: a husband, wife, and eleven children, all living in two rooms. There were lots of smiles, laughter, and affection, but I noticed exhaustion on the face of the mother. She carried a two-month-old baby in her arms while pointing to the one-and-a-half-year-old girl on the bed. I tried to get a smile from her, but found little response. Pete told me she was just diagnosed as having Down syndrome.

I spent the day visiting Maureen, a Dominican nurse, walking around the area, attending a mass during which the sick were anointed, talking to Sister Vivian, a Maryknoll doctor, and just wondering what it would be like to live here.

During the evening, I picked up some of Gustavo Gutiérrez's early writings. My visit to Ciudad de Dios makes his words sound very real. This, indeed, is a theology born out of solidarity with the people. The people speak about God and his Presence in ways I must slowly come to understand. It will take time, much time, but a willingness to learn is one thing I can bring here.

Before leaving for Bolivia, I would like to make some notes about Maryknoll and its role in Latin America. The first objective of the Maryknoll Society, as expressed by the General Chapter in 1979, is: "To recognize and elaborate a mission of spirituality which integrates community, prayer, a simple life-style, apostolic work, and commitment to the poor." I like the word "recognize." A true spirituality cannot be constructed, built, or put together; it has to be recognized in the daily life of people who search together to do God's will in the world.

I am impressed by the documents written about Peru by the Maryknollers. Their socioeconomic, political, and religious analyses are well-documented, clearly explained, and skillfully integrated into their self-understanding as missioners. A few simple facts are worth remembering. The present population of Peru is about 17 million (54% mestizo [mixed Indian and white], 33% Indian, 13% white). The main perspective of the Maryknoll missioners in Peru is summarized well in the following quote:

> The vast majority of Peruvians are classified as poor or "lower class" workers, campesinos or unemployed. This class is distinguished by race: it is composed of Indians, blacks and mestizos. It is dominated by the "upper class" and it is considered inferior. The Peruvian "middle-class" is composed of professionals who are generally either white or mestizos and though economically and politically it is gaining strength, it is numerically small and no rival to the power of the "upper class." The "upper class" is white and though minute it controls the wealth and the political power of the country.
>
> One fourth of one percent of the population receives more than 33% of all income in the country. The predominant social dynamic in Peru is the structural oppression and domination of the "lower class" and the emerging resistance of the poor to this domination (*Peru Regional Directory*, 1980, p. 3).

This is the context of the work of the Maryknoll Society, and the background against which its commitment to the poor needs to be understood. There are about forty-eight people directly connected with the work of the Maryknoll fathers in Peru (priests, associate priests, brothers, and lay missioners). Their activities are varied: parish work, religious training and formation, counseling, teaching, small group work, publishing, research, and so forth. They work in the Juli Prelature, in Arequipa, Huacho, and Lima. Maryknoll came to Peru in 1943, and has focused in different ways on the development of the local church. "To create self-directing, self-sustaining, and self-propagating Christian Communities captures the thrust of Maryknoll work in Peru from the beginning but the manner and emphasis have changed over the years."

The change in "manner and emphasis" of the missionary activities of Maryknoll over the years is of crucial importance. One Maryknoll priest, Ralph Davila, remarked during dinner: "It is the change from selling pearls to hunting for the treasure." Indeed, not too long ago, the main task was seen as selling the pearls of good news to the poor and ignorant people. Now a radically new perspective dominates the Maryknoll activities: to search with the poor for the treasure hidden in the ground on which they stand. It is this shift from spiritual colonialism to solidarity in servanthood that explains the style of life, the way of speech, the kind of literature, and the overall mood that I have become part of during the last few days.

I really feel that I am welcome here, not just as a guest who can learn a lot from Maryknoll, but also as someone from whom some contribution is expected. At this moment I cannot think of myself as someone who has anything to offer—I feel like someone surrounded by experts— but I am willing to live with the supposition that he who truly receives also gives. It is encouraging to feel part of a true community of apostolic love and fervor so soon. I now am ready to go to Bolivia for language training, because I now know that I will be welcome here when I return.

Thursday, October 22
Cochabamba, Bolivia

Today I flew from Lima to La Paz and from La Paz to Cochabamba. It was a magnificent flight over Lake Titicaca and over the wild and desolate mountain ranges of Bolivia. In the plane I talked with Henry Perry, a surgeon from Duke University, who hopes to set up elaborate health services in Achacachi, and with a young woman from San Francisco, who is dedicated to studying the intricate weaving techniques of the Indians in Ecuador, Peru, and Bolivia.

Warm summer weather engulfed me when I stepped off the plane, and the taxi ride to the Instituto de Idiomas, the language school, showed me clearly that Cochabamba is, indeed, the garden city of Bolivia. The great wealth of flowers reminded me that it is spring here, and that it will be midsummer when December comes.

Gerald McCrane, the director of the institute, welcomed me warmly and invited me to look with some of the students of the institute at a video-tape of a CBS report on El Salvador. And thus, staying in one of the most lovely towns of Latin America, I am reminded that violence, oppression, persecution, torture, and indescribable human misery are all around. The film showed the civil war in El Salvador in gruesome detail. The Bolivians who watched it with us remarked that similar things were happening here.

Latin America: impressive wealth and degrading poverty, splendid flowers and dusty broken roads, loving people and cruel torturers, smiling children and soldiers who kill. It is here that we have to hunt for God's treasure.

I pray that my stay in Bolivia will teach me much more than Spanish.

Friday, October 23

Today was a day of getting used to my new environment. This seems easy: friendly people, beautiful gardens, and a smoothly run school. But when I reflect on what is going on underneath this comfortable exterior, I realize that I probably will never get used to my new world.

Chris Hedges, a Harvard Divinity School student, told me about the drug traffic in Bolivia. A Maryknoller visiting the institute explained to me how the military pushes Bolivia into bankruptcy, creates terror all through the country, and imprisons, kills, and tortures at random.

At lunch I met the Archbishop of La Paz, Monsignor Manrique. A short man with dark, Indian features, he impresses me as a simple and humble person. As the many stories indicate, he is one of the few people who dare to resist the regime. His faith gives him the moral power to speak out forcefully against the oppression of his people. In 1978, twelve hundred people staged a three-week-long hunger strike to reinforce their demands for an amnesty for all political prisoners and exiles. The government of General Banzer was forced to capitulate, but only after Manrique threatened to close all the churches of the diocese. He once said to the military: "You play tigers in La Paz in front of unarmed citizens, but you are cowards on the borders when you are facing the Chileans. You haven't won one war yet." Archbishop Manrique is undoubtedly one of the most courageous Christian leaders in Latin America, deeply loved by the miners and workers of Bolivia for his consistent demands for justice. I asked him if there were any priests in prison. He said: "At this moment, no. The human rights committee of the UN is coming to Bolivia today, and that helps."

Bolivia desperately wants recognition from the United States as a way to prevent total economic chaos. The Reagan administration requires an end to the drug traffic as a condition for recognition. The military, however, is so heavily involved in this illegal business, which brings in more money than all the mining industries put together, that any significant action can hardly be expected. So now there are some sporadic antidrug actions in the Beni (Bolivian lowlands). The victims—as always—are not the big cocaine traffickers, but some innocent *campesinos.* Meanwhile, the United States government seems to be placated with these gestures, and the newspapers expect a speedy recognition from Reagan.

I guess it is better not to get used to my new environment too soon.

Saturday, October 24

Although it is only a week ago that I came to Latin America, I have been here for a long time. The many new things I saw and heard during the last seven days must have intensified my mental activity. At the same time, I have had more time for myself than I have had for a long time—more time to pray, more time to read, more time to talk to people, more time to relax and just look around.

Today was a day in which prayer was uppermost on my mind. Last night the Franciscan priest, Justus Wirth, said in his reflection on the Gospel that the new commitment to the poor and the new emphasis on prayer were both signs of the action of the Holy Spirit in our time. When he said this, I suddenly realized that, indeed, prayer and work with the poor belong together and that the need to pray had grown in me ever since I have been confronted with the oppression and exploitation of the poor in Peru and Bolivia.

The several times I awoke last night, I found myself saying: "Lord, give me a true desire to pray"; and today I found it easier than before just to sit in the presence of God and listen quietly. I am grateful for this experience, and I am slowly becoming aware that something new is happening in me.

One image has been with me ever since I saw Pamplona Alta in Lima. It is the image of living as a hermit in the midst of the poor. That image must have been vague and subconscious, since I never wrote or spoke about it. But when a visiting priest from the St. Louis, Missouri, diocese said to me: "I am living in a poor section of La Paz as a hermit among the people," I immediately understood him. Yes—indeed, just to pray for, with, and among the poor spoke to me as a true missionary vocation. Wouldn't that be an authentic way of entering into solidarity with those who have nothing to lose?

True prayer always includes becoming poor. When we pray we stand naked and vulnerable in front of Our Lord and show him our true condition. If one were to do this not just for oneself, but in the name of the thousands of surrounding poor people, wouldn't that be "mission" in the true sense of being sent into the world as Jesus himself was sent into the world? To lift up your hands to the Lord and show him the hungry children who play on the dusty streets, the tired women who carry their babies on their backs to the marketplace, the men who try to forget their misery by drinking too much beer on the weekends, the jobless teenagers and the homeless squatters, together with their laughter, friendly gestures, and gentle words—wouldn't that be true service? If God really exists, if he truly cares, if he never leaves his people alone, who is there to remind him of his promises? Who is there to cry out: "How long will you frown on your people's plea? . . . Turn again, we implore, look down from heaven and see. Visit this vine and protect it, the vine your right hand has planted. . . . Let your face shine on us, and we shall be saved" (Ps. 80)? I feel that in a world rushing to the abyss, the need for calling God to the task, for challenging him to make his love felt among the poor, is more urgent than ever.

There were many wars, conflicts, and much poverty and misery in the thirteenth century, but we do not remember the political struggles and the socioeconomic events of that century. We remember one man who lived in the midst of it and prayed, prayed, and prayed until his hands and feet were pierced with the wounds of Christ himself. Who will be the St. Francis of our age? Many are asking themselves this question again. Who will lift up the world of today to God and plead for his mercy? Why does God still allow this world to continue? Because of Ronald Reagan, Begin, Brezhnev, Thatcher, Marcos, Belaúnde, or Torrelio? Or perhaps because of the few hermits hidden in the forests of Russia, on the roofs of New York City, and in the *favelas* of Brazil, Peru, and Bolivia? When the Lord looks down on us, what does he see? He sees his son Jesus in the faces of the few who continue to cry out in the valley of tears. For Jesus' sake he will save us from total destruction.

Prayer is the ongoing cry of the incarnate Lord to the loving God. It is eternity in the midst of mortality, it is life among death, hope in the midst of despair, true promise surrounded by lies. Prayer brings love alive among us. So let us pray unceasingly.

Sunday, October 25

Donald Stoker, an English priest, said to me last night: "Did you notice the night sounds here? When you go to bed you hear the bull-frogs croak. When you wake up at two in the night you hear the dogs bark. When you wake up at four you hear the cocks crow, and when you get up at six you hear the birds sing." Indeed, there are no silent nights in Bolivia. And during the day the voices of playing children join the birds in their chatter. All these sounds come together to form a single unceasing prayer to the Creator, a prayer not of thoughts and words but of sounds and life. How sad it is that thinking often makes prayers cease.

Monday, October 26

Chris Hedges gave me an article to read called, "Up to Our Steeple in Politics." It is written by Will D. Campbell and James Holloway and published in *Christianity and Crisis* on March 3, 1969. In it, the authors explore the issue of exactly how far the Church can become involved in politics without being corrupted by it, how far one can go into the world of Caesar before one loses sight of God.

The questions Campbell and Holloway raise are as important for the Latin American upheavals as they were for the civil rights movement in the United States, about which they were writing. Will we ever know whether we are living witnesses to the light or serving the prince of darkness? That is the question for the four priests who participated in the revolution in Nicaragua and are now members of the new Sandinista cabinet. That, too, is the question for Christians active in agrarian reform, in the development of cooperatives for the *campesinos,* and in programs for better health and better housing.

The Christian is called to live in the world without being of it. But how do we know whether we are just in it, or also of it? My feeling is that every Christian who is serious about his or her vocation has to face this question at some point.

How, then, are we to find the right answer for ourselves? Here we are called to discern carefully the movements of God's Spirit in our lives. Discernment remains our lifelong task. I can see no other way for discernment than a life in the Spirit, a life of unceasing prayer and contemplation, a life of deep communion with the Spirit of God. Such a life will slowly develop in us an inner sensitivity, enabling us to distinguish between the law of the flesh and the law of the spirit. We certainly will make constant errors and seldom have the purity of heart required to make the right decisions. We may never know whether we are giving to Caesar what belongs to God. But when we continuously try to live in the Spirit, we at least shall be willing to confess our weakness and ask for forgiveness every time we find ourselves again in the service of Baal.

Tuesday, October 27

This is my second day of language training, frustrating and exhilarating at the same time. It is frustrating, since I make the same mistakes I made nine years ago and continue to have the feeling that I should be much more advanced after the many weeks and months I have worked on Spanish in the past. There are frequent moments during which I say to myself: "I will never master this language." But the same experience is also refreshing. I can be a student again. I can spend many hours doing simple exercises that often appear as little puzzles, and I can be with other people who go through the same frustrations as I do. The teachers are dedicated and are always in a good mood and willing to help inside and outside of classes. The institute is equipped with the best possible facilities and everything is well organized. I can hardly think of a better place to learn a new language.

During the sixties, I spent two weeks in Madrid and a month in Cuernavaca with the conviction that Spanish was essential for my future work. But I never practiced it outside the formal training periods. Then I came here in the summer of 1972 and gave it another try. Again my acquired knowledge slipped away and now—nine years later—I feel that again I am beginning from scratch.

As I reflect on this fragmented approach to mastering Spanish, I can only say that I never gave up the deep conviction that I must learn it somehow, sometime. I never have been able fully to explain this conviction to myself or to anyone else. But the urge always was there and still is there; my desire to know Spanish and to know it well is as strong as ever. Why? I don't know. I hope that I will know before I die. There must be a meaning to such a strange passion!

I just read Paul Blustein's article about the Maryknollers in Peru. It gave me a strong sense of *déjà vu*. Blustein speaks about his encounter with Pete Ruggere and about his visit to Pete's neighbors:

On a urine-soaked bed near the entrance lies an infant girl who, Father Ruggere says, suffers from malnutrition and almost certainly won't live beyond her fifth birthday. When the priest swoops the baby into his arms, gurgling endearments in Spanish, the child neither laughs nor cries, but merely gazes blankly at him through filmy brown eyes . . . (*Wall Street Journal*, August 14, 1981).

When I read this I saw it all over again, and realized that he was speaking about my future neighbors. The article is a masterful piece of reporting and one of the most balanced descriptions of the Maryknoll work I have read or heard.

Wednesday, October 28

This afternoon at three o'clock, my sister called from Holland to tell me that my sister-in-law had given birth to a daughter who was diagnosed as suffering from Down syndrome. A week ago I wrote about having seen a Down syndrome child in the house of Pete Ruggere's neighbors; yesterday I read about that child in the *Wall Street Journal*; today I have a niece who suffers from the same disease. I called Holland and talked to Heiltjen, my sister-in-law. The baby, she told me, had been born five hours previously, and the doctors had told her immediately about the child's handicap. "With Laura, our lives will be very different from now on," she said. My brother Laurent was not in the hospital when I called, but my sister as well as Heiltjen told me how distressed he was.

I still find it hard to appropriate this news. I cannot think about much else than this little child who will become the center of my brother and my sister-in-law's lives and will bring them into a world of which they have never dreamt. It will be a world of constant care and attention; a world of very small progressions; a world of new feelings, emotions, and thoughts; a world of affections that come from places invisible in "normal" people.

I know that Laurent and Heiltjen's love is being tested, not only their love for their new child but even more their love for each other and for their two-year-old daughter Sarah. I pray tonight for them that they will be able to grow in love because of Laura, and that they will discover in her the presence of God in their lives.

Laura is going to be important for all of us in the family. We have never had a "weak" person among us. We all are hardworking, ambitious, and successful people who seldom have had to experience powerlessness. Now Laura enters and tells us a totally new story, a story of weakness, brokenness, vulnerability, and total dependency. Laura, who always will be a child, will teach us the way of Christ as no one will ever be able to do.

I hope and pray that I can be of some support to Laurent and Heiltjen in their long journey with Laura, and that Laura will bring all of us closer together and closer to God.

Thursday, October 29

Tonight the Dominican priest, John Risley, spoke at the institute about the Puebla Documents. These are the public statements that were the result of the 1978 Latin American Bishops' Conference in Puebla, Mexico. The main point he made was that the Church had made a definite choice for the poor. Thus, he said, Puebla brought good news for the poor but bad news for those who hold power and do not want to give it up. The lively discussion that followed revealed various opinions about the implications of such a "preferential option" and about the theology of liberation in general.

One thought hit me in the midst of all the viewpoints, opinions, and ideas that were expressed. It was the thought that the poor themselves are the best evangelizers. I have already met a few very simple people here who revealed to me God's presence in life in a way nobody else could. During breakfast this morning I spoke to Lucha, one of the maids working in the institute. We did not speak about God or religion, but her smile, her kindness, the way she corrected my Spanish, and her stories about her children created a sense of spiritual jealousy in me. I kept thinking: "I wish I had the purity of heart of this woman, I wish I could be as simple, open, and gentle as she is. I wish I could be as in touch." But then I realized that maybe even she didn't know what she was giving me. Thus my ministry to her is to allow her to show me the Lord and gratefully to acknowledge what I am receiving.

True liberation is freeing people from the bonds that have prevented them from giving their gifts to others. This is not only true for individual people but also—particularly—for ethnic groups. What does mission to the Indians really mean? Isn't it foremost to discover with them their own deep religiosity, their profound faith in God's active presence in history, and their understanding of the mystery of nature that surrounds them?

It is hard for me to accept that the best I can do is probably not to give but to receive. By receiving in a true and open way, those who give to me can become aware of their own gifts. After all, we come to recognize our own gifts in the eyes of those who receive them gratefully. Gratitude thus becomes the central virtue of a missionary. And what else is the Eucharistic life than a life of gratitude?

Friday, October 30

Today Gerry McCrane, the director of the language school, gave a presentation to the newcomers. In his gentle and pastoral way he offered us an opportunity to share our struggles in adapting ourselves to a new culture.

One theme that came up was the re-emergence of long-forgotten conflicts. In displacing ourselves into a new and unfamiliar milieu, old, unresolved conflicts often start asking for attention. When our traditional defense systems no longer are available and we are not able to control our own world, we often find ourselves experiencing again the feelings of childhood. The inability to express ourselves in words as well as the realization that everyone around us seems to understand life much better than we do, puts us in a situation quite similar to that of a child who has to struggle through a world of adults.

This return to childhood emotions and behavior could be a real opportunity for mental and spiritual growth. Most of the psychotherapies I have been exposed to were attempts to help me relive those times when immature ways of coping with stress found their origin. Once I could re-encounter the experience that led me to choose a primitive coping device, I was also able to choose a more mature response. Thus I could let go of behavior that was the source of my suffering. A good psychotherapist is a person who creates the environment in which such mature behavioral choices can be made.

Going to a different culture, in which I find myself again like a child, can become a true psychotherapeutic opportunity. Not everyone is in the position or has the support to use such an opportunity. I have seen much self-righteous, condescending, and even offensive behavior by foreigners towards the people in their host country. Remarks about the laziness, stupidity, and disorganization of Peruvians or Bolivians usually say a lot more about the one who makes such remarks than about Peruvians or Bolivians. Most of the labels by which we pigeonhole people are ways to cope with our own anxiety and insecurity. Many people who suddenly find themselves in a totally unfamiliar milieu decide quickly to label that which is strange to them instead of confronting their own fears and vulnerabilities.

But we can also use the new opportunity for our own healing. When we walk around in a strange milieu, speaking the language haltingly, and feeling out of control and like fools, we can come in touch with a part of ourselves that usually remains hidden behind the thick walls of our defenses. We can come to experience our basic vulnerability, our need for others, our deep-seated feelings of ignorance and inadequacy, and our fundamental dependency. Instead of running away from these scary feelings, we can live through them together and learn that our true value as human beings has its seat far beyond our competence and accomplishments.

One of the most rewarding aspects of living in a strange land is the experience of being loved not for what we can do, but for who we are. When we become aware that our stuttering, failing, vulnerable selves are loved even when we hardly progress, we can let go of our compulsion to prove ourselves and be free to live with others in a fellowship of the weak. That is true healing.

This psychological perspective on culture shock can open up for us a new understanding of God's grace and our vocation to live graceful lives. In the presence of God, we are totally naked, broken, sinful, and dependent, and we realize that we can do nothing, absolutely nothing, without him. When we are willing to confess our true condition, God will embrace us with his love, a love so deep, intimate, and strong that it enables us to make all things new. I am convinced that, for Christians, culture shock can be an opportunity not only for psychological healing but also for conversion.

What moves me most in reflecting on these opportunities is that they lead us to the heart of ministry and mission. The more I think about the meaning of living and acting in the name of Christ, the more I realize that what I have to offer to others is not my intelligence, skill, power, influence, or connections, but my own human brokenness through which the love of God can manifest itself. The celebrant in Leonard Bernstein's *Mass* says: "Glass shines brighter when it's broken. . . . I never noticed that." This, to me, is what ministry and mission are all about. Ministry is entering with our human brokenness into communion with others and speaking a word of hope. This hope is not based on any power to solve the problems of those with whom we live, but on the love of God, which becomes visible when we let go of our fears of being out of control and enter into his presence in a shared confession of weakness.

This is a hard vocation. It goes against the grain of our need for self-affirmation, self-fulfillment, and self-realization. It is a call to true humility. I, therefore, think that for those who are pulled away from their familiar surroundings and brought into a strange land where they feel again like babies, the Lord offers a unique chance not only for personal conversion but also for an authentic ministry.

Saturday, October 31

During the last few days, I have been thinking about the significance of gratitude in mission work. Gratitude is becoming increasingly important for those who want to bring the good news of the Kingdom to others. For a long time, the predominant attitude of the missioners was that they had to bring the knowledge of the Gospel to poor, ignorant people and thus offer light in their darkness. In such a view, there is not much room for gratitude.

As the missionary attitude changed, however, and more and more missioners came to see their task as helping others to recognize their own God-given talents, and thus to claim the good news for themselves, gratitude became much more than an occasional "thanks be to God." Gratitude is the attitude which enables us to receive the hidden gifts of those we want to serve and to make these gifts visible to the community as a source of celebration.

There is little doubt that jealousy, rivalry, anger, and resentment dominate our society much more than gratitude. Most people are afraid to make themselves available to others. They fear that they will be manipulated and exploited. They choose the safe way of hiding themselves and thus remaining unnoticed and anonymous. But in such a milieu of suspicion and fear, no community can develop and no good news can become visible.

True missioners are people who are hunting for the Divine treasure hidden in the heart of the people to whom they want to make the Good

News known. They always expect to see the beauty and truth of God shining through those with whom they live and work.

The great paradox of ministry, therefore, is that we minister above all with our weakness, a weakness that invites us to receive from those to whom we go. The more in touch we are with our own need for healing and salvation, the more open we are to receive in gratitude what others have to offer us. The true skill of ministry is to help fearful and often oppressed men and women become aware of their own gifts, by receiving them in gratitude. In that sense, ministry becomes the skill of active dependency: willing to be dependent on what others have to give but often do not realize they have. By receiving in gratitude what we have helped others to discover in themselves, we enable them to claim for themselves full membership in the human and Christian community. Only those who truly believe that they have something to offer can experience themselves as spiritually adult. As long as someone feels that he or she is only an object of someone else's generosity, no dialogue, no mutuality, and no authentic community can exist.

As ministers, we share with all other human beings—especially those who have elaborate education and training—the desire to be in control, to tell others what to do and how to think. But if we want to follow Christ and "have his mind," we are called to empty ourselves of these privileges and become servants of the people. True servants depend on those whom they serve. They are called to live lives in which others guide them, often to places they would rather not go.

In different ways, these thoughts have been part of my understanding of ministry for over a decade. But here in Bolivia, in a different milieu, these ideas have taken deeper root; I no longer consider them romantic or sentimental. There is a danger of interpreting these thoughts about gratitude as a requirement to have certain concrete emotions towards others. But how can I feel grateful when I see so many poor, tired, and often apathetic people? My first response is: "How can I give them food, a house, an education, and a job?"

What then is it that we do receive in ministry? Is it the hidden insights and skills of those to whom we want to bear witness? Maybe so . . . but that can never be the true source of our own growth. Seeing how a person slowly becomes aware of his or her own capacities might make us happy for awhile, but that is not enough for a grateful life. A grateful life is a life in which we come to see that the Lord himself is the gift. The mystery of ministry is that the Lord is to be found where we minister. That is what Jesus tells us when he says: "Insofar as you did this to one of the least of these brothers of mine, you did it to me" (Matt. 25:40). Our care for people thus becomes the way to meet the Lord. The more we give, help, support, guide, counsel, and visit, the more we receive, not just similar gifts, but the Lord himself. To go to the poor is to go to the Lord. Living this truth in our daily life makes it possible to care for people without conditions, without hesitation, without suspicion, or without the need for immediate rewards. With this sacred knowledge, we can avoid becoming burned out.

The goal of education and formation for the ministry is continually to recognize the Lord's voice, his face, and his touch in every person we meet. As long as we live, the Lord wants to reveal to us more of himself. As long as we minister, we can expect the Lord to make himself known to us in ways we have not yet experienced. God himself became flesh for us so that we would be able to receive him every time we find ourselves serving another human being.

The question, however, is not only what are we receiving, but who is the receiver? Is it just *I*, with my unique capacity to see or hear, while others remain blind and deaf? No, because to see or to hear God is not a human possibility. It is a divine sensitivity. It is the Spirit of God in us who gives us eyes to see and ears to hear, who allows us to see and hear God in every person we serve. God is thus not only the gift, but also the receiver. Just as it is not we who pray, but the Spirit in us, so it is not we who receive but the Spirit in us.

Gratitude is not just a psychological disposition, but a virtue. Gratitude is an intimate participation in the Divine Life itself. The Spirit of God in us recognizes God in the world. The eyes and ears by which we can see God in others are in fact spiritual sensitivities that allow us to receive our neighbor as a messenger of God himself.

This theological perspective on gratitude makes it clear why it is so crucial that we pray: through prayer we become aware of the life of God within us and it is this God within us who allows us to recognize the God among us. When we have met our Lord in the silent intimacy of our prayer, then we will also meet him in the *campo,* in the market, and in the town square. But when we have not met him in the center of our own hearts, we cannot expect to meet him in the busyness of our daily lives. Gratitude is God receiving God in and through the human interaction of ministry. This viewpoint explains why true ministers, true missionaries, are always also contemplatives. Seeing God in the world and making him visible to each other is the core of ministry as well as the core of the contemplative life.

Today, Reformation Day, a group of North American Lutheran ministers is visiting the institute. They are traveling through Latin America in order to evaluate their mission work. They come with open minds and hearts. Their vision is very much in tune with the vision of Maryknoll, and their main question is: "How can we work together to make and fulfill our common call to evangelize the nations?"

I was invited to attend the meeting, and I felt part of an extremely important new form of ecumenism: cooperation in the missions between the Roman Catholic and the Lutheran communities. To set the tone, Gerry McCrane gave all of us the following words, written by a third world bishop for those who come as missioners to Latin America.

Walk with Us in Our Search

Help us discover our own riches; don't judge us poor because we lack what you have.

Help us discover our chains; don't judge us slaves by the type of shackles you wear.

Be patient with us as a people; don't judge us backward simply because we don't follow your stride.

Be patient with our pace; don't judge us lazy simply because we can't follow your tempo.

Be patient with our symbols; don't judge us ignorant because we can't read your signs.

Be with us and proclaim the richness of your life which you can share with us.

Be with us and be open to what we can give.
Be with us as a companion who walks with us—neither behind nor
    in front—in our search for life and ultimately for God!

These words not only point toward a contemporary missionary spirituality, but also offer a base for true ecumenism in Latin America. Because, whether we are Lutherans or Roman Catholics, we first of all must
listen to the people to whom we come; it is they who will show us the way
to Christian unity.

2

November

New Faces and Voices

Sunday, November 1, All Saints Day

THIS MORNING I went with Brian Clark, a journalist for the *Modesto* [California] *Bee*, and with Simon, a Redemptorist brother, to Mass in the Church of Santa Ana. The Dominican priest, Oscar Uzin, celebrated the Eucharist. In a simple, clear, and convincing way, he explained the meaning of All Saints Day: "We do not concentrate today on spiritual heroes, but on people who are saints by loving one another, caring for one another, forgiving one another in their normal, everyday lives. We are celebrating the saints among us who do not have haloes above their heads but who, formed and inspired by the gospel, can make the interest of others more important than their own."

I felt at home in this simple Sunday liturgy. The church was packed with people, young and old, men and women, Cochabambinos and foreigners. Everybody was attentive and many went to communion. It was easy to feel part of this celebration, and, as always in situations like this, I marvel at the universal appeal of the words of Our Lord.

Tonight I was looking at the new moon and the bright stars decorating the wide skies of Bolivia. The air was cool and pleasant. Ernie, an eighty-two-year-old man from Rhode Island, joined me. After a moment of silence, he said: "Nice climate here; if the government were the same, everything would be all right."

Monday, November 2, All Souls Day

Throughout Latin America, All Souls Day is a special feast, the day in which people pay tribute to and enter into communion with those who have died. The place where this celebration of the lasting bonds with the dead can be experienced is the cemetery.

For me, the day started quietly. I spent an hour in the early morning in silent prayer for my mother and all the family members and friends who had died over the last years. From that intimate center, I let the eyes of my mind wander into wider and wider circles. I first saw the many acquaintances in my own little world who are no longer with me, then I thought about the many whose deaths I had learned of through newspapers, radio, and television, and finally I saw the thousands and thousands who had lost their lives through hunger and violence and whose names would always remain unknown to me. Suddenly, I found myself surrounded by a crowd of people who had been cruelly snatched away from life without a prayer, a word of consolation, or even a kiss on the forehead. To all of these I was intimately linked—so intimately that their total freedom had come to depend more and more on this ongoing connection stretching out far beyond the boundary of death. Indeed, part of the meaning of life for the living is our opportunity to pray for the full liberation of those who died before us.

With these thoughts, I began a busy day, which included a visit to the doctor and four classes in Spanish. At 2:30 P.M. I was free to join some friends for a visit to the cemetery of Cochabamba. What I saw there I will never forget. Thousands of people were sitting and walking around the graves as though they were camping with their beloved ones who had died. All types of sounds were mingled together: the sound of boys praying aloud, the sound of a trumpet, the sound of friendly conversations, the sounds of laughter and tears. Was this a gigantic picnic, a massive wake, a city-wide prayer service, a feast, a reunion, a day of repentance, or a celebration of continuing brotherhood and sisterhood? It obviously was all of that and much, much more. Something became visible at that cemetery that defied our usual distinctions between sorrow and joy, mourning and feasting, eating and fasting, praying and playing, and, most of all, living and dying. The people who came together at the cemetery revealed a reality that cannot be grasped by any of the categories that we use to define our daily experiences.

One sad exception remained: the distinction between the rich and the poor. We entered the cemetery through a large gate inscribed with the words, *Fiat Voluntas Tua* ("Your Will Be Done"); but after having passed the large monumental graves and the huge walls with square niches, we soon found ourselves in an open field covered with small wooden crosses that marked the rudimentary graves of the poor. And when we left the official cemetery through a small gate in the back wall, we came upon a large sandy stretch of land where hundreds of people who could not pay for even the simplest spot had claimed a place where they could bury their relatives and visit them. Sister Jeri Cashman, who had lived in Cochabamba for quite some time, explained that after five years the bodies of the poor are removed and burned to make a place for others. A large pit in which you could see pieces of skulls and bones showed that this burning of the poor was a daily event.

Somehow, I felt much more at home in the open field than between the monuments and the walls with niches. Wherever we walked people looked at us with friendly smiles, as if they were grateful that we had come. They appeared to be at a party. Each grave was surrounded by people who had spread a blanket over the grave and covered it with food: bananas, oranges, and all forms of *urpo*, a special bread baked for this day. Often the centerpiece was a cake in the form of a man or woman, representing the one who was buried under the blanket. At one place I saw a large bread, standing up in the form of a man with uniform and gun, indicating that the family was mourning the death of a soldier. Sister Jeri explained: "The people bring all sorts of food to the graves, often the food their deceased relatives most liked, and then they have a meal with them and thus continue to stay in touch."

What caught my attention most of all were the praying boys. In pairs, ten-to twelve-year-old boys walked all over the cemetery with large white sacks over their shoulders. One of each couple had a small booklet. They went from grave to grave asking if the people would let them pray. When the answer was yes, they knelt down in front of the grave, one boy loudly reciting the litany printed in his booklet, the other responding even more loudly every ten seconds: "Let us praise the Lord in the Blessed Sacrament of the altar and the Virgin Mary conceived without original sin." It was clear that the boys had hardly any idea what they were saying, but their eyes were tightly closed and their hands devoutly folded. All over the cemetery the boys' voices sounded in a strangely pleasant rhythm that seemed to unite all that was happening into one great prayer. The members of the family themselves did not utter a word; that was the boys' task. After they had finished their booklet, the boys rose from their knees and opened their sacks to receive the pay for their prayers: a banana, a few cookies, a piece of cake, or whatever they could get. Then they went on to the next grave, while another couple of boys took their place. And so it went on the whole day. When the fruit and the bread had vanished from the blankets into the boys' sacks, fresh food was brought and put on the grave, often arranged in a decorative way.

At one place, I saw an old and inebriated man urging a family to let him pray for their dead. After some pleading, he received permission. He started to say an Our Father and a Hail Mary, but he was so drunk that he could hardly finish it. When he received only one cookie for his prayers, he said with some indignation in his voice: "Is that all?" The head of the family said "Yes," and signaled two boys to take over his poorly performed task. Having watched this scene for a while, I introduced myself to the family. When they heard I was a Dutch priest, they lost all their initial reservation and told me all I wanted to know. "Who is buried here?" I asked. "My sister-in-law," answered a dark young man. "She died five months ago in childbirth." Then he introduced me to his widowed brother and three little children, who were sitting quietly around the grave. The other members of the family just looked on. After some more exchanges, I knelt down on the graveside, said some silent prayers, and blessed the living and the dead. When I rose, the two brothers asked me with some anxiety: "What did you pray?" I said: "I prayed that the Lord will lead your wife and sister-in-law into his home, that he will give new strength and courage to all the members of your family, and that he will bring peace to your country." Everyone expressed a sense of relief and gratitude. "Thank you very much, thank you, thank you," they said as they shook my hand with affection.

When I left the cemetery, many thoughts ran through my mind. What had I witnessed? What did all of this mean? Most central to all the impressions I had received was the impression that I had seen something very deep, old, basic, and human. The gatherings around the graves, the food on the blankets, the human-shaped breads, the praying boys, the exchange of gifts, and the all-pervading spirit of gentleness and hospitality: all of that seemed to come from ages past, even from far beyond the time when the Gospel of Jesus was first brought to Latin America. Most of the inhabitants of Cochabamba are Quechua Indians, and their Christianity is pervaded with the religious convictions and practices of the Quechua culture. Although Our Fathers and Hail Marys are constantly recited, it seemed that they only partially express the power of Indian spirituality.

I felt very much part of a mystery that cannot simply be observed and understood, and I started to sympathize even more with the sisters and priests who, after many years in Bolivia, say: "We still can only partially grasp the depth of the Quechua soul." One image stayed uppermost in my mind. It was the image of the boys receiving food for their prayers. The food put on the graves to be eaten with the dead was given to those who prayed for them. In front of my eyes I saw how prayers became food and food became prayers. I saw how little boys who had to struggle to survive received life from the dead, and how the dead received hope from the little children who prayed for the salvation of their souls. I saw a profound communion between the living and the dead, an intimacy expressed in words and gestures whose significance easily escapes our practical and often skeptical minds. The little children, as well as some of the older blind and crippled people, were allowed to enter into communication with the dead, while the adults remained silent, watched, and handed out gifts. "Out of the mouths of babes" we hear the truth, and by them the mysteries of life are revealed to us.

When I returned home, I knew that the Indians had given me a glimpse of a reality that mostly remains hidden in my rational, well-planned, and well-protected life. I had heard voices, seen faces, and touched hands revealing a divine love in which the living and the dead can find a safe home. In the evening I celebrated the Eucharist with friends in the language school. It seemed to me that all who had been part of this day—my family members and friends for whom I had prayed in the early morning, the medical doctor, the students and teachers, the Indian people of Cochabamba and their dead, as well as all the people who live and die on this earth—were gathered around the table. When the bread and the cup, the body and blood of Our Lord, were shared, I felt even more a part of the mysterious interchange I had witnessed in the cemetery. Yes, we all are one people loved by One Lord who became food and drink for us all and thus took away whatever may separate the living from the dead.

Tuesday, November 3

Tonight I saw the movie *All Quiet on the Western Front*, which shows how the members of a German platoon are physically and mentally destroyed in the trenches of the First World War. It brought home the insanity of young German men killing young French men without knowing why.

Meanwhile, the world powers are preparing for a war so massive and devastating that there won't be many left to tell the story or make a movie of it. Samuel Cohen, the father of the neutron bomb, does not believe that a third world war can be avoided. In an interview published on the first of November in *Los Tiempos*, the Catholic daily newspaper printed in La Paz, Cohen expresses his pride in having invented this instrument that "kills but does not destroy." He says, "I never think 'my God, what did I invent?' I am conscious that this bomb is the most selective weapon ever invented. A weapon such as this never existed." In response to the question: "Do you believe that we will have another war?" he says: "Yes . . . I consider this simply to be part of human nature: struggle, death and war . . . and in all wars both parties will take in hand all the possible arms. . . . Nuclear weapons will be used in their total potential."

Reading this after having seen *All Quiet on the Western Front*, I try to imagine the horrible quiet that will hover over our planet if Cohen's prediction comes true. Will there be anyone to mourn the dead or to consider the rebuilding of a human community? The only words that can offer comfort are the words Jesus spoke: "Stay awake, praying at all times for the strength to survive all that is going to happen, and to stand with confidence before the Son of Man" (Luke 21:36). O Lord, have mercy on us.

Wednesday, November 4

Tonight Ed Moore, a Maryknoll priest who was involved in leadership training in Guatemala, and Tom Henehan, a Maryknoller who is doing similar work in Santiago, Chile, shared their ideas and experiences with the students of the language school. One thing was clear to me: those who are trained in leadership roles quickly become targets of the oppressors. When politicians realize that the Indians are no longer passive, dependent beings who can be exploited, but have become a people educated to speak with a clear voice, they respond with oppression, torture, and murder. I was struck with the fact that often education means preparation for martyrdom. This is no argument for not educating. Those who have become aware of the nature of their captivity and have seen what is necessary to change the system never regret what they have learned, even though their knowledge may cost them their lives.

One of Ed's observations helped me see how quickly politics enters the picture. Many young people who have been trained as evangelizers, health promotors, or social-change agents soon become aware of the political nature of the physical, mental, and spiritual poverty of their people. This awareness frequently leads them to enter directly into the political arena; they strive to become mayor of their town or to acquire other political offices.

Another observation made by Tom explained why foreign missioners are so frequently accused of political involvement. In general, they are the ones who work most closely with the poor, the homeless, and the jobless, because they are the only ones who can afford to do so. The local pastoral workers need to earn money to survive, not only for themselves but also for parents and siblings who look to them for support. Thus they are forced to accept income-producing jobs such as teaching in grade school, high school, or university. Foreign missioners, on the other hand, are supported by their congregations at home, and thus have the freedom to live and work with the poor. Thus it is quite understandable that many oppressive governments make the foreign priests, sisters, and lay missioners the target of their hostility and condemn them as communist subversives.

Meanwhile, I try to remember that Jesus was killed as a subversive. God, who became human, submitted himself to the manipulation and oppression of the political powers of his time. He died under the accusation of being the enemy of the ruling class. It was not without reason that Pilate placed above Jesus' head the charge: "This is Jesus, the King of the Jews." Can we be true Christians without being considered to be subversives in the eyes of the oppressors?

Thursday, November 5

I am reading a fascinating chapter from Jerry Mander's book *Four Arguments for the Elimination of Television*. The main idea is: "We evolve into the images we carry in our minds. We become what we see. And in today's America, what most of us see is one hell of a lot of television."

I had heard stories about Vietnam veterans who, during their first real battle, thought that it was just another war movie and were shocked when those they killed did not stand up and walk away. I had read that Vincent van Gogh saw the real world as an imitation of the paintings he saw in the museum. I had noticed how children often are more excited about the repeated advertisements on television than about the movie they interrupt. But I had never fully thought through the enormous impact of the artificially imposed images on my thoughts, feelings, and actions. When it is true that the image you carry in your mind can affect your physical, mental, and emotional life, then it becomes a crucial question as to which images we expose ourselves or allow ourselves to be exposed.

All of this is important to me because it has profound spiritual implications. Prayer also has much to do with imagining. When I bring myself into the presence of God, I imagine him in many ways: as a loving father, a supporting sister, a caring mother, a severe teacher, an honest judge, a fellow traveler, an intimate friend, a gentle healer, a challenging leader, a demanding taskmaster. All these "personalities" create images in my mind that affect not only what I think, but also how I actually experience myself. I believe that true prayer makes us into what we imagine. To pray to God leads to becoming like God.

When Saint Ignatius proposes that we use all our senses in our meditation, he does more than offer a technique to help us concentrate on the mysteries of God's revelation. He wants us to imagine the reality of the divine as fully as possible so that we can slowly be divinized by that reality. Divinization is, indeed, the goal of all prayer and meditation. This divinization allows St. Paul to say: "I live now not with my own life but with the life of Christ who lives in me" (Gal. 2:20).

The more we come to depend on the images offered to us by those who try to distract us, entertain us, use us for their purposes, and make us conform to the demands of a consumer society, the easier it is for us to lose our identity. These imposed images actually make us into the world which they represent, a world of hatred, violence, lust, greed, manipulation, and oppression. But when we believe that we are created in the image of God himself and come to realize that Christ came to let us re-imagine this, then meditation and prayer can lead us to our true identity.

These considerations reveal the intimate bond between ministry and the life of prayer and meditation. Because what else is ministry than witnessing to him whom "we have heard, and we have seen with our own eyes; . . . watched and touched with our hands" (1 John 1:1)? Ministry is the manifestation in our own person of the presence of Christ in the world. The more fully we have imagined who we truly are and the more our true identity becomes visible, the more we become living witnesses of Jesus Christ. This means much more than speaking and acting in the Name of Him who came to us long ago. It means that our words and actions themselves become a manifestation of the living Christ here and now.

Latin America offers us the image of the suffering Christ. The poor we see every day, the stories about deportation, torture, and murder we hear every day, and the undernourished children we touch every day, reveal to us the suffering Christ hidden within us. When we allow this image of the suffering Christ within us to grow into its full maturity, then ministry to the poor and oppressed becomes a real possibility; because then we can indeed hear, see, and touch him within us as well as among us. Thus prayer becomes ministry and ministry becomes prayer. Once we have seen the suffering Christ within us, we will see him wherever we see people in pain. Once we have seen the suffering Christ among us, we will recognize him in our innermost self. Thus we come to experience that the first commandment to love God with all your heart, with all your soul and with all your mind, resembles indeed the second: "You must love your neighbor as yourself" (Matt. 22:39–40).

Friday, November 6

Tonight the students and staff of the language school celebrated a special Eucharist of solidarity with the Church in the prelature of Juli in Peru. Bill McCarthy, the Maryknoller who came from Lima to attend a conference here, was the main celebrant; and Sister Lourdes, who works in Juli and is currently studying Aymara (the language of the Aymara Indians, who live in the Altiplano), gave the homily and sang a Spanish song, which she composed herself. A small sculpture of an Indian carrying a heavy load on his back, a plate with incense, flowers, and a candle were placed in the center of the circle to symbolize the suffering, the prayers, and the hope of the poor in Juli. There also was a broken glass and a stone to remind us of the violence that has occurred there recently.

The main reason for this celebration was to call attention to the day of prayer that will take place in Juli on November fifteenth. On that day, Christians from all over Peru will come to Juli to make a prayerful response to the first signs of persecution of the Church in Peru. Sister Lourdes herself was present at the Institute for Rural Education when it was attacked by forty masked men.

As I listened to Bill's explanation of the symbols and to Lourdes' words about fear, hope, and the importance of being faithful, I could not prevent myself from thinking that all of this might be the beginning of a confrontation that can take on dimensions much greater than we now can imagine. What will result from the demonstration on November fifteenth? There are many people who hate the Church because of its support for the poor. Will they see the day of prayer as a reason to intensify the oppression or as a challenge to conversion? It is hard to say. Protest is required by our faithfulness to the poor. But nobody knows if things will become better or worse. I fear the worst, but hope that November fifteenth will make it clear that the Church won't back off from its promises to support the poor at all times.

The songs were joyful, the readings hopeful, and the sharing of the Body and Blood of Our Lord a true expression of community. The celebration allowed us to remind ourselves that we are already part of the kingdom even though we are still living in the valley of tears. It is becoming clearer to me every day that one of the greatest gifts offered to Christians is the possibility of celebrating not only their newly found freedom, but also the captivity to which they are still subjected. In the Christian community, joy and sorrow are never separated. Our joy witnesses to the awareness that nothing can separate us from the Lord of life, our sorrow reminds us that the way of the Lord of life is the way of the cross.

Saturday, November 7

Today was a day filled with letter writing. I wrote to my brother and his wife to express to them my support and love as they struggle to offer a safe and loving home to their little daughter Laura. I wrote to my aunt and uncle to offer them a word of comfort as they grieve for the death of their daughter Rosemarie, who died a few years after they lost their daughter Magdaleen. I wrote to my priest friend, Henry, who lost both of his parents within a few weeks. I wrote to my cousin who lost her husband shortly before she gave birth to her second child.

I now feel tired and emotionally drained. As I let all these pains in the lives of my family and friends enter into my heart, I wondered how I could offer true comfort. How could I ever enter into their pain and offer hope from that place? How could I enter into real solidarity with them? But then I slowly realized that I do not have to be like them or to carry their burdens, but that our Lord, my Lord and their Lord, has carried all human burdens and was crushed by them, so that we could receive his Spirit, the comforter. I realize now that my first task is to pray that this comforting Spirit will reach the hearts and minds of all those to whom I have written today. I hope that my halting and stuttering letters will be received as an expression of my sincere prayer that what is beyond my ability to touch can be touched by the consoling and healing power of the God whose name is Love.

Monday, November 9

Today I found new living quarters. During the weekend I had become aware that I was speaking too much English and that I needed a total immersion in the Spanish language.

The Quiroga family, who live about a half-hour walk from the institute, offered me their generous hospitality. It is a joy to be here. Mr. and Mrs. Quiroga are very kind and quite willing to correct my Spanish, and their twelve-year-old son, Rodolfito, is excited to have someone in the house with whom he can practice his English.

Rodolfo Senior and his wife, Nancy, lived for eight years in Miami. During that time they learned some English, although the predominantly Cuban population did not encourage them to practice it. But because their son went to school there, he became much more fluent in English than his parents. When the family returned to Bolivia more than four years ago, Rodolfito continued in an English-speaking grade school. Although he now goes to the Spanish-speaking Catholic high school in Cochabamba, he continues to practice his English on the American guests who come to his home. Rodolfo is a businessman in Cochabamba, and Nancy is an enthusiastic shortwave radio amateur, who speaks daily with people from all over the world: Indonesia, Thailand, Poland, Holland, the States, and many other countries.

One of the best parts of living with the Quiroga family is that they all like to talk. I am always surrounded by Spanish sounds, and I hope that these sounds will become more and more familiar to me.

Tuesday, November 10

Last night Rodolfo Quiroga told me the story of his life. He was born in Oruro, the city of the tin mines. His parents were simple, hardworking people. Five of their nine children died during their first months. "Poor climate and poor medical help," Rodolfo explained.

When Rodolfo was eight years old, the son of the owner of the house in which they lived, a seventeen-year-old boy known for his morbid desire to hurt animals, walked into the house with a pistol and killed Rodolfo's ten-year-old brother. Rodolfo's parents were out of their minds with grief. For many days his father woke up during the night, walked around the house with a gun, and spoke wildly about revenge. But when he realized that he still had a caring wife and three boys who needed him, he slowly became a different man. While he had always been a fervent atheist and was married under the condition that the Church would have nothing to do with him and his family, he suddenly turned to God in his grief and became a man who committed his life to prayer, charity, and the spiritual well-being of his family. Both he and his wife started to go to church every day. Soon afterwards, their three sons were baptized and received their first communion. The house of this simple family became a place of faith and hope.

Alex, one of the sons, studied philosophy with the Jesuits for some years and contemplated joining their Society; but he had to leave because of poor health. Alex is currently a professor of Spanish literature in Massachusetts, a very active Christian who introduced the Marriage Encounter movement in Cochabamba. Max, the second son, is an accountant, who after many years in La Paz moved to Cochabamba to give his sickly wife a better climate in which to live. Rodolfo, my host, joined the religious congregation of the Servites for a few years, but had to leave them to support his family when his mother became ill. He married Nancy soon after his return home. Their first two children died. A few years after Rodolfito was born, they adopted a boy who died unexpectedly in his third month of life. Now their twelve-year-old son Rodolfito is the center of their life.

I was moved by this story and the simple and loving way in which Rodolfo told it. For him it was God's story as much as his own. It was a story about suffering, but a suffering in which God had become present and shown his love. When Rodolfo told me his life, he seemed to be speaking more about God's love than about his own struggles. His voice was full of gratitude and praise. No anger, no resentment, no feelings of revenge. He spoke with the quick knowledge that God has guided his life and will continue to do so, no matter what happens.

Last night Rodolfo celebrated his fifty-second birthday. To me it seemed like an old-fashioned Dutch birthday party. Family and friends kept coming during the evening to congratulate Rodolfo and his wife. As it got later, the circle became larger, the conversation more animated and the voices louder. Everyone was happy and everyone was everyone else's entertainment. No television, radio, music, or slides; just good lively exchanges of home news, town news, and family news, real or made up for the occasion. The food and wine led to the traditional birthday cake which was—to my surprise—welcomed with the American song "Happy Birthday to You."

The evening was of special interest to me because I had a long conversation with Peter, the recently ordained Polish priest who is studying with me at language school and had become a friend of the Quiroga family. Peter's story moved me and awoke in me emotions that had remained hidden for a long time.

During all of his life, Peter had lived in Poland. As a teenager he was not very religious, but he was a good youth leader. A Dominican priest evoked in him the desire for the priesthood. First he thought about becoming a Dominican; but a short time before entering the Dominican novitiate, he met a priest of the Divine Word Society who spoke to him about their missions. Peter felt that this was a providential encounter and he decided to join the Divine Word Society in the hope that one day he could be a missionary in Japan, Korea, or Taiwan. Six months ago, Peter was ordained. But instead of being sent to any of the countries he hoped for, his superiors sent him to Bolivia to learn Spanish in preparation for three years of mission work in Paraguay.

Peter impressed me deeply from the moment I first saw him among the other students of the language school. He has a fine, youthful face that makes him look like a very tender boy; he does not speak one word of English, but his Spanish is remarkable for the short time he has been studying it. Although there is one other Polish priest and two Polish sisters in the institute, he avoids them; he is determined not to utter one Polish word before Christmas. As a result, he learns Spanish faster than anyone else I know.

The first thing Peter expressed to me was a deep sadness that mothers in Poland no longer have the necessary food for their newborn babies. There is such a lack of milk, butter, and other crucial nutrients that the number of abortions in Catholic Poland is staggering. "It is terrible," Peter kept saying. "It is the great sin of our nation. In the few months since I have been a priest, I have heard the confession of so many men and women who agonize over their inability to care for children. But abortion is no solution."

And slowly Peter revealed to me his deep faith, which is intimately connected with his love for his people. "We in Poland desire only two types of freedom: freedom from sin and freedom from foreign domination. Every father and every mother speaks to their children about these freedoms, which are more important for us than food, a house, or material success." With strong emotion, Peter spoke about the faith of his people. "Being Polish and being Catholic is the same for us. We are not interested in politics, in war, in power. We have never started a war. What we desire is to live a life close to God and the Virgin Mother. There is no house in Poland without a picture of Our Lady of Czestochowa, and, I tell you, miracles happen every day to those who bring their sufferings to her. And the Communists? They have the power, they give away the key positions, they make all the decisions, they rule the country. But the heart of the thirty million Poles is not with them. The people pray, the people go to Mass, the people come together in their houses for religious instruction, and that is where you come to understand the Polish soul."

When Peter spoke about John Paul II, I could sense strong feelings surge up in him. John Paul was given to his people to offer them new courage and a new hope for freedom. I came to see in Peter's eyes that John Paul was indeed the mysterious answer of God to decades of fervent Polish prayers. Since John Paul had become Pope, hundreds of young people had entered seminaries and religious life. Now there are thirty major seminaries and each has at least one hundred students. Talking about John Paul, Peter said: "When he was shot, most people in the world were reading the papers or watching television to follow the events, but the Poles all went to their churches and prayed." Moreover, Peter was convinced that without John Paul there would probably have been no Solidarity movement. Peter said: "The Poles listened to every word John Paul said during his visit to Poland. He always spoke about the Spirit of God that all of us have received and that is the basis of our true freedom. His words gave us strength, self-confidence, and the courage to claim our own rights. I think indeed that John Paul had a lot to do with the origin of Solidarity, not directly, but certainly indirectly."

There was not a trace of triumphalism in Peter's voice. It was clear that he spoke as a man who had suffered oppression, exploitation, and hunger although I felt that at times he overlooked some important questions (such as the suffering of Polish Jews in the past and the present), he radiated a simple solid faith that allowed him to speak about God, Jesus, Mary, the Church, and the Pope with an intimacy and familiarity that made me jealous.

He told me about his departure. His father and mother told him: "You are a priest now; be sure to pray always, wherever you are; never let a day go by without saying the rosary." Peter had tears in his eyes when he told me this. "If I just had a little bit of my parents' faith! They are such simple, poor, and faithful people. They truly know what counts. They do not want me to be important, powerful, successful. The only thing they hope is that I will be a man of prayer who leads others closer to God. They know nothing about Bolivia or Paraguay, but they pray for me and for all the people I am sent to."

Peter opened deep places in me. His whole being radiated commitment to God and to his Church, and I sensed that I was in the presence of a man of faith, a faith that I had not seen for a long time. And somewhere, too, Peter gave me a new glimpse of that remarkable—and often disturbing—holy man, John Paul II.

Thursday, November 12

It suddenly hit me. The United States wants war! It is frightening to write this sentence down, but during the last week the thought that the Reagan Administration is not only preparing for the possibility of a war, but is even directly moving towards it, kept haunting me. For a few days, the idea of an approaching war in which a destruction of life and culture would take place such as history has never witnessed kept me restless during the day and sleepless during the night. Looking at the movements of the U.S. government from the perspective of this utterly poor, helpless, and dependent country is a quite different experience than looking at it from within the United States. Living in the United States allows you to maintain the illusion that the arms race, the joint military exercises in Egypt, the sale of the AWACS planes to Saudi Arabia, and especially the Cancun conference in Mexico, are all movements to keep the peace. But living here in Bolivia, surrounded by increasing poverty and human misery, the face of the United States becomes uglier and uglier as the days progress.

What frightens me most is the shift in the popular expectation of war. Although there is no Hitler raving about the superiority of the Aryan race, although there is no visible advantage to any country to become involved in an international conflict, the majority of the American people expect a world war in the near future and few believe that an all-out nuclear holocaust can be avoided.

During the last few weeks, most of the U.S. weeklies as well as the major foreign publications have filled their pages with speculations about an impending war. What most frightens me is the predominantly military responses of the U.S. government to the main problems in the world. *Newsweek* (November 9, 1981) writes: "Reagan had relied mainly on a display of military might: his White House has struck arms deals with El Salvador, Venezuela, and Pakistan, promised to speed up arms shipments to Egypt and the Sudan and invited China to shop at America's weapons bazaar." Behind this show of power is the desire to give the American people the sense of being in control. One of Reagan's top advisers says: "The bottom line is that America is tired of being shoved around and [Reagan has] taken care of that." But the more I think about the lack of genuine diplomacy between Moscow and Washington, the growing tensions in Poland, the extremely fragile situation in the Middle East, the increasing U.S. support to South Africa, and the blatant U.S. help to the "authoritarian" right-wing military regimes in the Southern hemisphere to counteract the so-called totalitarian influence of Cuba in Central America—all of this in the context of the biggest "peacetime" military buildup in the history of the United States—the more I wonder whether there is any serious attempt to ensure peace. I fear that the increasing economic problems not only of the third world countries but also of the United States and Europe may become the occasion to try out some of the apocalyptic toys on which the Pentagon relies so much. Even after Vietnam, we seem to believe that weapons can make peace. They can certainly make war, but today a war no longer can have peace at the other end, only total annihilation.

Meanwhile, words remain extremely dangerous. We now hear words about a nuclear warning attack, words about occupying Cuba or invading Nicaragua. Such words by people in power, with their subsequent denials, create an ongoing atmosphere of anxiety and may eventually lead to mistakes, the consequences of which cannot be overestimated.

It is in the context of this international situation that Christians have to make their choice for peace. Personally, I sometimes feel so engulfed by the political realities that I wonder if a world conflict can be avoided. The main question for me is: Do I "have the strength to survive all that is going to happen, and to stand with confidence before the Son of Man" (Luke 21:36)? Or will I allow myself and others to be so overwhelmed by all these wars and rumors of war that we will die of fear as we await what menaces the world? Am I really ready to encounter my Lord when he comes in a "cloud with power and great glory" (Luke 21:26–27)?

How much time and energy we spend in understanding, analyzing, discussing, and evaluating the socioeconomic and political status of our globe, and how little of our hearts and minds is occupied to prepare ourselves for the day of the Lord, which will be sprung on us suddenly, "like a trap" (Luke 21:35). Prayer, meditation, fasting, communal life, care for the sick, the dying, the hungry, and the fearful, are they really in the center of our lives as Christian people? The world is coming to an end, probably by our own doing, and this will happen this week, this decade, this century, or millions of years in the future; but the certainty of an end should give us the strength to announce boldly and fearlessly that those who hold on to the Lord of life will not be harmed but have eternal life. But woe to us when, on the day of the Lord, "hearts will be coarsened with debauchery and drunkenness and the cares of life" (Luke 21:34).

All of this suggests to me the urgent need for a spirituality that takes the end of things very seriously, not a spirituality of withdrawal, nor of blindness to the powers of the world, but a spirituality that allows us to live in this world without belonging to it, a spirituality that allows us to taste the joy and peace of the divine life even when we are surrounded by the powers and principalities of evil, death, and destruction. I wonder if a spirituality of liberation does not need to be deepened by a spirituality of exile or captivity. I wonder if a spirituality that focuses on the alleviation of poverty should not be deepened by a spirituality that allows people to continue their lives when their poverty only increases. I wonder if a spirituality that encourages peacemaking should not be deepened by a spirituality that allows us to remain faithful when the only things we see are dying children, burning houses, and the total destruction of our civilization. May God prevent any of these horrors from taking place, may we do all that is possible to prevent them, but may we never lose our faith when "great misery [descends] on the land and wrath on this people, . . . [when there are] signs in the sun and moon and stars, . . . [when] nations [are] in agony, bewildered by the clamor of the ocean and its waves" (Luke 21:24–26). I pray that we will not be swept away by our own curiosity, sensationalism, and panic, but remain attentive to Him who comes and will say: "Come, you whom my Father has blessed, take for your heritage the kingdom prepared for you since the foundation of the world" (Matt. 25:34–35).

Friday, November 13

One of the best articles I have read about the plight of the Latin American Church was published in Lent 1981 in the *National Catholic Reporter.* It is written by an anonymous American priest working in Bolivia. The author preferred to remain anonymous in order to prevent reprisals against himself and those with whom he works. From the depth of his heart he cries out to his fellow Christians in the United States, begging them to listen, to understand and to act. He writes:

What we see is this. The documents of the Latin American bishops' meetings at both Medellin and Puebla . . . condemn "liberal capitalism" by name along with atheistic communism and ideologies of national security. Neither the U.S. Catholic bishops nor priests, with rare exceptions, teach the implications of this doctrine in the ethical formation of U.S. Catholics. We think this is a grave dereliction of duty which has terrible human consequences.

We see these consequences every day. Assassination, physical and psychological torture and rape are the ordinary judicial means of inquiry in our countries. These intelligence skills have been taught for 35 years to more than 80,000 Latin American military and police forces as counter-insurgent and anti-terrorist tactics to keep the "Communists" from invading our economic sphere of influence. You would want proof? Get names and addresses from the bishops of Chile, Brazil, Argentina, Bolivia, El Salvador, etc., as well as from Amnesty International.

Latin Americans do not want to be satellites of the superpowers, neither of Russia nor the United States. They want to be free of economic and political colonialism. And they are not permitted to be. By force and physical violence, every normal avenue of social and political change is closed to them. Or must we accept the opinion that violence is the only "normal" path to a healthy human society? . . .

For the first time in their tortured history, Salvadoreans, Guatemalans, Peruvians, Brazilians, etc., want the right to be themselves. They want the right to make their own mistakes in their own path to maturity as a people with identity and responsibility. No one can stop this march of history. . . .

Latin America in the year 2000 will have 500 million people, half of them under 21 with creative energy and youthful aspirations. The United States, with its own anti-life culture which considers children as the enemy of conspicuous consumption, will be a nation of old people and old ideas, spent, sterile, wasted and without a future. . . .

The coming generations of young Latin Americans will hate the people of the United States if we continue our greedy ways. How long can we keep these hordes controlled to provide us with our more than comfortable lifestyle if they learn how to read and write?

After these words, this anonymous author addresses himself to parishioners, bishops, and priests, theologians and intellectuals, men and
women religious, union members and workers, and finally to the young:

> Do not sell your faith or your freedom to maintain the antique shop
> called "western civilization." Whatever it may have been in the 18th
> and 19th centuries, it has not been for the 20th. And it offers no hope
> to youth for their century, the 21st. . . . The political and economic
> systems, theories and practices we have seen for 35 years offer noth-
> ing but a musty nostalgia. The smell of death is upon them. . . .
>
> We, your mission representatives, do not ask you to wallow in
> unproductive guilt. We ask you to change your priorities. And the
> priorities of our nation. You will then be free. And so will millions of
> others whose slavery and poverty are now the basis of your good life.
> How can people of conscience and faith be at peace with themselves
> or their society knowing what their comfort costs others?

And he concludes with these powerful words:

> As for ourselves, we know that we now have, no security and no pro-
> tection from either our host countries or the colonial power of the
> United States government always acting behind the scenes. We have
> no arms except the armor of faith and the shield of hope. We are free
> as never before to give witness to the life of Jesus as did the sisters in
> El Salvador. "We are cursed and we bless. . . ." We are condemned as
> "subversives," "agitators," "Communists," "foreigners" wherever we
> unmask the idolatry of money and power. We are imprisoned, tor-
> tured, expelled, or killed for living the gospel. . . . Our mission task
> now is to tell the Americans to convert, to "let my people go," to seek
> a just and fraternal human life with the poor of Latin America and
> the world. Or to see the United States destroy itself, its youth and its
> future, by stupid, selfish, useless, endless greed and violence. There
> is no liberation, no resurrection without conversion and the death
> of old ways ("A Cry for Latin America," *National Catholic Reporter*,
> April 17, 1981).

Living here in Bolivia, seeing the tired faces of the women who carry their heavy burdens to the market, seeing the undernourished children, seeing miserable fruit vendors and beggars and realizing that things are getting worse and worse day after day, I know that this cry from and for Latin America doesn't hold any sentimentality, sensationalism, or false rhetoric.

Saturday, November 14

As the days and weeks pass by and I come to know the students of the language school better, I realize more and more how insecure, fearful, and often lonely many of us are. Not only do we continue to hope for mail from "home," but we also continue to be submerged by the powers around us. At home we at least had our own niche in life, our own little place where we could feel useful and admired. Here none of that is present. Here we are in a world that did not invite us, in which we can hardly express ourselves and which constantly reminds us of our powerlessness. And still, we know that we are sent here, that God wants us here, and that it is here that we have to work out our salvation.

The more these strong and often conflicting feelings come to the surface, the more I realize how much we need each other. Mission work is not a task for individuals. The Lord sent his disciples into the world in small groups, not as individual heroes or pioneers. We are sent out together, so that together—gathered by One Lord—we can make him present in this world.

Many of us are eager to go out and to start working as soon as possible, with or without words! It is certainly a sign of zeal, good will, great energy, and generosity. But maybe we should first of all look at each other, recognize each other's suffering and come together as a living body to pray, and to share our joys and hopes, our fears and pains. This experience of belonging to each other by our common love for Our Lord and our common awareness of our task can create the space where God's Spirit will descend and from where we can go out in many directions without ever feeling alone. After all, the first and most important witness is to them who can say of us: "See how they love each other."

Tuesday, November 17

I spent the afternoon with the children of the Catholic orphanage called Gotas de Leche (Drops of Milk). The children were so starved for affection that they fought with each other for the privilege of touching me.

How little do we really know the power of physical touch. These boys and girls only wanted one thing: to be touched, hugged, stroked, and caressed. Probably most adults have the same needs but no longer have the innocence and unself-consciousness to express them. Sometimes I see humanity as a sea of people starving for affection, tenderness, care, love, acceptance, forgiveness, and gentleness. Everyone seems to cry: "Please love me." The cry becomes louder and the response so inaudible that people kill each other and themselves in despair. The little orphans tell more than they know. If we don't love one another, we kill one another. There's no middle road.

Wednesday, November 18

My move to the Quiroga family hasn't made my prayer life easier. I spend much time going back and forth to the language institute, have a hard time keeping up with my four classes every day, and feel more tired than usual. The last two weeks I was not able to spend much time in prayer and had to limit myself to my breviary and the Eucharist. Life without prayer weakens my spirit. I have to start looking for a new rhythm. At least I know the difference between days with ample time for prayer and days that are hurried and restless.

Nobody has to prove to me that prayer makes a difference. Without prayer I become irritable, tired, heavy of heart, and I lose the Spirit who directs my attention to the needs of others instead of my own. Without prayer, my attention moves to my own preoccupation. I become cranky and spiteful and often I experience resentment and a desire for revenge.

I am surprised that I allow the language training to become so important that my prayer life takes a second place to it. It seems that when there are no urgent things to do, I create them myself, and when there are no deadlines to meet, I organize them for myself. That is a clear form of self-deception. The powers that try to keep me from simply being with God have a seductive quality. Something as simple as a language course can play demon with me. Why speak different languages if my heart remains dry and angry, upset and lonely? Everything is so obvious. To reach the obvious, I have to struggle. It is the struggle that Our Lord himself came to share.

Thursday, November 19

In times of testing, God and the demon seem close together. Today I felt this more strongly than on other days. After classes I went to downtown Cochabamba to pick up Rodolfo's bicycle, which he was willing to lend me. As I biked through town and saw groups of young men loitering around the street corners and waiting for the next movie to start; as I walked through the bookstores stacked with magazines about violence, sex, and gossip; and as I saw the endless advertisements for unnecessary items imported mostly from Germany and the United States, I had the feeling of being surrounded by powers much greater than myself. I felt the seductive powers of sin all around me and got a glimpse of the truth that all the horrendous evils which plague our world—hunger, the nuclear arms race, torture, exploitation, rape, child abuse, and all forms of oppression—have their small and sometimes unnoticed beginnings in the human heart. The demon is very patient in the way he goes about his destructive work. I felt the darkness of the world all around me.

After some aimless wandering, I biked to the small Carmelite convent on Avenida America, close to the house of my hosts. A friendly Carmelite sister spoke to me in the chapel and told me that I would be welcome at any hour to come there to pray or celebrate the Eucharist. She radiated a spirit of joy and peace. She told me about the light that shines into the darkness without saying a word about it. As I looked around, I saw the statues of St. Teresa of Avila and St. Thérèse of Lisieux. Suddenly it seemed to me that these two women were talking to me as they had never before. They spoke of another world. As I knelt down in the small and simple chapel, I knew that this place was filled with God's presence. I felt the prayers that had been said there day and night.

After returning from the Carmelite sisters, I read the life of St. Thérèse of Lisieux in *Ten Christians,* a book that I had taken with me on my journey. Thérèse's unconditional love for Christ spoke to me in a new way. She dedicated her life to the missions and she considered herself a missionary in her hidden convent. She reminded me that true mission means being sent into the world as Christ was sent into the world: in total surrender to God's will.

My visit to the Carmelite sisters helped me realize again that where the demon is, God is not far away; and where God shows his presence, the demon does not remain absent very long. There is always a choice to be made between the power of life and the power of death. I myself have to make that choice. Nobody else, not even God, will make that choice for me.

Friday, November 20

This morning at 8:30 Gerry McCrane and Sister Lourdes gave a report to the students at the language school about their journey to Peru. They participated in the day of prayer in Juli on November fifteenth organized in response to the recent attacks on the local church. It was a moving report. Gerry and Lourdes told how five thousand poor *campesinos* walked from the house where the first attack took place to the cathedral. They showed how the Church of Juli had truly become the Church of the people. The people had grown aware over the years that the Church had become something other than a wealthy institution that tries to maintain the status quo. This transition was not as obvious as it might seem. Many of the organizers of the day of prayer had wondered what the response would be. Would people come and join in the pilgrimage? Would there be violence from those who had already shown their hostility by destruction and death threats? Would people get hurt in the crowds? What would be the response of those bishops who like to keep things quiet and who consider such actions provocative? These and many other questions had occupied the mind of Alberto Koenigsknecht, the prelate of Juli, and of his collaborators. The issue had been: "Are we doing more harm than good by calling the people of Peru to a public manifestation of their religious commitment in the face of a beginning persecution?"

But Sunday, November fifteenth, had been a day of solidarity for the poor, a day of sincere prayer, a day of mutual encouragement, and a day of recommitment to the work in Juli. Gerry, who had been pastor in Juli for many years, showed great joy as he gave his report: "It was such a source of gratitude to see that, after many years of hard pastoral work, the people had come to see and believe that they themselves are the Church and that they were willing to offer up a day good for planting to show it." And Lourdes told with excitement how hundreds of *campesinos* had worked together to prepare this day. Small pamphlets about the meaning of this special pilgrimage had been studied in the different parishes during the weeks preceding the day of prayer, and many hours had been spent to make this day not so much a protest against hostile behavior as a witness for Christ living in the people of the Juli prelature. The Eucharist, celebrated on the square in front of the cathedral, had been a true Aymara feast. Many Aymara symbols had been integrated into the celebration; this was not a Latin ritual imposed on poor Indians, but a true manifestation of the spirituality of the Aymara people.

I was glad to hear this story of faith and hope. For awhile I had thought about going with Gerry and Lourdes myself, but felt that language training had to remain my priority for the short time I am in Bolivia. Meanwhile, I wonder with some apprehension if this is the last word we will hear about the prelature of Juli. Where God's love becomes very visible, the forces of evil usually do not long remain hidden. Is the day in Juli the end of a short experience of persecution or the beginning of a long road of suffering on which the faith of many will be tested? I pray that all who work there and will work there will have the strength and the courage to be faithful.

Saturday, November 21

God exists. When I can say this with all that I am, I have the "gnosis" (the knowledge of God) about which St. John speaks and the "Memoria Dei" (the memory of God) about which St. Basil writes. To say with all that we have, think, feel, and are: "God exists," is the most world-shattering statement that a human being can make. When we make that statement, all the distinctions between intellectual, emotional, affective, and spiritual understanding fall away and there is only one truth left to acclaim: God exists. When we say this from the heart, everything trembles in heaven and on earth. Because when God exists, all that *is* flows from him. When I want to know if I ever have come to the true knowledge, the gnosis, of God's existence, I have simply to allow myself to become aware of how I experience myself. It doesn't take much to realize that I am constantly with myself. I am aware of all of the various parts of my body, and I "know" when I am hurting and when not. I am aware of my desire for food and clothing and shelter. I am aware of my sexual urges and my need for intimacy and community. I am aware of my feelings of pity, compassion, and solidarity, my ability to be of service and my hope to give a helping hand. I am aware of my intellectual, physical, and artistic skills and my drive to use them. I am aware of my anger, my lust, my feelings of revenge and resentment, and even at times of my desire to harm. Indeed, what is central to me is: *I exist.* My own existence fills me, and wherever I turn I find myself again locked in my own self-awareness: I exist. Although experiences of hatred are different from experiences of love, and although a desire for power is different from a desire to serve, they all are the same insofar as they identify *my* existence as what *really* counts.

However, as soon as I say, "God exists," my existence no longer can remain in the center, because the essence of the knowledge of God reveals my own existence as deriving its total being from his. That is the true conversion experience. I no longer let the knowledge of my existence be the center from which I derive, project, deduct, or intuit the existence of God; I suddenly or slowly find my own existence revealed to me in and through the knowledge of God. Then it becomes real for me that I can love myself and my neighbor only because God has loved me first. The life-converting experience is not the discovery that I have choices to make that determine the way I live out my existence, but the awareness that my existence itself is not in the center. Once I "know" God, that is, once I experience his love as the love in which all my human experiences are anchored, I can only desire one thing: to be in that love. "Being" anywhere else, then, is shown to be illusory and eventually lethal.

All of these reflections have taken a new urgency for me, during these weeks in Bolivia. It slowly dawned on me that so much, if not most, of our energy and attention goes to the question of our own existence. We wonder how we are doing, how we feel, how we will serve in Latin America, and how we will organize our next day, weekend, year, or decade. We try hard to make responsible and moral choices that give us a sense that at least we are searching in the right direction. But all of this, the good as well as the bad, the responsible as well as the irresponsible, the acts of lust as well as the acts of service, lose their power over us when we realize that God exists, before and after, in the past and in the future, now and forever, and that in and through the knowledge of that divine existence I might get a small glimpse of why there is an I and a he, she, we, and they. Then all questions have only one answer: God. What am I supposed to think about? About God, because all thoughts find their creative power in him. What am I supposed to say? His Word, because all my words are fruitful to the degree that they are a reflection of his. What am I supposed to do? His will, because his will is the loving desire that gave existence to all that is, myself included.

Is it better to be in Bolivia, in Peru, in the United States, or in Holland? Is it better to give a glass of water to a thirsty child or to work on a new world order in which children will no longer beg for water? Is it better to read a book or to walk on the street, to write a letter or bind the wounds of a dying man? Is it better to do this or that, say this or that, think about this or that? All these questions suddenly appear to me as false preoccupations, as a captivity in the illusory concern about my own existence, as an expression of my sick supposition that God depends on me, that his existence is derived from mine.

Nothing is real without deriving its reality from God. This was the great discovery of St. Francis when he suddenly saw the whole world in God's hands and wondered why God didn't drop it. St. Augustine, St. Teresa of Avila, St. John Vianney, and all the saints are saints precisely because for them the order of being was turned around and they saw, felt, and—above all—knew with their heart that outside God nothing is, nothing breathes, nothing moves, and nothing lives.

This makes me aware that the basis of all ministry rests not in the moral life but in the mystical life. The issue is not to live as well as we can, but to let our life be one that finds its source in the Divine Life.

God exists, and the meaning of all that I am depends totally on that knowledge. I wonder constantly if I am genuinely allowing my life to be determined by that truth. Maybe part of my reason for hesitating to embrace this truth fully is that it challenges me to give up all control over my life and to let God be God, my God, the God of my neighbor, and the God of all creation. But I also realize that as long as I do not "do" this, my life is an illusion and most of my energy is spoiled in trying to keep that illusion going.

Does all of this mean that my thoughts, plans, projects, and ideas no longer matter? That conclusion has been drawn by people who used the spiritual life as a way to manipulate others and that conclusion has led, sadly enough, to false views on asceticism, obedience, surrender to God's will, and certain forms of self-denial. The converted person does not say that nothing matters anymore, but that everything that is happens in God and that he is the dwelling place where we come to know the true order of things. Instead of saying: "Nothing matters any more, since I know that God exists," the converted person says: "All is now clothed in divine light and therefore nothing can be unimportant." The converted person sees, hears, and understands with a divine eye, a divine ear, a divine heart. The converted person knows himself or herself and all the world in God. The converted person *is* where God is, and from that place everything matters: giving water, clothing the naked, working for a new world order, saying a prayer, smiling at a child, reading a book, and sleeping in peace. All has become different while all remains the same.

Somehow I feel that all these reflections are important for me in a time during which I have to make some very concrete decisions. The "nothing matters" and the "everything matters" should never be separated in a time such as this. What brings them together is the unceasing cry coming from the heart: "God exists."

Sunday, November 22

This morning for two hours I played with the little boys and girls at the state orphanage. This orphanage is much worse than Drops of

Milk, the Catholic orphanage. About a hundred little kids were running around in a poorly kept stony yard surrounded by a large fence. The kids jumped all over me trying to be touched, to attract attention, to play, and to be lifted up. What struck me most was their explicit interest in my body. They kept stroking my forehead, saying, "What a large forehead!" They wanted to see my teeth, my tongue, and kept comparing the size of their hands and fingers with mine. Their fascination with a large person moved me. One six-year-old looked at me and said, "A grown man!" For her I symbolized a world from which she is excluded. These children see mostly other children. They have very few adults around who can help them see beyond themselves. Very soon I was transformed into a climbing tree. The kids tried to climb over my knees, chest, and shoulders to the top, and at one point there was a line of ten little ones waiting for their turn to climb the big man.

I fell in love with a little deaf-mute boy who was able with his expressive hands and eyes to explain to me whatever he wanted me to do. Everytime I did something—connecting a cord to his toy, making a knot in his piece of rope, tying his shoes—he gave me a big smile and put his arms around me.

None of these children has a home. The food they receive is minimal, the attention meager, and the education poor. What will become of them? Who will give them what they need? In a poor country the children always suffer the most.

In the afternoon I celebrated the feast of Christ the King with the Carmelite sisters. The children were on my mind when I took the bread and wine and said: "This is my body, this is my blood." The Lord became flesh and blood for these children; so they could touch him, hug him, kiss him, stroke him. And thus he is their friend, their brother. Jesus died naked on the cross with the words above his head: "This is the King of the Jews." Many of the kids walked around naked, jumping in and out of a cement tub of water, and running up to me to be hugged and kissed and to let my hands touch their skin and squeeze their little bodies. The naked King on the Cross and the naked kids in Cochabamba belong together. The God who is love stands with the children who crave love. I knew that I had seen my King again. He seems to say: "Come back. I will be here every day, every week, every year. I stay here because I became body and blood for them. Come and touch me."

Monday, November 23

Rodolfo Quiroga could hardly be a less political man. He never attends any meetings other than those of the Christian Family Movement, and he spends all his free time with his wife and son. He enjoys taking care of his flowers, making little repairs in his house, and joining his wife in her ham radio hobby. He is one of the most homebound men I have ever met and his conversations focus on his family, his religion, and occasionally—and somewhat reluctantly—on his business.

And yet a little over a year ago, at two o'clock one morning, a group of armed men appeared at his door and asked for entrance. When Rodolfo refused to let them in, they broke open his front door, forced him into their car, and took him off to prison. Nancy, Rodolfito, and the maid, Marcelita, were left in fear and confusion. Early the next day, with the influence of her friends, Nancy got access to the head of the police and was able to find out what had happened and where Rodolfo was. It turned out that a family member with whom they had a long-standing personal conflict had called the military authorities and told them that Rodolfo was a Communist and was using his house for a conspiracy with his leftist friends to overthrow the government. The reaction had been immediate. The paramilitary police—mostly Argentinians trained in sinister duties and hired by the Bolivian government—were called and sent off to arrest Rodolfo. With brute force, they entered his house and took him to an overcrowded prison cell.

When Nancy spoke to the head of the police, one of his first questions was, "Do you know anyone who might like to harm your husband?" When Nancy told him about the conflict with the family member, the officer recognized that this was the same story he had already heard from Rodolfo himself and he told her about the phone call and the accusations. Since the Quirogas have many influential friends in Cochabamba, excuses were quickly made and within two hours Rodolfo was set free. The police officer even offered Nancy breakfast, but nobody offered to pay for the damage to the house.

This story might be read as a comedy of errors, but it illustrates one of the most familiar aspects of Latin American politics, the intimate connection between political and family conflicts. I think it will be hard ever to understand the complex political situations in Latin America without realizing how often old and bitter family conflicts are intermingled with the uses of political power. Objectively, nobody could be less likely to be considered a Communist, a political agitator, a conspirator, or even a public figure than Rodolfo, but he came close to being tortured or killed because of his alleged involvement in a fictitious political event.

All of this reminded me of the story of Dr. Joel Filártiga, my Paraguayan friend, whose seventeen-year-old son was tortured to death in 1976 to silence his own political resistance. Dr. Filártiga is a long-time opponent of the dictatorship of General Alfredo Stroessner. He publicly—through writing and drawing—criticizes his government. But his son would never have been abducted and cruelly murdered if the police inspector Americo Peña, who supervised the torture of the boy with electric shocks, had not also had a long-standing conflict with the Filártiga family.

In small countries such as Paraguay and Bolivia, there are only a few candidates for political office, and these few frequently have as many personal conflicts between themselves as political differences. Often it is difficult to figure out who is against whom and for what reason. The word "Communist" always comes in as a handy word to get the guns out of the closet, but it might well be that an unpaid loan or an offensive word is the real reason for destroying someone's life.

Little Rodolfito now is terribly afraid to be alone in the house. He bites his nails and worries about going away from home without his parents. The sight of his father being dragged out of his home continues to haunt him. Meanwhile, Nancy and Rodolfo endure many sleepless nights wondering what the next move of their enemy will be. I have begun to see why they both spend so many hours during the weekend playing with their ham radio and talking to friendly people from other parts of the world: it is safe company and a good distraction.

Tuesday, November 24

Tonight Sister Maria Rieckelman spoke about the problems of acculturation. She gave a fine presentation about the many psychological struggles we can experience when we try to find a home in a new culture.

She mentioned Erich Fromm's remark that our two main fears are of losing control and of becoming isolated. I keep experiencing these fears every time I make a move, major or minor, and I wonder if I am getting any better in dealing with them. I find myself with the same old struggles every time I am in a new and unfamiliar milieu. In particular, the experience of isolation keeps returning, not in a lessening but in an increasing degree. Becoming older makes the experience of isolation much more familiar—maybe simply because of sheer repetition—but not less painful.

So, maybe the question is not how to cope better, but how slowly to allow my unchanging character to become a way of humility and surrender to God. As I recognize my fears of being left alone and my desire for a sense of belonging, I may gradually give up my attempts to fill my loneliness and be ready to recognize with my heart that God is Emmanuel, "God-with-us," and that I belong to him before anything or anyone else.

And so a new vision of maturity may emerge; not a vision in which I am more and more able to deal with my own pains, but in which I am more willing to let my Lord deal with them. After all, maturation in a spiritual sense is a growing willingness to stretch out my arms, to have a belt put round me and to be led where I would rather not go (John 21:18).

Wednesday, November 25

For two weeks the workers in the tin mines in Huanuni have been on strike to force recognition of their union. Solidarity strikes in other mines soon followed and finally, two days ago, about twelve women from the families of arrested labor leaders went on a hunger strike.

The response of the government was harsh and violent. Many workers were picked up during the night and put in prison, gas and food supplies to the city of Huanuni were cut off, newspapers were kept from circulating, striking workers were fired, and *campesinos* in need of work were sent into the mines. Since it was evident that the workers were not going to give up easily, it seemed for a while that the government was losing control over the situation and that there might be a new coup to break the deadlock. The miners asked the church to mediate. Archbishop Manrique and the Apostolic Nuncio agreed. Finally, a settlement was reached in which all arrested miners would be set free. A government commission will study the issue of recognition of the unions.

Today the Bolivian newspapers announced that the conflict has been solved. Neither the miners nor the government seems to have won. The emphasis during the strike shifted from the recognition of the union to the release of its leaders. The labor leaders will be free, but recognition of the unions will probably be long in coming. The only good thing is that more violence and repression were avoided. The oppressed and exploited miners will most likely not be better off than before. Hundreds of people have suffered terribly during the last few weeks, a suffering that will be kept out of the papers and yet will become part of the quiet and anonymous suffering of this country.

Thursday, November 26

Thanksgiving Day! There is probably no day I liked so much in the United States as this day. I can remember clearly all the Thanksgiving Days I celebrated in the last ten years. It was always a day of being together with friends, and truly a day of saying thanks. In many ways, it struck me as a more spiritual or religious day than Christmas: no gifts, few commercial preparations, just a coming together to express gratitude for life and all the blessings we have received.

Today I miss being in the United States, as do many people here at the language institute. I could feel it at the dinner table and also in the mood during the breaks between classes.

Still, what is important is to be grateful today and to give thanks. I am more and more convinced that gratitude is one of the most sublime of human emotions. It is an emotion that reaches out far beyond our own self to God, to all of creation, to the people who gave us life, love, and care. It is an emotion in which we experience our dependencies as a gift and realize that in the celebration of our dependencies we become most aware of who we truly are: a small but precious part of creation and above all of the human family. On this day we can say: It is good "just" to be human and it is in our common humanity that we can recognize God's love.

Friday, November 27

A psychology of education must exist which describes the up and down phases a student experiences in learning a new language. This week I felt as though I had not learned a thing since I came here. I experienced myself as stuttering worse than ever, as making the same basic mistakes as when I came here five weeks ago, and as still unable to know what people are talking about when they are not talking to me. I also noticed that expressions and constructions that a few weeks ago seemed quite obvious and even simple to me suddenly became real problems again. A small comfort was the realization of how terribly hard the English language is for Spanish-speaking people. Nancy Quiroga made me aware that *una cerveza* (a beer), *un pájaro* (a bird), and *un oso* (a bear) sounded to her all the same in English.

Saturday, November 28

Today is the last day of the liturgical year and tonight at the language school we will have a three-hour prayer vigil for justice and peace to start the advent season. I am happy for the occasion to pray together with the students and teachers. Though our only reason for being together is to become more able to reveal the presence of God in this world, we seldom have expressed this publicly in common worship.

We all know how far we are from a just and peaceful world. Ireland is on the brink of a civil war, Poland is uncertain whether the Russians will invade, Iran is tortured by weekly executions of hundreds of its own people and its war with Iraq, Guatemala is flooded with terror, El Salvador is being destroyed by oppression and civil war, Nicaragua is more and more insecure about its future, the United States is selling arms all over the world, Europe is in turmoil about the increase of nuclear arms on its territory, the Middle East is more explosive than ever, and the peoples of many Asian, African, and Latin American countries are threatened by malnutrition and starvation. The four beasts of which the Prophet Daniel speaks in his vision are running wild over this world.

There is a good reason to pray, especially for us who have come together from all parts of this world to be peacemakers. We know we cannot make peace with our own hands. We know that we are in the service of the King of Peace who one day will appear on the clouds. To him the kingdom, the power, and the glory will be given, and people of all languages and nations will serve him. We know that he will defeat all the beasts and that his power will be eternal and that his kingdom will never be destroyed (see Daniel 7:14). But we, too, are subject to the temptations of this world, the temptations of greed and lust, violence and revenge, hatred and destruction. We are not immune to the powers of the beasts. Therefore we have to help each other to keep our hearts and minds directed toward the Son of Man, so that we will recognize him when he comes and will be free to stand with confidence before him (see Luke 21:36). We have to keep ourselves and each other anchored in his words, because "heaven and earth will pass away, but my words will never pass away" (Luke 21:33). It is on that eternal Word, who became flesh and lived among us, that our hope is built.

Sunday, November 29

It is Advent again. In his sermon this morning, Oscar Uzin said: Be alert, be alert, so that you will be able to recognize your Lord in your husband, your wife, your parents, your children, your friends, your teachers, but also in all that you read in the daily papers. The Lord is coming, always coming. Be alert to his coming. When you have ears to hear and eyes to see, you will recognize him at any moment of your life. Life is Advent; life is recognizing the coming of the Lord.

In Bolivia the Advent symbols are different from those I am used to. In the past, Advent always meant to me the shortening of days, the approach of winter, and the time in which nature became darker and colder until the day of light. But now I have to learn to wait for the coming of the Lord while spring becomes summer and the light increases day by day. Now Advent means the coming of hot days with their fertile showers. Now Advent is the time during which schools are closed and children play on the streets. Now Advent means a time of blossoming trees and first fruits. And so the symbols of Easter become symbols of Christmas. Maybe my first Advent in the southern part of our planet will reveal to me new things about the mystery of God's becoming flesh among us. Until now, nature has only told me half of the story of God's incarnation; now the other half can be told.

But I have to listen, quietly, patiently, and with inner expectation. Nature can only tell me its other half of the story when I am ready to hear it, when my heart is not so full of false images and unnecessary preoccupations that there is no place left to receive the good news I have not yet heard.

Still I keep making my mistakes. Tonight I went with Richard and Theresa to *The Stuntman*, a movie about the making of a film. The movie was so filled with images of greed and lust, manipulation and exploitation, fearful and painful sensations, that it filled all the empty spaces that could have been blessed by the spirit of Advent. The film showed me how human beings are willing to waste their money, time, energy, and most precious intellectual and emotional talents to create a product that will fill the eyes and ears of thousands of people with images that can only damage the gentleness that lies dormant in our innermost being and asks to be awakened by a Divine touch.

Why did I go to this spectacle with Richard and Theresa? Richard is a kind Englishman who just returned from years of work with cooperatives in Africa, and Theresa is an Australian woman with great interest in music and handicrafts. Both hope to work together in Latin America and come to know better the beauty of this land and its people.

To be together, why did we need this violent and intrusive film? We could have spent our time so much better listening to each other's stories than watching the stuntman's tricks. Why do we keep missing the most obvious signs of God's coming and allow our hearts to be filled with all those things that keep suggesting, not that the Lord is coming, but that nothing will happen unless we make it happen.

I hope and pray that Advent will not be filled with stuntmen, but with the Spirit of him who invites us to listen carefully to the sounds of the New Earth that are manifesting themselves in the midst of the old.

Monday, November 30

St. Ignatius of Loyola was converted by reading the lives of the saints. I can understand this quite well, because everytime I read the life of a saint I experience a powerful call to conversion. Every man or woman who lives the Christian life to the full cannot but exercise a deep influence on everyone he or she meets. What continues to fascinate me is that those whose whole mind and heart were directed to God had the greatest impact on other people, while those who tried very hard to be influential were quickly forgotten.

When I met Mother Teresa in Rome, I saw immediately that her inner attention was focused constantly on Jesus. It seemed that she saw only him and through him came to see the poorest of the poor to whom she has dedicated her life. She never answers the many psychological and socioeconomic questions brought to her on the level they are raised. She answers them with a logic, from a perspective, and in a place that remains unfamiliar to most of us. It is a divine logic, a divine perspective, a divine place. That is why many find her simplistic, naive, and out of touch with the "real problems." Like Jesus himself, she challenges her listeners to move with her to that place from where things can be seen as God sees them.

When I explained to her all my problems and struggles with elaborate details and asked for her insights, she simply said: "If you spend one hour a day in contemplative prayer and never do anything which you know is wrong, you will be all right." With these words she answered none as well as all of my problems at the same time. It was now up to me to be willing to move to the place where that answer could be heard.

All these thoughts have come to me since I have been reading Boniface Hanley's book *Ten Christians,* In this book, Hanley offers simple but penetrating portraits of Pierre Toussaints, Damien de Veuster, Frederic Ozanam, Maximilian Kolbe, Teresa of Calcutta, St. Francis of Assisi, St. John Bosco, Rose Hawthorne Lathrop, Joseph Cardinal Cardijn, and St. Thérèse of Lisieux.

Reading these short biographies is like stepping out of this world and back into it again under the guidance of these concrete human beings. They all are much like me, but also different. They all know the struggles I know, but they are living with them in a different way. They all loved the world, but it was a world they came to see through God's eyes.

After having read such biographies, Ignatius could no longer continue his old life. He had seen how he could live when he was willing to take the risk of total surrender to the love of God.

3

December

A Land of Martyrs

Tuesday, December 1

LIVING WITH THE Quiroga family has helped me understand the struggle of Bolivian life. Every day I see more pain and tears under the surface of this seemingly happy and successful family. A few days ago, Nancy told me that little Rodolfito was not their biological son, but their adopted child. After her miscarriage, Nancy and Rodolfo wanted to adopt a child; but in Bolivia this is not easy. Nancy mentioned her desire to one of her ham radio friends, a medical doctor from another Latin American country with whom she had regular radio contacts. One day he told her that he knew of a little baby boy who needed caring parents. Nancy and Rodolfo went to visit the doctor and took the little boy home.

In Bolivia, however, having an adopted child, or being one, is looked down on as something unusual and strange. Soon Nancy and Rodolfo became fearful that their enemies would use their knowledge of the adoption to harm them. Their greatest concern was that the boy would find out from hostile people that he was not his parents' real child. They wanted to be sure that they themselves would explain to their son how and why they adopted him. This was the main reason for which Nancy and Rodolfo left the country and settled with their son in Miami, to give the boy a peaceful and quiet youth. Only when Rodolfito was old enough to understand that he had a truly safe home and that he was chosen by his parents out of love did they return to their country.

Their return did not bring them the peace they desired. Since their enemies had not left, they soon were exposed to the attack and imprisonment I wrote about on November twenty-third. Although Nancy and Rodolfo clearly want to live in their own country, I doubt that they will do so for long. Their son was so Americanized during his six years in the United States that he not only prefers hamburgers, french fries, soft drinks, and pancakes above anything Bolivian, but also dreams about a future in the land of his childhood memories.

All these things—the intense dedication to the short-wave radio, the six years in the United States, the nighttime intrusion of the paramilitary forces, the boy's fear of being away from his parents and Nancy and Rodolfo's intense concern for the well-being of their son—seem to fit together like the pieces of a strange puzzle.

Wednesday, December 2

"A shoot shall sprout from the stump of Jesse, and from his roots a bud shall blossom. The spirit of the LORD shall rest upon him . . ." (Isa. 11:1–2).

These words from last night's liturgy have stayed with me during the day. Our salvation comes from something small, tender, and vulnerable, something hardly noticeable. God, who is the Creator of the Universe, comes to us in smallness, weakness, and hiddenness.

I find this a hopeful message. Somehow, I keep expecting loud and impressive events to convince me and others of God's saving power; but over and over again, I am reminded that spectacles, power plays, and big events are the ways of the world. Our temptation is to be distracted by them and made blind to the "shoot that shall sprout from the stump."

When I have no eyes for the small signs of God's presence—the smile of a baby, the carefree play of children, the words of encouragement and gestures of love offered by friends—I will always remain tempted to despair.

The small child of Bethlehem, the unknown young man of Nazareth, the rejected preacher, the naked man on the cross, *he* asks for my
full attention. The work of our salvation takes place in the midst of a
world that continues to shout, scream, and overwhelm us with its claims
and promises. But the promise is hidden in the shoot that sprouts from
the stump, a shoot that hardly anyone notices.

I remember seeing a film on the human misery and devastation
brought by the bomb on Hiroshima. Among all the scenes of terror and
despair, emerged one image of a man quietly writing a word in calligra-
phy. All his attention was directed to writing that one word. That image
made this gruesome film a hopeful film. Isn't that what God is doing?
Writing his Word in the midst of our dark world?

Thursday, December 3

Tonight we celebrated the first anniversary of the martyrdom of Ita
Ford, Maura Clark, Jean Donovan, and Dorothy Kazel, the American
churchwomen who were raped, tortured, and murdered in El Salvador.
Many sisters and priests from the United States, along with their Bolivian
and American friends, came together in the parish church of Cala Cala
to pray for their sisters who died such a violent and cruel death. It was
a moving service in which faith and hope dominated the sadness about
the tragic loss.

For me, the most moving part of the service was the reading of the
martyrology by Father Jon Sobrino, one of the leading theologians in
Latin America. He lives in El Salvador and is deeply involved in the
struggle of the Church there. With restraint, he called out the names of
the men and women who have been murdered in Latin America during
the last decade. As he let the years pass in front of our minds, the num-
bers of martyrs increased. And every time he finished the list of victims
of one particular year, all the people in church responded with a loud:
"Presente." Yes, indeed, those who had given their lives for the liberation
of the poor were still present in the minds and hearts of the people they
came to serve. As the list of names grew—1971, 1972, 1973 . . . until
1981—the word *presente* became louder and clearer.

As I listened I realized that Ita, Maura, Dorothy, and Jean were just a few in the growing number of Christians who died as witnesses for the suffering Christ in Latin America. Hundreds and thousands of men and women in El Salvador, Guatemala, Nicaragua, Chile, Argentina, Brazil, Bolivia, as well as in the other countries of Central and South America, have died violent deaths during the last decade—and, for the most part, we do not even know their names. It suddenly struck me that with the thousands of Latin Americans who died, there are few with Anglo-Saxon names. The courage of those few North Americans who came to live and die with their brothers and sisters in South and Central America is a hopeful reminder that God's love transcends all human-made boundaries.

Friday, December 4

After last night's service in memory and honor of the martyrs of El Salvador, Jon Sobrino came to the language school for an informal discussion.

There were about fifteen people sitting in a circle listening to Jon's story. Seldom have I heard a story that touched me so deeply. Most of the facts he told I had heard about at one place or another, and most of the explanations he offered were familiar to me. But to hear the story of the horrendous suffering of the Salvadoran people, told by a man who witnessed it all and was involved in the struggle, is an experience that cannot be compared to reading news reports.

The first thing Jon Sobrino did was simply to state the facts. He kept stressing how tempting it is to deny the truth, to deal with it only partially or to present it in a soft way. We need to face the truth of the mass murders that destroy the lives of thousands of civilians, men, women, and children; of the indiscriminate killings to terrorize the poor; and of the selective and well-planned elimination of the leaders of the opposition, whether they are church leaders or political leaders. At least thirty thousand people have been killed in El Salvador during the last two years, and this is a conservative estimate.

The Church in El Salvador is far from united in the face of these barbarities. Jon Sobrino worked closely with Archbishop Oscar Romero, and now he is in close touch with his successor, Acting Bishop Arturo

Rivera y Damas. He spoke with great love and sympathy about these men, but left no doubt that they were exceptions. Most of the Salvadoran bishops show little sympathy for Romero's prophetic behavior, which cost him his life. The people might revere him as a saint, but his fellow bishops certainly do not. When some people asked one of the bishops to protest against the torture of one of his priests, he said: "I cannot do this, since he is not tortured as a priest but as a leftist." This bishop is also *vicarius castrensis,* army bishop, and continued to be present as the Church's representative at military functions.

Hearing this, I felt a profound sadness. It is precisely this inner division of the Church that makes a united confrontation of the powers of evil so hard.

I asked Jon Sobrino to say a little more about himself. "Why are you still alive?" I asked. He confessed that his international notoriety was probably his best safeguard. "The military resent deeply all the publicity around their actions in the international press. I am the only theologian of El Salvador who is known outside the country, and my death would create more problems than it would solve. The great indignation in the United States that followed the death of the four American women in December 1980 was very embarrassing to them. They do not want to see this repeated."

Jon Sobrino encouraged me to come to El Salvador and visit his community. "We won't have much time for you," he said, "because there are fewer and fewer priests and sisters to do the work that needs to be done. But we certainly appreciate visits from foreigners, because it is a way of being protected."

I was impressed by Jon Sobrino. His directness, his honesty, his deep faith, his fidelity to the Church, and his great openness to everyone who shows interest in the Church of El Salvador were signs of hope. But the many tensions of the last years have also wounded him. He told us, "People often speak about the beautiful and spiritual victory of the martyrs in El Salvador, but don't forget that the Church in El Salvador is systematically being destroyed and nobody knows how it will end. The only thing we have is our naked hope."

Saturday, December 5

This morning Sister Fran, a Maryknoll Sister who has lived in Bolivia for many years, invited me to celebrate the Eucharist for the blind people with whom she works regularly. With ten blind women and one blind man, we sat in a circle around a table. The first two readings and the responsory psalms were read by the women from their braille sheets, which Fran had prepared for them. After the Gospel reading, there was a lively discussion about baptism and confirmation in response to the story about the baptism of John and the baptism of Jesus. We sang to the accompaniment of an accordian. We listened to words about God's love spoken by those who have inner eyes. Their faith gave me strength and comfort. "Happy the pure in heart: they shall see God" (Matt. 5:8).

Monday, December 7

After seven weeks at the language institute, I am distressed at how superficial the interaction between students and teachers remains. Maybe this is just my own feeling, but I have not experienced an increase in community between the people at the institute. The atmosphere is pleasant, friendly, and mostly sympathetic, but it is clear that everyone has his or her own agenda and thinks primarily about what lies beyond the institute. Students come to learn a new language as quickly as possible and then move on to the "real thing." In that sense, the institute is very much like a seminary where students endure their studies in order to enter the professional world.

I experienced it in my own seminary years and saw it at Notre Dame, at the North American College, at Yale Divinity School, and at many other places. Everywhere there was the tendency to live, act, and think as if the real life is not here but there, not now but later. This tendency makes the formation of community so difficult, if not impossible. Community develops where we experience that something significant is taking place *where we are*. It is the fruit of the intimate knowledge that we are together, not because of a common need — such as to learn a language — but because we are called together to help make God's presence visible in the world. Only to the degree that we have this knowledge of God's call can we transcend our own immediate needs and point together to him who is greater than these needs.

I do not know if I will be alive tomorrow, next week, or next year. Therefore today is always more important than tomorrow. We have to be able to say each day, "This is the day the Lord has made, let us rejoice and be glad." If we all would die on the last day of our language training, nobody should have to say, "I wasted my time." The language training itself should have enough inner validity to make its usefulness secondary.

There are people from all over the world at this school, and together we represent a treasure house of knowledge, experience, human struggle, and, most of all, of faith, hope, and love. If these mental and spiritual talents could be brought into the light we all would have a beautiful space in which our life together could become an ongoing expression of worship and gratitude. Indeed, we could then experience the kingdom of God among us and thus find the strength to go out to serve people in pain.

But our own fears, insecurities, anxieties, and suspicions continue to interfere with our vocation and push us into small cliques of people in which we find some alleviation of our inner tensions. We quickly fall into the temptation of gossip and divisive words and actions, and before we know it we are imitating all the patterns of the world that we want to change by our ministry. This is the irony and tragedy of most theological and ministerial education. It is therefore not surprising that few will find "out there" what they could not find "right here."

Tuesday, December 8

During the celebration of the Eucharist in honor of the Immaculate Conception of Mary, the mother of God, Sister Lourdes offered a moving meditation. She helped me see Mary through the eyes of the poor people of the third world. Mary experienced uncertainty and insecurity when she said yes to the angel. She knew what oppression was when she didn't find a hospitable place to give birth to Jesus. She knew the sufferings of the mothers who see their children being thrown in the air and pierced by bayonets; she lived as a refugee in a strange land with a strange language and strange customs; she knew what it means to have a child who does not follow the regular ways of life but creates turmoil wherever he goes; she felt the loneliness of the widow and the agony of seeing her only son being executed. Indeed, Mary is the woman who stands next to all the poor, oppressed, and lonely women of our time. And when she continues to speak to people it is the simple and the poor to whom she appears: Juan Diego, the simple old Mexican Indian of Guadalupe; Bernadette, the poor sickly girl in Lourdes; Lucia, Jacinta, and Francesco, the unspectacular children in Fatima.

Every word in Scripture about Mary points to her intimate connection with all who are forgotten, rejected, despised, and pushed aside. She joyfully proclaims: "He has cast down the mighty from their thrones, and has lifted up the lowly. He has filled the hungry with good things, and the rich he has sent away empty" (Luke 1:52–53). These words today have taken on so much power and strength that, in a country like El Salvador, they are considered subversive and can lead to torture or death. Mary is the mother of the living, the new Eve, the woman who lives deeply in the heart of the Latin American people. She gives hope, inspires the fight for freedom, and challenges us to live with an unconditional trust in God's love.

Wednesday, December 9

Psalm 42 remains a source of strength to me. I prayed this psalm many, many times while my mother was dying, and every time since that week in October 1978 it has returned to me in times of distress.

> Like the deer that years
> for running streams,
> so my soul is yearning
> for you, my God. . . .
> Why are you cast down my soul,
> Why groan within me?
> Hope in God; I will praise him still,
> my savior and my God.

When I read this psalm last Monday during my morning prayer, I noticed that the psalm-prayer that followed it entered into my soul with an unusual power, so much so that it has stayed with me during the last few days. The prayer says:

Father in heaven, when your strength takes possession of us we no longer say: Why are you cast down, my soul? So now that the surging waves of our indignation have passed over us, let us feel the healing calm of your forgiveness. Inspire us to yearn for you always, like the deer for running streams, until you satisfy every longing in heaven.

The words "let us feel the healing calm of your forgiveness" are words that I want to hold onto, because if I desire anything, it is the healing calm of God's forgiveness. The longer I live, the more I am aware of my sinfulness, faithlessness, lack of courage, narrow-mindedness; the more I feel the surging waves of greed, lust, violence, and indignation roaring in my innermost self. Growing older has not made life with God easier. In fact, it has become harder to experience his presence, to feel his love, to taste his goodness, to touch his caring hands. Oh how much do I pray that he will let me know through all my senses that his love is more real than my sins and my cowardice, how much do I want to see the light in darkness, and how much do I wait for the day that he will order the surging waves to calm down, and how much do I wait to hear his voice, which says: "Why are you afraid, man of little faith? I am with you always."

Friday, December 11

Every morning at 6:45 I go to the small convent of the Carmelite Sisters for an hour of prayer and meditation. I say "every morning," but there are exceptions. Fatigue, busyness, and preoccupations often serve as arguments for not going. Yet without this one-hour-a-day for God, my life loses its coherency and I start experiencing my days as a series of random incidents and accidents.

My hour in the Carmelite chapel is more important than I can fully know myself. It is not an hour of deep prayer, nor a time in which I experience a special closeness to God; it is not a period of serious attentiveness to the divine mysteries. I wish it were! On the contrary, it is full of distractions, inner restlessness, sleepiness, confusion, and boredom. It seldom, if ever, pleases my senses. But the simple fact of being for one hour in the presence of the Lord and of showing him all that I feel, think, sense, and experience, without trying to hide anything, must please him. Somehow, somewhere, I know that he loves me, even though I do not feel that love as I can feel a human embrace, even though I do not hear a voice as I hear human words of consolation, even though I do not see a smile as I can see a human face. Still the Lord speaks to me, looks at me, and embraces me there, where I am still unable to notice it. The only way I become aware of his presence is in that remarkable desire to return to that quiet chapel and be there without any real satisfaction. Yes, I notice, maybe only retrospectively, that my days and weeks are different days and weeks when they are held together by these regular "useless" times. God is greater than my senses, greater than my thoughts, greater than my heart. I do believe that he touches me in places that are unknown even to myself. I seldom can point directly to these places; but when I feel this inner pull to return again to that hidden hour of prayer, I realize that something is happening that is so deep that it becomes like the riverbed through which the waters can safely flow and find their way to the open sea.

Saturday, December 12

Today we celebrated with Sister Lourdes and Sister Martha the 150th anniversary of the Sisters of Mercy. It was an important celebration for me, since it reminded me of the fact that "the preferential option for the poor," about which we speak so much today in the missionary circles of Latin America, is nothing new and original.

A reading from *Trinity*, by Leon Uris, offered a vivid description of the hunger, illness, misery, and agony of the Irish people in the year 1831, the year in which Catherine McAuley founded the Sisters of Mercy. Catherine's main purpose in those days was to assist the poor, the ill, and the dying, and offer some relief to the victims of Ireland's famine. To help the poor, and preferably the poorest of the poor, is not an invention of Mother Teresa nor a new idea that has been propagated by the church of Latin America since Medellin or Puebla. This call has lived in the heart of the Church ever since the Lord died in total poverty on the cross. Time and time again this call is revitalized and lived out in new ways. St. Basil heard this call when he organized communities to work for the sick and the poor in the fourth century. St. Francis heard this call in the thirteenth century, St. Vincent de Paul heard it in the sixteenth century, and many others have heard it since.

It was good to realize that the Sisters of Mercy, who now form the largest English-speaking congregation of religious women in the world, find their origin in Catherine McAuley's desire to serve the poorest of the poor. Her fervent hope was to make God's mercy visible to the people by simple, direct, and efficient service to those in need.

No congregation today attracts as many people as the Missionaries of Charity of Mother Teresa, who is for the twentieth century what Catherine McAuley was for the nineteenth, St. Vincent de Paul for the sixteenth, St. Francis for the thirteenth, and St. Basil for the fourth century. Every time we see the crucified Lord again in the wretched of our cities, in the refugee camps, and on the desolated deserts and plains of our world, our faith becomes new again.

Sunday, December 13

Newspapers and radio broadcasts are all announcing the frightening news that the government of Poland has declared a state of martial law. The leaders of Solidarity, Poland's new labor movement, have been arrested; churches, cinemas, and theaters closed; people cannot leave their houses during most hours of the day; the military controls the streets of Warsaw; telephone, radio, and television communications have been broken off; and the whole country lives anxiously awaiting what will come next.

Will the Russians invade? What will be the response of China and the United States? Will the people of Poland rise up in protest? Will this be the beginning of a long suffering of the Polish people or even of many peoples? Will this be the beginning of the third World War?

I saw Peter, the young Polish priest, for a moment. He was nervous, tense, and especially angry at the Communists who without hesitation had accused Solidarity and the Church of causing all the problems. He realized that he was excluded, that he would not be able to call his family, to hear any reliable news, or to get any idea about the fate of his many Polish friends. How powerless and isolated he must feel.

I pray that we all will be able to know what God wants us to do in the midst of this increasing tension and anxiety. I pray for Peter and his people, I pray for John Paul II, to whom many look for leadership in this critical moment, and I pray that we will be faithful to Our Lord and to each other in this hour of darkness.

Monday, December 14

Today is the feast of St. John of the Cross, the sixteenth-century Spanish mystic who speaks to me with great power. Not only did St. John experience oppression, humiliation, and imprisonment in his attempts to reform the Carmelite Order, but in the midst of his agony he experienced God's love as a purifying flame and was able to express this love in the most profound mystical poetry.

St. John reveals the intimate connection between resistance and contemplation. He reminds us that true resistance against the powers of destruction can be a lifelong commitment only when it is fed by an ardent love for the God of justice and peace. The ultimate goal of true resistance is not simply to do away with poverty, injustice, and oppression, but to make visible the all-restoring love of God. The true mystic always searches for this Divine knowledge in the midst of darkness. St. John sings "the Song of the Soul Delighted by the Knowledge of God" *(el cantar del alma que se huelga de conocer a Dios)*. He sings this song "though it is night" *(aunque es noche)*.

In the midst of our darkness—darkness in Poland, Ireland, Afghanistan, Iran, and in most Latin American countries; darkness in the broken, hungry, and fearful families; darkness in the hearts of millions who feel impotent and powerless in the face of the powers and principalities; and spiritual darkness in the countless souls who cannot see, feel, or understand that there is any love for them—in the midst of this darkness, St. John of the Cross sings of a light too bright for our eyes to see. In this divine Light we find the source of our whole being. In this Light we live, even when we cannot grasp it. This Light sets us free to resist all evil and to be faithful in the darkness, always waiting for the day in which God's presence will be revealed to us in all its glory.

Tuesday, December 15

Yesterday, a group of twelve Bolivian workers started a hunger strike in the cathedral. They are asking for a general amnesty for all the Bolivian workers who have been exiled from the country or jailed as political prisoners, for the recognition of their unions, and for the implementation of the human rights guaranteed by the national constitution.

The workers have refused to leave the cathedral to enter into dialogue with the prefect of Cochabamba. Afraid of being arrested, they seek the protection of the Church. A commission representing the prefect is now shuttling between the cathedral and *prefectura*, but so far nothing has been accomplished.

The hunger strikers are supported by large groups of workers. In La Paz and other cities, similar hunger strikes are being organized. The frustration, disappointment, and hostility of the Bolivian workers have been growing ever since the miners' strike. Large general strikes may follow and may prompt violence and oppression by the military regime. Christmas may be far from peaceful this year.

There are many parallels between the situations in Poland and Bolivia. The Bolivian workers have not been able to organize themselves in the way the Polish workers have, but with their determination it is unlikely they will give up their demands easily. In the coming days, the tension and anxiety most likely will increase. In a bankrupt country with a corrupt government, all this will probably lead to more repression, more poverty, and more misery for those who are already close to the bottom.

Wednesday, December 16

Tonight I gave the last of three advent meditations on compassion. During a meeting in November, Ralph Davila had asked for more student initiatives to strengthen the community life of the institute. On that occasion I offered to lead a series of reflections that might be of help to people in their preparation for Christmas.

When I look back at the three meetings, I know that I made a mistake. I should not have offered to give these meditations, but should have stuck to my decision to be a student and not to give any lectures, talks, courses, or presentations during my stay in Latin America. These meditations came forth more from my need to be useful than from any real need existing in the students or staff of the institute.

The three evenings never created any spiritual enthusiasm, and I experienced them in the way I had experienced many obligatory clerical days of recollection in the past, when people came more to please the bishop, the superior, or the speaker than to renew their own spirit. Some few people expressed an honest appreciation; but nothing really "happened." Events like these are little more than ways to maintain the status quo. They do not really help us take a step forward in our committed life together. I have seldom felt so little contact with people as with those who came to these meetings. The fact that Gerry and others expressed their concern that I not let the meetings last longer than the scheduled hour symbolized for me that there was little participation from the heart. As so often happens in clerical circles, obligation won out over desire.

My words remained words coming from far away and did not become life-giving words. I am learning that I am in another world, and that words that can renew minds and hearts at one time and place might have a dulling and even deadening effect at another time and place. I have learned that this is not a time for speaking but for listening; not a time for initiatives but for waiting; not a time to offer leadership but a time to let go of old and cherished ideas and to become poor in spirit. Since we can learn from our mistakes, I might as well use this experience as a way to recall that these are times to be silent.

Thursday, December 17

In preparation for my language classes I had to analyze a short story by the Spanish poet and novelist Carmen Corde. In this story a young mother discovers shortly after the birth of her baby boy that the child is blind. She calls her family together and says, "I do not want my child to know that he is blind!" She insists that from that point on everyone use a language in which words such as "light," "color," and "sight" are avoided. The child grows up believing that he is like everyone else until a strange girl jumps over the fence of the garden and uses all the forbidden words.

I think that this story symbolizes much of our behavior. We all seek to hide what is strange and painful and to act as if things are as usual. We say, "Let us act as if there were no problems, no abnormalities, no pains, no wounds, no failures, no illnesses." In my own life I have experienced the power of this urge to hide, an urge that often is more harmful than what it tries to conceal.

Every time I have had the courage or gave others the courage to face their blindness, their mental anguish, or their spiritual agony and let others become part of the struggle, new creative energies became available and the basis of community was laid. Fear, shame, and guilt often make us stay in our isolation and prevent us from realizing that our handicap, whatever it is, can always become the way to an intimate and healing fellowship in which we come to know one another as humans.

After all, everyone shares the handicap of mortality. Our individual physical, emotional, and spiritual failures are but symptoms of this disease. Only when we use these symptoms of mortality to form a fellowship of the weak can hope emerge. It is in the confession of our brokenness that the real strength of new and everlasting life can be affirmed and made visible.

Friday, December 18

This was my last day of language school. When I think about my eight weeks of classes, I have reason enough to be grateful. I do not think that there is any better way to learn Spanish than the way the institute has worked it out. Most impressive are the competence, the dedication, and the flexibility of the teachers. Every two weeks I worked with a different team of four teachers. Daily I had two individual classes with sophisticated language drills, one conversation class together with Brian Clark, and one grammar class with a small group of six students. It was a nice balance between intense individual work and more relaxing work with other students. After I finished the three basic textbooks, I asked for more attention for my personal language problems and thus my last two weeks were even more tailored to my needs than the first six weeks.

I was impressed by the way the teachers prepared their classes. They prepared the material of the lessons well, but they also tried to help the individual students with their personal struggles with the language. Ernestina, for instance, gave me a series of special exercises to train me in the use of the different past tenses, and made up many complicated sentences to help me distinguish between the use of *por* and *para*, two words I kept mixing up.

During my short time here I had fourteen different teachers. With this helpful change of teachers every two weeks, I never had a chance to get bored. Different teachers had different styles of working, different ways of expressing themselves, different personal interests, and often also a different way of relating to me. Some were formal and stayed close to the book, others enjoyed little mental excursions. Some used the blackboard a lot and appealed to my desire to see things written down. Others tried hard to train my ear and help me hear Spanish sounds better. Some kept the conversation to familiar household matters; others didn't hesitate to become involved in controversial political, social, and religious subjects. But everyone had something significant to offer and did so with great generosity and dedication. One of the most impressive traits of all the staff members of the institute — teachers, librarians, and secretaries — was their insistence on correcting students on the spot. Since I seldom uttered a sentence without at least two mistakes, I offered them all many opportunities to do their work.

Did I learn the language? I can only say that I gave it a good start, and that another three months is probably necessary to approach fluency in it. On the other hand, I do not have the energy or the motivation to continue at this moment. Eight weeks of intensive training is about as much as I can take in one stretch. I am happy that I am not returning to an English-speaking world but can go to Peru and continue to practice Spanish every day.

If I decide to dedicate a few years of my life to full-time work in Latin America, I probably will have to return to the institute for a few more months of language training. I especially would like to be able to write in Spanish. That certainly would take some extra work. For the time being, however, it seems better to leave the school and let the people of Peru become my teachers.

Saturday, December 19

This morning I went to the cathedral to meet the hunger strikers. I expected that it would be hard to get close to them and to have a conversation, yet I found the church open and unguarded with plenty of people going in and out. In a small sectioned-off area of the large cathedral, the hunger strikers lay on mattresses and blankets, slept, read the newspaper, or talked with visitors and medical aides. During the last few days their number had increased from twelve to forty-eight and about a thousand other workers of MANACO, the largest factory of Cochabamba, had joined them in a separate, supportive hunger strike.

Two men in their late twenties were eager to talk to me. "We are not giving up until the government takes our request seriously," they said. "It is not enough that the government recognizes the unions, we won't stop this hunger strike until the government offers a general amnesty. Thousands of Bolivians live as exiles outside their country since the coup of Garcia Meza on July 18, 1980. We want them to be free to return to their homes and families."

Just a few days earlier, the government had declared that there would be no amnesty this Christmas; but the workers and students in the cathedral made it clear that they would not eat anything until they had accomplished their goals. "Monday our families will join us in the strike if nothing has changed by then. It is going to be very serious."

Meanwhile, aides were walking around giving liquids to the strikers. Sister Mary-Jean, the Vincentian nun from the States who is the newly elected head of the school of nursing in Cochabamba, goes regularly to the cathedral to take the blood pressure of the strikers and to keep an eye on their physical condition. She told me yesterday that the liquid they gave the strikers contained sugar to reduce danger to their health. Nevertheless, the strike is now already five days old, and some of the men are visibly weakening.

"Are you a priest?" they asked. "Yes," I replied. It was clear that the workers had put all their hope in the support of the Church and in the religious sensitivities of the Bolivian people. They said: "The new church (they mean the church that made a preferential option for the poor) gives us much support. Many priests and sisters are on our side and Monsignor Walter Rosales (Vicar General of the Diocese and the highest church authority until the newly appointed bishop is installed) comes regularly to visit us." When I left them they thanked me for my visit and added jokingly: "Write about us in the Dutch papers."

How will Christmas be in Bolivia this year? The rumors are that all the banks will be on strike on Monday to show support for the strikers. Meanwhile, I am struck by the irony that President Reagan offers words of support and sympathy to the Polish labor union Solidarity but refuses any support for the workers in Latin America. The power that criticizes and condemns oppression of the working class when it comes from the Communist regimes ignores, denies, or even encourages the same oppression when it results from the military regimes in Latin America. The issue for Reagan is obviously not, "When are people oppressed?" but, "Who is the oppressor?" The oppressors of the exploitative regimes in Latin America are called "our friends," the oppressors in Poland and Russia are called "our enemies." It seems indeed that the Church today is one of the few institutions in the world willing to defend human rights regardless of who the oppressor is.

Sunday, December 20

The Church is speaking loudly today. Pope John Paul II sent a delegation to Poland to visit Church and government leaders in order to find a nonviolent solution to the increasing conflict. It seems, from the latest newscasts, that the Pope is seriously considering going to Poland himself.

Meanwhile, the bishops of Bolivia wrote a strong Christmas message asking the government to restore the confidence of the Bolivian people in their leaders and to offer a broad political amnesty. "We ask those responsible for the public cause, to restore the faith of the people, which they lost after so many deceptions. The Spirit of justice and true love for the country which transcends the interests of individuals and groups has to be able to return to the people a renewed hope in those who have the responsibility in concrete circumstances. We ask the supreme government for a broad political amnesty, that will open the way to reconciliation of all the Bolivians."

In the midst of all the conflicts, wars, and rumors of war, these strong voices offer hope and encouragement. Although we have to admit that peace and justice have not won the field during the last ten years, we can rejoice in the fact that the voice of the Lord of peace and justice is heard clearer than ever. I pray that many people who are poor and oppressed

will find comfort and consolation when they hear this voice, and will find
the strength to work together for a better world.

Monday, December 21

The hunger strikers gave up. Nothing has changed. During the
weekend, it became clear that there was absolutely no chance that the
government would give in, and that the only possible outcome would
be bloodshed and the useless loss of lives. The political analysts, who
are trusted by the strikers, persuaded them that the continuation of their
hunger strike would only bring misery to themselves and their families.

I tried to understand this sudden change by talking to different
people. I concluded from all the comments that the position of the government is so weak that a general amnesty would simply mean suicide
for the present government. Bringing the many Bolivian exiles back into
the country would change the balance of power so drastically that the
present government would have no chance of surviving.

Meanwhile, the economic situation of the country is so bad that
any promise to offer better financial conditions to the workers would be
empty. Many industries lack the funds to offer the expected Christmas
bonus and everyone expects the Bolivian peso to drop in value significantly during the first week of January. The official exchange rate is 25
pesos for a dollar, but at any exchange office I can easily get 35 pesos or
more. Meanwhile, it remains impossible for the Bolivians to buy dollars.
For those who have debts in the States—as the Quiroga family has—
this means a growing financial crisis. Rodolfo bought many goods in the
States to sell in his store. Now the Bolivians have no money to buy his
articles, and his debts to the U.S. banks increase by the rapid devaluation
of the peso. This is a quick way to bankruptcy.

I am sad to witness yet another example of the powerlessness of the
poor. The military personnel have large salaries and are allowed to buy
goods in special military stores for very low prices. Meanwhile, the poor
get less and less for their money and most have to let Christmas pass without being able to give any presents to their children. While the president
of the country gives patriotic speeches about love of country, unity of the
people, and cooperation between all to save the country from disintegra-

tion, it is clear that he and his political friends are protecting their wealth gathered by cocaine traffic and other forms of contraband by giving money and guns to those who are willing to protect their privileged position. The Bolivian army exists not to defend the country against outside invaders, but to defend the wealthy few against the poor and the hungry.

Many of the intelligent people who could provide leadership and change the situation give up, leave the country, and become doctors, lawyers, and businessmen in the United States or in Europe. It is a tragedy that today, in Chicago alone, there are a large number of Bolivian M.D.s while the most basic medical care is lacking in large parts of their own country.

Where is the peace and joy of Christmas? In the United States, in Russia, in Poland, in Ireland, in El Salvador, Guatemala, Nicaragua, or Bolivia? Indeed, "The word was the true light that enlightens all men; and he was coming into the world. He was in the world that had its being through him and the world did not know him. He came in his own domain and his own people did not accept him" (John 1:9–11).

Tuesday, December 22

In the midst of all the bad news from Poland and Bolivia, the familiar words from the Song of Zechariah suddenly have an unusual power:

> The God of Israel has raised up for us
> a savior who will free us from our foes,
> from the hands of all who hate us.
> He will give light to those in darkness,
> those who dwell in the shadow of death
> and guide us into the way of peace.

How often have I spoken these words as if they were little more than the expression of an ancient and pious Jew! But here in Bolivia, with the alarming news from Poland covering the front pages of the newspapers, they sound as a call to rebellion, as an invitation to follow a new leader who will throw off the yoke of oppression.

I should not forget that when Zechariah raised his voice Judea and

Samaria were occupied territories and that the Jews felt about the Romans as the Dutch felt about the Germans during World War II, and as most Poles feel about the Russians today. Zechariah's song doesn't leave politics behind. In fact, it was difficult for the Jews of Jesus' time to make a distinction between religion and politics. Jesus himself was executed as a political enemy, as someone who claimed to be King of the Jews.

In Latin America, the Good News of the Gospel is a threat to those who oppress and exploit the people. To take the words of the Gospel seriously would mean political suicide for most rulers. The words "God has raised up for us a savior who will free us from our foes" ring out less a note of piety than a call to resistance.

Wednesday, December 23

It has been raining the whole day. I had expected a hot Christmas with cloudless skies and a burning sun, but heavy clouds hang over the Cochabamba valley and people walk hastily in raincoats and with umbrellas, jumping over pools of water and trying to escape the splashes of water caused by the fast-driving buses.

I did my Christmas shopping today: two books about jet planes and space travel for Rodolfito, a Spanish metal cross for Rodolfo and Nancy, a brooch and bracelet for Marcelita, and a few things for the Christmas guests in the Quiroga home.

I also wanted to do something special for Christmas. In Rodolfo's store, I had seen little cars and dolls that would make good presents for the boys and girls of the state orphanage I visited last month. So I asked a friend for the telephone number of the orphanage and called the director to tell her about my plan to give all the kids a Christmas gift. The director was very excited about my plan, but when I asked her, "How many kids do you have?" she said, "Seventy-seven girls between twelve and eighteen." Suddenly, I realized that my friend had given me the number of the wrong orphanage. The cars and dolls from Rodolfo's store probably would not please the teenage girls of the orphanage I now was talking with. But I decided to be brave. I acted as if all were normal and promised the unknown director to appear on Christmas afternoon with gifts for seventy-seven teenage girls.

As soon as I told Rodolfo about my mistake and challenged him to be inventive, he and his staff went to work and came up with games, perfumes, mirrors, brushes, and all sorts of other things that—as they assured me—would certainly please girls between twelve and eighteen. On the twenty-fifth we all will go to the orphanage, and I wonder what the response will be.

Meanwhile, I am looking forward to my first Christmas in the summer.

Thursday, December 24

The most important part of this day for me was the celebration of Vespers and Mass of the Vigil of Christmas. At five o'clock in the afternoon, Sister Fran and I went to the small Carmelite convent and experienced the quiet joy of Christmas with the sisters. It was very quiet and peaceful, a simple and restful service. In the midst of the many activities in preparation for Christmas and surrounded by so many political and socioeconomic anxieties, this celebration was a true oasis. The joyful alertness of the twelve sisters offered Fran and me an opportunity to come in touch with the still and deep presence of God in our lives. I read the genealogy of Jesus Christ as St. Matthew gives it in the first chapter of his Gospel. The many names from Abraham to Jesus are certainly not names of saints. They are names of men and women who struggled hard with the powers of evil, sometimes more successfully than others, and who have experienced love, hatred, joy, pain, reward, and punishment, like ourselves. It is these men and women who form the story of which God himself wanted to become part. God, so it seems, inserted himself in our own tiresome and often exhausting journey and became a fellow traveler. When Jesus joined the sad and deeply disappointed disciples on their road to Emmaus and opened their eyes so that they could see what was happening, he revealed what it means that God is a God with us.

God came to us because he wanted to join us on the road, to listen to our story, and to help us realize that we are not walking in circles but moving towards the house of peace and joy. This is the great mystery of Christmas that continues to give us comfort and consolation: we are not alone on our journey. The God of love who gave us life sent us his only

Son to be with us at all times and in all places, so that we never have to feel lost in our struggles but always can trust that he walks with us.

The challenge is to let God be who he wants to be. A part of us clings to our aloneness and does not allow God to touch us where we are most in pain. Often we hide from him precisely those places in ourselves where we feel guilty, ashamed, confused, and lost. Thus we do not give him a chance to be with us where we feel most alone.

Christmas is the renewed invitation not to be afraid and to let him — whose love is greater than our own hearts and minds can comprehend — be our companion.

Friday, December 25

Peter, the Polish priest, and I presided together over the midnight Mass in Temporal. Temporal is a section of Cochabamba that does not have its own church. The Marist brothers have a large school there and on Sundays and feastdays they convert their auditorium into a worship hall. Over the years, the brothers have developed quite a parish. Although they have no regular priest, they usually manage to convince one of the priest-students of the language institute to do the fixed parts of the Mass, while they take care of everything else: preparations, music, sermon, and all the details necessary for a good liturgy. The only thing they require of the priest is that he can read Spanish in an acceptable way.

We all gathered on the playground of the school. As I looked out from the steps of the auditorium over the more than three hundred people gathered there, I realized again how mysteriously God keeps calling us together from so many parts of the world. Although most people were Bolivians, and most of them from Temporal, there were brothers from Spain, visitors from the United States, Peter from Poland, and myself from Holland. And while we all are so aware of the conflicts and wars that result from the ethnic and geographic divisions between people, a celebration like this reveals again that God did not create these divisions but wants his people to come together in unity and peace.

This joyful celebration unfolded with mystery and a few surprises, the first of which announced itself as a mechanical bird hidden in the Christmas tree! A large silver ball produced loud bird calls at regular intervals and the layman who acted as deacon during the liturgy was so enchanted with this gadget that he turned it on at the most unusual moments. Just before the Marist brother started his sermon, the deacon walked up to the tree and made the "metal bird" sing its songs. The brother didn't seem to mind. He just raised his voice and competed happily with the bird, who interrupted every second sentence of his sermon with its calls. When the brother invited me to add a few words to his, I first sent the deacon up to the tree to shut the bird up. My Spanish is bad enough; I don't need an artificial bird to punctuate it.

The lights went out during communion, a second surprise. The electricity fails regularly in Bolivia, but this interruption created more confusion than usual. Luckily, many people had Christmas candles with them, and thus we were able to continue and finish the service without many problems. The singing of *"Noche de Paz"* ("Silent Night") by candlelight added to the Christmas mood.

The third surprise—at least for me—was that quite a few boys and girls made their first communion during the Mass. They were festively dressed and looked happy in their new suits and dresses and with their large candles and white rosaries in their hands. I found it difficult to combine the celebration of Christmas with the celebration of the first communion, and to pay sufficient attention to both celebrations during the service, but nobody else seemed to share my problem and thus I tried to go with it as best I could.

Finally there were the *"niños"* (baby Jesus dolls). While celebrating the Eucharist, Peter and I were surrounded by baby dolls, small and large, naked and elaborately dressed, lying on simple cushions or hidden in large glass cases. I never saw so many Jesus-babies together in my life. I soon found out that it belongs to the folk tradition that the baby Jesus has to hear Mass on Christmas day. Therefore families take their Christmas child out of his stable and bring him to church. After Mass, Peter and I were busy for quite awhile blessing all the dolls and giving ample attention to the different ways the baby Jesus looked.

But whatever the surprises were, all the people were happy, joyful, and pleased with this holy night, and everyone went home saying or shouting to each other: *"Feliz Navidad!"* or *"Felices Pascuas de Navidad!"*

When I looked up to the sky, I saw a splendid firmament richly decorated with bright stars singing their praises to the newborn child. And we, little people with our candles, rosaries, and dolls, smiled at the heavens and heard the song again: "Glory to God in the highest heaven, and peace to men and women and children who enjoy his favor."

This afternoon we went to the state orphanage, taking with us our gifts from Rodolfo's store. Rodolfo had decided to make his own contribution, and had added to the gifts seventy-seven yellow T-shirts that a Japanese perfume factory had sent him as a form of advertisement. At 5 P.M. Rodolfo, Nancy, Rodolfito, and I drove to the outskirts of Cochabamba and, after a few wrong turns, located the orphanage.

We were greeted with enthusiasm, for the girls had been waiting with great expectation. Immediately Rodolfo began to give everybody in the house one of his yellow T-shirts. One went to a little eight-year-old boy who happened to be visiting his sister that afternoon. Raphaelito was so tiny that I lifted him up and stood him on the table to put on his T-shirt, which went all the way down to his bare feet. With his brown face and big dark eyes staring out from above his long yellow dress he looked like a little cupid. When the girls saw him standing there rather forlornly on top of the table they all began to laugh. At that moment big tears came rolling down Raphaelito's round cheeks and he burst out in sobs. It took us a while to console him, and he needed a few more presents to dry his tears.

What an irony! Here I was trying to make everybody happy and the first result was a tearful boy surrounded by seventy-seven laughing girls. But soon all was forgotten and everyone was excited with the gifts. We talked, sang songs, and played games. When we left we were escorted by Raphaelito and all the girls to the gate and lavishly thanked with handshakes, embraces, and kisses. As we drove away we saw a happy crowd with waving arms wishing us good-bye.

The laughter of Raphaelito and the girls also made us mindful of their unmentioned rejection and loneliness. This joyful interruption in their lives had brought us closer to the sadness of their permanent condition. As we returned to our comfortable home, they stayed in their lonely house; as we are surrounded by the care of family and friends, they wonder if anyone cares.

True ministry goes far beyond the giving of gifts. It requires giving of self. That is the way of him who did not cling to his privileges but emptied himself to share our struggles. When God's way becomes known to us, and practiced by us, hope emerges for Raphaelito and the girls in the orphanage.

Saturday, December 26

At three o'clock Sister Mary-Jean picked me up with her Toyota jeep to take me to the Quechua town of Morochata for the weekend. Her friends Sister Ann and Sister Delia, who run the parish in Morochata, had asked her urgently to look for a priest to hear confessions, to celebrate the Eucharist for the children who were receiving their first communion, and to assist in seven marriages. Sister Mary-Jean, whom I had come to admire as a forthright, courageous, and very lively person, convinced me that to accept her invitation would not only be good for the parish of Morochata, but even more so for me. "You will see fabulous landscapes, you will be excited about the llamas in the high mountains, you will love the people of Morochata, and most of all you will discover what the missionary life is really about." Well, this certainly was an invitation I could not refuse! By three thirty we had left the highway and were slowly curving our way up to the top of the mountains. After a while we could overlook the valley of Cochabamba. What a magnificent view! Dark clouds hung above the city, but the sun found enough space between them to throw floods of radiant light into the valley. As we came higher, we gradually entered into the clouds until we were driving in a heavy mist. As soon as we passed the large cross planted on the top, we could see the clouds breaking and had some glimpses of the little villages below on the other side of the mountain. Mary-Jean drove her jeep carefully through the seemingly endless hairpin turns marked by many small crosses, reminding us of the people who had lost their lives on this dangerous road.

It took us about an hour to make our descent into Morochata. "I am sorry that we didn't see many llamas," Mary-Jean said, "but I promise you will see a lot of them tomorrow on your way back." I hoped she was right.

The priests of the diocese of Dubuque, Iowa, who live and work at St. Raphael's parish in Cochabamba had often mentioned Morochata to me. It was the place where their friend Raymond Herman was murdered six years ago. In different places I had seen pictures of Ray Herman, a young-looking, handsome priest. Why was he murdered? Nobody could answer that question satisfactorily, but everyone agrees that his four years of pastoral work for the poor *campesinos* was the main cause.

About thirty years ago, Morochata was a small, flourishing town. Many wealthy landowners had their houses and managed the *campesinos* from there. The large church and the pleasant central square remind visitors of these old days. There was so much going on in this little town that the rich citizens decided to build a small hotel to accommodate their many visitors. But all of that changed when Victor Paz Estenssoro came to power in Bolivia and initiated a radical agrarian reform in 1952, making the *campesinos* owners of their land and terminating the ages-old system of *latifundios* (large landholdings), on which the farmers were little more than slaves.

Soon the wealthy landowners realized that Morochata could no longer offer them the comfort they desired. Gradually, they all moved away, leaving the town to the poor *campesinos*, who discovered that the land reform did not bring them the promised prosperity. The little pieces of land they now owned soon were divided between their many children. The *campesinos* lack of experience and education, combined with the failure of the government to provide adequate loans for machinery and fertilizer, prevented them from developing a decent economic base.

The hotel, which was under construction when the land reform started, was never finished, and its skeleton only reminded the people of Morochata that their town was once a center of attraction for those who had money and power. In 1971, Raymond Herman came to Morochata to become its pastor. Ray was a diocesan priest from Iowa who had worked for many years in Cochabamba. Hardworking, fully dedicated to his people, concerned for nothing but their physical and spiritual well-being, Ray was as apolitical as one can be, and stayed far from the intrigues that characterize the history of Bolivia. He was deeply loved by his people, by the poor and destitute, and also by those who euphemistically could be called middle class.

When Ray saw the half-finished hotel, he immediately thought: "This should be a hospital." For many years he worked hard to collect funds and find support for his plan, and finally, in October 1975, the building was finished and ready to be opened to receive its first patients.

On the morning of October 20, 1975, the day after the dedication of the hospital, Don Pascual Villaroel, Ray's sacristan, bookkeeper, and teacher of cathechetics, was waiting for Ray to say Mass. Noticing the absence of the jeep, he thought that Ray had probably gone on an errand and would soon be back; but when he found his alarm clock on the ground outside of the rectory, he started to feel very nervous. Finally, he went to Ray's bedroom, knocked on the door, and entered. At first he thought that the priest lay in deep sleep, since he could see only his hair outside the sheet. When he could not wake him up, he carefully pulled away the sheet, and saw an unspeakable horror. Ray had been strangled and two bullets were shot through his head; he had been brutally tortured.

Four hours later, Don Pascual reached Cochabamba to tell Leon, the pastor of St. Raphael, the tragic news. It took him a long time before he was able to say that something demonic had happened. Don Pascual hardly could say what he really had seen.

The autopsy performed on Ray's body made it clear that the murder could never have been done by one man. A group of people must have entered his bedroom around 2:00 A.M., torturing and killing him. They took the jeep and many things from his room and made it look like an "ordinary" robbery; but if anything is clear, it is that this was a well-planned assassination that had little to do with robbing a priest.

When I saw Ray's bedroom and heard the story, I asked again: "Why?" The answer to that question, summarized from different people's remarks, was: "We don't know. Some people say that the truck drivers did it because Ray was trying to find cheaper ways for the *campesinos* to bring their products to town. Others say that Ray's serious attempt to help raise the standard of living of the poor—the hospital was a symbol of that—had made him the enemy of those who are in control, and that the order to kill him came from very high up."

I asked what happened afterwards. "Nothing really," one of the people said. "Two men were arrested and put in jail, but soon they were allowed to escape. The Bolivian as well as the American governments have covered up the whole event and even today, six years later, nobody knows the true story."

I walked around the church and the little square. The young people sitting on benches greeted me in a friendly way. From the house in which the sisters live, I had a splendid view of Morochata and the mountains that surrounded it. Everything looked so peaceful and serene. But the demonic force of evil had reached this little town too. People knew it. Next Friday would have been Ray's birthday, and people from all directions have come to be sure that there will be a celebration in his memory. He was very much loved; but here those who are loved as he was are seldom destined to live very long. They are reminders of a world that has not yet been realized.

Sunday, December 27

This morning at eight o'clock I celebrated the Mass for Cecilio, Bernardo, Rolando, Linder, and Alejandro, who were receiving their first communion. Well-dressed and well-groomed, they sat in the first pew with rosaries and candles in their hands while parents, godparents, friends, and parishioners filled the church to be part of the occasion.

Most of the boys were twelve or thirteen years old. So the story of Jesus who went with his parents to Jerusalem and stayed there "among the doctors, listening to them and asking them questions," seemed appropriate for the occasion. I enjoyed explaining this story to them, asking them questions about it, and giving them some idea of the great mystery that this Jesus who once was a boy like them, now comes to them as their lasting guide and support in the sacrament of bread and wine. Everyone was radiant, joyful, and grateful; and when the boys came to the house of the sisters for the traditional cup of hot chocolate, they all looked like little princes, even though their real status was more like that of the poor shepherds of Bethlehem.

The weddings took place at ten o'clock. Don Pascual had placed the seven couples and their *padrinos* (the best men and maids of honor) in a large circle around the altar. Since practically no one spoke Spanish, Don Pascual led the service of the word and the whole wedding ceremony in Quechua. I just tried to follow the ceremony as well as I could and did whatever Don Pascual asked me to do.

After the traditional questions and the exchange of vows, some special rites took place. First there was the blessing and exchange of rings. This proved more complicated than I expected, since it took a while to find a finger on which the rings would fit. (Obviously, these rings had known other couples.) Then I took a handful of coins from a plate and gave them to the groom to make him aware of his responsibility to provide for his family. The groom let all these coins fall into the hands of his bride to show her that he would share all his wealth with her, and the bride then flung the coins back on the plate to make it clear that after all money was not the most important thing in their life together.

After this ritual, the *padrinos* put a thin chain around their heads, which Don Pascual then covered with a red velvet cloth. I handed them a burning candle.

Seven times these rituals were repeated. During all of this, the seven couples looked extremely serious; I could not get one little smile from any of them. They had waited in great anticipation for this moment, and for them this was certainly not a moment for smiles or laughter. One couple must have been in their forties. They never had been able to afford a wedding and had to wait many years before they had the money to offer to their friends the fiesta that forms an essential part of the event.

In the Indian culture, no couple will marry in the church without having lived together for some time and without being sure that the woman will be able to bear children. The church ceremony is more an affirmation by the community of their relationship than a beginning of a new life together. When the church becomes involved, the couple has already proven to each other, their friends, and their community that there is a real basis to their union.

What struck me most before, during, and after the event was the lack of any expression of affection whatsoever between the grooms and the brides. They hardly talked to each other; they did not touch each other except when the ritual demanded it. Not one kiss was ever exchanged. Pascual had to remind them repeatedly during the exchange of vows to look at each other, and even that seemed hard for them. When I asked

Ann about this later, she said: "Even in their homes, husband and wife seldom show affection to each other, but both are expressive in their love for their children: they play with them, hug them, kiss them, and touch them constantly."

After the wedding ceremony, I celebrated the Eucharist in Spanish and gave to all who were just married and to their *padrinos* the Body and Blood of Christ. Everyone participated intensely in all that took place, even though probably none of them would be able to explain anything about the Eucharist. But their belief in God's presence during this sacred hour could be read from their dark faces.

At twelve o'clock, when I thought that it was all over, Ann said to me: "I have a little surprise for you: there are thirteen little babies to be baptized! Their parents and godparents are waiting for you in the church. I decided to surprise you with it, because if I had told you before, you might not have come!" There was a lot of action and noise around the baptismal font. Every time a baby cried too loudly for Ann's taste, she asked the godmother to give the baby back to the mother, who then immediately gave her breast to the little one. It always worked. Meanwhile, I went from baby to baby with oil and signed their chests with the sign of the cross. Then, one by one they came to the font and, as I poured the water over their heads, they usually protested with loud cries. After thirteen baptisms, we had quite a noisy crowd! But everyone smiled and laughed and showed their gratitude.

"There is one more thing I want you to do," said Ann, when the people had left the church. "There is a lady here who lost her only son of sixteen years last month. His name was Walter. She wants you to go with her to the cemetery, pray with her, and bless the grave." I found the woman sitting on a bench in the village square. As I touched her, she started to cry bitterly. It was a sad story. Last month, Walter went to Cochabamba with a truck loaded with produce and people. As usual, the younger boys were standing on the running board of the truck holding onto the door. At one point, Walter lost his balance and fell from the truck without the driver noticing. He fell between the wheels and was crushed by the back tires of the truck. They took him in the truck in the hope of reaching the hospital in Cochabamba in time, but he died on the way.

Ann and I drove with Walter's mother in the jeep to the small ceme-tery behind the hospital. There we found the little niche where Walter's body was laid. We prayed and I sprinkled the place with holy water and we cried. "He was my only son, and he was such a good boy," his mother said with tears in her eyes. Ann told me how helpful Walter had been in the parish and how everyone was shocked by his death.

I couldn't keep my eyes from the woman's face, a gentle and deep face that had known much suffering. She had given birth to eight chil-dren: seven girls and Walter. When I stood in front of the grave I had a feeling of powerlessness and a strong desire to call Walter back to life. "Why can't I give Walter back to his mother?" I asked myself. But then I realized that my ministry lay more in powerlessness than in power; I could give her only my tears.

At four o'clock, we were on our way back around the many curves, and at five we reached the top again. And there they were! A large herd of beautiful llamas. We stopped the jeep and walked close to where they stood. They stretched their large necks and looked at us with curious eyes. It was a moving encounter, high up in the mountains where there are hardly any human beings. The llamas stared at us, making it clear that we really didn't belong there.

When we descended into the Cochabamba valley, we noticed how the heavy rain had washed away parts of the road. But Mary-Jean kept her jeep on the path, and at six o'clock we rolled into the city again.

I was very tired, but happy. Mary-Jean had been right when she said that I would see fabulous landscapes, would be excited about the llamas in the high mountains, would love the people of Morochata, and most of all would discover what the missionary life is really about.

Monday, December 28

Although the house of the Quiroga family is richly decorated during this Christmas season, and although Rodolfo and Nancy offered a festive dinner to their family and friends, these days have not been peaceful for them.

On the morning of December 24, when Rodolfo and Rodolfito came to the store to start their day of work, hoping that this last day before Christmas would give them some good business, a man was waiting for them with a court order. At first, Rodolfo thought it was a customer who wanted to buy Christmas gifts; but he soon realized that the family member who had sent him to prison last year was trying to do the same again. The hatred of this man must be of a satanic quality; he had chosen Christmas Eve to do as much harm as possible to Rodolfo. The court order contained many accusations; but since most offices are closed on the day before Christmas, and lawyers and judges do not work during these feast days, there was a real chance that Rodolfo would have to go to prison until the authorities could hear his case.

The man who confronted Rodolfo at his store did not allow him to call Nancy or to warn anybody. He and another man took him immediately to the courthouse, leaving little Rodolfito crying in the street with the keys of the store in his hands. When the personnel of the store arrived, the boy told them what had happened. They immediately called Nancy, who rushed to their lawyer; together they went quickly to the courthouse. Meanwhile, other influential friends were informed, and they all soon appeared at the same place to keep Rodolfo out of prison. By noon, things had been "clarified," and Rodolfo could return to his work.

"This is the third Christmas he has tried to destroy," said Nancy. Although Rodolfo was spared from having to spend the holidays in prison, the whole event robbed him of his inner tranquility and made it hard for him to celebrate freely the feast of Christ's birth. He had to spend much of his time contacting lawyers, witnesses, and friends to convince the court that the whole thing was another attempt of his enemy to destroy his family life, and his peace.

Today the tension finally diminished. Rodolfo and Nancy came home with smiles on their faces, telling me that the lawyers had been able to convince the court that this was a setup without any other basis than personal hatred.

"How can this man get court orders to arrest you?" I asked. "He is very wealthy," Rodolfo said, "and here in Bolivia you can buy anything, even judges and witnesses."

Wednesday, December 30

Tonight I visited the Albergue San Vicente with Gerry McCrane. It is a shelter for young boys of Cochabamba who live on the streets, shine shoes, wash cars, and steal to survive. For many years the Vincentian Sister Anne Marie Branson, who has spent most of her religious life in Bolivia, dreamt about a house where these street urchins could find a home. She felt strongly that this is the type of work Vincent de Paul, the founder of the Vincentians, would have been most interested in. She had seen many of these little boys in the streets in Cochabamba, had talked with them, and had become aware of their dehumanized existence.

Finally, in April of this year, some old buildings and some money became available, and Sister Anne Marie started her new work. She went to the boys and invited them to come to her Albergue San Vicente. Within a few weeks, she had thirty regulars. The boys come in the evening, get a warm meal, receive some personal attention, stay for the night, and go back on the streets after a decent breakfast. The stories of these boys are tragic. An eight-year-old boy was simply thrown out of the house when his mother remarried. He was able to get on a truck and come to Cochabamba. He had been roaming the streets for three years until Sister Anne picked him up and gave him a home. Another boy, ten years old, said: "My mother took me to the market, went to the bathroom, and never came back." Every boy has a painful story to tell.

Sister Anne Marie said: "There must be at least two hundred of these boys on the streets of Cochabamba, but I have room for only thirty. Often the boys come home at night with a street friend, and then I try to give him a mattress for the night. My dream is to build a larger dormitory, so I can help more of these poor kids."

The building where Sister Anne Marie works is simple and poor: one large room filled with beds, a small place to eat, and a kitchen. Sister Anne Marie does the cooking—mostly soup with bread—and tries to help the boys live together in some peace. It is a hard job. These boys are so preoccupied with surviving that they do not afford themselves the luxury of being kind, generous, or peaceful. "The whole world is their enemy," Anne Marie says. "What can you expect? Now they at least eat together without fighting, and I am trying to give them some tranquility and quiet during the night."

As soon as Gerry and I came in, two boys noticed our dirty shoes, pulled out their shoeshine boxes, and gave us a free shoeshine. I was moved when they adamantly refused to accept money for their work. Anne Marie was trying to teach them that some people are your friends and you want to help them without asking for money. "I am trying to get some of them to go to school again," Anne Marie said, "but it is hard for them. They are not used to any discipline, and many of them have so little ego that it is hard for them to apply themselves to any task that asks for endurance. Moreover, it is practically impossible for them to trust anyone. They have no experience of a trusting relationship. For as long as they can remember the world has been hostile to them. I am hoping to get some more professional help, a mental health team, that could assist these boys to develop some confidence in themselves and others."

One boy came in with a bleeding foot. Anne Marie gave him some instructions on how to wash his feet with hot water and disinfectants and how to put on a bandage.

As we walked through the dormitory, a little boy of seven years old stood on his bed neatly dressed in blue jeans and a colorful shirt. He had received these clothes as a Christmas gift and was trying them on before going to bed, because the next day he had to help serve at a dinner being given by some rich people. Eagerly he was looking forward to the occasion.

"Oh, it is just band-aid work," Anne Marie said. "We do not even touch the real problem, but at least we may help a few boys."

I had heard a lot about the street boys in Lima, and they had often been on my mind. I was happy to see at least one place and to meet one person who had responded to the inexhaustible needs of these children and had shown them that not everyone is an enemy.

4

January

In Pablo and Sophia's House

TODAY WAS FILLED with packing, saying goodbye, paying quick visits to people to say thanks, returning books, umbrellas, raincoats, and the many other little things that I had borrowed.

At eleven-thirty, we celebrated a liturgy with a few old and a few new students. Gerry McCrane was there with Antonio, his close friend. Happily, Lucha and Albina and the two cooks of the institute also joined. So here we were: five Bolivian women, one Bolivian man, a few Americans, two Irishmen, a Filipino, and a Dutchman. For some, Spanish was their only language. For some, Spanish was a second language. For others, Spanish was just becoming their language. And for a few, Spanish was the great unknown. So we made it a bilingual event with readings both in English and in Spanish and with a dialogue homily and prayers in whatever language the person most easily could speak.

All in all, it was a good last day in Bolivia. I spent a quiet evening with Gerry in his room and felt grateful for his friendship and generous hospitality. As I go to bed I can truly say thank you to the friends in the institute, to the Quirogas, to the Carmelite Sisters, and most of all to the Lord of all people who brought me here.

Saturday, January 2
Lima, Peru

Peter, Gerry, and Fran came with me to the airport to be with me at the hour of departure. Peter will soon start his work in Paraguay, while still suffering from the news that comes from Poland. Gerry will continue to work hard at the institute to make it more and more a center for missionary formation, and Fran will continue to explore pastoral work with the blind and will become an active worker in the parish of Cala Cala. They are three committed people whom I now know as true friends.

Now I am back again in the house where I lived for a week in October. The first person I met was Raymond Brown, the biblical scholar, who is here to attend the Faith and Order Conference of the World and Council of Churches. Next week he will come to the house to give a series of talks to the Maryknollers in Lima.

Sunday, January 3

This afternoon I had tea in downtown Miraflores (a section of Lima) with John and Kathy Goldstein. John is a Lutheran minister, Kathy is a nurse; and both are preparing themselves to work as Lutheran missionaries in Cuzco. Our conversation made me aware of how spoiled I am. I am living with a supportive missionary community, well-equipped to help newcomers in getting settled. But John and Kathy had to find their way into a new culture, a new country, and a new type of work all by themselves. They studied Spanish and Quechua in Cochabamba, and now are struggling to find their way to Cuzco. For the last two months, they have been trying to get through all the red tape to obtain permanent residency in Peru, to have their Land Rover fixed, to find good doctors for Kathy (who is expecting a baby in February), and to find an apartment in Cuzco. The months have been very tiring for both, but now it seems that they are ready to move from Lima to Cuzco; Kathy by plane and John with a friend in the Land Rover. Next Sunday, they hope to start their missionary work in Cuzco. "What are you going to do there?" I asked. "We don't know yet," John replied. "It is a totally new place for us. We have to see what others are doing there and see where we can fit in. Kathy can always find work as a nurse, but I, as a pastor, will have to wait and see what is the best way to start a Lutheran mission."

I suddenly realized how lonely they both must feel. Two young people, just out of school, in an unfamiliar country, sent to start a new mission. "It is so frustrating to have to wait so long to get anything done," John said. "Yes," Kathy agreed. "Especially since we are expecting our first baby in a few weeks. It would be so good to have a place that we could call home. Now we live in a small hostel and eat out every night in a different place."

When we said farewell, they said: "Be sure to come to Cuzco to see the baby!" After all I had heard about their struggle, I felt especially eager to celebrate their new joy with them. "You can expect me in Cuzco soon," I said. I feel it is a firm promise.

Monday, January 4

Today Claude Pomerleau and Don McNeill arrived. While I was at breakfast, Claude appeared. I knew he was coming, but somehow he surprised me, as he always does, with the easygoing, smiling way in which he walked into the house. Claude is a Holy Cross priest who teaches political science at Notre Dame University. We have been friends for many years, and whenever there is a chance to meet we grab it. Claude was asked to come to Chile for a month to explore the possibility of starting a Notre Dame extension program in Santiago. He is exceptionally well-informed about the social, economic, and political situation in Latin America. He has been central in the development of my interests here.

Around midnight Don, who heads the Center for Experiential Learning at Notre Dame, arrived. He has just spent two weeks in Chile visiting the Holy Cross Associates, laymen and laywomen who give two years of their lives to work in the missions. Don is a strategist and planner. Without his concrete recommendations and suggestions, I would never have come here. It was he who first suggested that I come to Peru, and he put me in touch with the Maryknoll community.

Claude and Don are close friends, and the idea of visiting me in Peru had captured their imagination. The three of us certainly have a lot to discuss. Yet, more important to me is the awareness of having two close friends who have come to help me start my new life.

Tuesday, January 5

At noon, Don, Claude, and I met Bob Plasker in downtown Lima. Bob, a Holy Cross priest and a close friend of Don's, works with a pastoral team in Canto Grande, a huge *barrio* on the outskirts of Lima.

What struck me most was the contrast between the two forms of ministry to which we were exposed. Bob took us to lunch in Le Sillon Missionaire, one of the most elegant restaurants I have ever seen. It is run by Les Travailleuses Missionaires de l'Immaculée (the Missionary Workers of the Immaculate Mother of God), a community of French women who have similar restaurants in Italy, Upper Volta, the Philippines, Argentina, and New Caledonia.

When we entered, we were greeted kindly by a tall, striking, black sister from Upper Volta who led us to our table and explained a little bit about their ministry. "We want to offer people a milieu where they can taste not only good food, but also something of true Christian hospitality." When I looked around, I soon realized that many bishops, priests, and religious people in Lima come there to enjoy this peaceful hospitality. The surroundings were pleasant. An old mansion with a lovely courtyard had been tastefully converted into a dining space, and while we ate a delicious lunch, baroque music filled the large area and gave us the impression of being transported from the busy streetlife of Lima to a peaceful garden. It was a form of ministry we had not anticipated but Claude, Don, Bob, and I felt grateful for this moment of luxury on our way to Canto Grande.

In Canto Grande, Bob showed us another type of ministry. It took us twenty minutes in a taxi to reach the center of the "desert-city." The word "desert-city" seems the best word to describe this huge new development at the outskirts of Lima; "About a hundred thousand people have come to live here during the last ten years," Bob explained. "Most of them came from the country, lived for some time with friends or relatives in town, and then settled here. You can see the different phases. First they build something like a hut of matted bamboo, and then, over the years, they start earning a little money. They buy bricks, build walls, and slowly transform their huts into small houses. It may take them many years to reach the luxury of a house. Sometimes a fire destroys it all. Fires are especially devastating when there is no water."

I kept thinking about a desert. Yellow sand was all you could see. Trucks, cars, and gusts of wind created a lot of hot dust. The dwellings lacked the two main commodities of modern living—electricity and running water. In front of most houses stone water containers were built to provide the families with washing and drinking water. Large water trucks came daily to Canto Grande to sell water. In many houses there were oil lamps or candles; but most people went to bed with the sun.

Bob and his fellow priests live in a small wooden house in the heart of Canto Grande. It is very simple, but with the help of some plants and a simple rug it looked quite cozy to me.

Bob's understanding of ministry was simply "living with the people, as the people." Instead of a church, he has used different places spread over a large area to celebrate Mass and to conduct other pastoral activities. There was a small pastoral center where the Sunday services are held and where the different work groups have their meeting spaces. The parish committee on human rights is very active and regularly publishes small folders on the rights and urgent needs of the people. On October 20, 1980, this committee, together with many other local groups, organized a march to the center of town to call the attention of the government to the serious problems of Canto Grande: health, energy, transportation, and education. On October 23, the Senate responded and declared the valley of Canto Grande a *zona de emergencia* (emergency zone).

Bob and his fellow workers see it as their main task to work with the people, to make them aware that the Gospel of Jesus Christ supports the poor in their struggle for basic human rights, and to join them in this struggle.

In the short time we were in Canto Grande, we met many good and generous people. They showed hope and a strong will to work for their future. When we walked home through the dark, guided by no other light than the moon, we were grateful to have been able to witness this ministry of solidarity.

Wednesday, January 6

Today Don, Claude, and I did some sightseeing in downtown Lima. One of the churches we saw was the Jesuit Church of San Pedro. A talkative Jesuit brother told us about the busy life of the parish. Daily Masses are celebrated at 7:00 A.M., 8:00 A.M., 9:00 A.M., 10:00 A.M., and every hour afterward until the final mass at 7:30 P.M. "Many people come here," the brother said. "And there are always long rows of people who want to go to confession." While we were standing there talking with the brother, people kept entering and leaving the church. It was clear that at this time of year the main attraction was not the confessional but the Nativity scene, built in one of the side chapels. It was quite a sight. Not only was there the manger with the child and his parents, but around it were landscapes with hills, rivers, waterfalls, and bridges. There were little village scenes with women washing their clothes in the river. There were large herds of sheep and llamas. There were houses in which the lights were going on and off. There were medieval castles and humble straw dwelling places. It was not surprising that many parents took their children there to see the Christmas event laid out in miniature in front of them. But this was not all. In front of a house in which the Angel Gabriel announced to Mary that she was going to become the Mother of God was an American police car, with a policewoman keeping an eye on Mary's house. "We put the car there five years ago," the Jesuit brother explained. "It gives a little touch of modern life. Jesus was born for all people and for all times, and in our time there are many police cars to protect us. We even have permanent police protection for the church." When we looked outside on the little square in front of the church, we saw indeed a white police car and two policemen watching the entrance of the church. It seemed, however, that the police car and the policewoman had not been enough to give the Christmas scene a contemporary flavor. This year a jet plane had been added to fly in circles above the Christmas landscape. By some ingenious mechanism the plane was able to come low and then pull up again, some-times coming quite close to the shepherds and the Magi, but never close enough to create an accident. "Some people feel that that plane is a little much," the brother said, "but others like it a lot. It is part of our time."

To me it all seemed a little strange, as it was so far from the world of Canto Grande, but it was a genuine expression of the mixture of the Indian, colonial, and technological worlds that underlies the predica-ment of Peruvian life. Piety and poverty, modern aspirations, realism and sentimentalism, humor and mystery—they all are part of the world of the Peruvian people who continue to celebrate the birth of their Savior.

Thursday, January 7

This morning Claude left for Chile and tonight Don went back to the States. It was good to be together, to deepen our friendship, and to reflect on the new directions our lives are taking. It is strange that after sixteen years of friendship we find ourselves together in Peru, a place none of us thought much about when we met for the first time at Notre Dame. It is a testimony to a radical change of thinking and feeling that has taken place in us all. It is a source of comfort to me to know that in the midst of our inner and outer changes, our friendship has grown. That offers hope for the future.

Friday, January 8

Four hundred and twelve years ago, on January 9, 1570, Servan de Cerezuela arrived in Lima to open a Tribunal of the Inquisition. My stay in Lima offers me my first direct confrontation with the reality of the Inquisition. The Inquisition in Lima was active over a period of two hundred and fifty years. Artifacts from its history are displayed in the Museum of the Inquisition, which I visited with Don and Claude. It shows large paintings of the autos-da-fé, displays lists with crimes and punishments, shows the dungeons in which the prisoners were held, and has a large torture chamber in which, with the help of lifesize mannequins, the visitor can witness the ecclesiastical cruelties of these days.

The museum, which is the only one in Lima where you can enter without paying, was set up to make a forceful anticlerical statement. The museum guard kept saying to us: "This was the work of the priests." All the torturers were dressed in Dominican habits. In one place we saw a plastic Dominican dismembering a prisoner stretched out on a table. At another place we met a Dominican forcing water into a prisoner's body, thus slowly choking him to death. In another scene a priest was flagellating a man, whose head was locked into a wooden block. Besides these cruelties we were exposed to a vivid presentation of hangings, feet burnings, and starvation, all executed by the "servants of God."

As the guard kept repeating that *"los curas"* (the priests) had done all this, Claude finally responded, "And today the military has taken over their job." He did not realize that just then a man in uniform had entered the museum and heard the remark. The man acted as if he had not heard but said politely: "Good afternoon."

Since my visit to this house of torture, I have been reading about the Inquisition. The evaluation of this shameful episode in the history of the Church varies widely. Henry Charles Lea writes, "The colony was kept [by the Inquisition] in a constant state of disquiet, the orderly course of government was well-nigh impossible, intellectual, commercial, and industrial development were impeded, universal distrust of one's neighbor was commanded by ordinary prudence, and the population lived with the sense of evil ever impending over the head of every one. That there was any real danger to the faith in Peru is absurd. Possibly the Tribunal may have been of some service in repressing the prevalence of bigamy among laymen and of solicitation among the clergy, but the fact that these two offenses remained to the last so prominent in its calendar would show that it accomplished little. In the repression of the practices which were regarded as implying a pact with the demon, the Inquisition may be said to have virtually accomplished nothing. It would be difficult to find, in the annals of human misgovernment, a parallel case in which so little was accomplished at so great a cost as by the Inquisition under Spanish institutions" (Frederick B. Pike, ed., *On the Conflict between Church and State in Latin America* [New York: Knopf, 1964], p. 52).

This evaluation stands in contrast with the evaluation of Salvador de Madariaga, who writes: "the Holy Office of the Inquisition kept its prestige intact with many of the learned, and its popularity alive with the masses, particularly in the capitals such as Lima and in Mexico, where its processions and autos-da-fé were eagerly awaited festivals. The auto-da-fé was above all a pageant of human drama and of colour—human drama because rich and poor alike, when guilty, could be seen under the eyes of poor and rich pass in the procession humbled and crushed under the weight of error and sin; colour because the ceremonies, processions, and settings were carefully staged sights, with the purple silk of the bishops, the black, white, and blue gowns of the monks, the scarlet velvets and blue damasks of viceroys and high officials. . . . The Inquisition was a part of that strange and wonderful life of the Indies, one of the rare periods of History which have succeeded in creating that elusive virtue—a style" (Pike, pp. 63–64).

Lea and de Madariaga are voices on the extremes of a wide spectrum of opinions about the Inquisition. Personally, I see the Museum of the Inquisition as a powerful reminder of how quickly we human beings are ready to torture each other and to do so often in the preposterous assumption that we are acting in the name of God.

Compared with the torture going on in many Latin American countries today, and compared with the thousands of people who have been mutilated and killed during the last few years, the victims of the Inquisition seem few. But the realization that the Church could encourage and participate in creating ways to cause an excruciating and slow death for those whom it considered dangerous, sinners, heretics, or apostates, can only be a reason for repentance and humble confession and a constant reminder that what we now condemn with strong voices was an intimate part of the Church's daily life only two centuries ago.

Saturday, January 9

Letters are gifts, often greater than the writers realize. Ever since I left the United States, I have experienced a deep hunger for lifegiving letters—letters from very close friends who have little to ask and little to inform me of, but who simply speak about bonds of friendship, love, care, and prayer. I am overwhelmed by a letter that says: "We think of you, pray for you, and we want you to know that we love you." I have never experienced the power of such letters as strongly as during these last months. They directly affect my spiritual, emotional, and even physical life. They influence my prayers, my inner feelings, and even my breathing and heartbeat.

"The Word was made flesh, he lived among us" (John 1:14). These words by St. John received new life for me during my last months here. A word of love sent to me by a friend can indeed become flesh and bridge long distances of time and space. Such a word can heal pains, bind wounds, and often give new life. Such a word can even restore a faltering faith and make me aware that in the community of love, the incarnation of the divine love can be realized wherever we are.

Monday, January 11

Yesterday Jim and Mary Ann Roemer arrived. Jim is dean of students at Notre Dame. He and Mary Ann are dear friends of Don McNeill, and they stopped by for a day on their way from Santiago to South Bend. Today Jim, Mary Ann, and I visited three of Lima's downtown churches. The manifold representation of the suffering Christ became an over-whelming impression. I saw many statues of Jesus sitting in a chair cov-ered with a velvet purple cloak, his head crowned with thorns, streaks of blood covering his face. I saw a painting of Jesus lying naked on the floor, his whole body covered with stripes from the flagellating whip. I saw one altar with a lifesize Jesus figure with the eyes of a man driven mad by torture. It was so frightening that I could not look at it longer than a few seconds. But most haunting of all was a huge altar surrounded by six niches in which Jesus was portrayed in different states of anguish: bound to a pillar, lying on the ground, sitting on a rock, and so on, always naked and covered with blood. All these niches were surrounded by rich golden ornaments—so much so that the whole wall became like a solid gold icon portraying the most abject forms of human suffering.

Men and women from all ages and backgrounds gazed at these mor-bid Christ figures, some kneeling, some standing, some with crossed fingers, some with their arms stretched out in a pleading gesture. This is the Christ the Spanish conquistadors introduced to the Indians. This is the Christ to whom the people of Peru have prayed during the last five centuries. This is the Christ to whom they bring their own pains and suffering.

Nowhere did I see a sign of the resurrection, nowhere was I reminded of the truth that Christ overcame sin and death and rose victorious from the grave. All was Good Friday. Easter was absent.

I asked a priest about all of this. "Yes," he said. "On Good Friday the churches are packed and thousands of people go to confession, but Easter here seems like a quiet, ordinary Sunday. This is a penitential people."

When we came to the third church, Mary Ann couldn't look at any more. The contrast between the abundance of gold and the tortured bodies of Jesus figures repulsed her. She left the church and waited outside until Jim and I had walked from altar to altar.

The nearly exclusive emphasis on the tortured body of Christ strikes me as a perversion of the Good News into a morbid story that intimidates, frightens, and even subdues people but does not liberate them. I wonder how much of this has also been part of my own religious history, although more subtly. Maybe deep in my psyche I too know more about the deformed Jesus than about the risen Christ.

Tuesday, January 12

At four o'clock in the morning, Jim and Mary Ann Roemer left the house to catch an early flight to Miami. Pete Byrne and I set our alarm clocks early so we could say goodbye. We both felt grateful for their visit and joyful to know them as friends.

This was Ray Brown's day. He gave two splendid lectures on the variety of Christian communities in the post-apostolic period. Ray carefully interpreted the post-Pauline literature (the pastoral letters, the letters to the Ephesians and Colossians, and the writings of Luke) in the morning, and First Peter, Matthew's Gospel, and John's writings in the afternoon. In a convincing and clear way, he presented us with the different styles of the common life at the end of the first century and showed us the various implications for our present-day ministry.

I had to come all the way to Lima, Peru, to hear Ray Brown, who was practically my neighbor in the United States. But it certainly was worth it. Ray made me aware of how much I had allowed the pastoral letters to determine my view of the Church, a church in which structure and good organization dominate. The church life as presented by the other biblical literature—more mystical, more spiritual, more egalitarian— had really never entered into my understanding of the Church during my formative years.

I hope and pray that those who prepare themselves for the priesthood will have incorporated more deeply and personally the different church styles that Ray presented today, and will give hope for an even more multiform life in the church.

Wednesday, January 13

Next week Pete Byrne is leaving for Hong Kong, where the regional superiors of Maryknoll will meet to report on the events in the different regions and to discuss issues of general importance for the society.

In preparation for his trip, Pete called the Maryknollers of Lima together. From this valuable meeting, I received an overview of the variety of missionary activities currently taking place in Peru.

Of most interest to me was the discussion about missioners participating in projects that were cosponsored by the Agency for International Development (AID). AID is a United States government agency that offers financial help to development projects in different countries. Obviously, such aid is given only when the project is in line with the general objectives of the State Department. It was clear from the discussion that Maryknoll did not in any way want its missionary goals to be connected with, or influenced by, the goals of United States foreign policy. Thus a strong statement was sent to the meeting in Hong Kong, declaring that the Maryknoll Missionary Society should not participate in any projects that received money from AID.

This important statement shows a growing hesitation on the part of U.S. church people to be connected with United States government policies. There was a time when being a good Catholic and being loyal to the U.S. government were closely connected. But today, being a Christian and being a loyal patriot are no longer necessarily the same, and the Catholic Church is less and less eager to identify itself with the American "cause." This is clear not only in the Maryknoll statement, but also in the recent statements of U.S. bishops concerning both United States foreign policy in Central America and the nuclear arms race.

It took a long time to move away from the "Constantinian connection," but the Reagan policies have certainly helped to speed up the process of disconnecting.

Thursday, January 14

Tonight I finally moved to Pamplona Alta. I have now been in Peru for twelve days, and I have needed all that time to get oriented, meet different Maryknollers, get a feel for the region, and organize my own affairs. It is good to move away from the comfortable American climate of the center-house into the Peruvian world.

Pete Ruggere drove me in his blue Volkswagen to my new living quarters with the Oscco-Moreno family. They are his neighbors, and with their help he has built a pleasant room on top of the roof of their house. The word "roof" is a euphemism since this house, like many of the houses in the area, is only half-finished. Construction continues at a variable rate depending on money, need, and time. My little room, therefore, might better be seen as the first room built on the second floor. Since nothing else is finished on the second floor, I have in fact a large terrace looking out over the many houses of the neighborhood. My room consists of four brick walls—painted pink ("the only color I had") by our neighbor Octavio—and a roof made of sheets of metal. There is a door and a window, but the wind and the dust have free access to my home since the builders left a lot of open spaces where walls, window, door, and roof meet. With virtually no rain here and with little cold weather, my small place seems quite comfortable and pleasant.

I often have thought about having a *poustinia* or small building for prayer on the marketplace, and this new place seems to be just that. It is like a monk's cell between a large sea of houses and people.

I was warmly welcomed by the downstairs family of Sophia and Pablo and their three children, Pablito, Maria, and Johnny. They all showed great kindness to me, and the kids were soon hanging on my arms and legs.

Pete Ruggere, Tom Burns, and Larry Rich live in the next house. There I can go at any time to wash, use the bathroom, eat, listen to music, or watch television. Their house is a section of the house in which Octavio and his wife and eleven children live. The space looks very small to me, and I wonder where and how they all live and sleep. But last night at ten o'clock nobody seemed to be sleeping. Kids of all ages kept walking in, out, and around, usually accompanied by a few dogs. Everyone is open, smiling, friendly, and obviously quite poor.

Friday, January 15

Today I came to know my new family a little better. I played with Johnny, Maria, and Pablito, took some photographs of them, let them show me the different neighborhood stores, and took them to Mass at night. I also talked a little with Pablo and his wife, Sophia. Pablo works as a butcher in the large market of Ciudad de Dios, and Sophia takes care of the family. The house consists of three dark rooms with walls of gray cement. One room functions as the kitchen, the other as the children's bedroom, and the third serves as living room, dining room, television room, and bedroom for Pablo and Sophia.

From talking with Pablo, I learned that the two most treasured items in the house are the television and the refrigerator. When I came home from Mass with the three children, Pablo was standing on the street corner talking with a neighbor. When he saw me, he said: "Father, we are talking about the robberies on our street. At night, robbers drive their cars up, climb on the roof, and enter the house from above. They are after our televisions and refrigerators. The few things we have, they try to take away from us! It is becoming an unsafe place here."

A noticeable fear could be heard in Pablo's voice. A little later Sophia joined in the conversation, saying: "Can you believe it? They steal from the poor, those *rateros*." For a moment, I thought that *rateros* meant "rats," but a rat is *una rata*. Usually *ratero* means pickpocket, but here it is used for thief.

The Oscco-Moreno family is poor, but not miserable. The children are well cared for, seem to be healthy, and are playful. Pablo has a job and seems to make enough to give his family the basics. The television and the refrigerator show that they make a little more than their neighbors. Their daily life is very simple. They seem to keep pretty much to themselves. Johnny is never far from his thirteen-year-old brother, Pablito, and always gives him a hand when they walk together. Maria, who is ten years old, spends more time with her mother. It is a simple, but happy family; but not without the fears and anxieties of most poor people. I do not think they are eager churchgoers, but the walls show many pictures of Jesus, Joseph, and Mary. I am glad to live with these people. They teach me about life in ways no books can.

Saturday, January 16

My home in Pamplona Alta is about a fifteen-minute walk from the church of Ciudad de Dios. When people say, "I am going to the city," they do not mean the center of Lima, but the place where the first invasion of poor people took place in 1954, and where Cardinal Cushing built the large church that is staffed by Maryknoll.

Tonight I walked to the church; and when I got there, I saw large groups of people in the parish office as well as in the church. The office was filled with people who came to register for baptism, first communion, or marriage; and the church was filled with parents, godparents, and children waiting for a baptismal ceremony. I attended the baptisms. At first, I thought that only babies were being baptized, but soon I saw teenagers walking up with their parents and godparents to the baptismal font. When people started to lift up these boys and girls like babies, "Padre Carlos"—the Maryknoller Charles Murray—told them that they could stand on their own feet and only needed to incline their heads to be baptized. Before doing so, however, Charles asked them some questions about their faith to make them aware that they were no longer babies, but could answer for themselves.

After Charles had baptized about twenty babies and children, Pete Ruggere walked up to him and said: "There is a wedding here at seven o'clock, and it is already ten past!" Ten minutes later, Charles had finished the baptisms and the church was again filled with the family and friends of the couple to be married. An hour later, another couple was married and the church filled anew with people. Meanwhile, the staff in the office was busy filling out forms, answering questions, advising about preparation for first communion and marriage, and trying to help with whatever problem came up.

To me it all seemed hectic, even chaotic. But for Charles, Pete, and Tom, the priests of Ciudad de Dios, it was just another Saturday night.

Talking about this seemingly busy parish, Pete said, "There are one hundred and twenty thousand people living in this parish. We reach only about 5 percent of them." There is room for at least ten churches within the boundaries of the present parish. Many invasions of people over the last thirty years have made this one of the most populated areas of Lima, and the long lines of people waiting at the parish office testify to the tragic lack of pastoral personnel and facilities in the "City of God."

Sunday, January 17

This morning at nine o'clock I celebrated the Eucharist in the Church of Ciudad de Dios and preached. Preaching for very poor people is an activity that forces you to be honest with yourself. I kept asking myself: "What do I really have to say to these people?" I had the feeling that they had more to say to me than I to them. I thought: "Who am I to think that I can say anything of value in this situation. I have never been poor, I have never had to struggle with survival as these people have, and I do not even know their language!" And yet I knew that I was here to preach and that none of my hesitations was a valid reason not to preach. That, I am sure, is part of the mystery of being sent. I prayed that somehow God would touch the hearts of the people through my own broken words.

The Gospel told the story about Andrew and another disciple of John who followed Jesus. Jesus said: "What are you looking for?" They said: "Rabbi, where do you live?" When Jesus said: "Come and see," they stayed with him. Later, Andrew shared what they had seen and heard with his brother Simon, and so Simon came to Jesus. This story offers three important verbs to reflect upon: to look for, to stay, and to share. When we search for God, stay with him, and share what we have seen with others, we become aware of the unique way that Jesus calls us. A vocation is not a privilege of priests and sisters. Every human being is called by Jesus in a unique way. But we have to be looking for God, we have to be willing to spend time with him, and we must allow others to become part of our spiritual discoveries. The three Spanish words— *buscar, quedar,* and *compartir*—helped me to articulate what I wanted to say.

I wanted to help the people realize that they are important in God's eyes, and that they are called as much as any other human being. I hope that—in between all my broken Spanish—people sensed at least that I took them seriously, and that God certainly does. But when I am honest

I have to confess that the youth choir with its liberation songs received a lot more attention that I did with my sermon. The powerful songs led by a fervent university student, Javier, seemed in this instance to express the spirit of the people better than the words of a foreigner.

Monday, January 18

Every day I see and hear a little more about the different forms of pastoral care in this immense parish. Today I saw the "parish kiosk" and "the library."

On Monday mornings from 9:00 to 12:00, Tom Burns goes to his little kiosk, which he built in one of the small markets in the parish. This market consists of about two hundred stalls where vegetables, fruit, and cloth are sold, and here people from the neighborhood come for their daily shopping. It is not a flourishing place. Since the vendors can only sell small quantities, their prices are high compared to those of the large market in Ciudad de Dios. Among all these little stalls, Tom has his *kiosko parroquial* (parish kiosk). With a smile, he tells me that his motto is: *"Aqui no se venden verduras, sino verdades"* ("Here we sell not vegetables but truths"). As we arrived at the *kiosko*, people greeted us with big smiles. Tom's first task is to unlock the place and open the wooden shutters. It looks just like a small newspaper stand, the only difference being that instead of buying newspapers, you can enter it and talk with a priest.

The loudspeaker of the market announces that "Padre Tomas" has arrived and welcomes visitors. It was a slow morning. One person came to talk about the first communion of his child. Another asked for help to get his daughter into high school, and someone else had marriage plans to talk about.

While Tom received his parishioners, I walked around the area with Sister Mary Kay, whom we met in the market. She offered to show me her library, a little old medical dispensary that was no longer used as such. "We had the building and wanted to put it to good use," Mary Kay explained. "We wondered if we could make it available to the schoolchildren, who have no books with which to study. We didn't realize that we had struck a pastoral gold mine. We often had wondered how to reach the youth, and we had not been very successful. But when we opened this little library, we suddenly found ourselves surrounded by hundreds of boys and girls eager to learn." It was a small operation, but very effective. Every day after school, the children come, take out the book that the teacher has recommended, and study it in the reading room. No book can be taken home; all the studying takes place in the library itself. The children themselves tell the staff what books they need most, and thus slowly a library has been formed geared to the needs of the children. History, geography, mathematics, and religion were well represented. There also were quite a few classic stories in comic strip form, which proved to be quite popular. The whole collection was kept in a small room and could fit on a dozen shelves, but more than a thousand young people are being helped by this mini-library.

I asked Sister Mary Kay, "How do students normally study?" She answered, "By taking notes in class and studying them. The children and the schools are too poor to have books. All education is note-taking." I asked again: "Was there any way for these kids to read books before this library existed?" "Yes," Mary Kay answered, "But they had to go to downtown Lima and stand in line for hours to use a book for awhile, and very few had the time, the opportunity, and the motivation to do so."

While we were talking, a group of teenagers was having a mathematics class in the reading room. Mary Kay told me, "Many students have problems with mathematics. So, during the summer, we hire a mathematics teacher to help the students catch up. It is a very popular class."

What most impressed me was the great eagerness to learn. Education was clearly seen as *the* way to get out of poverty and to move ahead in life. I could see on the faces of the students how seriously they took their classes. Keeping order was obviously no problem for the teacher.

"We never were fully aware of this need," Mary Kay said. "We have worked here for many years and only accidentally hit on this ministry. When we started this library, we wondered if anyone would use it. Now we have more than one thousand regular users, and we meet more young people than ever before. We are very excited about it."

As we walked back to the marketplace, we heard the loudspeaker announce a course for adults in Peruvian history: seven lectures and a trip to the anthropological Museum in Lima. Price: 100 *soles* (20 cents). "That is one of the courses we have organized. It is quite popular," Mary Kay said.

We found Tom alone in his kiosk reading a book about the Kingdom of God. It suddenly hit me that Tom and Mary Kay had given me a better understanding of Jesus' words, "The Kingdom of God is among you."

Tuesday, January 19

Tomorrow a two-day conference on El Salvador starts in Lima, organized by the Social Democrats. Although they are almost unknown in the United States, the Social Democrats are a powerful political force throughout Europe and the third world. There are more than seventy social democratic parties, and about twenty-five of these are exercising power—among them, the parties of Helmut Schmidt in Germany and François Mitterrand in France. The Social Democrats have nothing to do with the Communists, who look at them as nothing more than another form of bourgeois political liberalism.

All of the world's social democratic parties have joined together in an organization called the Socialist International. Under its president, Willy Brandt, it has made a great effort in recent years to give support to democracy and liberation movements throughout the third world. It supported, for instance, the Sandinista struggle against the dictatorship of Anastasio Somoza. In Europe and in many circles of the third world, the Social Democrats are well known and greatly respected. It is for these reasons that the Lima meeting is so important.

Some members of the United States delegation to the conference visited the parish this afternoon. Robert Drinan, S.J., former United States congressman; Joe Eldridge, director of the Washington Office in Latin America (WOLA); and Larry Burns, the key person of the Council of Hemispheric Affairs (COHA). WOLA and COHA are two highly regarded human rights organizations that work out of Washington, D.C. Regrettably, the visitors did not have enough time to come to my neighborhood, so I missed meeting them. Tom Burns, who will attend the conference as a representative of Maryknoll, showed them a little of Ciudad de Dios and answered some of their questions.

Wednesday, January 20

Can we truly live with the poor? Although I live with them and share their life to some extent, I am far from poor. During the noon hour, I walk to the rectory in Ciudad de Dios and eat a good meal prepared by a good cook, and one day a week I go to the Maryknoll center house in Miraflores to take a shower, sleep in, and have a day of relaxation.

So my living with the poor hardly makes me poor. Should it be different? Some say yes, some say no. Some feel that to be a priest for the poor, you should be no different from them, others say that such is not realistic or even authentic.

I have been here only one week, and thus am unable to have an opinion, but I know one thing: right now I would be physically, mentally, and spiritually unable to survive without the opportunity to break away from it all once in awhile. All the functions of life, which previously hardly required attention, are complicated and time-consuming operations here: washing, cooking, writing, cleaning, and so on. The winds cover everything with thick layers of dust; water has to be hauled up in buckets from below and boiled to be drinkable; there is seldom a moment of privacy, with kids walking in and out all the time, and the thousands of loud sounds make silence a faraway dream. I love living here, but I am also glad that I can escape it for two hours a day and for one day a week. Living here not only makes me aware that I have never been poor, but also that my whole way of being, thinking, feeling, and acting is molded by a culture radically different from the one I live in now. I am surrounded by so many safety systems that I would not be allowed to become truly poor. If I were to become seriously ill, I would be sent back to the United States and given the best possible treatment. As soon as my life or health were really threatened, I would have many people around me willing to protect me.

At this moment, I feel that a certain realism is necessary. I am not poor as my neighbors are. I will never be and will not ever be allowed to be by those who sent me here. I have to accept my own history and live out my vocation, without denying that history. On the other hand, I realize that the way of Christ is a self-emptying way. What that precisely means in my own concrete life will probably remain a lifelong question.

I am writing all this from my comfortable room in the center house in Miraflores, where I have a day off. I enjoyed my shower, I am glad to receive mail and have a dust-free desk on which to answer it, and I look forward to reading a book, seeing a movie, and talking to friends about religion, politics, and "home." But I am also happy that tomorrow I can return to Pablito, Johnny, and Maria and play with them in Pamplona Alta.

Thursday, January 21

The conference of the Social Democrats on El Salvador ended today. Tom Burns, who attended all the meetings as a Maryknoll representative, and Larry Rich, who attended as a journalist for *Noticias Aliadas* (Latin American Press), both felt optimistic about the strong statement issued against United States military intervention and against elections without negotiations. Moreover, a feeling emerged that this conference had created a powerful human rights platform in Latin America.

Friday, January 22

This afternoon Sister Pam and I visited several families with retarded children. Trained in special education, Pam has worked for many years with the physically and mentally handicapped.

Pam came to Pamplona Alta to continue the work that Sister Mariana had started. After many years of patient work, Sister Mariana had built a small school for children who need special education and had identified the families with handicapped children. While doing this difficult and often ungratifying ministry, she herself was fighting cancer in her own body. Finally, she realized that she was losing the battle and had to return to the United States. In July 1981 she died.

One of the consolations during her last months of life was that someone would continue her work. When Sister Pam arrived, she found a well-organized card system with all the names and addresses of the families who needed special attention.

As we walked through the sandy streets, Pam said: "I am only visiting those children who are too handicapped to be able to go to the school." We visited a twelve-year-old girl who is unable to speak, hardly able to walk, and totally dependent for all basic life functions on her mother and two brothers. We visited a little six-year-old boy, one of eleven children, who suffers from cerebral palsy and cannot speak. We visited a three-year-old boy who has regular convulsions and seems to be getting worse as he grows older. We visited an extremely retarded thirteen-year-old girl who, as a result of the dysfunction of her glands, had grown so fat that a huge chair had to be built for her. And so we went from house to house.

All these people lived in extreme poverty. Many of the dank, humid hovels looked worse than stables; they were filled with naked children and terrible smells, and lacked any sanitary facilities. In one house, a four-year-old retarded girl who refused to wear clothes kept ripping off any dress they tried to put on her. She was living naked on a cement floor surrounded by chickens and dogs, making strange, inarticulate noises.

"One of the problems I have," Pam said, "is to get the cooperation of the family in the treatment of these retarded children. It is so hard to convince the parents to do regular exercises with their children and thus to help them in the development of their muscles." I soon saw how right she was. When we visited an eighteen-month-old child with Down syndrome, we realized that the baby always lay on her back and was not developing the muscles necessary to lift her head, to reach out her arms, or to strengthen her legs. Pam said: "I keep telling her mother and older sisters to teach her to walk and to help her lift up her head, but they simply don't do it. Every time I come here, I find the little girl again on her back in bed. As you can see, she is less developed than her five-month-old brother. It is so hard to convince people that something can really be done for retarded children. Parents tend to give up soon and neglect their retarded children. They do not really believe that any help is possible."

My walks with Sister Pam gave me a glimpse of the larger dimensions of poverty. Poverty is so much more than lack of money, lack of food, or lack of decent living quarters. Poverty creates marginal people, people who are separated from that whole network of ideas, services, facilities, and opportunities that support human beings in times of crisis. When the poor get sick, have handicapped children, or are the victims of an accident, no help seems available. The poor are left to their own minimal resources.

It suddenly hit me how crucial it is for the poor to organize themselves into supportive communities. But for people who struggle day after day just to survive, little energy remains to build these necessary networks.

Saturday, January 23

Pam and I continued our visits today. In one house we met a little two-year-old girl whose face and left hand were terribly deformed as a result of a fire. While the mother was away from home, her bamboo-matted house caught on fire and the burning roof fell on the baby, who was lying alone on the bed. The doctors were able to save the child's life, but they did not perform surgery to restore her face and hand. The mother, an energetic and intelligent woman, went many times to the hospital to ask for further treatment but was sent back again and again with the message that there was no bed available.

Pam said: "When I saw this girl, I realized that a further delay of surgery would make it more and more difficult to restore her face and hand. So I went to a group of wealthy women in Lima who want to help poor sick children and pleaded with them to accept this child. They finally promised to take her on and now I hope that we can find a private clinic where surgery can be done. Without ample financial support, nothing is going to happen."

This seemed to be a typical story. Good medical care is out of the reach of the poor, and many poor people do not even try to find it. Often they do not have the time, the opportunity, or the transportation to go to a good hospital; and frequently they cannot pay for the medicines the doctors prescribe.

Parents simply do not have the time and energy to give the necessary attention to their handicapped child. In one of the houses we found a totally paralyzed three-year-old boy lying on his parents' bed. His little brothers and sisters were playing around the house. Both parents were absent. The father works from 7:00 A.M. to 11:00 P.M. on odd jobs to earn enough to keep his family alive, and the mother goes far distances every day to bring her husband his lunch and to do the necessary errands for the family. When Pam told the mother that she had to do daily exercises with her little boy to help him develop his leg, arm, and neck muscles, she simply said: "I cannot do it. I do not have the time for that work."

In another house, Pam had come across a fourteen-year-old boy, Alfredo, who had had meningitis when he was twelve and had been in the hospital for one year. He was partially paralyzed but had a good mind. Since he had come home, however, he stayed in bed watching television all day. He had become totally passive. Pam said: "It took me endless visits to get the boy to talk, to read, and to do some schoolwork." When Pam and I entered the house, he was sitting in a chair with a book. It was more than Pam had expected. With some difficulty, Alfredo talked with me. Together we read a story about David and Absalom and tried to discuss some of the questions at the end of the story. Alfredo had no difficulties in grasping the content of the story; but I realized that, without constant personal support, he would probably not be motivated enough to do regular homework. With both parents absent most of the time, it is unlikely that he will come far in developing his muscles as well as his mind.

Wherever we went, we came across similar situations: poor, overburdened people unable to give the members of their family the basic help they need and unable to afford the help that is available to the happy few.

Sunday, January 24

Today I became fifty years old. I am glad that I can celebrate this birthday in the parish of Ciudad de Dios and with my family in Pamplona Alta. I hope that by concluding here half a century of living, I am perhaps moving toward a new way of living and working in the future.

There were small celebrations at different moments during the day. Father Charles announced my birthday to the people in church at the nine o'clock Mass, which I celebrated. As a result, I received several hundred kisses and embraces from the people after Mass. At noontime Father John Eudes, the abbot of the Genesee Abbey, and Kay, Eileen, and Virginia, friends from New Haven, surprised me with their congratulations by phone. After dinner there was the traditional birthday cake with candles, and at 6:00 P.M. I brought a cake to my family to have a little *fiesta* with them. Pablito, Johnny, and Maria sang "Happy Birthday," I blew out the candle (which I had put into the cake myself), and Sophia made some coffee. Together we watched the cartoons on television, and Johnny beat me in a game of checkers.

Later Charles, Pete, Tom, Larry, and I went out for a pizza; and there Charles asked me the difficult question: "How does it feel to be fifty?"

"How does it feel?" It feels quiet and peaceful. I am here with good, simple, and affectionate people; I sense that God wants me to be here; and this fills me with a simple joy. The words of Paul to the Corinthians, which we read during Mass today, expressed my feelings very well: "Our time is growing short. . . . Those who mourn should live as though they had nothing to mourn for; those who are enjoying life should live as though there were nothing to laugh about . . ." (1 Cor. 7:29–30).

I felt a little of this "spiritual indifference." Within a few years (five, ten, twenty, or thirty) I will no longer be on this earth. The thought of this does not frighten me but fills me with a quiet peace. I am a small part of life, a human being in the midst of thousands of other human beings. It is good to be young, to grow old, and to die. It is good to live with others, and to die with others. God became flesh to share with us in this simple living and dying and thus made it good. I can feel today that it is good to be and especially to be one of many. What counts are not the special and unique accomplishments in life that make me different from others, but the basic experiences of sadness and joy, pain and healing, which make me part of humanity. The time is indeed growing short for me, but that knowledge sets me free to prevent mourning from depressing me and joy from exciting me. Mourning and joy can now both deepen my quiet desire for the day when I realize that the many kisses and embraces I received today were simple incarnations of the eternal embrace of the Lord himself.

Monday, January 25

This afternoon Betty Evans presented a lecture on the history of Peru, the first in a mini-course offered to the women of Pamplona Alta and organized by the women's commission of the Center of the People's Culture.

Betty Evans—a Peruvian teacher married to an Englishman—gave a lively presentation with slides about the formation of the Inca culture in Peru. The thirty or so women, who had come from different sections of Pamplona Alta to the public soup kitchen in the little market where Tom has his kiosk, showed great interest in Betty's talk and a strong desire to learn about their own past. Some came because their children had questions they couldn't answer, others because they simply felt a need to know more about their own history. Everyone came to meet other women and to become aware of common interests, needs, and roots. Betty designed the course to help the women understand better why they live the way they live, and what factors have played a role in the development of their present socioeconomic situation.

After the lecture, Mary Kay told me that when the children were asked to draw pictures of their families, many depicted the father drunk or fighting, and the mother doing all the heavy work. Mary Kay said: "Betty is going to talk with these children to get a better idea of the way they experience their parents." I began to see how a course for women about their own history could be an important tool in the slow process of human liberation.

Wednesday, January 27

Anyone who has lived awhile in one of the poor sections of Lima tends to warn visiting friends against robbers and pickpockets. "Do not wear your watch visibly on the bus, someone will rip it off;" "Be sure to have a second pair of glasses, someone might pull your glasses from your head to sell the frame;" "Do not let your purse hang loosely from your shoulders, someone might cut the straps and run away with all your money and your papers;" and so on. Such warnings can be heard every day, often coupled with dramatic stories to show that the warnings are necessary.

Today, however, I heard a story about the consequences not of carelessness but of hypervigilance. A nun who had lived in Lima for quite some time had a friend visiting her. One afternoon, when this friend wanted to go shopping in the market, her experienced host said: "Now, be careful on the buses and in the market place. Before you know it, they will grab your money, your purse, and your watch. Be sure to take your watch off and put it in your purse and hold your purse tight under your arm."

Thus warned, the sister went on her way. The bus was crowded as always, and she had to push her way into it, always conscious of the potential robbers around her. While the bus was moving, and the sister was holding on to the handle to keep her balance, she suddenly noticed her watch on the bare arm of a young man leaning against her.

Overcome by the awareness that after all the warnings she had not been able to avoid being robbed, and furious at the shameless thief, she screamed: "You stole my watch, give it back immediately." While saying this, she pulled out her pen and pushed it right into the man's cheek. The reaction was quick. The man, frightened by the aggressive nun, and realizing (without understanding her English) that she meant business, quickly took off the watch and gave it to her.

Meanwhile, the bus had come to a stop and this gave the sister the opportunity to get off immediately. She had become so nervous that her only desire was to get home. When she returned to her friend's house with her watch still tightly grasped in her hand, her friend said: "But how, in heaven's name, did this man ever get into your purse?" "I don't know," was the puzzled answer.

Then the sister opened her purse and found her watch tucked safely between her notebooks and papers. In total consternation, she cried out: "My God, now I have two watches—and one of them I stole!" Her hypervigilance had turned her into a robber.

Sometimes we may be more frightened of people than we need to be. Maybe on her next trip to the market, the sister should wear a watch on each arm so that at least one will be stolen.

Thursday, January 28

If anything has affected me deeply since I have been living in Pamplona Alta, it has been the children. I have realized that since my eighteenth year I have not been around children. The seminary, the university, and all the teaching positions that followed were the worlds of young adults, worlds in which children and old people hardly entered. Yet here I am surrounded by boys and girls running up to me, giving me kisses, climbing up to my shoulders, throwing balls at me, and constantly asking for some sign of interest in their lives.

The children always challenge me to live in the present. They want me to be with them here and now, and they find it hard to understand that I might have other things to do or to think about. After all my experiences with psychotherapy, I suddenly have discovered the great healing power of children. Every time Pablito, Johnny, and Maria run up to welcome me, pick up my suitcase, and bring me to my "roof-room," I marvel at their ability to be fully present to me. Their uninhibited expression of affection and their willingness to receive it pull me directly into the moment and invite me to celebrate life where it is found. Whereas in the past coming home meant time to study, to write letters, and to prepare for classes, it now first of all means time to play.

In the beginning, I had to get used to finding a little boy under my bed, a little girl in my closet, and a teenager under my table, but now I am disappointed when I find my friends asleep at night. I did not know what to expect when I came to Pamplona Alta. I wondered how the poverty, the lack of good food and good housing would affect me; I was afraid of becoming depressed by the misery I would see. But God showed me something else first: affectionate, open, and playful children who are telling me about love and life in ways no book was ever able to do. I now realize that only when I can enter with the children into their joy will I be able to enter also with them into their poverty and pain. God obviously wants me to walk into the world of suffering with a little child on each hand.

Friday, January 29

Charles, Tom, Pete, Sister Marge, and I went to the beach today. Charles explained: "When there are five Fridays in a month, we cancel our team meeting on the fifth Friday and go to the beach to swim and to have a good meal." We drove to Punta Hermosa, about a half-hour north of Lima. Huge waves came rolling up to the beach in rapid succession. Compared with the waves of the Atlantic Ocean, these waves were immense. It was great fun to try to "catch a wave" at the right time and to be carried in on its crest. I failed most of the time, and often found myself spinning under a wall of water, wondering where I would emerge. I found that not only the children but the waves of the Pacific have healing

power! They wash away my preoccupations and make me smile in gratitude to him who led his people through the Red Sea and the Jordan and
calmed the storms on the lake.

Saturday, January 30

Dust is probably my greatest physical problem here. Wherever I turn,
I encounter dust. Walking on the sandy street, I am always surrounded
by small clouds of dust, and when a car passes the dust becomes like a
heavy fog that vanishes only slowly. Everything in my room is covered
with a layer of fine dust. When I want to write a letter, I first blow the
dust away; when I want to drink tea, I have first to wash the dust off the
cup; and when I want to go to sleep, I have first to shake the dust from
the covers and the sheets. It settles in my hair, ears, and nose. It crawls
into my socks, shirts, and pants; and it creeps in between the pages of the
books I am reading. Since it is quite humid here, the dust sticks easily
to whatever it lands on. This gives me a nearly permanent desire for a
shower. Only the realization that the pleasure of feeling clean would
probably not last longer than five minutes has helped me to develop a
certain indifference to this dustbowl.

For the many people who like to keep their houses, their bodies, and
their small children clean and fresh-looking, dust remains a resolute enemy. The only hope is that the water pipeline that has recently been built
to Pamplona Alta will enable trees, plants, and grass to grow fast enough
so that within a decade its people will win the war against the dust.

Sunday, January 31

The Gospel of this Sunday touches a sensitive nerve in me. It speaks
about the authority with which Jesus speaks, heals, and exorcises demons. People who saw Jesus said: "What is this? A new teaching, taught
with authority!" When Jesus addressed the people, his words had healing
power and even were able to make evil spirits obey.

All of this stands in contrast to my own experience in preaching
here. I wonder if anyone is really listening, and I often experience my
words as totally powerless. This morning, while I was trying to say a
few things with conviction, I found myself face to face with a man who

was sound asleep. He was sitting in the corner of the first pew and kept reminding me, in his passive state, that my words had absolutely no authority for him.

The most important question for me is not, "How do I touch people?" but, "How do I live the word I am speaking?" In Jesus, no division existed between his words and his actions, between what he said and what he did. Jesus' words were his action, his words were events. They not only spoke about changes, cures, new life, but they actually created them. In this sense, Jesus is truly the Word made flesh; in that Word all is created and by that Word all is recreated.

Saintliness means living without division between word and action. If I would truly live in my own life the word I am speaking, my spoken words would become actions, and miracles would happen whenever I opened my mouth. The Gospel of today thus confronts me not so much with a question about pastoral tactics or strategy, but with an invitation to deep personal conversion.

5

February

An Inner and Outer Struggle

Monday, February 1

THE NIGHTS IN Pamplona Alta are filled with loud sounds. Until late at night, music from different parties pours through the many holes in my little room. Around 2:00 A.M., buses come to the neighborhood to pick up the merchants to take them to the warehouses where they buy the products which they will sell later in the day in the market. Since the people are afraid to wait outside of their houses with money in their pockets, the bus drivers blow their horns loudly to tell the people of their arrival. From 2:00 to 3:00 A.M., these loud sounds of the dilapidated buses fill the air. Shortly after 4:00 A.M., the roosters start their calls; and by 6:00 A.M. the bread-carrying boy blows his whistles to sell his fresh-baked loaves. Strangely enough, it is quite peaceful between 6:00 and 8:00 A.M. But then the huge loudspeaker of a neighboring school blasts the national anthem over the roofs and makes everyone part of the first instructions to the children.

Parties, buses, roosters, breadboys, and loudspeakers keep the sounds floating through the night and the early morning. During my first weeks here, I thought I would never get used to it; but now these sounds have become a familiar background noise that no longer interrupts my sleep, my prayers, or my reading, but simply reminds me in my roof-room that I am in the middle of a world of people who have to struggle not only hard, but also loudly in order to survive.

Tuesday, February 2

Today we celebrate the presentation of our Lord in the temple. I have been thinking about this mysterious event. Mary and Joseph took Jesus to Jerusalem "to present him to the Lord" and to offer the Lord the sacrifice of the poor, "a pair of turtledoves or two young pigeons." There in the temple they met two old people, Simeon and Anna, who sensed the sacredness of the moment and spoke words about the child that astounded his parents.

Every time I try to meditate on a sacred event such as this, I find myself tempted to think about it in an intellectual way. But today I realized more strongly than ever before that I simply have to be there. I have to travel with Mary and Joseph to Jerusalem, walk with them on the busy temple square, join the thousands of simple people in offering their simple gifts, feel somewhat lost and awed by it all, and listen to two unknown old people who have something to say, something that sounds very strange and even frightening. Why do I want more? Why do I want to add a comment to it all? It is as if I want to keep some distance. But the story is so simple, so crystal clear, so unpretentious. I do not have to do anything with it. I do not have to explain or examine these events. I simply have to step into them and allow them to surround me, to leave me silent. I do not have to master or capture them. I have only to be carried by them to places where I am as small, quiet, and inconspicuous as the child of Mary and Joseph.

Something of that happened to me as I went through the day. I kept seeing Simeon and Anna; and instead of disregarding them as two pious old church mice who disturbed me with their aggressive predictions, I sat down for a while and allowed them to speak and me to listen. I heard Simeon and Anna many times over during the day, and I suddenly realized that they have been trying to speak to me for a long time.

Wednesday, February 3

Writing letters has become extremely important for me during this long absence from home. I have discovered in myself a growing freedom to express to my friends my feelings simply and directly. A deep change is taking place in me as I write down what is most joyful and most painful for me. I find myself hardly interested in telling about the daily events of my outer life, but strongly compelled to share openly, even nakedly, what is happening within me. I no longer feel that I have anything to lose: all I have I can give. Writing letters is becoming a way of self-emptying, of being nothing more and nothing less than someone who wants to give and receive love. It seems that the poor people of Pamplona Alta have taught me this. They keep telling me without words: "All you have is yourself, so do not hide it from those you love."

Thursday, February 4

When I first came to Lima, Bill McCarthy invited me to visit his house in Andahuaylas. I met Bill for the first time a few years ago at Yale, when he spent a sabbatical year there. Bill McCarthy is a Maryknoller who spent most of his professional life teaching church history at the Maryknoll seminary in New York state. Although he entered the Maryknoll society to become a missioner, he found himself for many years teaching future missioners at home. But after his sabbatical at Yale, Bill asked to be sent to the missions. He went to Cochabamba for language training and after that joined Joe, a young Maryknoller, to start a new mission in Andahuaylas, a seven-year-old *barrio* in eastern Lima.

Today I saw Bill's new house and got some impressions of the neighborhood and the pastoral work Bill and Joe are developing. Ten years ago, Andahuaylas was still a large hacienda at the outskirts of Lima. Now it is a *pueblo joven* (young town) with hundreds of small houses under construction. It looks very much like Pamplona Alta but as yet has neither running water nor electricity. Most of the people try to earn their living as *ambulantes*, walking vendors in the market place.

Bill and Joe, with the help of Lucho, the catechist, are trying to develop small Christian "base" communities. They go around visiting people in their homes and encouraging them to meet regularly with people from their block, discussing common problems in the light of the Gospel, studying the Scriptures, and praying.

"How do you motivate people to form such a community?" I asked. Bill answered: "Well, we first explain to people that the Church started in the homes of people and not in church buildings. We read from the Acts of the Apostles and suggest that just as the apostles built the Church in the first century in the Middle East, so we can build the Church now, in the twentieth century."

It was an effort that required much patience and perseverance. "It is very slow work," Bill said. "The people who live here work long hours and when they come home from the market, they often are so tired that they do not have the energy to have meetings and to study and pray. On their few free days, they like to rest and play soccer. It is important for us to understand their condition." In addition to the different basic communities, which were slowly developing, Bill, Joe, and Lucho also started two liturgical centers for the Sunday Eucharist. One was in the chapel of the former owner of the hacienda, and the other was in an open lot that was set aside for the future church. Attendance was low: thirty people at one place, ten at the other. "We are just beginning," Bill said, "and we are still groping for the right way to be pastors here."

This short visit created in me a desire to learn how to build a church from the ground up, to let the people themselves give shape and form to their own Christian life. This approach is far from the old triumphalism of the gold-decorated churches in downtown Lima, far from the church of great visibility and power. A very humble and inconspicuous church builds upon the rock of faith, hope, and love.

Friday, February 5

Unexpectedly, I am experiencing a deep depression. Perhaps the days of friendly greetings and introductions have kept me on an artificial level of contentment that prevented me from acknowledging my deep-seated feeling of uselessness. The depression seems to hit me from all sides at once. I have very little strength to deal with it. The most pervasive feeling is that of being an outsider, someone who doesn't have a home, who is tolerated by his surroundings but not accepted, liked but not loved. I experience myself as a stuttering, superfluous presence and the people around me as indifferent, distant, cold, uninterested, and at times hostile.

The men, women, and children I see on the streets seem to be so far from me that I despair when I think of them as people to whom I am sent. I crave personal attention and affection. The life in a parish suddenly strikes me as cool, mechanical, and routine. I cannot find a person with whom I can go beyond asking informative questions. I desire friendships, a moment of personal attention, a little interest in my individual experiences. The world around me appears to me as a complex pattern of words, actions, and responses in which I am caught, an entrapping net of baptisms, weddings, masses, and meetings. Meanwhile, I keep hearing: "This is the way we do things here. You should just try to become part of it. If you have problems, just stay with it and you will find out that our ways are the best."

The fact that my feelings are so general and touch practically everything I see, hear, or do, shows that I am dealing with a genuine depression and not with critical observations. I have little control over it. It feels like a form of possession. I try to pray for deliverance, but prayer does not bring any relief. It even appears dark and frightening. What else can I do but wait?

Saturday, February 6

The emotions of loneliness, isolation, and separation are as strong today as they were yesterday. It seems as if the depression has not lost any of its intensity. In fact, it has become worse. My mind keeps asking: "Why does nobody show me any personal attention?" My sensation that my feelings, experiences, history, and character are irrelevant to the people I meet, and that I am primarily used as a body that can take over routine functions, keeps ripping me apart from the inside. What I am craving is not so much recognition, praise, or admiration, as simple friendship. There may be some around me, but I cannot perceive or receive it. Within me lies a deadness that leaves me cold, tired, and rigid.

I attended a small workshop given by Pete Ruggere and Tom Burns about the basic meaning of being a Christian, but little of what was said reached my heart. I realized that the only thing I really wanted was a handshake, an embrace, a kiss, or a smile; I received none. Finally, I fell asleep in the late afternoon to escape it all.

Sunday, February 7

In times of depression, one of the few things to hold onto is a schedule. When there is little inner vitality, the outer order of the day allows me to continue to function somewhat coherently. It is like a scaffolding put around a building that needs restoration.

I got up at 6:30 A.M. and assisted Charles in the 7:00 o'clock Mass. At 9:00 A.M. I celebrated Mass myself and gave a sermon. From 10:30 to 12:30, I wrote a few letters. After lunch, at 2:00 P.M., Tom took me to a little fund-raising fiesta in Los Angeles, one of the sections of Pamplona Alta. The small Christian community there wants to build a chapel and decided to have a mini-fiesta on one of the street corners. They had games to play and food to buy. I picked up Pablito, Johnny, Maria, and her little girlfriend so they could try out the food and the games. They had a good time.

At 7:00 P.M. I was back at the parish and attended a short meeting in which two couples who had just finished a marriage encounter were welcomed home by other couples. Around 9:00 Charles, Tom, Pete, Larry, Patricia, a visiting Mercy Sister, and I went out to have a pizza. At 11:00 I was back home. I prayed my evening prayers and went to bed. The events of this "uneventful" day kept me mentally alive. I feel I am simply waiting for the day and the hour that the cloud of depression will pass by and I can see the sun again.

Monday, February 8

Today a two-week summer course in theological reflection began in downtown Lima. It is the twelfth time that this course, inspired and directed by Gustavo Gutiérrez, has been held. It is one of the most significant yearly events in the church in Lima. This year, three thousand "pastoral agents" are participating. People come not only from all the districts of Peru, but also from Chile, Brazil, Colombia, Ecuador, Paraguay, Uruguay, Argentina, Panama, and Nicaragua. It is a young, vital, and enthusiastic student body.

The summer course has three levels. The first level is an introductory theology course. The second and third levels have different emphases each year. This year, the second-level course deals with Christology and the third-level course with Spirituality.

I decided to take the course on Spirituality. From 3:00 to 5:00 P.M. there are discussion groups, and from 5:30 to 8:00 P.M. lectures. Gustavo Gutiérrez gave the first two lectures tonight. He discussed Christian spirituality under three headings: (1) living according to the Spirit; (2) the encounter with Christ; and (3) a global way of life.

Gustavo is a lively teacher. Holding a microphone in one hand and gesturing vigorously with the other, he takes his audience through theological hills and valleys and shows one fascinating panorama after the other. Impatiently, he shuffles his papers and complains that he cannot say it all in a few hours. He gives the impression of a man who has an enormous treasure to share and is continually frustrated that he cannot show his gifts all at once. But in a short time he is able to give his listeners a desire for theological understanding, offer them challenging perspectives, and make them aware of the privilege of being a Christian today. One of the points that stuck with me was his view on the interior life. The interior life, Gustavo said, does not refer to the psychological reality that one reaches through introspection, but is the life lived free from the constraining power of the law in the Pauline sense. It is a life free to love. Thus the spiritual life is the place of true freedom. When we are able to throw off the compulsions and coercions that come from outside of us and can allow the Holy Spirit, God's love, to be our only guide, then we can live a truly free, interior, and spiritual life.

Tuesday, February 9

Gustavo's lecture today was entitled "The Journey of a People in Search of God." It was a brilliant treatment of a spirituality of leaving, walking, and entering: the people of God are called to leave their situation of slavery and walk through the desert in order to enter the land of freedom, where they can own the land and live in justice and peace.

In the light of many biblical texts, Gustavo explored the meaning of this journey of freedom. His main assertion was that the search for God *is* the search for freedom, and that the search for freedom *is* the search for God. Many people who are deeply involved in the struggle for water, for light, for schools, and for health care do not perceive this as a search for God. And many who attend churches, walk in processions, and bless their houses with holy water do not experience this as part of a struggle for freedom. This is not uncommon. Even the Hebrews who left Egypt did not fully understand the meaning of the events in which they were participating. It is precisely in the reflection on the events of the people that the search for God and the struggle for liberty are connected and can deepen each other.

Of particular importance to me was Gustavo's notion that the journey of the people is not a journey from nothing to something, but from something to something. When we speak about a movement from slavery to freedom, from scarcity to possession, and from exploitation to justice, we should not think and act as if freedom, possession, and justice are only on one end of the polarities. In fact, in Egypt there existed freedom, possessions, and justice. That is why at times the Hebrews wanted to return to Egypt, and that too is the reason why a desire for full freedom, possession, and justice could grow. You can only desire what you already know or have in some measure.

This, therefore, also means that the search for God is a search for him whom we have already met, and who has already shown us his mercy and love. The desire for God makes us aware that we already know him.

For me, these thoughts are important because they point to a ministry that first of all recognizes the gifts of God that are already present. It is by acknowledging these gifts and lifting them up as signs of God's presence in our midst that we can start leaving, walking, and entering. The journey is not a journey of despairing people who have never seen God nor tasted freedom; rather, it is a journey of hopeful people, who know that God is with them and will lead them to a freedom of which they have already tasted the first fruits.

Wednesday, February 10

I continue to be impressed by the thousands of people who are actively participating in the summer course. They are not only people from all parts of Latin America, but also from very different stages and walks of life. There are quite a few priests and sisters, mostly Americans, British, and Irish; but the majority of this assembly is made up of people who have been born and raised in the poor *barrios* and have become active pastoral agents in the process of liberation. They know their own people and they have learned to think with one eye on the Gospel and one eye on the plight of their compatriots. In the Latin American Church, the people themselves are showing the direction in which to go. They are open and hospitable to strangers who want to participate, but the struggle is theirs and they themselves provide the leadership.

Many of these people are very young. They work in their different districts as catechists, social workers, project coordinators, and so on. All of them are steeped in the Bible; with it they live and struggle. They have come to think of themselves as the people of God called to the promised land. They all know it will be a long, arduous, and often painful journey; but they also know that no worldly powers can make them give up their struggle and return to the state of submission and resignation from which they came.

In his lecture today, Manuel Diaz Mateos, S.J., developed a spirituality of the marginal person and the stranger. He pointed to Abel (the weak one), Noah, Job, Ruth, the innocent children, the widows, the publicans, and the Samaritans as proof of God's special love and attention for those who live on the periphery of society and who are considered weak. For me, this presentation opened up a vision of ministry that I keep losing, although I am constantly called back to it. It is the vision that ministry means first of all searching for God where people are lost, confused, broken, and poor. Often I have gone to such people to bring them back to God, to the sacraments, and to the church. But that is acting and living as if God is where I am, and as if my first task is to bring others to my place. When, however, God is with the poor and marginal, then I have to dare to go there, live there, and find him there. I now realize that I can be with people without having to make them think my thoughts and say my words. I can be free to listen and slowly to discern where God shows his merciful face to me.

Thursday, February 11

Every day of the summer course, the students meet for two hours in "commissions," discussion groups in which the lectures of the previous day are discussed and appropriated. I am a member of a discussion group with twenty participants. We are a very interesting little community. The majority are Peruvians, but there are two Chileans, a Uruguayan, a Nicaraguan, a Swiss, and myself. All of these people are active in some form of pastoral care, and most of them are leaders in their own communities.

The discussions are extremely poignant, with little abstract thinking going on. People constantly test the ideas presented in the lectures against their own daily experiences and try to let these experiences be their source of ongoing theological reflections. Some of these experiences are harsh. They are experiences of harassment, exploitation, imprisonment, and torture. Everyone is aware that the road to liberation is rough and uncharted, asking for a commitment that goes as far as the willingness to sacrifice one's life. It is overwhelming for me to hear these young men and women speak so directly and articulately about their love for Jesus Christ, their desire to give everything to the realization of his Kingdom, their willingness to be and remain poor with the poor, and their joy to be chosen for this great task of liberation. There is little sentimentality and little piety. The word that dominates all the discussions is *la lucha*, the struggle.

Today the main topic was prayer. Within a few minutes, the growing charismatic movement (Neo-Pentecostalism) became the main subject. Most participants considered the charismatic movement as appealing primarily to the middle-and upper-class youth; as offering a spiritual experience without social consequences; as closely linked to other conservative organizations such as the *cursillistas*, as a spiritual weapon in the hands of the oppressing classes. People didn't hesitate to say that prayer, as seen and practiced in many charismatic groups, was not Christian prayer since it does not come from nor lead to the *lucha* for the liberation of God's people.

Reflecting on this discussion, I feel quite uncomfortable. The sweeping generalizations about the charismatic movement seem to deny the need of many people to find a still point in their lives where they can listen to the voice of God in the midst of a sad and war-ridden world. This desire for inner tranquility and the direct experience of God's Spirit can become a form of escape from the struggle for liberation, but it does not have to be that way.

During my one-semester stay in Rome, I participated actively in a charismatic prayer group at the Gregorian University. In many ways it kept me spiritually alive during that time. I never experienced this prayer group as an escape mechanism, but as a source of spiritual revitalization that freed me from many fears and compulsions and allowed me to dedicate myself more generously to the service of others.

I even have the feeling that those who want to be active in the struggle for freedom for a lifetime will need an increasingly strong and personal experience of the presence of the Spirit of God in their lives. I would not be surprised if, within a few years, a search for new disciplines of prayer were to occupy the minds of many Christians who struggle with the poor for liberation. I hope that the division between the charismatic movement and the liberation movement will not grow so wide that it creates a *lucha* within the Christian community.

Friday, February 12

The lectures given yesterday and today were disappointing; they consisted of many words but few connections with daily experiences. One speaker spoke eloquently about compassion as the most important attribute of Jesus, and another talked about the centrality of contemplation in the history of Christian spirituality. Each covered a huge area of Christian thought, but neither was able to touch his audience. It was sad to see how everyone had a hard time staying awake during lectures on such life-giving realities as compassion and contemplation.

The discussion group showed a lot more vitality. We were asked to list core traits of a Latin American spirituality. Fifteen aspects of Christian spirituality were written on the blackboard and everyone was asked to choose three that were most important for Latin America today. Everyone agreed that "compassion" had too many passive connotations. Some argued that, in a world in which the largest part of the population is oppressed and exploited, the word compassion sounds too personalistic and suggests a sentimental acceptance of the status quo. However, when people started to choose the three most important traits, many still considered compassion an essential quality in the struggle for liberation. After much discussion, we came to the conclusion that every

Christian is called to a radical commitment to establish the Kingdom of God on earth, and that for the Latin American Christian this means a compassionate struggle to liberate the poor. Everyone stressed that this formulation was inadequate and did not cover the whole of a Christian spirituality for Latin America, but nobody denied that this formulation captured the main thrust of the "New Church."

I was struck by the repeated use of the word *lucha*. This word is used to counteract a passive and fatalistic stance towards the misery of the masses and to stress the urgency of an active—even aggressive—involvement in the war against poverty, oppression, and exploitation. However, I tried to locate a concrete idea of this *lucha* in the daily life of the Christian community, and of the Christian strategy of this struggle. In the absence of such a concrete idea and strategy, there is a danger that the struggle for the full liberation of the people will be narrowed down to a "fight for rights." This type of *lucha* can easily lead to a fanaticism no longer guided by the joy and peace of God's Kingdom, but by a human instinct seeking to replace one form of oppression with another.

Saturday, February 13

Over the week, my depression has worn off a bit. It has not been lifted or healed, but it has lost its most painful edges in the midst of the summer course. I was helped by the insight that I had to move directly and aggressively in the direction I want to go. Waiting to be shown the best people to meet, the best places to visit, the best events to become part of, only feeds my depression. I am sure that I will find my direction in life when I search actively, move around with open eyes and ears, ask questions, and—in the midst of all that—pray constantly to discover God's will. The Lord searches for me, I am sure, but only when I search for him too will I encounter him and will his word for me become clear. Every time I slip into another depression, I notice that I have given up the struggle to find God and have fallen back into an attitude of spiteful waiting.

Sunday, February 14

In Peru, people celebrate Carnival by throwing water at each other. Innocent passersby are often surprised by a shower, and buses and cars with open windows make attractive targets for water-throwers. A few years ago, this was causing so many accidents that the government decided that the only Carnival days were the four Sundays of February, disregarding the date of Ash Wednesday.

My friends had instructed me to wear old clothes on these wet Sundays. Wherever I went today I saw little groups of teenagers on the street corners ready to attack any dry person with anything that can hold water: balloons, pots and pans, and even large buckets. I also noticed eager water-throwers perched on the roofs to surprise people entering and leaving the buildings. Some people simply decide to stay home during Carnival. One of the parish choirs decided not to sing today, because they don't like to sing in church while soaking wet.

I took a bus to Las Flores, a large *barrio* on the southern outskirts of Lima, to visit a community of English Benedictines. Unlike many other buses I had ridden on here, there were few broken windows on this bus, but at every stop people getting on or off were thoroughly drenched. Everyone seemed to enjoy the game, although even well-dressed people looked like drowned cats as they stepped on the bus. The driver tried to escape the water-throwing youths by stopping between official stops to let people off and by letting people on at any place they raised their hands. He played the game with a good spirit. He lost a few and won a few.

Most people, from very young to very old, take it all with good-natured laughter. "As long as they don't put paint in the water," a woman said to me, "it's a lot of fun. It is so hot here anyhow that you are dry again before you are home." I made it to the monks moist but not wet.

Monday, February 15

During the last few years, I have received several letters from Marist Sister Teresa asking for money to help some Peruvian ex-prisoners. Today Sister Teresa took me to Lurigancho, the huge prison where she works. It is hard to describe what I saw, heard, and smelled during my four hours in Lurigancho. I want to record at least some of my impressions.

Lurigancho is a world within a world. About four thousand men live inside a small area surrounded by huge walls and watchtowers. They are there for reasons varying from murder to buying cocaine on the street.

The majority of these men have never been sentenced and have no idea when their case will come to court or how long they will have to stay behind those walls. Some have been there for a few months, others for more than seven years; some are there for the first time, others old regulars for whom Lurigancho has become a second home. Some seem friendly and gentle, others silent and menacing.

Lurigancho impressed me as a microcosm of the extremes in life. Within the prison I visited several small libraries with helpful librarians. Everywhere were men weaving baskets, playing ball, sleeping in the sun, and standing on corners talking together. Less visible but no less real are the knives, guns, and drugs hidden in the corners, closets, and cells. What do these men do? For most of them there is no work, no way to keep busy except weaving baskets. Yet much activity goes on. Gangs fight each other, prisoners kill each other, groups pray together, men study together. There are meek, quiet, and unassuming people; there are also aggressive and dangerous men who are feared, avoided, or kept under control.

What struck me first was the enormous chaos. Once we had made our way through the gates, it seemed that all discipline was gone. Since most of the thirteen huge cellblocks were open, we could walk freely in, out, and through. Prisoners were walking around with little restriction and behaved as if they were in charge. Most of them were naked from the waist up; many just wore swimming trunks. Some showed big scars on their bodies, the result of self-inflicted cuts that had put them in the hospital and allowed them to escape from torture. The food consists of bread in the morning, rice and beans in the afternoon, and soup in the evening. It is brought in huge containers and put on the patio of the cellblock for anyone who wants it. But many feed themselves in other ways. They get money from their visitors and buy food from the different black market stores or bars.

There is as much horror, cruelty, and violence as there is friendliness, human play, and simple village life. One of the most surprising things to me was that all the prisoners can receive visitors two times a week. During visiting days the population practically doubles. Women come with large baskets of food, some to bring it to their imprisoned relatives, others to sell it to those who have money. One cellblock looked like a lively market place. There were different food stands, and all over the place groups of people were sitting on the floor, talking or playing cards. It was not all that different from the marketplace in Ciudad de Dios.

Prisoners can take their wives or girlfriends to their cells with them. Cellmates simply stay away for a few hours, and when one of them has a visitor the favor is returned. Most prisoners live together according to the area of town or the district they come from. The nature of their crime seems to have little to do with the company they keep; first offenders often live together with experienced killers.

Often cellblocks fight with each other. Walls get broken down, windows smashed, and when there is enough alcohol around, people get wounded or killed. Once in a while things get so far out of hand that the *guardia republicana*, the police force, moves in. On February 2 the police carried out a wild and indiscriminately brutal assault on one cellblock. Tear gas was used and random shooting took place. During the four-hour rampage prisoners were severely beaten, tortured, and wounded. When it was all over, three men were dead.

While talking about all this, one of the prisoners brought me to a little flower garden he had carefully cultivated. Proudly he showed me the lovely roses that had just come out. It was hard for me to put it all together. But that is Lurigancho.

On our walk, we passed a pavilion that we could not enter. "That is where the homosexuals live together," one of my prisoner-guides told me. I saw a lot of prisoners hanging around the building and gazing through the fence into the open lot. I suddenly felt as though I were at a zoo. One prisoner said: "Look, those are the gays." It was clear to me that they were really talking about transvestites. There is a lot of sex between men in Lurigancho, but in this section lived the real "queens," who had asked to be together to have some degree of freedom from harassment. They were locked up by their own wish more than by that of any prison authority. I have never seen humans look at caged people in such a way. It made me feel something very dark and evil.

Finally, Teresa led me to the pavilion of the foreigners. It was located at some distance from the other cellblocks we had just seen. When we went in, I had the strange sensation of walking into an exclusive country club. On the open patio, blond young men in tiny swimming suits were playing racketball or sunbathing on a towel. Their tanned and well-fed bodies were a stark contrast to the dark, scarred bodies of the poor Peruvians I had just visited. These were prosperous, middle-class Europeans, Americans, or Australians who came from a world light-years away from the dark, dirty cells of the other pavilions. A minute after I entered, I met a young Dutchman who was glad to meet a fellow countryman and to speak his mother tongue. He gave me the grand tour. The main living space consisted of a huge, open hall where people spent most of their time. The atmosphere was that of an exposition hall. In the center stood workbenches where people could do a little carpentry. Scattered about were stands where food and drinks were sold, and all over the place people were playing cards, chess, and checkers. The place looked clean and well-kept—more like an amusement park than a prison. My Dutch guide showed me his bedroom. It was a small wooden room with two bunkbeds. "I paid $200 for it," the Dutchman explained. "You can get anything here when you pay for it." He introduced me to his roommate, a tall, good-looking American from Washington, D.C. "It doesn't look too bad here," I said. "Oh no," they responded. "In fact it's quite all right here, except that you're locked up and don't know for how long."

I soon found out that they both were arrested because of drugs. "I sold some drugs to an undercover policeman, and that got me here," the Dutchman said. As he and his American friend talked more, I got the picture. Since they had been arrested on drug charges, they now have to buy their way out, and legal help is extremely expensive. Every step of the way can cost a fortune. But money came from Holland or the United States through the embassies. The American was lucky to have his wife in Lima, who could visit two times a week and bring in all the food they wanted. "We don't touch the prison food," the Dutchman said. "My American friend's wife brings us steaks and good soup, and we make our own meals." I asked how they spend their time. "We read a lot and play games, talk and sit in the sun," they said. "And here we can get any drugs we want."

I had never expected this strange island of decadence in the center of the Lurigancho prison. If I ever saw discrimination, it was here. The poor lived in miserable poverty, the wealthy built their own country club, and these two worlds lived side by side behind the prison walls.

But this living side by side was not as simple as it might seem. At night the foreigners had to protect their domain against attacks from the poor pavilions. My hosts explained: "We had to organize our own guard to keep the others from our roof and to prevent them from breaking in and stealing our stuff."

When we were let out through the heavy gates and stepped onto the bus to go home, I knew that only a very simple, pure, and holy person would be able to work with these men for any length of time. Just being there for four hours had made me see that Teresa must be such a person. She moved in this world without fear, open, practical, unsentimental, and with a deep sense of God's love. She saw it all clearly, but was not entangled in it. The men knew that she was one of the few who had no second motives. She was just there to be of help and that was all. Surrounded by the complexity of the dark world, the simple love of God can easily be discerned.

Tuesday, February 16

Today I went to the airport to pick up some galley proofs that were sent to me by my publisher through one of the airlines. Naively, I thought that it would be a matter of a few minutes. But when I got to the cargo area I received some papers to take to a network of offices, officials, cash registers, and desks that was more complex than I have experienced before in my life. Every time I had made it through one hoop, another awaited me. A sea of people, as nervous and confused as I, added to the endless waiting. Meanwhile, young boys offered to do it all for me for some money, trying to convince me that they knew the right way to the package. However, I clung to my growing stack of documents with the anxiety of a man whose life is in danger. Finally, after three hours, I made it to the warehouse where I could see the package. An hour later, a man from customs came with some more documents and let me open the package and identify the galleys. For a moment I thought that now I could take them home with me, but I soon found out that I was only halfway through the process. Two more payments had to be made, and at least three more offices with long waiting lines had to be visited. At that time, I gave in to the boys and gave them the money to do the work for me. They took my papers and gave me their I.D., and I left the airport with their promise that tomorrow morning I would get my package.

David Ritter, a Jefferson City, Missouri, priest who has worked in Peru for three years and who drove me to the airport for this "quick errand," prevented me from going crazy in the midst of it all. He smiled and laughed about it and explained how this way of doing things gave work and money to many Peruvians, and gave me a chance to practice my patience.

I am amazed how hard it is to just take things the Peruvian way, use my time to talk with people, practice my Spanish, and simply flow with the stream. After all, I might profit more from waiting than from being waited on. My frustration, anger, anxiety, and impatience, however, clearly showed me how far I truly am from enjoying solidarity with the poor!

Wednesday, February 17

After two more hours of running from office to office, talking to an endless succession of people, and paying more tips, I finally got my package. Then I returned to the course on spirituality and listened to Gustavo Gutiérrez's lecture on the "traits of a contemporary spirituality in Latin America." It was the most impressive presentation of the course so far, and it brought together many of the themes that have occupied our minds during the last ten days.

Gustavo stressed the "eruption of the poor into the history of Latin America." The suffering poor have become the pastoral agents who point to a new way of being Christian, a new spirituality, characterized by a call to conversion not only of individual people, but of the church as a whole. This conversion promises a way of living in which effectiveness is sought in a climate of grace. Such a climate allows us to experience a real joy that comes forth from suffering, helps us to live as "spiritual infants" with the poor while fighting against poverty, and makes it possible to find freedom in a communal life. Although all of these are among the classical themes of a Christian spirituality, they have found new articulation and meaning in the context of the eruption of the poor.

What struck me most was Gustavo's ability to integrate a spirituality of struggle for freedom with a spirituality of personal growth. He placed great emphasis on the importance of personal friendship, affective relationships, "useless" prayer, and intimate joy as essential elements of a true struggle for liberation.

The method Gustavo used was of special interest to me. As the source for his spirituality, he used documents that came forth from the suffering church in Latin America. A text written by a Christian community in Lima, declarations by the bishops of Guatemala and Chile, sermons of Bishop Romero of El Salvador, letters by Rutilio Grande, Nestor Paz, and Louis Espinal, and statements by the mothers of the "vanished ones" all formed the sources from which Gustavo developed a spirituality for Latin America. It was a powerful example of reflection on the suffering experienced in persecution and martyrdom. I was not surprised, therefore, with the warm and enthusiastic reception that Gustavo's vision met. He is a genuine theologian, a man who breaks the bread of God's word for thousands of people and offers hope, courage, and confidence.

Thursday, February 18

What does it mean to live a religious life in Latin America? During the last months I have often asked myself: Would it be possible to live with a small group of dedicated people in the midst of a *pueblo joven* and practice there the disciplines of prayer and meditation in such a way that the group would become a center of hope for the neighborhood?

What I see now are many dedicated and generous people involved in different projects. They are very busy, distracted, pressured, and restless, and often very tired. They hardly have time and space for each other, let alone for spiritual reading, theological reflection, sharing of religious experiences, mental prayer, the liturgy of the hours, or any other religious practice.

But how would it be if, in the midst of the very poor, a small group of men and women created a space for people to celebrate God's presence? How would it be if, instead of running in all directions, these men and women could draw others into prayer, silence, reflection, sharing of experiences, and singing God's praise? Maybe it is just a romantic dream, but it is a dream that continues to press itself on me.

Friday, February 19

This was the last day of the summer course. At seven-thirty, Bishop German Schmitz celebrated a festive liturgy with the three thousand students and teachers of the course. There was a general mood of gratitude. All the people I spoke with communicated a real excitement about having been part of this event and a desire to go back to work and share with others the new insights and experiences that the course had offered.

Among the hundreds of ideas that passed through my mind in the past days, one in particular has stayed with me. It is the simple thought that true theological reflection can convert a paralyzing experience into an experience of hope. That seemed to me what this course had done for many. Most of the students work with the poor, often in depressing, discouraging, and even agonizing circumstances. The reflections of the course gave us a consciousness of a divine and liberating presence in the midst of it all and freed us from fatalism and despair. We came to experience that agony really means struggle, and that God is in that struggle with us. And so a new joy could grow, and we could become aware that it is a privilege to work with the poor and suffer with them for a new world.

Thus the final liturgy could be a genuine celebration, a lifting up of God's presence among us and among the poor, and an expression of gratitude for what we had seen with our own eyes, heard with our own ears, and touched with our own hands (1 John 1:1).

Saturday, February 20

Gratitude is one of the most visible characteristics of the poor I have come to know. I am always surrounded by words of thanks: "thanks for your visit, your blessing, your sermon, your prayer, your gifts, your presence with us." Even the smallest and most necessary goods are a reason for gratitude. This all-pervading gratitude is the basis for celebration. Not only are the poor grateful for life, but they also celebrate life constantly. A visit, a reunion, a simple meeting are always like little celebrations. Every

time a new gift is recognized, there are songs or toasts, words of congrat-
ulation, or something to eat and drink. And every gift is shared. "Have a
drink, take some fruit, eat our bread" is the response to every visit I make,
and this is what I see people do for each other. All of life is a gift, a gift to
be celebrated, a gift to be shared.

Thus the poor are a eucharistic people, people who know to say
thanks to God, to life, to each other. They may not come to Mass, they
may not participate in many church celebrations. But in their hearts they
are deeply religious, because for them all of life is a long fiesta with God.

Sunday, February 21

After more than a month in Pamplona Alta, I have come to believe
strongly that a "pastoral presence" is more important than any plan or
project. This conviction has grown out of the observation that, more than
anything else, people want you to share their lives. This afternoon I simply walked to where I heard music. About six blocks from where I live, I
soon saw people dancing around a tree and cutting it down bit by bit. It
proved to be a carnival celebration that is popular in the jungle of Peru,
and that some emigrants had transported to Pamplona Alta.

Although nobody knew me, it didn't take long for people to offer me
a drink and to make me part of their fiesta. One member of the band told
me without blinking an eye that he was a drug dealer and had just imported a kilo of "cocaine pasta" from Colombia. He said: "I look simple
and poor, but I have a good business and make enough money to go to
the World Cup games in Spain." When I told him that I had met a lot
of drug buyers and drug dealers in the Lurigancho prison, he was hardly
impressed. It seemed that he worked for the drug underworld, and that
he was so well protected that his frankness about this business was not
any real risk for him.

Besides this drug dealer, there were many others who wanted to tell
me their stories, some jokingly, others seriously, some heavily inebriated,
others with a clear mind. What struck me most of all was the easy way in
which these Peruvians received me and let me be one of them.

More and more, the desire grows in me simply to walk around, greet
people, enter their homes, sit on their doorsteps, play ball, throw water,

and be known as someone who wants to live with them. It is a privilege to have the time and the freedom to practice this simple ministry of presence. Still, it is not as simple as it seems. My own desire to be useful, to do something significant, or to be part of some impressive project is so strong that soon my time is taken up by meetings, conferences, study groups, and workshops that prevent me from walking the streets. It is difficult not to have plans, not to organize people around an urgent cause, and not to feel that you are working directly for social progress. But I wonder more and more if the first thing shouldn't be to know people by name, to eat and to drink with them, to listen to their stories and tell your own, and to let them know with words, handshakes, and hugs that you do not simply like them, but truly love them.

If I ever decide to live in Peru for a long time, I think I should stay in one place and spend the first year doing little more than participating in the daily Peruvian life. A ministry of word and sacrament has to grow from a deep solidarity with the people. Contemplation is essential to ministry, and listening to people's lives and receiving them in a prayerful heart is true contemplation. I have little doubt that out of this contemplation it will become clear how the good news of the Gospel has to be announced, and how the healing presence of God needs to be made manifest among his people.

The greatest news of all is that God is with his people, that he is truly present. What greater ministry, then, can be practiced than a ministry that reflects this divine presence? And why worry? If God is with his own, his own will show me the way.

Monday, February 22

I am still fascinated with the question of what it would be like to be living with two or three brothers or sisters in the midst of one of the *barrios* of Lima, praying together at regular hours, walking the streets, visiting the homes, spending one day in study and reflection, practicing hospitality whenever possible, and celebrating the mysteries of God's presence. The core of this idea is that of living among the people to learn from them. This might sound romantic and sentimental, but in fact it requires discipline to allow the people to become our teachers. With such discipline, all that we see and hear can become a rich source for locating the presence of God among his people.

It would be a ministry of presence, but an active, articulate, considered presence. It would be a mutual ministry of continuous receiving and giving. It would be contemplation and action, celebration and liberation, study and work, ascetic and festive, fraternal and hospitable. I am convinced that there are at this moment young, idealistic, well-trained theological students who would be very open to such a ministry. Is this idea a dream, a fantasy, an illusion, or something worth pursuing? I will let it rest for a while and see what happens with this little seed that I put into the ground of my own search to serve God.

Tuesday, February 23

Villa Salvador is a section of Lima that in 1971 was nothing but a bare desert, dry, sandy, isolated, and inhospitable. Now, eleven years later, three hundred thousand people have found a home there. It has been a hard and painful struggle for the people to make the desert into a city, but now they are proud of what they have accomplished. There is a water supply, electricity, many schools, and a slowly improving transportation system that takes the workers to their factories and offices.

Today I visited Eugene Kirk, an Irish priest who has lived in Villa Salvador for the last eight years. I also visited two "little brothers of Jesus," the Frenchman Jacinto and the Basque José, who founded one of their fraternities there. What most struck me during the long conversations with Eugene, Jacinto, and José was that they considered the simple act of staying with the people the core of their ministry. Eugene began in Villa Salvador by living in a small shack and setting up a little carpentry shop. Slowly but surely he got to know many people and was able to build a Christian community that today is strong and vital. Jacinto works in a small furniture factory and commutes two hours a day with thousands of others. José works in a carpenter's shop in the neighborhood. During the weekends, Jacinto and José stay around the house to receive visitors and help the neighbors with whatever needs they have. Eugene, Jacinto, and José have small chapels in their houses and live as contemplatives in the midst of a sea of humans.

It was a joy to spend a day with these men. They are simple, good men who enjoy their life with the people immensely. They work hard, yet they seem to have time for anyone and anything. They feel at home in this desert-city and they speak easily about the great privilege of being allowed to live and work as members of the community of Villa Salvador.

There is a great and holy mystery here, the mystery of the incarnation lived in simple ways. I saw an Irishman, a Basque, and a Frenchman thanking and praising God daily for being given the opportunity to be with the people of God. The many little children walking in and out of their dwellings made me realize how close the Lord is to all of them.

Wednesday, February 24

Ash Wednesday. During the last weeks, I have slowly become aware of what my Lenten practice might be. It might be the development of some type of "holy indifference" toward the many small rejections I am subject to, and a growing attachment to the Lord and his passion.

I am constantly surprised at how hard it is for me to deal with the little rejections that people inflict on each other day by day. I feel this even more strongly now that I am living in a country where I am so dependent on introductions and invitations. It is hard to meet people, to see projects, or to learn about current issues if you are not explicitly brought in touch with them. During the last month, I kept hearing about many interesting events only when they were past! Why didn't anyone tell me about them? Why wasn't I invited? Why was nobody willing to make me aware of them? How should *I* know? I do not think that there is any hostility towards me. Everyone thinks that everyone knows, and nobody takes the initiative to extend a personal invitation. Thus I feel welcome and not welcome at the same time. Nobody objects to my presence, but nobody is very glad about it either.

This atmosphere often leaves me with a feeling of being rejected and left alone. When I swallow these rejections, I get quickly depressed and lonely; then I am in danger of becoming resentful and even vengeful. But it is such an institutional problem that I can hardly imagine that I can ever be without it. The Catholic Church, wherever I have seen it operate, from the Vatican to the parishes in the *barrios* of Peru, tends to make the personal subservient to the institutional. There is always a need for priests to say Masses, baptize, and marry, and anyone who can do that in a responsible way is always "welcome." There are so many things to do that good workers can easily be placed. At the same time, there are so many people asking for services, so many activities to participate in and meetings to attend, that it is difficult to pay attention to the intimate interpersonal aspects of existence. And thus the paradox becomes that those who preach love and defend the values of family life, friendship, and mutual support find themselves often living lonely lives in busy rectories.

Is there a solution to this? When I see the people I am working with, I doubt there is one. They are all deeply committed, hardworking, and caring people. They will all give their lives for their people. They are full of enthusiasm and pastoral energy. But they too are part of an enormous institution that has such a pervasive influence on their way of being that it is practically impossible to escape the loneliness it breeds.

But maybe all of this is the other side of a deep mystery, the mystery that we have no lasting dwelling place on this earth and that only God loves us the way we desire to be loved. Maybe all these small rejections are reminders that I am a traveler on the way to a sacred place where God holds me in the palm of his hand. Maybe I do have to become a little more indifferent towards all these ups and downs, ins and outs, of personal relationships and learn to rest more deeply in him who knows and loves me more than I know and love myself.

Thursday, February 25

Today, I realized that the question of where to live and what to do is really insignificant compared to the question of how to keep the eyes of my heart focused on the Lord. I can be teaching at Yale, working in the bakery at the Genesee Abbey, or walking around with poor children in Peru and feel totally useless, miserable, and depressed in all these situations. I am sure of it, because it has happened. There is not such a thing as the right place or the right job. I can be happy and unhappy in all situations. I am sure of it, because I have been. I have felt distraught and joyful in situations of abundance as well as poverty, in situations of popularity and anonymity, in situations of success and failure. The difference was never based on the situation itself, but always on my state of mind and heart. When I knew that I was walking with the Lord, I always felt happy and at peace. When I was entangled in my own complaints and emotional needs, I always felt restless and divided.

It is a simple truth that comes to me in a time when I have to decide about my future. Coming to Lima or not for five, ten, or twenty years is no great decision. Turning fully, unconditionally, and without fear to the Lord *is*. I am sure this awareness sets me free to look around here without much worrying and binds me to the holy call to pray unceasingly.

Friday, February 26

Rose Dominique and Rose Timothy, two Maryknoll sisters, are the directors of a small downtown office, the Centro de Creatividad y Cambio (The Center for Creativity and Change). Their work could be seen as a nonecclesiastical ministry through which they reach many different groups of people, non-Christians as well as Christians. This center is a grass-roots organization to work for a new society. Its members publish pamphlets and booklets to draw attention to urgent problems concerning health, education, and youth, and to suggest strategies for change. The "Roses" pay special attention to the plight of Peruvian women. They felt that working within the traditional church structures was not the best way to strive for the liberation of women; so they set up shop for themselves while continuing to offer their services to parishes and church groups when asked.

This morning I talked for an hour with Sister Rose Dominique. Her sharp and compassionate understanding of the Peruvian situation helped me to articulate some of my own feelings of which I had been only vaguely aware. What impressed me most was her observation that the leaders in the theology of liberation had little sympathy with or understanding of the issues that touch the oppressed situation of the women in the church. Rose remarked: "In this Catholic country, it is very hard to change the predominantly clerical way in which the Church works. The liberation theologians are very much Church people, and they have a hard time considering our concern for women as a real part of their struggle for liberation."

I feel that she was talking about something that I had noticed but had found hard to pinpoint. The obvious and overwhelming need for socio-economic liberation and the undeniable presence of immense poverty creates a situation in which women's issues are easily seen as a distraction, especially in a clerical, male-dominated Church. I had felt this in many little ways. After living for many years in an interdenominational and interconfessional setting, I could feel the strong dominating influence of a Church that is the only real religious power. And even the most progressive and liberated people in that Church are still marked, mostly unconsciously, by this clerical, male-dominated way of thinking and living.

Saturday, February 27

During the last few weeks I have been asking myself and others if I was learning enough about pastoral ministry during my stay in Pamplona Alta. I love the family I live with, I enjoy celebrating the Eucharist with the people, I am moved when I bring Communion to the sick, and I appreciate my weekly meetings with the lectors, but I have not really become a part of the pastoral team. Most things that happen remain unknown to me, and somehow I am getting the message that it is more a bother than a help to make me part of the daily life of the parish. I had hoped to participate in youth-group meetings, to visit the little communities in some of the sections of the parish, to help out in preparations for the sacraments of baptism and matrimony and — in general — to share actively in the ministry of the parish. Now I feel that I am standing in the center of a busy square wondering in which direction everyone is going. Last week I discussed my feelings with Tom, but it seems hard to make me part of things.

The whole situation is quite understandable. People are busy, and there are so many short-term visitors that it becomes fatiguing to keep introducing them over and over again to the daily goings-on in the parish. I have come to the conclusion that I have learned as much as I can and that I had better try to discover some new areas of ministry outside of Pamplona Alta before I leave Peru. In order to be able to make a responsible decision about my future, I need more experience than I can get here.

So this afternoon I explained to Charles and Tom that I felt it was better to move back to the center house in Miraflores and to start visiting people and places from there. It was hard to say good-bye to Sophia, Johnny, Pablito, and Maria. Living with them was, undoubtedly, the most important experience of my time here. Their affection and friendship were gifts for which I will always remain grateful. We ate some ice cream together, and Johnny and Pablito helped me carry my suitcases to the bus. When I stood on the steps of the bus and saw them waving good-bye, I felt a real pain and prayed that somehow I would be able to see them again as happy and mature adults. I waved back and shouted: "*Adiós, hasta la vista, gracias por todo.*"

Sunday, February 28

This morning at 11:00 I had a good visit with Bishop German Schmitz, one of the auxiliary bishops of Lima. His main responsibility is the young towns in the southern part of Lima. I wanted to express to him some of the ideas that have developed in my mind during the last month and get his response. I explained my desire to live in a poor section of Lima—alone or with a few others—and to try to articulate the rich spiritual gifts of the people. My short stay with Sophia, Pablo, and their children had given me a glimpse of the presence of God with the poor. What a joy it would be to make this divine presence visible not only to them but also to the many nonpoor people who sincerely search for light in their darkness! A life of prayer and hospitality among the poor, to discover and express their gifts, is slowly presenting itself as a vocation to me.

Bishop Schmitz responded warmly, even enthusiastically, to this idea. But he felt that something more was needed. He said: "There is such a need for spiritual growth and formation among the poor that you would offer a real service with retreats and days of recollection for the people. They are too tied down to their homes to travel far for days of reflection and study. But if an opportunity for this arose in their own neighborhood, they would gladly respond." Bishop Schmitz kept stressing that his idea was not really different from mine. He only wanted to "complete the picture" based on his own understanding of the need of the people.

I felt affirmed in this conversation, and I have a sense that something is becoming visible that might prove to be more than just a fantasy. Bishop Schmitz suggested that I discuss my ideas a little more with others, and then present them to the Cardinal of Lima. He made it clear that he could not yet give his permission and that the Cardinal needed to be consulted before any action was taken. But that is not my problem at this time. I am far from that phase. At this moment I was happy to have a sympathetic response from a Peruvian bishop.

6

March

The Outlines of a Vision

Monday, March 1

SISTER REBECCA, ONE of the Marist sisters, took me this morning to Larco Herrera, a huge mental hospital in Lima. Rebecca had worked in the Lurigancho prison, and also had access to the pavilion of the mentally ill prisoners who are sent to this hospital.

We spent most of the morning with Manuel and Luis, two prisoner-patients. Both are intelligent and articulate people who in no way showed any signs of being criminals or mentally ill. They took us around their pavilion, introduced us to their fellow inmates, and explained everything we wanted to know. We also spoke with the psychologist of the section, a friendly man who received us and our guides with great hospitality and discussed the difficult situation of his patients. Most of them were never sentenced, and nobody could say how long they would remain locked up. We also talked a bit to the *guardia republicana*, the armed guards who surround this little section of the hospital, since it is a prison as well.

Although the place, which houses thirty-eight patients, was extremely poor; although the patients had nothing to keep them busy; although the justice system in Peru is so bureaucratic and complex that these men may be there for many years without any attention to their case, the atmosphere was very humane. Guards, doctors, and patients treated each other amiably, talked freely, and showed a remarkable openness to each other. Somehow, the Peruvian friendliness and hospitality have taken some of the sharp edges off the suffering of these men. One of the guards even allowed Luis to bring us to the main gate. He walked along with us and was as much a part of the party as Rebecca, Luis, and myself.

Poverty, injustice, misery, and loneliness were all present; but in the midst of it all I saw an expression of humanity I have never seen in any mental hospital before. While we walked to the gate, I noticed that Luis was playing with scissors and a piece of silver paper from a pack of cigarettes. Just before we said good-bye, he offered me a lovely silver flower that he had quickly made while walking. This gesture captured the poignancy and paradox of my visit. I embraced him and for a moment all was good, very good.

Tuesday, March 2

This morning I visited the Centro Bartolome de las Casas with Bill McCarthy. A three-story building on Ricardo Bentin street in Rimac, it is the heart of the liberation theology movement. I had heard so much about it that I expected a large building, with many people and classrooms, full of activity. Instead, I saw a very simple house in a suburb of Lima. Gustavo Gutiérrez, who founded the center, was not in; but Alberto Maguina, one of the staff members, received us kindly and told us all we wanted to know.

The center is an independent institute with a small staff of sociologists and theologians who dedicate themselves to sociotheological studies and to the formation and continuing education of pastoral agents in Peru. Their work is divided into four main areas: (1) popular religiosity; (2) the daily life of the poor; (3) the poor as protagonists of their own history; and (4) Church and Society. Under these four titles, different subjects are studied.

One of the subjects under the heading of "popular religiosity" is "the moral sense of the poor." Such a theme is prepared by the staff in a pre-workshop, in which all the available literature is studied and methodological questions are dealt with. Then a year-long workshop is set up, in which about forty people participate. These people are mostly grass-roots workers, men and women who live and work with the poor and can offer their observations and experience as sources for reflection. After a year, the results of the workshops are summarized and made available to a larger circle of pastoral workers. Some of the work of the center finds its way into *Páginas*, the widely read monthly magazine edited by Carmen Lora, or in the publications of Centro de Estudios y Publicaciones (CEP), directed by Pedro de Guchtenere.

What is most striking about this center of higher studies is that it stays close to the daily life of the people. It practices theology by reflecting critically on socioeconomic, political, and ecclesiastical events, and by evaluating these events in the light of the Gospel and the teachings of the Church. There is a large library of classical theological sources and documents of past and present events in Church and state. It is clear that these are continually consulted and studied with the concrete problems of the day in mind.

What makes liberation theology so original, challenging, and radical is not so much its conceptual content as its method of working. A true liberation theologian is not just someone who thinks about liberation, but someone whose thought grows out of a life of solidarity with those who are poor and oppressed. The most impressive aspect of the Centro Bartolome de las Casas is that those who come and work there are men and women whose knowledge has grown from an intimate participation in the daily life of the people who struggle for freedom. Thus the center reveals one of the oldest of truths: that *theologia* is not primarily a way of thinking, but a way of living. Liberation theologians do not think themselves into a new way of living, but live themselves into a new way of thinking.

Wednesday, March 3

This morning I had a pleasant discussion with David Molineau, the new director of *Noticias Aliadas* (Latin American Press). I mentioned to David how impressed I had been with the way the Peruvian people express their faith, their gratitude, their care, their hopes, and their love.

I told him that it might be a special task for me to give words to much of the spiritual richness that I saw, but of which the people themselves are hardly aware. David agreed, but added: "Living with the poor not only makes you see the good more clearly, but the evil as well." He told me some stories from his own experience in a Peruvian parish, and illustrated the truth that in a world of poverty, the lines between darkness and light, good and evil, destructiveness and creativity, are much more distinct than in a world of wealth.

One of the temptations of upper-middle-class life is to create large gray areas between good and evil. Wealth takes away the sharp edges of our moral sensitivities and allows a comfortable confusion about sin and virtue. The difference between rich and poor is not that the rich sin more than the poor, but that the rich find it easier to call sin a virtue. When the poor sin, they call it sin; when they see holiness, they identify it as such. This intuitive clarity is often absent from the wealthy, and that absence easily leads to the atrophy of the moral sense.

David helped me see that living with the poor does not keep me away from evil, but it does allow me to see evil in sharper, clearer ways. It does not lead me automatically to the good either, but will help me see good in a brighter light, less hidden and more convincing. Once I can see sin and virtue with this clarity, I will also see sadness and joy, hatred and forgiveness, resentment and gratitude in less nebulous ways.

Thursday, March 4

Not far from the Maryknoll center house is the secretariat of the Latin American section of Pax Romana. This large Catholic student organization is hardly known in the United States, but in Latin America it is one of the most creative and influential forces in recent developments in the Church. Many of the leaders of the liberation theology movement, laymen, laywomen, and priests, received their spiritual formation and inspiration through membership in Pax Romana. For many years, Gustavo Gutiérrez has been the chaplain of UNEC, the Peruvian section of Pax Romana, and layleaders such as Manuel Piqueras, Javier Iguiniz, and Rolando Ames had and still have intimate ties with this Catholic student movement.

I had lunch with the staff today. There were representatives from Brazil, Ecuador, the Dominican Republic, Chile, Spain, and Peru. They told me that I would never understand the meaning and influence of liberation theology without seeing the Catholic student movement as an integral part of its growth. After lunch I talked to Luis Maria Goicoechea, a Basque priest. He told me about the history of Pax Romana, showed me its publication, and gave me some idea of the preparations for the upcoming assembly in Montreal, where the emphasis will be on the poor in the world.

The core of the spirituality of Pax Romana is *La Revisión de Vida*, an ongoing process of evaluation of one's daily life in the light of the Gospel. It is an important discipline that challenges the members to explore how they live out their Christian commitment in the concrete events of each day. The question, "How did I put my life in service of the Kingdom of God today?" invites the active members of the movement (they call themselves *militantes*) to continue to develop, and search for new directions. It is this spiritual flexibility that made it possible for the Latin American Pax Romana to play such a crucial role in the years that followed Vatican II.

Friday, March 5

It is far from easy to be a missioner. One has to live in a different culture, speak a different language, and get used to a different climate, all at great distances from those patterns of life which fit most comfortably. It is not surprising that, for many missioners, life is full of tension, frustration, confusion, anxiety, alienation, and loneliness.

Why do people become missioners? Why do they leave what is familiar and known to live in a milieu that is unfamiliar and unknown? This question has no simple answer. A desire to serve Christ unconditionally, an urge to help the poor, an intellectual interest in another culture, the attraction of adventure, a need to break away from family, a critical insight into the predicament of one's own country, a search for self-affirmation—all these and many other motives can be part of the making of a missioner. Long and arduous formation offers the opportunity for re-alignment and purification of these motives. A sincere desire to work in the service of Jesus Christ and his kingdom should become increasingly central in the mind and heart of a future missioner, although nobody can be expected to be totally altruistic. Not seldom do we come in touch with our hidden drives only after long and hard work in the field. Preparatory formation and training cannot do everything. The issue is not to have perfectly motivated missioners, but missioners who are willing to be purified again and again as they struggle to find their true vocation in life.

The two most damaging motives in the makeup of missioners seem to be guilt and the desire to save. Both form the extremes of a long continuum, both make life in the mission extremely painful. As long as I go to a poor country because I feel guilty about my wealth, whether financial or mental, I am in for a lot of trouble. The problem with guilt is that it is not taken away by work. Hard work for the poor may push my guilt underground for a while, but can never really take it away. Guilt has roots deeper than can be reached through acts of service. On the other hand, the desire to save people from sin, from poverty, or from exploitation can be just as harmful, because the harder one tries the more one is confronted with one's own limitations. Many hardworking men and women have seen the situation getting worse during their missionary career; and if they depended solely on the success of their work, they would quickly lose their sense of self-worth. Although a sense of guilt and a desire to save can be very destructive and depressive for missioners, I do not think that we are ever totally free from either. We feel guilty and we desire to bring about change. These experiences will always play a part in our daily life.

The great challenge, however, is to live and work out of gratitude. The Lord took on our guilt and saved us. In him the Divine work has been accomplished. The human missionary task is to give visibility to the Divine work in the midst of our daily existence. When we can come to realize that our guilt has been taken away and that only God saves, then we are free to serve, then we can live truly humble lives. Clinging to guilt is resisting God's grace, wanting to be a savior, competing with God's own being. Both are forms of idolatry and make missionary work very hard and eventually impossible.

Humility is the real Christian virtue. It means staying close to the ground *(humus)*, to people, to everyday life, to what is happening with all its down-to-earthness. It is the virtue that opens our eyes for the presence of God on the earth and allows us to live grateful lives. The poor themselves are the first to help us recognize true humility and gratitude. They can make a receptive missioner a truly happy person.

Saturday, March 6

Today I met Javier Iguiniz. During the last few weeks, I had heard his name mentioned different times, always with great respect and sympathy. Javier is professor of Economics at the Catholic University in Lima, and a very committed and active collaborator of the Centro Bartolome de las Casas. He has known Gustavo Gutiérrez since his years as a student, and has become increasingly involved in the liberation theology movement.

One of the most interesting things Javier said to me was that liberation theology was a way of thinking and working in close relationship with and in obedience to the *movimiento popular*, the movement of the people. He contrasted the individualistic academic world that I come from, characterized by the principles of competition and "publish or perish," with the slow, patient, and communal way of working of the people who meet at the Centro Bartolome de las Casas.

"We are not interested in creating a new theology, we are not trying to confront traditional church structures. We are not hoping for quick radical changes. No, we want to listen carefully and patiently to the movement of the people and slowly identify those elements that lead to progress. We want to work as church participants in an age-old process of living, thinking, celebrating, and worshiping, and then give form and shape to what really belongs to the movement of God's people."

Javier was very aware of the fact that he belonged to the Church, which works slowly and gradually but in which sudden eruptions can make drastic change possible. Such eruptions, although they cannot be organized, need to be recognized, understood, evaluated, and made part of the larger movement of the Church. "We have thousands of ideas, insights, and visions. We talk about them, exchange them, and play with them. Often they seem very significant, but most of them are shelved, usually for many years. A few of these ideas, insights, and visions may later reappear and prove to be substantial. But it can be a long time before we know if we are in touch with something that really belongs to the movement."

Javier showed me—without explicitly saying so—a theology of doing theology. He was extremely critical of "theological heroism." He did not believe in simply publishing all the good ideas that come up. He kept stressing the need for humble, slow, faithful work in obedience to the people who are to be served. He said: "Many of the poor are still very close to the Council of Trent in their spirituality. If we do not understand this, our concern for their liberation cannot be a true Christian service."

Javier was sympathetic to my desire to live with the people, but strongly urged me to continue my academic work. The greatest need, he felt, was not for more pastoral workers but for people who could help articulate, evaluate, systematize, and communicate what is going on in the pastoral field. "We need people who can conceptualize what they live and connect it with the larger tradition of the Church." He warned me against romanticism: "It is quite possible to live with the people without being part of the movement of the people, and that movement you might find as much in the university as in the *barrio*."

My general impression was that Javier did not discourage me in my desire to come to Peru, but he did want to make me aware that the way of doing theology here would require a great faithfulness to the slow-moving Church of the people.

Sunday, March 7

Rose Timothy and Rose Dominique invited me to come to Caja de Agua, a large barrio in the North Zone of Lima where they live. I arrived at 8:00 A.M. and went straight to the rectory. There I met Matias Sienbenaller, the pastor of Caja de Agua and the Vicar of the whole North Zone. Matias is a diocesan priest from Luxembourg who has worked in Lima for the last sixteen years. He is highly respected and admired by many and has been a creative and patient leader since he arrived in Peru.

Matias had not the faintest idea who this poorly-Spanish-speaking stranger was that walked into his house at 8:00 A.M. on Sunday morning. He seemed suspicious in the beginning, and didn't know how to respond. He offered me a cup of coffee and asked many questions. After awhile, he relaxed and showed interest in my search for a vocation in Peru. He said that he had very little time for me at this moment, but invited me to come back and stay with him for a few days so that he could give me a better perspective on the possibilities of coming to Peru. He felt that my experience so far had been far too limited, and that I needed a broader vision to be able to make a responsible decision.

I immediately realized that I had met a man who has much to offer. Since he is a diocesan priest from Europe—as I am—with much experience in Peru, I felt a strong desire to spend more time with him.

Monday, March 8
Cuzco, Peru

During these last weeks, the Maryknollers Michael Briggs and Paul Kavanaugh were staying in the Center house. Both are working in the Altiplano, the high mountain plane around Lake Titicaca, and have come to Lima for their altitude leave, a much needed time to recuperate from the physical stresses of "high living."

Talking with them has increased my desire to see more of Peru than Lima. They convinced me that to know only Lima would give me a very one-sided impression, not only of Peru, but also of the pastoral work in Peru. Before returning to their missions, Mike and Paul planned to attend a two-week course in Cuzco for all the pastoral workers of the region of the Southern Andes. They invited me to join them.

So this morning we flew from Lima to Cuzco and settled in at the Instituto de Pastoral Andina (the Pastoral Institute of the Andes). Since the course does not start until tomorrow morning, I had the whole day to look around Cuzco. Cuzco is like a precious pearl set in a lovely green valley. The many trees, the fresh pastures, and the green-covered mountains offered a dramatic change from the dry and dusty hills of Pamplona Alta. Set in the pure blue sky, a bright sun threw its light over the small city. The central square of Cuzco is of unusual beauty. The imposing facades of the cathedral and the Church of the Compañía are flanked by pleasant galleries with shops, restaurants, bars, and bookstores.

Paul and I walked around town for a few hours and enjoyed the busy life in this Quechua town. The dark faces of the people, the stores with beautiful Indian handicrafts, the old Inca walls in which huge stones interlock with meticulous precision, and the many memories of the Inca empire all made me aware that Cuzco explains much of the glory and agony of present-day Peru.

In the late afternoon we took a cab to the Indian ruins surrounding the city. We saw the old Inca fortress of Sacsahuamán, the sculpted rock of Quenkko, and the ritual baths of Tambomachay. These solemn and sacred sights in the midst of splendid green mountains gave me the desire to spend some quiet days there meditating on the mystery and misery of human history. I soon realized that the splendid churches in downtown Cuzco were built with the stones from these old Indian temples and fortresses. The main concern of the Spaniards had been to destroy the pagan world and to show triumphantly the victory of the Christian faith. The Indian people were only reluctantly recognized as human beings. It would take centuries to acknowledge their rich spiritual heritage. Only recently has mission come to mean something other than a spiritual conquest.

In Cuzco, all can be seen together: the solemn faces of the Inca gods, the glory and the shame of a Christianity proclaimed with the support of the sword, the living faith of the people who have brought their Indian heritage and their new religion together into a deeply rooted spirituality, and the poverty and oppression of a people that has never fully regained its freedom.

Tuesday, March 9

Rolando Ames, a political scientist at the Catholic University in Lima, is leading the first three days of the course. The lectures are on the *Coyuntura Política-Eclesiástica*, the status of Church and politics in Peru.

In his brilliant lectures, Rolando brought together many of the pieces of information, insight, hearsay, and gossip that I had gathered during the last two months. Many things fell into place. Rolando described the years 1976 to 1978 as the period during which a new revolutionary consciousness developed that affected the whole nation. This new consciousness

provided the climate for a new way to preach the gospel and deeply influenced the pastoral work of the Peruvian Church. This period has now
passed. Today the Church has to continue to work in a different political
climate. With the popular movement no longer as clearly visible, an increasing pragmatism has emerged that makes the poor less militant and
the left less clear about its direction.

Rolando affirmed in a concrete way what Xavier told me on Saturday, namely that it is crucial for every pastoral worker to keep in close
touch with the political ups and downs of Peru. The problems of 1971
and those of 1982 might look much the same; there is still poverty, malnutrition, lack of educational facilities, poor medical care, and a great
need for a more developed knowledge of the Christian faith. Why, then,
is there a need to enter into the complexity of daily politics? Rolando's
answer is that even when the problems seem the same, the spiritual tone
can be very different. The understanding of this tone is essential for the
work of a Christian who really wants to serve the people. To ignore the
political movements of a country such as Peru is to ignore the realities
that determine the hope or despair of the people.

During the past few years, Peru has shifted toward a growing dependence on international capitalism. All the emphasis is on promoting
export of those materials that serve the needs of the large transnational
corporations. This means less support for local and national enterprises,
and thus less work and money for Peruvian workers and companies.
Since the transnational corporations don't see any profit coming from
capital invested in people's projects (educational, agrarian, or industrial) these "economics" offer little optimism to the people.

How then can we form true communities of hope in the midst of this
political reality? That is the question that touches the heart of pastoral
care in this country.

Wednesday, March 10

Rolando Ames helped us to identify today the major developments
within the Peruvian Church over the last thirty years. In many ways,
they reflect the tumultuous events within the Church in all of Latin
America.

Three main phases can be distinguished. First of all, the Church distanced itself from the ruling class—or the oligarchy, as it is called in Latin America. Until the fifties, the Latin American Church lived and worked hand in glove with the ruling class. The *haciendas*, where owner and priest were both considered as bosses by those who worked the land, were vivid manifestation of the connection between the Church and the oligarchy. But in 1958, an official church document appeared in which the *orden oligárquico* (rule by oligarchy) was called unjust. It was the first sign of a movement in the Church that called attention to the plight of the poor and oppressed.

In the second phase, the Church moved from a general sympathy for the poor to an active defense of their rights. The Vatican Council had set the tone which made this development possible, but the Conference of the Latin American Bishops in Medellin in 1968 gave it shape. In Medellin, the Church formulated the "preferential option for the poor" and thus defined itself as a Church that supports oppressed people in their struggle for liberation. In many ways, the statements of Medellin went far beyond the psychological state of mind of most of the bishops there present. But the decision by the Church as a body to speak directly and officially in defense of the poor, oppressed, and exploited peoples of Latin America meant the birth of a new Church. By calling the order that causes the rampant injustices "sinful," the Church had committed itself—at least in principle—to the struggle for a new social order.

This radical change in self-definition made the Latin American Church of the seventies a Church drenched by the blood of martyrs. In Argentina, Brazil, Chile, El Salvador, Guatemala, and many other countries, thousands of Christians lost their lives as a consequence of their commitment to this new Church. Although direct persecution did not take place in Peru, the option for the poor has led to many conflicts between the Church and the Peruvian ruling class.

The third phase has just begun, the phase in which an ecclesial counter-reaction is taking shape. During the seventies, the opposition within the Church itself against a new direction had remained dormant. But in the beginning of the eighties, a new and well-organized conservatism that divides the Church into two camps has become visible. One of the preparatory documents for the Latin American Bishops' Conference in Puebla, published in 1979, opened this third phase. The document describes the task of the Church as guiding the unavoidable transition of the Latin American society from a rural to an industrial society. It stressed the necessity of preventing the secularism that resulted from a similar transition in France during the last century, and it pointed to the bishops of Latin America as those who have to secure the faith in this time of change.

Today, the conservative forces in the Church in Peru are well-established. Because the hierarchy can no longer follow one line, the episcopal documents have become compromises between two opposing directions. Whereas, a few years ago, the Peruvian bishops could still issue strongly prophetic statements in the spirit of Medellin, the latest publications of the Peruvian Bishops' Conference show ambiguity, ambivalence, and paralysis.

Rolando showed how hard it will be for many who found their faith in the new church to continue in the struggle and not become discouraged. But he was convinced that the new conservatism is a passing phase to test and purify the new commitment to the poor, from which there is no return.

Friday, March 12

Tonight George-Ann Potter, assistant director of Catholic Relief Services in Peru, invited me to dinner. She also invited Rolando Ramos, a Peruvian priest who works in Amparaes (Calca province). Although I had never met (or even heard of) Rolando, an immediate sense of friendship developed between us. It seemed to me that here was the priest I had been looking for. He combined a deep, contemplative spirit with a strong commitment to service among the poor. He radiated faith in the presence of God among the people, hope for the liberation of the poor, and love for all he meets. Being in his presence felt like being in the presence of a man of God, a pastor and prophet.

Rolando's parish is four hours away from Cuzco. He serves a large group of small villages that can be reached only on horseback or on foot. He lives the life of the poor and participates fully in their daily struggles.

He lives this hard life with gladness, because he can see, hear, and touch the Lord in his people and feels deeply grateful for that privilege.

I guess that my joy in knowing Rolando has something to do with my difficulties in relating to the people in the course. I find the participants tough and even harsh. They have so identified themselves with the *lucha* that they permit little space for personal interchange. They are good and honest people, but difficult to get to know. They work diligently, not only in their parishes but also in this course. They are serious, intense, and deeply concerned men and women.

When I met Rolando and experienced his personal warmth, his kindness, and his spiritual freedom, I was suddenly able to come in touch with the feelings of oppression that I myself was experiencing in the course. Rolando invited me to come to his parish and to live with him for as long as I wanted. There I would be able to experience that it was possible to be fully involved in the struggle for the poor while at the same time remaining sensitive to the personal and interpersonal quality of life. That explains my immediate feelings of closeness to him.

Saturday, March 13

For the last few days, the course has dealt primarily with the new agricultural law. A lawyer from Lima came to explain the law, and triggered a lively debate about the way the poor *campesinos* would be affected by it. Most pastoral workers felt that this law was simply one more way in which the poor would be made poorer. The law opened the way for rich people who had lost their land during the agrarian reform to reclaim it. One of the French pastoral workers presented an alternative law that would serve the poor farmer. This law had been formulated by the *campesinos* themselves, with the help of leftist lawyers and economists.

When I reflect on these legal debates and discussions, I become strongly aware of the new style of this liberation-oriented Church. It would have taken an outsider a long time to find out that this was a group of priests, nuns, and Catholic laymen and laywomen dedicated to the preaching of the Gospel. The style of the dialogue, the fervor of the discussions, and the ideological language suggested a meeting of a political party rather than a church group. I feel that this is true not only for the formal sessions, but also for the informal relationships between the participants—during meals and coffee breaks. Yet these men and women from France, Spain, Italy, and the United States have left their countries to serve the poor of Peru in the name of the Lord Jesus Christ. Their religious dedication has led them into the lives of the poor. Therefore the sophisticated and highly critical analysis of the new agrarian law was for them not purely political but a necessary step in the struggle for freedom for the people of God.

Yet two Churches are gradually developing in Peru, and they are at the point where they are no longer able to talk to each other. On the one side is the Church that speaks primarily about God, with little reference to the daily reality in which the people live; on the other side is the Church that speaks primarily about the struggle of the people for freedom, with little reference to the Divine mysteries to which this struggle points. The distance between these Churches is growing. This morning I went to the Cathedral of Cuzco, and when I walked from altar to altar and statue to statue and listened to the monotone voice of a priest saying Mass, I suddenly felt a deep pain. I would never feel at home any more in this traditional Church, but will I ever in the Church of the *lucha*?

Sunday, March 14

George-Ann Potter and her guest, Anne Lise Timmerman, vice-president of Caritas in Denmark, invited me to join them on a trip to the sacred valley of the Incas.

The majestic beauty of this valley impressed me; the Urubamba River, surrounded by fertile cornfields and green-covered mountain ranges, filled me with awe. Along the road small groups of Indians guiding cattle carried their loads of wood. These small, dark, silent people with faces carved by nature and hard work evoked in me a sense of the sacred.

In their silence, they spoke of centuries of care for the land, of a mysterious intimacy with nature, of an unceasing prayer to the God who has made their land fertile, and of a knowledge that we in our Volkswagen would never be able to grasp. The valley was filled with a holy silence: no advertisements along the roads, no factories or modern houses, no loudspeakers or shouting vendors. Even the busy market of the little town of Pisac seemed covered with this sacred quietness.

We bought a few artifacts in the marketplace, attended Mass in the Pisac Church, and visited an agricultural school for *campesinos*. We talked about all sorts of things, had a pleasant dinner, and struggled for an hour to change a tire. But none of our activity could disturb the sacred silence of this valley of the Incas. When we came back to Cuzco I felt refreshed, renewed, and grateful to the Indian people for this healing gift of silence.

Monday, March 15

Today the last part of the course began. After three days about the political and ecclesial state of affairs in Peru, and two days about the new agrarian law and its possible alternatives, the emphasis now shifts to a spirituality of liberation. Gustavo Gutiérrez flew into Cuzco from Lima this morning, and will be our guide in a four-day workshop. Just as in the summer course in Lima, Gustavo's presence had a vitalizing effect. Many of us showed signs of fatigue after six days of intense discussions, but Gustavo unleashed new energies and engendered new enthusiasm.

Two ideas in Gustavo's presentations impressed me deeply. The first focused on the Gospel terms, which have passed through the filter of individualism and thus have been spiritualized and sentimentalized. The word "poor" has come to mean "humble," the word "rich," "proud." Terms like "the children," "the blind," "the sinner" have lost their historical meaning and have been "translated" into ahistorical, asocial and apolitical words. Thus, "child," which in the New Testament refers to an insignificant, marginal, and oppressed human being, has become an expression for simplicity, innocence, and spontaneity. Jesus' call to become "like children" has been passed through the filter of individualism and has thus been romanticized.

This explains how the idea of a spiritual combat has lost its social, political, and economic quality and now refers only to an inner struggle. Gustavo showed us as an example of how the Magnificat is mostly read in a very individualistic way and has lost its radical, social dimensions in the minds of most contemporary Christians. In the Magnificat, Mary proclaims: "[The Lord God] has shown the strength of his arm, he has scattered the proud in their conceit. He has cast down the mighty from their thrones and has lifted up the lowly." These words have a concrete historical, socio-economic, and political meaning; the interpretations that relate these words exclusively to the inner life of pride and humility rob them of their real power.

A second idea that touched me in Gustavo's presentation was that affection, tenderness, solitude are not to be rejected by those who struggle for the freedom of the people. There is a danger that these important realities of the Christian life are considered by the "revolutionaries" as soft and useless for the struggle. But Gustavo made it clear that love for the people is essential for a true Christian revolution. Those who do not value tenderness and gentleness will eventually lose their commitment to the struggle for liberation.

This observation was extremely important to me, especially in the context of my earlier feelings about the participants in this course. Someone mentioned to me that "new fighters" in the struggle for liberation often are tense, harsh, and unfeeling, but that those who have been in the struggle for a long time are gentle, caring, and affectionate people who have been able to integrate the most personal with the most social. Gustavo himself is certainly an "old fighter."

Tuesday, March 16

Today Gustavo showed how the eruption of the poor has dramatic implications for our spirituality. The new and concrete pastoral concerns that came out of the involvement with the poor have dramatically challenged the traditional ways of living the spiritual life. But those who have gone through this crisis and tasted it to the full have also come to realize that, even though the experience of a break with the past remains a reality, so too does continuity. In fact, as Gustavo remarked, the full immersion in the struggle makes us rediscover the basic spiritual values that also undergirded the "old-fashioned" seminary spirituality. Humility, faithfulness, obedience, purity—these and many other traditional values are being rediscovered in the midst of the work with the poor.

One example of this rediscovery of traditional values is the renewed understanding of humility. In the spirituality of the past there was little place for conflict; but anyone who really becomes involved in the daily lives and struggles of the poor cannot avoid moments and periods of conflict. Experiences of abandonment, despair, and deep anguish can enter into the spiritual life itself. It can even lead to a struggle and confrontation with God, who does not seem to make his presence known. Thus a spirituality marked by the struggle for liberation can lead to an experience of deep darkness, which will require true humility. It is this humility that enables us to continue in the struggle, even when we see little progress, to be faithful even when we experience only darkness, to stay with the people even when we ourselves feel abandoned.

I am moved by this new understanding of humility, precisely because it is so old! It has deep connections with the humility of Jeremiah, who confronts God in the midst of his confusion, and with the humility of John of the Cross, who stays faithful in the darkness. Thus the new spirituality of liberation opens us to the mystical life as an essential part of the pastoral task given to us by the people themselves.

Wednesday, March 17

After lunch, I had an opportunity to spend some time with Gustavo Gutiérrez and to ask his advice about a possible long stay in Peru. He was extremely concrete in his advice. He said that it would be a good thing for me to come to Peru for a long time, live in a parish in Lima, do some pastoral work, get to know as much as possible the pastoral people of the city, and join a theological reflection group in the Centro Bartolome de las Casas. In many ways, his suggestions were similar to those of Xavier Iguiniz and Rolando Ames.

I feel far from making a decision of this nature. The many shifts in my emotions and my feelings of being a lonely bystander indicate that this is not the right time to accept Gustavo's invitation.

I am happy that I do not have to decide now, and that I can take more time to let things develop in me. It probably will be a gradual process of discernment. I will be at home here only when I experience my stay as a vocation, a call from God, and from the people. At this moment, the call is not clear. I will have to bring my search more directly into the presence of God and pray more fervently for light.

Thursday, March 18

Yesterday I read the so-called Santa Fe document. It is an analysis written in 1980 by a group of Latin American experts of the Republican Party, to formulate the new policy for the United States towards Latin America in anticipation of Ronald Reagan's presidency.

The third proposition of the second part reads: "The foreign policy of the United States must start to confront (and not simply respond after the facts) the theology of liberation as it is used in Latin America by the clergy of the 'liberation theology'."

This proposition is clarified by the following explanation:

In Latin America, the role of the Church is vital for the concept of political freedom. Regrettably, the Marxist-Leninist forces have used the Church as a political weapon against private property and the capitalist system of production, by infiltrating the religious community with ideas which are more Communist than Christian (Translated from the French publication *Dial: diffusion de l'information sur l'Amérique Latine*, January 28, 1982).

Although these words show a lack of understanding of liberation theology, they disclose that those who were setting the guidelines for the greatest power in the world consider theology a real threat. The simple fact that theology is taken that seriously by people whose primary concern is to obtain and maintain first place among all the powers of the world is among the greatest compliments to theology I have ever heard.

There is a little man in Peru, a man without any power, who lives in a *barrio* with poor people and who wrote a book. In this book he simply reclaimed the basic Christian truth that God became human to bring good news to the poor, new light to the blind, and liberty to the captives. Ten years later this book and the movement it started are considered dangerous by the greatest power on earth. When I look at this little man, Gustavo, and think about the tall Ronald Reagan, I see David standing before Goliath again with no more weapon than a little stone, called *A Theology of Liberation*.

Friday, March 19

The Cuzco course is over. Last night we celebrated the Eucharist together in a way I will never forget. It was a celebration in which all the joys and the pains of the struggle for the liberation of the poor were brought together and lifted up together with the bread and the wine as a sacrifice of praise. It was a powerful spiritual experience, serious yet glad, realistic yet hopeful, very militant yet peaceful. It was for me the most prayerful moment of the course.

During his last presentation, Gustavo made an interesting observation. He remarked that the Christians of Latin America had passed from a traditional to a revolutionary understanding of their faith without going through a modernistic phase. One person in whom this process could be seen was Archbishop Oscar Romero of El Salvador. This traditional churchman became a true revolutionary through his direct contact with the suffering people without ever rejecting or even criticizing his traditional past. In fact, his traditional understanding of God's presence in history was the basis and source of his courageous protest against the exploitation and oppression of the people in El Salvador. What is true of Bishop Romero is true of most Latin American Christians who joined the movement for liberation. Their traditional understanding of the teachings of the Church was never a hindrance to their conversion. On the contrary, it was the basis for change.

Here we see an important difference between the Latin American situation and the situation in Western Europe and in some parts of the United States. Latin America did not go through a stage of secularization. In Europe, many liberation movements have an antireligious, antichurch, and anticlerical character. That is not the case today in Latin America. Most people who have joined liberation movements in Latin America are deeply believing Christians who look to the Church for guidance and support. Many Europeans who come to Latin America to know more about the people's movement for liberation are surprised and often impressed by the Christian commitment they encounter in the revolutionaries with whom they speak. Europeans often feel that the Church has lost credibility and relevance in the struggle for a new world. But here they discover that the Church is one of the main sources of inspiration in the struggle.

The closing Eucharist of the course made this clear to me. The texts of Scripture, the prayers of petition and thanks, the offering of the gifts, the sharing of the bread and the cup, and the hymns of praise were an integral part of all that had been said during the last two weeks. The Eucharist was not tacked on to the course because all the participants were Christians. No, the Eucharist was the most powerful and the most radical expression of what this whole course was about. It became a powerful call to go out again and continue in the struggle of the people of God.

Saturday, March 20

Now that the course is finished, I am living with my Lutheran friends John and Kathy Goldstein in Cuzco.

It is wonderful to stay with friends in a "homey" house, to have a good bed, good conversation, and free time to write, to play with John and Kathy's five-week-old son, Peter Isaac, and to make little trips to the center of Cuzco. The difference between the intense atmosphere at the Pastoral Institute and the relaxed and friendly family atmosphere in the Goldstein's home has really struck me. It is the difference between quick meals on long tables with eighty people and leisurely meals around the kitchen table, between introducing yourself every moment to a new person and being in a familiar place, between always talking about Church and society and talking about the little things of daily life, between the hectic eagerness of celibates and the sustained concern of a father and a mother for their newborn child. All these differences make me very glad to be with my friends and to take it easy for a while.

Monday, March 22

During the last few days, I have been deeply disturbed by the news of the murder of four fellow Dutchmen in El Salvador. Koos Koster, Hans Lodewijk, Jan Kornelius Kuiper, and Johannes Willemsen were members of a Dutch television team sent to El Salvador to report on the political situation in the weeks before the elections. The radio mentions the official explanation of the Salvadoran government, which says that the four Dutchmen were caught in a crossfire between government troops and guerrilla fighters. The radio also mentions that another Dutch reporter refutes this explanation and says that the four were murdered by a military unit.

The Peruvian paper *El Diario* gives a detailed report of the murders. It says that the four Dutchmen had just finished their work and were on the way to the airport of Lloapango in their car, loaded with equipment and just-finished films. Near the detour of Santa Rosa, before the turn to Chalatenango, they were intercepted by a military truck. A group of soldiers of the fourth brigade of the infantry forced the four Dutchmen to board their truck, hitting them with the butts of their rifles. A little further, the prisoners were let out and machine-gunned down with total disregard for the astonished guides who accompanied the four Dutchmen and the people who witnessed the murder from the surrounding thicket. When the soldiers arrived in the *cuartel* of El Paisnal with the four bodies, they reported to their superiors. All the cameras, as well as films showing the daily agony of the Salvadoran people, were immediately destroyed.

In a long analysis of the murders, *El Diario* is of the opinion that "the Argentinian Colonels, who offer their intelligence service to the armed forces of El Salvador could finally rest since they had finished a hunt that had started nine years ago." With the help of Anibal Aguilar Penarrieta, the president of the Association of Lawyers for Human Rights in Bolivia, *El Diario* was able to reconstruct the journeys through Latin America of the Dutch television team during the last decade. Koos Koster was in Chile during the 1973 coup of General Augusto Pinochet and made an extraordinary film of the attack on the Palace de la Moneda, where President Salvador Allende died. During 1973, 1974, and 1975, Koster was in Peru with his colleagues and made films about the life of the *campesinos*. Later the team came to Argentina, where they made the best available documentary about the thirty thousand "disappeared ones" and the mothers of the Plaza de Mayo. When their shocking film appeared on European television, the Argentinian military started to look for an opportunity to kill them, according to *El Diario*. In 1980, the television crew was in Bolivia documenting the violations of human rights during the military occupation of the Bolivian tin mines. They also revealed the role of Argentina in the Bolivian coups of Garcia Meza and Arce

Gomez. But when Arce Gomez ordered their arrest, they had already left Bolivia.

A few weeks ago, *El Diario* says the head of the Salvadoran armed forces traveled to Argentina to work out a plan for selective terrorism. Part of the conversation is supposed to have dealt with the way to eliminate the Dutch reporters in El Salvador. The plan was to authorize the Dutchmen to travel to the interior of El Salvador and to give them apparent freedom of movement. Then they would be arrested under the pretense that their names were found as contact persons on the dead body of a guerrilla fighter. *El Diario* concludes: "With this puerile proof the execution did not have to be delayed long and on the 17th of March they fell, in the same month that two years ago Bishop Oscar Arnulfo Romero was assassinated."

This tragedy has made Holland suffer with the poor and oppressed people of Central America. I hope and pray that this painful compassion will bring the people of El Salvador at least one step closer to peace.

Tuesday, March 23

This is my last day in Cuzco. John, Kathy, and I made a trip to the splendid Inca ruins in the area and to some churches and a museum in town. More than ever before, I was impressed by the majestic beauty of the buildings of the Inca Empire. The gigantic temples, the watchposts, and ritual baths were the work of a people guided by the rule, "Do not lie, do not steal, and do not be lazy," and inspired by a powerful devotion to the Sun God and many other divinities. But, more than before, I was stunned by the total insensitivity of the Spanish conquerors to the culture and religion they found here.

It suddenly hit me how radical Gustavo Gutiérrez's liberation theology really is, because it is a theology that starts with the people and wants to recognize the deep spirituality of the Indians who live in this land. How different from what we saw today on our trip. There we witnessed a centuries-long disregard for any Indian religiosity, and a violent destruction of all that could possibly be a reminder of the Inca Gods. What an incredible pretention, what a cruelty, what a sacrilegious sin committed by people who claimed to come in the name of a God of forgiveness, love, and peace.

I wished I had the time to spend a whole day just sitting on the ruins of Sacsahuamán. These temple ruins overlooking the city of Cuzco, with its many churches built from its stones, make me ask the God of the sun, the moon, the stars, the rainbow, the lightening, the land, and the water to forgive what Christians did in his name.

Maybe the new spirituality of liberation is a creative form of repentance for the sins of our fathers. And I should not forget that these sins are closer to my own heart than I often want to confess. Some form of spiritual colonialism remains a constant temptation.

Wednesday, March 24
Lima, Peru

Today I flew back from Cuzco to Lima. I arrived just in time to commemorate the second anniversary of the martyrdom of Archbishop Oscar Romero of El Salvador. Since his death, tens of thousands of other Salvadorans have been murdered. They are the anonymous martyrs of our day. They are men and women who were killed because, in some way or another, they witnessed for freedom, human dignity, and a new society.

Often we think of martyrs as people who died in defense of their consciously professed faith, but Jesus' words, "What you did for the least of mine, you did for me," point to a true martyrdom in the service of God's people.

In a strange way, I am grateful that it is not only poor anonymous people who are losing their lives, but also well-known churchmen and churchwomen. The death of people like Bishop Romero allows us to lift up the martyrdoms of thousands of unknown *campesinos,* cathechists, youth leaders, teachers, priests, and guerrilla fighters, and to make them fruitful for the whole Christian community in Latin America. Bishop Romero's solidarity in death with the poor and oppressed of his country makes him a true bishop, not only in life, but also in death.

We celebrated Bishop Romero's death in the Church of Ciudad de Dios. I am increasingly impressed by the Christian possibility of celebrating not only moments of joy but also moments of pain, thus affirming God's real presence in the thick of our lives. A true Christian always affirms life, because God is the God of life, a life stronger than death and destruction. In him we find no reason to despair. There is always reason to hope, even when our eyes are filled with tears.

Many priests of the southern part of Lima joined Bishop Herman Schmidt in the celebration of the Eucharist. It was good to be back in these now-familiar surroundings. Many parishioners came up to me to express their joy at seeing me again after a few weeks of absence. I felt consoled by those whom I had known only for a short time. This mysterious experience in which grief and joy, gladness and sadness merged brought me to a new understanding of the unity of the death and resurrection of Christ.

Thursday, March 25

John Goldstein had asked me to take a letter to Troy Baretta, the coordinator of the ministry of the Lutheran Church in America (LCA) in Peru. John and Kathy had already made me aware of how hard it is for Protestant missionaries to live and work in Peru. In the beginning of this century, Protestants were still outlawed, and the history of Protestantism shows periods of harsh persecution. Under the influence of a greater religious tolerance in the western world, and of a greater appreciation of the Protestant churches by the Second Vatican Council, outright persecution has stopped and some creative ecumenical dialogue has started. But from my own impressions, it seems that many Catholics have remained suspicious of Protestants, and some even overtly hostile toward them.

Such anti-Protestantism is partly understandable. Most priests have had disturbing experiences with different fundamentalist sects which are known for their fierce anti-Catholic preaching and for their divisive practices. Various evangelical sects—Jehovah's Witnesses, Mormons, Israelites, and similar groups—tend to create divisions between people, arouse an atmosphere of suspicion towards Catholics, and isolate people from their natural bonds with their relatives and friends. The great proliferation of these sometimes fanatic sects has certainly not built an ecumenical atmosphere between Catholics and Protestants.

But this being the case, there remains the fact that Protestantism has as much "right" to be in Peru as Catholicism and that there is, in fact, a relatively large, well-established Peruvian Protestant community. I am

shocked by the argument that Catholicism is so much a part of the Peruvian culture that Protestantism, even in its most orthodox forms, can be
seen only as robbing people of their own heritage. In the light of the way
in which the Spanish destroyed the Indian cultures in Peru and imposed
their religion on the people with the force of weapons—and this less than
four hundred years ago—it seems quite preposterous to consider Protestantism a threat to the Peruvian culture. Moreover, the historic Catholic missionaries have never hesitated to evangelize alien cultures and to
bring the Gospel to people for whom accepting the Good News of Jesus
required a radical break with their traditions and customs. The history of
the missions to China, Japan, and other well-integrated cultures shows
clearly that cultural integrity has certainly not been the main concern of
Catholic evangelizers in the past.

My discussions with John and Kathy, with Troy and Anne, and with
many other Protestant missionaries from mainline denominations (Lutherans, Methodists, and Episcopalians) in Latin America have convinced
me of the urgent need for a new ecumenism in the area of mission and for
a much greater humility on the part of Catholics in their relationship with
their Protestant brothers and sisters. It seems that there are now enough
people on both sides who are open and ready for a creative collaboration.

Friday, March 26

This proved to be a very important day for me. As I had planned
before going to Cuzco, I met again with Matias Sienbenaller, the Lux-
embourgian priest who is pastor in Caja de Agua, one of Lima's *barrios*.
This morning as we talked I felt that many pieces of my puzzle began to
come together.

I explained to Matias my dream about living among the people, praying with and for them, visiting them in their homes, offering days of
retreat and recollection, and gradually helping them to articulate their
own spiritual gifts. I asked him if he felt there was a place for me in Peru,
how to relate all this to my past in Holland and the United States, and
in which way to envision my future. I also shared with him my feelings
about the clericalism in Peru, my need for a supportive community, and
my search for ways to live a somewhat structured spiritual life with others.

Matias responded with great warmth and concrete suggestions. He gave me a true sense of being called. He offered his own parish as a good place to try out what I was dreaming about. There is a good pastoral team that would offer support, encouragement, and constructive criticism; there is a daily life of communal prayer in the "rectory," a friendly home, and a strong spirit of working together. Moreover, the *barrio* Caja de Agua is close to the center of town and would make it easy to work closely with the people of Centro Bartolome de las Casas and to keep in touch with other pastoral events in town. Important for me was Matias's insistence that I not cut off from all contact with the academic world in the United States. While he stressed that I should commit myself firmly to the Peruvian Church and be willing to work in the service of that Church, he also felt that it would be good to continue to communicate through writing and lecturing to the world from which I come. He therefore encouraged me to stay in touch with the places of theological formation in the States. Some part-time teaching there might be good for me, for the Church in Peru, and for students in the United States. Finally, we talked a little about introductions to the Cardinal of Lima, letters of recommendation, time schedules, and other such things.

It was quite a morning. Just three days before my return to the United States, an appealing, clear, and convincing vocation has started to take form. Many of the things Matias proposed had a certain obviousness to me. The more I thought about them during the day, the more I felt that things fit very well and that I have as much clarity and certainty as I probably will ever have.

I now have to return to my friends in the States and to my bishop in Holland to ask for their responses and advice. Then I should soon be able to make a decision that has a solid basis and that is, I hope, not just an expression of my own will.

Saturday, March 27

My discussion with Matias gave me a sense of closure. My stay in Peru is coming to an end, my impressions of ministry in Peru are starting to show patterns and my future plans are slowly taking some identifiable shape.

As I walked through Lima today, I had the strong sense that this city would become an important place for me in the future. I felt the desire to pray in this city at the different holy places and to ask God's guidance for my future. So I decided to go to the Church of the Lord of the Miracles. I still have vivid memories of my first Sunday in Peru, when I joined the crowd on the Plaza de Armas to welcome the procession of the Lord of the Miracles. This time I had a chance to see the painting on the main altar of the Church. Many people, young and old, men and women, were praying and I felt grateful that I could be there with them. As I looked up to the painting of the crucified Lord and felt the deep devotion of the people surrounding me, I had the feeling of being accepted in Peru. This, indeed, could become my country, my home, my church, and these people could become my fellow Christians, my friends, and my co-workers in the ministry. As my thoughts wandered to the future, I saw myself coming to this Church many times, asking the Lord of the Miracles to bless the people, to give me strength and courage, and to fill me with a spirit of joy and peace.

I also visited the house of St. Rose of Lima, observing where she lived her harsh and ascetic life, and the Church of La Merced, where the Cross of Pedro Urrarte is venerated. The streets and churches of Lima were all filled with people. I felt embraced by a welcoming city, and enjoyed just being carried along from place to place by the crowds. I did not feel like a stranger anymore. I felt more like a guest who was being invited to stay longer. My prayers became part of the murmuring sounds of the thousands who paraded through the streets and in and out of the churches. There was a sense of harmony, of belonging, yes, maybe even of vocation. To find that vocation, I had to come to Peru.

Sunday, March 28

Today during the Eucharist, we read in the letter to the Hebrews: "In the days when [Christ] was in the flesh, he offered prayers and supplications with loud cries and tears to God, who was able to save him from death, and he was heard because of his reverence. Son though he was, he learned obedience from what he suffered; and when perfected, he became the source of eternal salvation for all who obey him" (Heb. 5:7–9).

Jesus learned obedience from what he suffered. This means that the pains and struggles of which Jesus became part made him listen more perfectly to God. In and through his sufferings, he came to know God and could respond to his call. Maybe there are no better words than these to summarize the meaning of the option for the poor. Entering into the suffering of the poor is the way to become obedient, that is, a listener to God. Suffering accepted and shared in love breaks down our selfish defenses and sets us free to accept God's guidance.

After my stay in Bolivia and Peru I think that I have seen, heard, and even tasted the reality of this theology. For me it is no longer an abstract concept. My time with Sophia, Pablo, and their children was an experience that gave me a glimpse of true obedience. Living, working, and playing with them brought me close to a knowledge of God that I had not experienced anywhere before.

But do I really want to know the Lord? Do I really want to listen to him? Do I really want to take up my cross and follow him? Do I really want to dedicate myself to unconditional service?

I look forward to going home tomorrow, to sitting in a comfortable airplane. I like to be welcomed home by friends. I look forward to being back again in my cozy apartment, with my books, my paintings, and my plants. I like showers with hot water, faucets with water you can drink, washing machines that work, and lamps that keep burning. I like cleanliness. But is it there that I will find God? I look forward to being back at the Trappist monastery in upstate New York, to feeling the gentle silence of the contemplative life, singing the psalmodies in the choir, and celebrating the Eucharist with all the monks in the Abbey church. I look forward to walking again in the spacious fields of the Genesee Valley and driving through the woods of Letchworth Park. But is it there that I will find God? Or is he in this dusty, dry, cloud-covered city of Lima, in this confusing, unplanned, and often chaotic conglomeration of people, dogs, and houses? Is he perhaps where the hungry kids play, the old ladies beg, and the shoeshine boys pick your pocket?

I surely have to be where he is. I have to become obedient to him, listen to his voice, and follow him wherever he calls me. Even when I do not like it, even when it is not a way of cleanliness or comfort. Jesus said to Peter: "When you were young you put on your own belt and walked where you liked; but when you grow old you will stretch out your hands, and somebody else will put a belt round you and take you where you would rather not go" (John 21:18). Am I old enough now to be led by the poor, disorganized, unclean, hungry, and uneducated?

Monday, March 29

I am at the Lima airport. It is close to midnight. My flight is leaving at 1:00 A.M. At 6:30 A.M. I will be in Miami, at 10:15 A.M. in Washington, D.C., and at 2:05 P.M. in Rochester, New York. If all goes well, I will be at the Abbey around 3:30 P.M., just in time to celebrate the Eucharist with the monks. It is hard for me to comprehend this huge step from a restless airport in Peru to the restful monastery in upstate New York. My mind cannot yet do what the plane will do.

I feel grateful, deeply grateful. George-Ann Potter and her friend, Stephanie, came to the Maryknoll Center house to say good-bye. That meant a lot to me. We decided to have a little farewell party in a nearby restaurant. John and Cheryl Hassan, Larry Rich, Betty-Ann Donnelly, and Phil Polaski, Maryknoll lay missioners who happened to be at the Center house, joined in the celebration.

Just before we left the house, the city lights went out. We found our way to the restaurant in the pitch dark and sat around a large table with a candle in the middle. It felt like a mysterious conspiracy of friends.

This spontaneous last-minute get-together was a significant conclusion to my journey that started six months ago. It was as if these good friends were telling me, without planning to do so, that it would be possible to feel truly at home in Peru, to have good friends, to pray together, to share experiences and hopes, and to work in unity for the Kingdom of God. I felt a stronger bond with this small group of people huddled around the candle than I had felt with any other group during my stay in Peru. It felt as if these friends were answering the question that had occupied me during most of my stay here: Will there be a community in Peru that can give me a sense of belonging? Nobody in the casual, unpretentious, and unplanned gathering talked about community, at-homeness, or a sense of belonging, but to me all those present spoke a language that maybe only I could fully interpret. It was in that language that I heard a true invitation to return.

It is midnight now. The plane from Buenos Aires and Santiago has just arrived. I am eager to get on board and head north; but I am also aware that something has happened to me. I sit here and wonder if going north still means going home.

CONCLUSION

A Call to Be Grateful

THE TITLE OF this journal summarizes what I found, learned, and heard. The word that I kept hearing, wherever I went, was: *Gracias!* It sounded like the refrain from a long ballad of events. *Gracias a usted, gracias a Dios, muchas gracias*—thank you, thanks be to God, many thanks! I saw thousands of poor and hungry children, I met many young men and women without money, a job, or a decent place to live. I spent long hours with sick, elderly people, and I witnessed more misery and pain than ever before in my life. But, in the midst of it all, that word lifted me again and again to a new realm of seeing and hearing: "*Gracias!* Thanks!"

In many of the families I visited nothing was certain, nothing predictable, nothing totally safe. Maybe there would be food tomorrow, maybe there would be work tomorrow, maybe there would be peace tomorrow. Maybe, maybe not. But whatever is given—money, food, work, a handshake, a smile, a good word, or an embrace—is a reason to rejoice and say *gracias*. What I claim as a right, my friends in Bolivia and Peru received as a gift; what is obvious to me was a joyful surprise to them; what I take for granted, they celebrate in thanksgiving; what for me goes by unnoticed became for them a new occasion to say thanks.

And slowly I learned. I learned what I must have forgotten somewhere in my busy, well-planned, and very "useful" life. I learned that everything that is, is freely given by the God of love. All is grace. Light and water, shelter and food, work and free time, children, parents and

454

grandparents, birth and death — it is all given to us. Why? So that we can say *gracias*, thanks: thanks to God, thanks to each other, thanks to all and everyone.

More than anything else, I learned to say thanks. The familiar expression "let us say grace" now means something very different than saying a few prayers before a meal. It now means lifting up the whole of life into the presence of God and all his people in gratitude.

As I was trying to find an answer to the question: "Does God call me to live and work in Latin America?" I gradually realized that the word *"gracias"* that came from the lips of the people contained the answer. After many centuries of missionary work during which we, the people of the north, tried to give them, the people of the south, what we felt they needed, we have now come to realize that our very first vocation is to receive their gifts to us and say thanks. A treasure lies hidden in the soul of Latin America, a spiritual treasure to be recognized as a gift for us who live in the illusion of power and self-control. It is the treasure of gratitude that can help us to break through the walls of our individual and collective self-righteousness and can prevent us from destroying ourselves and our planet in the futile attempt to hold onto what we consider our own. If I have any vocation in Latin America, it is the vocation to receive from the people the gifts they have to offer us and to bring these gifts back up north for our own conversion and healing. The Maryknoll community in Peru speaks about "reverse mission," suggesting that the movement God wants us to learn is the movement from the south to the north. In the Latin America where countless martyrs have made the suffering Christ visible, a voice that we need to hear more than ever cries out. That voice calls us anew to know with heart and mind that all that is, is given to us as a gift of love, a gift that calls us to make our life into an unceasing act of gratitude.

ACKNOWLEDGMENTS

THIS JOURNAL WOULD never have been written without the generous hospitality and skillful assistance of many friends in Latin America. Therefore my gratitude extends first to my many hosts. Pete Byrne, the Superior of the Maryknoll fathers in Peru, was the first to greet me when I came to Latin America. His faithful friendship became the context for many enriching experiences. In the months to follow, many other members of the Maryknoll community offered me a warm welcome, especially Alex Walsh, Bill McCarthy, Pete Ruggere, Tom Burns, and Charles Murray. They made me feel at home in the Maryknoll Center house in Lima and let me become part of their ministry in Ciudad de Dios. I am especially grateful to Pablo and Sophia Oscco-Moreno for letting me live with their family during my time in the parish.

My stay at the language institute in Bolivia would not have been such a good experience without the great care and attention that I received from the director, Gerry McCrane. Even if I had not learned much Spanish, just coming to know him as a friend would have made the trip worthwhile. I am also deeply grateful to Nancy and Rodolfo Quiroga, who made me a true member of their family during my two months in their home in Cochabamba. I fondly remember their kindness and great patience in correcting my mistakes in Spanish.

Two dear friends, Fran Kersjes in Bolivia and Anne Marie Tamariz in Peru, deserve a special word of thanks. They typed and retyped the text as it was first written, making it possible for me to send it to friends who wanted to know how things were going. It was a joy to work with them.

This journal would never have been published without the dedicated help of friends in the United States. I owe a deep gratitude to Bobby Massie, who spent many hours, days, and weeks editing the manuscript, suggesting cuts and changes, and helping me to separate the wheat from the chaff. His personal interest and his many words of encouragement have been essential for the progress of this project. Phil Zaeder and Peggy Schreiner generously offered their time and talents when the text needed a final critical reading. For their countless literary suggestions I am very grateful. I also want to say thanks to Richard Alan White, Robert Durback, and Fred Bratman for their insightful criticisms. Mabel Treadwell, June Hagan, and Carol Plantinga did much of the hard administrative and secretarial work during the last stages of this journal. Their generous help in sending the text to different readers and in typing and retyping it was indispensable. I cannot say "thanks" to them often enough.

John Shopp, my editor at Harper & Row, has been a great support all along the way. His personal interest in this journal and his great availability in discussing even minute details have been a real source of encouragement to me.

Finally, I want to say thanks to Joseph Núñez. He gave this journal its title and, by so doing, helped me see its main theme more clearly than ever before. When he said, "Why don't you call it *Gracias*—isn't that what you heard and said most of all?" I knew that he had made me aware of the main experience of my journey to Latin America.

Thus I can say to all who are mentioned in this journal, to all who helped it to be written and published, and to all who stand around it without being mentioned by name: *Gracias a Dios, gracias a ustedes, muchísimas gracias.*

Letters to Marc About Jesus

Living a Spiritual Life in a Material World

LETTERS TO MARC ABOUT JESUS
CONTENTS

PREFACE

SOME YEARS AGO Herman Pijfers, a publisher friend of mine, asked me: "Why don't you, for once, write a book in Dutch?" My answer at the time was, "I've been living in the United States for so long and been in my own country so seldom that I feel no longer in a position to sense the spiritual climate in the Netherlands fairly or to say anything about it." To this Herman replied, "Even so, write some letters, based on your personal situation, to a Dutch person to whom you really would like to convey something about the life of the spirit." It was that simple, but fascinating proposition that touched off these letters to Marc.

Marc van Campen is my sister's son, now nineteen years of age. When I asked him whether he might feel inclined to share the task of writing a "book of letters" about the spiritual life, he turned out to be keen on it and promised his full cooperation. After that, it was some while before I could find the time and the quiet to begin writing; but in 1986, when I did at last get down to it, writing letters to Marc became such a source of inspiration for me that it proved easy to keep going.

So these are not letters which turned out, in retrospect, to be worth publishing. They were written with publication in mind. I make a point of this because it explains their style and tone. From the beginning, and despite the fact that these letters were indeed written for Marc, I had in mind a readership far wider than those of his age and upbringing. That may be why the "epistolary" aspect has here and there gone by the board. Still, it would not have been possible to write these texts at all had Marc

461

not been open to receiving them as an interested and critical party. From beginning to end he was the center of my concern.

In the course of writing I became aware that I was engaged not only in telling Marc what I thought about Jesus and the meaning of our existence, but also in rediscovering Jesus and the meaning of my existence for myself. When I began these letters I had no precise idea as to how I should write about the spiritual life. I was often surprised to find that places where I was staying, events that were happening in the world, and people whom I met were providing me with new ideas and new perspectives. These letters, then, have come to be a logbook of spiritual discoveries that I want to share with Marc and others. Although my initial intention was to write something helpful to Marc himself, it soon became evident that my main concern was to convey to him the enthusiasm I was feeling about my own discoveries. The letters in this book witness first and foremost, therefore, to my personal dealing with the life of faith. It was in that spirit also that Marc himself has received and valued them.

The original plan had been to record Marc's reactions as well. I eventually dropped that idea because it suited me better to use his reactions, which were mostly requests for clarification, in my reworking of the text. That made it possible to achieve a greater degree of internal unity and clarity.

I am especially grateful to Herman Pijfers and to Marc for the parts they have played in the writing of this book. Without them it would never have seen the light of day. I would also like to thank Mrs. B. van Breemen for her secretarial assistance, Pieter Janssens and Margreet Stelling for their stylistic corrections, and Lieven Sercu for being of such great help to me on the editorial side.

I very much hope that those who are asking themselves what it means to lead a spiritual life will be helped by this book.

Jesus: The Heart of Our Existence

Tuesday, 11th February

My dear Marc,

Well now, I've got round to it at last. It must be a year or so since I promised to write you some letters about the spiritual life. Over the past twelve months you've reminded me frequently of my promise. "When are those letters of yours going to arrive?" It was difficult to get down to it because there always seemed to be something more urgent to attend to. However, if I were to let my life be taken over by what is urgent, I might very well never get around to what is essential. It's so easy to spend your whole time being preoccupied with urgent matters and never starting to live, really to live.

But is writing letters to you essential? Of course not, at least in the usual sense of the word. Even without any letters from me you have two dear parents, a lovely sister, a caring brother, a comfortable home, good food, a congenial school, and plenty of relaxation. You're well looked after, in good health, and intelligent. At eighteen you've already seen a good deal of the world: France, Germany, Switzerland, Italy, and the United States. You've also got plenty of hobbies—stamp collecting, film, music, Egyptian art—and lots to talk about. You've not only got a very inquiring mind, but you're also very gifted. There's really very little you can't do or can't acquire. So why do you need any letters from me?

When we spoke together about these letters, you said that you really did need them. That need, I think, is partly a consequence of your stay in the United States. When you attended that summer course in Concord, New Hampshire, and saw young men and women as intelligent as yourself genuinely concerned with religion in their lives, it raised some new questions in your mind. You asked yourself, "What do I really believe? What kind of role does the church play in my life? Who is Christ for me? Does the Eucharist make sense to me?" All those questions were more or less mixed up together; but it was clear that a new area had been opened up within you and asked for your attention. You might say that in the last year or so a new need has been brought to birth inside you: the need to look in the midst of everything you have and are doing, for the meaning and purpose of your life.

You yourself know that if you keep fit, if nothing goes wrong, if no war breaks out, and so on, then you probably won't have much trouble in becoming a prosperous lawyer or a well-heeled businessman. I haven't forgotten what you said to me in Boston: that you would probably come back to America later on to make a career. When I pointed out that a lot of people in America fail to make it, you replied with considerable self-confidence, "Not the clever ones!" So you're evidently not worried about your financial prospects. Still, you're asking yourself, "Even if I am a big success, so what?"

It may actually be your self-assurance that allows you to raise frankly the question about the meaning of your life. A lot of people have to expend so much energy on overcoming their low opinion of themselves that they seldom get round to asking about the purpose of their existence. And if they do, it is often out of fear.

It's not like that for you. For you the question has a different significance because many problems that other people are intensely aware of are scarcely problems at all for you. Invariably, you sail through your homework and still get high marks for it. You're good at sports, have good friends, and many interests. Everything comes easily for you. That is why, I think, you have room and time to ask yourself questions that to many of your classmates seem irrelevant. Your American experience has given you the confidence to pose these questions quite directly and not bother about what your friends are going to think. In that sense your self-assurance would seem to be an advantage where the development of a spiritual life is concerned. For it is indeed the life of the spirit with which we are dealing here: that is what these letters must be about. Now, if you set out to confront issues that affect the meaning of your life, you can't adopt an approach based purely on reason. Questions about the meaning of your life affect your whole person. They are connected not only with the way you think and act; but also, and even more so, with the way you are a human being, and with the bond between you and everything that is.

Living spiritually is more than living physically, intellectually, or emotionally. It embraces all that, but it is larger, deeper, and wider. It concerns the core of your humanity. It is possible to lead a very wholesome, emotionally rich, and "sensible" life without being a spiritual person: that is, without knowledge or personal experience of the terrain where the meaning and goal of our human existence are hidden.

The spiritual life has to do with the *heart* of existence. This is a good word. By heart I do not mean the seat of our feelings as opposed to the seat of our thoughts; I mean the center of our being, that place where we are most ourselves, where we are most human, where we are most real. In that sense the heart is the focus of the spiritual life. I shall have more to say about that later on; but here and now I want to make sure you understand the word 'heart' because for me it is such an important word in the life of the spirit. There are times when I would like to substitute the expression 'life of the heart' for 'the spiritual life'; but that smacks of sentimentality, and so I shall stick to the more traditional 'spiritual'—as long as you realize that 'spiritual' is not the opposite of physical or emotional or intellectual. I haven't yet found a good word for the opposite of 'spiritual'; but the 'unspiritual' is that which does not affect the heart of our being, that which remains on the surface, or that which belongs to the margins of existence rather than to its core.

There are many contexts for discussions about 'the spiritual life.' Buddhists, Hindus, Muslims are all living a spiritual life. Even people who see themselves as nonreligious can have a profound spiritual life. However, when I write to you about the spiritual life, I do so as a Christian whose experience is that of living his Christianity in union with the

Catholic tradition. For me, this is the sole possibility, in as much as it's only as a Catholic Christian that I know the spiritual life, to some extent, from the inside. And I want to write only about what I myself have lived out and lived through.

I want to give you a taste of the richness of life as a Christian as I know it, experience it, and continue to discover it. I really do believe that I have something of importance to tell you and I am very happy that I can do so. It is so good to be able to set what is most precious to me before someone who is happy to listen and who is also ready to take a very personal interest in it.

As you know, I'm thirty-six years older than you. When I was your age I was at the Aloysius College in The Hague. At the time I found it very difficult to study, much more difficult than you do. I was a keen Boy Scout and later a Rover. You probably find that hard to imagine. I used to attend daily Mass and was a diligent altar boy. In that, too, our backgrounds differ. Along with other fellow students intending to become priests, I belonged to a group dedicated to self-examination with much discussion of prayer. This must sound strange to you now. Despite all the differences between those times and the present, the question of the spiritual life is no less relevant today. The difference is that you don't have the support that I did. You have to face the question alone and must make a concerted effort to grapple with it on your own. It's not forced on you. For me it has been a lifelong preoccupation.

Back in 1957 when I became a priest, I may have thought I knew what it was to live spiritually. If that's what I thought then, I certainly don't think so now. My studies in psychology at Nijmegen and my years spent teaching in the Netherlands, the United States, and Latin America have taught me that raising questions about the spiritual life leads more to a new way of living than to a new way of thinking. These questions have to be lived rather than developed intellectually. I have tried to live them myself in various ways: with Catholics and Protestants, with Christians and humanists, with radical revolutionaries and traditional patriots, with the resentful and the resigned, with rich and poor, with the healthy and the sick. Time after time I've learned something new and have discovered how much more there is to live.

In every phase of my search I've discovered also that Jesus Christ stands at the center of my seeking. If you were to ask me point-blank, "What does it mean to you to live spiritually?" I would have to reply, "Living with Jesus at the center."

Countless questions, problems, discussions, and difficulties always demand one's attention. Despite this, when I look back over the last thirty years of my life, I can say that, for me, the person of Jesus has come to be more and more important. Increasingly, what matters is getting to know Jesus and living in solidarity with him. At one time I was so immersed in problems of church and society that my whole life had become a sort of drawn-out, wearisome discussion. Jesus had been pushed into the background; he had himself become just another problem. Fortunately, it hasn't stayed that way. Jesus has stepped out in front again and asked me, "And you, who do you say that I am?" It has become clearer to me than ever that my personal relationship with Jesus is the heart of my existence.

It is about Jesus, above all, that I want to write to you in these letters, and I want to do so in a personal way. I don't want to lecture you about Jesus, but to tell you about him as I have come to know him. I am not trying to avoid the many questions about religion and church-life, war and peace, poverty and wealth, which you and I raise today; but I do want to subordinate them to the question: "Who is Jesus for you and for me?" So, what I intend is to start from my conviction that Jesus is the heart of my existence and, on that basis, to take a look at the world we live in. These letters can also help me to intensify my own experience of being a Christian and so prepare me for the Feast of the Resurrection, which we shall be celebrating in forty days time, when Easter comes.

I do hope that with this letter we are on to something really good.

My warmest greeting to you,
Henri

Jesus: The God Who Sets Us Free

Thursday, 13th February

My dear Marc,

At the moment I'm in Freiburg-im-Breisgau, a charming little town in South Germany that was completely rebuilt after the big air raid of 27th November 1944. As luck would have it, or thanks to instructions given to the officer commanding the bomber squadron, the beautiful cathedral remained undamaged. The Münster's slender tower stands like a resplendent jewel at the heart of the town and gives you a feeling of reassurance. Every time I visit this cathedral church I feel more centered and serene. The simple thought that construction on this church began in the year 1200 and went on until 1513 is reason enough to calm down and not behave as though everything has to be wrapped up this very afternoon. Freiburg today is a quiet, altogether peaceful little place. Everything runs like clockwork. The people are friendly, the shops full, the streets clean, the trains run on time, and you can see that no one goes short of anything. As there isn't much industry, the town has kept its intimate and homely character. This is reinforced by the way the center has been reconstructed. Water burbles along the runnels laid down in the streets. Cars aren't admitted; only a few colorful streetcars. In the evening, the finest buildings are floodlighted; and from the open tower of the Münster there streams a warm, amber glow. It makes for a very inviting atmosphere.

Walking around here like this, I have the feeling that this world of ours must be all right. Things are going well. But you yourself know that Freiburg doesn't tell the whole story. The papers are full of dictator "Baby Doc" Duvalier's flight from Haiti and of the violent disorder accompanying the elections in the Philippines. From everywhere there comes news of violence and oppression. The new leader in Uganda, Yoweri Museveni, shows journalists the mass graves of the victims of his predecessor, Milton Obote. Museveni claims that between 1980 and 1985 some 200,000 people in his country were murdered. And you have only to think of South Africa, Northern Ireland, Iran and Iraq, Central America, and many other places in the world to know beyond a doubt that the peace and quiet of Freiburg tell a good deal less than half the truth.

I'm also reminded of this by two priests with whom I have breakfast every morning. One is a refugee from Czechoslovakia, and the other is a Croat. Their stories confirm what the newspapers tell us in all sorts of ways; for most people freedom is a dream. It's a lot easier to find evidence of oppression in this world than of freedom. And from what I know of history I get the impression that it has never been much different.

I'm mentioning all this to help you appreciate the first story I want to tell you about Jesus. It's the story of Cleopas and his friend who, with heavy hearts, had set out on the road from Jerusalem to Emmaus. They were going home, disillusioned, dejected, and downcast. We don't know much about these two friends, but Luke in his Gospel intimates quite clearly how they felt: beaten and oppressed. For a long time past, the Romans had been masters in their country; there was little genuine freedom and, as anyone would be, they were impatient to be free. When they came to know Jesus, their hopes were raised that this man from Nazareth would be able to give them the freedom they had been looking forward to for so long. But it had all come to nothing. The Jesus of whom they had expected so much had been arrested, condemned to death, and crucified by the Romans. Everything was just as it had been before: a life in which you could be picked up at any moment and put in jail. Freedom had not returned. Cleopas and his friend had lost heart. In their despair they were making their way back home. It was not a way of hope. It was a cheerless way, a despairing way.

It will not be easy for you to identify with these two men. You've had no experience of being oppressed. I can still remember vaguely what it is like. I was thirteen when the Second World War ended. I can still recall the infamous winter of hunger and the victorious entry of the Canadians in May 1945. I've personally experienced the difference between "being occupied" and "being free," and so I know what a privileged individual I've been since 1945. For you, being oppressed is an unknown experience. Nevertheless, you are, I think, somewhat able to put yourself in the shoes of people who above all else long to be completely and utterly free, and you are able to understand to some degree how they must feel.

Jesus joins the two men, but they fail to recognize him. What does he do? First he listens to their sad story in a very personal, you might say intimate, fashion. He enters right into their sense of disappointment. He shares their feelings with them. He is prepared to be where they are.

Here you have to remember what had happened to Jesus himself. He had been hideously tortured to death and then buried. People often talk about Jesus as though his death had been followed immediately by his resurrection, but that's not what is reported to us by the gospels. Jesus lay in the tomb for three days. That means not only that he had been, like many people today, the victim of oppression; but also that his body, like everyone else's, proceeded to decay. When Lazarus had been lying in the tomb for four days, his sister Martha said to Jesus: "Lord, by now he will smell." The grave is a place of putrefaction. Jesus lay in the tomb for three days; and there his body putrefied. I mention this because decomposition is surely the most telling symbol of human desperation. Whatever we do or say, however learned we are, however many our friends or great our wealth—in ten, thirty, fifty, seventy years' time—we shall rot. That's why we are so deeply affected by life's disappointments and setbacks. They remind us that, sooner or later, everything decays. Despair is our inner conviction that, in the end, it is utterly impossible to prevent anything from coming to nothing.

Left with the impression that their great expectations had once again been shattered, Cleopas and his friend were grief-stricken. Yet again, it had become painfully clear to them just how meaningless their lives really were. They had already caught a whiff of the decay afflicting their own lives. So it was with bowed heads that they were making for home. It wasn't just their adventure with Jesus that was over, everything else had come to nothing in the end.

So when Jesus joins these two dejected men, he knows very well what is in their hearts. He knows from experience what human despair is. He knows death and the tomb; he knows what it means to be mortal. Cleopas and his friend must, I think, have perceived that this stranger was really no stranger at all. He understood them too well to remain strange to them for long. They saw that this man was not going to offer them easy words of comfort. When it is Jesus' turn to speak, he speaks with an authority based not on power, but on personal experience of living. That's why they listen to him so attentively.

What does Jesus tell them? Not that death and the dissolution of life are unreal. Nor that their yearning for freedom is unreal. No: in what he says he takes seriously not only death and dissolution, but their longing for freedom as well. He tells them that the Jesus in whom they had placed all their hopes, the Jesus who was indeed dead and buried, this Jesus is alive. He tells them that for the Jesus whom they had admired so much, death and dissolution have become the way to liberation. And he says this in such a way that they sense in their innermost selves that his way can become their way too.

As Jesus was talking to them, they experienced in their hearts the arrival of something new. It was as if their hearts were burning with a flame that came not from without but from within. Jesus had kindled in them something for which they had no words but which was so authentic, so real, that it overcame their depression. Jesus had not said, "It isn't nearly as bad as you think." He had said something entirely new: "The most tragic, the most painful, the most hopeless circumstances can become the way to the liberation you long for most of all."

It's very difficult for you and me to grasp much of this. In fact, it goes against logic. You and I as rational people say, "Death is death. Death and all that approaches it or leads to it must be avoided at all costs. The further away we can stay from death and everything connected to it— pain, illness, war, oppression, poverty, hunger and so on—the better for us." That's a normal, spontaneous human attitude. But Jesus makes us see human existence from a quite different angle, one that is beyond the reach of our ordinary common sense.

Jesus makes us see existence in terms of his own experience that life is stronger and greater than death and dissolution. It's only with our hearts that we can understand this. Luke doesn't write: "Then it dawned on them" or "Then they saw the light." No, he says, "Their hearts burned within them." The burning heart revealed something completely new to Cleopas and his friend. At the center of their being, of their humanity, something was generated that could disarm death and rob despair of its power; something much more than a new outlook on things, a new confidence, or a new joy in living; something that can be described only as a new life or a new spirit. Nowadays we would say: "In their hearts the spiritual life had begun"; but it's better not to use these terms at this point. Otherwise, we shall stray too far from the actual story and there's too much still to be told.

When the three men reached Emmaus, so much had happened between them that the two companions were unwilling to let the stranger go. Between these two and Jesus there had arisen a bond which had given them new hope, even though they scarcely knew why. They felt that this unknown individual had given them something new. They didn't want to go indoors without him. So they said, "Stay with us. It is nearly evening, and the day is almost over." Luke, in his account, even says that they implored him to be their guest. Jesus accepted the invitation and went in with them.

And now there happens something which, for you and me, is of major significance. It touches the very core of the spiritual life. When they sit down to eat, Jesus takes some bread, speaks a blessing over it, breaks it and offers it to them. And as he does so, they know suddenly and with unshakeable certainty that this stranger is Jesus, the same Jesus who had been put to death and laid in a tomb. But at the precise moment this certainty is given to them, he becomes invisible to them.

So much is going on here that it's difficult to get its full significance across to you; and so I shall limit myself to what is, for me, a very crucial aspect of this incident. What matters here is that the moment Cleopas and his friend recognized Jesus in the breaking of bread, his bodily presence was no longer required as a condition for their new hope. You might say that the bond between them and the stranger had become so intimate that everything strange about him vanishes, and, in the most literal sense, he becomes their bosom friend. So close does he come to them that they no longer need a bodily manifestation in order to hope. They realize now that the new life born in them as they talked with him on the road will stay with them and give them the strength to return to Jerusalem and tell the other people why it isn't true that "It's all over." That's why Luke reports that they went off straightaway to tell Jesus' other friends about their experience.

Are you beginning to see what I'm getting at? Cleopas and his friend had become different people. Because they had experienced for themselves that the Jesus whom they had mourned for was alive and closer to them than ever, their hearts were born again, and their inner life was made radically new. That's something quite different from coming to a new conviction or acquiring a new outlook on things or undergoing a change of opinion. Something much more profound than that had happened to these two. The Jesus they had seen had come not only into their home, but into their hearts as well, so that they were enabled to share in the new life he had won through his death and disintegration.

What you see here is a process of fundamental liberation. Because Jesus joined them, the two men who walked from Jerusalem to Emmaus made a spiritual journey too. When they first set out, liberation still meant shaking off the Roman yoke. They had hoped that Jesus would help them, and they were deeply dismayed when their great hero, their liberator, was put to death. But then, when Jesus offered them the bread and their eyes were opened, they became conscious of a freedom they had never thought possible. It was a freedom which they could hardly anticipate because they had no conception of it. It was a freedom unknown to them and, therefore, beyond their asking. It was a freedom that went much further and deeper than the freedom for which they had hoped and dreamed; a freedom that invaded their hearts to the very depths; a freedom that no earthly power, Roman or Jewish, could take from them. It was a freedom of the spirit: a freedom from any specific political, economic, or social expectations for the future, a freedom to follow the Lord now, anywhere, even if it should mean suffering.

Let me take these thoughts about the freedom Jesus gives to Cleopas and his friend a little further. The better you understand that spiritual freedom and get the feel of it for yourself, the greater the chance that you will come to discover who Jesus is. A number of people in this century have written about spiritual freedom: Dietrich Bonhoeffer, in *Letters and Papers from Prison*; Etty Hillesum, in her diary, *An Interrupted Life*; Titus Brandsma, in his letters from a Dutch jail. Amid the most frightful forms of oppression and violence these people discovered within themselves a place where no one had power over them, where they were wholly free. Although very different from one another, they had in common an awareness of spiritual freedom that enabled them to stand on their own two feet in the world, without being manipulated by that world. Their freedom was such that they had even overcome, to a great extent, the fear of death. They knew in their heart of hearts that those who might be able to destroy their bodies would never be able to deprive them of their freedom. Jesus himself spoke of that freedom when he told his disciples: "Do not be afraid of those who kill the body but cannot kill the soul."

What I personally find so fascinating is that this *spiritual* freedom is something quite different from a *spiritualized* freedom. The freedom Jesus gives doesn't imply that oppressors can go on oppressing, that the poor can stay poor and the hungry stay hungry, since we are now, in a spiritual respect, free. A true spiritual freedom that touches the heart of our being in all its humanity must take effect in every sphere: physical, emotional, social, and global. It is meant to be everywhere visible; but the core of this spiritual freedom doesn't depend on the manner in which it is made visible. A sick, mentally handicapped, or oppressed person can still be spiritually free, even if that freedom cannot as yet manifest itself in every area of life.

I became sharply aware of this when I visited Nicaragua. In a small village, Jalapa, I talked with the women whose husbands or sons had been brutally murdered by the so-called Contras. These women knew all too well that the Contras were being backed by the United States, and yet there was no detectable trace of hatred or vindictiveness in them. They remembered the words of Jesus on the cross: "Father, forgive them; they do not know what they are doing" and were ready, like Jesus, to pray for their enemies to be forgiven.

When I was with them, I sensed their deep spiritual freedom. Amid all the oppression no one had been able to deprive them of that. Their hearts had remained free, and their indescribable suffering had not broken their spirits. For me, that was an unforgettable experience. There, on the border between Nicaragua and Honduras, I saw something of that same freedom which Cleopas and his friend knew after they had recognized Jesus and admitted him into their hearts.

Freedom belongs to the core of the spiritual life; not just the freedom which releases us from forces that want to oppress us, but the freedom also to forgive others, to serve them, and to form a new bond of fellowship with them. In short, the freedom to love and to work for a free world.

I should really leave it at that. But I still want to tell you something else concerning Luke's Emmaus story, something which has quite concrete consequences for your day-to-day life, something that will bring the event a bit closer to you.

The story was written when the first Christian congregations had already been formed. So it speaks to us not only about Jesus and the spiritual life, but also about life in the very early church. In fact, it was written within the context of a believing community and its lived experience. That gives the story a whole new dimension. It tells us something about the different aspects of communal worship: owning up to our confusion, depression, despair, and guilt; listening with an open heart to the Word of God; gathering around the table to break the bread and so to acknowledge the presence of Jesus; and going out again into the world to make known to others what we have learned and experienced. You've probably seen already that these are the various components of a Eucharistic celebration. It's there that you find confession of sin, proclamation and exposition of the Word, partaking of the Lord's Supper, and being sent out into the world. Thus you can say that each time you celebrate the Eucharist you once again make the journey from Jerusalem to Emmaus and back. You can say, too, that each time you celebrate the Eucharist you are able to achieve a bit more spiritual freedom. Freedom from the subjugating powers of this world, powers that forever try to entice you to become rich and popular, and freedom to love friend and foe.

So here you are, very nearly back on home ground after all. You've often asked me about the meaning of the Eucharist. Insofar as you get to know Jesus, you will begin to understand better the significance of the Eucharist. This letter will, I hope, help you to appreciate the connection.

This has turned out to be a long letter. I have worked on it, though not without a good deal of joy, for quite some time. It's now half past five on a Saturday afternoon, and I want to get back into the center of Freiburg once more to visit the cathedral. It's always very quiet on a Saturday afternoon in Münster square. By the time I get there it will be dark, and that warm, amber light will be glowing again through the spire. I wish you were here so we could go together. That can't be, alas! So I'm enclosing a few post cards. They will give you some idea of the place at any rate.

Greetings and love to your parents, and to your sister and brother, Frédérique and Reinier.

Till next time,
Henri

Jesus: The Compassionate God

Monday, 17th February

My dear Marc,

Yesterday I went with some friends to Colmar, a French town in Alsace an hour from Freiburg by car. We went there to take a look at the Isenheimer Altar. You've probably heard about it already. You may even have seen it. For me it proved to be a very profound experience.

The Isenheimer Altar was painted between 1513 and 1515 for the chapel at the hospital for plague victims in the small village of Isenheim, not far from Colmar. The artist was a man of such a retiring disposition, some say very melancholic as well, that historians are still unable to agree who he actually was. According to most authorities, Matthias Grünewald was the creator of this masterpiece. In it the whole pictorial art of the late Middle Ages is summed up and brought to its highest point. This work is not only the most spectacular altarpiece ever made, but also the most moving.

The altarpiece is a multiple series of panels. The front panel depicts Jesus' death on the cross. On the second, Grünewald has painted the Annunciation, the birth of Jesus, and his resurrection. On the third, which actually consists of two panels on each side of a group of sculpted figures, you can see the temptations of St. Anthony and his visit to the hermit Paul.

Although I had read two booklets by Wilhelm Nyssen before visiting this altar, the reality surpassed any description or reproduction. When I saw the body of Jesus on the cross, tortured, emaciated, and covered with abscesses, I had an inkling of the reaction of the plague-stricken and dying sufferers in the sixteenth century. On this altar they saw their God, with the same suppurating ulcers as their own, and it made them realize with a shock what the Incarnation really meant. They saw solidarity, compassion, forgiveness, and unending love brought together in this one suffering figure. They saw that, in their mortal anguish, they had not been left on their own.

But they saw too, when the front panel was opened out, that the tortured body of Jesus, born of Mary, had not only died for them, but—also for them—had risen gloriously from death. The same ulcerated body they saw hanging dead on the cross exudes a dazzling light and rises upward in divine splendor—a splendor which is also in store for us.

The two Anthony panels on both sides of the dramatic statuary reminded the plague-ridden sufferers that sharing in the divine glory of Jesus demands a readiness to share in his temptations as well. Anthony was the patron of the monastic order that nursed the plague victims, and his life showed, without any cheap sentimentality, that those who would follow Jesus are bound to have a narrow and frequently rocky road to tread.

I remained at the Isenheimer Altar for more than three hours. During that time I learned more about suffering and resurrection than from many days of reading. The crucified and risen Christ of Matthias Grünewald is carved so deeply into my memory and imagination now that wherever I go or stay I can call him to mind. I know now in a completely new way that if I am to succeed in fully living my life, in all its painful yet glorious moments, I must remain united to Jesus.

As we drove back through the vine-covered hills of the Kaiserstuhl, in Germany, I also came to understand better what Jesus meant when he said to his friends: "I am the vine, you are the branches. Whoever remains in me, with me in him, bears fruit in plenty; for cut off from me you can do nothing."

Remarkably enough, I'd already made up my mind last week to write to you this week about the suffering and resurrection of Christ. At that time I hadn't yet seen the Isenheimer Altar. Now I have a feeling that I had to see it in order to find the words I need for this letter.

The record of the suffering and resurrection of Jesus forms the kernel of the "good news" which Jesus' disciples intended to make known to the world. Jesus is the Lord who has suffered, died, was buried, and rose again on the third day. Everyone had to know about that. These were the "glad tidings"; and so they still are. You could say that everything else the four Gospels have to say about Jesus is intended to bring out the full significance of his suffering, death, and resurrection.

When I saw the Isenheimer Altar yesterday, this became clear to me again. Without the death and resurrection of Jesus the gospel is a beautiful tale about an exceptionally saintly person, a tale that might inspire good thoughts and great deeds; but there are other stories of that sort. The gospel is, first and foremost, the story of the death and resurrection of Jesus, and that story constitutes the core of the spiritual life. Grünewald understood this and wanted to make it plain to the dying men and women of his time.

It won't be easy to write to you about the death and resurrection of Jesus in a way that will affect you deeply. True, you've had scarcely any proper instruction in religion and have taken only a sporadic interest in the gospel, but the story of Jesus' death and resurrection is such a familiar part of the milieu in which you've grown up that it can hardly surprise, astound, or shock you any more. You're more likely to say, "Oh yes. I know about that; let's talk about something else." Yet somehow I have to alert you to the truth that what this is all about (the suffering, death, and resurrection of Jesus) is the most fundamental, the most far-reaching event ever to occur in the course of history. If you don't see and feel that for yourself, then the gospel can be, at most, interesting; but it can never renew your heart and make you a reborn human being. And rebirth is what you are called to—a radical liberation that sets you free from the power of death and empowers you to love fearlessly.

When I saw Grünewald's paintings of the tortured, naked body of Jesus, I realized anew that the cross isn't just a beautiful piece of art decorating the living rooms and restaurants of Freiburg; it is the sign of the most radical transformation in our manner of thinking, feeling, and living. Jesus' death on the cross has changed everything. What is the most spontaneous human response to suffering and death? The words that spring immediately to my mind are these: preventing, avoiding, denying, shunning, keeping clear of, and ignoring. All of these words indicate that suffering and death don't fit into our program for living. We react to them as uninvited, undesirable, and unwelcome interlopers, and we want to show them the door as soon as we can. If we get sick, our primary concern is to get better as quickly as possible. If that doesn't happen, then we try to persuade ourselves or each other that it may not be as bad as it looks and to convince one another, often against all odds, that everything will be all right again. If, nevertheless, death does come, we are often surprised, taken aback, deeply disappointed, or even angry.

Fortunately, Elisabeth Kübler-Ross and others have worked hard to bring about a change in this attitude and to offer a more realistic view of suffering and death; but my own experience has been that, for most people, these are still the chief enemies of life. They really ought not to exist. We must try, somehow, to get them under control as well as we can and, if that doesn't work the first time, we must try to do better the second time.

Many sick people don't have much understanding about their sickness, and often they die without ever having given much thought to their death. About a year ago a friend of mine died of cancer. Six months before his death, it was already obvious that he hadn't long to live. Even so, it was very difficult to prepare him properly for his death. He was so surrounded with tubes and hoses and busy nurses, that one got the impression that he had to be kept alive at any price. No one did anything wrong—it was all according to the rules. But so much attention was given to keeping him alive that there was hardly time to prepare him for death.

The result of this for us is that we no longer pay much attention to the dead. We do little to remember them, to make them a part of our interior life. How often do you visit your grandmother's grave? How often do your mother and I visit the graves of our deceased grandparents, uncles, aunts, and friends? In fact, we behave as though they no longer belong to us, as though we have nothing more to do with them. They no longer have any real influence on our lives. Not only have they gone from us physically, but they have also left the world of our thoughts and feelings.

Jesus' attitude was quite different. He encountered suffering and death with his eyes wide open. Actually, his whole life was a conscious preparation for them. Jesus doesn't commend them as desirable things; but he does speak of them as realities we ought not to repudiate, avoid, or cover up.

On a number of occasions he foretold his own suffering and death. Quite soon after Jesus had commissioned his twelve disciples, he was already telling them: "The Son of man is destined to suffer grievously, to be rejected by the elders and chief priests and scribes and to be put to death, and to be raised up on the third day." Not so long after, he repeated this prophecy with the words: "Have these words constantly in mind: The Son of man is going to be delivered into the power of men." That even in those days people wanted to ignore reality is surely evident from Peter's reaction. "Taking Jesus aside, Peter started to rebuke him. 'Heaven preserve you, Lord,' he said, 'this must not happen to you.'" Jesus' reply is cutting. It would even appear that he regards Peter's reaction as the most dangerous of all for those in quest of a truly spiritual life: "Get behind me, Satan! You are an obstacle in my path, because you are thinking not as God thinks but as human beings do." After that he tells his disciples yet again, and very plainly, that a person who wants to lead a spiritual life cannot do so without the prospect of suffering and death. Living spiritually is made possible only through a direct, uncushioned confrontation with the reality of death. Just listen to what Jesus has to say: "If anyone wants to be a follower of mine, let him renounce himself and take up his cross and follow me. Anyone who wants to save his life will lose it; but anyone who loses his life for my sake will find it."

Finding new life through suffering and death: that is the core of the good news. Jesus has lived out that liberating way before us and has made it the great sign. Human beings are forever wanting to see signs: marvelous, extraordinary, sensational events or people that can distract them a little from hard reality. It isn't without reason that we keep on looking for signs among the stars, whether they are stars in the skies or stars in the movies. We would like to see something marvelous, something exceptional, something that interrupts the ordinary life of every day. That way, if only for a moment, we can play at hide-and-seek. But to those who say to Jesus: "Master . . . we should like to see a sign," he replied, "It is an evil and unfaithful generation that asks for a sign! The only sign it will be given is the sign of the prophet Jonah. For as Jonah remained in the belly of the sea-monster for three days and three nights, so will the Son of man be in the heart of the earth for three days and three nights."

From this you can see what the authentic sign is; not some sensational miracle but the suffering, death, burial, and resurrection of Jesus. The great sign, which can be understood only by those who follow Jesus, is the sign of Jonah, who also wanted to run away from reality but was summoned back by God to fulfill his arduous task to the end. To look suffering and death straight in the face *and* to go through them oneself in the hope of a new God-given life: that is the sign of Jesus and of every human being who wishes to lead a spiritual life in imitation of him. It is the sign of the cross: the sign of suffering and death, but also of the hope for total renewal.

That's why Matthias Grünewald had the courage to confront the dying patients in the Isenheim hospital so directly with the terrible suffering of Jesus. He dared to show them what we all prefer to shut our eyes to, because he believed that suffering and death no longer barred the way to the new life but had become, through Jesus, the way to it. If you look carefully you see that the cross painted by Grünewald looks like a drawn bow with an arrow. That is in itself a sign of hope. The tortured body of Jesus is bound to an arrow pointing toward the new life.

So what, in concrete terms, are we to make of Jesus' suffering and death? In telling you the story of Cleopas and his friend in the previous letter, I wanted to show you that freedom is an essential aspect of the spiritual life. From the story of Jesus' suffering and death it will be clear to you now that compassion must be added to freedom. The spiritual life is a free life that becomes visible in compassion. I now want to help you to see and feel this more clearly.

God sent Jesus to make free persons of us. He has chosen compassion as the way to freedom. That is a great deal more radical than you might at first imagine. It means that God wanted to liberate us, not by removing suffering from us, but by sharing it with us. Jesus is God who-suffers-with-us. Over time, the word *sympathizing* has become a somewhat feeble way of expressing the reality of "suffering with" someone. Nowadays, if someone says, "I have sympathy for you," it has a rather distant ring about it. The feeling, at least for me, is of someone looking down from above. The word's original meaning of "suffering together with someone" has been partly lost. That's why I've opted for the word compassion. It's warmer, more intimate, and closer. For me, it's taking part in the suffering of the other, being totally a fellow-human-being in suffering.

God's love, which Jesus wants to make us see, is shown to us by his becoming a partner and a companion in our suffering, thus enabling us to turn it into a way to liberation. You're probably familiar with the questions most frequently raised by people who find it difficult or impossible to believe in God: How can God really love the world when he permits all that frightful suffering? If God really loves us why doesn't he put an end to war, poverty, hunger, sickness, persecution, torture, and all the other misery that we see everywhere? If God cares about me personally why am I in such bad shape? Why do I always feel so lonely? Why am I still without a job? Why do I feel my existence to be so pointless?

I've been preoccupied continually with these questions myself, especially since I got to know the poverty that exists in Central and South America and saw how innocent Indians are kidnapped, tortured, and killed in the most cruel fashion.

Paradoxically, it was there that I found the beginning of an answer! I discovered that the victims of poverty and oppression are often more deeply convinced of God's love than we middle-class Europeans are, and that the question of the why of suffering was raised less by the people who had tasted suffering themselves than by you who had only heard and read about it. Seldom have I seen so much trust in God as among the poor and oppressed Indians of Central and South America. While it seems to be getting more and more difficult for a lot of people in the Netherlands, who have become increasingly well off during the last few years, to have a sense of the nearness of God in their day-to-day lives, many men and women in Latin America, whose suffering can be read on their faces, are filled with the Spirit when they tell how God gives them hope and courage.

You will appreciate, of course, the deep impression this has made on me. I've gradually come to see that these people have learned to know Jesus as the God who suffers with them. For them, the suffering and dying Jesus is the most convincing sign that God really loves them very much and does not leave them uncared for. He is their companion in suffering. If they are poor, they know that Jesus was poor too; if they are afraid, they know that Jesus also was afraid; if they are beaten, they know that Jesus too was beaten; and if they are tortured to death, well then, they know that Jesus suffered the same fate. For these people, Jesus is the faithful friend who treads with them the lonely road of suffering and brings them consolation. He is with them in solidarity. He knows them, understands them, and clasps them to himself in their moments of greatest pain.

The statues of Jesus that I saw in the churches of San Pedro in Lima, and in those of Santiago at the lake of Atitlán in Guatemala, present an exhausted man, scourged, crowned with thorns, and covered with wounds. I often found it horrible to look at; but for the Peruvians and Guatemalan Indians, this broken human being was their greatest source of hope.

Perhaps all of this seems a bit remote, yet you and I too have experiences that make us sensitive to the compassion of Jesus. A real friend isn't someone who can solve all your problems or who has an answer to every question. No, a real friend is someone who doesn't walk off when there are no solutions or answers, but sticks by you and remains faithful to you. It often turns out that the one who gives us the most comfort is not the person who says, "Do this, say that, go there"; but the one who, even if there is no good advice to give, says, "Whatever happens, I'm your friend; you can count on me." The older you become, the more you discover that your joy and happiness depend on such friendships. The great secret in life is that suffering, which often seems to be so unbearable, can become, through compassion, a source of new life and new hope.

God has become human so as to be able to live with us, suffer with us, and die with us. We have found in Jesus a fellow human being who is so completely one with us that not a single weakness, pain, or temptation has remained foreign to him. Precisely because Jesus is God and without any sin, he is able to experience our sinful, broken human condition so thoroughly that we may say he knows us better than we know ourselves and loves us more than we love ourselves. No one else, however well disposed, is ever in a position to be with us so completely that we feel ourselves to be understood and loved without limit. We humans remain too self-centered to be able to forget ourselves fully for the other person's sake. But Jesus does give himself fully, he holds nothing back for himself; he wants to be with us in so total a fashion that we can never again feel alone.

Jesus is the compassionate God who comes so close to us in our weakness that we can turn to him without fear. The Letter to the Hebrews puts it in incomparably profound words: "He has been put to the test in exactly the same way as ourselves, apart from sin. Let us, then, have no fear in approaching the throne of grace, to receive mercy and to find grace when we are in need of help."

I hope that you can grasp something of all this and take it to heart. In the end, I think it is only through prayer that you can come to understand it. When you stand before God, vulnerable as you are, and let him see all there is of you, you will begin gradually to experience for yourself what it means that God has sent Jesus to be, in all things, God-with-you. Then you will begin to know that, by becoming a human being in Jesus, God is offering you his divine life. Then you can ask yourself in a new way how you wish to conduct your own life.

In my previous letter the key word was freedom. In this one it is compassion. When you come to see Jesus more and more as the compassionate God, you will begin increasingly to see your own life as one in which you yourself want to express that divine compassion. What can happen then is that you feel a deep longing grow within you to make your own life a life for others. The better you learn to know and love Jesus, the more you find yourself longing to lead your life in conformity with his. You already discovered some of that for yourself when you read Thomas à Kempis's *Imitation of Christ*. You observed then that it involved something quite radical, but also very inviting. Living for other people in solidarity with the compassionate Jesus: that's what it means to live a spiritual life. In that way you too achieve true freedom.

Before I finish this letter I want to show, as in my previous letter, that the account of Jesus' suffering, death, and resurrection is not just a story about the past. Like the Emmaus story, it was written from within the Christian community. In this community the Eucharist was and is celebrated. That's why the account of the Last Supper belongs to the Passion story. It's there you read that before his suffering and death Jesus took the bread and the wine and said to his friends: "This is my body which is given for you. Do this in memory of me."

You've heard these words so often already that, for you, they no longer carry their full and proper weight. But consider what is taking place here. Jesus is saying, "I want to give myself to you totally. As intimately as food and drink are united with your body, so would I be united with you. I don't want to keep anything for myself. I want to be eaten and drunk by you." You could best translate Jesus' words, therefore, as: "Eat me, drink me." What you have to hear and feel in this is the completely self-giving love of Jesus. The suffering and death that follow the Last Supper are a way of making visible that self-giving love. The agony, scourging, mocking, crowning with thorns, the crucifixion and death of Jesus allow us to see in the most drastic manner possible how utterly Jesus gives himself to us when he says, "Eat me, drink me." In that sense, you might say that the account of the Passion makes plain to us what has already taken place at the Last Supper.

The Eucharist was and is the center of the fellowship of those who put all their trust in Jesus. It was within the setting of the Eucharistic celebration that the first Christians retold to one another the story of Jesus' suffering and death. It was also from within this Eucharistic community that it was recorded by the gospel writers. This is so very important for you and me because we are able to celebrate the Eucharistic day by day. With every celebration, the suffering, death, and resurrection of Jesus are made present. The best way to put it might be like this: every time you celebrate the Eucharist and receive the bread and wine, the body and blood of Jesus, his suffering and his death become a suffering and death for you. Passion becomes compassion, for you. You are incorporated into Jesus. You become part of his "body" and in that most compassionate way are freed from your deepest solitude. Through the Eucharist you come to belong to Jesus in the most intimate way. Jesus suffered for you, died for you, and is risen for you so that you may suffer, die, and rise with him.

Do you understand better now why Matthias Grünewald chose the altar at Isenheim as the appropriate place for his moving portrayal of Christ's suffering, death, and resurrection? He was showing these mortally ill people what it was that the Eucharist really gave them. They had no more need to endure their plague alone. They were incorporated into the suffering of Jesus and so could trust also that they would be allowed to share in his resurrection.

I will leave it at that for now. There's so much more still to be said. As I was writing this letter I became aware of how much I would have to restrict myself; but then it is not necessary to get everything down on paper. In the end my desire is just to get you to read the Bible and develop your spiritual life for yourself. My letters are only meant to spur you on a bit.

A friend of mine arrived yesterday from Boston to spend a few days' vacation with me. His name is Jonas, and he arrived at the very moment I was writing to you about the prophet Jonah. Today we're going to look around Freiburg; tomorrow we're off to the Black Forest; and the day after that we go via Paris to Trosly, a small French village where I am staying until the end of August. So I shall send you my next letter from France and tell you something of my work and my life there.

Greetings and love to all the family.

Until next time,
Henri

Jesus: The Descending God

Tuesday, 25th February

My dear Marc,

So here I am, writing from France. My friend Jonas and I had a good journey, with a stop at Strasbourg. Along with two other priests I was invited to celebrate the holy Eucharist in the cathedral there. It was an extraordinary experience to be able to look from the high altar into the majestic Gothic nave and see the sunlight pouring in through the beautiful rose window. During his sermon, the preacher pointed to that huge round window of stained glass and said, "It is a work of art made by human beings. But unless God's sun shines through it we see nothing."

The enormous cathedral impressed Jonas and me deeply. We felt at one with the many generations who have lived and prayed in Strasbourg. But now I'm "home" again in Trosly, where everything is small and very unpretentious. Jonas has gone back to Boston, and I'm sitting here writing to you in the small but cosy room where I've been living since August.

In this letter I want to speak to you about the love of God made visible by Jesus in his life. When I asked myself how I could best do this, I began to realize that my life here in this French village would be the most obvious starting point. Trosly, close to Compiègne, in northern France, is an undistinguished little place. It would never have occurred to me to come and spend a year here, were it not for the fact that in August 1964 a Canadian, Jean Vanier, purchased a small house here, invited two handicapped men to come and live with him, and thus started a new community, which he called "The Ark." Now "L'Arche" is known and loved in many countries.

Initially, all that Jean Vanier himself wanted was just to live in poverty with poor people. He had grown up in an aristocratic environment; from 1959 to 1967 his father was Governor General of Canada. After having served five years in the navy, Jean went on to study philosophy in Paris and then became a visiting professor at St. Michael's College in the University of Toronto. He soon was quite popular there, but success left him unsatisfied. He felt called to another kind of life: simpler, poorer, and more centered on prayer and commitment to service. He thought of becoming a priest; but shortly before his ordination he realized that Christ was asking something else of him. At first he didn't know what the "something else" was; but gradually, under the direction of his spiritual counselor, the French Dominican Thomas Philippe, he realized that he was being asked to give up his career at the university, to return to France, and to start living there with mentally handicapped people. He asked Raphael and Philippe, who for most of their lives had stayed in an institution without any family to visit them, to join him in a simple life in imitation of Jesus.

When he took these two men out of the institution and brought them to his "Ark" in Trosly, he knew he had done something for which there could be no going back. Raphael and Philippe had no parents or family who could look after them. Sending them back to the institution from which they had been released was unthinkable. He was committed to these two mentally injured people for the rest of his life. He himself felt it to be a bond with the poor in spirit, a bond that demanded of him the loyalty of a lifetime.

In August of 1964 Jean Vanier had no other idea than to devote his whole life to Raphael and Philippe. Although he was deeply convinced (to the dismay, at first, of his parents) that he was being called to give up his very promising academic career for these two poor people, he knew little or nothing about caring for the handicapped. He relied on his intuition and the support and encouragement offered by Thomas Philippe. However, when word of Jean Vanier's decision got out, young people from various countries began arriving in Trosly to help him. Quite contrary to what Jean had expected, his small Ark soon grew into a worldwide movement with homes for mentally handicapped people not only in Western Europe, but in Asia, Africa, and the Americas as well.

A few years ago, when I was still teaching at Yale University, Jean sent one of his coworkers to invite me, in the way of friendship, to get in touch with him. That was the first step of a journey of spiritual discovery which eventually made me decide to leave the academic life and go to Trosly with the possibility of making L'Arche my new home.

So, here I am in my new surroundings. I may say that the contrast between my university life and my life here in L'Arche is greater than I realized at the outset. The contrast isn't so much between intelligent students and mentally handicapped people as in the "ascending" style of the university and the "descending" style of L'Arche. You might say that at Yale and Harvard they're principally interested in upward mobility, whereas here they believe in the importance of downward mobility. That's the radical difference; and I notice in myself how difficult it is to change direction on the ladder.

When Jean Vanier moved from Toronto to ronto to Trosly, he made a radical change of direction in his life. He renounced a career that would take him higher and higher up the ladder of success for a vocation that brought him down to the level of the poor, the weak, the sick, and those in distress. It has become very clear to me now that the further you descend, the more your eyes are opened to the brokenness of our humanity.

I said at the beginning of this letter that I wanted to write to you about the love of God become visible in Jesus. How is that love made visible through Jesus? It is made visible in the descending way. That is the great mystery of the Incarnation. God has descended to us human beings to become a human being with us; and once among us, he descended to the total dereliction of one condemned to death. It isn't easy really to feel and understand from the inside this descending way of Jesus. Every fiber of our being rebels against it. We don't mind paying attention to poor people from time to time, but descending to a state of poverty and becoming poor with the poor—that we don't want to do. And yet that is the way Jesus chose as the way to know God.

In the first century of Christianity there was already a hymn being sung about this descending way of Jesus. Paul puts it into his Letter to the Philippians in order to commend to his people the descending direction on the ladder of life. He writes:

Make your own the mind of Christ Jesus: Who, being in the form of God, did not count equality with God something to be grasped. But he emptied himself, taking the form of a slave, becoming as human beings are; and being in every way like a human being, he was humbler yet, even to accepting death, death on a cross.

Here, expressed in summary but very plain terms, is the way of God's love. It is a way that goes down further and further into the greatest destitution: the destitution of a criminal whose life is taken from him. You may wonder, at this point, whether Jesus isn't a masochist in search of misery. The opposite is true. The gospel of Jesus is a gospel of peace and joy, not of self-disdain and self-torment. The descending way of Jesus is the way to a new fellowship in which we human beings can *reach new* life and celebrate it happily together.

How is it possible for the descending way of Jesus to give rise to a new kind of community, grounded in love? It's very important that you come to understand this from the inside, so that a desire to follow Jesus in his descending way can gradually grow in you.

As you know, I come to the Netherlands only occasionally and so changes strike me more forcibly than if I were living there all the time. I have noticed one thing in particular: increasing prosperity has not made people more friendly toward one another. They're better off; but that new-found wealth has not resulted in a new sense of community. I get the impression that people are more preoccupied with themselves and have less time for one another than when they didn't possess so much. There's more competitiveness, more envy, more unrest, and more anxiety. There's less opportunity to relax, to get together informally, and enjoy the little things in life. Success has isolated a lot of people and made them lonely. It seems sometimes as though meetings between people generally happen on the way to something or someone else.

There's always something else more important, more pressing, of more consequence. The ordinary, simple, little, homely things have to make way for something you really ought to be doing: that film you really should see, that country you simply must visit, and this or that event which you've got to attend. And the higher up you get on the ladder of prosperity, the harder it becomes to be together, to sing together, to pray together, and to celebrate life together in a spirit of thanksgiving.

Is it so astonishing, then, that in the Netherlands as in other prosperous countries there are so many people who are lonely, depressed, and anxious and are never genuinely happy? At times, I get the feeling that, under the blanket of success, a lot of people fall asleep in tears. And the question that perhaps lies hidden most deeply in many hearts is the question of love. "Who really cares about me? Not about my money, my contacts, my reputation, or my popularity, but just me? Where do I really feel at home, secure, and cherished? Where can I freely say and think what I like without the fear of losing out on love? Where am I really safe? Where are the people with whom I can simply be, without having to worry about the impression I make on them?

When I was visiting in Bolivia and Peru, I got to know a fair number of poor people. For two months I lived in Lima with Pablo and Sofia and their children, Pablito, Maria, and Johnny. Their house was dark and damp, their food inadequate, good clothes too expensive, a good school too far away, and good work, generally speaking, not to be found. And yet . . . it was there that I learned what joy and thankfulness are. It was in that house that I learned to laugh, even to laugh fit to burst. There I learned how to be sociable and to have a really good time, and in that little house I learned something new about love.

When I returned from that visit to rejoin my students in North America, I sensed once again their anxiety about the future, the extent of their inner desperation, their suicidal melancholy. I had to ask myself once more why it is that God shows his love for us in the descending way of Jesus. The more I thought about it, the more I realized what Jesus was getting at when he said, "Many who are first will be last, and the last, first." I was even worried lest my success with the careermakers should in the end deprive me of the love and affection I most longed for. For that reason I decided to seek another way, and that's why I've ended up here in Trosly, in the hope of staying closer to the love that lies concealed in poverty.

In the gospel it's quite obvious that Jesus chose the descending way. He chose it not once but over and over again. At each critical moment he deliberately sought the way downwards. Even though at twelve years of age he was already listening to the teachers in the Temple and questioning them, he stayed up to his thirtieth year with his parents in the little-respected town of Nazareth and was submissive to them. Even though Jesus was without sin, he began his public life by joining the ranks of sinners who were being baptized by John in the Jordan. Even though he was full of divine power, he believed that changing stones into bread, seeking popularity, and being counted among the great ones of the earth were temptations.

Again and again you see how Jesus opts for what is small, hidden, and poor, and accordingly declines to wield influence. His many miracles always serve to express his profound compassion with suffering humanity; never are they attempts to call attention to himself. Often he even forbids those he has cured to talk to others about it. And as Jesus' life continues to unfold, he becomes increasingly aware that he has been called to fulfill his vocation in suffering and death. In all of this it becomes plain to us that God has willed to show his love for the world by descending more and more deeply into human frailty. In the four accounts of Jesus' life and death you can see very clearly that the more conscious he becomes of the mission entrusted to him by the Father, the more he realizes that that mission will make him poorer and poorer. He has been sent not only to console poor people, but also to give this consolation as one of them himself. Being poor doesn't just mean forsaking house and family, becoming a homeless wanderer, and being increasingly persecuted; it also means parting company with friends, with success, and even with the awareness of God's presence. When, finally, Jesus is hanging on the cross and cries out with a loud voice: "My God, my God, why have you forsaken me?" only then do we know how far God has gone to show us his love. For it is then that Jesus has not only reached his utmost poverty, but also has shown God's utmost love.

Here we're confronted with a mystery which we can apprehend only in silent prayer. If you try to speak about it, you fall into absurdities that can only sound ridiculous. Who is going to condemn himself to torture and death if he can prevent it? At the moment of his arrest, Jesus said, "Do you think that I cannot appeal to my Father, who would promptly send more than twelve legions of angels to my defense?" But he does no such thing, for God's way of making love visible is not our way.

God's way can only be grasped in prayer. The more you listen to God speaking within you, the sooner you will hear that voice inviting you to follow the way of Jesus. For Jesus' way is God's way, and God's way is not for Jesus only, but for everyone who is truly seeking God. Here we come up against the hard truth that the descending way of Jesus is also the way for us to find God. Jesus doesn't hesitate for a moment to make that clear. Soon after he has ended his period of fasting in the wilderness and calls his first disciples to follow him, he says

How blessed are the poor in spirit . . .
Blessed are the gentle . . .
Blessed are those who mourn . . .
Blessed are those who hunger and thirst for uprightness . . .
Blessed are the merciful . . .
Blessed are the pure in heart . . .
Blessed are the peacemakers . . .
Blessed are those who are persecuted in the cause of uprightness . . .

Jesus is drawing a self-portrait here and inviting his disciples to become like him. He will continue to speak in this way to the very end. Jesus never makes a distinction between himself and his followers. His sorrow will be theirs; his joy they too will taste. He says, "If they persecuted me, they will persecute you too; if they kept my word, they will keep yours as well." As he speaks, they too must speak; as he behaves, they too must behave; as he suffers, they too must suffer. In all things Jesus is their example, and even more than that: he is their model. In his last great prayer to his Father Jesus prays for his disciples: "They do not belong to the world any more than I belong to the world. . . . As you sent me into the world, I have sent them into the world."

It is love that moves Jesus to send the disciples as the Father has sent him. Jesus loves his disciples with the same love that the Father loves him; and as this love makes Jesus one with the Father, so too does it make the disciples one with Jesus. Thus it is indeed Jesus himself who continues his work in his disciples. Just as that love is made visible in the descending way of Jesus, so too will it become visible in our descending way.

It is so difficult to express the richness of the gospel. I would really like to write down every saying of Jesus because again and again, each time in a different way, he presents to us the great mystery of the descending way. It is the way of suffering, but also the way to healing. It is the way of humiliation, but also the way to resurrection. It is the way of tears, but of tears that turn into tears of joy. It is the way of hiddenness, but also the way that leads to the light that will shine for all people. It is the way of persecution, oppression, martyrdom, and death, but also the way to the full disclosure of God's love. In the gospel of John, Jesus says: "As Moses lifted up the snake in the desert, so must the Son of man be lifted up." You see in these words how the descending way of Jesus becomes the ascending way. The "lifting up" that Jesus speaks of refers both to his being raised up on the cross in total humiliation and to his being raised up from the dead in total glorification.

The descending way of love, the way to the poor, the broken, and oppressed becomes the ascending way of love, the way to joy, peace, and new life. The cross is transformed from a sign of defeat into a sign of victory, from a sign of despair into a sign of hope, from a sign of death into a sign of life.

Every time I see a crucifix, I think about this mystery. Imagine someone setting up a gallows in his living room and getting a feeling of joy from it. You would judge such a person to be sick. Yet for us the cross, a means of execution, has become a sign of liberation. God himself has made the descending way the way to glory. Only when you are prepared to experience this in your own life of prayer and service will you get an inkling of the mystery of God's love.

You are probably wondering how, in imitation of Jesus, you are to find that descending way. That's a very personal and intimate question, and in the end I don't think that anyone can answer it but you. It's not simply a matter of renouncing your money, your possessions, your intellectual formation, or your friends or family. For some people it has indeed meant this, but only because they felt personally called to take that road. Each one of us has to seek out his or her own descending way of love. That calls for much prayer, much patience, and much guidance. It has nothing at all to do with spiritual heroics or dramatically throwing everything overboard to "follow" Jesus. The descending way is a way that is concealed in each person's heart. But because it is so seldom walked on, it is often overgrown with weeds. Slowly but surely we have to clear the weeds, open the way, and set out on it unafraid.

For me this weeding-out process is always related to prayer, because to pray is to make free time for God—even when you're very busy with important matters of one kind or another. Every time you make free time for God, you clear up a bit of the descending path, and you see where you can plant your feet, on the way of love. It doesn't have to be spectacular or sensational. It may simply be a matter of what you say, what you read, to whom you speak, where you go on a free afternoon, or how you regard yourself and other people. What's fascinating is that the first step invariably makes the second one easier. You begin to discover that love begets love, and step by step you move further forward on the way to God. Gradually, you shed your misgivings about the way of love; you see that "in love there is no room for fear," and you feel yourself drawn to descend deeper and deeper on the way that Jesus walked before you.

This leads me back to the Eucharist. I have written about the Eucharist in my previous letters and I want to do the same here; because the Eucharist is the sacrament of love, given to us as the means of finding that descending way of Jesus in our hearts. Jesus himself says, "I am the living bread which has come down from heaven. Anyone who eats this bread will live forever." You see here how the descending way of Jesus can become your way too. Whenever you eat the bread of heaven you not only become more profoundly united with Jesus, but you also learn gradually to walk his descending way with him.

Jesus wants to give himself to us so much that he has become food for us, and whenever we eat this food the longing is aroused in us also to give ourselves away to others. The self-surrendering love which we encounter in the Eucharist is the source of true Christian community. Paul makes that very clear when he presents the descending way of Jesus to us as the model for living in community. He says, "make my joy complete by being of a single mind, one in love, one in heart and one in mind. Nothing is to be done out of jealousy or vanity; instead, out of humility of mind everyone should give preference to others, everyone pursuing not selfish interests but those of others."

This mind-set gives concrete form to the descending way of Jesus, who "did not count equality with God something to be grasped. But he emptied himself, taking the form of a slave." This is the eucharistic mind. Whenever we eat the body of Jesus and drink his blood, we participate in his descending way and so become a community in which competitiveness and rivalry have made way for the love of God.

If you yourself are seriously searching for the specific way which you must walk to follow Jesus, then I beg you not to do so on your own, but within a eucharistic community. I feel more and more certain that the way of Jesus can't be found outside the community of those who believe in Jesus and make their belief visible by coming together around the eucharistic table. The Eucharist is the heart and center of being-the-church. Without it there is no people of God, no community of faith, no church. Often enough, you see that people who abandon the church have trouble in holding on to Jesus. This becomes understandable when you consider that the church is the eucharistic community in which Jesus gives us his body and blood as gifts that come to us from heaven and help us to find the way of love in our own lives.

It is time to bring this letter to an end. I hope that I've been able to bring Jesus a little closer to you. Here in Trosly we talk about Jesus a lot. Every evening the community of handicapped people and their helpers come together to celebrate the Eucharist. Then Père Thomas preaches a lengthy sermon which is not always easy to follow. Invariably, everyone listens with great attention, even those who, because of their mental handicap, don't understand a thing. Yet these people feel themselves very much involved. Full of affection and deeply trusting, they watch this elderly spirit-filled priest. It's as though they understand very well what he's saying, even though it's hard for them to follow his thinking. And then, when they all come to receive the body and blood of Jesus, their eyes are filled with joy. They feel privileged to belong to the people of God and don't hesitate to show their gratitude.

I'd be delighted if, in the coming months, you could come and spend a few days here. I'd love to introduce you to the friends I've made and give you a taste of the day-to-day life of the handicapped people and their assistants. It might, perhaps, be the best way to get you to feel something of God's love. Anyway, think about it.

Lots of love to everybody at home.

Until next time,
Henri

Jesus: The Loving God

My dear Marc,

When I started writing to you Lent had just begun. I thought then that I'd be able to send you one letter a week. But I seem to have so much to do here in Trosly that I've not been able to live up to my good intentions. It took me five weeks in all to write my letter about the descending way of Jesus. In the meantime Easter has come again. It makes me realize how much I am influenced by the liturgical seasons!

During Lent I was so full of the descending way of Jesus which led him to his death that it would have been hard for me to write about anything else. But now that the daily Bible readings speak of Jesus' victory over death, I notice that I too am thinking differently about Jesus and want to speak of him to you in another way. I now see Jesus more in his state of glory, and my thoughts are more concerned with the joy of being his disciple. Each part of the liturgical year makes us see Jesus in a different way.

What happened in the Philippines last month alerted me in a new way to the fact that Jesus has come to conquer death. When I was writing my second letter to you the papers were full of the elections in the Philippines, and I was convinced at the time that the massive electoral fraud designed to keep President Marcos in power would lead to a bloody civil war. Now, a few weeks later, Cory Aquino is president; and she has come to power without any resort to violence. For me, this is a hope-filled event, a clear sign that a nonviolent victory over a dictatorship is possible.

From various friends who've been following recent events in the Philippines at close quarters, I've heard that we really can speak of a spiritual victory. What happened there involved much more than a political strategy which chanced to be successful. For years Christian people, bishops, priests, and leading figures in the political life of the country familiarized themselves with the practice of nonviolence. Members of the Fellowship of Reconciliation organized retreats aimed at teaching people how to rely on the power of love, and with that power, to defeat the dictatorship. The words of Jesus that go right to the heart of nonviolence are well known. Let me write them down for you:

> Love your enemies, do good to those who hate you, bless those who curse you, pray for those who treat you badly. To anyone who slaps you on one cheek, present the other cheek as well; to anyone who takes your cloak from you, do not refuse your tunic. Give to everyone who asks you, and do not ask for your property back from someone who takes it. Treat others as you would like people to treat you . . . love your enemies and do good to them, and lend without any hope of return.

These sayings express not only the essence of nonviolent resistance, but also the heart of Jesus' preaching. If anyone should ask you what are the most radical words in the gospel, you need not hesitate to reply: "Love your enemies." It's these words that reveal to us most clearly the kind of love proclaimed by Jesus.

In these words we have the clearest expression of what it means to be a disciple of Jesus. Love for one's enemy is the touchstone of being a Christian.

Cory Aquino's struggle against the dictatorship in her country was rooted in love for one's enemy. Before she presented herself as a candidate for the presidency she prayed the whole night for her opponent, Ferdinand Marcos. She knew that hatred would lead to violence. The Filipino bishops and priests supported her and summoned the whole nation to nonviolent resistance. When Marcos ordered his tanks to crush his opponents, the soldiers refused to drive over the people who were praying. Priests wearing their vestments approached the soldiers, embraced them, and invited them to drop their weapons and pray with the people for reconciliation and peace.

Now that Cory Aquino is herself president, the issue is whether she will be in a position to make love for one's enemy the basis of her government. Many forces will make this extremely difficult for her. But whatever happens, we've seen something in the Philippines which a lot of people believed impossible: a resistance to the enemy which was full of love and through which a bloody civil war was prevented.

I've dwelt on the Philippine situation in some detail because it helps me to write concretely about love for one's enemy. As you know, my hope is that through these letters you will get to know Jesus better. I've already described him as the one who descended to us to make God's love visible to us. In this letter I want to say something about the nature of that love. We human beings use the word 'love' in so many ways that it's hard to talk about God's love without creating confusion. Still, the command of Jesus to love our enemies is, I think, a good starting point for entering more deeply into the mystery of God's love.

The most important thing you can say about God's love is that God loves us not because of anything we've done to earn that love, but because God, in total freedom, has decided to love us. At first sight, this doesn't seem to be very inspiring; but if you reflect on it more deeply this thought can affect and influence your life greatly. We're inclined to see our whole existence in terms of quid pro quo. We assume that people will be nice to us if we are nice to them; that they will help us if we help them; that they will invite us if we invite them; that they will love us if we love them. And so the conviction is deeply rooted in us that being loved is something you have to earn. In our pragmatic and utilitarian times this conviction has become even stronger. We can scarcely conceive of getting something for nothing. Everything has to be worked for, even a kind word, an expression of gratitude, a sign of affection.

I think it's this mentality that lies behind a lot of anxiety, unrest, and agitation. It's as though we're forever on the go, trying to prove to each other that we deserve to be loved. The doubt we harbor within us drives us on to ever-greater activity. In that way we try to keep our heads above water and not drown in our ever-increasing lack of self-respect. The enormous propensity to seek recognition, admiration, popularity, and renown is rooted in the fear that without all this we are worthless. You could call it the "commercialization" of love. Nothing for nothing. Not even love.

The result is a state of mind that makes us live as though our worth as human beings depends on the way others react to us. We allow other people to determine who we are. We think we're good if other people find us to be so; we think we're intelligent if others consider us intelligent; we think we're religious if others think so too. On the other hand, if we're despised we think at once that we must be contemptible; if we're laughed at we immediately think we must be ridiculous; if we're ignored we jump to the conclusion that we're not worth being noticed. And so we submit the most intimate awareness of who we are to the fickle opinions of those around us. Thus we sell our souls to the world. We're no longer master in our own house. Our friends and enemies decide who we are. We've become the playthings of their good or bad opinions.

We can go further and say that something else, something quite different even, is amiss. Love has not only come to be an emotional bargaining counter, it has also become coercive. One can speak nowadays of coercive love. I'll elaborate on that a little, to show how revealing are Jesus' words: "Love your enemies." The more constricted our self-confidence, the greater our need to be reassured. A low opinion of ourselves reinforces our desire to receive signs and tokens of love. In a world in which so many people feel lonely, isolated, and deserted, the longing for love can often take on "inhuman" proportions. People come to expect more of each other than it is possible to give. When loneliness and low self-esteem become the main source of the longing to be loved, that longing can easily lead to a kind of desperation. Then it's as though one person says to another: "Love me so that I won't feel lonely anymore. Love me so that I can believe in myself again, at least a little bit."

The tragic thing, though, is that we humans aren't capable of dispelling one another's loneliness and lack of self-respect. We humans haven't the wherewithal to relieve one another's most radical predicament. Our ability to satisfy one another's deepest longing is so limited that time and time again we are in danger of disappointing one another. Despite all this, at times our longing can be so intense that it blinds us to our mutual limitations and we are led into the temptation of extorting love, even when reason tells us that we can't give one another any total, unlimited, unconditional love. It is then that love becomes violent. It is then that kisses become bites, caresses become blows, forgiving looks become suspicious glances, lending a sympathetic ear becomes eavesdropping, and heartfelt surrender becomes violation. The borderline between love and force is frequently transgressed, and in our anxiety-ridden times it doesn't take very much to let our desire for love lead us to violent behavior.

When I look about me and see the many forms of coercion present in human relationships, I often have a sense of seeing here, there, and everywhere people who want nothing more or less than to be loved, but who have been unable to find any way to express that longing other than through violence, either to others or to themselves. I sometimes get the impression that our prisons are crammed full of people who couldn't express their need to be loved except by flailing about furiously and hurting others. At the same time, many of our psychiatric institutions are filled with people who, full of shame and guilt, have given a form to the self-same need by inflicting damage on themselves. Whether we do violence to others or to ourselves, what we long for in our heart is a nonviolent, peaceful communion in which we know ourselves to be secure and loved. But how and where are we to find that noncoercive, nonviolent love?

In what I've been describing as coercive love, you will, I hope, have detected something of yourself or of the people around you. If so, you will the more readily understand what Jesus means when he speaks of love. Jesus is the revelation of God's unending, unconditional love for us human beings. Everything that Jesus has done, said, and undergone is meant to show us that the love we most long for is given to us by God— not because we've deserved it, but because God is a God of love.

Jesus has come among us to make that divine love visible and to offer it to us. In his conversation with Nicodemus he says, "For this is how God loved the world: He gave us his only Son . . . For God has sent his

Son into the world not to judge the world, but so that through him the world might be saved." In these words the meaning of the Incarnation is summed up. God has become human, that is, God-with-us in order to show us that the anxious concern for recognition and the violence among us spring from a lack of faith in the love of God. If we had a firm faith in God's unconditional love for us, it would no longer be necessary to be always on the lookout for ways and means of being admired by people; and we would need, even less, to obtain from people by force what God desires to give us freely and so abundantly.

The descending way of Jesus, painful as it is, is God's most radical attempt to convince us that everything we long for is indeed given us. What he asks of us is to have faith in that love. The word 'faith' is often understood as accepting something you can't understand. People often say, "Such and such can't be explained, you simply have to believe it." However, when Jesus talks about faith, he means first of all to trust un-reservedly that you are loved, so that you can abandon every false way of obtaining love. That's why Jesus tells Nicodemus that, through faith in the descending love of God, we will be set free from anxiety and violence and will obtain eternal life. It's a question of trusting in God's love. The Greek word for faith is *pistis*, which literally means "trust." Whenever Jesus says to the people he has healed, "Your faith has saved you," he is saying that they have found new life because they have surrendered in complete trust to the love of God revealed in him.

Trusting in the unconditional love of God: that is the way to which Jesus calls us. The more firmly you grasp this, the more readily will you be able to perceive why there is so much suspicion, jealousy, bitterness, vindictiveness, hatred, violence, and discord in our world. Jesus himself interprets this by comparing God's love to the light. He says,

> . . . though the light has come into the world people have preferred darkness to light because their deeds were evil. And indeed, every-body who does wrong hates the light and avoids it, to prevent his actions from being shown up; but whoever does the truth comes out into the light, so that what he is doing may plainly appear as done in God.

Jesus sees the evil in this world as a lack of trust in God's love. He makes us see that we persistently fall back on ourselves, rely more on ourselves than on God, and are inclined more to love of self than to love of God. So we remain in the darkness. If we walk in the light, then we are enabled to acknowledge in joy and gratitude that everything good, beautiful, and true comes from God and is offered to us in love.

If you come to see this, you'll also understand why Jesus' words "Love your enemies" are among the most important in the gospel. These words bring us to the heart and center of love. As long as love is a matter of quid pro quo, we can't love our enemies. Our enemies are those who withhold love from us and make life difficult for us. We are inclined spontaneously to hate them and to love only those who love us.

Jesus, however, will have no part in such bartering. He says,

> If you love those who love you, what credit can you expect? Even sinners love those who love them. And if you do good to those who do good to you, what credit can you expect? For even sinners do that much. And if you lend to those from whom you hope to get money back, what credit can you expect: Even sinners lend to sinners to get back the same amount.

Jesus shows us that true love, the love that comes from God, makes no distinction between friends and foes, between people who are for us and people who are against us, people who do us a favor and people who do us ill. God makes no such distinction. He loves all human beings, good or bad, with the same unconditional love. This all-embracing love Jesus offers to us, and he invites us to make this love visible in our lives.

If our love, like God's, embraces friend as well as foe, we have become children of God and are no longer children of suspicion, jealousy, violence, war, and death. Our love for our enemies shows to whom we really belong. It shows our true home. Jesus states it so clearly: ". . . love your enemies, and do good to them, and lend without any hope of return. You will have a great reward, and you will be children of the Most High, for he himself is kind to the ungrateful and the wicked."

There you have it: the love of God is an unconditional love, and only that love can empower us to live together without violence. When we know that God loves us deeply and will always go on loving us, whoever we are and whatever we do, it becomes possible to expect no more of our fellow men and women than they are able to give, to forgive them generously when they have offended us, and to respond to their hostility with love. By doing so we make visible a new way of being human and a new way of responding to our world problems.

Cory Aquino realized that hatred for President Marcos could not lead to peace in the Philippines; Martin Luther King understood that hating whites could not lead to true equality among Americans. Mohandas Gandhi knew that hating the British could not bring about genuine independence in India. A new world without slaughter and massacre can never be the fruit of hatred. It is the fruit of the love of "your Father in heaven, for he causes his sun to rise on the bad as well as the good, and sends down rain to fall on the upright and the wicked alike." It is the fruit of God's love, which we limited humans are to make visible in our lives in accordance with the words of Jesus: "You must therefore set no bounds to your love, just as your heavenly Father sets none to his."

Whenever, contrary to the world's vindictiveness, we love our enemy, we exhibit something of the perfect love of God, whose will is to bring all human beings together as children of one Father. Whenever we forgive instead of letting fly at one another, bless instead of cursing one another, tend one another's wounds instead of rubbing salt into them, hearten instead of discouraging one another, give hope instead of driving one another to despair, hug instead of harassing one another, welcome instead of cold-shouldering one another, thank instead of criticizing one another, praise instead of maligning one another . . . in short, whenever we opt for and not against one another, we make God's unconditional love visible; we are diminishing violence and giving birth to a new community.

I hope you feel that we are touching here the heart of the gospel. Jesus challenges us to move into a totally new direction. He asks for conversion—that is to say, a complete interior turn-around, a transformation. Not an easy thing, as is certainly evident from his words: "But it

is a narrow gate and a hard road that leads to life, and only a few find it."
Everything within us seems set against this way. And yet . . . every time we
take a few steps along it, we become aware that something new is happening within us and experience a desire to try yet another step forward. And
so, step by step, we come closer to the heart of God, which is the heart
of an undiscriminating, always-forgiving, inexhaustible love. This might
look like a very tall order, especially when you're facing it alone. You've
often told me about your classmates' cynical reactions whenever you talk
about Jesus. It is, indeed, very difficult to look for the way to the heart of
God without the support of your friends. That's why it's important to ask
yourself with whom you intend to look. You need a community, even if
it's a fairly small one. For myself, I've enjoyed a lot of support from one
or two friends with whom I was able to share my spiritual adventure. It's
practically impossible to lay yourself open to other people who are ill-
disposed or indifferent toward you. Real vulnerability can only be fruitful
in a community of people who are searching for God together. So one of
your most important tasks is to find friends who want to walk with you on
the long road of conversion.

Still, there are a number of concrete steps which you yourself can
take here and now in order to arrive at this conversion.

In this letter I want to limit myself to just two of these and to give you
a few thoughts about prayer and the Eucharist. If you wish to learn the
love of God, you have to begin by praying for your enemies. That's not as
easy as it may sound. Prayers for people entail wanting the best for them;
and that's far from easy if it has to do with a fellow student who speaks ill
of you, a girl who finds someone else more attractive than you, a "friend"
who gets you to do all those awkward little chores for him, or a colleague
who's trying his best to get your job. But each time you pray, really pray,
for your enemies, you'll notice that your heart is being made new. Within
your prayer, you quickly discover that your enemies are in fact your fellow human beings loved by God just as much as yourself. The result is
that the walls you've thrown up between "him and me," "us and them,"
"ours and theirs" disappear. Your heart grows deeper and broader and
opens up more and more to all the human beings with whom God has
peopled the earth.

I find it difficult to conceive of a more concrete way to love than by praying for one's enemies. It makes you conscious of the hard fact that, in God's eyes, you're no more and no less worthy of being loved than any other person, and it creates an awareness of profound solidarity with all other human beings. It creates in you a world-embracing compassion and provides you in increasing measure with a heart free of the compulsive urge to coercion and violence. And you'll be delighted to discover that you can no longer remain angry with people for whom you've really and truly prayed. You will find that you start speaking differently to them or about them, and that you're actually willing to do well to those who've offended you in some way.

To end, I want to return to the subject of the Eucharist. In the Eucharist God's love is most concretely made present. Jesus has not only become human, he has also become bread and wine in order that, through our eating and our drinking, God's love might become our own. The great mystery of the Eucharist is that God's love is offered to us not in the abstract, but in a wholly concrete form; not as an example or a theory, but as food for our daily life. The Eucharist opens the way for us to make God's love our own. Jesus himself makes that clear to us when he says,

> . . . my flesh is real food and my blood is real drink. Whoever eats my flesh and drinks my blood lives in me and I live in that person. As the living Father sent me and I draw life from the Father, so whoever eats me will also draw life from me.

Whenever you receive the body and blood of Jesus in the Eucharist his love is given to you—the same love that he showed on the cross. It is the love of God for all people of all times and places, all religions and creeds, all races and classes, all tribes and nations, all sinners and saints.

On the cross Jesus has shown us how far God's love goes. It's a love which embraces even those who crucified him. When Jesus is hanging nailed to the cross, totally broken and stripped of everything, he still prays for his executioners: "Father, forgive them; they do not know what they are doing." Jesus' love for his enemies knows no bounds. He prays even for those who are putting him to death. It is this, the enemy-loving love of God, that is offered to us in the Eucharist. To forgive our enemies doesn't lie within our power. That is a divine gift. That's why it's so important to make the Eucharist the heart and center of your life. It's there that you receive the love which empowers you to take the way that Jesus has taken before you: a narrow way, a painful way, but the way that gives you true joy and peace and enables you to make the nonviolent love of God visible in this world.

I began this letter by discussing events in the Philippines. The nonviolent resistance to President Marcos's dictatorship made a big impression on me and prompted me to write to you about love for one's enemy as the core of Jesus' preaching. That the events in the Philippines were exceptional is evident from the fact that, as I conclude this letter, the papers are full of the American attack on Libya. Muammar Qaddafi's terrorism has resulted in the use of force by the United States. Violence on the one side has provoked it on the other. Now everyone is afraid that the violence may spread like an oil slick on the water. It's the endless chain of hatred and retaliation. Despite the fact that those who wield power in our world persist in thinking that they can counter force with force, the opposite proves to be the case over and over again. Violence invariably breeds violence. Mrs. Aquino's example of nonviolent resistance is not emulated. It is still an exception, but, nevertheless, it is a sign of hope.

I earnestly pray and hope that you will cling to those small signs of hope and not let yourself be led astray by the noise and clamor of those who persist in relying on violence. The way of Jesus is not self-evident, but it is the only way that leads to life and can save our world from total destruction. Let us hope and pray with all our hearts that we may have the courage and the confidence to follow the way of Jesus to the end.

My warmest greetings to your father and mother, and to Frédérique and Reinier.

With much affection, till next time,
Henri

Jesus: The Hidden God

Friday, 18th April

My dear Marc,

This letter comes to you from Châteauneuf de Galaure, a small village in the Drôme region, south of Lyons and east of the Rhône. I'm surprised at myself for being here, because before I went to France I'd never heard of Châteauneuf de Galaure, and now, eight months later, it's become for me one of the most important places in the world. That probably sounds exaggerated to you, but I hope you'll understand by the time you've finished this letter.

During my first month in Trosly I kept hearing the name of someone entirely unknown to me: Marthe Robin. Often, when someone tried to tell me how he or she had come to have a deep faith in Jesus, I would hear, "It was Marthe who set me on the right path." I discovered, too, that her name was associated with a number of new spiritual movements in France. Wherever I turned to get a better insight into the development of French spirituality, I heard the name of Marthe Robin.

As you can imagine, I became increasingly curious. I began reading books about her and asking for more and more information. Then, one day, Thérèse Monique, a friend of mine in Trosly, said to me, "Marthe Robin was born, lived, and died in Châteauneuf de Galaure. If you want to discover the deeper significance of her life, you should go and spend a week there. Two good friends of mine, Bernard and Claudine, live very near Châteauneuf, and they'll be glad to put you up. I will be glad to take you there in the car." She was as good as her word.

It's now April 18th, a Friday. I've been with Bernard and Claudine since last Sunday, and throughout the week I've had time and opportunity to find out about Marthe Robin's life and to understand why she's had and still has such an influence on the spiritual life inside France and, to an increasing extent, outside France as well.

Now I'd like to tell you one or two things about her, not just because I happen to be here but because, all along, I've been wanting to write to you about Jesus as the hidden God. I don't think you'll ever be able to penetrate the mystery of God's revelation in Jesus until it strikes you that the major part of Jesus' life was hidden and that even the "public" years remained invisible as far as most people were concerned. Whereas the way of the world is to insist on publicity, celebrity, popularity, and getting maximum exposure, God prefers to work in secret. You must have the nerve to let that mystery of God's secrecy, God's anonymity, sink deeply into your consciousness because, otherwise, you're continually looking in the wrong direction. In God's sight, the things that really matter seldom take place in public. It's quite possible that the reasons why God sustains our violent and homicidal world and continues giving us new opportunities for conversion will always remain unknown to us. Maybe while we focus our whole attention on the VIPs and their movements, on peace conferences and protest demonstrations, it's the totally unknown people, praying and working in silence, who make God save us yet again from destruction. I often think that I've succeeded in staying true to my Christian and priestly calling thanks to the prayers and magnanimity of people who remain completely unknown to me during my lifetime. Perhaps the very greatest of saints remain anonymous.

Marthe Robin is one of the most impressive examples of God's hidden presence in our world. She was born in 1902. At sixteen she fell ill, and her illness, for which the doctors could find no explanation, grew worse and worse. Slowly but surely she became aware that God was calling her to a life in which she would be linked in a special way to the suffering of Jesus. When she was twenty-three, she wrote an "act of abandonment." In it she gave to the God of love all that she had: her memory, her reason, and her will; her body with all its senses, her mind with all its faculties, her heart with all its feelings. "I belong to you without any reservations, forever. O Beloved of my soul! It is you only whom I want, and for your love I renounce all."[1]

When she was twenty-six her legs became totally paralyzed, and soon afterwards her arms. From then on she did not eat, drink, or sleep. From 1928 to her death in 1981 she took no food other than weekly Holy Communion. When I first heard about this it sounded to me like a pious fairy tale, but now that I've talked to a lot of people who knew Marthe Robin personally, I realize that God can achieve a great deal more in a human being than we who are of little faith are prepared to believe possible. The total "abstinence" of Marthe is one of the ways in which Jesus showed his love to her.

In September 1930 Jesus appeared to Marthe and asked her, "Do you wish to become as I am?" She replied, "Yes," and soon afterwards she received the wounds of Jesus in her hands, feet, and side. She also received the crown of thorns. From that time on, week by week, Marthe began to enter fully into the Passion of Jesus. Her suffering with Jesus was so intense that tears of blood flowed from her eyes and the marks of invisible thorns appeared across her head.

Every Friday she entered so fully into the death of Jesus that only on Saturday did she come to herself again; and then until Sunday or Monday she remained in a state of total exhaustion. As the years passed her suffering grew deeper. In the beginning she suffered *with* Jesus, but little by little she *became* the suffering Jesus. To Jean Guitton, a well-known French philosopher who visited her several times, she said:

> At the start, I recognized in my visions people along the road that Jesus took to Calvary. But now I've gone beyond that. What occupies me now is the Passion, uniquely Jesus. I don't know how I am to explain it. . . . Things like that are so grievous that you would die if God did not support you. And yet it's exquisite.[2]

---

1 Raymond Peyret, *Marthe Robin* (New York: Alba House, 1983), 39.
2 Jean Guitton, *Portrait de Marthe Robin* (Paris: Grasset, 1985), 199.

I am not telling you all this for the sake of relating something un-canny or gloomy or weird. I want to show you that in the midst of our warring world there are people who, in a very hidden way, enter into the mystery of Jesus' suffering, a suffering for the world's sake. This happened back in the thirteenth century with St. Francis of Assisi, and it has hap-pened in our lifetime with Marthe Robin.

A number of times now, I've been to pray in the room where for fifty-one years Marthe experienced the suffering of Jesus. Many of those who knew her say that there has probably never been anyone who has lived out so directly and so fully in their own body the suffering and death of Jesus. Every time I walk into that little room, I experience what I have so far never experienced anywhere else: a peace which the world cannot give; a joy which doesn't conflict with suffering; a total surrender which makes true freedom possible; and a love which comes from God himself, but which often remains unknown to us human beings. There I discover quite concretely what life is about and what is asked of me if I want to spread the love of God. It's a life in which joy and the cross are never separated. It's a life which doesn't seek influence, power, success, and popularity, but trusts that God is secretly at work and, in secret, is causing something new to grow. It's a life of mortification, that is to say, of dying to old ways of being so as to make it possible for us to bear new fruit.

Many people came to visit Marthe during her lifetime to seek her advice and counsel. In utter simplicity and often with a great sense of humor, she would chat with them. It was extremely rare for her to talk about herself. Her concern and compassion were always directed toward her guests. Not infrequently, she would understand them even before they'd asked her anything. Sometimes she would give quite explicit in-structions, sometimes she only asked questions, but always people left her room with a profound feeling of inner peace.

It's no exaggeration to say that the renewal of the French church be-gan, to a great extent, with Marthe. In God's name she provided a man-date for setting up new Christian schools and building retreat houses; she stressed the importance of the laity in the church; she inspired priests to initiate new religious communities; and she helped people decide whether to marry or to enter a religious order. The renewal and deepening of religious life in France is inconceivable apart from her. After her death on 6th February 1981, her influence became greater than ever. Jesus says: ". . . unless a wheat grain falls into the earth and dies, it remains only a single grain; but if it dies it yields a rich harvest." Only now, after Marthe's death, is the significance of her life becoming apparent.

Whenever I see the small French homestead where Marthe spent her days, and talk with the two elderly women who looked after her year by year and even now still welcome the people who come to pray in her room, I'm bound to be reminded of Jesus's words: "I bless you, Father, Lord of heaven and earth, for hiding these things from the learned and the clever and revealing them to little children." While the most frightful things were happening in Europe, and while two world wars were unveiling the demonic dimensions of evil, Jesus disclosed to a frail countrywoman in France his unfathomable love for humankind.

You see here an aspect of Jesus that we can so easily forget. Jesus is the hidden God. He became a human being among a small, oppressed people, under very difficult circumstances. He was held in contempt by the rulers of that country and was eventually put to an ignominious death between two criminals.

There was nothing spectacular about Jesus' life—far from it! Even when you look at Jesus' miracles, you find that he did not heal or call back to life people in order to get publicity. He frequently forbade them even to talk about it. His resurrection too was a hidden event. Only his disciples and a few of the women and men who had known him well before his death were allowed to see him as the risen Lord.

Now that Christianity has become one of the major world religions and millions of people utter the name of Jesus every day, it's hard for us to believe that Jesus revealed God in hiddenness. But neither Jesus' life nor his death nor his resurrection were intended to astound us with the great power of God. God became a lowly, hidden, almost invisible God.

I'm constantly struck by the fact that wherever the gospel of Jesus bears fruit, we come across this hiddenness. The great Christians throughout history have always been lowly people who sought to be hidden. Benedict hid himself in the vale of Subiaco, Francis in the Carceri outside Assisi, Ignatius in the grotto of Manresa, and the little Thérèse in the Carmel of Lisieux. Whenever you hear about saintly people, you sense a deep longing for that hiddenness, that seclusion. We so easily forget it, but Paul too withdrew into the wilderness for two years before he started on his preaching mission.

The initial reaction of someone who has a really personal encounter with Jesus is not to start shouting it from the rooftops, but to dwell secretly in the presence of God. It is very important for you to realize that perhaps the greater part of God's work in this world may go unnoticed. There are a number of people who in these days have become widely known as great saints or influential Christians: Mother Teresa in Calcutta, Bishop Romero in El Salvador, Padre Pio in Italy, and Dorothy Day in New York; but the greatest part of God's work in our history could well remain completely unknown. That's a mystery which is difficult to grasp in an age that attaches so much value to publicity. We tend to think that the more people know and talk about something, the more important it must be. That is understandable considering the fact that great notoriety often means big money, and big money often means a large amount of power, and power easily creates the illusion of importance. In our society it is often statistics that determine what's important: the best-selling record, the most popular book, the richest man, the highest building, the most expensive car. With the enormous spread and growth of advertising, it's become nearly impossible to believe that what's really important happens in secret. Yet . . . we do possess some intimations of this. A human life begins in the seclusion of the womb, and the most determinative experiences occur in the privacy of the family. The seedling grows in the seclusion of the soil, and the egg is hatched in the seclusion of the nest. Like creativity, intimacy too needs seclusion. We know intuitively that everything which moves us by its delicacy, vulnerability, and pristine beauty can stand only very little public exposure. The mass media, which magnify creativity and intimacy, are proof of that. What is precious and sacred in hiddenness often becomes cheap and even vulgar when exposed to the public by the mass media. Publicity standardizes, hardens, and not infrequently suffocates what it exposes.

Many great minds and spirits have lost their creative force through too early or too rapid exposure to the public. We know it; we sense it; but we easily forget it because our world persists in proclaiming the big lie: "Being unknown means being unloved." If you're ready to trust your intuition and so preserve a degree of healthy skepticism in the face of the current propaganda, you are more likely to detect the hidden presence of God. It strikes me again and again that, in our publicity-seeking world, a lot of discussions about God take it as their starting point that even God has to justify himself. People often say, "If that God of yours really exists, then why doesn't he make his omnipotence more visible in this chaotic world of ours?" God is called to account, as it were, and mockingly invited to prove, just for once, that God really does exist. Again, you often hear someone say, "I've no need whatever for God. I can perfectly well look after myself. As a matter of fact, I've yet to receive any help from God with my problems!" The bitterness and sarcasm evident in remarks of this sort show what's expected of God: that God should at least be concerned about his own popularity. People often talk as though God has as great a need for recognition as we do.

Now look at Jesus, who came to reveal God to us, and you see that popularity in any form is the very thing he avoids. He is constantly pointing out that God is revealed in secrecy. It sounds very paradoxical, but accepting and perhaps even entering into that paradox sets you on the road of the spiritual life.

With these thoughts about the hidden revelation of Jesus, is it now possible for you to start moving spiritually? I think you can, because the truth that Jesus makes himself known to you in secret, requires that you start looking for him in your own seclusion. It is *his* seclusion, *his* hiddenness, that invites you to enter into your own.

And here we're back again with the mystery of our own heart. Our heart is at the center of our being human. There our deepest thoughts, intuitions, emotions, and decisions find their source. But it's also there that we are most alienated from ourselves. We know little or nothing of our heart. We keep our distance from it, as though we were afraid of it. What is most intimate is also what frightens us most. Where we are most ourselves, we are often strangers to ourselves. That is the painful part of our being human. We fail to know our hidden center; and so we live and die often without knowing who we really are. If we ask ourselves why we think, feel, and act in a certain way, we often have no answer, thus proving to be strangers in our own house.

The mystery of the spiritual life is that Jesus desires to meet us in the seclusion of our own heart, to make his love known to us there, to free us from our fears, and to make our own deepest self known to us. In the privacy of our heart, therefore, we can learn not only to know Jesus, but through Jesus to know ourselves as well. If you reflect on this a bit more you will see an interaction between God's love revealing itself to you and a constant growth in self-knowledge. Each time you let the love of God penetrate deeper into your heart, you lose a bit of your anxiety; and every time you shed a bit of your anxiety, you learn to know yourself better and long all the more to be known by your loving God.

Thus the more you learn to love God, the more you learn to know and to cherish yourself. Self-knowledge and self-love are the fruit of knowing and loving God. You can see better now what is intended by the great commandment to "love the Lord your God with all your heart, with all your soul, and with all your mind, and to love your neighbor as yourself." Laying our hearts totally open to God leads to a love of ourselves that enables us to give whole-hearted love to our fellow human beings. In the seclusion of our hearts we learn to know the hidden presence of God; and with that spiritual knowledge we can lead a loving life.

But all of this requires discipline. The spiritual life demands a discipline of the heart. Discipline is the mark of a disciple of Jesus. This doesn't mean, however, that you must make things difficult for yourself, but only that you make available the inner space where God can touch you with an all-transforming love. We human beings are so faint-hearted that we have a lot of trouble leaving an empty space empty. We like to fill it all up with ideas, plans, duties, tasks, and activities.

It strikes me increasingly just how hard-pressed people are nowadays. It's as though they're tearing about from one emergency to another. Never solitary, never still, never ever really free, but always busy about something that just can't wait. Amid this frantic hurly-burly we lose touch with life itself. We have the experience of being busy, while nothing real seems to happen. The more agitated we are, the more compacted our lives become and the more difficult it is to keep a space where God can let something truly new take place.

The discipline of the heart helps us to let God into our hearts and become known to us there, in the deepest recesses of our own being. This is not so easy to do; we like to be master in our own house and don't want to admit that our house is God's house too. God wants to be together with us where we really live and, by loving us there, show us the way to become a complete human being. God's love is a demanding love, even a jealous love; and when we let that love speak within us, we are led into places where we often would rather not go.

And yet we know that everyone who has allowed God's love to enter into his or her heart has not only become a better human being, but has also contributed significantly to making a better world. The lives of the saints show us that. And so I say, make room in your heart for God and let God cherish you. There you can be alone with God. There heart speaks to heart and there in that holy seclusion the new person will be born in you. Jesus said to Nicodemus: "No one can see the Kingdom of God without being born from above." It is this rebirth that is made possible when you dare to be alone with God. It takes place in the deepest secrecy, but its effect reaches to the ends of the earth. Where God's heart speaks to your heart, there everything is made new.

In this letter too I want to come back for a moment to the Eucharist; for the Eucharist is preeminently the sacrament of God's hiddenness. What is more ordinary than a piece of bread and a sip of wine? What is simpler than the words: "Take and eat, take and drink. This is my body and blood . . . Do this in remembrance of me?"

I've often stood with friends around a small table, taken bread and wine, and said the words which Jesus spoke when he took leave of his disciples; nothing pretentious, nothing spectacular, no crowd of people, no stirring songs, no formality. Just a few people eating a piece of bread and drinking a little wine, not bread enough to make a meal and not enough wine to quench a thirst. And yet . . . in this hiddenness the risen Jesus is present, and God's love is revealed. Just as God became a human being for us in hiddenness, so too in hiddenness God becomes food and drink for us. That anyone can pass by, unheeding, is actually the greatest event that can happen among us human beings. In the course of my stay at L'Arche in France I discovered how closely Jesus' hiddenness in the Eucharist is bound up with his hiddenness in all people.

I still remember Mother Teresa once saying to me that you can't see Jesus in the poor unless you can see him in the Eucharist. At the time, that remark seemed to me a bit high-flying and pious, but now that I've spent a year living with handicapped people, I'm beginning to understand better what she meant. It isn't really possible to see Jesus in human beings if you can't see him in the hidden reality of the bread that comes down from heaven. In human beings you can see this, that, and the other: angels and devils, saints and brutes, benevolent souls and malevolent power-maniacs. However, it's only when you've learned from personal experience how much Jesus cares for you and how much he desires to be your daily food, that you can learn to see that every human heart is a dwelling place for Jesus. When your heart is touched by the presence of Jesus in the Eucharist, then you will receive new eyes capable of recognizing that same presence in the hearts of others. Heart speaks to heart. Jesus in our heart speaks to Jesus in the hearts of our fellow men and women. That's the eucharistic mystery of which we are a part.

We want to see results, and preferably instantly. But God works in secret and with a divine patience. By taking part in the Eucharist you can come gradually to understand this. Then your heart can begin to open up to the God who suffers in the people around you.

I began this letter by talking about Marthe Robin. For more than fifty years the only food she took was the eucharistic bread, brought to her once a week. Jesus was indeed her whole being. Because of this she could teach her visitors how to discover Jesus in their own hearts. For many of them that discovery was the beginning of a radical spiritual transformation. When we know through personal experience that God does indeed live in us, we are able, like Jesus himself, to work miracles and to change the face of the earth. We do this not by seeking publicity, but by constantly seeking Jesus in the hidden center of our lives and the lives of our fellow men and women.

Dear Marc, I hope that in this letter I've been able to bring you a little closer to Jesus as the hidden God. I shall leave it at this. In my next letter, a final one, I want to offer you some suggestions for living, day by day, a life in which Jesus is, and will always be, at the center.

Warmest greetings to your mother and father, and to Frédérique and Reinier.

Yours affectionately,
Henri

LETTER VII

Listening to Jesus

Thursday, 18th September

My dear Marc,

It was more than seven months ago that I began writing these letters about the spiritual life. I sent you the first three from West Germany, the three later ones from France. That now seems far away and long ago.

In mid-August I went to Canada to live and work at Daybreak, the L'Arche community near Toronto. This morning I read through my letters to you once more, and I realized that I'd probably written them as much for myself as for you. My year in Europe was meant to be a period of searching for a new direction in my life. I had a vague notion that Jesus was calling me to leave the university and to go and live with mentally handicapped people. My meeting with Jean Vanier and my stay in the L'Arche community at Trosly awoke in me something new which I couldn't continue to ignore. The burning question was, "How best am I to follow Jesus?"

In my letters I've tried to bring you closer to Jesus. But I now realize that I've also "used" these letters to get to know Jesus better myself and so become better able to hear the invitation to follow him. It's good, I think, that these letters have a purpose for both of us, because it's only with what touches my heart that I am able to touch yours.

In my first letter, I said that I could write to you only what I've lived through and experienced myself. In this final letter I can honestly say that everything I have written to you has sprung directly from my own search for God. I hope this will prove more of a help than a hindrance for you. My greatest desire was to awaken in you a deep love for Jesus. I've told you of the Jesus who liberates, of the suffering Jesus and his compassion; of the Jesus who in his humility chose the descending way; of the loving Jesus who challenges us to love even our enemies; and finally of the Jesus of Nazareth who reveals to us the mystery of God's hiddenness. As you see, I've begun with the end of the gospel and ended with the beginning. In doing that I've tried to stay close to the church's proclamation, which approaches the mysteries of God's incarnation and redemption from the perspective of its faith in the risen Lord.

In the course of writing I've discovered for myself the great extent to which I'm inclined to "secularize" Jesus. Instinctively, I look to Jesus for a cheap liberation, a solution to my problems, help with my desire for success, getting even with my opponents, and a good measure of publicity. It's not always easy to see Jesus as the gospel presents him: as the Lord who calls us to spiritual freedom, shares our suffering, shows us the descending way, challenges us to love our enemies, and secretly reveals God's love to us. And yet, each time I catch a glimpse of the real Jesus, I'm conscious of a new inward peace, and it is again possible to recognize his voice and follow it.

So I can tell you that these letters have helped me to see the real Jesus and have strengthened my decision to go to Canada and live and work there with mentally handicapped people.

Spiritual life is life lived in the spirit of Jesus. I've spoken of the Eucharist as being the center of that life. Jesus is more, much more, than an important historical figure who can still inspire us today. In the Eucharist he sets us free from constraint and compulsion, unites our suffering with his, forms a fellowship in shared vulnerability, offers us a love that forgives even our enemies, and helps us to see God in the seclusion of the human heart. Where the Eucharist is, there Jesus really is present; there too the church really is a body, and there we really do share, even now, in eternal life.

You and I both are called to be disciples of Jesus. The differences between us in age, circumstances, upbringing, and experience are small matters compared with the calling we have in common. What counts is being attentive at all times to the voice of God's love inviting us to obey, that is, to make a generous response.

How can we keep listening to this voice in a world which does its best to distract us and get our attention for seemingly more urgent matters? In this last letter I want to put before you, by way of a conclusion, three forms of listening that for me have proven to be the most productive.

First of all, listen to the church. I know that isn't a popular bit of advice at a time and in a country where the church is often seen more as an obstacle in the way than as the way to Jesus. Nevertheless, I'm deeply convinced that the greatest spiritual danger for our times is the separation of Jesus from the church. The church is the body of the Lord. Without Jesus there can be no church; and without the church we cannot stay united with Jesus. I've yet to meet anyone who has come closer to Jesus by forsaking the church. To listen to the church is to listen to the Lord of the church. Specifically, this entails taking part in the church's liturgical life. Advent, Christmas, Lent, Easter, Ascension, and Pentecost: these seasons and feasts teach you to know Jesus better and better and unite you more and more intimately with the divine life he offers you in the church.

The Eucharist is the heart of the church's life. It's there that you hear the life-giving gospel and receive the gifts that sustain that life within you. The best assurance that you'll go on listening to the church is your regular participation in the Eucharist.

Second, listen to the book. By that I mean read the Bible; read books about the Bible, about the spiritual life, and the lives of "great" saints. I know you read a good deal; but a lot of what you read distracts you from the way that Jesus is showing you. The secondary school and university offer you little in the way of "spiritual reading." That's why it's very important for you to read regularly books which will help you in your spiritual life. Many people are brought to God through spiritual literature that they chance or choose to read. Augustine, Ignatius, Thomas Merton, and many others have been converted through the book. The challenge, however, is not to read a "spiritual" book as a source of interesting information, but rather to listen to it as to a voice that addresses you directly. It isn't easy to let a text "read" you. Your thirst for knowledge and informa-tion often makes you desire to own the word, instead of letting the word own you. Even so, you will learn the most by listening carefully to the Word that seeks admission to your heart.

Finally, listen to your heart. It's there that Jesus speaks most intimately to you. Praying is first and foremost listening to Jesus, who dwells in the very depths of your heart. He doesn't shout. He doesn't thrust himself upon you. His voice is an unassuming voice, very nearly a whisper, the voice of a gentle love. Whatever you do with your life, go on listening to the voice of Jesus in your heart. This listening must be an active and very attentive listening, for in our restless and noisy world Jesus' loving voice is easily drowned out. You need to set aside some time every day for this active listening to Jesus, if only for ten minutes. Ten minutes each day for Jesus alone can bring about a radical change in your life.

You'll find that it isn't easy to be still for ten minutes at a time. You'll discover straightaway that many other voices—voices that are very noisy and distracting, voices which are not God's—demand your attention. But if you stick to your daily prayer time, then slowly but surely you'll come to hear the gentle voice of love and will long more and more to listen to it.

These three ways of listening will guide you to an ever-deepening spiritual life. They will help you to get to know Jesus in a very intimate way, make you aware of the unique manner in which he is calling you, and give you the courage to follow him even to places where you would rather not go. Living with Jesus is a great adventure. It's the adventure of love. When you admit Jesus to your heart nothing is predictable, but ev-erything becomes possible. I pray that you will venture on a life with Je-sus. He asks everything of you, but gives you more in return. With all my heart I wish you much hope, much courage, and abounding confidence.

Affectionate greetings to your parents, and to Frédérique and Reinier.

Henri

A Letter of Consolation

A LETTER OF CONSOLATION
CONTENTS

INTRODUCTION

THIS LETTER WAS written six months after the death of my mother. I wrote it to my father as a letter of consolation. When I wrote it I did not think of making it public, but now, three years later, I feel a certain urge to do so. Because now I have a real desire to offer this letter to all those who suffer the pain that death can bring and who search for new life. During the last few years I have come to realize in a new way what it means to live and die for each other. As this awareness grew in me, I began to wonder if the fruits of our grief are to be tasted only by ourselves.

Like other letters, this letter has its own history and I would like to introduce its publication by offering some explanation of why I decided to write it.

Very shortly after my mother's funeral in October 1978, I returned from Holland to the United States. A few days later I was busy again, as always, teaching, counseling students, attending faculty meetings, answering mail, and doing the many things that fill the daily life of a university teacher. There had been little or no opportunity to let mother's suffering and death enter deeply into my innermost self.

During the days that my mother was dying and during the days immediately after her death, I tried to pay as much attention as I could to my family and to anyone who offered friendship and love. And then, back in the United States, far away from home, the busy school life certainly did not encourage me to listen to my own inner cries. But one day, when I paused for a while in my office between appointments, I suddenly realized that I had not shed a single tear before or after mother's death. At that moment I saw that the world had such a grasp on me that it did not allow me to fully experience even the most personal, the most intimate, and the most mysterious event of my life. It seemed as if the voices around me were saying, "You have to keep going. Life goes on; people die, but you must continue to live, to work, to struggle. The past cannot be recreated. Look at what is ahead." I was obedient to these voices: I gave my lectures with the same enthusiasm as ever; I listened to students and their problems as if nothing had happened; and I worked with the same compulsiveness that had characterized my life since I started to teach. But I knew then that this would not last if I really took my mother and myself seriously. By a happy coincidence—no, by a gracious gift of God—I had planned a six months' retreat with the Trappist monks at the Abbey of the Genesee, which during the past years had become a second home to me.

When I arrived at the monastery in January I knew that this was going to be my time of grief. On several occasions, while sitting in my little room surrounded by the deep silence of the monastery, I noticed tears coming from my eyes. I did not really understand this. I was not thinking about mother, I was not remembering her illness, her death, or her funeral, but from a place in me deeper than I could reach, grief welled up and manifested itself in soft weeping.

As the days and weeks passed I experienced a growing urge to live through more fully and more directly the loss of which my tears reminded me. But I did not want to do this alone. I wanted to do it with someone who could really understand what was happening inside me. And who could better understand me than my own father? It was an obvious and easy decision, because ever since my mother's death his letters had become my greatest source of comfort. In these letters he had told me about his own grief and his struggle to build a new, meaningful life without her. Maybe I could offer him consolation and comfort by uniting my pain with his.

Thus, I started to write this letter to my father, a letter to speak with him about her whom we had both loved so much, a letter to show him my love and affection, a letter to offer him some of my reflections on mother's death—in short, a letter of consolation. I wrote and wrote and wrote. Once I started to write I realized how much I felt, how much I wanted to say, and how much had remained hidden during the six months since mother had died.

To whom did I write this letter? To my father, surely. But I was also writing to myself. Who was consoled? My father was, I know, but when I finally wrote down the last words, I knew that I had received as much and maybe more comfort and consolation than he would. Many letters are that way: they touch the writer as much as the receiver.

I now realize that this letter had to be written for my father, for me, and maybe, too, for many others who are asking the same questions that we were asking. When I asked my father, two and a half years after the letter was written, how he would feel about making it available to others in the form of a small book, he said, "If you think that your writing about mother's death and about our grief can be a source of hope and consolation to more people than just ourselves, do not be afraid to have it printed."

And thus, after some thought and much encouragement from friends, I felt that it would be good to take the letter out of the privacy of my life and that of my father and offer it to those who know the same darkness and are searching for the same light.

I hope and pray that I made the right decision.

Henri J. M. Nouwen
December 29, 1981

DEAR FATHER

NEXT MONDAY IT will be half a year since mother died. It will be Holy Week and both of us will be preparing ourselves to celebrate Easter. How will this Easter be for us? You will be in the parish church of our little Dutch town listening to the story of Christ's resurrection. I will read that same story to monks and guests in a Trappist monastery in upstate New York. Both of us will look at the Easter candle, symbol of the risen Christ, and think not only of him but also of her. Our minds and hearts will be flooded with ideas and feelings that are too deep, too complex, and too intimate to express. But I am sure that we both shall think about last year's Easter, when she was still with us. We both shall remember how she loved this great feast and how she decorated the house with flowers and the dinner table with purple and yellow ribbons. Somehow it seems long, long ago. Isn't that your experience also? The last six months could as well have been six years. Her death changed our experience of time; the short period between last October and this April seemed a very strange time in which the days, weeks, and months were as long as they are for a small child who is taking his first steps. We had to relearn life. Every "normal" experience became for us like a new experience. It had the quality of a "first time." How often have we used these words! The first Christmas without mother, the first New Year without mother, the first wedding anniversary without mother. And now it will be the first Easter without mother. I know that you have been asking yourself often, as I have, "How will it be without her?" We can hardly remember any of these events without her being part of them. We can no longer predict how we will feel on these familiar days and occasions. They are, in fact, no longer familiar. They have become unknown to us. We have become suddenly aware how intimately our ideas, feelings, and perceptions were determined by her presence. Easter was not only an important day to celebrate, but a day to celebrate with her, a day on which her voice was heard, her letters anticipated, her active presence felt—so much so that we could not distinguish between the joys brought to us by the feast and the joys brought to us by her presence at the feast. They had become one and the same. But now we are forced to make a distinction, and now we have become like children who have to learn to do things for the first time on their own.

New experiences such as these have made the last six months a strange time for us. Her death became an ongoing death for us. Every time we lived through another event without her, we felt her absence in a new way. We became aware of deep connections with her that we had forgotten for a while but that were brought back to consciousness by the forward movement of history. And each time, she died again in us. Memories of what she would have done, said, or written on certain occasions made us more aware of her not being with us and deepened our grief.

Real grief is not healed by time. It is false to think that the passing of time will slowly make us forget her and take away our pain. I really want to console you in this letter, but not by suggesting that time will take away your pain, and that in one, two, three, or more years you will not miss her so much anymore. I would not only be telling a lie, I would be diminishing the importance of mother's life, underestimating the depth of your grief, and mistakenly relativizing the power of the love that has bound mother and you together for forty-seven years. If time does anything, it deepens our grief. The longer we live, the more fully we become aware of who she was for us, and the more intimately we experience what her love meant for us. Real, deep love is, as you know, very unobtrusive, seemingly easy and obvious, and so present that we take it for granted. Therefore, it is often only in retrospect—or better, in memory—that we fully realize its power and depth. Yes, indeed, love often makes itself visible in pain. The pain we are now experiencing shows us how deep, full, intimate, and all-pervasive her love was.

Is this a consolation? Does this bring comfort? It appears that I am doing the opposite of bringing consolation. Maybe so. Maybe these words will only increase your tears and deepen your grief. But for me, your son, who grieves with you, there is no other way. I want to comfort and console you, but not in a way that covers up real pain and avoids all wounds. I am writing you this letter in the firm conviction that reality can be faced and entered with an open mind and an open heart, and in the sincere belief that consolation and comfort are to be found where our wounds hurt most.

When I write to you, therefore, that, in our remembering, not only the full depth of mother's love but also the full pain of her leaving us will become known to us, I do so with the trying question in mind: "Why is it that she died before we did and why is it that we are the ones who have to carry the burden of grief?" You must have asked yourself this question many times. You have lived your life with the unquestioned assumption that you would die before mother. You felt this way not simply because you were three years older than she or because her health always seemed better than yours, but because you sensed that she would be more capable of living on without you than you without her. Why then are you the one who has to relearn life without her, and why are you the one who came to know her not only in the joy of her presence but in the pain of her absence? She has been spared the sorrow of your death; she never had to experience life without you. All the sorrow has been given to you to bear, and you have been entrusted with that awesome task of discovering her love not only in life but in death. Why? Although I am twenty-nine years younger than you are, and although the "logic of life" says parents die before their children, for me the question is no different, because love does not know "clock time."

I am writing this letter to you conscious of this great question. I want to explore with you and for you the meaning of her death and our life, of her life and our death. In your letters to me since her death—letters richer and fuller than any you wrote to me before—you have raised the question of death yourself. Ever since we saw her still face in the hospital, we have wondered what death really is. It is a question mother has left us with, and we want to face it, enter it, explore it, and let it grow in us. By doing so we may be able to console one another. It will be a hard road to travel, but if we travel it together we may have less to fear. I am glad, therefore, that in this quiet and peaceful Trappist monastery I have the opportunity to write you this letter, and I am especially glad that I can write to you during the days when both of us are preparing ourselves to celebrate the resurrection of our Lord Jesus Christ.

I

OFTEN I FEEL sad about the great distance between us. Although I have always been content with living in the United States, since mother's death I have sensed more than before the distance that prevents me from being of more help and support to you during these difficult months. Regular letters and occasional phone calls are a very limited substitute for being together. And yet the paradox of it all is that the distance between us may prove after all to be a blessing in disguise. If I were still living in Holland and were able to visit you every weekend and call you every day, I should probably never have been able to let you know my deeper feelings about mother and you. Isn't it true that it is much harder to say deep things to each other than to write them? Isn't it much more frightening to express our deeper feelings about each other when we sit around the breakfast table than when the Atlantic Ocean separates us? We have spent many hours watching television together since mother died. We have often had a meal together at home or in a restaurant. We have taken little rides together through the woods. But seldom, very seldom, have we spoken about what was closest to our hearts. It was as if the physical closeness prevented the spiritual closeness we both desired. I am not sure if I fully understand this myself, but it seems that we are not the only people for whom this holds true. Physical and spiritual closeness are two quite different things, and they can—although they do not always—inhibit each other. The great distance between us may be enabling us to develop a relationship that you might not be able to develop with your other children and their families who live so close to you.

One obvious result of our distance is that you have started to write letters to me. Since mother died you not only write more often, but your letters are different. That has meant a lot to me during the last six months. I had become so used to mother's weekly letters, in which she told about all the family events, big and small, and kept showing her interest in my own life with all its ups and downs, that I feared their sudden absence. You used to write very seldom, and when you did, your letters consisted mostly of general, almost philosophical, reflections; they did not reveal much about your actual work, concerns, or feelings. It always seemed as though you felt that mother was the one who took care of personal relationships. I remember how often you used to say, as I left the house to return to the United States, "Don't forget to write mother." It was almost as if you were not very interested in hearing from me and were primarily concerned that mother and I would stay in close touch. I do not think that this was true. On the contrary, I think that you were very interested in hearing from me, but you usually left it to mother to express the affection, concern, and interest that you shared with her. Sometimes it was even humorous. Whenever I called you by phone, I was surprised that you took it for granted that I really called for mother. I always had the hardest time keeping you on the line for more than a few seconds. After reassuring me that everything was fine with you, you always said quickly, "Well, here's mother." I knew a call made you happy, but your happiness seemed to be derived from mother's joy and gratefulness.

But now she is no longer there for you to hide behind. And you have indeed stepped forward! You have written me letters as warm and personal as those of mother. In fact, even more so. And just as I once looked forward to receiving mother's letters, I now long for yours. Now I not only know—as I did before—that you are interested in my life, but I can also see it expressed in your written words. And now you accept the simple and true fact that I write to you for yourself alone and call you for yourself alone.

The more I think about this, the more I realize that mother's death caused you to step forward in a way you could not before. Maybe there is even more to say than that. Maybe I have to say that you have found in yourself the capacity to be not only a father, but a mother as well. You have found in yourself that same gift of compassion that brought mother so much love and so much suffering. You have started to see more clearly the loneliness of your friends and to sympathize more with their search for company; you have begun to feel more deeply the fears of your widowed colleagues and to experience more sharply the mystery of death. And—if I may say so—you have discovered that you have a son who has been alone since he left your house. Becoming a priest for me has in fact meant to enter the road of "the long loneliness," as Dorothy Day called it, and my many physical and spiritual journeys have deepened that experience even further. That long loneliness is what had made me feel so especially close to mother and has made me feel so lost by her death. But isn't this now also the basis for a unique solidarity between the two of us? Am I right when I suppose that you, who are known and feared for your irony and sarcasm, for your sharp wit and critical analysis—all qualities that made you such a good lawyer—are now allowing your tender side to come more to the center and are now experiencing a new bond with those who are dear to you?

There is always that strange tendency in marriage to divide roles, even psychological roles. And our culture certainly encourages that: mother for the children, you for earning a living; mother to be gentle and forgiving, you to be strict and demanding; mother hospitable and receptive, you reserved and selective. In fact, you even liked to play with these differences and point them out in your comments at dinner. But now there are no longer any qualities to divide, and you are challenged to let develop more fully in yourself what you so admired in mother. I even sense that the memory of mother, and the way she lived her life with you, makes you consciously desire to let her qualities remain visible for your children and your friends—visible in you.

You are not imitating mother. You are not saying, "I will do things the way mother used to do them." That would be artificial and certainly not an honor to her. No, you are becoming more yourself, you are exploring those areas of life that always were part of you but remained somewhat dormant in mother's presence. I think that we both have a new and honorable task. It is the task to be father, son, and friend in a new way, a way that mother made possible not only through her life, but through her death. When Jesus said that if a grain of wheat dies it will yield a rich harvest, he not only spoke about his own death but indicated the new meaning he would give to our death. So we have to ask ourselves, "Where do we see the harvest of mother's death?" There is no doubt in my mind that this harvest is becoming visible first of all in those who loved her most. Our deep love for her allows us to be the first to reap the harvest and to share with others the gifts of her death.

Isn't it here that we have to start if we want to discover the meaning of mother's death? Before anything else, we have to come into touch with — yes, even claim — the mysterious reality of new life in ourselves. Others might see it, feel it, and enjoy it before we do. That is why I am writing to you about it. We may help each other to see this new life. That would be true consolation. It would make us experience in the center of our beings that the pain mother's death caused us has led us to a new way of being, in which the distance between mother, father, or child slowly dissolves. Thus our separation from mother brings us to a new inner unity and invites us to make that new unity a source of joy and hope for each other and for others as well.

AS I SAID earlier, mother's death has made us raise more directly and explicitly the question of death itself. The question about death, however,
is mostly asked by someone who is himself not dying. You yourself made
me aware of this when you reminded me how much mother spoke about
her death when there was no real danger and yet hardly mentioned it
at all when she was actually dying. It seems indeed important that we
face death before we are in any real danger of dying and reflect on our
mortality before all our conscious and unconscious energy is directed
to the struggle to survive. It is important to be prepared for death, very
important; but if we start thinking about it only when we are terminally
ill, our reflections will not give us the support we need. We enjoy good
health now. We are asking about death, mother's death and our own, not
because we are dying, but because we feel strong enough to raise the
question about our most basic human infirmity.

I want to take up the challenge of this question. This indeed seems to
be the opportune time not only for you, but also for me. We both have to
ask ourselves what mother's death means, and we both are confronted in
a new way with our own deaths. The fact that you are "already" seventy-
six and I am "only" forty-seven is not a real hindrance to a common
meditation on death. I think, in fact, that mother's death has taken away
much of the age difference between us, so that the prospect of dying and
death is not really different for you and for me. Once you have reached
the top of the mountain, it does not make much difference at which

point on the way down you take a picture of the valley—as long as you are not in the valley itself.

I think, then, that our first task is to befriend death. I like that expression "to befriend." I first heard it used by Jungian analyst James Hillman when he attended a seminar I taught on Christian Spirituality at Yale Divinity School. He emphasized the importance of "befriending": befriending your dreams, befriending your shadow, befriending your unconscious. He made it convincingly clear that in order to become full human beings, we have to claim the totality of our experience; we come to maturity by integrating not only the light but also the dark side of our story into our selfhood. That made a lot of sense to me, since I am quite familiar with my own inclination, and that of others, to avoid, deny, or suppress the painful side of life, a tendency that always leads to physical, mental, or spiritual disaster.

And isn't death, the frightening unknown that lurks in the depths of our unconscious minds, like a great shadow that we perceive only dimly in our dreams? Befriending death seems to be the basis of all other forms of befriending. I have a deep sense, hard to articulate, that if we could really befriend death we would be free people. So many of our doubts and hesitations, ambivalences and insecurities are bound up with our deep-seated fear of death that our lives would be significantly different if we could relate to death as a familiar guest instead of a threatening stranger.

In the book *Nacht und Nebel*, the Dutchman Floris Bakels writes about his experiences in the German prisons and concentration camps of the Second World War. He makes very clear what power a man can have who has befriended his own death. I know how much this book has moved you, and I was very happy with the copy I just received. Wouldn't you say that Floris Bakels was able to survive the horrors of Dachau and other camps and write about it thirty-two years later precisely because he had befriended death? It seems, at least to me, that Floris Bakels said in many different ways to his SS captors, "You have no power over me, because I have already died." Fear of death often drives us into death, but by befriending death, we can face our mortality and choose life freely.

But how do we befriend death? During the last few years you have seen many deaths—even of people you knew quite well. They have touched you, shocked you, surprised you, and even caused you grief, but when mother died it seemed as if death came to you for the first time. Why? I think because love—deep, human love—does not know death. The way you and mother had become one, and the way this oneness had deepened itself during forty-seven years of marriage, did not allow termination. Real love says, "Forever." Love will always reach out toward the eternal. Love comes from that place within us where death cannot enter. Love does not accept the limits of hours, days, weeks, months, years, or centuries. Love is not willing to be imprisoned by time.

That is why mother's death was such a totally different experience for you from the deaths of so many other people you have known. In the core of your being, you—your love—could not accept her leaving you so drastically, so radically, so totally, and so irretrievably. Her death went directly against your most profound intuitions. And so I could well understand your writing to me that mother's death had led you to the general question of death's meaning. Someone might say, "Why did it take him so long to raise that question? He is seventy-six years old—and only now does he wonder about the meaning of death." But someone who says this does not understand that only mother could raise that question for you, because in her dying the real absurdity of death revealed itself to you. Only her death could really make you protest in your innermost being and make you cry out, "Why could our love not prevent her from dying?"

Yet, the same love that reveals the absurdity of death also allows us to befriend death. The same love that forms the basis of our grief is also the basis of our hope; the same love that makes us cry out in pain also must enable us to develop a liberating intimacy with our own most basic brokenness. Without faith, this must sound like a contradiction. But our faith in him whose love overcame death and who rose from the grave on the third day converts this contradiction into a paradox, the most healing paradox of our existence. Floris Bakels experienced this in a unique way. He came to see and feel that the power of love is stronger than the power of death and that it is indeed true that "God is love." Surrounded by people dying from hunger, torture, and total exhaustion, and knowing quite well that any hour could be his hour to die, he found in the core of his being a love so strong and so profound that the fear of death lost its power over him. For Floris Bakels, this love was not a general feeling or emotion, nor an idea about a benevolent Supreme Being. No, it was the very concrete, real, and intimate love of Jesus Christ, Son of God and redeemer of the world. With his whole being he knew that he was loved with an infinite love, held in an eternal embrace and surrounded by an unconditional care. This love was so concrete, so tangible, so direct, and so close for him that the temptation to interpret this religious experience as the fantasy of a starved mind had no lasting hold on him. The more deeply and fully he experienced Christ's love, the more he came to see that the many loves in his life—the love of his parents, his brother and sisters, his wife, and his friends—were reflections of the great "first" love of God.

I am convinced that it was the deeply felt love of God—felt in and through Jesus Christ—that allowed Floris Bakels to face his own death and the deaths of others so directly. It was this love that gave him the freedom and energy to help people in agony and made it possible for him to resume a normal life after he returned from the hell of Dachau.

I am writing so much about Bakels because I know that you, being of the same generation and the same profession, can understand him quite well and will lend him a sympathetic ear. He can indeed show you better than psychologists or psychoanalysts what it means to befriend death.

Although you and I also tasted the terror of the Nazis, you as a young man who had to hide yourself to escape from deportation and I as a fearful child, and although we all had to struggle hard to keep alive during the horrible "winter of hunger" in 1944–45, we were spared the horrors of the concentration camps and did not have to face death in the way Floris Bakels did. Thus, we were not forced to befriend death at such an early age. But mother's death invites us to do so now. Many people seem never to befriend death and die as if they were losing a hopeless battle. But we do not have to share that sad fate. Mother's death can bring us that freedom of which Bakels writes; it can make us deeply aware that her love was a reflection of a love that does not and cannot die—the love that we both will affirm again on Easter Sunday.

I I I

IN NO WAY do I want to suggest that you have been repressing or denying your mortality. In fact, I know few people who have been so open
about their own death. At different times you have spoken about your
own death publicly and privately, to strangers and to friends, mockingly
and seriously. Sometimes you even embarrassed mother and your guests
with your directness! I remember your mentioning on several occasions
how quickly our "great lives" are forgotten and how short-lived are the
pious memories of our friends and colleagues. I remember how you told
me, before you left on a long trip to Brazil, what I should do in case a
fatal accident took the lives of you both. And I remember your very concrete wishes about the way you hoped your children and friends would
respond to your death. Sometimes your words about your death had a
sarcastic quality, and conveyed a desire to unmask sentimentalism and
false romanticism. You even enjoyed gently shocking the pious feelings
of your friends and testing your and their sense of reality. But mostly,
your words were serious and showed that you were indeed reflecting on
the end of your own life. Thus it is quite clear that you have not been
living as if your life would go on forever. You are too intelligent and too
realistic for that.

Still, hidden in us there are levels of not-knowing, not-understanding
and not-feeling that can only be revealed to us in our moments of great
crisis. For some people such moments never come, for others they come
frequently. For some they come early, for others they come quite late. We

might think that we have a certain insight into "what life is all about" until an unexpected crisis throws us off balance and forces us to rethink our most basic presuppositions. In fact, we never really know how deeply our lives are anchored, and the experience of crisis can open up dimensions of life that we never knew existed.

Mother's death is certainly one of the most crucial experiences of both our lives, perhaps even the most crucial. Before her death, it was impossible to know even vaguely what it would do to us. Now we are beginning to sense its impact. Gradually we are able to see where it is leading us. A new confrontation with death is taking place, a confrontation that we could never have created ourselves. Whatever we felt, said, or thought about death in the past was always within the reach of our own emotional or intellectual capacities. In a certain sense, it remained within the range of our own influence and control. Remarks and ideas about our own deaths remained *our* remarks and *our* ideas and were therefore subject to our own inventiveness and originality. But mother's death was totally outside the field of our control or influence. It left us powerless. When we saw how slowly she lost contact with us and fell away from us, we could do nothing but stand beside her bed and watch death exercise its ruthless power. This experience is not an experience for which we can really prepare ourselves. It is so new and so overpowering that all of our previous speculations and reflections seem trivial and superficial in the presence of the awesome reality of death. Thus mother's death changes the question of death into a new question. It opens us to levels of life that could not have been reached before, even if we had had the desire to reach them.

What did mother's death do to you? I do not know and cannot know since it is something so intimate that nobody can enter fully into your emotions. But if your experience of her death is in any way close to mine, you were "invited"—as I was—to re-evaluate your whole life. Mother's death made you stop and look back in a way you had not done before. Suddenly you entered into a situation that made you see your many years of life—your life as a student, a young professional, a successful lawyer, a well-known professor—with a bird's-eye view. I remember your telling me how you could capture your long and complex history in one clear picture, and how from the point of view of mother's death, your life lost much of its complexity and summarized itself in a few basic lines. In that way her death gave you new eyes with which to see your own life and helped you to distinguish between the many accidental aspects and the few essential elements.

Death indeed simplifies; death does not tolerate endless shadings and nuances. Death lays bare what really matters, and in this way becomes your judge. It seems that we both have experienced this after mother's death and funeral. During the last six months we have been reviewing our life with mother. For you this meant opening drawers that had not been opened for years; looking at photographs whose very existence you had forgotten; reading old letters now yellow and wrinkled with age; and picking up books that had collected much dust on the shelves. For me this meant rereading her letters to me; looking again at the gifts she brought to me on visits; and praying with renewed attention the psalms we so often prayed together. Long-forgotten events returned to memory as if they had taken place only recently. It seemed as if we could put our whole lives in the palms of our hands like small precious stones and gaze at them with tenderness and admiration. How tiny, how beautiful, how valuable!

I think that from the point of view of mother's death and our own mortality, we can now see our lives as a long process of mortification. You are familiar with that word. Priests use it a lot during Lent. They say, "You have to mortify yourself." It sounds unpleasant and harsh and moralistic. But mortification—literally, "making death"—is what life is all about, a slow discovery of the mortality of all that is created so that we can appreciate its beauty without clinging to it as if it were a lasting possession. Our lives can indeed be seen as a process of becoming familiar with death, as a school in the art of dying. I do not mean this in a morbid way. On the contrary, when we see life constantly relativized by death, we can enjoy it for what it is: a free gift. The pictures, letters, and books of the past reveal life to us as a constant saying of farewell to beautiful places, good people, and wonderful experiences. Look at the pictures of your children when you could play with them on the floor of the living room. How quickly you had to say goodbye to them! Look at the snapshots of your bike trips with mother in Brittany in the mid-thirties. How few were the summers in which those trips were possible! Read mother's letters when you were in Amalfi recuperating from your illness and my letters to you from my first trip to England. They speak now of fleeting moments. Look at the wedding pictures of your children and at the Bible I gave you on the day of my ordination. All these times have passed by like friendly visitors, leaving you with dear memories but also with the sad recognition of the shortness of life. In every arrival there is a leavetaking; in every reunion there is a separation; in each one's growing up there is a growing old; in every smile there is a tear; and in every success there is a loss. All living is dying and all celebration is mortification too.

Although this was happening all the time during our rich and varied lives, we did not notice it with the same acuteness as we do now. There was so much life, so much vitality, and so much exuberance that the presence of death was less striking and was only acknowledged in the way we acknowledge our shadows on a sunny day. There were moments of pain, sadness, disillusionment; there were illnesses, setbacks, conflicts, and worries. But they came and went like the seasons of the year, and the forces of life always proved victorious. Then mother died. Her death was a definitive end, a total break that presented itself with a finality unlike any other. For a while, we kept living as if she were only gone for a time and could return at any moment. We even kept doing things as if we were preparing for the moment when she would appear again on our doorsteps. But as the days passed, our hearts came to know that she was gone, never to return. And it was then that real grief began to invade us. It was then that we turned to the past and saw that death had been present in our lives all along and that the many farewells and goodbyes had been pointing to this dark hour. And it was then that we raised in a wholly new way the question of the meaning of death.

IV

WHEN WE EXPERIENCED the deep loss at mother's death, we also experienced our total inability to do anything about it. We, who loved mother so much and would have done anything possible to alleviate her pain and agony, could do absolutely nothing. All of us who stood around her bed during her last days felt powerless. Sometimes we looked at the doctors and nurses with the vain hope that maybe *they* could change the course of events, but we realized that what we were witnessing was the inevitable reality of death, a reality we shall all have to face one day soon.

I think it is important for us to allow this experience of powerlessness in the face of mother's death to enter deeply into our souls, because it holds the key to a deeper understanding of the meaning of death.

Father, you are a man with a strong personality, a powerful will, and a convincing sense of self. You are known as a hard worker, a persistent fighter for your clients, and a man who never loses an argument, or at least will never confess to losing one! You have achieved what you strove for. Your successful career has rewarded your efforts richly and has strengthened you in your conviction that success in life is the result of hard work. If anything is clear about your life-style, it is that you want to keep your hands on the tiller of your ship. You like to be in control, able to make your own decisions and direct your own course. Experience has taught you that displaying weakness does not create respect and that it is safer to bear your burden in secret than to ask for pity. You never strove for power and influence, and even refused many positions that would have given you national recognition, but you fiercely guarded your own spiritual, mental, and economic autonomy. Not only did you in fact achieve an impressive amount of autonomy for yourself, but you also encouraged your children to become free and independent people as soon as possible. I think it was this great value you put on autonomy that made you proud to see me leave for the United States. I am sure you did not want me to be so far from home, but this inconvenience was richly compensated for by the joy you drew from my ability to "make it" independently of the support of my family and friends. One of your most often repeated remarks to me and to my brothers and sister was, "Be sure not to become dependent on the power, influence, or money of others. Your freedom to make your own decisions is your greatest possession. Do not ever give that up."

This attitude—an attitude greatly admired by mother and all of us in the family—explains why anything that reminded you of death threatened you. You found it very hard to be ill, you were usually a bit irritated with the illnesses of others, and you had very little sympathy for people whom you considered "failures." The weak did not attract you.

Mother's death opened up for you a dimension of life in which the key word is not autonomy, but surrender. In a very deep and existential way, her death was a frontal attack on your feeling of autonomy and independence, and in this sense, a challenge to conversion, that is, to the profound turning around of your priorities. I am not saying that mother's death made your autonomy and independence less valuable, but only that it put them into a new framework, the framework of life as a process of detachment.

Autonomy and detachment are not necessarily opposites. They can be if they confront each other on the same level of existence. But I sincerely believe that a healthy autonomy can give you the real strength to detach yourself when it is necessary to do so. Let me try to explain what I mean.

Even when we are trying to be in control and to determine our own course in life, we have to admit that life remains the great unknown to us. Although you worked quite hard in life to build up a successful career and to give your family a happy home, some of the main factors that made things develop the way they did were totally out of your hands. Many things that happened *to* you were as important as the things that happened *through* you. Fifty years ago, neither you nor anyone else could have predicted your present situation. And how futile it is for us to predict our own immediate or distant future. Things that made us worry greatly later prove to be quite insignificant, and things to which we hardly gave a thought before they took place turn our lives around. Thus our autonomy is rooted in unknown soil. This constitutes the great challenge: to be so free that we can be obedient, to be so autonomous that we can be dependent, to be so in control that we can surrender ourselves. Here we touch the great paradox in life: to live in order to be able to die. That is what detachment is all about. Detachment is not the opposite of autonomy but its fruit. It takes a good driver to know when to use his brakes!

This is far from theoretical, as you well know. We have both seen how some of our friends could not accept unforeseen changes in their lives and were unable to deal with an unknown future. When things went differently than they had expected or took a drastic turn, they did not know how to adjust to the new situation. Sometimes they became bitter and sour. Often they clung to familiar patterns of living that were no longer adequate and kept repeating what once made sense but no longer could speak to the real circumstances of the moment. Death has often affected people in this way, as we know too well. The death of husband, wife, child, or friend can cause people to stop living toward the unknown future and make them withdraw into the familiar past. They keep holding on to a few precious memories and customs and see their lives as having come to a standstill. They start to live as if they were thinking, "For me it is all over. There is nothing more to expect from life." As you can see, here the opposite of detachment is taking place; here is a re-attachment that makes life stale and takes all vitality out of existence. It is a life in which hope no longer exists.

If mother's death were to lead us onto that road, her death would have no real meaning for us. Her death would be or become for us a death that closes the future and makes us live the rest of our lives in the enclosure of our own past. Then, our experience of powerlessness would not give us the freedom to detach ourselves from the past, but would imprison us in our own memories and immobilize us. Thus we would also lose the autonomy you have always held so dear.

I think there is a much more human option. It is the option to re-evaluate the past as a continuing challenge to surrender ourselves to an unknown future. It is the option to understand our experience of pow-erlessness as an experience of being guided, even when we do not know exactly where. Remember what Jesus said to Peter when he appeared to him after his resurrection: "When you were young you put on your own belt and walked where you liked; but when you grow old you will stretch out your hands, and somebody else will put a belt round you and take you where you would rather not go." Jesus said this immediately after he had told Peter three times to look after his sheep. Here we can see that a growing surrender to the unknown is a sign of spiritual maturity and does not take away autonomy. Mother's death is indeed an invitation to surrender ourselves more freely to the future, in the conviction that one of the most important parts of our lives may still be ahead of us and that mother's life and death were meant to make this possible. Do not forget that only after Jesus' death could his disciples fulfill their vocation.

I am constantly struck by the fact that those who are most detached from life, those who have learned through living that there is nothing and nobody in this life to cling to, are the really creative people. They are free to move constantly away from the familiar, safe places and can keep moving forward to new, unexplored areas of life. I am not suggesting to you that you are called to do something unusual or spectacular in your old age—although there is no telling to what you might be called! But I am thinking primarily of a spiritual process by which we can live our lives more freely than before, more open to God's guidance and more willing to respond when he speaks to our innermost selves.

Mother's death encourages us to give up the illusions of immortality we might still have and to experience in a new way our total dependence on God's love, a dependence that does not take away our free selfhood but purifies and ennobles it. Here you may catch a glimpse of the answer to the question of why mother died before you and why you have been given new years to live. Now you can say things to yourself, to others, and to God that were not disclosed to you before.

V

IN ALL THE previous reflections, dear father, an idea has emerged that was only vaguely in my mind when I started to write. It is the idea that the meaning of death is not so much the meaning our death has for us as the meaning it has for others. That explains why the meaning of mother's death and the meaning of our death are so closely related. I have a feeling that to the degree we can experience the fact that mother died for you, for her children, and for many others, our own death will have more meaning for us. I will try to explain this to you in such a way that you can find a certain obviousness in this idea.

Let me start with your own observation, which you have often made since mother's death, namely, that she lived her life for others. The more you reflected on her life, looked at her portraits, read her letters, and listened to what others said about her, the more you realized how her whole life was lived in the service of other people. I too am increasingly impressed by her attentiveness to the needs of others. This attitude was so much a part of her that it hardly seems remarkable. Only now can we see its full power and beauty. She rarely asked attention for herself. Her interest and attention went out to the needs and concerns of others. She was open to those who came to her. Many found it easy to talk with her about themselves and remarked how much at ease they had felt in her presence. This was especially noticeable during her visits to me in the United States. Often she knew my students better after one evening than I did after a year, and for many years to come she would keep asking about them. During the last six months I have grown painfully aware of how accustomed I had become to her unceasing interest in all that I did, felt, thought, or wrote, and how much I had taken it for granted that, even if nobody else cared, she certainly did. The absence of that caring attention often gives me a deep feeling of loneliness. I know that this is even truer for you. You no longer hear her ask how well you slept, what your plans are for the day, or what you are writing about. You no longer hear her advise you to be careful on the road, to eat more, or to get some extra sleep. All these simple but so supportive and healing ways of caring are no longer there, and in their absence we begin to feel more and more what it means to be alone.

What I want to say now, however, is that she who lived for others also died for others. Her death should not be seen as a sudden end to all her care, as a great halt to her receptivity to others. There are people who experience the death of someone they love as a betrayal. They feel rejected, left alone, and even fooled. They seem to say to their husband, wife, or friend, "How could you do this to me? Why did you leave me behind in this way? I never bargained for this!" Sometimes people even feel angry toward those who die, and express this by a paralyzing grief, by a regression to a state of total dependence, by all sorts of illnesses and complaints, and even by dying themselves.

If, however, mother's life was indeed a life lived for us, we must be willing to accept her death as a death for us, a death that is not meant to paralyze us, make us totally dependent, or provide an excuse for all sorts of complaints, but a death that should make us stronger, freer, and more mature. To say it even more drastically: we must have the courage to believe that her death was good for us and that she died so that we might live. This is quite a radical viewpoint and it might offend the sensitivities of some people. Why? Because, in fact, I am saying, "It is good for us that she left us, and to the extent that we do not accept this we have not yet fully understood the meaning of her life." This might sound harsh and even offensive, but I believe deeply that it is true. Indeed, I believe even more deeply that we will come to experience this ourselves.

Although the time is past when widows were burned with their dead husbands—even a contemporary Phileas Fogg would not encounter such a scene on a trip around the world—still, in a psychological sense, many widows and widowers end their lives with that of their spouse. They respond to the death of husband or wife with a sudden lack of vitality and behavior that turns life into a gruesome waiting room for death. I am aware of the fact that the other extreme—living on as if one had never been married—can also be seen. But since that is not within the horizon of your capacities, I do not need to talk about that here. What is important for us to recognize is that mother's own life invites us to see her death as a death that can bring us not only grief but also joy, not only pain but also healing, not only the experience of having lost but also the experience of having found.

This viewpoint is not just my personal viewpoint as against the viewpoint of others. It is the Christian viewpoint, that is, a viewpoint based on the life and death and resurrection of Jesus Christ. I need to be very clear about this, or you might not really understand what I am trying to express.

Five days have passed since I began this letter and it is now the evening before Holy Thursday. During this Holy Week we are confronted with death more than during any other season of the liturgical year. We are called to meditate not just on death in general or on our own death in particular, but on the death of Jesus Christ who is God and man. We are challenged to look at him dying on a cross and to find there the meaning of our own life and death. What strikes me most in all that is read and said during these days is that Jesus of Nazareth did not die for himself, but for us, and that in following him we too are called to make our death a death for others. What makes you and me Christians is not only our belief that he who was without sin died for our sake on the cross and thus opened for us the way to his heavenly Father, but also that through his death our death is transformed from a totally absurd end of all that gives life its meaning into an event that liberates us and those whom we love. It is because of the liberating death of Christ that I dare say to you that mother's death is not simply an absurd end to a beautiful, altruistic life. Rather, her death is an event that allows her altruism to yield a rich harvest. Jesus died so that we might live, and everyone who dies in union with him participates in the life-giving power of his death. Thus we can indeed say that mother, who died under the sign of the cross, died so that we might live. Therefore, under that same sign, each of our deaths can become a death for others. I think that we need to start seeing the profound meaning of this dying for each other in and through the death of Christ in order to catch a glimpse of what eternal life might mean. Eternity is born in time, and every time someone dies whom we have loved dearly, eternity can break into our mortal existence a little bit more.

I am aware that I am barely touching the great mystery I want to give words to. But I think that the mystery is so deep and vast that we can enter it only slowly and with great care.

As we enter more deeply into the mysteries of this Holy Week and come closer to Easter, it will become clear what needs to be said. But now it seems of first importance to realize that when we begin seeing that mother died for us, we can also catch an insight into the meaning of our own death. Initially this insight might well be that the meaning of our death cannot be expressed in an idea, a concept, or a theory. Rather, it must be discovered as a truth less visible to us than to those for whom we die. This is perhaps why the meaning of mother's death is slowly revealing itself to us even though it remained hidden from her, and why the meaning of our death will remain more concealed from us than from those who will miss us most. To die for others implies that the meaning of our death is better understood by them than by ourselves. This requires of us great detachment and even greater faith. But most of all, it calls us to an ever increasing surrender to the ways in which God chooses to manifest his love to us.

VI

TODAY IS HOLY Thursday or, as you would say, White Thursday. As I continue this letter, I realize that this day enables me to write about death in a way that I could not before. As you know, Holy Thursday is the day of the Eucharist, the day on which Jesus took bread and wine and said to his intimate companions: "Take . . . eat . . . drink . . . this is my body . . . this is my blood . . . do this as a memorial of me." On the night before his death, Jesus gave us the gift of his lasting presence in our midst in order to remind us in the most personal way that his death was a death for us. That is why Paul remarks in his letter to the Corinthians, "Every time you eat this bread and drink this cup, you are proclaiming his death."

I am glad that I can write to you about mother's death and about our own death on this holy day because now I can see more clearly than ever how much the mystery of this day binds us together. My whole being is rooted in the Eucharist. For me, to be a priest means to be ordained to present Christ every day as food and drink to my fellow Christians. I sometimes wonder if those who are close to me are sufficiently aware of the fact that the Eucharist constitutes the core of my life. I do so many other things and have so many secondary identities—teacher, speaker, and writer—that it is easy to consider the Eucharist as the least important part of my life. But the opposite is true. The Eucharist is the center of my life and everything else receives its meaning from that center. I am saying this with so much emphasis in the hope that you will understand what I mean when I say that my life must be a continuing proclamation of the death and resurrection of Christ. It is first and foremost through the Eucharist that this proclamation takes place.

What has all of this to do with mother's death and with our death? A great deal, I think. Certainly much more than we might realize. You know better than I how important the Eucharist was for mother. There were few days in her adult life when she did not go to Mass and Communion. Although she did not speak much about it herself, we all knew that her daily participation in the Eucharist was at the center of her life. There were few things that remained so constant in her daily routine. Wherever she was or whatever she did, she always tried to find a nearby church to receive the gifts of Christ. Her great desire for this daily spiritual nourishment frequently led you to plan your trips in such a way that you both could attend Mass each day before resuming your travels.

I do not think I am exaggerating when I say that it was mother's deep and lasting devotion to the Eucharist that was one of the factors, if not the main factor, in my decision to become a priest. That is why this Holy Thursday is such an important day. It unites us in a very intimate way. The death of Christ as proclaimed in the Eucharist has given meaning to our lives in a way too deep for us to explain. What is important is the realization that through participation in the Eucharist, our lives and our deaths are being lifted up in the life and death of Christ. This is an enormously mysterious reality, but the more deeply we enter into it the more comfort and consolation we will find during these months of grief. Long before you, mother, or I was born, the death of Christ was celebrated in the Eucharist. And it will be celebrated long after we have died. During our few years of conscious participation in the Eucharist, our lives and deaths become part of this ongoing proclamation of the life and death of Christ. Therefore I dare to say that every time I celebrate the Eucharist and every time you receive the body and blood of Christ, we remember not only Christ's death but also her death, because it was precisely through the Eucharist that she was so intimately united with him.

This illuminates more fully that, in and through Christ, mother's death was a death for you and for me. By being united with Christ in the Eucharist, she participated in his life-giving death. Only Christ, the Son of God, could die not for himself but for others. Mother's brokenness and sinfulness did not make it possible for her to die for others in complete self-surrender. But by eating the body and drinking the blood of Christ, her life was transformed into the life of Christ, and her death was lifted up into his death so that, living with Christ, she could also die with him. Thus, it is the death of Christ that gives meaning to her death. Hence we can say quite boldly that she died for us. Perhaps the sentence, "Christ died for us," has never before touched us in its full significance and has remained a rather abstract idea for both of us. But I think that mother's death can give us new insight into this central mystery of our faith. Once it starts making sense to us that mother died for our sake, and once we see that this was possible because of her intimate union with Christ through the Eucharist, we may also discover in a more personal way the ultimate meaning of Christ's death. Mother's death, then, directs our attention to the death of Christ and invites us to find in him the source of all our consolation and comfort.

I do not think that you would have said any of the things I have tried to say today. The language I have used does not come easily to you and the words are probably not the words you yourself would use. But on the other hand, I know that what I have written is not unfamiliar to you. Although you shared in mother's devotion to the Eucharist during her lifetime and joined her regularly in receiving the body and blood of Christ, during the last six months you have come to realize that you can experience a lasting bond with her through this great sacrament. It is my great hope that you will find an increasing strength from the Eucharist. Since you are living alone and often experience painful loneliness, the gifts of Christ, who died for you, can unite you in a very intimate way with him and so reveal to you the deeper meaning of mother's death. The Eucharist can never be fully explained or understood. It is a mystery to enter and experience from within. Every event of life can lead us to a deeper knowledge of the Eucharist. Marriage enables us to understand more deeply God's faithful love as it expresses itself in his lasting presence among us; illness and inner struggle can bring us more closely in touch with the healing power of the Eucharist; sin and personal failure can lead us to experience the Eucharist as a sacrament of forgiveness. What I am trying to say today is that mother's death can open our eyes to the Eucharist as a sacrament by which we proclaim Christ's death as a death for us, a death by which we are led to new life. Thus it can also help us to prepare for our own deaths. The more we see the Eucharist as a proclamation of Christ's death, the more we start seeing that our own deaths in communion with Christ cannot be in vain.

Thus the Eucharist brings us together in a very profound way. It is the core of my priesthood; it reveals the deeper meaning of mother's death; it helps us to prepare ourselves for our own deaths; and it points above all to Christ, who gives us his body and blood as a constant reminder that death is no longer a reason for despair but has become in and through him the basis of our hope. Therefore we will have the boldness to sing tomorrow in the liturgy, "We greet you cross, our only hope."

VII

IT MIGHT BE that after all my words about the meaning of death you will get the impression that death is something to be desired; something that we can journey toward with expectation; something for which all of life prepares us; something, therefore, that is more or less the high point of life. If I have created such an impression, I need to correct it as soon as I can. Although I think it is possible to speak about the meaning of death, I also think that death is the one event against which we protest with all our being. We feel that life belongs to us and that death has no place in our basic desire to live. It is therefore not so surprising that most people, even older people, do not think much about death. As long as we feel healthy and vital, we prefer to keep our minds and bodies busy with the things of life. German theologian Karl Rahner calls death "the absurd arch-contradiction of existence," and indeed death does not make sense for anyone who can only make sense out of what he or she can understand in some way. But our total powerlessness in the face of death, in which any possibility of controlling our destiny is taken away from us, can hardly be perceived as having any value. Our whole being protests against the threat of non-being.

I am writing this on Good Friday. I have just participated in the liturgy, in which the death of Christ is remembered in the most moving way. I was asked to read the words Christ spoke during his passion. As I was pronouncing them in a loud voice so that all the monks and guests would be able to let them enter deeply into their hearts, I came to realize that Christ himself entered with us into the full experience of the absurdity of death. Jesus did not want to die. Jesus did not face his death as if he considered it a good to be striven for. He never spoke about death as something to be accepted gladly. Although he spoke about his death and tried to prepare his disciples for it, he never gave it morbid attention. And the Gospels contain no evidence that death was attractive to him. What we see in them is, rather, a deep inner protest against death. In the garden of Gethsemane, Jesus was gripped with fear and distress, and he prayed loudly to his Father: "Everything is possible for you. Take this cup away from me." This anguish became so intense that "his sweat fell to the ground like great drops of blood." And as he died on the Cross he cried out in agony: "My God, my God, why have you deserted me?"

Much more than the pain of his death, I think, it was death itself that filled Jesus with fear and agony. For me this is a very important realization, because it undercuts any sentimentalizing or romanticizing of death. We do not want to die, even if we have to face—yes, befriend— our own death with all possible realism. Although we must befriend our death, that is, fully recognize it as a reality that is an intimate part of our humanity, death remains our enemy. Although we can and must prepare ourselves for death, we are never prepared for it. Although we have to see how death has been part of our life since birth, it remains the greatest unknown in our existence. Although we have to search for the meaning of death, our protest against it reveals that we will never be able to give it a meaning that can take our fear away.

Mother's death has made this very clear to us. You know how much her life was filled with the thought of God and his mysteries. Not only did she receive the Eucharist every day, but she spent many hours in prayer and meditation and read the holy Scriptures eagerly; she was also deeply grateful to everyone who supported her in her spiritual life. She had a very deep devotion to Mary, the Mother of God, and never went to sleep without asking for her prayers at the hour of her death. Indeed, mother's life was a life of preparation for death. But this did not make death easy for her. She never hesitated to say that she was afraid to die, that she did not feel prepared to appear before God, and that she was not yet ready to leave this world. She loved life, loved it to the full. She loved you with an unwavering devotion. You are the person she always thought of and spoke about first; she would never allow anyone to distract her attention from you. Her children and grandchildren were her perennial concern and delight. Their joys were her joys, and their pains were her pains. And how she loved beauty: the beauty of nature with its flowers and trees, mountains and valleys; the beauty of the French cathedrals or old village churches; the beauty of the Italian cities, Ravenna, Florence, Assisi, and Rome. She could walk through these towns and cities and say with amazement, "Look, isn't it beautiful, look at that house, look at that church, look at those balconies with bougainvillea — isn't it lovely!" And she would be filled with joy and amazement. Yes, mother loved life. I still remember how she said to me, "Although I am old, I would like so much to live a few more years."

Death was hard and painful for her. In fact, I often think that it was precisely because her life of prayer had given her such a profound appreciation of all that is created, that it was so very hard for her to let it all go. The God she loved and for whom she wanted to give her life had shown her both the splendor of his creation and the complete finality with which death would cut her off from all she had learned to love.

As I reflect on mother's death, something that I could not see as clearly before is now becoming more visible to me. It is that death does not belong to God. God did not create death. God does not want death. God does not desire death for us. In God there is no death. God is a God of life. He is the God of the living and not of the dead. Therefore, people who live a deeply spiritual life, a life of real intimacy with God, must feel the pain of death in a particularly acute way. A life with God opens us to all that is alive. It makes us celebrate life; it enables us to see the beauty of all that is created; it makes us desire to always be where life is. Death, therefore, must be experienced by a really religious person neither as a release from the tension of life nor as an occasion for rest and peace, but as an absurd, ungodly, dark nothingness. Now I see why it is false to say that a religious person should find death easy and acceptable. Now I understand why it is wrong to think that a death without struggle and agony is a sign of great faith. These ideas do not make much sense once we realize that faith opens us to the full affirmation of life and gives us an intense desire to live more fully, more vibrantly, and more vigorously. If anyone should protest against death it is the religious person, the person who has increasingly come to know God as the God of the living.

This brings me back to the great mystery of today, the day we call Good Friday. It is the day on which Jesus, the Son of God, light of light, true God of true God, one in being with the Father, died. Indeed, on that Friday nearly two thousand years ago, outside the walls of Jerusalem, God died.

I hope you can feel with me that here lies the source of our consolation and hope. God himself, who is light, life, and truth, came to experience with us and for us the total absurdity of death. Jesus' death is not a memorable event because a good, holy prophet died. No, what makes the death of Jesus the main—and in a sense the only real—event in history is that the Son of God, in whom there was no trace of death, died the absurd death that is the fate of all human beings.

This gives us some idea of the agony of Jesus. Who has tasted life more fully than he? Who has known more intimately the beauty of the land in which he lived? Who has understood better the smiles of children, the cries of the sick, and the tears of those in grief? Every fiber of his being spoke of life. "I am the Way, the Truth and the Life," he said, and in him only life could be found. How will we ever be able to grasp what it must have meant for him to undergo death, to be cut off from life and to enter into the darkness of total destruction! The agony in the garden, the humiliation of the mockery, the pains of the flagellation, the sorrowful way to Calvary, and the horrendous execution on the Cross were suffered by the Lord of life.

I write this to you not to upset you but to console you in your grief. The Lord who died, died for us—for you, for me, for mother, and for all people. He died not because of any death or darkness in him, but only to free us from the death and darkness in us. If the God who revealed life to us, and whose only desire is to bring us to life, loved us so much that he wanted to experience with us the total absurdity of death, then—yes, then there must be hope; then there must be something more than death; then there must be a promise that is not fulfilled in our short existence in this world; then leaving behind the ones you love, the flowers and the trees, the mountains and the oceans, the beauty of art and music, and all the exuberant gifts of life cannot be just the destruction and cruel end of all things; then indeed we have to wait for the third day.

VIII

I AM LOOKING at the photograph you took of mother's grave. I look at the simple light brown wooden cross. The two heavy beams speak of strength. I read the words "In Peace," her name, "Maria," and the dates of her birth and death. They summarize it all. It is a lovely picture. What an exuberance of flowers! They really are splendid. With their white, yellow, red, and purple colors, they seem to lift up the cross and speak of life. Oh, how well I remember the 14th of October, six months ago today. What a beautiful morning that was! How gently the sun's rays covered the land when we carried her to this place! Do you remember? It was a sad day, but not only sad. There was a feeling of fulfillment, too. Her life had come to its fulfillment, and it had been such a gracious life. And there was gratitude in our hearts for her and for all who came to tell us what she had meant to them. It was a peaceful, quiet, and intimate day. I know you will never forget that day. Neither will I. It was the day that gave us strength to live on in quiet joy, not only looking backward but also forward.

Every time I look at that photograph of her grave, I experience again the new emotion that came to me after we buried her, an emotion so different from the emotion of seeing her again after a long absence, so different too from the emotion of watching her suffer and die. It is a new, very precious emotion. It is the emotion of a quiet, joyful waiting. Surely you know what I mean. There is a quiet contentment in this emotion. She has finished her life with us. She no longer has to suffer as we do;

she no longer has to worry as we do; she no longer has to face the fear of death as we do. More than that, she will be spared the many anxieties and conflicts we still have to face. Nobody can harm her any more. We no longer have to protect her and be concerned about her health and safety. Oh, how we should love to have that concern again! But we have laid her to rest and she will not return. The rich soil in which we have buried her, the green hedges behind her grave, and the high lush trees around the small cemetery all create a feeling of safety, of being well received. But there is another side to this emotion. It includes waiting, quiet waiting. The solid, simple cross that stands above her grave speaks of something more than her death. Every time we go to that place, we sense that we are waiting, expecting, hoping. We wish to see her again and be with her once more, but we know that she has left us not to come back. At times, we wish to die and join her in death, but we know that we are called to live and to work on this earth. Our quiet, joyful waiting is much deeper than wishful thinking. It is waiting with the knowledge that love is stronger than death and that this truth will become visible to us. How? When? Where? These questions keep rushing into our impatient hearts. And yet, when we experience that quiet, joyful waiting, they cease troubling us and we feel that all is well.

You may have guessed, dear father, that I am writing this part to you on Holy Saturday. I have lived through this day many times, but this Saturday, April 14, 1979, is unique because today I have a new insight into what the quiet silence of this day means.

You know the story. They had laid him in the tomb that was in the garden close to the place where he was crucified. Joseph of Arimathea "rolled a stone against the entrance to the tomb" and "Mary of Magdala and Mary the mother of Joset were watching and took note of where he was laid." "Then they returned and prepared spices and ointments. And on the sabbath day they rested."

This is the quietest day of the year: no work, no great liturgical celebration, no visitors, no mail, no words. Just a very, very deep repose. A silent, in-between time. Lent is over but Easter has not yet come. He died, but we do not yet fully know what that means. The anxious, fearful tension of Good Friday is gone but no bells have yet been heard. A brother calls me to prayer with a wooden clapper. It has stopped raining. The raging storm that came over the valley last night has withdrawn, but clouds still cover the sky. Yes, a silent, joyful waiting. No panic, no despair, no screams, no tears or wringing of hands. No shouts of joy, either. No victorious songs, no banners or flags. Only a simple, quiet waiting with the deep, inner knowledge that all will be well. How? Do not ask. Why? Do not worry. Where? You will know. When? Just wait. Just wait quietly, peacefully, joyfully . . . all will be well.

Sacred Saturday! The day on which we buried mother; the day on which we sit near Jesus' tomb and rest; the day on which monks look at each other as if they know something about which they are not yet allowed to speak. It is the day when I understand what your life has been like since you laid mother in her grave.

Do you feel what I am writing about? There are many, many questions, and we would like answers to them now. But it is too early. Nobody knows what to say. We saw that death is real. We saw that death took away from us the one we loved most. We stand by the grave. Let us not ask questions now. This is the time to let that inner quietude grow in us. The disciples thought that it was all over, finished, come to an end . . . if they thought much at all. The women wanted to take care of the grave. They prepared spices and ointments. But on Saturday, they all rested.

Doesn't this Holy Saturday give us a new insight into what our new life without mother can increasingly become? Doesn't this Holy Saturday tell us about this new emotion of quiet, joyful waiting in which we can grow steadily and securely? No longer do we have to cry; no longer do we have to feel the painful tearing away. Now we can wait, silencing all our wishes and fantasies about what will be, and simply hope in joy.

I X

AFTER I BEGAN to write this letter to you something happened that at first seemed rather insignificant to me. In the days following, however, it took on more and more importance. Therefore, I want to tell you about it before I finish this letter. It is a weather story. The weather here in upstate New York was lovely up until ten days ago. The winter was over, the spring had begun. The climate was mild and sunny, and the monks enjoyed walking through the woods and observing the first signs of the new season. Yellow, white, and blue crocuses decorated the yard, and everybody seemed happy that another cold season had come to an end. But not so! On the day I finally got myself organized enough to begin writing you this letter, a violent storm broke over the land, bringing with it heavy rains. Buckets appeared under the leaks in the roof, windows were shut securely, and no one ventured forth from the house. The temperature dropped sharply, and soon the rain turned into snow. The next day we were back in winter. It kept snowing the whole day, and I felt strangely disoriented. My whole body had been anticipating bright flowers, green trees, and songbirds, and this strange new weather felt totally incongruous. When the storm was over, the landscape seemed idyllic, like a Christmas card. The snow was fresh and beautiful and had settled on the green fields and fir trees like a fresh white robe. But I could not enjoy it. I simply kept saying to myself, "Well, one week from now it will be Easter and then it will be spring again." I discovered in myself a strange certainty that Easter would change the weather. And when everything was still pure white on Wednesday of Holy Week, I continued to feel, "Only three more days and everything will be green again!" Well, on Good Friday stormy winds rose up, a miserable rain began to come down, and it poured for the rest of the day. The next morning all the snow was gone. In the afternoon the clouds dissolved and a brilliant sun appeared, transforming everything into a joyous spectacle. When I looked out of my window and saw the fresh, clear light covering the meadows, I had a hard time not breaking the monastic silence! I walked out and went up to the ridge from which I could overlook the valley. I just smiled and smiled. And I spoke out loudly to the skies, "The Lord is risen; he is risen indeed!"

Never in my life have I sensed so deeply that the sacred events that we celebrate affect our natural surroundings. It was much more than the feeling of a happy coincidence. It was the intense realization that the events we were celebrating were the real events and that everything else, nature and culture included, was dependent on these events.

You will probably want to know now what the weather was like on Easter morning. It was gentle and cloudy. Nothing very unusual. No rain, no wind; not very cold, not very warm. No radiant sun, only a gentle, soft breeze. It did not really matter much to me. I would probably have been happy even if there had been snow again. What mattered to me was that I had come to experience during this holy season that the real events are the events that take place under the great veil of nature and history. All depends on whether we have eyes that see and ears that hear.

This is what I so much want to write to you on this Easter of 1979. Something very deep and mysterious, very holy and sacred, is taking place in our lives right where we are, and the more attentive we become the more we will begin to see and hear it. The more our spiritual sensitivities come to the surface of our daily lives, the more we will discover— uncover—a new presence in our lives. I have a strong sense that mother's death has been, and still is, a painful but very blessed purification that will enable us to hear a voice and see a face we had not seen or heard as clearly before.

Think of what is happening at Easter. A group of women go to the tomb, notice that the stone has been moved away, enter, see a young man in a white robe sitting on the righthand side, and hear him say, "He is not here." Peter and John come running to the tomb and find it empty. Mary of Magdala meets a gardener who calls her by name, and she realizes it is Jesus. The disciples, anxiously huddled together in a closed room, suddenly find him standing among them and hear him say, "Peace be with you." Two men come hurrying back from Emmaus and tell their puzzled friends that they met Jesus on the road and recognized him in the breaking of the bread. Later on, Simon Peter, Thomas, Nathanael, James, and John are fishing on the lake. A man on the shore calls to them, "Have you caught anything, friends?" They call back, "No." Then he says, "Throw the net out to starboard and you'll find something." They do, and when they catch so many fish that they cannot haul in their net, John says to Peter, "It is the Lord." And as these events are taking place, a new word is being spoken, at first softly and hesitatingly, then clearly and convincingly, and finally loudly and triumphantly, "The Lord is risen; he is risen indeed!"

I wonder how this story, the most important story of human history, speaks to you now that you know so well what it means to have lost the one you loved most. Have you noticed that none of the friends of Jesus, neither the women nor the disciples, had the faintest expectation of his return from death? His crucifixion had crushed all their hopes and expectations, and they felt totally lost and dejected. Even when Jesus appeared to them, they kept hesitating and doubting and needing to be convinced, not only Thomas but others as well. There was no trace of an "I-always-told-you-so" attitude. The event of Jesus' resurrection totally and absolutely surpassed their understanding. It went far beyond their own ways of thinking and feeling. It broke through the limits of their minds and hearts. And still, they believed—and their faith changed the world.

Isn't this good news? Doesn't this turn everything around and offer us a basis on which we can live with hope? Doesn't this put mother's death in a completely new perspective? It does not make her death less painful or our own grief less heavy. It does not make the loss of her less real, but it makes us see and feel that death is part of a much greater and much deeper event, the fullness of which we cannot comprehend, but of which we know that it is a life-bringing event. The friends of Jesus saw him and heard him only a few times after that Easter morning, but their lives were completely changed. What seemed to be the end proved to be the beginning; what seemed to be a cause for fear proved to be a cause for courage; what seemed to be defeat proved to be victory; and what seemed to be the basis for despair proved to be the basis for hope. Suddenly a wall becomes a gate, and although we are not able to say with much clarity or precision what lies beyond that gate, the tone of all that we do and say on our way to the gate changes drastically.

The best way I can express to you the meaning death receives in the light of the resurrection of Jesus is to say that the love that causes us so much grief and makes us feel so fully the absurdity of death is stronger than death itself. "Love is stronger than death." This sentence summarizes better than any other the meaning of the resurrection and therefore also the meaning of death. I have mentioned this earlier in this letter, but now you may better see its full meaning. Why has mother's death caused you so much suffering? Because you loved her so much. Why has your own death become such an urgent question for you? Because you love life, you love your children and your grandchildren, you love nature, you love art and music, you love horses, and you love all that is alive and beautiful. Death is absurd and cannot be meaningful for someone who loves so much.

The resurrection of Jesus Christ is the glorious manifestation of the victory of love over death. The same love that makes us mourn and protest against death will now free us to live in hope. Do you realize that Jesus appeared only to those who knew him, who had listened to his words and who had come to love him deeply? It was that love that gave them the eyes to see his face and the ears to hear his voice when he appeared to them on the third day after his death. Once they had seen and heard him and believed, the rest of their lives became a continuing recognition of his presence in their midst. This is what life in the Spirit of the risen Christ is all about. It makes us see that under the veil of all that is visible to our bodily eyes, the risen Lord shows us his inexhaustible love and calls us to enter even more fully into that love, a love that embraces both mother and us, who loved her so much.

It is with this divine love in our hearts, a love stronger than death, that our lives can be lived as a promise. Because this great love promises us that what we have already begun to see and hear with the eyes and ears of the Spirit of Christ can never be destroyed, but rather is "the beginning" of eternal life.

Today is the third day of Easter. Easter Tuesday. Here in the Trappist monastery it is the last day of the Easter festivities. For three days we have celebrated the resurrection of Jesus Christ, and it has been a real feast. Although the monks speak with each other only when necessary, and although there are no parties or parades, the Easter days have been more joyful than any I have celebrated in the past. The liturgies have been rich and exuberant with their many alleluias; the readings have been joyful and affirmative; the music has been festive; and everyone has been filled with gratitude toward God and each other.

On Easter Sunday I read the Gospel story about Peter and John running to the tomb and finding it empty. There were more than a hundred visitors in the abbey church, some from far away and some from nearby, some young and some old, some formally and some casually dressed. Sitting with forty monks around the huge rock that serves as the altar, they gave me a real sense of the Church. After reading the Gospel, I preached. I had seldom preached on Easter Sunday during my twenty-two years of priesthood, and I felt very grateful that I could announce to all who were present: "The Lord is risen; he is risen indeed." Everyone listened with great attention and I had a sense that the risen Christ was really among us, bringing us his peace. During the Eucharist, I prayed for you, for mother, and for all who are dear to us. I felt that the risen Christ brought us all together, bridging not only the distance between Holland and the United States but also that between life and death. Lent was long, sometimes very hard, and not without its dark moments and tempting demons. But now, in the light of the resurrection of Christ, Lent seems to have been short and easy. I guess this is true for all of life. In darkness we doubt that there will ever be light, but in the light we soon forget how much darkness there was.

Now there is light. In fact, the sun has even broken through and the large stretches of blue sky now visible behind the clusters of clouds remind me again that often what we see is not what is most enduring.

Dear father, this seems the most natural time to conclude not only the Easter celebration but also this letter. For twelve days I have been reflecting on mother's death in the hope of offering you and myself some comfort and consolation. I do not know if I have been able to reach you in your loneliness and grief. Maybe my words often said more to me than to you. But even if this is so, I still hope that the simple fact that these words have been written by your son about her whom we have both loved so much will be a source of consolation to you.

Our Greatest Gift

A Meditation on Dying and Caring

To Marina Nouwen-San Giorgi,
my sister-in-law,
whose courage and joy
were a great inspiration.
She died in the early morning of
May 8, 1993.
May this book honor her.

OUR GREATEST GIFT
CONTENTS

Befriending Death

ON DECEMBER 31, 1992, at three o'clock in the afternoon, Maurice Gould died. He died in York Central Hospital in Richmond Hill, near Toronto, Canada, after a long struggle with Alzheimer's disease.

Maurice—"Moe," as we called him—had been a member of L'Arche. Founded in 1964 by the Canadian Jean Vanier, L'Arche is a worldwide network of communities where people with mental disabilities and their assistants create home for one another. Maurice had made his home in the L'Arche Daybreak community in Toronto for fourteen years. He was known for his joyfulness, gentleness, and love of home. The countless people who met him over the years speak about him with much endearment. Somehow his condition—Down's syndrome—seemed only the other side of his great gift: to give and receive love.

During the last days of Moe's life, I was in Freiburg, Germany. Daybreak had sent me there to take a few months away from my pastoral work in the community and focus exclusively on my writing. When Nathan Ball, the director of our community, called me to tell me about Moe's death, I knew at once that I must return to Toronto as soon as possible to be with Moe's family and many friends and to experience with them the sorrow of his leaving, as well as the joy of his fifty-eight fulfilling years of life.

The next day, during my flight home, I thought a great deal about life and death and began to wonder how our dying can be as much our own as our living.

As the Air Canada plane took me from Frankfurt over Germany, Holland, England, the Atlantic Ocean, and Nova Scotia, Canada, to Toronto, I had ample time to think about dying: Maurice's dying, my own dying, and the dying of so many people every day all over the world.

Is death something so terrible and absurd that we are better off not thinking or talking about it? Is death such an undesirable part of our existence that we are better off acting as if it were not real? Is death such an absolute end of all our thoughts and actions that we simply cannot face it? Or is it possible to befriend our dying gradually and live open to it, trusting that we have nothing to fear? Is it possible to prepare for our death with the same attentiveness that our parents had in preparing for our birth? Can we wait for our death as for a friend who wants to welcome us home?

During the eight-and-one-half-hour flight, I thought not only about Maurice and these questions, but also about my other dying friends and my aging father. Just over a month earlier, on November 24, I had been with Rick in Bethany House, the Catholic worker house in Oakland, California. Bethany House was recently founded by Michael Harank to provide a place to care for people living with AIDS. Rick has AIDS and knows that he has only a short time left to live. As I sat on his bed and held his hand, he said, "What can I still do in the months that are left to me? My friend, who I love so much, can make all sorts of plans for his future, but I have no future anymore." Tears flowed from his eyes as he tightened his grip on my hand.

Then I thought of Marina, my sister-in-law, who had struggled for five full years with intestinal cancer, had survived three horrendous surgeries, and finally, when all further therapy had proved useless, had allowed things to take their natural course. Marina had spoken openly about her death to her doctors, to the nurses, to her many friends, to her mother, to her husband, Paul, and to me. In her poems, she had expressed her feelings about her approaching death, even while those around her hardly dared mention it in her presence.

Meanwhile, my father, in Holland, would celebrate his ninetieth birthday within ten days. He is full of energy, still writing, still lecturing, still making plans. But to me he says, "Son, my body is spent, my eyes are no longer able to focus, my stomach doesn't tolerate much food any-more, and my heart is very, very weak."

People are dying. Not just the few I know, but countless people ev-erywhere, every day, every hour. Dying is the most general human event, something we all have to do. But do we do it well? Is our death more than an unavoidable fate that we simply wish would not be? Can it somehow become an act of fulfillment, perhaps more human than any other hu-man act?

When I arrived that day in January at Terminal II at Pearson Inter-national Airport in Toronto, Nathan Ball was waiting for me. In the car, he told me about Moe's death. Family and friends had been with Moe during his last hours. Both sadness and gladness had been there. A beau-tiful friend had left us. A long suffering had come to a gentle end. "Moe was so much loved by everyone," Nathan said. "We will miss him, but it was time for him to go."

The days that followed were full of sorrow and joy. Moe was dead, but it seemed as if new life became immediately visible. Telephone calls were made to friends far and wide; letters were written. Most of all, people came together to pray, to eat, to tell stories, to look at pictures — to remember with smiles and tears. Of all the days that I have lived at Day-break, those after Moe's death belong to the most intimate, the most uniting, and, in a strange way, the most sacred. A man who, through his fragility and weakness, had helped us create community during his life did so even more through his death. As we came together in our chapel, visited the funeral home, sang and spoke in gratitude in the Anglican Church of Richmond Hill, and carried the coffin to the grave in King City's cemetery, we shared a deep sense that not only does life lead to death, but death leads to new life. The spirit of gentleness and kindness that surrounded and pervaded our conversation, the spirit of forgiveness and healing that touched each of us, and most of all the spirit of unity and communion that bound us together in a new way — that spirit was gratefully received as a gift of Moe, who was dead and yet very much alive.

On the evening before my return to Europe to celebrate my father's birthday and to continue my writing in Freiburg, I had dinner with Nathan, a friend and longtime member of Daybreak, and Sue Mosteller. During the meal, Nathan asked me, "Where and how do you want to die?" He raised the question in a gentle way. It was a question that came from our new awareness that, like Moe, we would soon die. Our awareness prompted us to ask ourselves: Are we preparing ourselves for our death, or are we ignoring death by keeping busy? Are we helping each other to die, or do we simply assume we are going to always be here for each other? Will our death give new life, new hope, and new faith to our friends, or will it be no more than another cause for sadness? The main question is not, How much will we still be able to do during the few years we have left to live? but rather, How can we prepare ourselves for our death in such a way that our dying will be a new way for us to send our and God's spirit to those whom we have loved and who have loved us?

Nathan's question, "Where and how do you want to die?" brought me face-to-face with a great challenge: not only to live well, but also to die well.

The next day, as we drove to the airport, Nathan thanked me for returning for Moe's funeral and wished me a happy celebration of my father's birthday and a creative month of writing in Freiburg. While flying to Amsterdam, I realized that I knew better than before what I would write about. I wanted to write about befriending my death so that it can become my best gift to the world I love so much.

Now—after many celebrations in Holland and a long train ride through Germany—I am alone again in my little, peaceful, and solitary apartment in Freiburg. What better place than this in which to befriend death?

Grace Hidden in Powerlessness

IT HAS NEVER been easy for me to find a quiet place to write. I have gone to convents, monasteries, and retreat centers and have even tried to stay home with the door closed. But wherever I have searched for solitude, I have soon become entangled again in the daily events of my surroundings. My own restlessness, my need for companionship, and my fear of rejection and abandonment have made me flee solitude as soon as I have found it. My resistance to solitude has proved as strong as my desire for it. Again and again I have found excuses to talk with people, give conferences, preach sermons, preside at liturgies, join in celebrations, or hang around in libraries. In short, I have found excuses not to be alone.

Still, I have always known that one day I would have to find the courage to go beyond my fear. I would have to trust that in solitude I would discover my true teacher, who would give me the words that I must write.

Now I have my chance. Franz and Reny Johna, my friends in Freiburg, have offered me the third story of their three-story house in the Schubert Strasse. The first story serves as their own home, the second is rented to an elderly couple, and the third is usually kept free for their two children, Robert and Irene. Robert, however, has moved to the United States, where he specializes in internal medicine, and Irene has moved to Frankfurt, where she works for the Bundesbank. "You can have the third-story apartment," Franz and Reny said to me. "It is a true hermitage, away from people and the events of every day, and definitely noise-and light-proof." Indeed, the third story of Franz and Reny's house is the ideal place for a city hermit. It has everything a solitary person can desire: a study, a bedroom, a small living room that I have made into a kitchen, and a bathroom.

So now I have what I have always dreamed of having: complete silence, complete solitude. When I let down the window blinds, my bedroom is pitch dark, and not even the sound of a passing car can be heard. All becomes completely still.

This stillness is purifying. Strange as it may seem, the outer quietude quickly reveals the inner restlessness. What am I going to do when there is nothing to do? What am I going to do when there is no one demanding my attention or inviting me to do something or making me feel valuable? Without phone calls, letters, and meetings, the minutes, hours, and days stretch out into horizonless deserts of solitude.

Is this not the most blessed place in which to befriend my death? Is this not the place where the outer silence can gradually lead me to an inner silence, where I can embrace my own mortality? Yes, silence and solitude invite me to gradually let go of the outer voices that give me a sense of well-being among my fellow humans, to trust the inner voice that reveals to me my true name. Silence and solitude call me to detach myself from the scaffolding of daily life and to discover if anything there can stand on its own when the traditional support systems have been pulled away.

While sitting alone in my little hermitage, I realize how unprepared I am to die. The silence and solitude of this comfortable apartment are sufficient to make me aware of my unwillingness to let go of life. Nevertheless, I will have to die soon. The ten, twenty, or thirty years left to me will fly by quickly. Gradually, my body will lose its strength, my mind its flexibility; I will lose family and friends; I will become less relevant to society and be forgotten by most; I will have to depend increasingly on the help of others; and, in the end, I will have to let go of everything and be carried into the completely unknown.

Am I willing to make that journey? Am I willing to let go of whatever power I have left, to unclench my fists and trust in the grace hidden in complete powerlessness? I don't know. I really don't know. It seems impossible, since everything alive in me protests against this journey into nothingness. I do know that the silence and solitude of my small apartment in Freiburg offer me the best opportunity I will ever have to explore my ability to surrender to death.

Somehow, I believe that this lonely task of befriending my death is not simply a task that serves me, but also a task that may serve others. I have lived my whole life with the desire to help others in their journey, but I have always realized that I had little else to offer than my own, the journey I am making myself. How can I announce joy, peace, forgiveness, and reconciliation unless they are part of my own flesh and blood? I have always wanted to be a good shepherd for others, but I have always known, too, that good shepherds lay down their own lives—their pains and joys, their doubts and hopes, their fears and their love—for their friends.

Now in my sixties, trying to come to terms with my own mortality, I trust that, like everything else I have lived, my attempt to befriend my death will be good not only for me, but also for others who face a similar challenge. I want to die well, but I desire also to help others to die well. In this way, I am not alone in my little apartment in the Schubert Strasse in Freiburg. In fact, I am surrounded by people who are dying and who hope to die well. I want my silence and solitude to be for my friends and for the friends of my friends. I want my desire to embrace my own mortality to help others embrace theirs. I want my little hermitage to be truly in and for the world.

I have five weeks ahead of me in this sanctuary: five weeks in which to pray, to think, and to write about dying and death—my own as well as that of others. My task has two sides to it. First, I must discover what it means to befriend my own death. Second, I must discover how I can help others befriend theirs. The inner life is always a life for others. When I myself am able to befriend death, I will be able to help others do the same. That is the work of this little book. I write first about dying well, then about caring well.

PART ONE

———

DYING WELL

Close to the Heart

AS CHILDREN, WE need parents, teachers, and friends to teach us the meaning of our lives. Once we have grown up, we are on our own. Then, we ourselves become the main source of knowledge, and what we say to others about life and death has to come from what is truly our own. Great thinkers and great saints have written and spoken about dying and death, but their words remain uniquely theirs. I must find my own words so that what I say comes from the depth of my experience. Although many people have deeply influenced that experience, nobody else has had it. In this lies its power, but in this too lies its weakness. I must trust that my experience of mortality will give me words that can speak to others who are struggling to give meaning to their own lives and deaths. I must also accept that many will not be able to respond to what I have to say, simply because they cannot see or feel the connections between their lives and mine.

In the first three chapters of this book, I deal with dying well. I explore in my own innermost being what it means that we human beings are children of God, brothers and sisters of each other, and parents of generations to come.

I stay close to my own heart, listening carefully to what I have heard and felt. I also stay close to the hearts of those whose joys and pains are touching me most at this time of my life. Most of all, I stay close to the heart of Jesus, whose life and death are the main source for understanding and living my own life and death.

1

We Are Children of God

WHEN I BECAME sixty, the Daybreak community gave me a big party. More than one hundred people came together to celebrate. John Bloss was there, eager as always to play an active role. John is full of good thoughts, but his disability makes it painfully difficult for him to express these thoughts in words. Still, he loves to speak, especially when he has a captive audience.

With everyone sitting in a large circle, Joe, the master of ceremonies, said, "Well, John, what do you have to say to Henri today?" John, who loves the theatrical, got up, put himself in the center of the circle, pointed to me, and began to search for words. "You . . . you . . . are," he said with a big grin on his face. "You . . . you . . . are . . . uh . . . uh . . ." Everyone looked at him with great expectation as he tried to get his words out while pointing ever-more directly at me. "You . . . you . . . are . . . uh . . . uh . . ." And then, like an explosion, the words came out. "An old man!" Everybody burst out laughing, and John basked in the success of his performance.

That said it all. I had become "an old man." Few people would say it so directly, and most would continue with qualifications about still looking young, still so full of energy, and on and on. John said it simply and truthfully: "You are an old man."

It seems fair to say that people between the ages of one and thirty are considered young; those between thirty and sixty are considered middle-aged; and those past their sixtieth birthday are considered old. But then you yourself are suddenly sixty, and you don't feel old. At least I don't. My teenage years seem only a short time ago, my years of studying and teaching feel like yesterday, and my seven years at Daybreak feel like seven days. Thinking of myself as "an old man" does not come spontaneously. I need to hear it announced loud and clear.

A few years ago a university student spoke to me about his father. "My dad doesn't understand me," he said. "He's so bossy, and he always wants to be right; he never allows any room for my ideas. It's difficult to be with him." Trying to comfort him, I said, "My dad is not very different from yours, but, you know, that's the older generation!" Then with a sigh, he said, "Yes, my dad is already forty!" I suddenly realized that I was speaking to someone who could have been my grandson.

Indeed, I somehow keep forgetting that I have become old and that young people regard me as an old man. It helps me to look at myself in a mirror once in a while. Gazing at my face, I see both my mother and my father when they were sixty years old, and I remember how I thought of them as old people.

Being an old man means being close to death. In the past, I often tried to figure out if I could still double the years I had lived. When I was twenty, I was sure that I would live at least another twenty years. When I was thirty, I trusted that I would easily reach sixty. When I was forty, I wondered if I would make it to eighty. And when I turned fifty, I realized that only a few make it to one hundred. But now, at sixty, I am sure that I have gone far past the halfway point and that my death is much closer to me than my birth.

Old men and old women must prepare for death. But how do we prepare ourselves well? For me, the first task is to become a child again — to reclaim my childhood. This might seem to be opposite to our natural desire to maintain maximum independence. Nevertheless, becoming a child — entering a second childhood — is essential to dying a good death. Jesus spoke about this second childhood when he said, "Unless you change and become like little children, you will never enter the Kingdom of Heaven" (Matthew 18:3).

What characterizes this second childhood? It has to do with a new dependence. For the first twenty or so years of life, we depend on our parents, teachers, and friends. Forty years later, we again become increasingly dependent. The younger we are, the more people we need so that we may live; the older we become, the more people we again need to live. Life is lived from dependence to dependence.

That's the mystery that God has revealed to us through Jesus, whose life was a journey from the manger to the cross. Born in complete dependence on those who surrounded him, Jesus died as the passive victim of other people's actions and decisions. His was the journey from the first to the second childhood. He came as a child and died as a child, and he lived his life so that we may claim and reclaim our own childhood and thus make our death—as he did his—into a new birth.

I have been blessed with an experience that has made all of this clear to me. A few years ago, I was hit by a car while walking along a roadside and brought to the hospital with a ruptured spleen. The doctor told me she wasn't sure that I would make it through surgery. I did, but the hours lived before and after the operation allowed me to get in touch with my childhood as never before. Bound with straps on a table that looked like a cross, surrounded by masked figures, I experienced my complete dependence. I realized not only that I fully depended on the skills of an unknown medical team, but also that my deepest being was a dependent being. I knew with a certainty that had nothing to do with any particular human insight that, whether or not I survived the surgery, I was safely held in a divine embrace and would certainly live.

This freak accident had led me into a childlike state in which I needed to be cared for as a helpless infant, an experience that offered me an immense sense of safety—the experience of being a child of God. All at once, I knew that all human dependencies are embedded in a divine dependence and that that divine dependence makes dying part of a greater and much vaster way of living. This experience was so real, so basic, and so all-pervasive that it changed radically my sense of self and affected profoundly my state of consciousness. There is a strange paradox here: dependence on people often leads to slavery, but dependence on God leads to freedom. When we know that God holds us safely— whatever happens—we don't have to fear anything or anyone but can walk through life with great confidence. This is a radical perspective; we are accustomed to thinking of the ways in which people are oppressed and exploited as signs of their dependence and therefore perceive of true freedom only as the result of independence. We can think about this in another way, however. When we claim our most intimate dependence on God not as a curse but as a gift, then we can discover the freedom of the children of God. This deep inner freedom allows us to confront our enemies, throw off the yoke of oppression, and build social and economic structures that allow us to live as brothers and sisters, as children of the one God whose name is love. This, I believe, is the way in which Jesus spoke about freedom. It is the freedom rooted in being a child of God.

We are fearful people. We are afraid of conflict, war, an uncertain future, illness, and, most of all, death. This fear takes away our freedom and gives our society the power to manipulate us with threats and promises. When we can reach beyond our fears to the One who loves us with a love that was there before we were born and will be there after we die, then oppression, persecution, and even death will be unable to take our freedom. Once we have come to the deep inner knowledge—a knowledge more of the heart than of the mind—that we are born out of love and will die into love, that every part of our being is deeply rooted in love and that this love is our true Father and Mother, then all forms of evil, illness, and death lose their final power over us and become painful but hopeful reminders of our true divine childhood. The apostle Paul expressed this experience of the complete freedom of the children of God when he wrote, "I am certain of this: neither death nor life, nor angels, nor principalities, nothing already in existence and nothing still to come, nor any power, nor the heights nor the depths, nor any created thing whatever, will be able to come between us and the love of God, known to us in Christ Jesus" (Romans 8:38–39).

So the first tasks in preparing ourselves for death are to claim the freedom of the children of God and, in so doing, to strip death of any further power over us. The word *child* has its problems. It suggests littleness, weakness, naïveté, and immaturity. But when I say that we must grow into a second childhood, I do not mean a second immaturity. To the contrary, I think of the maturity of the sons and daughters of God, of the sons and daughters chosen to inherit the Kingdom. There is nothing little, weak, or naïve about being a child of God. In fact, this election allows us to keep our heads erect in the presence of God even while we walk through a world falling apart on every side. As sons and daughters of God, we can walk through the gates of death with the self-confidence of heirs. Paul again proclaimed this loudly as he said, "All who are guided by the Spirit of God are sons [and daughters] of God: for what you received was not the spirit of slavery to bring you back into fear; you have received the spirit of adoption, enabling us to cry out, 'Abba, Father.' The Spirit himself joins with our spirit to bear witness that we are children of God. And if we are children, then we are heirs, heirs of God and joint-heirs with Christ, provided we share his suffering, so as to share his glory" (Romans 8:14–17).

This is not the voice of a small, timid child. This is the voice of a spiritually mature person who knows that he is in the presence of God and for whom complete dependence on God has become the source of strength, the basis of courage, and the secret of true inner freedom.

Recently, a friend told me a story about twins talking to each other in the womb. The sister said to the brother, "I believe there is life after birth." Her brother protested vehemently, "No, no, this is all there is. This is a dark and cozy place, and we have nothing else to do but to cling to the cord that feeds us." The little girl insisted, "There must be something more than this dark place. There must be something else, a place with light where there is freedom to move." Still, she could not convince her twin brother.

After some silence, the sister said hesitantly, "I have something else to say, and I'm afraid you won't believe that, either, but I think there is a mother." Her brother became furious. "A mother!" he shouted. "What are you talking about? I have never seen a mother, and neither have you. Who put that idea in your head? As I told you, this place is all we have. Why do you always want more? This is not such a bad place, after all. We have all we need, so let's be content."

The sister was quite overwhelmed by her brother's response and for a while didn't dare say anything more. But she couldn't let go of her thoughts, and since she had only her twin brother to speak to, she finally said, "Don't you feel these squeezes every once in a while? They're quite unpleasant and sometimes even painful." "Yes," he answered. "What's special about that?" "Well," the sister said, "I think that these squeezes are there to get us ready for another place, much more beautiful than this, where we will see our mother face-to-face. Don't you think that's exciting?"

The brother didn't answer. He was fed up with the foolish talk of his sister and felt that the best thing would be simply to ignore her and hope that she would leave him alone.

This story may help us to think about death in a new way. We can live as if this life were all we had, as if death were absurd and we had better not talk about it; or we can choose to claim our divine childhood and trust that death is the painful but blessed passage that will bring us face-to-face with our God.

2

We Are Brothers and Sisters of Each Other

TWO OF THE greatest joys experienced are the joy of being different from others and the joy of being the same as others. The first of these I saw while watching the 1992 Summer Olympics in Barcelona on television. Those who stood on the rostrum and received their bronze, silver, and gold medals experienced joy as the direct result of being able to run faster, jump higher, or throw farther than others. The difference might have been extremely small, but it had great significance. It was the distinction between defeat and victory, between rueful tears and ecstatic joy. This is the joy of the hero and the star, the joy that comes from successfully competing, winning the prize, receiving the honor, and walking into the limelight.

I know this joy myself. I know it from getting an award at school, from being chosen the leader of my class, from receiving tenure at the university, and from seeing my books published and receiving honorary degrees. I know the immense satisfaction that comes from being considered different from others. These types of achievements dispel self-doubts and bestow self-confidence. This is the joy of having "made it," the joy of being recognized for making a difference. We all wait for this joy somewhere, somehow. It remains the joy of the one who said, "I thank you God, that I am not like everyone else" (Luke 18:11–12).

The other kind of joy is harder to describe but easier to find. It is the joy of being the brother or sister of all people. Although this joy is closer at hand—more accessible—than the joy of being different, it is not as obvious, and only a few people ever truly find it. This is the joy of being a part of that vast variety of people—of all ages, colors, and religions—who together form the human family. This is the immense joy of being a member of the human race.

At several times in my life, I have tasted this joy. I felt it most acutely in 1964, when I walked with thousands of people in Alabama from Selma to Montgomery in a civil rights march led by Martin Luther King, Jr. I will never forget the joy I experienced during that march. I had come by myself. Nobody knew me—nobody had ever heard of me—but when we walked together and put our arms around each other's shoulders and sang "We shall overcome one day," I experienced a joy I had never experienced before in my life. I said to myself, "Yes, yes, I belong; these are my people. They may have a differently colored skin, a different religion, a different way of life, but they are my brothers and sisters. They love me, and I love them. Their smiles and tears are my smiles and tears; their prayers and prophecies are my prayers and prophecies; their anguish and hope are my anguish and hope. I am one with them."

In an instant, all differences seemed to melt away as snow in the sun. All my comparing disappeared, and I felt surrounded by the welcoming arms of all humanity. I was aware that some of the people with whom I held hands had spent years in prison, were addicted to drugs or alcohol, suffered from loneliness and depression, and lived lives radically different from mine, but they all looked to me like saints, radiant with God's love. They were indeed God's people, immensely loved and radically forgiven. All I felt was a deep sameness, a profound communion with all people, an exhilarating sense of brotherhood and sisterhood.

I am convinced that it is this joy—the joy of being the same as others, of belonging to one human family—that allows us to die well. I do not know how I or anyone else could be prepared to die if we were mainly concerned about the trophies we had collected during our best years. The great gift hidden in our dying is the gift of unity with all people. However different we are, we were all born powerless, and we all die powerless, and the little differences we live in between dwindle in the light of this enormous truth. Often this human truth is presented as a reason to be sad. It is not seldom called a "sobering truth." Our great challenge is to discover this truth as a source of immense joy that will set us free to embrace our mortality with the awareness that we will make our passage to new life in solidarity with all the people of the earth.

A good death is a death in solidarity with others. To prepare ourselves for a good death, we must develop or deepen this sense of solidarity. If we live toward death as toward an event that separates us from people, death cannot be other than a sad and sorrowful event. But if we grow in awareness that our mortality, more than anything else, will lead us into solidarity with others, then death can become a celebration of our unity with the human race. Instead of separating us from others, death can unite us with others; instead of being sorrowful, it can give rise to new joy; instead of simply ending life, it can begin something new.

At first this might sound absurd. How can death create unity instead of separation? Isn't death the ultimate separation? It is, if we live by the norms of a competitive society always concerned with the question, Who is the strongest? But when we claim our divine childhood and learn to trust that we belonged to God before we were born and will belong to God after we have died, then we experience that all people on this planet are our brothers and sisters, and we are all making the journey together through birth and death to new life. We are not alone; beyond the differences that separate us, we share one common humanity and thus belong to each other. The mystery of life is that we discover this human togetherness not when we are powerful and strong, but when we are vulnerable and weak.

The experiential knowledge that we will all die can fill us with a profound joy and make it possible for us to face death freely and fearlessly. We can say not only, "It is good to live like everyone else," but also, "It is good to die like everyone else." Some of us die earlier, others later; some after a short life, others after a long life; some after an illness, others suddenly and unexpectedly. But all of us will die and participate in the same end. In light of this great human sameness, the many differences in how we live and die no longer have to separate us but can, to the contrary, deepen our sense of communion with one another. This communion with the whole human family, this profound sense of belonging to each other, takes the sting out of dying and points us far beyond the limits of our chronology. Somehow, we know that our bond with one another is stronger than death.

We touch here the core of Jesus' message. Jesus didn't come to simply point us away from this world by promising a new life after death. He came to make us aware that, as children of his God, we are all his brothers and sisters, all brothers and sisters of each other; we can, therefore, live our lives together without fear of death. He wants us not only to participate in his divine childhood, but also to enjoy fully the brotherhood and sisterhood that emerges from this shared childhood. He says to us, "Just as the Father has loved me, so I have loved you" (John 15:9), and "You must love one another, just as I have loved you" (John 13:34).

The gospel writer John, writing many years after Jesus' death, clearly showed the intimate connection between our being children of God and our being brothers and sisters of one another. He said, "Let us love, then, because God loved us first. Anyone who says I love God and hates his brother or sister, is a liar, since whoever does not love the brother or sister that can be seen, cannot love God who cannot be seen. Indeed this is the commandment we have received, that whoever loves God, must also love his brother and sister" (1 John 4:19–21). The joy of this brotherhood and sisterhood allows us to die well, because we no longer have to die alone but can die in intimate solidarity with all people on this planet. This solidarity offers hope.

In a mysterious way, the people dying all over the world because of starvation, oppression, illness, despair, violence, and war become our teachers. In Somalia and Ethiopia, children are dying. As their brothers and sisters, we must help them live, but we also must understand that we will die as they do. In Bosnia, Muslims, Croats, and Serbs are dying. As their brothers and sisters, we must do everything to prevent them from killing each other, but we also must remain aware that we will die as they do. In Guatemala, Indians are dying. As their sisters and brothers, we must work hard to stop their oppressors in their murderous work, but we also must face the fact that we will die as they do. In many countries, young and old people are dying of cancer and AIDS.

As their brothers and sisters, we must care for them as well as we can and keep looking for cures, but we should never forget that we will die as they do. Countless men and women are dying through poverty and neglect. As their brothers and sisters, we must offer them our resources and support. But we must remind ourselves continually that we will die as they do.

In their immense pain and grief, these people ask for solidarity, not only in life, but in death as well. Only when we are willing to let their dying help us to die well will we be able to help them to live well. When we can face death with hope, we can live life with generosity.

We all die poor. When we come to our final hours, nothing can help us survive. No amount of money, power, or influence can keep us from dying. This is true poverty. But Jesus said, "Blessed are you who are poor; the kingdom of God is yours" (Luke 6:20). There is a blessing hidden in the poverty of dying. It is the blessing that makes us brothers and sisters in the same Kingdom. It is the blessing we receive from others who die. It is the blessing we give to others when our time to die has come. It is the blessing that comes from the God whose life is everlasting. It is the blessing that reaches far beyond our birth and death. It is the blessing that carries us safely from eternity to eternity.

A friend who was very ill had a great devotion to Mary, the mother of Jesus, and decided to make a pilgrimage to Lourdes, France, to ask for healing. When she left, I was afraid that she would be disillusioned if no miracle happened. But on her return, she said, "Never did I see so many sick people. When I came face-to-face with that human suffering, I no longer wanted a miracle. I no longer wanted to be the exception. I experienced a deep desire to be one of them, to belong to these wounded people. Instead of praying for a cure, I prayed that I would have the grace to bear my illness in solidarity with them. And I trust that the mother of Jesus will bring my prayer to her Son."

I was deeply moved by this radical change in my friend's prayers. She who had hoped to be different from all those who are ill now wanted to be like them and to live her pain as their sister in suffering.

This story reveals the healing power of the experience of human solidarity. This healing power helps us not only to live our illness well, but also to die well. Indeed, we can be healed from our fear of death, not by a miraculous event that prevents us from dying, but by the healing experience of being a brother or sister of all humans—past, present, and future—who share with us the fragility of our existence. In this experience, we can taste the joy of being human and foretaste our communion with all people.

3

We Are Parents of Generations to Come

MARINA, MY SISTER-IN-LAW, is only forty-eight years old. She is dying. Five years ago, her doctor told her that she has cancer. Ever since, her life has been a long, painful attempt to fight the illness and to survive the many medical interventions. With three major surgeries and much chemotherapy, medical experts tried to remove the cancer and to prolong Marina's life.

My brother Paul did everything possible to offer his wife hope that there was a chance to beat the enemy. But finally he realized, as others with him realized, that the battle was lost. As I write this, Marina is preparing herself for death.

During the last few years, I have often had the opportunity to talk with Marina about her illness and even about her death. Marina is a strong, unsentimental woman. She likes to look at things as they are and has no time for people who try to comfort or console her with white lies. Although she has cooperated fully with the doctors and nurses who have helped her to fight her cancer, she does not want anyone to make any decision of which she is not fully a part. Nor does she want any spiritual support based on religious convictions that she does not hold. She often questions my spiritual viewpoints and has strong opinions about life and death—her own death as well as the deaths of others.

As the years go by and Marina's illness gets worse, she has expressed herself more and more through painting and poetry. These activities started as hobbies but have gradually become her primary activity. The weaker she has become physically, the stronger, more direct, and less adorned her artistic style has become. Her poems especially are the direct fruit of her struggle to befriend death.

Marina has lived an active and productive life. As a teacher and codirector of a language school, she built a career for herself and introduced creative new educational methods. But her illness has cruelly interrupted all of that and forced her to let go of the world she loved so much. Since her illness began, her art has replaced her many educational activities and become a new source of life for her. Often, when I am with her, she recites her poems by heart and asks me what I think of them. Many of them are playful and written with a humorous twist, but all express her increasing awareness that each day she has something more to let go of and that she is entering a time of many farewells.

As I have seen Marina prepare herself for her death, I have gradually realized that she is making her own dying a gift for others—not only for my brother Paul, not only for her family and friends, but also for the nurses and doctors and the many circles of people with whom she has spoken and shared her poems. Having taught all her life, she now teaches through her preparation for death. It strikes me that her successes and accomplishments will probably soon be forgotten, but the fruits of her dying may well last a long time. Marina is childless and has often wondered what her unique contribution to our society could be. Not having had the joy of motherhood, she has become the parent of many through the way she lives toward her death. The last five years might well prove to belong to the most fruitful of her life. She has shown me, in a whole new way, what it means to die for others. It means to become the parent of future generations.

Few of Jesus' words have affected me personally so much as his words about his own approaching death. With great directness, Jesus spoke to his closest friends about the end. Although he acknowledged the sorrow and sadness it would bring, he continued to announce his death as something good, something full of blessing, full of promise, full of hope. Shortly before his death, he said, "Now I am going to the one who sent me. No one of you asks, 'Where are you going?' Yet you are sad at heart because I have told you this. Still, I am telling you the truth: it is for your own good that I am going, because unless I go, the Spirit will not come to you; but if I go, I will send him to you. . . . I shall have many things to say to you but they would be too much for you to bear now. However, when the Spirit of truth comes he will lead you to the complete truth, since he will not be speaking of his own accord, but will say only what he has been told; and he will reveal to you the things to come" (John 16:4–7, 13).

At first, these words may sound strange, unfamiliar, even far away from our daily struggle with life and death. But after my conversations with Marina and with many other friends facing death, Jesus' words strike me in a new way and express the deepest significance of what these people are experiencing. We may be inclined to view the way Jesus prepared himself and his friends for his death as unique, far beyond any "normal" human way. But in fact, Jesus' way of dying offers us a hopeful example. We, too, can say to our friends, "It is for your own good that I am going, because if I go I can send the Spirit to you, and the Spirit will reveal to you the things to come." Isn't this what Marina wants to say when she makes poems and paintings that will give new life to those who will mourn her death? Isn't "sending the Spirit" the best expression for not leaving those you love alone but offering them a new bond, deeper than the bond that existed in life? Doesn't "dying for others" mean dying so that others can continue to live, strengthened by the Spirit of our love?

Some people might protest, saying, "Jesus, the only Son of the Father, did send his Holy Spirit to us . . . but we are not Jesus, and we have no Holy Spirit to send!" But when we listen deeply to Jesus' words, we realize that we are called to live like him, to die like him, and to rise like him, because the Spirit—the Divine Love, which makes Jesus one with his Father—has been given to us. Not only the death of Jesus, but our death, too, is destined to be good for others. Not only the death of Jesus, but our death, too, is meant to bear fruit in other people's lives. Not only the death of Jesus, but our death, too, will bring the Spirit of God to those we leave behind. The great mystery is that all people who have lived with and in the Spirit of God participate through their deaths in the sending of the Spirit. Thus God's Spirit of Love continues to be sent to us, and Jesus' death continues to bear fruit through all whose death is like his death, a death for others.

In this way, dying becomes the way to everlasting fruitfulness. Here is the most hope-giving aspect of death. Our death may be the end of our success, our productivity, our fame, or our importance among people, but it is not the end of our fruitfulness. In fact, the opposite is true: the fruitfulness of our lives shows itself in its fullness only after we have died. We ourselves seldom see or experience our own fruitfulness. Often we remain preoccupied with our accomplishments and have no eye for the fruitfulness of what we live. But the beauty of life is that it bears fruit long after life itself has come to an end. Jesus said, "In all truth I tell you, unless a wheat grain falls into the earth and dies, it remains only a single grain; but if it dies it yields a rich harvest" (John 12:24).

This is the mystery of Jesus' death and of the deaths of all who have lived in his Spirit. Their lives yield fruit far beyond the limits of their short and often localized existence. Years after my mother's death, she continues to bear fruit in my life. I am deeply aware that many of my major decisions since her death have been guided by the Spirit of Jesus, which she continues to send me.

Jesus lived less than forty years; he didn't travel outside his own country; the people who knew him during his life scarcely understood him; and when he died, only a few of his followers remained faithful. In every respect, his life was a failure. Success had left him, popularity had dwindled, and all his power was gone. Still, few lives have been so fruitful; few lives have affected the thinking and feeling of other people so deeply; few have so profoundly shaped future cultures; few have influenced so radically the patterns of human relationships. Jesus himself referred constantly to the fruitfulness of his life that would only become manifest after his death. Often he stressed that his disciples did not comprehend what he said or did, but that one day they would understand. When Jesus washed Peter's feet, he said, "At the moment you do not know what I am doing, but later you will understand" (John 13:7). When Jesus spoke about his return to the Father, he said, "I have said these things to you while still with you, but . . . the holy Spirit whom the Father will send in my name, will teach you everything and remind you of all that I have said to you" (John 14:25–26). The full meaning of Jesus' life was only revealed after his death.

Isn't this also true of many of the great men and women in history? For many of them, the full meaning of their lives became clear long after they died. Some were barely known during their lives, and some were known for completely different things than the things they are remembered for today. Some were successful and famous; others suffered from endless failures and rejections. But all truly great men and women who have shaped our ways of thinking and acting have borne fruit that they themselves couldn't see or predict.

Brother Lawrence is only one of many examples of this. This simple lay brother lived as a cook and shoemaker in a French Carmelite house of studies from 1614 to 1691. After his death, his letters and reflections about "walking in the presence of God" were made public, and even today they continue to affect the spiritual lives of many people. The life of Brother Lawrence was unspectacular but fruitful. Lawrence himself never thought much about influencing other people's lives. His only wish was to do all that he did in the presence of God.

The real question before our death, then, is not, How much can I still accomplish, or How much influence can I still exert? but, How can I live so that I can continue to be fruitful when I am no longer here among my family and friends? That question shifts our attention from doing to being. Our doing brings success, but our being bears fruit. The great paradox of our lives is that we are often concerned about what we do or still can do, but we are most likely to be remembered for who we were. If the Spirit guides our lives—the Spirit of love, joy, peace, gentleness, forgiveness, courage, perseverance, hope, and faith—then that Spirit will not die but will continue to grow from generation to generation.

In pondering Marina's death and my own, I realize the great challenge of life. While the society in which I live keeps asking for the tangible results of my life, I must gradually learn to trust that those results may or may not prove to be significant. What really counts are the fruits that my life bears. As I grow older and weaker, I will be able to do less and less. Both my body and my mind will become weaker. My eyes will move closer to the book I want to read and my ears closer to the neighbor I am trying to understand. My failing memory will lead me to repeat my jokes more often, and my decreasing ability to reflect critically will turn me into a less interesting conversationalist. Nonetheless, I trust that God's Spirit will manifest itself in my weakness and move where it wants and bear fruit from my deteriorating body and mind.

So my death will indeed be a rebirth. Something new will come to be, something about which I cannot say or think much. It lies beyond my own chronology. It is something that will last and carry on from generation to generation. In this way, I become a new parent, a parent of the future.

I think of my friends with AIDS every day. Some of these people I know personally; some I know as friends of friends; many I know by what is written by them or about them. From the outset of this horrendous epidemic, I have felt close to the many young men and women who live with AIDS. They all know that they cannot live long and that they will die difficult and often painful deaths. I want so much to help them, to be with them, to console and comfort them. I am overwhelmed by the tragedy that, in their desperate desire to be embraced and cared for, many have found illness and death instead. I cry out to heaven, saying, "Why, O God, does the human search for communion and intimacy lead to separation and anguish? Why are so many young people who simply want to be loved languishing in hospitals and lonely rooms? Why are love and death so close to each other?" Maybe the why is not what is important. Important are the men and women with their beautiful names and beautiful faces who wonder why they didn't find the love they yearned for. I feel close to these people because their pain is not far from mine.

I, too, want to love and be loved. I, too, must die. I, too, know that mysterious connection between my heart's yearning for love and my heart's anguish. In my heart, I want to embrace and hold all these people who are dying—hungry for love.

Recently I read Paul Monette's deeply moving book *Borrowed Time*. In it, he describes in pain-filled detail his battle against the AIDS of his friend Roger Horwitz. The whole book is like one battle cry: "We will beat the enemy. We will not let this evil force destroy our lives." It is a heroic battle, in which every means of survival is tried. But it is a lost battle. Roger dies, and Paul remains alone. Is death finally stronger than love? Are we finally all losers? Is all our struggle to survive, in the end, a silly struggle, as silly as the struggle of a fox attempting to gnaw its way out of a leg trap?

Many must feel that way. Only their deep, human self-respect in the face of the unbeatable power of death makes them put up an honest fight. I admire strongly the way Paul and Roger fought their grim battle. But after a life of reflection on the death of Jesus and many of his followers, I want to believe that beyond the fatal battle for survival is a hopeful battle for life. I want to believe—indeed, I do believe—that, ultimately, love is stronger than death. I have no argument to present. I have only the story of Jesus and the stories of those who trust in the life-giving truth of his life and his word. These stories show me a new way of living and a new way of dying, and I have a profound desire to show that way to others.

When I visited Rick in Bethany House—the Catholic worker house for people with AIDS in Oakland, California—I wanted to say something to him that Paul hadn't been able to say to Roger. In Paul's experience, the churches had nothing significant to say to people with AIDS. He could only think of churches as hypocritical, oppressive, and rejecting. He found more comfort in Greek mythology than in the Christian story. But when I held Rick's hand and looked into his fear-filled eyes, I felt deeply that the short time he had still to live could be more than a brave but losing battle for survival. I wanted him to know and believe that the meaning of the time left lay not in what he could still do but in the fruits he could bear when there was nothing left to do. When we were together, Rick said, "My friends shall have a future. I have only death to wait for." I didn't know what to say, and I knew that a lot of words wouldn't do him much good. Instead, I took his hand in mine and laid my other hand on his forehead. I looked into his tearful eyes and said, "Rick, don't be afraid. Don't be afraid. God is close to you, much closer than I am. Please trust that the time ahead of you will be the most important time of your life, not just for you, but for all of us whom you love and who love you." As I said these words, I felt Rick's body relax, and a smile came through his tears. He said, "Thank you, thank you." Then he reached out his arms and pulled me close to him and whispered in my ear, "I want to believe you. I really do, but it is so hard."

As I think of Rick and the many young people who are dying like him, everything in me rises in protest. I know that it is a temptation to think of people with AIDS as fighting a losing battle. But with all the faith I can muster, I believe that their deaths will be fruitful and that they are indeed called to be the parents of generations to come.

The Choice to Die Well

TO BEFRIEND DEATH, we must claim that we are children of God, sisters and brothers of all people, and parents of generations yet to come. In so doing, we liberate our death from its absurdity and make it the gateway to a new life.

In our society, in which childhood is something to grow away from, in which wars and ethnic conflicts constantly mock brotherhood and sisterhood among people, and in which the greatest emphasis is on succeeding in the few years we have, it hardly seems possible that death could be a gateway to anything.

Still, Jesus has opened this way for us. When we choose his way to live and die, we can face our death with the mocking question of the apostle Paul: "Death, where is your victory? Death, where is your sting?" (1 Corinthians 15:55). This is a choice, but a hard choice. The powers of darkness that surround us are strong and easily tempt us to let our fear of death rule our thoughts, words, and actions.

But we *can choose* to befriend our death as Jesus did. We *can choose* to live as God's beloved children in solidarity with all people, trusting in our ultimate fruitfulness. And in so doing, we can also become people who care for others. As men and women who have faced our mortality, we can help our brothers and sisters to dispel the darkness of death and guide them toward the light of God's grace.

Let us turn now to the subject of care.

PART TWO

CARING WELL

At the Heart of Being Human

BEFRIENDING OUR DEATH is a lifelong spiritual task but a task that, in all its different nuances, deeply affects our relationships with our fellow human beings. Every step we take toward deeper self-understanding brings us closer to those with whom we share our lives. As we learn, over time, to live the truth that death does not have a sting, we find within ourselves the gift to guide others to discover the same truth. We do not first do one of these things and later the other. Befriending our own death and helping others to befriend theirs are inseparable. In the realm of the Spirit of God, living and caring are one.

Our society suggests that caring and living are quite separate and that caring belongs primarily to professionals who have received special training. Although training *is* important, and although certain people need preparation to practice their profession with competence, caring is the privilege of every person and is at the heart of being human. When we look at the original meaning of the word *profession* and realize that the term refers, first of all, to professing one's own deepest conviction, then the essential spiritual unity between living and caring becomes clear.

In the following three chapters, I reflect on caring for the dying. First, I look at caring for the dying as helping our fellow human beings to befriend their own deaths. In these reflections, I hope to make clear that, to the degree that we befriend our own death, we can become truly caring people. Paralleling the first three chapters of this book, I look at care as helping others to claim for themselves the spiritual truth that they are — as we are — children of God, brothers and sisters of each other, and parents of generations to come.

4

You Are a Child of God

MAURICE GOULD, WHO died ten days before I began writing this book, was one of the first people I met at Daybreak. He was a member of the "Green House," the house where I spent my first week. Moe was born with Down's syndrome. For many years, he lived with his parents and sister, who cared for him lovingly. When he was in his early forties, he came to Daybreak. Two years ago, Maurice began to show signs of Alzheimer's disease. From then until his death, the community tried to care for him in the special way that Alzheimer patients require. The doctors told us that Moe would not be able to live long and that we must prepare him, as well as ourselves, for his death.

For those who were close to Moe—his family, his friends, and those who lived with him in the Green House—caring for him became a great challenge, a challenge at once painful and joyful. As Moe gradually lost his memory, his ability to recognize people, his sense of orientation, and his ability to feed himself, he became increasingly anxious and could no longer be his old good-humored self. Seeing him slip into a state of complete dependence, needing more help than we could offer him, was difficult. Finally Moe was taken to the nearby hospital, where a competent staff, together with the members of the Green House, cared for him during the last months of his life.

Among the things I remember most about Moe are his generous hugs. Often he would walk up to me with both hands stretched out and ready for a big embrace. As he held me, he would whisper in my ear,

"Amazing Grace," his cue for me to sing his favorite song with him. I also remember his love for dancing, his love of food, and his love for making people laugh with his imitations. When he imitated me, he put his glasses upside down on his nose and made wild gestures.

As I sit in Freiburg, far away from my community, and think of Moe, I realize more than ever that Moe was, and became evermore, a child of God. Because his friends were allowed to be so close to his "second childhood," they were able to care for him with great patience and lavish generosity.

Moe's illnesses—Down's syndrome and Alzheimer's disease—showed in a dramatic way the journey we all must make somewhere, somehow. But at the end of that journey, what do we finally see? Do we see a person who has lost all human abilities and has become a burden for everyone, or do we see a person who has become evermore a child of God, a pure instrument of grace? I cannot help but think about the countless times Moe looked me in the eyes and said, "Amazing Grace." I was not always ready to sing the old song again, and often I would say, "Next time, Moe." Now that Moe is gone, I keep hearing his persistent words—"Amazing Grace, Amazing Grace"—God's way of announcing to me the mystery of Moe's life and of all people.

Many of the people in Daybreak cannot do what most people outside the community can do. Some cannot walk, some cannot speak, some cannot feed themselves, some cannot read, some cannot count, some cannot dress themselves, and a few can do none of these things. No one is waiting for a cure. We only know that things will get harder as we get older and that the difference between people with a disability and those without a disability will become ever smaller. What are we ultimately growing toward? Are we simply becoming less capable people, returning our bodies to the dust from which they came, or are we growing into living reminders of that amazing grace that Moe always wanted to sing about?

We must choose between these two radically different viewpoints. The choice to see our own and other people's decreasing abilities as gateways to God's grace is a choice of faith. It is a choice based on the conviction that we see not only failure on the cross of Jesus but victory as well, not only destruction but new life as well, not only nakedness but glory as well. When John, the beloved disciple, looked up to Jesus and saw blood and water flowing from Jesus' pierced side, he saw something other than proof that all was over. He saw fulfillment of the prophecy "They will look up to the one whom they have pierced," a glimpse of God's victory over death, and a sign of God's amazing grace. John wrote, "This is evidence of the one who saw it—true evidence, and he knows that what he says is true—and he gives it so that you may believe as well" (John 19:35).

That is the choice of faith. It is the choice we make when we say that Moe, with his body and mind completely depleted by Alzheimer's disease, brought to us, through his dying and death, an amazing grace. It's the choice we make when we care for dying people with all the tenderness and gentleness that God's beloved children deserve. It's the choice that allows us to see the face of Jesus in the poor, the addicted, and those who live with AIDS and cancer. It's the choice of the human heart that has been touched by the Spirit of Jesus and is able to recognize that Spirit wherever people are dying.

Recently I attended a meeting of the leaders of several Christian institutions responsible for the supervision of homes for people with mental disabilities. In our free market economy, they told me, human care is spoken of in terms of supply and demand. In this context, the suffering person becomes the buyer of care, and the care professional becomes the merchant of care. It seems to me that this language and the vision that underlies it reduce the human person to nothing but a commodity in the competitive world of high finance. In this language, a vision has been chosen that no longer encourages us to celebrate the dying and the death of people like Maurice Gould. Amazing grace has been replaced by not-so-amazing business considerations.

Care, as I speak of it here, is the loving attention given to another person—not because that person needs it to stay alive, not because that person or some insurance company is paying for it, not because care provides jobs, not because the law forbids our hastening death, and not because that person can be used for medical research, but because that person is a child of God, just as we are.

To care for others as they become weaker and closer to death is to allow them to fulfill their deepest vocation, that of becoming ever-more fully what they already are: daughters and sons of God. It is to help them to claim, especially in their dying hours, their divine childhood and to let the Spirit of God cry out from their hearts, "Abba, Father" (Galatians 4:9). To care for the dying is to keep saying, "You are the beloved daughter of God, you are the beloved son of God."

How do we say this? The ways are countless: through words, prayers, and blessings; through gentle touch and the holding of hands; through cleaning and feeding; through listening and just being there. Some of these forms of care may be helpful, some not. But all are ways of expressing our faith that those we care for are precious in God's eyes. Through our caring presence, we keep announcing that sacred truth: dying is not a sweet, sentimental event; it is a great struggle to surrender our lives completely. This surrender is not an obvious human response. To the contrary: we want to cling to whatever is left. It is for this reason that dying people have so much anguish. As did Jesus, dying people too often experience their total powerlessness as rejection and abandonment. Often the agonizing cry "My God, my God, why have you abandoned me?" (Matthew 27:47) makes it difficult to say, "Father into your hands I commend my Spirit" (Luke 23:46).

Moe was not spared this struggle. As Alzheimer's disease took away his already-limited abilities to direct his own life, a great anguish grew within him. He often cried out in agony, and he experienced an ever-growing fear of aloneness. Often, during the night, he wanted to get up and go to work. Among the last words he could say were, "Call me . . . call me . . . call me."

Moe's fear was no different from my own. It was the fear of being rejected or left alone; of being found a burden or a nuisance; of being laughed at or considered useless. It was the deep fear of not belonging, of excommunication, of final abandonment. The more intimately I come to know people with mental disabilities, the more I am convinced that their deepest suffering is not in their inability to read, study, speak, or walk but in their deep fear of rejection, of being a burden; in this respect, they do not differ from me. Our greatest suffering comes from losing touch with my/ our belovedness and thinking of ourselves only as a useless, unwanted presence.

Caring for others is, first of all, helping them to overcome that enormous temptation of self-rejection. Whether we are rich or poor, famous or unknown, disabled or fully abled, we all share the fear of being left alone and abandoned, a fear that remains hidden under the surface of our self-composure. It is rooted much more deeply than in the possibility of not being liked or loved by people. Its deepest root lies in the possibility of not being loved at all, of not belonging to anything that lasts, of being swallowed up by a dark nothingness—yes, of being abandoned by God.

Caring, therefore, is being present to people as they fight this ultimate battle, a battle that becomes evermore real and intense as death approaches. Dying and death always call forth, with renewed power, the fear that we are unloved and will, finally, be reduced to useless ashes. To care is to stand by a dying person and to be a living reminder that the person is indeed the beloved child of God.

Mary's standing under the cross is the most moving expression of that care. Her son died in agony. She was there: not speaking, not pleading, not crying. She was there, reminding her son by her silent presence that, while she could not keep him for herself, his true sonship belongs to the Father, who will never leave him alone. She helped him recall his own words: "The time will come . . . when you will leave me alone. And yet I am not alone, because the Father is with me" (John 16:32). Mary encouraged Jesus to move beyond his experience of abandonment and to surrender himself into the embrace of his Father. She was there to strengthen his faith that, even in the midst of darkness, where he can feel nothing but loss and rejection, he remains the beloved Son of God, who will never leave him alone. It was this motherly care that finally allowed Jesus to win the battle against the demonic powers of rejection, to ward off the temptation of abandonment, and to surrender his whole being to God, with the words, "Father into your hands I commend my Spirit" (Luke 23:46).

Can we care as Mary did? I don't believe we can care in this way on our own. Even Mary was not alone. John, the beloved disciple, was with her beneath the cross. Reminding people in their agony of their divine childhood is not something we can do on our own. The powers of darkness are strong, and we can easily be pulled into the darkness ourselves and drawn into enormous self-doubts. To stand by a person who is dying is to participate in the immense struggle of faith. It is a struggle no person should take on alone. Before we realize it, the anguish of our dying friend becomes ours, and we become the victim of the same powers our friend is struggling with. We become overwhelmed by feelings of helplessness, powerlessness, self-doubt, and even guilt linked to our often-unacknowledged wish that it all would end soon.

No, we shouldn't try to care by ourselves. Care is not an endurance test. We should, whenever possible, care together with others. It is the community of care that reminds the dying person of his or her belovedness. It is Mary *and* John, Lori *and* Carl, Loretta *and* David, Carol *and* Peter, Janice *and* Cheryl, Geoff *and* Carrie, Lorenzo *and* many others who together can stand at the foot of the cross and say, "You are the beloved child of God, now as always." This circle of love surrounding our dying friends has the power to expel the demons of self-rejection and abandonment and bring light in the midst of darkness. I saw it happening around Moe, and I see it happening in the AIDS community and in the networks of support for cancer patients. Together, as a body of love, as a community that cares, we can come close to the dying and discover there a new hope, a new life, and a new strength to live. There can be smiles and stories, new encounters and new knowledge about ways to help, beautiful moments of silence and prayer. There can be the gift of people being together, waiting patiently for death to come. Together we can create that place where our dying friends can feel safe and can gradually let go and make the passage knowing that they are loved.

Caring together is the basis of community life. We don't come together simply to console each other or even to support each other. Important as those things may be, long-term community life is directed in other ways. Together we reach out to others. Together we look at those who need our care. Together we carry our suffering brothers and sisters to the place of rest, healing, and safety.

I have always been impressed with the thought that people are only ready to commit themselves to each other when they no longer focus on each other but rather focus together on the larger world beyond themselves. Falling in love makes us look at each other with admiration and tenderness. Committing ourselves to one another in love makes us look together toward those who need our care: the child, the stranger, the poor, the dying. That commitment lies at the heart of every community.

When I reflect on my own community, the L'Arche Daybreak community in Toronto, I realize increasingly that what keeps us faithful to each other is our common commitment to care for people with mental disabilities. We are called to care together. No one in our community could care single-handedly for any one of our disabled members. Not only would it be physically impossible, but it would quickly lead to emotional and mental exhaustion. Together, however, we can create a caring space that is good, not only for those who receive care, but also for those who give it. In this space, the boundaries between receiving and giving vanish, and true community can start to exist. It is essential to the weakest members of our community that those who care for them do so together. These members say to us, "For me to live, you must love not just me, but each other, too."

When I reflect on community life through the ages, I can easily see how the "ups" are closely connected to the vibrancy of caring together and the "downs" to absorption in internal matters. Even the most contemplative, seemingly hidden community could stay alive and well only when its life remained a life reaching out beyond the boundaries of the community. Even a life dedicated to prayer and meditation needs to maintain a quality of caring together for others. The mystery of this caring together is that it not only asks for community, but also creates it.

Those who cared for Moe realized after his death that he had brought them closer than they were before. Just as the dying Jesus brought Mary and John closer to each other by giving them to each other as mother and son, so too did Moe bring his friends closer to each other as sons and daughters of the same God. All true care for the dying person brings new awareness of the bonds that create a community of love.

The Flying Rodleighs are trapeze artists who perform in the German circus Simoneit-Barum. When the circus came to Freiburg two years ago, my friends Franz and Reny invited me and my father to see the show. I will never forget how enraptured I became when I first saw the

Rodleighs move through the air, flying and catching as elegant dancers. The next day, I returned to the circus to see them again and introduced myself to them as one of their great fans. They invited me to attend their practice sessions, gave me free tickets, asked me to dinner, and suggested I travel with them for a week in the near future. I did, and we became good friends.

One day, I was sitting with Rodleigh, the leader of the troupe, in his caravan, talking about flying. He said, "As a flyer, I must have complete trust in my catcher. The public might think that I am the great star of the trapeze, but the real star is Joe, my catcher. He has to be there for me with split-second precision and grab me out of the air as I come to him in the long jump." "How does it work?" I asked. "The secret," Rodleigh said, "is that the flyer does nothing and the catcher does everything. When I fly to Joe, I have simply to stretch out my arms and hands and wait for him to catch me and pull me safely over the apron behind the catchbar."

"You do nothing!" I said, surprised. "Nothing," Rodleigh repeated. "The worst thing the flyer can do is to try to catch the catcher. I am not supposed to catch Joe. It's Joe's task to catch me. If I grabbed Joe's wrists, I might break them, or he might break mine, and that would be the end for both of us. A flyer must fly, and a catcher must catch, and the flyer must trust, with outstretched arms, that his catcher will be there for him."

When Rodleigh said this with so much conviction, the words of Jesus flashed through my mind: "Father into your hands I commend my Spirit." Dying is trusting in the catcher. To care for the dying is to say, "Don't be afraid. Remember that you are the beloved child of God. He will be there when you make your long jump. Don't try to grab him; he will grab you. Just stretch out your arms and hands and trust, trust, trust."

5

You Are Brothers and Sisters of Each Other

ONE DAY, SALLY, a good friend of mine, said, "It has been five years since my husband, Bob, died, and I would like to visit his grave with my children. Would you be willing to come with us?" When I said, "Of course, I would love to come with you," she told me what had happened. Bob had died unexpectedly from heart failure, and Sally had suddenly been faced with the hard task of helping her children, Mitchell and Lindsay, who were four and five at the time, to respond to their father's death. She had felt then that it would be too difficult for the children to see their father being put into the ground and covered with sand. "They are much too young to understand," Sally had thought.

As the years went by, the cemetery became a fearful place for Sally, Lindsay, and Mitchell. Intuitively, Sally felt that something was not right. And so she invited me to go with her and the children to Bob's grave. It was still a little too scary for Lindsay, because she had such concrete memories of Bob, so only Mitchell came along.

It was a beautiful, sunny day. We soon found Bob's grave: a simple stone engraved with the words "A kind and gentle man." We sat on the grass around the stone, and Sally and Mitchell told stories about Bob. Mitchell remembered how his dad had played ball with him. When his memory became hazy, Sally filled in the details. I just asked questions.

As we began to feel more at ease, I said, "Wouldn't it be nice to have a picnic here? Maybe one day we could all come back, bring food and drinks with us, and celebrate Bob's life, right here at his grave. We could eat together in his memory." At first Sally and Mitchell were puzzled with the idea, but then Mitchell said, "Yes, why not? Then I am sure Lindsay will come, too."

When Sally and Mitchell went home, they told Lindsay that it hadn't been scary at all but had been quite all right. A few days later, Lindsay asked Sally to take her to the grave. They went and talked together about Bob. Gradually, Bob became less a stranger and more a new friend, and having a picnic on his grave became something to look forward to. After all, Jesus, too, had asked his friends to remember him with a meal.

This story shows how easily we distance ourselves from those who have died and treat them as fearful strangers who remind us of things we don't want to be reminded of—especially our own mortality. But it also shows how easily we can bring those who have died back into the circle of the living and make them gentle friends who can help us to face our own death.

How often do we see someone die? How often do we see a dead person? How often do we throw sand on top of a coffin that has been lowered into the grave? How often do we go to the cemetery and stand, kneel, or sit in front of the place where our spouse, parents, brothers, sisters, aunts, uncles, or friends have been buried? Are we still in touch with those who have died, or are we living our lives as if those who lived before us never really existed?

In Geysteren, the little village where my father lives in the southern part of Holland, the dead are still part of the daily life of the people. The cemetery, close to the village square, is a beautifully kept garden. The gate is freshly painted, the hedges well trimmed, the walkways raked clean, and each grave well cared for. Many of the memorial crosses or stones are decorated with fresh flowers or evergreen plants. The cemetery feels like a place where visitors are welcome and where it is good to spend time. The villagers love their cemetery. They go there, often, to pray and to be with their family or friends who have left them. During each service in the village church, "those who rest in [the] cemetery" are mentioned and included in the prayers of the community.

Whenever I visit my father in Geysteren, I go to that little cemetery. Close to the entrance, on the left side, is my mother's grave, marked with a simple brown wooden cross on which her name and the dates of her birth and death are painted in white. In front of the cross, evergreen plants outline the place where her body is laid to rest, and newly planted violets cover the center. When I stand before that simple grave, look at the cross, and hear the wind play with the leaves of the tall poplars surrounding the cemetery, I know that I am not alone. My mother is there, and she speaks to me. There is no apparition, no mysterious voice, but there is the simple, inner knowledge that she who died more than fourteen years ago is still with me. Embraced by the solitude of the beautiful cemetery, I hear her say that I must be faithful to my own journey and not be afraid to join her someday in death.

As I stand in front of my mother's grave, the circles of the dead surrounding me become ever wider. I am surrounded not only by the villagers who lie buried there, but also by family members and friends. Even wider is the circle of those whose actions and words have shaped my life and thoughts. Beyond are the many circles of the countless men and women whose names I do not know but who have, in their own unique way, made the journey that I am making and shared in the pains and joys of being human.

The poplars of the little cemetery in Geysteren sing their songs for all these people buried wide and far. Some were buried with the same gentleness as my mother was, some simply put away and forgotten, many dumped into mass graves of which few know the location and where no one ever comes to pray. For all of these people, the poplars sing, and standing in that cemetery, I feel grateful for being human as all of these people were and for being called to die as they did.

What a gift it is to know deeply that we are all brothers and sisters in one human family and that, different as our cultures, languages, religions, lifestyles, or work may be, we are all mortal beings called to surrender our lives into the hands of a loving God. What a gift it is to feel connected with the many who have died and to discover the joy and peace that flow from that connectedness. As I experience that gift, I know in a new way what it means to care for the dying. It means to connect them with the many who are dying or have died and to let them discover the intimate bonds that reach far beyond the boundaries of our short lives.

Going with Sally and Mitchell to Bob's grave and standing silently in the Geysteren cemetery in front of the place where my mother is buried have strengthened my conviction that all who are dying should know about the deep communion among all men and women on this planet. We human beings belong together, whether we live now or lived long ago, whether we live close by or far away, whether we have biological ties or not. We are brothers and sisters, and our dying is truly a dying in communion with each other.

But when we look at the world around us, the question arises: Do we really live as brothers and sisters? Every day, the newspapers and television remind us that human beings are fighting each other, torturing each other, killing each other. All over the world, people are the victims of persecution, war, and starvation. All over the world there is hatred, violence, and abuse. For a while, we lived with the illusion that the period of concentration camps was far behind us, that a holocaust such as that which occurred during the Second World War would no longer be humanly possible. But what is happening today shows how little we have really learned. The true sin of humanity is that men and women created to be brothers and sisters become again and again each other's enemies, willing to destroy each other's lives.

God sent Jesus to restore the true human order. Jesus is called the Redeemer. He came to redeem us from our sins and to remind us of the truth that we are sons and daughters of God, brothers and sisters of one another. How did Jesus redeem us from our sins? By becoming one of us: being born as we are born, living as we live, suffering as we suffer, and dying as we die. Indeed, Jesus became our brother, God-with-us. When the angel of God came to Nazareth and spoke to Joseph in a dream, he said, "Joseph, son of David, do not be afraid to take Mary home as your wife because she has conceived what is in her by the Holy Spirit. She will give birth to a son and you must name him Jesus, because he is the one who is to save his people from their sins." The evangelist Matthew, who wrote this, added, "Now all this took place to fulfill what the Lord had spoken through the prophet: 'Look! the virgin is with child and will give birth to a son whom they will call Immanuel,' a name which means 'God-with-us'" (Matthew 1:20–23).

God became God-with-us, our brother, so that we might claim for ourselves our brotherhood and sisterhood with all people. That is the story of Jesus, the story of our redemption. The heart of that story is that, in and through Jesus, God wanted to share not only our life, but our death. Jesus' death is the most radical expression of God's desire to be God-with-us. Nothing makes all human beings so similar to each other as their mortality. Our common mortality shows the illusion of our differences, the falseness of the many divisions among us, and the sins of our mutual enmities. By dying with and for us, Jesus wanted to dispel our illusions, heal our divisions, and forgive our sins so that we can rediscover that we are each other's brothers and sisters. By becoming our brother, Jesus wanted us to become once again brothers and sisters for one another. In nothing but sin did he want to differ from us. That is why he died for us. As one who was as mortal as we are, Jesus called us to stop living in fear of each other and to start loving one another. And this was more than his wish. It was his commandment, because it belongs to the essence of our being human. Jesus said, "This is my commandment, love one another as I have loved you. No one can have greater love than to lay down his life for his friends. You are my friends, if you do what I command you, . . . I shall no longer call you servants, because a servant does not know his master's business; I call you friends because I have made known to you everything that I have learned from my Father. . . . My command to you is to love one another" (John 15:12–17).

This great mystery of God becoming God-with-us has radical implications for the way we care for the dying. When God wants to die with and for us, we too must die with and for each other. Tragically, however, we think about our death first as an event that separates us from others. It is departing. It is leaving others behind. It is the ending of precious relationships, the beginning of loneliness. Indeed, for us, death is primarily a separation and, worse, an irreversible separation.

But Jesus died for us so that our death no longer need be just separation. His death opened for us the possibility of making our own death a way to union and communion. That's the radical turn that our faith allows us to make, but making that turn does not happen spontaneously. It requires care.

To care for the dying means to help them live their dying as a way to gather around them not only those who come to visit, not only family and friends, but all of humanity, the living as well as the dead. When we say that it is not good for a human being to die alone, we touch a deep mystery. In our death, we need to be, more than ever, in communion with others. The passage of our life is the passage that, more than any other passage, needs to be made with others.

There is something so obvious about this that no one would ever question the importance of being with someone at the moment of death. One of our worst fears about dying is that we might die without anyone at our side. We want someone to hold our hand, someone to touch us and speak gently to us, someone to pray with us. And that's what we want to do for others.

But there is more—much more—that is less obvious. To care also means to gently encourage our dying friend to die with and for others. Somehow, we who care need to have the courage to bring together around our dying friends the saints and sinners of all times: the starving children, the tortured prisoners, the homeless, the wanderers, the AIDS-afflicted, and the millions who have died or are now dying. At first, this might seem harsh, even cruel, but the opposite is true. It lifts our dying friends out of their isolation and makes them part of the most human of all human events. When those who are dying begin to realize that what they are experiencing, though painful, unites them with the worldwide and centuries-old family of humanity, they may be able to let go and gradually let that human family carry them through the gate of death.

For this reason, through the course of Christian history, dying people have been encouraged to look at the cross. On the famous sixteenth-century Isenheimer Altar in Colmar, France, Christ is portrayed hanging on the cross in unspeakable agony. His body is covered with sores caused by the black plague. When those who were dying of the plague looked up at that suffering Christ, they saw not only Jesus, who died with and for them long ago, but also all their dying brothers and sisters. There they found consolation. They realized that, as Christ had died for them, they too could die for their brothers and sisters and so make their dying an act of human solidarity.

Recently, in San Francisco, I saw a cross on which Jesus was dying of AIDS. There, too, all men, women, and children of the world with AIDS were portrayed, not to frighten, but to offer hope. The dying people of our century can look up to this cross and find hope.

Caring, then, is different from protecting dying people from seeing the larger picture. To the contrary, it is helping these people to grow in their awareness that their individual, painful condition is embedded in the basic condition of human mortality and, as such, can be lived in communion with others.

This care can be seen today in the many AIDS communities. In North American cities, young people are supporting each other as they live their illness in solidarity with each other and with others who are dying. They may seldom think or talk about this solidarity as an expression of God's solidarity with us, but even so, they do help each other to die in the same spirit in which Jesus died, the spirit of communion with the larger human family.

Is there anything practical to say about care for the dying in this perspective? Maybe only that dying people can face the reality of life much better than caregivers often realize. We have a tendency to keep the "bad news" of our world hidden from those who are dying. We want to offer these people a quiet, undisturbed, "peaceful" end. To accomplish that, we are inclined to avoid telling them about other people who are sick or dying, to avoid speaking with them about the victims of war and starvation in other places of the world. We want to keep them separated from the terrible realities of life. But do we offer them a service in doing so? Or do we prevent them from living their illness in solidarity with their fellow human beings and making their death a death with and for others?

Illness, and especially terminal illness, tends to narrow a person's vision, because people quickly become preoccupied with their own medical ups and downs and the daily events connected with their health. The often repeated question "How are you doing?" encourages people to tell and retell their own story, often against their desire.

I think many people desire to remain part of the larger world and would be glad to hear and speak about things outside their home or hospital. I remember vividly how grateful I was during my hospital stay after my accident for visitors who didn't ask or speak about me but rather focused my attention on something larger than myself. In fact, I felt grateful *not* to be separated from the world. I felt encouraged and strengthened by the assumption of my friends that my illness did not prevent me from being truly interested in the struggles of other people. Being connected and constantly reconnected with the larger suffering of my brothers and sisters in the human family did not paralyze me. To the contrary, this connection had a healing effect. Healing came not from being infantilized but from being treated as a mature adult able to live pain together with others.

I am not suggesting that we care for dying people simply by telling them about all the misery in the world. That would be unwise and unhelpful. I am not suggesting that we cause our dying friends to worry about the suffering of others. I *am* suggesting that, when we ourselves have befriended our own mortality, we will have no need to isolate our dying friends and will intuitively know how to maintain their communion with the larger, suffering human family. When we who care are not afraid to die, we will be better able to prepare the dying for death and deepen their communion with others instead of separating them.

A few years ago, the IMAX company made a short film, called *The Blue Planet*, from a space shuttle. The film is shown on a huge, concave screen with sounds coming from all sides. The viewers feel as if they are, in fact, sitting in the shuttle. The most remarkable part of this film is that it allows us to see what astronauts see: our own planet. For the first time in human history, we are able to see the earth from a distance. As we look at our earth, we realize that the beautiful blue ball moving through the universe is our own home. We can say, "Look! That's where we live, where we work, where we have our family. That's our home. Isn't it a beautiful place to live?"

As we look at that beautiful, majestic blue planet as our home, we suddenly have a completely new understanding of the word *our*. *Our* means all people, from all the continents, of all colors, religions, races, and ages. Seen from the space shuttle, the many differences among people that cause hatred, violence, war, oppression, starvation, and mutual destruction seem ridiculous. From the distance of the space shuttle, it is crystal clear that we have the same home, that we belong together, that together we must care for our beautiful blue planet so that we will be able to live here, not just now, but for the long future. Our space age has made it possible for us to grow into a new consciousness of the basic unity of all people on earth and the common responsibility of all people to care for each other and, together, for our home. Seeing our blue planet from a distance, we can say in a new way, "We are indeed brothers and sisters, as Jesus told us long ago. We all are born as fragile beings; we all die as fragile beings. We need each other and our beautifully made home to live well and to die well."

The distant view of our home may make it possible for us to live and die with a deeper knowledge of being children of one God and brothers and sisters of each other and to truly care.

6

You Are Parents of Generations to Come

LAST YEAR, DURING Holy Week, while having dinner with some friends in downtown Toronto, I received a phone call that Connie Ellis, my secretary and close friend for the past six years, had suddenly become ill and been taken to the hospital. Until late that afternoon, she had tried hard to finish work on a text that I needed to take with me to Europe after Easter. She had gone home tired and suddenly had felt disoriented and anxious. Happily, she was still able to call her daughter-in-law, Carmen. When Carmen heard Connie's slurred and barely understandable speech, she became worried and hurried to see her at Connie's home.

Tests the next day showed that Connie had suffered a stroke caused by a large brain tumor. On Good Friday, she underwent extensive surgery. Although the surgery was "successful," it left her paralyzed on her left side, unable to walk by herself, and in constant danger of falling. After extensive radiation therapy, doctors told Connie that the cancer was in remission. But she remained fragile, without much prospect that things would ever be "normal" for her again.

For years, Connie had been known for her great vitality, her competence, and her ability to accomplish a lot in a short time. She had become both my right and my left hand. She knew all the people who came to the office, phoned in, or wrote and had developed a warm relationship with many of them. The help, support, and advice she had given to countless people during the six years we worked together had made her a friend of many. Her ministry had become as important as my own.

Then, in an instant, all that was over. She who had always been eager to help others now needed others to help her. In one day, a strong, healthy, active, efficient woman had become fully dependent on family and friends. It was painful for me to see my close friend and co-worker suddenly lose her ability to do many things and help many people. But I was also hopeful in seeing that this radical change had not affected her trusting and loving disposition. Often Connie would say to me, "I feel deep inner peace. I am sure God will perform a miracle for me, but if not, I am ready to die. I have had a beautiful life."

As I reflect on this dramatic event in Connie's life and realize that she is, in fact, one of many people who have similar experiences, I wonder what meaning to give it. We human beings cannot live without meaning. Whatever happens to us, we ask, "Why is this happening to me? What does it mean?"

Much of the meaning in Connie's life has come from her relationships with her two sons, John and Steve, and their families. Her close friendships with Steve's wife, Carmen, and with her two grandchildren, Charles and Sarah, especially, have given her great joy and satisfaction. One of Connie's joys before her illness was to take Charles to play hockey and to encourage him from the sidelines. I could be critical about anyone else in Connie's presence, but not about "Carm and the kids," who were simply beyond criticism.

Much meaning also has come from Connie's work in the office. To the last minute of her working life, she enjoyed immensely what she was doing and did it with a never-abating dedication. I remember how happy she was that she had been able to transcribe all my interviews with the five trapeze artists in the circus. She fervently supported me in my "crazy" idea to write a book about them and wanted to be sure that I had all the necessary texts before returning to Germany for more interviews. Our work together, in all its variety and hecticness, gave meaning to her life. Few people realized that she was already past seventy and getting tired at times.

When, suddenly, everything changed, the question of meaning returned in full force. For a while, the emphasis was on getting better and being independent again. "Once I can drive my car again," Connie would say, "I won't be so dependent on John, Steve, Carm, and the kids anymore and will be able to manage by myself again." But she gradually came to see that this might never be possible. For the rest of her life, she might need others to help her.

To care for Connie and for the many who can no longer expect to return to their work, who can no longer be of service to their families and friends, is to search together for new meaning, a meaning no longer drawn from activities to get things done. Somehow, meaning must grow out of the "passivities" of waiting.

Jesus moved in his life from action to passion. For several years, he was extremely active preaching, teaching, and helping, always surrounded by large crowds and always moving from place to place. But in the Garden of Gethsemane, after his last supper with his disciples, he was handed over to those who resented him and his words. He was handed over to be the object of actions by others. From that moment, Jesus no longer took initiatives. He no longer did anything. Everything was done to him. He was arrested, put in prison, ridiculed, tortured, condemned, and crucified. All action was gone. The mystery of Jesus' life is that he fulfilled his vocation not through action but through becoming the subject of other people's actions. When he finally said, "It is fulfilled" (John 19:30), he meant not only "All I needed to do I have done," but also "All that needed to be done to me has been done to me." Jesus completed his mission on earth through being the passive subject of what others did to him.

What Jesus lived we also are called to live. Our lives, when lived in the spirit of Jesus, will find their fulfillment in a similar kind of dependence. Jesus made this clear when he said to Peter, "When you were young, you put on your belt and walked where you liked, but when you grow old, you will stretch out your hands and somebody else will put a belt round you and take you where you rather would not go" (John 21:18). We, too, must move from action to "passion," from being in control to being dependent, from taking initiatives to having to wait, from living to dying.

Painful and nearly impossible as this move seems to be, it is in this movement that our true fruitfulness is hidden. Our years of action are years of success and accomplishment. During these years, we do things about which we can speak with pride. But much of this success and many of these accomplishments will soon lie behind us. We might still point to them in the form of trophies, medals, or artistic products. But what is beyond our success and productivity? Fruitfulness lies beyond and that fruitfulness comes through passion, or suffering. Just as the ground can only bear fruit if broken by the plow, our own lives can only be fruitful if opened through passion. Suffering is precisely "undergoing" action by others, over which we have no control. Dying is always suffering, because dying always puts us in the place where others do to us whatever they decide to do, good or bad.

It is not easy to trust that our lives will bear fruit through this sort of dependence because, for the most part, we ourselves experience dependence as uselessness and as burdensome. We often feel discomfort, fatigue, confusion, disorientation, and pain, and it is hard to see any fruit coming from such vulnerability. We see only a body and a mind broken to pieces by the plow that others hold in their hands.

Believing that our lives come to fulfillment in dependence requires a tremendous leap of faith. Everything that we see or feel and everything that our society suggests to us through the values and ideas it holds up to us point in the opposite direction. Success counts, not fruitfulness—and certainly not fruitfulness that comes through passivity. But passion is God's way, shown to us through the cross of Jesus. It's the way we try to avoid at all costs, but it is the way to salvation. This explains why it is so important to care for the dying. To care for the dying is to help the dying make that hard move from action to passion, from success to fruitfulness, from wondering how much they can still accomplish to making their very lives a gift for others. Caring for the dying means helping the dying discover that, in their increasing weakness, God's strength becomes visible.

The well-known words of the apostle Paul, "God chose those who by human standards are weak to shame the strong" (1 Corinthians 1:27), take on new meaning here because the weak are not only the poor, the disabled, and the mentally ill, but also the dying—and all of us will be dying one day. We must trust that it is also in *this* weakness that God shames the strong and reveals true human fruitfulness. That's the mystery of the cross. When Jesus was on the cross, his life became infinitely fruitful. There, the greatest weakness and the greatest strength met. We can participate in this mystery through our death. To help each other die well is to help each other claim the fruitfulness in our weakness. Thus our dying enables us to embrace our cross with the trust that new life will emerge. Much of this becomes concrete when we are with people who must come to terms with their approaching death.

After her brain surgery, Connie always expressed a double desire: the desire for "a miracle," as she called it—to be completely cured and to be able to resume a normal life—and the desire to die peacefully, without causing too much grief to her children and grandchildren. As it became clear that a full cure was unlikely to occur, she began to think and speak more about her death and how to prepare herself and her family for it.

I remember vividly how she said to me one day, "I am not afraid to die. I feel safe in God's love. I know that you and many others pray for me every day and that nothing bad can happen to me. But I worry about the kids." As she said this, she began to cry. I knew how close she felt to her grandchildren, Charles and Sarah, and how much their lives, their happiness, and their future concerned her. I asked her, "What are you thinking?" She said, "I don't want the kids to suffer because of me. I don't want them to become sad and sorrowful as they see me dying. They always knew me as the strong grandmother they could count on. They don't know me as a paralyzed woman whose hair is falling out because of radiation therapy. I worry when I look into their faces and see them so anxious and sad. I want them to be happy children now and after I am gone." Connie didn't think about herself. She thought first of others. She wanted to be sure that I would find a good person to take over her work in the office. She wanted to be sure that her illness would not interrupt the life of her children and their families. Most of all, she wanted her grandchildren to be happy people. She worried that her sickness and death would prevent that.

As I saw Connie's pain, I saw more than ever what a beautiful, generous, caring person she is. She deeply cares for all the people who are part of her life. *Their* well-being is more important for her than her own. *Their* work, *their* pleasures, and *their* dreams concern her more than her own. In this society, in which most people are so self-centered, Connie is a true ray of light.

Still, I wanted Connie to move beyond her worries and to trust that her love for her family and friends would be fruitful. I wanted her to believe that what was important was not only what she did or still could do for others, but also—and ever-more so—what she lives in her illness and how she lives it. I wanted her to come to see that, in her growing dependence, she is giving more to her grandchildren than during the times when she could bring them in her car to school, to shops, and to sports fields. I wanted her to discover that the times when she needs them are as important as the times when they need her. In fact, in her illness, she has become their real teacher. She speaks to them about her gratitude for life, her trust in God, and her hope in a life beyond death. She shows them real thankfulness for all the little things they do for her. She doesn't keep her tears or fears hidden when they suddenly well up, but she always returns to a smile.

Connie herself can't see most of her own goodness and love. But I and the many other people who visit her can see it. Now, in her growing weakness, she who lived such a long and productive life gives what she couldn't give in her strength: a glimpse of the truth that love is stronger than death. Her grandchildren will reap the full fruits of that truth.

In our dying, we become parents of generations to come. How true this is of many holy people. Through their weakness, they have given us a view of God's grace. They are still close to us: St. Francis of Assisi, Martin Luther, John Henry Newman, Thérèse de Lisieux, Mahatma Gandhi, Thomas Merton, John XXIII, Dag Hammarskjöld, Dorothy Day, and many who have belonged to our own little circle of family and friends. Our thoughts and feelings, our words and writings, our dreams and visions are not just our own, they belong also to the many men and women who have died already and are now living within us. The lives and deaths of these people are still bearing fruit in our lives. Their joy, hope, courage, confidence, and trust haven't died with them but continue to blossom in our hearts and the hearts of the many who are connected with us in love. Indeed, these people keep sending the Spirit of Jesus to us and giving us the strength to be faithful in the journey we have begun.

We, too, must see to it that our deaths become fruitful in the lives of those who will live after us. Without care, however, it is difficult, if not impossible, to let our lives bear fruit in the generations to come. Devoid of care, our society makes us believe that we are what we have, what we do, or what people think about us. With such a belief, our death is, indeed, the end because, when we die, all property, success, and popularity vanishes. Without care for each other, we forget who we truly are— children of God and each other's brothers and sisters—and so cannot become parents of generations to come. But as a community of care, we can remind each other that we will bear fruit far beyond the few years we have to live. As a community of care, we trust that those who live long after we have lived will still receive the fruits of the seeds we have sown in our weakness and find new strength from them. As a community of care, we can send the Spirit of Jesus to each other. Thus we become the fruit-bearing people of God who embrace past, present, and future and thus are a light in the darkness.

Our meals in the Daybreak community show something about fruit-fulness born in weakness. Meals in our houses are the high points of our daily life. They are like small celebrations. Food is eaten slowly, because many of us cannot eat by ourselves and need to be fed. Conversations around the table are simple, because many of us cannot speak, and those who can don't use many words. Prayers are always for others; each person is mentioned by name because, for people with mental disabilities, other people are what really count. Often there are candles and flowers, and on special occasions there are banners and balloons.

Whenever I am part of such a meal, I become acutely aware that the gifts of the Spirit of Jesus are given to us in weakness. Even while many of us experience much physical or emotional pain, while quite a few cannot make a move without assistance, and while some have few ways to communicate needs and desires, the spiritual gifts of peace, joy, gentleness, forgiveness, hope, and trust are very much present. Our shared vulnerability seems to be the favorite climate for Jesus to show us his love, for it is certainly not we who have created these gifts of love. We wouldn't even know how to go about doing such a thing. Many of us are too preoccupied with just surviving or helping others to survive. As in all families and communities, there are tensions and conflicts, too. Still, it seems that around this table of poverty, Jesus becomes powerfully present, generously sending his spirit.

During the time of prayer at the end of each meal, it becomes clear that these Daybreak meals have the quality of a memorial. We lift up not only our own life to God in gratitude, but also the lives of those of whose weaknesses we are aware, and especially the lives of those who are dying or have died. Thus we make all part of our "fellowship of weakness."

These memorial meals are also ways in which we care for each other and prepare each other to accept our final vulnerability. There is little chance that anyone will ever talk about our evening dinners as "last suppers," but still we want to say to each other, "When I am no longer here, keep remembering me whenever you come together to eat, drink, and celebrate, and I in return will send you the Spirit of Jesus, who will deepen and strengthen the bonds of love that bind you together." So every meal in which we remember Jesus and those who have died in him also prepares us for our own death. Thereby we not only feed ourselves, but also nurture each other, and so we become, each day, a little more the community of care to which we always will belong.

The Choice to Care Well

TO CARE WELL for the dying, we must trust deeply that these people are loved as much as we are, and we must make that love visible by our presence; we must trust that their dying and death deepen their solidarity with the human family, and we must guide them in becoming part of the communion of saints; and finally, we must trust that their death, just as ours, will make their lives fruitful for generations to come. We must encourage them to let go of their fears and to hope beyond the boundaries of death.

Caring well, just as dying well, asks for a choice. Although we all carry within us the gift to care, this gift can become visible only when we choose it.

We are constantly tempted to think that we have nothing or little to offer to our fellow human beings. Their despair frightens us. It often seems better not to come close than to come close without being able to change anything. This is especially true in the presence of people who face death. In running away from the dying, however, we bury our precious gift of care.

Whenever we claim our gift of care and choose to embrace not only our own mortality, but also other people's, we can become a true source of healing and hope. When we have the courage to let go of our need to cure, our care can truly heal in ways far beyond our own dreams and expectations. With our gift of care, we can gently lead our dying brothers and sisters always deeper into the heart of God and God's universe.

CONCLUSION

The Grace of the Resurrection

NEARLY THREE WEEKS have passed since I started to write this book on dying well and caring well. Although I have, for the most part, kept to my hermitage on the third floor of Franz and Reny's house, I have traveled far and wide in my mind. I have been with Maurice and Connie in Canada, Richard in the United States, and Marina in Holland. I have "visited" countless people in Europe, Asia, Africa, and Latin America who are dying as the result of war, starvation, and oppression, and I have tried to embrace with my heart those who have lived and died but continue to inform and inspire me with their actions and words.

During all these extensive mental travels, I have tried to claim for myself as well as for others that we are children of God, sisters and brothers of each other, and parents of generations to come. I have attempted to explore the ways in which this spiritual identity offers us a vision not only of how to die well ourselves, but also of how to care well for others who are dying.

Now as I sit behind my desk writing this conclusion, I realize a question may have come to those reading these words: "What of the resurrection?" It surprises me that so far I have neither written about the resurrection nor felt a need to do so. This simply didn't seem an urgent question as I was writing. But the fact that the resurrection didn't present itself with great urgency does not mean that it isn't important. To the contrary, the resurrection is more important than any of the things of which I have written so far because the resurrection is the foundation of my faith. To write about dying and death without mentioning the resurrection is like writing about sailing without mentioning the wind. The resurrection of Jesus and the hope of our own resurrection have made it possible for me to write about dying and death in the way that I have. With Paul the apostle, I dare to say, "[I]f Christ is proclaimed as raised from the dead, how can some of you be saying that there is no resurrection of the dead? For, if the dead are not raised, neither is Christ, and if Christ has not been raised, your faith is pointless and you have not, after all, been released from your sins. In addition, those who have fallen asleep in Christ are utterly lost. If our hope in Christ has been for this life only, we are of all people the most pitiable" (1 Corinthians 15:12–19).

It hardly seems possible to have a stronger opinion about the resurrection than Paul expresses in these words, and I want to make Paul's words my own. Still, I have not yet written about the resurrection of Jesus and of ourselves. I think that my hesitation in writing about this is connected with my conviction that the resurrection of Jesus is a hidden event. Jesus didn't rise from the dead to prove to those who had crucified him that they had made a mistake or to confound his opponents. Nor did he rise to impress the rulers of his time or to force anyone to believe. Jesus' resurrection was the full affirmation of his Father's love. He showed himself only to those who knew about this love. He made himself known as the risen Lord only to a handful of his close friends. Probably no other event in human history has had such importance while at the same time remaining so unspectacular. The world didn't notice Jesus' resurrection; only a few knew, those to whom Jesus had chosen to show himself and whom he wanted to send out to announce God's love to the world just as he had done.

The hiddenness of Jesus' resurrection is important to me. Although the resurrection of Jesus is the cornerstone of my faith, it is not something to use as an argument, nor is it something to use to reassure people. It somehow doesn't take death seriously enough to say to a dying person, "Don't be afraid. After your death you will be resurrected as Jesus was, meet all your friends again, and be forever happy in the presence of God." This suggests that after death everything will be basically the same, except that our troubles will be gone. Nor does it take seriously Jesus himself, who did not live through his own death as if it were little else than a necessary passage to a better life. Finally, it doesn't take seriously the dying, who, like us; know nothing about what is beyond this time-and place-bound existence.

The resurrection does not solve our problems about dying and death. It is not the happy ending to our life's struggle, nor is it the big surprise that God has kept in store for us. No, the resurrection is the expression of God's faithfulness to Jesus and to all God's children. Through the resurrection, God has said to Jesus, "You are indeed my beloved Son, and my love is everlasting," and to us God has said, "You indeed are my beloved children, and my love is everlasting." The resurrection is God's way of revealing to us that nothing that belongs to God will ever go to waste. What belongs to God will never get lost—not even our mortal bodies. The resurrection doesn't answer any of our curious questions about life after death, such as, How will it be? How will it look? But it does reveal to us that, indeed, love is stronger than death. After that revelation, we must remain silent, leave the whys, wheres, hows, and whens behind, and simply trust.

On the occasion of his ninetieth birthday, my father gave an interview to a Dutch radio station. After the reporter had asked him many questions about his life and work, and even more about the current Dutch tax system—since that was my father's professional interest—he finally wanted to know what my father thought would happen to him after his death.

My father and I were both listening to the program as it was broadcast a week after it was made. I was obviously quite curious about what my father's answer would be to that last question. I heard him say to the reporter, "I have very little to say about it. I don't really believe that I will see my wife or friends again as we see each other now. I don't have any concrete expectations. Yes, there is something else, but when there is no time and space anymore, any word about that 'something else' wouldn't make much sense. I am not afraid to die. I don't desire to become one hundred years old. I just want to live my life now as well as I can and . . . when I die, well, then we will see!"

Our Greatest Gift 643

Maybe my father's belief, as well as his lack of belief, is best summarized in these last words: "Well, then we will see." His skepticism and his faith touch each other in these words. "Well, then we will see" can mean "Well, it's all up in the air" or "Well, we finally will see what we always wanted to see!" We will see God, we will see one another. Jesus was clear about that when he said, "Do not let your hearts be troubled. You trust in God, trust also in me. In my Father's house there are many places to live in. . . . I am going now to prepare a place for you and after I have gone and prepared you a place, I shall return to take you to myself, so that you may be with me where I am" (John 14:1–3). When Jesus appeared to Mary of Magdala near the empty tomb, he sent her out with the words "Go and find my brothers and tell them: I am ascending to my Father and your Father, to my God and your God" (John 20:17).

The risen Jesus, eating and drinking with his friends, revealed that God's love for us, our love for each other, and our love for those who lived before and who will live after us is not just a quickly passing experience, but an eternal reality transcending all time and space. The risen Jesus, showing his pierced hands, feet, and side to his friends, also revealed that all we have lived in our body during our years on earth—our joyful as well as our painful experiences—will not simply fall away from us as a useless cloak but will mark our unique way of being with God and each other as we make the passage of death.

"Well, then we will see" will probably always have a double meaning. As the father of the epileptic boy, who asked Jesus to heal his child, we will always have to say, "I believe. Help my unbelief" (Mark 9:25). Still, when we keep our eyes fixed on the risen Lord, we may find not only that love is stronger than death, but also that our faith is stronger than our skepticism.

Death: A Loss and a Gift

YESTERDAY AFTERNOON, JUST as I was finishing the conclusion of this book, Jean Vanier called me from Trosly, France. In a gentle way, he said, "Henri, Père Thomas died this morning." Père Thomas Philippe, a French Dominican priest, was Jean's spiritual father and the cofounder of L'Arche. He was a man aflame with love of Jesus, Jesus' Mother Mary, and all the "little" people of this world. Père Thomas, who inspired his student and friend Jean Vanier and encouraged Jean to leave his teaching position in Toronto and start a life with disabled people—this holy and humble Dominican priest is now dead.

Listening to Jean, I heard the voice of a man who had lost his mentor and has now to continue alone. "What a loss for you!" I said. He replied, "Yes, a great loss for me and for L'Arche . . . but also a great gift."

Père Thomas's death is indeed a loss and a gift. A loss, because so many people, including myself, can no longer visit him and find new hope by just being with him. During the most difficult period of my life, when I experienced great anguish and despair, he was there. Many times, he pulled my head to his chest and prayed for me without words but with a spirit-filled silence that dispelled my demons of despair and made me rise up from his embrace with new vitality. Countless people have been willing to wait for hours in the vestibule of his little room to be with him. People in despair, people with great mental suffering, people agonizing about the choices they have had to make, people not knowing how to pray, people who couldn't believe in God, people with broken relationships, and, recently, people living with AIDS and looking for someone to help them die well. We all have lost our good shepherd, our "crook and staff" in this valley of darkness and wonder how to keep going without him.

But as Jean said, Père Thomas's death is a gift, too. Now his life can bear full fruit. Père Thomas suffered immensely. He suffered for the church he loved so much, especially when the church closed the international community of students he had founded and no longer allowed him to continue his work as university chaplain. He suffered great loneliness when he came to the little village of Trosly in the north of France and began to minister there to a group of young men with mental disabilities. He suffered during the long hours he spent in front of the blessed sacrament in his little chapel, wondering what Jesus wanted of him. And after having started L'Arche with Jean Vanier, he often suffered from feelings of being misunderstood and even rejected, especially when he saw developments taking place that were quite different from what he had expected. As he became older, he entered into an ever-deeper communion with Jesus on the cross and suffered with him great anguish and feelings of abandonment.

When, finally, Père Thomas could no longer be with so many people, he withdrew to the south of France, where he lived for a few years in hiddenness. There he died a few days after Jean had visited him and a few hours after his brother, Père Marie Dominique, had given him the Eucharist. That was yesterday, February 4, at one o'clock in the morning. As Jean said, Père Thomas's death is not only a loss, but a gift, too. It is the end of a great suffering and the beginning of a new fruitfulness in L'Arche, in the church, in society, and in the hearts of the many who mourn his death.

When I began to write this book, I wasn't thinking about Père Thomas, even though he has been my main spiritual guide since I came to L'Arche. Since his leaving Trosly, he had become so hidden that even I didn't always fully realize that he had not yet made the final passage. Now it dawns on me how immensely lonely he must have been during these last years, alone as Jesus was alone on Golgotha, "the place of the skull" (John 19:17). But since Jean's telephone call, he is here with me.

He is so much God's beloved child, brother of all those he cared for, and father of so many who will receive life from hearing about him, listening to his tapes, and reading his books. Seldom have I met a man who loved so deeply and intensely. He was truly on fire with love. So much did he love that he dared to say to me, "When you can't sleep during the night, just think of me and you will be fine." He had such confidence in the Spirit of Jesus blazing in him that he didn't say, "Think of God" or "Think of Jesus" or "Think of the Spirit," but rather he said, "Think of me." It was this burning love that made him heal so many and suffer so much. It was this love that penetrated every part of his being and made him into a living prayer: a prayer with eyes, hands, and a mouth that could only see, touch, and speak of God. This love consumed him as it consumed Jesus and gave life as it was consumed. This love could not and cannot die, but can only grow and grow.

The death of Père Thomas is given to me today to end this book. Père Thomas was a great gift to Jean, to me, and to many others. Now he is a gift to all people. Now he can send the Spirit of Jesus to everyone, and the Spirit can blow where and when it pleases.

Tomorrow, Saturday, I will leave Freiburg to go to France. I had not thought I would leave so soon—I have only been here three weeks—but after Jean's call, I want to be in Trosly, where Père Thomas's body will be brought and buried. I no longer want to be by myself in my little apartment writing about dying well and caring well. I want to be with that great community of people, poor and rich, young and old, strong and weak, gathered around the body of the man who loved so much and has been loved so much. As I travel from Freiburg to Strasbourg, from Strasbourg to Paris, from Paris to Compiègne, and from there to Trosly, I will think my thoughts and pray my prayers in communion with Moe, Rick, Marina, Connie, and my father, but I will feel especially close to Thomas Philippe, that beautiful man in whom the Spirit of Jesus was so fully alive and active. And in that large crowd of people mourning and giving thanks while breaking bread together in his memory, I will know as never before that God indeed is love.

ACKNOWLEDGMENTS

THIS LITTLE BOOK would never have been written without the warm friendship and generous hospitality of my German friends Franz and Reny Johna. In their home, I found not only a quiet place to write, but also the lively company to discuss my thoughts and bounce off my ideas. My gratitude to them is deep and lasting.

I also thank all the friends who are mentioned in this book. Not only did they allow me to write about them, but many took the time to critically read the manuscript and make suggestions for changes and additions.

A special word of thanks goes to my secretary, Kathy Christie, for typing and retyping the text and for offering me much-needed encouragement and support during the final phases of writing this book. I am also grateful for Conrad Wieczorek's and Terri Goff's careful editing work.

Finally I want to express my deep gratitude to Peggy McDonnell, her family, and friends. Their faithful encouragement and generous financial support in memory of Murray McDonnell have enabled me to find the quiet time and space to write *Our Greatest Gift*.

INDEX

HENRI J. M. NOUWEN (1932–1996) was the author of *With Open Hands, Reaching Out, The Wounded Healer, Making All Things New,* and many other bestsellers. He taught at Harvard, Yale, and Notre Dame universities before becoming the senior pastor of L'Arche Daybreak in Toronto, Canada, a community where men and women with intellectual disabilities and their assistants create a home for one another.